THE Official GREAT BRITISH

FACTORY SHOP GUIDE

HUNDREDS OF FACTORY SHOPS

✓ *Where they are*
✓ *When they open*
✓ *What they sell*
✓ *How to get there*

THE ESSENTIAL
GUIDE TO VALUE-FOR-MONEY SHOPPING

**by Gillian Cutress
& Rolf Stricker**

Personally researched, written & published by
Gill Cutress & Rolf Stricker
1 Rosebery Mews, Rosebery Road,
London SW2 4DQ
Phone 0181-678 0593 *Fax* 0181-674 1594
E-mail factshop@macline.co.uk

The Official Great British Factory Shop Guide 1996–97
Updated and reprinted summer 1996
Updated and reprinted autumn 1996

This is the 61st edition published in this series

Please do not have a wasted journey!

The vast majority of the entries in this guide were checked by the companies just before we went to press.
But – especially so in the current economic climate – organisations change, shops open at new times, holidays alter, shops decide to close for stocktaking and, from time to time, a shop ceases to trade altogether.
We deeply regret any inconveniences such changes cause, but it is a fact of life that these things do happen.

Therefore we cannot recommend strongly enough that you should phone the shop first if you are going a long way or making a special journey.

Changes and mistakes

We have done our best to ensure that all the information in this guide is correct. However, as we deal with thousands of details, it is possible that an error has occasionally slipped in. Do please let us know of any error you notice. As every reasonable care has been taken in the preparation of this book, we can accept no responsibility for errors, omissions, or damage, however caused.

CONTENTS

to the second edition of *The Official* **Great British Factory Shop Guide.** The first edition was so successful that it had to be reprinted twice, and, much to our delight, became a popular Christmas present!

Factory shopping is a world wide phenomenon which has gathered pace over the last few years. What used to be a simple concept of the on-site factory shop has become infinitely more complex, and the purpose of this book is to lead you through the maze. The next few pages aim to give you a few items of background information.

This new edition contains nearly 800 factory shops of all kinds. To help you find your way around the book (and plan your shopping journey around the country) we have added a much improved system of indexing. The book also contains all the essential information which readers of our regional guides have come to appreciate: clear instructions on how to get to each shop (with many useful maps, too), public transport if you have no car, wheelchair and pushchair access, what tours and facilities for shopping groups are on offer, and, not least, where to get meals or refreshments in the area.

It is useful to remember that famous high street chainstores are not manufacturers. They use a large number of manufacturing companies in the UK and abroad to make goods for them. As you tour factory shops, you may recognise the goods, but they are almost always unidentified. Chainstores are not very keen to have their 'seconds', ends of lines and samples promoted. For this reason we cannot give all the brand names sold by many of the factory shops, but we feel certain that you will know what you are buying!

We hope this book will help you to save money, and we wish you many enjoyable and successful shopping expeditions.

Gill and Rolf

Who are the authors?

We believe we are the ultimate British factory shoppers.

We have made several thousand factory shop visits over recent years, have saved a great deal of money and – together with all our relations – we are clad from head to foot in factory shop purchases. Our house and garden are brimming with bargains we could not resist.

Moreover, Rolf and I are so addicted that we have researched factory shops in France, Switzerland, the USA, South Africa and Australia. Once we travelled to Jersey for a weekend off – only to be greeted in the arrivals lounge by a stack of leaflets for a factory shop in Jersey too.

When we began our research, accidentally after wandering into a factory shop in Derbyshire ten years ago, factory shops were a little known aspect of retailing. Our proposal to write a guidebook about this type of shopping was met with incredulity in some quarters – and not a little alarm from manufacturers who felt that factory shops should remain a well kept secret for local residents.

How things have changed! Factory shopping has gained an ever increasing profile over the last ten years and canny shoppers tour the country especially to find value for money.

We have done our utmost to visit every single shop featured in this book (unfortunately some contacted us only at the last moment and we have not yet had the pleasure of making their acquaintance). We believe it is important for us to know the shops, to be aware of their atmosphere, to see the quality of the goods, and – which gives us enormous pleasure – to talk to the shop managers. The drawback is that we are on the road a great deal; the big bonus is that we have the pick of the bargains around the country.

Several people give us invaluable help in compiling our books. Pete, who began as a dedicated non-shopper, enjoyed a spending spree at Bicester Village. Yanka, accustomed to more academic activities than shopping, joined us on a tour of factory shops in Manchester and quickly became a convert. Emma is a natural shopper. Lee is discriminating in her factory shop purchases. Michelle thought it was a great reason for visiting France. Debbie is decidedly warm towards the idea of saving money (especially at one of the chocolate shops). Nick attempts to reconcile the theme of shopping with his love of ancient history. Sincere thanks to them all for wonderful help in our venture.

What are Factory Shops?

Ten years ago when we began our research, the definition of a factory shop was fairly simple: it was a shop, almost always on the factory site, where the manufacturer sold off samples, excess and returned items, ends of lines and goods which failed to meet stringent quality controls. Rather than carry such dead stock, the manufacturer sold these goods direct to the public at very worthwhile prices.

Over the years the definition has become much less precise, in part because manufacturers have begun to lease high street or shopping mall premises, in part because non-manufacturing brand names now sell their surplus stock in 'factory shops' and in part because genuine manufacturers' shops buy in more stock than they did in the past. As an example of how things have changed, 70% of the stock which a large Nottingham factory shop carried ten years ago was its own make. That figure has decreased to just 20%.

Brand names in the UK tend to belong to the retailer rather than to the manufacturer. Many brand names, however, now have 'factory shops' too – especially in the new 'outlet villages' which have opened recently.

Another new type of 'factory shop' is also appearing in Britain – a chain of stores in which British manufacturers will lease space on three-month contracts.

The link is that all these shops – including the shops owned by mail order catalogue companies – sell off surplus goods directly to the public.

What shoppers seek varies. Some shoppers patronise only 'genuine' on-site factory shops. Other people delight in finding wide selections of good value shops in the new shopping malls, especially as they offer other facilities such as restaurants. Others simply seek reduced prices, regardless of the type of shop.

This book leads people to a wonderful assortment of shops and items to buy. Whatever their preferences, we hope readers will find great value for money.

How much can you save?

The essence of factory shopping is saving money. How much you save depends on how much you spend. By this we mean that if you spend several hundred pounds on a carpet, they you might well save several hundred pounds too. If you buy a pair of socks at a good discount, the maximum you can save will be a pound or two. But both items represent impressive value at 50% off. On the whole we estimate that you will save 30% on everything you buy. On occasions you will save 50%, and it is a rare event when you come across even greater savings. Act fast! Other people will be keen to snap up such a bargain too.

Some advertisements which appear in the national press give the impression that savings in the range of 70–80% are regular occurrences. In our experience this is not the case.

Finding your way there

Preparing directions for finding the shops takes an inordinate amount of time. What might seem on the surface like a straightforward undertaking can become very complicated and very time-consuming, especially in city centres, in heavy traffic and when you simply cannot avoid the almost inevitable one-way system. How simple life was when you could go *up* and *down* each street!

Recognising that some shoppers prefer to navigate by maps, while other people find it much easier to follow verbal directions, we aim to give accurate details in the clearest way possible. Densely built urban areas present the greatest challenge to preparing directions (so that anyone can track down each shop from any direction). We presume that the reader has basic maps and a road atlas of the country.

We are constantly taken aback by the frequency with which roads, road numbers, road signs, roundabouts and one-way systems change, and how often petrol stations alter brand. If you notice such changes, we will be very grateful if you will let us know.

Why are some factory shops missing?

A year is a long time in the life of a manufacturing company in the current economic climate and some companies have been unable to commit themselves to giving details which might change over coming months ... managers may move on; the company may be subject to a management buyout or takeover, or be 'rationalised'; the shop may change hours or alter its sales policy, move site – or even close down. With so many unknown factors, it is not surprising that some companies asked us not to include their shops. Other shops which feature in our regional guides have specifically stated that they prefer not to appear in the national book. This is usually for one of three reasons: because their shops are already at full stretch and cannot cope with more customers, or because their aim is to meet the needs of the *local* population, or because they bear such well known brand names that they cannot risk upsetting their normal retail shops throughout the country. We respect these wishes – and point out that our regional editions include some gems which do not, unfortunately, appear in these pages!

We need your help!

We are a very small and very personal venture and we have gained a great many friends around the country over the last ten years. Precisely because we are so small, we need your help. Mainline publishers organise expensive and impressive publicity campaigns; we rely on personal contact. This is especially important when it comes to shops in this book. They need to know that the book works for them, that they benefit by appearing in it.

So, each time you visit a factory shop in this book, and especially if you have an enjoyable and worthwhile shopping trip,

PLEASE TELL THE FACTORY SHOP MANAGER THAT YOU USE THE FACTORY SHOP GUIDE.

Thank you very much.

Glass & Cutlery

This book begins with beautiful items for the table.

The term 'crystal' has come into use this century and invokes the resemblance of glass to precious stones. In Britain 'full lead' contains 30–34% lead. Lead adds a rich lustrous appearance and a fine ringing tone. Glass with a high lead content is a pleasure to hold, to look at and to use.

Most continental and American glass contains 24% lead, which explains why it is cheaper. At the shops in this book you should be able to find fine cut wine glasses, tumblers, whisky tumblers, vases, decanters and bowls for considerably less than you would pay elsewhere. Some interesting coloured glass is also made by the companies featured here. During recent visits, we have invariably found extra value special sales on certain ranges and have bought quite a few pieces for as little as half the usual factory shop price. We have also made the most of on-the-spot chip repair services which some shops offer. Knowing that such services exist makes you feel less suicidal when you knock the edge of your favourite glass or vase.

British glass makes a welcome present for friends abroad. It is easy to carry, but there is one drawback to transporting it. You must be prepared to be stopped at Customs when the lead content sets off the X-ray alarms.

Make sure you allow enough time to join a tour round a glass factory, and take any opportunity to see cutlery being forged, or silver chased. When you have watched the demanding skills involved in producing these beautiful items, you will want to own them.

CUTLERY & GLASS

Derwent Crystal	6	**Ashbourne**	Derbys
Edinburgh Crystal	327*	**Bicester**	Oxon
Oneida	347*	**Bicester**	Oxon
House of Marbles/Teign Valley Glass	276*	**Bovey Tracey**	Devon
Edinburgh Crystal	365*	**Brighton**	E Sussex
Nazeing Glassworks	7	**Broxbourne**	Herts
Gleneagles Crystal	8	**Broxburn**	Lothian
Abbey Horn of Lakeland	241*	**Carnforth**	Lancs
Dema International	9	**Chesterfield**	Derbys
Dartington Crystal	10	**Denby**	Derbys
Derwent Crystal	11	**Derby**	Derbys
Edinburgh Crystal	384*	**Ellesmere Port**	Cheshire
BRK Crystal	12	**Gildersome**	S Yorks
Dartington Crystal	13	**Great Torrington**	Devon
Edinburgh Crystal	413*	**Hartlepool**	Cleveland
Royal Brierley	419*	**Hartlepool**	Cleveland
David Mellor Cutlery	1	**Hathersage**	Derbys
Hornsea Freeport	430*	**Hornsea**	Humberside
Dartington Crystal	434*	**Kendal**	Cumbria
Caithness Crystal	14	**King's Lynn**	Norfolk
Arthur Price of England	2	**Lichfield**	Staffs
Villeroy & Boch	43*	**London : Wandsworth**	
Crystal Art	15	**Luton**	Beds
Oban Glass Studio	16	**Oban**	Strathclyde
Edinburgh Crystal	17	**Penicuik**	Lothian
Caithness Glass	18	**Perth**	Tayside
Royal Worcester & Spode	46*	**Porth**	Mid Glamorgan
Lightwater Village Factory Outlets	447*	**Ripon**	N Yorks
Selkirk Glass	19	**Selkirk**	Borders
George Butler of Sheffield	3	**Sheffield**	S Yorks
Hiram Wild	4	**Sheffield**	S Yorks
Osborne Silversmiths	5	**Sheffield**	S Yorks
Schott-UK	20	**Stafford**	Staffs
Wedgwood Group Factory Shop	62*	**Stoke-on-Trent : Fenton**	Staffs
Royal Worcester	64*	**Stoke-on-Trent : Hanley**	Staffs
Staffordshire Crystal	21	**Stoke-on-Trent : Longton**	Staffs
Royal Doulton Crystal	22	**Stourbridge area : Amblecote**	W Mids
Brierley Hill Glass Co.	23	**Stourbridge area : Brierley Hill**	W Mids
Royal Brierley Crystal	24	**Stourbridge area : Brierley Hill**	W Mids
Staffordshire Crystal	25	**Stourbridge area : Brierley Hill**	W Mids
Dennis Hall Tudor Crystal	26	**Stourbridge : Brierley Hill**	W Mids
Dartington Crystal	462*	**Street**	Somerset
Royal Brierley	477*	**Street**	Somerset
Royal Brierley Crystal	27	**Tipton**	W Mids
Royal Scot Crystal	28	**Toddington**	Beds
Georgian Crystal (Tutbury)	29	**Tutbury**	Staffs
Tutbury Crystal Glass	30	**Tutbury**	Staffs
Caithness Glass	31	**Wick**	Highlands and Islands
Royal Worcester Porcelain	51*	**Worcester**	Worcs

* Please see full details in respective chapter

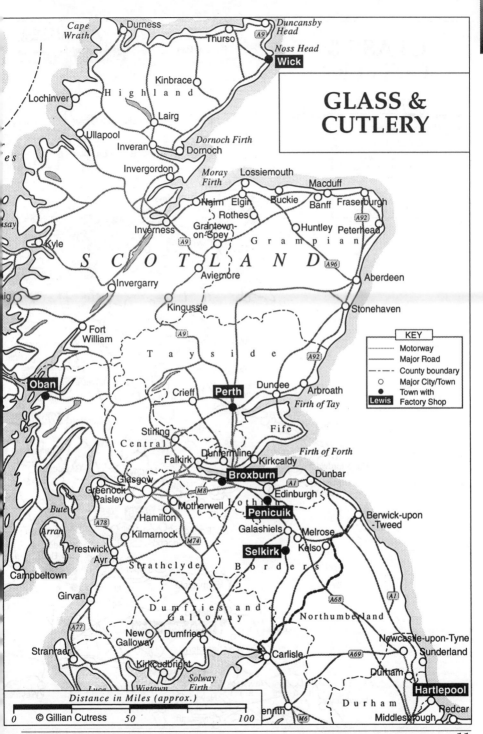

GLASS & CUTLERY

KEY

··········	Motorway
————	Major Road
—·—·—	County boundary
○	Major City/Town
●	Town with Factory Shop
Lewis	Factory Shop

Distance in Miles (approx.)

0   © Gillian Cutress   50   100

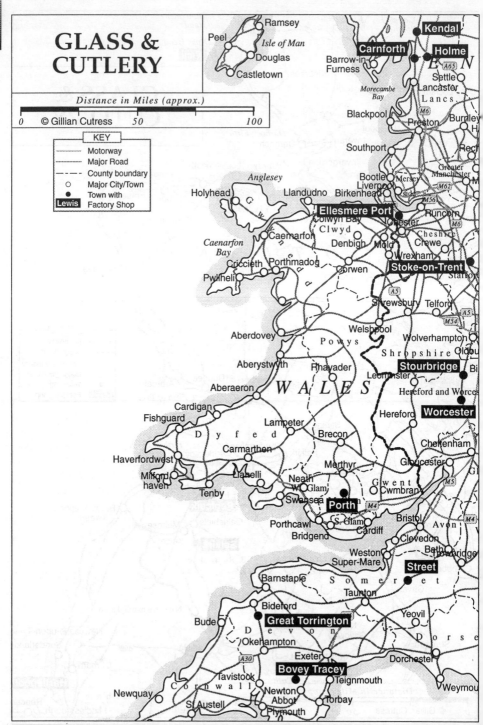

GLASS & CUTLERY

Distance in Miles (approx.)

© Gillian Cutress

| 0 | 50 | 100 |

KEY
.... Motorway
—— Major Road
—·—·— County boundary
○ Major City/Town
● Town with
Lewis Factory Shop

Ramsey
Peel
Isle of Man
Douglas
Castletown

Kendal
Carnforth
Holme
Barrow-in-Furness
Settle
Lancaster
Morecambe Bay
L a n c s .
Blackpool
Preston
Burnley
Southport
Greater Manchester
Bootle
Liverpool
Birkenhead
Mersey side
Runcorn
Holyhead
Anglesey
Llandudno
Ellesmere Port
Colwyn Bay
Chester
C l w y d
Caernarfon
Denbigh
Mold
Crewe
Caenarfon Bay
Wrexham
Cheshire
Criccieth
Porthmadog
Stoke-on-Trent
Pwllheli
Corwen
Stafford
Shrewsbury
Telford
Aberdovey
Welshpool
P o w y s
Wolverhampton
S h r o p s h i r e
Oldbu
Aberystwyth
Rhayader
Stourbridge
Bi
Leominster
Aberaeron
W A L E S
Hereford and Worce
Cardigan
Worcester
Fishguard
Lampeter
Hereford
D y f e d
Brecon
Cheltenham
Carmarthen
Gloucester
Haverfordwest
Merthyr
Gl
Milford haven
Neath
G w e n t
Llanelli
Glam
Cwmbran
M5
Tenby
Swansea
Porth
M4
Porthcawl
S. Glam
Bristol
Avon
Bridgend
Cardiff
M4
Clevedon
Bath
Weston-Super-Mare
Trowbridge
Street
S o m e r s e t
Barnstaple
Taunton
Bideford
Yeovil
Bude
Great Torrington
D e v o n
D o r s e
Okehampton
Exeter
Dorchester
A30
Bovey Tracey
Tavistock
Teignmouth
Newquay
C o r n w a l l
Newton Abbot
Torbay
Weymou
St Austell
Plymouth

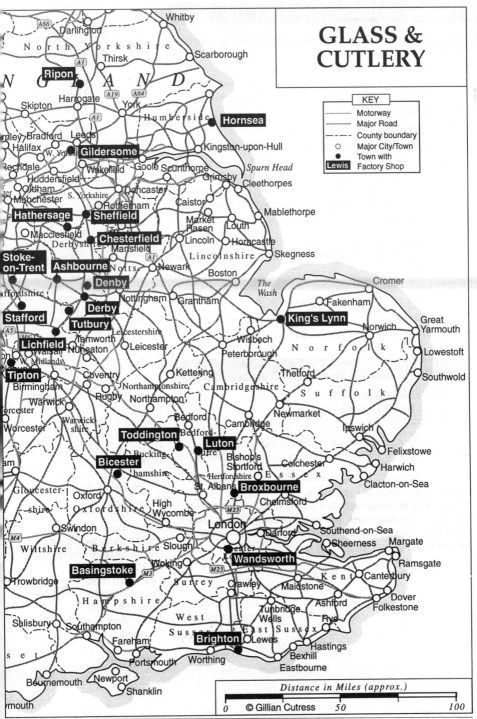

GLASS & CUTLERY

KEY

··········	Motorway
————	Major Road
– – – –	County boundary
○	Major City/Town
● Lewis	Town with Factory Shop

Distance in Miles (approx.)

0   © Gillian Cutress   50   100

Cutlery in Britain

Britain has led the world in cutlery design and production for centuries. This chapter leads you to sparkling displays of British craftsmanship at very good value. It would appear however that 1990s families do not boast as much tableware as in earlier times. A compendium of household hints published in 1800 recommended at least 48 spoons, 24 forks and 24 knives for a typical (genteel) household.

Nothing compares with silver cutlery! We are always surprised that the French, who take such pride in their cooking, are so uncaring of their table settings. How often have you eaten a delicious meal in a good restaurant across the Channel using bent, unmatched cutlery and cheapo glassware?

Cutlery companies are centred in the north Derbyshire/ South Yorkshire area and we list another shop in Staffordshire. Take care when you visit Sheffield because major road works during construction of the new transport system are causing traffic disruptions and diversions.

Lichfield Tourist Office *phone (01543) 252109*
Sheffield Tourist Office *phone (0114) 273 4671/2*

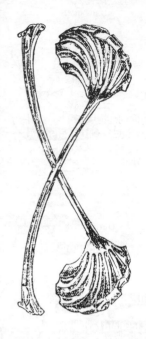

1   Hathersage   Derbys

David Mellor Cutlery
The Round Building S30 1BB
(01433) 650220

David Mellor's famous modern cutlery made here. Country shop sells superb kitchen equipment and finest English crafts.

....

On B6001 just south of Hathersage.
   From A625 in Hathersage: turn on to B6001 towards Grindleford. Go underneath railway bridge and go left at bottom of hill into drive to David Mellor. Well signposted to remarkable circular building.

Open: Mon–Sat 10–5; Sun 11–5; Bank Holidays.
Closed: Christmas, Boxing and New Year's Days.
Cards: Access, Visa.
Cars: Beside shop.
Toilets: No.
Wheelchairs: Ask for access through side door.
Teas: In Hathersage.
Tours: Brief tours of this award-winning factory sometimes possible. Groups please book in advance.
Transport: Local buses from Sheffield. Also BR station in Hathersage.
Mail order: Yes.
Catalogue: Free.

Arthur Price of England

Britannia Way, Britannia Enterprise Park WS14 9UY
(01543) 257775

Silver-plated and stainless steel Sheffield cutlery; tableware
and gifts, including tea and coffee sets, trays, tankards,
goblets, picture frames, candelabras, condiment sets etc.

*'All products British-made in own factories in Birmingham
and Sheffield. Items are seconds, ends of ranges or exhibition-
soiled.'*

....

On an industrial estate east of town.
   **From town centre: go towards Burton; pass Tesco on left; at
roundabout with County Council depot on right, go right for
Birmingham (A38).***
   **Going south from Stone/Stafford on A51: turn left for Burton,
Birmingham (A38), Britannia Enterprise Park into Eastern
Avenue (A5192). Keep going to roundabout; go straight over.***
   **Going south on A38: take first exit to Lichfield. Go over
railway, turn left at the roundabout.***
   *At next roundabout turn left.**
   **Going north on A38/A5148: exit for A5192, turn left. At
roundabout go right.**
   **Keep left for Britannia Way. Company on left.

Open: Mon–Fri 8.30–5;
Sat 9–1.
Closed: Bank Holidays;
Christmas–New Year.
Cards: Access, Visa.
Cars: Own spacious car-park.
Toilets: Yes.
Wheelchairs: Unfortunately
no access as shop is on first
floor.
Teas: Tea shops in Lichfield.
Groups: Pre-booked groups
welcome to shop. Special films
of cutlery and silverware
manufacture gladly shown to
groups by prior appointment.
Transport: None.
Mail order: No.
Catalogue: Free.

George Butler of Sheffield

12 Orgreave Drive S13 9NP
(0114) 269 4607

Sheffield made stainless steel and silver plated cutlery.
Many low priced loose items, as well as complete sets of
cutlery in attractive cabinets. A good variety of cutlery
patterns are generally available including cutlery serving
items.

*'All items are either discontinued, shop soiled or slightly
imperfect.'*

....

Just off the A57, about five miles east of Sheffield town centre.
   **From town centre: take A57 towards Worksop. Go through
Handsworth then after end of dual carriageway section turn left
on to B6066 Rotherham Road.***
   **From M1 exit 31: take A57 towards Sheffield. Go through
Woodhouse, then turn right onto B6066 Rotherham Road.***
   ***In Rotherham Road take first right, Orgreave Road, then at
T-junction turn right into Orgreave Place, which becomes
Orgreave Drive and shop is immediately on the right.**

Open: Mon–Fri 9–4;
Sat please check.
Closed: Bank Holidays.
Cards: Access, Visa and other
major cards.
Cars: Large private car-park
on site.
Toilets: Adjacent.
Wheelchairs: Ground level,
easy access.
Teas: Nearby.
Groups: Not suitable for
shopping groups.
Transport: Buses along the
A57 within 1/4 mile.
Mail order: Yes.
Catalogue: Free brochure.
No restrictions.

Hiram Wild Ltd.

64–70 Solly Street S1 4BA   *(0114) 272 3568*

Wide range of cutlery, silver plated and stainless. Loose and in canteens. Specialise in high quality stag and buffalo horn cutlery. Scissors (left-handed versions too), kitchen knives, carvery sets. Pocket knives, silver plated gallery trays, brides' cake knives, children's cutlery, christening mugs. Cutlery repair service.

'Genuine factory shop – HEAR cutlery being forged. Firsts and seconds.'

On north side of city centre. Best to approach via A61 or inner ring road.

From western side of ring road: follow sign to Jessop Hospital. Pass hospital; at bottom of hill, go left at roundabout for Chapeltown.*

From A61: turn off at roundabout to Glossop, City Centre, City Hospital, Museum on to dual carriageway. At next roundabout, double back.*

From city centre (front of City Hall): bear left into Leopold Street, go straight over first roundabout and downhill to second roundabout. Turn right to Chapeltown.*

*After 150 yds go left after Hallamshire Motors into Solly Street. Clearly marked shop 100 yds on right.

Open: Mon–Thur 8–5; Fri 8–4.30; Sat please phone to check.
Closed: Bank Holidays; late Spring Bank Holiday week; Christmas–New Year.
Cards: No.
Cars: Limited outside; nearby roads.
Toilets: No.
Wheelchairs: Five steps, so please phone first.
Teas: In town.
Tours: Groups welcome to see cutlery forged. For tours and shopping groups ring Michael Rodgers.
Transport: 10 minutes' walk from city centre. Nearest bus at West Bar.
Mail order: Yes.
Catalogue: Free catalogue, showing most of range, and price list gladly sent if you phone.

Osborne Silversmiths Ltd.

West Wick Works, Solly Street S1 4BA
(0114) 272 4929

Made in Sheffield top quality cutlery: silver plated, sterling silver and stainless steel in wide range of styles.

'Perfects and slight imperfects at up to 50% reduction on retail prices. We are only 8 miles from Derbyshire boundary.'

On north side of city centre. Best approach via A61 or inner ring road.

From western side of ring road: follow sign to Jessop Hospital. Pass hospital; at bottom of hill, go left at roundabout for Chapeltown.*

From A61: turn off at roundabout to 'Glossop, City Centre, City Hospital, Museum' on to dual carriageway. At next roundabout, double back.*

From city centre (front of City Hall): bear left into Leopold Street, go straight over first roundabout and go downhill to second roundabout. Turn right to Chapeltown.*

*After 150 yds go left after Hallamshire Motors into Solly Street. Clearly marked shop 50 yds on left.

Open: Mon–Fri 8.30–4; Sat by prior arrangement.
Closed: Bank Holidays; Christmas–New Year; Spring Bank Holiday week; last week July and first week Aug (phone to check first).
Cards: Access, Eurocard, Mastercard, Visa.
Cars: Public parking adjacent.
Toilets: Ask if desperate.
Wheelchairs: Access via despatch bay on request.
Teas: In Sheffield.
Groups: Shopping groups welcome, please phone first.
Transport: 10 minutes' walk from city centre. Nearest bus at West Bar.
Mail order: Yes.
Catalogue: Yes.

Although glass is blown, moulded, coloured, cut and etched across Britain, Scotland has become synonymous with paperweights. Outstanding examples are displayed, and available, at Scottish companies described here. Once you start studying paperweights, you become completely absorbed in their intricacy, colours and by the imagination which goes into their construction. Such items are highly collectible but the problem lies in deciding which to choose!

Fine glass collections are found in Glasgow and Edinburgh.

The Museum of the British Glass Industry (01384 273011), 'celebrates glass and the history of British glassmaking'. At Broadfield House in Kingswinford in the West Midlands, it is close to the heart of the English glass industry in Stourbridge. Recently restyled and expanded, this museum has a unique glass entrance pavilion which is the largest glass structure in the world. You can watch glass blowing and decoration, see a multi-screen presentation, learn about techniques, and indulge yourself in the shop. *Open afternoons, closed Monday.*

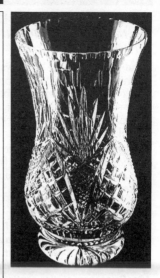

6   Ashbourne   Derbys

Derwent Crystal Ltd.
Shaw Croft Car Park DE6 1GH
(01335) 345219

English full-lead crystal glassware: wine glasses, tumblers and fancy gift items. Sandblasting and hand engraving.
'Factory shop prices. Special offers always available.'

This is the major car-park in the centre of Ashbourne. The company is clearly visible and well marked.

Open: Mon–Sat 9–5. Bank Holidays.
Closed: Christmas–New Year.
Cards: Access, Amex, Diners, Switch, Visa.
Cars: Own small car-park and huge public car-park.
Toilets: In car-park.
Wheelchairs: Easy access to small shop.
Teas: Several tea-shops within easy walking distance.
Groups: Always welcome to shop. Free tours for individuals around glassworks in the mornings. Coach parties (maximum 50 people) welcome but must book in advance.
Transport: Take any bus to Ashbourne.
Mail order: Yes.
Catalogue: Phone for free price list.

Nazeing Glassworks Ltd.
New Nazeing Road EN10 6SU
(01992) 464485

Hand-made hand-cut lead crystal glasses, vases, glass ashtrays, candle-holders, decanters etc. Unusual items: wine carafes with own ice coolers; zodiac paperweights, apple-shaped apple sauce boats; melon, avocado, corn cob dishes. Range of items in black and coloured glass, especially Bristol Blue glass.

'Huge range of perfects and seconds, 50p–£70, usually 30% less than normal retail price. Welcome special commissions, including engraving and ceramic decoration. Specialise in Ladies' Nights presents.'

Just outside M25 (exit 25) between Cheshunt and Hoddesdon.

From A10 (Great Cambridge Road): turn east for Broxbourne and get on to A1170 (NB if you are going north on A10, don't turn left for New River Trad. Est. but take next left). At traffic lights go east on to B194 for Nazeing/Lee Valley Park Lido. After Broxbourne station continue for 1/2 mile to small industrial estate on left; follow signs.

From Nazeing on B194: go under pylons then over canal; after 1/4 mile follow clear signs into estate on right.

Open: Mon–Fri 9.30–4.30; Sat 9.30–3.
Closed: Bank Holidays; Christmas–New Year.
Cards: Access, Visa.
Cars: Own car-park facing shop.
Toilets: Yes.
Wheelchairs: One step to large shop.
Teas: Broxbourne.
Tours: Thurs and Fri 11 am. Groups of 10–30 must book in advance. Adults 90p; children (must be over 5) and pensioners 60p; local school parties (within 5 mile radius) free. £2 refundable deposit for safety goggles.
Transport: Broxbourne station 1/2 mile. Broxbourne–Harlow buses stop outside.
Mail order: Yes.
Catalogue: Free: send large sae. A selected range is available.

Gleneagles Crystal
37 Simpson Road, East Mains Industrial Estate EH52 5AU
(01506) 852566

Wide range of crystal glass hand-cut here, including wine glasses, tumblers, decanters, bowls and vases, many in attractive gift boxes. Selected china, ceramic tableware and giftware from other leading manufacturers.

'Everything at factory prices. Slight seconds always available – from about £2.95 a glass. Designer label sweaters and shirts also available at realistic prices.'

Nearly 6 miles west of Edinburgh.

From Edinburgh: take A8 to junction with M8; then take A89 for Broxburn. After 2 miles fork right at next roundabout on to A899.*

From Glasgow coming east on M8: take exit 3A. At Boghall roundabout go right (A89) for Broxburn. At roundabout with A899, go left.*

***Take first right into East Mains Industrial Estate. Go right at first roundabout and left at second. Clearly marked factory is on left.**

Open: Mon–Sat 10–5; Sun 12–5. Bank Holidays.
Closed: Christmas, Boxing and New Year's Days; 2 Jan.
Cards: Access, Amex, Diners, Style, Switch, Visa.
Cars: In front of shop; also 100 spaces behind shop.
Toilets: Yes.
Wheelchairs: One small step into large shop.
Teas: Free coffee for visitors.
Groups: Groups welcome to shop: please book with shop manageress. Small groups (up to 6) can see glass-cutting any weekday (no charge).
Transport: Bus or train to Broxburn (East Mains Industrial Estate).
Mail order: No.

Dema International

Pottery Lane West S41 9BI   *(01246) 274201*

Plain and decorated moulded glassware made here. Also sell wide range of lead crystal *(Edinburgh Crystal* and continental), ceramics, *Denby* tableware – oven-to-tableware, china and silverware.

'Ends of ranges, discontinued lines, some seconds. Sales usually held at Easter (including Easter Monday), August and early November.'

....

About 2 miles north of Chesterfield.

    From town: take A61 north for Sheffield: go left at first round-about (Tesco superstore) for Newbold/Stonegavels. Keep straight for 1/2 mile to mini-roundabout; go right on to B6057.*

    Coming south on A61T: at roundabout with Tesco, go right for Newbold/Stonegavels. Keep straight for 1/2 mile to round-about; go right on to B6057.*

    Can also take old Sheffield Road (B6057), following signs to Whittington Moor.*

    *Pass fire station on left, go right into Pottery Lane, a small cul-de-sac. Shop, with clear sign, is at far right.

Open: Mon, Tues, Wed, Fri 9.30–4; Thur 9.30–8; Sat 9.30–1.30.
Closed: Bank Holidays; Christmas–New Year.
Cards: Access, Switch, Visa.
Cars: Outside shop.
Toilets: Yes.
Wheelchairs: Easy access, large shop and warehouse area.
Teas: Little Chef nearby.
Tours: Please contact Mrs Shaw, mentioning this Guide, for Thursday evening visits to factory/shop (light refreshments included). 18.45–20.45. Min 20, max 25 people. Min age 16 (for legal reasons). Also please book group visits to shop.
Transport: Bus nos. 19, 20, 21, 22 and 36 every 5 minutes from Chesterfield; X11 from Sheffield.
Mail order: No.

Dartington Crystal

Denby Pottery DE5 8NX
(01773) 513116

Wide selection of second quality *Dartington* crystal: clear crystal wine glasses, matching decanters, bowls, vases and gift ideas.

'All crystal at discounted prices.'

....

Within the Visitors Centre at Denby Pottery.

    Not in Denby village but on main B6179 (old A61 Derby Road), 2 miles south of Ripley and 8 miles north of Derby. Pottery is on sharp bend in road and is clearly visible (on right if you come from Derby or Belper, on left from Ripley).

    From A38: Pottery is signposted where B6179 turns off.

    From Belper: take A609 for Ilkeston. Go under A38 and at traffic lights go left on to B6179 to Ripley. Then on right as above.

Open: Mon–Sat 9–5; Sun 10–5. Bank Holidays.
Closed: Christmas, Boxing and New Year's Days.
Cards: Access, Visa.
Cars: Large car/coach park.
Toilets: Yes.
Wheelchairs: Easy access, large shop, no steps.
Teas: Restaurant in complex.
Groups: Shopping groups welcome.
Transport: Bus nos. 243 and 245 from Ripley
Mail order: No.
Catalogue: Free.

Derwent Crystal Ltd.

Little Bridge Street DE1 3LF
(01332) 360186

English full-lead crystal glassware: wine glasses, tumblers and fancy gift items. Sandblasting and hand engraving.
'Factory shop prices. Always special offers.'

....

1/3 mile north-west of Derby Museum/Art Gallery.

Little Bridge Street is a tiny lane off Bridge Street, part of which now comprises a one-way system on the A52 main Derby–Ashbourne road.

From Derby: aim for Ashbourne; go right off Friar Gate (A52) just outside inner ring road as if coming back into Derby (to Matlock A6).*

From Ashbourne via A52: as you come into town, go left into one-way system.*

*Go 100 yds along Bridge Street then keep straight where main road bends right into Agard Street; take little lane to right (Factory Shop sign) – a narrow cul-de-sac leading to canal. At canal, go sharp left into yard.

Open: Mon–Sat 9–5.
Closed: Bank Holidays; Christmas–New Year.
Cards: Access, Amex, Diners, Visa.
Cars: In nearby streets.
Toilets: In town centre.
Wheelchairs: Rough ground to small showroom so a little tricky.
Teas: Café round the corner.
Tours: Not here, but you can see the action at Ashbourne glassworks of same company.
Transport: 20 minutes' walk from city centre.
Mail order: Yes.
Catalogue: Phone for free price list.

BRK Crystal Ltd.

Treefield Estate LS27 7LB
(0113) 253 4277

Range of crystal items: vases, salad bowls, glasses, decanters etc.
'All items perfect. Excellent quality at low prices.'

....

Between Leeds and Bradford, about 4.5 miles south-west of Leeds. North of M62 exit 27, just off A62.

From M62 exit 27: take the A62 north for Leeds, cross the A650 at the roundabout and take the second right (signed 'Factory Crystal Shop').*

Going south from Leeds on the A62: cross the B6126, pass the petrol station and take the first left (after about 400 yds).*

*BRK is in the outside of the bend at the bottom.

Open: Mon–Fri 9–5, Sat–Sun 10–3.
Closed: Easter and Spring Bank Holiday; Christmas–New Year. Open other holidays.
Cards: Access, Visa.
Cars: Own car-park.
Toilets: Yes.
Wheelchairs: Easy access to small shop.
Teas: In town. Can be arranged for groups if booked in advance.
Groups: Shopping groups are welcome if they phone first. Can also arrange evening presentations for parties.
Transport: On Huddersfield–Leeds , Dewsbury–Pudsey and Bradford–Wakefield bus routes.
Mail order: Yes.
Catalogue: Phone for free brochure.

13   Great Torrington   Devon

Dartington Crystal Ltd.

Linden Close EX38 7AN
(01805) 622321

Wide choice of slightly imperfect *Dartington* crystal: clear crystal wine glasses, decanters, bowls, vases, plenty of gifts. Wide selection of china, kitchenware, cards and gifts. Also Tarka Mill Shop (Edinburgh Woollen Mill) for family knitwear and clothing.

'Items slightly below normal first quality; good discounts. Please phone for details of mail order.'

....

Six miles south-east of Bideford.
   From Bideford (A386): enter Great Torrington along New Street, look for church on right and go left into School Lane.*
   From Barnstaple (B3232) and South Molton (B3227): look for hospital at a roundabout. Go west along New Street, go right into School Lane opposite church.*
   ***Linden Close is second turning on left. Factory clearly marked.**

Open: All year: Mon–Sat 9.30–5; Sun 10.30–4.30. Bank Holidays.
Closed: Christmas and Boxing Days.
Cards: Access, Visa.
Cars: Large car-park.
Toilets: Yes.
Wheelchairs: Easy access to shop. Please arrange in advance for tours.
Teas: Licensed restaurant.
Groups: Tours (including Visitor Centre) to see glass blown and crafted from overhead galleries: Mon–Fri 9.30–3.30 (not Bank Holidays). £2.50 adults, children free when accompanied by full-paying adult. Groups (£1.80 pp) of 15+ must book in advance. School parties £1 pp.
Transport: Local bus service to New Street.
Mail order: Yes.
Catalogue: No.

14   King's Lynn   Norfolk

Caithness Crystal

11 Paxman Road, Hardwick Industrial Estate PE30 4NF
(01553) 765111

Large range of hand-made crystal glass. Coloured glass eg wine glasses, tumblers, decanters, vases etc. Coloured paperweights.

'Super bargains in well stocked shop. Personalised engraving. Factory seconds, discontinued lines. Christmas sale in Nov/Dec.'

....

Easy to find on southern outskirts of town.
   From town centre: go south towards A10 and Downham Market. Look for Campbell Soups on right; Caithness Crystal is in industrial estate on left.
   From south on A10 or Norwich on A47: get on to King's Lynn southern bypass (A47/A149); exit for King's Lynn at large roundabout.*
   From west: continue on southern bypass to major roundabout where A10 joins.*
   From north: go left on to the southern bypass from wherever you hit the ring road. At major roundabout go to King's Lynn.*
   ***Go along Hardwick Road. Take second right (Hansa Road). Pass Comet on right and take second left (phone box on far corner). Shop is on the left.**

Open: Mon–Sat 9–5; also Easter–Christmas Sun 11–4.30.
Closed: Christmas and New Year.
Cards: Access, Amex, Visa.
Cars: Free for cars and coaches.
Toilets: Yes, also for disabled.
Wheelchairs: No steps to large complex.
Teas: Own restaurant for light lunches, homemade cakes. Shop hours.
Tours: Self-conducted glass-making demonstrations Mon–Fri 9.15–4.15; *also 27 May–7 Sept*: Sat and Sun 11–4. No booking needed. See the skill of the glassmaker at close quarters. Free admission.
Transport: Swaffham and Downham Market buses.
Mail order: Yes.
Catalogue: Free. Only factory seconds sold by mail order.

Crystal Art

320 Selbourne Road LU4 8NV　　　　*(01582) 494904*

Cut and polished crystal figures of animals and flowers in 30% full lead Austrian crystal and English hand-worked glass; crystal trees and hanging window decorations; glass mirrored display cabinets.

'Firsts, seconds and discontinued lines. Many chainstore items made here. Special commissions accepted. Also many one-off prototype designs that are not available anywere else.'

On the north-west side of the town centre.

From M1 exit 11: aim for Luton town centre along Dunstable Road (A505). After 1/2 mile, go straight at roundabout; take next left (Waller Avenue) at traffic lights. *

From town centre and other directions: aim for Dunstable/M1 along Dunstable Road (A505). By Lex car showroom, go right at traffic lights into Waller Avenue. *

*Before the road goes over the railway, go right (Selbourne Road). Company is shortly on left.

Open: Mon–Fri 10–5; *also Nov–Dec Sat 10–4.*
Closed: Bank Holidays; Christmas–New Year period.
Cards: Access, Visa.
Cars: Own car-park.
Toilets: Yes.
Wheelchairs: One step.
Teas: Town centre (1 mile).
Tours: Shopping groups welcome – please book with sales department. Factory tours also arranged for groups – £2 per person (free crystal oyster given to each person).
Transport: Luton BR and bus nos. 31, 37, 38, 61 and 238.
Mail order: Yes.
Catalogue: £2 for full colour catalogue. Only firsts available by mail order. Please send payment with order (plus £2 for p+p).

Oban Glass Studio (Caithness Glass Ltd.)

Heritage Wharf, Railway Pier PA34 4PK
(01631) 563386

Glass and crystal glass, giftware and tableware in assorted colours and designs. Bowls, vases, paperweights, jewellery, engraving and tableware. Also *Colour Box* miniatures, giftwrap and artificial flowers.

'First and second qualities. Vases and bowls from £4.99, perfume flasks from £9.99, paperweights from £8.99; prices subject to change.'

In town centre on Railway Pier on Heritage Wharf, beside the railway station and ferry pier.

Open: All year: Mon–Sat 9–5 (late nights June–Sept). *also Easter–end Oct:* Sun 11–5. Bank Holidays.
Closed: Three days at Christmas and three days at New Year.
Cards: Access, Amex, Diners, Switch, Visa.
Cars: Large public car-park nearby.
Toilets: Yes, within Heritage Wharf.
Wheelchairs: Easy access.
Teas: Tea room within Heritage Wharf.
Groups: Groups welcome. No booking required.
Transport: Next to taxi rank and bus point.
Mail order: No.

17 Penicuik Lothian

Edinburgh Crystal

Eastfield EH26 8HA
(01968) 675128

World's largest collection of *Edinburgh Crystal:* cut crystal tumblers, decanters, wine glasses, vases, giftwear of first and second quality. Craft, gift and knitwear shop.

'Second quality crystal at least 30% off RRP. Always promotional offers. Items discounted up to 75%.'

....

Off the A701 near Edinburgh end of town.

From Edinburgh on A701 (Peebles Road): turn left about 50 yds into the town at the 'Crystal Visitor Centre' sign. Take next right to Visitor Centre.

From the south on A701/702 and A703: go into Penicuik, stay on A701 towards Edinburgh. Turn right immediately after BP petrol station, take next right for 'Crystal Visitor Centre'.

Open: Mon–Sat 9–5; Sun 11–5. Bank Holidays.
Closed: Christmas, New Year.
Cards: Access, Amex, Visa.
Cars: Car and coach parking.
Toilets: Yes, also for disabled.
Wheelchairs: Yes, rampway to first floor. Vast shop.
Teas: Coffee shop/light meals – licensed. Picnic and children's play areas (outside).
Tours: Free crystal exhibition and audio visual theatre 7 days a week. Factory tours Mon–Fri 9–3.30. Adults £2, concessions £1, disabled free. No children under 8 (safety reasons). Weekend tours May–mid Sept 11–2.30. Group rates (15+). Phone tours organiser for tours/shopping groups.
Transport: Edinburgh bus nos. 62, 64, 65, 81, 87. Free bus in summer (phone for details). BR station: Edinburgh Waverley.
Mail order: Yes. Free catalogue.

18 Perth Tayside

Caithness Glass

Inveralmond Industrial Estate PH1 3TZ
(01738) 637373

Glass and crystal in giftware and tableware in assorted colourways; vases, bowls, paperweights, jewellery, wine suites. Engraving. Also artificial flowers, *Colour Box* miniatures and gift wrapping.

'First and second qualities. Bud vases from £4.99, wine glasses from £4.99, perfume bottles from £9.99, paperweights from £8.99 (prices subject to change).'

....

At north end of Perth.

From Edinburgh via M90, Dundee via A85 or Stirling via A9: get on to or stay on A9 for Inverness. This bypasses Perth and takes you to large roundabout: exit into Inveralmond Industrial Estate, signposted 'Glassmaking Visitor Centre'.

From the north: turn into Inveralmond Industrial Estate at first roundabout in Perth, then take first left, following signs to 'Glassmaking Visitor Centre'.

Open: *June–Aug:* Mon–Sat 9–5; Sun 10–5; *April, May, Sept, Oct:* Mon–Sat 9–5; Sun 11–5; *Nov–Mar:* Mon–Sat 9–5; Sun 12–5
Closed: 24–26 Dec and 31 Dec–2 Jan.
Cards: Access, Amex, Diners, Switch, Visa and auto-teller.
Cars: Large car-park.
Toilets: Yes.
Wheelchairs: Easy access to huge complex.
Teas: Licensed restaurant for snacks and meals.
Tours: Viewing gallery. Free self conducted tours to see glassmaking Mon–Fri 9–4.30. Groups welcome to shop, booking not essential but helpful – please phone Mrs Sheenah Shepherd. Paperweight Collectors Gallery.
Transport: Perth BR and bus stations 3 miles.
Mail order: No.

Selkirk Glass Ltd.

Dunsdale Haugh TD7 5EE
(01750) 20954

Wide range of unique coloured glass paperweights, animals, artglass, perfume bottles, animal sculptures etc. Some locally made wooden furniture and hand-painted pottery.

'Perfects and seconds. Many items at factory prices.'

On north side of town.
 From Peebles/Innerleithen on A707 and Moffat on A708: cross river and go left immediately into Buccleuch Road. Continue for 1.5 miles; factory is clearly signed at far end of estate.
 From Hawick on A7: go through Selkirk; pass Exacta on left; this large company is on far left corner of next left turning.
 From Edinburgh & Galashiels on A7: look for Selkirk Glass on right as you come into town (just before left turning to Moffat). Clear car-park entrance.

Open: Mon–Fri 9–5; Sat 10–4.30; Sun 12–4.
Closed: 18 June; Christmas–New Year.
Cards: Access, Visa.
Cars: Own car and coach park.
Toilets: Yes, and for disabled.
Wheelchairs: Easy access to large shop and tour.
Teas: Own café for light snacks.
Groups: Free tours of glass-works, Mon–Fri 9–4.30 (not weekends). Any numbers, no need to book in advance. Regret no unaccompanied children. Parties also welcome to shop; please book in advance with Ron Hutchinson.
Transport: Edinburgh–Carlisle bus route.
Mail order: No.

SCHOTT-UK

Drummond Road, Astonfields Ind. Est. ST16 3EM   (01785) 223166

Over 20 complete suites of stemmed glasses in cut, plain and coloured crystal, boxed presentation sets, decanters, jugs, a range of exclusive hand-made crystal, barware and some heat-resistant glassware. Wide selection of crystal giftware – vases, bowls and ornaments.

'Perfect quality unless otherwise stated. Continuous special offers. Wedding list service available.'

See our display advertisement opposite.

On the east side of Stafford.
 *From north, south, west: approach from M6 exit 14. Follow A513. After 3/4 mile, go straight over roundabout for Uttoxeter. After 1/2 mile go right at sign to Common Road/Astonfields Industrial Estates. After one mile the road swings left into Astonfields Road. Drummond Road is first left. ***
 *From east: approach via A518 from Uttoxeter. At the round-about by Staffordshire University go right on to A513 for M6. After 1.3 miles go left just after traffic lights by the RAF into B5066 (Sandon Road). After 1/2 mile go right into Astonfields Road. Drummond Road is first right. ***
 **The shop is on right at end of Drummond Road.*

Open: Mon–Fri 10–4.30; Sat 10–3. Please enquire for Bank Holidays.
Closed: Christmas, Boxing and New Year's days.
Cards: Access, Visa.
Cars: Free large parking area with coach access.
Toilets: Yes.
Wheelchairs: One step to sizeable shop; willing assistance given.
Teas: In Stafford.
Groups: No factory tours but coach parties welcome to shop by prior arrangement: please contact Mrs Sue Cope, mentioning this book.
Transport: Bus no. 72 from Gaol Square every 30 minutes.
Mail order: No.

21 Stoke-on-Trent : Longton Staffs   *map p. 51*

Staffordshire Crystal

Uttoxeter Road ST3 1NY
(01782) 334194 (fax 01782 599863)

Attractive range of hand-cut and engraved stemware, glasses, vases,

'All items competitively priced. Gladly undertake special commissions for clubs, companies etc. Occasional seconds.'

See our display advertisement on p. 29

Just south of Longton town centre, on Uttoxeter Road (A50) opposite the Gladstone Pottery Museum.

   From Longton: take A50 for Uttoxeter, following Museum signs. After you emerge from one-way system, shop (formerly Aynsley) is on left.

   From Uttoxeter/Meir coming north on A50: pass Burmah petrol station on left and look for this shop on right as you go downhill into Longton.

For more details see page 52

Open: Mon–Thur 9–5;
Fri 9–4; Sat 10–4.
Closed: Bank Holidays;
Christmas–New Year.
Cards: None.
Cars: Local side streets.
Toilets: In Longton.
Wheelchairs: Small step to medium sized shop.
Teas: Cafés, pubs and fish & chip shops in Longton. In summer there is a café in the Gladstone Pottery Museum across the road.
Groups: No.
Transport: Easy walking from the bus and railway stations in Longton. China Link stop 8.
Mail order: No.

22 Stourbridge : Amblecote W Mids *map p. 28*

Royal Doulton Crystal
Coalbourn Lane DY8 4HS
(01384) 552900

Royal Doulton crystal, stemware and giftware.

....

About 1/2 mile north of Stourbridge ring road, in a little lane off the A491 (Stourbridge–Wolverhampton road).
  Going north on A491 from Stourbridge: Coalbourn Lane is on left.
  Going south on A491 from Amblecote/Kingswinford: cross the traffic lights at Collis Street (the A4102 [Dudley/Brierley Hill–Wollaston/Bridgnorth road]) and turn into the first little lane on right (large brown 'Royal Doulton' sign opposite).
  [Coaches please use the Wollaston Road entrance round the corner.]

Open: Mon–Sat 9–5.30.
Closed: Easter Monday; Christmas, Boxing and New Year's Days.
Cards: Access, Amex, Diners, Visa.
Cars: Own car-park in front of shop.
Toilets: Yes.
Wheelchairs: Good access for shop.
Teas: Hot-drink machine.
Groups: Free tours at 10 and 11.15 am. Maximum 52 people; advisable to book in advance with Mrs Oakes. No children under 10. No tours on Saturdays, in Easter week, Spring BH week, August BH or third week September, Christmas–New Year.
Transport: Bus stop 60 yds.
Mail order: Yes.
Catalogue: No.

23   Stourbridge : Brierley Hill *map p. 28*

Brierley Hill Glass Co. Ltd.
Mount Pleasant, Quarry Bank DY5 2YT
(01384) 77486/79264

Hand-cut lead crystal glassware: wine suites, tumblers, vases, jugs etc. Huge range of highly cut punch bowls, vases, bowls, ashtrays etc. Seconds, and first quality at manufacturer's prices.

'There is a large showroom, with one room for perfects and one for seconds. Special sales are held in March, November and December when opening times might be longer.'

....

A short distance due south of the Merry Hill Centre.
  From Merry Hill: go towards Bromsgrove (A491) and 'Quarry Bank A4036'. Go uphill to traffic lights, turn right for Brierley Hill into Mount Pleasant (A4100). Large shop is at far end on right.
  From Brierley Hill High Street (A461): turn into Mill Street and stay on the A4100; at the roundabout turn left, large shop is then on left.

Open: Mon–Thur 9–5; Fri, Sat 9–4; Bank Holidays.
Closed: Christmas, Boxing and New Year's Days.
Cards: Access, Eurocard, Visa.
Cars: Large car-park outside shop.
Toilets: Yes.
Wheelchairs: No steps to large showroom and shop.
Teas: In Brierley Hill.
Groups: Please contact Mrs J. Taylor if you would like to see how glass is cut. Tours are free and last one hour.
Transport: Birmingham bus nos. 137 and 138 pass through Mount Pleasant.
Mail order: No.

26   *The Official Great British Factory Shop Guide*

24   Stourbridge : Brierley Hill   *map p 28*

Royal Brierley Crystal Ltd.
Moor Street DY5 3SJ
(01384) 573580

Huge selection of hand-made, hand-cut crystal such as stemware, tumblers, decanters, jugs, vases.

'Huge shop – you get a trolley! Stock does not meet company's high standards so prices reduced. Sales in February; mid June–mid July; mid November.'

See our display advertisement above.

Five minutes' drive from the Merry Hill Shopping Centre, 3 miles north-east of Stourbridge and 3 miles south-west of Dudley in the heart of the British glass-making area.

Moor Street links Brierley Hill High Street (A461, Dudley–Amblecote road) with Brierley Hill Road (B4180, Dudley–Wordsley road). Shop is at Brierley Hill High Street end.

From Brierley Hill High Street (A461): turn off at traffic lights with sign to this company. Go downhill to the huge shop on left.

From Stourbridge: take the A491 north; turn right at traffic lights in Amblecote into Brettell Lane (A461). Turn left at signs to the shop.

Open: Mon–Fri 9.30–5.30; Sat 9–5; Sun 10–4. Bank Holidays.
Closed: Christmas, Boxing and New Year's Days.
Cards: Access, Amex, Visa.
Cars: Large car-parks, with coach area.
Toilets: Yes.
Wheelchairs: Easy access to huge spacious shop but tour difficult for wheelchairs.
Teas: Coffee Shop, for light meals, coffee, wine etc in nearby North Street. Mon–Fri 9–2.30; weekends by arrangement.
Tours: Coach parties, small groups or individuals please contact Visits Administrator to arrange. Groups to shop need not book.
Transport: Bus no. 137 from Birmingham goes along this road.
Mail order: Yes.
Catalogue: Yes.

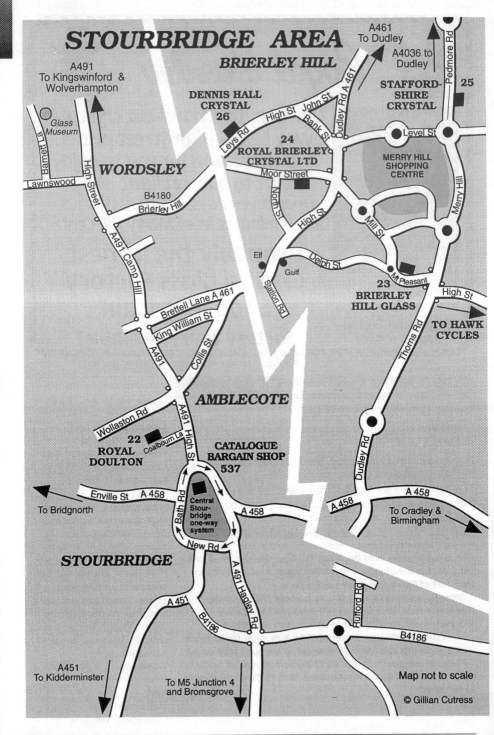

STOURBRIDGE AREA

BRIERLEY HILL

A491
To Kingswinford &
Wolverhampton

A461
To Dudley

A4036 to
Dudley

Pedmore Rd

Glass
Museum

Barnett La

DENNIS HALL
CRYSTAL
26

Leys Rd

High St

John St

Dudley Rd A 461

STAFFORD-
SHIRE
CRYSTAL

25

WORDSLEY

High Street

Bank St

Level St

MERRY HILL
SHOPPING
CENTRE

Merry Hill

Lawnswood

B4180
Brierley Hill

24
ROYAL BRIERLEY
CRYSTAL LTD

Moor Street

North St

High St

Mill St

A491 Camp Hill

Elf

Gulf

Delph St

Station Rd

M.Pleasant

23
BRIERLEY
HILL GLASS

High St

Brettell Lane A 461

King William St

Collis St

Thorns Rd

**TO HAWK
CYCLES**

A491

AMBLECOTE

Wollaston Rd

22
ROYAL
DOULTON

Coalbourn La

A491 High St

CATALOGUE
BARGAIN SHOP
537

Dudley Rd

Enville St   A 458

Bath Rd

Central
Stour-
bridge
one-way
system

A 458

A 458

A 458

To Bridgnorth

New Rd

To Cradley &
Birmingham

STOURBRIDGE

A 491 Hadley Rd

A 451

B4186

Rufford Rd

B4186

A451
To Kidderminster

To M5 Junction 4
and Bromsgrove

Map not to scale

© Gillian Cutress

Fine English Crystal blown and crafted on the premises

Staffordshire Crystal

Pedmore Road, Brierley Hill
West Midlands DY5 1TJ
Telephone (01384) 77701

See our entries nos. 21 and 25 (below)

Staffordshire Crystal

Pedmore Road, Brierley Hill DY5 1TJ (01384) 77701

33% lead oxide crystal melted in the furnace and mouth-blown on premises: tableware, stemware, tankards, bowls, vases etc. Cutting and engraving. Speciality: glass decanters cut like golf and tennis balls, footballs or bowls etc – ideal for club prizes.

'Everything hand-made. Prices about 50% less than normal high street prices. Perfects and seconds. Welcome special commissions for clubs, companies. Can engrave while you wait. Repair glass chips on the spot.'

See our display advertisement above.

....

On A4036 Pedmore Road close to Merry Hill Shopping Centre.
   From Dudley: take A461 for Stourbridge but turn on to A4036 following signs to Merry Hill Centre. Factory and shop clearly signed on the left about 250 yds before the roundabout.
   From Stourbridge: take the A461 to Brierley Hill. Go along the High Street and turn right at the traffic lights with signs to Merry Hill Centre. Go straight at the first roundabout and left at the second. Staffordshire Crystal is clearly visible on the right but you have to go up to the next roundabout and backtrack as this is a dual carriageway.

Open: Mon–Sun 9–5; Bank Holidays
Closed: Christmas and Boxing Days.
Cards: No.
Cars: Large car and coach park.
Toilets: Yes.
Wheelchairs: Easy access. One small step to shop.
Teas: Teas, restaurants etc in Merry Hill.
Tours: Yes, you are welcome to see the glass blown from the Visitor Area.
Transport: Any buses to Merry Hill.
Mail order: No.

Dennis Hall Tudor Crystal Ltd.

Chiltern House, Leys Road, Brockmoor DY5 3UR
(01384) 485254

English hand-made full lead (33%) crystal, blown, made and decorated here: wine suites, vases, bowls, glass animals, bells, compotes, christening cups, tankards, sweet dishes, witch bowls.

'First quality, discounted seconds and discounted lines. Special commissions undertaken. Repairs and replacements a speciality. Sherry glasses from £3.75, small bud vases from £4.75, salad bowls from £14.95, 8" vases from £14.75.'

On the B4180 (Leys Road).
At the traffic lights at the northern end of Brierley Hill High Street (A461 Stourbridge–Dudley road): turn on to B4179 for Pensett/Wordsley. Then turn left immediately after The Bridge pub on the left on to B4180 for Wordsley. Shop is on the right, just past West Midland Fabrications Engineering, opposite The Woodman.
From the A491 (Stourbridge–Wolverhampton road): turn on to B4180 at traffic lights in Wordsley. Shop is about a mile on left, 300 yds after BOC on the left, and opposite The Woodman.

Open: Mon–Fri 9–5;
Sat and Bank Holidays 10–4.
Closed: Christmas-New Year.
Cards: Access, Visa.
Cars: Outside shop.
Toilets: Yes.
Wheelchairs: Three steps.
Teas: The Woodman opposite shop for meals.
Tours: Please contact Gordon Noble or John Kimberley. Visitors can see glass blowing and glass cutting. Tours on Mon and Thur 10–12 & 1–3; Tues and Fri 10–12. No restrictions on numbers or ages.
Transport: Local buses.
Mail order: No restrictions on mail order.
Catalogue: Free.

Royal Brierley Crystal Ltd.

Bedford Street, Dudley Port DY4 7PM
(0121) 520 4429

Glass lampshades and lamp bases. 'Studio' range of informal shaped lead crystal glasses, carafes etc. Hand-made and hand-cut crystal, stemware, giftware, tumblers, decanters etc.

'All items seconds. Sales throughout February and mid June–mid July.'

See our display advertisement on p. 27

Just off Horseley Heath, the A461 leading from West Bromwich to Dudley. Turn north into Lower Church Lane (A4163 to Tipton) near Dudley Port station. Bedford Street is the second road on the right and the shop is at the far end on the right.

Open: Mon–Sat 9–5;
Bank Holidays.
Closed: Christmas–New Year.
Cards: Access, Amex, Visa.
Cars: Own car-park.
Toilets: Yes.
Wheelchairs: One small step to medium sized shop.
Teas: In town.
Groups: Groups of shoppers welcome; prior phone call appreciated. Glassworks tours available at the other factory in Brierley Hill.
Transport: Local buses.
Mail order: No.
Catalogue: Retail catalogue available from head office.

Royal Scot Crystal Factory Shop

Poplars Nursery
Garden Centre
Harlington Road
Toddington
LU5 6HE
(01525) 875897
Open 7 days 10–5

---

28 Toddington Beds

Royal Scot Crystal

Poplars Nursery, Harlington Road LU5 6HF
(01525) 875897

Hand-cut lead crystal glasses, decanters, vases etc. Specially engraved items. Crystal animals, paperweights and perfume bottles. Golf prizes.

'Most items made in own factory (not at this location). Sell first quality, some seconds and discontinued lines at substantially reduced prices.'

See our display advertisement above.

Clearly visible on A5120.
From M1 exit 12: go north-east towards Flitwick (not Toddington) on the A5120. After 1/2 mile turn right into nursery. The shop is at the rear of the building next to the tearoom.
From Flitwick: go south towards M1. This nursery is on the left, 1/2 mile before the motorway.

Open: Mon–Sun 10–5.
Closed: Christmas, Boxing and New Year's Days.
Cards: Access, Visa.
Cars: Garden centre car-park.
Toilets: Yes.
Wheelchairs: No steps.
Teas: Available in garden centre. Children's play area.
Groups: Small shopping groups welcome with prior phone call. Visit the garden centre at the same time.
Transport: None.
Mail order: Yes.
Catalogue: Free.

Georgian Crystal (Tutbury) Ltd.
Silk Mill Lane DE13 9LF
(01283) 814534 fax (01283) 520186

English full-lead crystal glassware: wine glasses, tumblers etc, honey pots, vases and small gift items.

'Firsts and seconds. Engraving service. Please mention this book if asking for a leaflet. Mail order service.'

....

This clearly signposted glassworks is in a small lane near the centre of Tutbury.

 From the High Street: turn right at the post office and then first left. Follow the sign to 'The Silkmill'.

Open: Mon–Sat 9–5; Sun 10–3; Bank Holidays.
Closed: Christmas and New Year.
Cards: Access, Amex, Diners, Switch, Visa.
Cars: Outside shop or car-park in village.
Toilets: Yes.
Wheelchairs: Access possible to sales area (from where you can see the furnace) but space is tight.
Teas: Tea rooms and pubs in the pleasant village of Tutbury.
Tours: Morning tours of the glassworks. Group visits very welcome. The shop is beside and above the glass-blowing area.
Transport: Trent bus no. 104 from Burton. Stephensons buses from Uttoxeter via Tutbury.
Mail order: Yes.
Catalogue: Price list available.

Tutbury Crystal Glass Ltd.
Burton Street DE13 9NC
(01283) 813281

Hand-made, hand-decorated full lead crystal glassware, stemware, tumblers, jugs, decanters, bowls, vases etc.

'All items on sale are seconds. Engraving service available.'

....

Almost in the centre of Tutbury, on the main road through the town where it makes a right-angle at the bottom of the hill. The company is clearly marked.

Open: Mon–Sat 9–5; Sun 11–4; Bank Holidays.
Closed: Christmas–New Year.
Cards: Access, Visa, Switch.
Cars: Own car-park.
Toilets: Yes.
Wheelchairs: Easy access via reception.
Teas: Own tea room on the premises Mon–Fri 9.30–4.30. Also tea shops in village.
Tours: Group visits to shop: please arrange in advance with reception. Glassworks tours: please book in advance, mentioning this guide. Tours Mon, Tues, Thur at 9.30, 11.30 and 1.30. Fri at 9.30 only. Tours for up to 60 people at 50p per person. Children must be accompanied.
Transport: Trent bus no. 104 from Burton. Stephensons buses from Uttoxeter via Tutbury.
Mail order: Yes.
Catalogue: Yes.

Caithness Glass

Airport Industrial Estate KW1 5BR
(01955) 602286

Glass and crystal tableware and giftware in assorted colours and designs: bowls, vases, paperweights, jewellery, engraving and tableware. Also *Colour Box* miniatures, gift wrap and artificial flowers.

'First and second qualities. Vases and bowls from £4.99, perfume flasks from £9.99, paperweights from £8.99 (prices subject to change).'

On the north side of the town on the main A9, by the airport, only 5 minutes from the town centre.

Open: Mon–Sat 9–5; (*also Easter–Dec* Sunday 11–5); Bank Holidays.
Closed: Three days at Christmas and three days at New Year.
Cards: Access, Amex, Diners, Switch, Visa.
Cars: Own large free car-park by main entrance.
Toilets: Super loos and mother/baby room.
Wheelchairs: Can be provided. Full access to all areas.
Teas: Licensed restaurant for snacks and meals.
Tours: Free self-conducted tours Mon–Fri. No booking needed. Groups welcome.
Transport: Wick rail and bus stations within walking distance.
Mail order: No.

MANUFACTURE OF GLASS.

Sheffield and Cutlery

Cutlery is indelibly linked with the city of Sheffield, where it has been produced for hundreds of years. The natural resources in this area allowed the industry to prosper over the centuries – rivers to drive the water wheels, coal to fuel the furnaces, iron ore to make the blades, and quarries with abundant millstone grit for the grinding wheels.

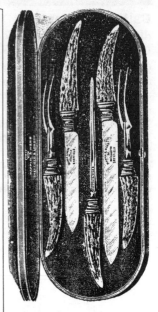

Edward III valued his Sheffield knife so highly that he bequeathed it as a separate item in his will; and in the late 1300s, Chaucer spoke of a Sheffield knife in The Reeve's Tale. The craft of blade making began with scythes and developed into kitchen knives, scissors and pocket knives, and finally into table cutlery and 'holloware' (tea and coffee pots and trays).

By the mid 1600s, small and delicate table knives were often decorated with silver, amber, ivory or agate. They were sometimes sold in pairs in a fancy leather sheath. In those days before the fork was known, one knife was used to cut and the other to hold the food.

Cutlery canteens made their appearance in Georgian times. Until then only a kitchen tool, the spoon now arrived on the table too. Design flourished and many of the famous Sheffield patterns, such as rattail and kings, developed in the 1700s, have been made ever since.

The Sheffield cutlers were at their peak in Victorian times, supplying the rest of the world with tableware. In 1869 one company alone produced 36,000 table knives and 7000 pairs of scissors per week. In the early 1900s, one company held 15 tons of ivory for handles.

Stainless steel (that is, iron which does not rust, and not a knife which didn't need washing up as the author thought when she was little) was developed by a Sheffield metallurgist called Harry Brearley. Sheffield cutlers were among the first to use this revolutionary material.

The British cutlery industry today is much reduced and has been hit hard by inferior overseas competition. Some famous English names are indeed Japanese owned. When you visit one of the English cutlery companies, inspect the quality of the work then compare it to a cheaper import. Once you have seen the difference you will be happy to pay for the luxury of a skilfully made item.

We appreciate the help of the British Cutlery and Silverware Association in providing these details.

China, Pottery, Models & Figurines

In this chapter you will find shops selling all kinds of china and pottery, from the useful to the ornamental, from the most delicate porcelain to stoneware. Some of the companies are small businesses producing hand-crafted pieces, other are large companies making everything from dinner services to sanitary ware. There are numerous factory tours on offer, which enable you to see the complexities of the manufacturing process.

The opportunities for bargains are enormous. 'Seconds' often have flaws undetectable to any but the most experienced eye; you can buy, at reduced prices, designs which no longer appear in the current catalogue. Many shops hold special sales, usually in January and July.

In the 18th century, it was considered a great joke to slip a live toad into a friend's beer; it didn't take long for an enterprising potter to realise that there was a market for beer mugs ready equipped with (ceramic) toads. To this day potters are turning out mugs containing beasties of varying degrees of repulsiveness to disgust one's friends! For an intriguing selection of these frog mugs visit the Ceramics Gallery in the City Museum in Hanley (01782 202173). You might also be interested in visiting the superb museums at Royal Worcester, Royal Doulton, Minton and Spode.

This chapter is set out alphabetically by town except that the many fascinating factory shops in the Stoke-on-Trent area are grouped together and are placed after all the shops elsewhere.

C H Brannam	83*	**Barnstaple**	Devon
John Jenkins	339*	**Bicester**	Oxon
Villeroy & Boch	359*	**Bicester**	Oxon
Park Rose Pottery Leisure Park	32	**Bridlington**	Humberside
Hornsea Pottery	368*	**Brighton**	E Sussex
Kemptown Terracotta	84*	**Brighton**	E Sussex
Goodwood MetalCraft	242*	**Chichester**	W Sussex
T G Green Pottery	33	**Church Gresley**	Derbys
Dartmouth Pottery	34	**Dartmouth**	Devon
Brookhouse Pottery Workshop	35	**Denbigh**	Clwyd
Denby Pottery	36	**Denby**	Derbys
Royal Crown Derby	37	**Derby**	Derbys
Dartington Crystal	13*	**Great Torrington**	Devon
Rookes Pottery	87*	**Hartington**	Derbys
China Ladies of Holmfirth, The	38	**Holmfirth**	W Yorks
Hook Norton Pottery	39	**Hook Norton**	Oxon
Chessell Pottery	40	**Isle of Wight : Yarmouth**	
Denby Pottery	41	**Kendal**	Cumbria
Suffolk Potteries	88*	**Kenninghall**	Norfolk
Highland Stoneware Pottery	42	**Lochinver**	Highlands and Islands
Villeroy & Boch	43	**London : Wandsworth**	London
Denby Factory Shop	44	**Matlock Bath**	Derbys
Dexam International	250*	**Midhurst**	W Sussex
Weston Mill Pottery	89*	**Newark**	Notts
Denby Factory Shop	45	**Nottingham**	Notts
Wetheriggs Country Pottery	90*	**Penrith**	Cumbria
Royal Worcester & Spode	46	**Porth**	Mid Glamorgan
Rye Pottery	47	**Rye**	E Sussex
Royal Doulton	52	**Stoke-on-Trent : Baddeley Green**	Staffs
Wedgwood Best	53	**Stoke-on-Trent : Barlaston**	Staffs
Crown Burslem Pottery	54	**Stoke-on-Trent : Burslem**	Staffs
Moorcroft, W	55	**Stoke-on-Trent : Burslem**	Staffs
Moorland Pottery	56	**Stoke-on-Trent : Burslem**	Staffs
Royal Doulton	57	**Stoke-on-Trent : Burslem**	Staffs
Wade Ceramics	58	**Stoke-on-Trent : Burslem**	Staffs
Churchill Tableware	59	**Stoke-on-Trent : Cobridge**	Staffs
Holland Studio Craft	60	**Stoke-on-Trent : Fenton**	Staffs
Royal Doulton	61	**Stoke-on-Trent : Fenton**	Staffs
Wedgwood Group Factory Shop, The	62	**Stoke-on-Trent : Fenton**	Staffs
Aynsley China	63	**Stoke-on-Trent : Hanley**	Staffs
Royal Worcester	64	**Stoke-on-Trent : Hanley**	Staffs
St George's Fine Bone China	65	**Stoke-on-Trent : Hanley**	Staffs
Aynsley China	66	**Stoke-on-Trent : Longton**	Staffs
Ceramic World	67	**Stoke-on-Trent : Longton**	Staffs
Gladstone Pottery Museum	68	**Stoke-on-Trent : Longton**	Staffs
Hadida, M R	69	**Stoke-on-Trent : Longton**	Staffs
Hudson & Middleton	70	**Stoke-on-Trent : Longton**	Staffs
John Beswick	71	**Stoke-on-Trent : Longton**	Staffs
Portmeirion Potteries	72	**Stoke-on-Trent : Longton**	Staffs
Queen's Fine Bone China	73	**Stoke-on-Trent : Longton**	Staffs
Royal Grafton Fine Bone China	74	**Stoke-on-Trent : Longton**	Staffs
Salisbury China	75	**Stoke-on-Trent : Longton**	Staffs
Sovereign Ceramics	76	**Stoke-on-Trent : Longton**	Staffs
Staffordshire Tableware	77	**Stoke-on-Trent : Meir Park**	Staffs
Blakeney Pottery	78	**Stoke-on-Trent : Stoke**	Staffs
Carlton House	79	**Stoke-on-Trent : Stoke**	Staffs
Minton	80	**Stoke-on-Trent : Stoke**	Staffs
Portmeirion Seconds Shop	81	**Stoke-on-Trent : Stoke**	Staffs
Spode	82	**Stoke-on-Trent : Stoke**	Staffs
Denby Pottery	48	**Street**	Somerset
Royal Worcester	478*	**Street**	Somerset
Clover Leaf Giftware	257*	**Swindon**	Wilts
Henry Watson's Potteries	49	**Wattisfield**	Suffolk
Bretby Art Pottery (Est. 1883)	50	**Woodville, Burton-on-Trent**	Staffs
Royal Worcester Porcelain	51	**Worcester**	Worcs

*Please see full
details in respective
chapter*

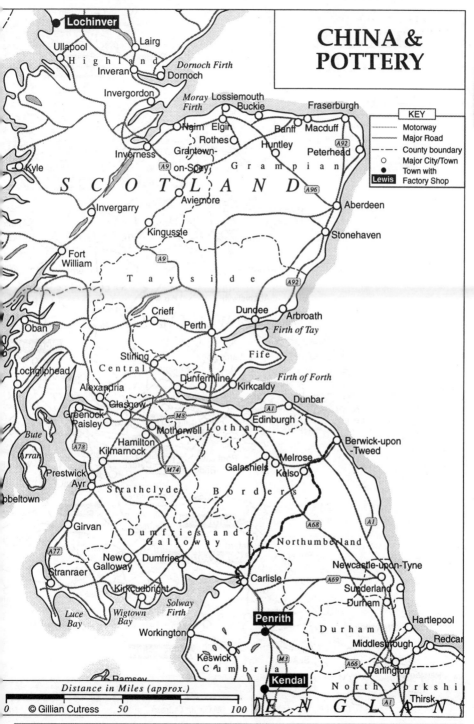

CHINA & POTTERY

KEY

...... Motorway
——— Major Road
-·-·- County boundary
○ Major City/Town
● Town with
Factory Shop
Lewis Factory Shop

Distance in Miles (approx.)

0   © Gillian Cutress   50   100

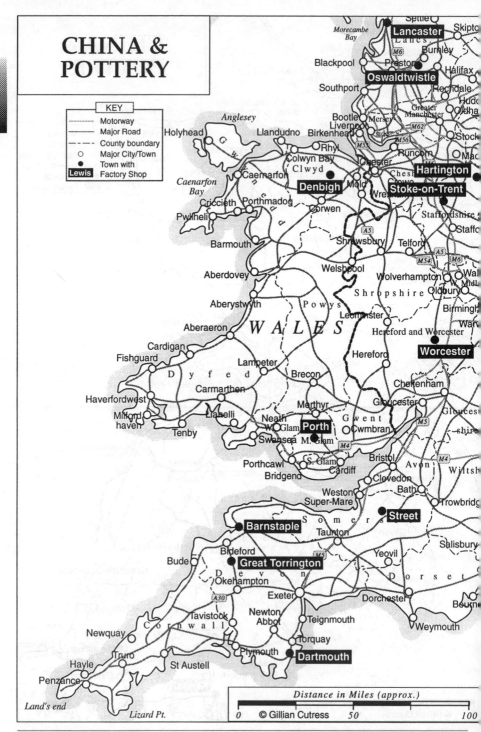

CHINA & POTTERY

KEY
- .... Motorway
- ———— Major Road
- – – – County boundary
- O Major City/Town
- ● Town with
- **Lewis** Factory Shop

Morecambe Bay

Settle · **Lancaster** · Skipton

Lancs.

M6

Blackpool · Preston · Burnley · Halifax

Oswaldtwistle

Southport · Rochdale

Anglesey · Bootle · Greater Manchester · Huddersfield · Oldham

Holyhead · Llandudno · Birkenhead · Liverpool · Mersey · M62 · Stockport

G.w. · Rhyl · Colwyn Bay · Chester · M56 · Runcorn · Mac

Caenarfon Bay · Caernarfon · Clwyd · Mold · **Hartington** · Chesh · **Stoke-on-Trent**

Criccieth · Porthmadog · Corwen · Wrexham · **Denbigh**

Pwllheli · Staffordshire · Stafford

Barmouth · Shrewsbury · Telford · A5

Aberdovey · Welshpool · Wolverhampton · Wal · W.Mid

Shropshire · Oldbury · Birmingham

Aberystwyth · *Powys* · Leominster · War

Aberaeron · Hereford and Worcester

Cardigan · *W A L E S*

Fishguard · Lampeter · Brecon · Hereford · **Worcester**

D y f e d · Cheltenham

Haverfordwest · Carmarthen · Merthyr · Gloucester · Glouces

Milford haven · Llanelli · Neath · W.Glam · **Porth** · *G w e n t* · Cwmbran · M5 · -shire

Tenby · Swansea · M.Glam · M4

Porthcawl · S.Glam · Bristol · *A v o n* · M4 · *Wiltsh*

Bridgend · Cardiff · Clevedon · Bath

Weston-Super-Mare · Trowbridge

S o m e r s e t · **Street**

Barnstaple · Taunton · Salisbury

Bideford · **Great Torrington** · Yeovil

Bude · *D e v o n* · *D o r s e t*

Okehampton · M5 · Bourne

Exeter · Dorchester

Tavistock · Newton Abbot · Teignmouth · Weymouth

Newquay · *C o r n w a l l* · Torquay

Truro · Plymouth · **Dartmouth**

Hayle · St Austell

Penzance

Land's end · *Lizard Pt.*

Distance in Miles (approx.)

0 © Gillian Cutress 50 100

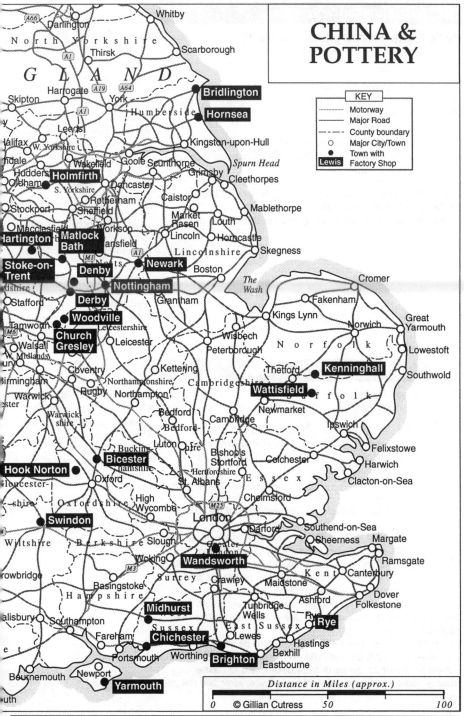

CHINA & POTTERY

KEY

.... Motorway
———— Major Road
- - - - County boundary
○ Major City/Town
● Town with
Lewis Factory Shop

Whitby
Darlington
A66
North Yorkshire
Thirsk
Scarborough
GLAND
Harrogate A19 A64
A1
York
Skipton
Bridlington
Hornsea
Humberside
Leeds
Kingston-upon-Hull
Halifax
W. Yorkshire
dale
Wakefield
Goole
Scunthorpe
Spurn Head
Hudders-
Oldham
Holmfirth
Doncaster
Grimsby
S. Yorkshire
Cleethorpes
Stockport
Rotherham
Caistor
Macclesfield
Sheffield
Market Rasen
Louth
Mablethorpe
Hartington
Matlock Bath
Worksop
Mansfield
Lincoln
Horncastle
Skegness
Lincolnshire
Stoke-on-Trent
Denby
Newark
Boston
Cromer
dshire
Stafford
Nottingham
Grantham
The Wash
Fakenham
Derby
Kings Lynn
Norwich
Great Yarmouth
Woodville
Leicestershire
Wisbech
Norfolk
Lowestoft
Tamworth
M6
Church Gresley
Leicester
Peterborough
Southwold
Walsall
W. Midlands
Coventry
Northamptonshire
Cambridgeshire
Thetford
Kenninghall
Wattisfield
Suffolk
birmingham
Rugby
Northampton
Newmarket
Ipswich
ster
Warwick
Warwickshire
Bedford
Cambridge
Felixstowe
Hook Norton
Bicester
Buckinghamshire
Luton
Oxford
Bishop's Stortford
Colchester
Harwich
Gloucester-shire
Oxfordshire
St. Albans
Hertfordshire
Essex
Clacton-on-Sea
Swindon
High Wycombe
Chelmsford
M25
London
Wiltshire
Berkshire
Slough
Dartford
Southend-on-Sea
Sheerness
Margate
rowbridge
Woking
M3
Greater London
Wandsworth
Crawley
Kent
Ramsgate
Canterbury
Basingstoke
Hampshire
Maidstone
Ashford
Dover
Folkestone
salisbury
Southampton
Midhurst
Tunbridge Wells
Surrey
Rye
Fareham
Chichester
Worthing
Lewes
Hastings
Bexhill
Bournemouth
Newport
Portsmouth
Brighton
Eastbourne
uth
Yarmouth
Sussex
East Sussex

Distance in Miles (approx.)
0   © Gillian Cutress   50   100

Park Rose Pottery Leisure Park

Carnaby Covert Lane YO15 3QF
(01262) 602823

Large range of hand decorated ceramics made here including co-ordinating lighting, planters, bedroom, bathroom and kitchenware accessories plus animal collectables and accessories range.

'Selected seconds on sale in the seconds warehouse, often at half normal high street prices. Pottery in 12 acres of beautiful parkland, ideal location for a family day out.'

··

Easy to find, 2 miles south of Bridlington between A166 (to Driffield) and A165 (to Beverley).
There are conspicuous brown signs on both these roads.

Open: Seven days a week, 10–5.
Closed: Christmas–New Year.
Cards: Access, Visa.
Cars: Huge free parking area for cars and coaches.
Toilets: Yes, including for disabled.
Wheelchairs: Easy access to all facilities. Everything on ground floor.
Changing rooms: Yes.
Teas: Own licenced café for snacks, meals etc.
Tours: Free pottery walkabout or detailed guided tour for nominal fee. Coach parties welcome for pottery or shopping.
Transport: Buses from Bridlington.
Mail order: No.

T G Green Pottery

John Street DE11 8EE   *(01283) 217981*

Large selection of decorated pottery; plain coloured cookware and tableware; catering pottery ex *Pearsons*. Table mats, trays, coasters, melamine food preparations, co-ordinated linens and small gifts.

'January and July sales. Ring for late night Christmas shopping.'

··

Five miles south-east of Burton upon Trent, just off the A50, on south side of Swadlincote.
  From Burton: take A50 south-east for Ashby. In Woodville, turn right on to A514 for Swadlincote; take first left to Church Gresley/Nuneaton A514; go left at roundabout for Measham B586. After 100 yds go left into private road; pottery is 200 yds on right.
  From Swadlincote: take B586 south for Measham. Go uphill, past artificial ski slope on left; go straight at roundabout. After 100 yds, go left through vehicle-welder's yard into private road; pottery is 200 yds on right.
  From Moira: go north on B586: pass Q8 petrol on left. After 1/3 mile, go right into private road (100 yds before roundabout at A514).
  From M42 exit 11: go north through Overseal to Castle Gresley. Take A514 east; go right on to B586; after 100 yds go left.

Open: Mon–Sat 9.30–4.15.
Closed: Easter Monday; two weeks at Christmas–New Year.
Cards: Access, Visa.
Cars: Own car-park.
Toilets: Yes.
Wheelchairs: Access to fairly spacious shop.
Teas: Own tea rooms.
Groups: To shop only by prior arrangement. Contact Brenda Maddock.
Transport: None.

Dartmouth Pottery – Seconds Shop

Warfleet TQ6 9BY
(01803) 832258

Cast earthenware pottery with a wide range of vases. Giftware. Exclusive range of hand-painted tableware. Photograph frames made by subsidiary company in wood, silverplate, leather or leatherex. Solid brass home furnishing accessories.

'Of special interest to florists. Extremely reasonably priced seconds.'

....

Warfleet is a short distance south of Dartmouth.

From Dartmouth: take B3205 coast road due south, follow signs to castle through Warfleet. Pottery well marked on left, just after turn to castle.

From Kingsbridge: follow A379 to Stoke Fleming. Go right along B3205, signposted to castle and Warfleet. Pottery in very attractive old 19th century mill on right.

Open: *April–Dec*: Mon–Sun 10–5.
Jan–March: Mon–Fri 10–5.
Closed: Christmas Eve–2 Jan.
Cards: No.
Cars: Limited parking outside in road.
Toilets: Yes.
Wheelchairs: Four steep steps, medium sized shop.
Teas: At the castle – Easter–October.
Groups: No pottery tours. Groups welcome to shop; please give advance notice.
Transport: 10 minute walk from Dartmouth.
Mail order: No.

Brookhouse Pottery Workshop

The Malt House, Brookhouse Lane LL16 4RF
(01745) 812805

Wide range of stoneware studio pottery, both production pieces and one-off items, such as jugs, dishes and bowls (including octagonal shapes) with special glazing. Unusual and large designs such as fountains. Celadon ware. Also some terracotta garden pots.

'Most items are perfects at prices lower than elsewhere. Some seconds on sale. Enjoy this specially designed showroom built over the stream.'

....

In a hamlet a short distance south of Denbigh.

From Denbigh town centre: go downhill to traffic lights, then right for Ruthin. At roundabout, continue following signs to Ruthin, A525. After 400 yds, go right for 'Brookhouse 1/4'.*

Coming north from Ruthin on A525: follow signs to Denbigh town centre. Immediately before the Denbigh town sign, go left into lane for 'Brookhouse 1/4'.*

*Specially designed gallery is 200 yds on left.

Open: Seven days a week 9–5.30. If travelling far at week-ends, worth phoning first as this is a family run business.
Closed: Phone to check Christmas opening times.
Cards: Access, Visa.
Cars: In lane outside gallery.
Toilets: No.
Wheelchairs: One step to small gallery.
Teas: Customers might be offered a cup of coffee!
Tours: Workshop is next to shop. Glad to show pre-arranged groups around pottery.
Transport: Ruthin–Rhyl buses (about once an hour).

Denby Pottery

Visitors Centre DE5 8NX
(01773) 570684 (Visitor centre)

Denby tableware, cookware and mugs – best, second quality and wedding list service available. Also a speciality cookshop, the *Dartington* crystal factory shop and gift and florist shop.

'Sales in January and July.'

....

On the B6179, 2 miles south of Ripley and 8 miles north of Derby. The pottery is clearly signposted on a sharp bend in the road (on the right if you come from Derby, on the left from Ripley).

From the A38: the pottery is signposted before the turning for Kilburn and Denby on the B6179.

The visitor centre is by the main entrance of Denby Pottery.

Open: Mon–Sat 9–5 (Tues 9.30–5); Sun 11–5. Bank Hols.
Closed: Xmas & Boxing Days.
Cards: Access, Connect, Switch, Visa.
Cars: Large car/coach-park.
Toilets: Yes.
Wheelchairs: Easy access to spacious shop, restaurant, Craftsman's Workshop, toilets. Regret wheelchairs cannot take part in full factory tour (safety).
Teas: Goodalls restaurant 9.30 –4.30: home-made lunches etc.
Groups: Mon–Thur 10.30 am and 1 pm; Fri 11. Adults £3.10; children/OAPs £2.10. Groups welcome, but advise booking for all factory tours. Craftsman's Workshop Mon–Sat 9.30–3.30, Sun 10–3.30. Adults £2.10; children/OAPs £1.60. Contact Tours Reception (01773 743644).
Transport: Bus nos. 243 and 245 from Derby.
Mail order: No.

Royal Crown Derby

194 Osmaston Road DE3 8JZ
(01332) 712833

Finely decorated bone china tableware; giftware such as paperweights. Wide selection of seconds.

'Some best quality but mainly seconds for sale.'

....

About 1/2 mile south of city centre.

From inner ring road: take A514 (Osmaston Road) signposted to Melbourne. The pottery is about 1/4 mile on right, set slightly back but clearly visible.

If you come into Derby on A514: go almost into city centre and look for this company set back on left.

Open: Mon–Fri 9–5; Sat 9–4; Sun10–4.
Closed: Most Bank Holidays – please check prior to visit.
Cards: Access, Amex, Diners, JCB, Visa.
Cars: Limited car-park, or in street.
Toilets: Yes (not weekends!).
Wheelchairs: Easy access to shop, but tour is unsuitable for the less-than-agile.
Teas: Drinks machine (except weekends). Refreshments for groups by prior arrangement.
Tours: Please arrange in advance mentioning this book. Up to 45 people (must be over 10 yrs). £3 pp, £2.75 OAP's & students. Tours at 10.30 & 1.45 Mon–Thur. None at weekends or late Spring Bank Hol week.
Transport: Many buses from Derby Market Place.
Mail order: No.

The China Ladies of Holmfirth

Bridge Mills, Huddersfield Road HD7 2TW
(01484) 687294

English bone china selected seconds from all the major
Staffordshire potteries plus range of imported porcelain.
'Probably the finest range of china in Yorkshire.'

*1/4 mile north of Holmfirth centre, on the Huddersfield road
(A6024).*

*From Huddersfield via A6024: as you come into Holmfirth,
pass hospital on right and mill is on far corner of next turn-off to
right (B6107 to Netherthong/Marsden). Go right here then left
into yard.*

*From town centre: take A6024 for Huddersfield; pass fire
station; after 250 yds pass this mill on left; go left on to B6107
to Netherthong/Marsden then go immediately left into yard.*

Open: Mon–Sat 10–4.30
including Bank Holiday
Mondays.
Closed: Christmas–New Year.
Cards: Access, Mastercard,
Visa.
Cars: Own car-park.
Toilets: Please ask in an
emergency!
Wheelchairs: Two small
steps after footbridge to spacious shop; assistance given.
Teas: Own small café for tea,
coffee and cold drinks.
Groups: Coach parties to
shop are most welcome; please
book by phone, mentioning
this Guide.
Transport: Five minutes'
walk from town centre. Bus
stop outside mill: nos. 309, 310,
311, 312 to Huddersfield; 334
and 335 to Meltham.
Mail order: No.

Hook Norton Pottery

East End Farmhouse OX15 5LC
(01608) 737414

Decorated and glazed stoneware: jugs, plates, mugs, cooking
dishes, pots, salt cellars etc.

At eastern end of this small village.

*Coming west from Banbury: go between old railway arches and
into village. Road bends sharp left then sharp right – castellated
farmhouse is on left in second bend. Entrance is to right of farmhouse, beside monkey puzzle tree (with clear white sign).*

*From all other directions: go into village then east towards
Banbury. Pottery on right where road turns sharp left.*

Open: Mon–Sat 9–5.
Closed: Bank Holidays;
Christmas–New Year.
Cards: Access, Visa.
Cars: Down drive, in front
of pottery.
Toilets: Yes.
Wheelchairs: Showroom up
flight of wooden stairs on first
floor.
Teas: Local pubs.
Tours: Welcome to see
potting on ground floor. Small
charge for groups, who should
book first with Mr Collins.
Transport: Infrequent buses
from Banbury and Chipping
Norton.

Chessell Pottery (Chessell Enterprises)

Chessell, Yarmouth PO41 OUF
(01983) 531248

Fine decorative, ornamental porcelain; vases, animals, fountains, dishes etc.

'Seconds available. Mail order service; please request a catalogue, mentioning this book. Collectors' Club with members' discounts.'

....

On the western end of the island.
 From Freshwater: take B3399 for Brighstone and Newport. After 3.5 miles fork left on to B3401 for Newport. Go right after 150 yds. *
 From Newport: take B3401 for Freshwater and the Needles. After 6 miles pass Calbourne Mill on right; after 1 mile go left. *
 ***Follow brown signs to pottery.**

Open: Mon–Sat 9–5.30; also April–Dec: Sun 10–5.
Closed: Christmas–New Year for two weeks.
Cards: Access, Diners, Switch, Visa.
Cars: Free car-park.
Toilets: Yes.
Wheelchairs: Full facilities for the disabled..
Teas: Own coffee shop: drinks and snacks.
Tours: Porcelain made and decorated Mon–Sat 9–5. Admission to studios: adults 40p, children (5–15) 20p.
Mail order: Yes.
Catalogue: Yes, free. No seconds sent.

Denby

K Village LA9 7BT
(01539) 735418

Denby tableware, mugs and cookware – best, second quality and wedding list service available.
'Sales in January and July.'

....

In the K Village on the A65 on south-east side of town.
 From town centre: take A6 south to M6. When you see signs to A65, follow these until you see K Village on right. Entrance at far end of complex.
 From south via A65: as you come into Kendal, clearly sign-posted complex is on left shortly after you reach river (on left).
 From A591(T) northbound (Kendal bypass): take A6 for Kendal and turn right at first traffic lights signpost to K Factories. Take first left after bridge then first left into car-park. (This is quickest way from M6 exit 36.)

Open: Mon–Sat 9.30–6; Sun 11–5. Bank Holidays.
Closed: Christmas Day.
Cards: Access, Connect, Switch, Visa.
Cars: Large free car and coach park outside shop; spaces for disabled drivers.
Toilets: Yes, also for disabled; baby changing facilities.
Wheelchairs: Easy access.
Teas: Riverside Restaurant.
Groups: Larger groups please phone first.
Transport: Ten minutes' walk from town centre or bus route 41/41A.
Mail order: No.

Highland Stoneware Pottery

Baddidarroch IV27 4LR
(01571) 844376

Huge range of high-fired stoneware. Tableware, cookware. Unusual gifts: fish dishes, bread crocks, ashets, wall plates, vases, jugs, mugs. Characteristic freehand painting (increasingly collectable).

'Selected seconds, prototypes, special exhibition pieces sold. Worldwide distribution and mail order service. Most things £10–£60.'

....

On the north side of the bay of Lochinver.
   The A837 is the main road in and out of Lochinver from south/east and from B869 from the north.
   Shortly after you enter Lochinver on A837: take second right (first is no entry): follow this road round until you see 'Pottery' sign off to the left. Pottery at end of drive.

Open: Mon–Fri 9–6; *also Easter–Oct* Sat 9–5. Bank Holidays. Other times by appointment.
Closed: Christmas–New Year (10 days).
Cards: Access, Switch, Visa.
Cars: Own car-park.
Toilets: Works toilets – access never refused!
Wheelchairs: Easy shop access, 3 steps to workshops: ramp and assistance available.
Teas: In town.
Tours: Welcome (please phone first, unsuitable for large coach parties) to walk around and watch potters at work: freehand painting, extruding, modelling. Free (charity box).
Transport: Lairg/Lochinver and Ullapool/Lochinver buses.
Mail order: Yes.
Catalogue: Free.

Villeroy & Boch

267 Merton Road SW18 5JS
(0181) 870 4168

Large range of *Villeroy & Boch* china tableware, cookware, crystal glassware, gifts, cutlery etc.

'Discontinued stock, seconds, samples, perfects at reduced prices.'

....

South of Wandsworth on A218, just off South Circular Road (A205).
   From all directions: go to Wandsworth then go clockwise round the one-way system. Pass town hall on right. Look for tall block of flats (Arndale Centre) ahead. Stay in left lane, go left after Arndale Centre. Continue for some distance along main road. Cross mini-roundabout, go over traffic lights. Shop in second building on left: large sign.
   Coming north into Wandsworth on Merton Road (A218) from South Wimbledon: look for this clearly signed building (set back from road) on the right, about 100 yds before traffic lights.

Open: Mon–Sat 10–5, Sun 10–4.
Closed: Phone about Bank Holidays, Christmas.
Cards: Access, Amex, Diners, Switch, Visa.
Cars: Own car-park in front of building.
Toilets: No.
Wheelchairs: Ramp from car-park to large shop.
Teas: Locally.
Groups: No pottery tours. Shopping groups welcome; check with shop first.
Transport: Local buses; Southfields tube station half mile (District Line).
Mail order: No.

Denby Factory Shop
44 North Parade DE4 3NS
(01629) 56408

Denby tableware, mugs and cookware – best, second quality and wedding list service available.
'Sales in January and July.'

....

The shop is situated in the long parade of shops on one side of the river, approximately 200 yds from BR station.

Open: Mon–Sat 10–5; Sun 11–5. Bank Holidays. Additional hours during summer, please ring for details.
Closed: Christmas, Boxing and New Year's Days.
Cards: Access, Connect, Switch, Visa.
Cars: Limited parking outside and nearby public car-parks.
Toilets: By the Tourist Office.
Wheelchairs: Small shop; access difficult.
Teas: Plenty of cafés along the parade.
Tours: Please see entry under 'Denby' for tours of the pottery.
Transport: Trains to Matlock Bath. Many buses to the area.
Mail order: No.

Denby Factory Shop
Drury Walk, Broadmarsh Centre NG1 7LL
(0115) 948 3932

Denby tableware, mugs and cookware – best, second quality and wedding list service available.
'Sales in January and July.'

....

Broadmarsh Centre is one of the two major shopping precincts in the centre of Nottingham.
The shop is on the upper level near The Caves exhibition.

Open: Mon–Sat 9–5.30 (Tues 9.30–5.30).
Closed: Bank Holidays; Christmas, Boxing and New Year's Days.
Cards: Access, Connect, Switch, Visa.
Cars: Huge public car-park in the Broadmarsh Centre.
Toilets: In Broadmarsh Centre.
Wheelchairs: Lifts & escalators in the shopping centre; limited access in the shop due to shortage of space.
Teas: Opposite shop.
Tours: Please see the company's entry under 'Denby' for details of factory tours.
Transport: Shop is above Broadmarsh bus station. Easy walk from BR station.
Mail order: No .

Royal Worcester & Spode

Unit D, Dinas Enterprise Centre, Cymmer Road CF39 9BS
(01443) 688120

Porcelain and fine bone china tableware, ornamental studies, figurines and giftware. Also *Spode, Dartington Crystal, Cloverleaf* mats, *Pimpernel* mats, *Stuart Crystal and Fo-Frames.*

'Seconds sold at 25% off high street price.'

Just outside (west of) Porth, on the road to Tonypandy.

From Porth (Pioneer Superstore, which is on the one-way system): with the superstore on your left, aim for Tonypandy. Stay in the left lane then fork left. At mini-roundabout go right for Tonypandy B4278. After about 350 yds, go right into the service road. Pass Integrasol and Remploy on right: Royal Worcester is in the next building, past the carpet shop.

From Tonypandy: go east to Porth, following signs to Pontypridd. Go along Dinas Road (B4278) which becomes Cymmer Road. Look for tyre company on the left: Royal Worcester is immediately past it.

Open: Mon–Sat 10–5. Some Bank Holidays – please phone to check.
Closed: Christmas and Boxing Days.
Cards: Access, Amex, Diners, Visa.
Cars: In access road leading to shop.
Toilets: Pioneer Superstore.
Wheelchairs: No steps.
Teas: Cafés in town.
Groups: Shopping groups and coaches welcome. Please book beforehand with the shop manager.
Transport: Porth BR station or buses to Porth then short taxi ride.
Mail order: Yes.
Catalogue: No. Any package, large or small, can be mailed world-wide.

Rye Pottery

Ferry Road TN31 7DJ
(01797) 223363

Wide range of decorated earthenware: some mugs, dishes, cake stands; selection of dogs, cats, owls, hares etc plus collector's range of figures from Chaucer's Canterbury Tales and American Folk Heroes.

'Perfects; and seconds reduced by 33%. Please mention this book when requesting catalogue. Special commissions accepted.'

On the west side of Rye.

By car: go round town till you see signs to 'Battle B2089' then follow them; go over level crossing; pottery is in large detached house 200 yds on right, just past The Ferry Boat Inn.

By train then foot: turn right outside station, go to end of road, turn right; go over level crossing; pottery is in large detached house 200 yds on right, just past The Ferry Boat Inn.

From Battle on B2089: go down Udimore Hill into Rye, pass the 'Cinque Ports' sign, then pottery is just over 1/2 mile on left, just before The Ferry Boat Inn.

Open: Mon–Fri 9–12 and 2–5; Sat 9.30–12.30 and 2.30–5.
Closed: Bank Holidays; Christmas–New Year.
Cards: Access, Visa.
Cars: Two car spaces beside pottery; town car-parks and local streets.
Toilets: In town.
Wheelchairs: Five steps and cobbled path so not possible for wheelchairs.
Teas: Lots of places in Rye.
Groups: No.
Transport: 5 minutes' walk from train station.
Mail order: Yes.
Catalogue: Free. Mail order service for firsts only.

Denby Pottery

Clarks Village, Farm Road BA16 0BB
(01458) 840940

Denby tableware, mugs and cookware – best, second quality and wedding list service available.
'Sales in January and July.'

Situated on the original Clarks factory site. Easy to find and clearly marked off the Street by-pass.

Open: Mon–Sat 9.30–6; Sun 11–5. Bank Holidays.
Closed: Christmas Day.
Cards: Access, Connect, Switch, Visa.
Cars: Large park for cars and coaches adjoining town centre car-park.
Toilets: Yes, plus baby changing facilities.
Wheelchairs: Easy access; wheelchairs available in complex by request.
Teas: Café, Burger King take-away, plus sandwich and pizza kiosks in complex; picnic area.
Groups: Larger groups please phone first.
Transport: Any bus to Street.
Mail order: No.

Henry Watson's Potteries Ltd.

IP22 1NI
(01359) 251239

Good quality seconds of terracotta storage jars (including large square jars with 1600 ml capacity), wine coolers, bread crocks, lasagne dishes, bread bakers, herb and spice jars, flan dishes etc at about 25% off. New range of glazed terracotta tableware in four colours (plates, bowls, teapots, salad bowls etc, all dishwasher-safe.)

'Lots of bargains, wonderful seconds. Many products at greatly reduced prices – from £1.25–£25.'

Wattisfield is a small village on the A143, 14 miles north-east of Bury St Edmunds and 9 miles south-west of Diss. The pottery is well signposted on A143.

From Bury: as you reach Wattisfield, pass the right turn-off to Wattisfield church; after several hundred yards, go right into well marked lane.

From Diss: pass the Suffolk Barn restaurant on left; after hundred yards go sharp left into well marked lane to pottery.

Open: Mon–Sat 9.30–4.30; Bank Holidays (except Good Friday).
Closed: Good Friday; Christmas Day and following week.
Cards: Access, Visa.
Cars: Large car-park.
Toilets: Yes, and for disabled.
Wheelchairs: No steps to shop, but no easy access for tours.
Teas: Own coffee shop now open.
Groups: Please phone to book 45-minute tour; see an original Roman kiln and the factory video. Groups welcome to shop.
Transport: None.
Mail order: No.

Bretby Art Pottery (Est. 1883)

Swadlincote Road DE11 8DF
(01283) 217434   Closed

Large range of earthenware pottery made on the premises: ex-chainstore lamp bases, vases, money boxes, bathroom accessories, equestrian figures etc.

'Seconds, perfects and end of line chainstore items for sale. Prices from 50p to £100!'

About 5 miles south-east of Burton-on-Trent, just off the A50.
From the roundabout in Woodville (on the A50): take the A514 signposted to Swadlincote. The shop is about 1/4 mile on left.

Open: 6 days a week 10–4. Bank Holidays, including Good Friday.
Closed: Two weeks at Christmas.
Cards: Access, Visa.
Cars: Large car-park (also for coaches).
Toilets: Yes.
Wheelchairs: Easy access to part of medium-sized shop on two levels.
Teas: Own tea room for teas, coffee, cream teas etc.
Groups: Shopping groups welcome; only need to book first if they are large, and require food and drink.
Transport: Burton–Ashby buses pass the door.

Royal Worcester Porcelain

Severn Street WR1 2NF   *(01905) 23221*

Four shops for bone china tableware, porcelain, oven-to-table ware, wall plates, gifts and souvenirs. Best ware shop for current range. Large seconds shop, including *Royal Brierley* and *Dartington Crystal*. Clearance shop for whiteware. Souvenir shop. Also sell *Spode, Caithness Glass, Country Artists, Arthur Price* cutlery, *Pimpernel* mats.

'January and July sales. Don't miss the wonderful Dyson Perrins Museum of Worcester porcelain.'

In city centre off A44 (Evesham–Leominster road) by the cathedral.
On foot or by car: aim for the cathedral.
If the cathedral is on your left (you come from Evesham/Upton/M5): go left at traffic lights into Edgar Street towards imposing cathedral archway.*
If you are going towards Evesham/Upton, the cathedral is on right. This main road is dual-carriageway so you must double back; then go left at traffic lights into Edgar Street towards imposing cathedral archway.*
From M5 exit 7: follow city centre signs. At third traffic lights, go left into Edgar Street towards imposing cathedral archway.*
*****Turn left in front of arch into Severn Street; company 150 yds on left.**

Open: Mon–Sat 9–5.30; Bank Holidays.
Closed: Xmas & Boxing Days.
Cards: Access, Amex, Diners, Visa.
Cars: Own car–park £1.50 (£1 redeemable against purchases over £5).
Toilets: Yes.
Wheelchairs: Easy access to shops and museum.
Teas: Own restaurant. Parties to book in advance.
Tours: 45 minute tours Mon–Fri (not Bank Holidays) £3. Book in advance with Mrs Savage. Unsuitable for elderly and disabled; no children under 8. 'Connoisseurs Tour' (£9.50) at 10.15 and 13.15 Mon–Thur (give 2 days' notice). Coaches to phone.
Transport: Easy walk city centre.
Mail order: Yes.
Catalogue: Any package can be mailed world-wide.

Detective Work Using Wedgwood Plates

When the National Trust embarked on the restoration of the grounds of Wimpole Hall near Cambridge, they little thought that a dinner service in the Hermitage Museum in St Petersburg would help provide the key to authenticity!

In 1774 Josiah Wedgwood had been commisioned to produce a dinner service for Catherine the Great of Russia. The 952-piece service depicted 1244 parkland and garden scenes of English country houses. Among them were six plates showing views of Capability Brown's original design for Wimpole Hall. Features such a Chinese bridge, a gothic folly, trees and lakes, now gone, were clearly illustrated.

During the Soviet regime access to the dinner service was difficult, but recently a Russian photographer gained permission to photograph the six plates and then flew to London with the pictures in his hand baggage!

Brown's original plan for Wimpole Hall are lost so these plates and some wartime RAF reconnaissance photographs were crucial source materials. A lake lost in a storm when a dam burst in the 1930s, a bridge and part of a circular walkway are among the features restored in phase one, which was opened in March 1995.

So, the work of Josiah Wedgwood, 220 years old, was the unlikely means of restoring that of another 18th century master craftsman.

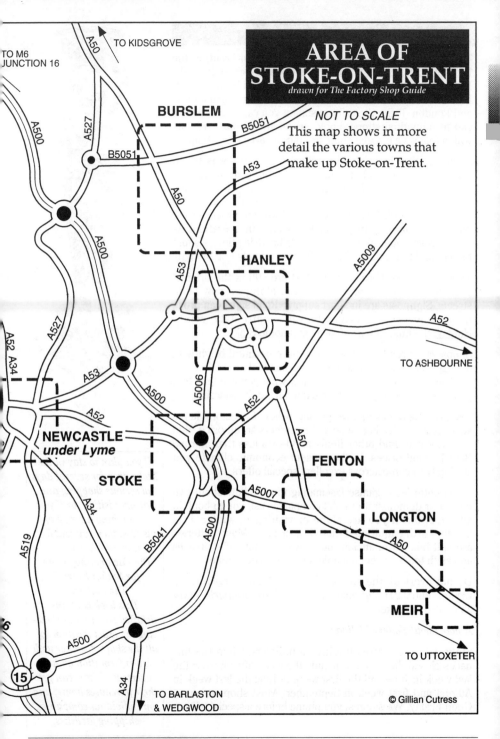

AREA OF STOKE-ON-TRENT
drawn for The Factory Shop Guide

NOT TO SCALE
This map shows in more detail the various towns that make up Stoke-on-Trent.

TO KIDSGROVE

TO M6
JUNCTION 16

BURSLEM

HANLEY

TO ASHBOURNE

NEWCASTLE
under Lyme

STOKE

FENTON

LONGTON

MEIR

TO UTTOXETER

TO BARLASTON
& WEDGWOOD

© Gillian Cutress

The area known as *The Potteries* in Stoke-on-Trent, in the heart of Staffordshire, is the mecca for chinaware enthusiasts. It takes about 3 1/2 hours by car or 2 hours by train from London to Stoke. Fast trains link Manchester, Birmingham and London. From the railway station you can take a bus or cab to individual shops. Look out for the *China Link* bus which follows a circular route around the area every hour.

Stoke-on-Trent is an agglomeration of six old towns which merge into one another. This can be confusing to visitors who may have a problem recognizing exactly where they are! Negotiating the busy roads takes longer than in the US or Australia, and heavy traffic slows down the process even more, especially as major roadworks are in operation. As most factory shops merit considerable browsing time, visitors tend to find that a day in The Potteries is simply not enough!

Many shops are hard to find. Most are still in the original potteries, off the beaten track and along narrow back streets. Signposts are in short supply. Road-signs can prove misleading, and road-signs to 'City Centre' take you to <u>Hanley</u>, the busiest part of town, and not to <u>Stoke</u>.

Shops vary greatly in style. Some have beautiful brightly lit displays; others have a less professional look and allow you to 'rummage'. You never quite know what you will find, but you *can* be certain you will have fun during the search!

Each company has its own pricing policy. Collectors' items such as character jugs tend to be perfects at full price. You can expect to find other items at 30–50% less than normal British retail prices. In the present economic climate you are likely to come across excellent special offers.

Some potteries organise fascinating tours (allow about two hours) or demonstrations. All companies ask you to book in advance; but if you are alone or visiting in winter, it is always worth enquiring if there is a vacancy. Many potteries are still housed in ancient buildings with lots of staircases and such tours are not suitable for the less-than-agile.

Do not overlook the shops for crystal items (*Staffordshire Crystal,* entry 21) and enamel (*Staffordshire Enamels,* entry 255), also in Stoke.

A note about Potters' Holidays

Stoke still recognizes traditional holidays, when the furnaces closed down. They include the week after Easter; the last week in June and the first week in July; the last week in August and first week in September. Most shops open on Good Friday. We suggest you phone before a special trip.

If you plan to stay in the Stoke area for several days of serious shopping and factory visiting, or if you are taking a group of visitors, then you will find it worthwhile to get The Factory Shop Guide for Staffordshire & The Potteries. This book contains detailed street maps showing the exact locations of all the shops, together with full information on how overseas visitors can get their purchases home, and on individual companies' shipping facilities.

Royal Doulton

Leek New Road ST2 7HR
(01782) 291700

Royal Doulton figures, character jugs, giftware, nursery items. Selection of seconds tableware and crystal.

'Good range of seconds in tableware.'

On the A53 north-west of Baddeley Green.
   From Leek on A53: pass left turn-off A5009 and Elf Petrol station on left. Pass the Victoria pub on the right then the shop is at the end of factory on the right.
   From Burslem: take A53 towards Leek. Enter Baddeley Green, pass large Partners (stationery) warehouse on left; shop is in next factory on left.

Open: Mon–Sat 9–5.30, Sun 10-4; Bank Holidays.
Closed: Christmas and New Year.
Cards: Access, Amex, Diners, Switch, Visa.
Cars: Car spaces next to shop. Coach parking available.
Toilets: Yes.
Wheelchairs: Easy access. No steps.
Teas: In town.
Groups: Coach parties welcome to shop, but for pottery tours and the Royal Doulton museum visit the Royal Doulton factory in Burslem.
Transport: PMT bus no. 218 (Hanley to Leek) every 30 minutes.
Mail order: Items gladly shipped.

Wedgwood Best

Wedgwood Visitor Centre ST12 9ES
(01782) 204218/204141

Perfect goods at normal retail prices – pottery and glass made by *Wedgwood Group* companies: fine china and glass tableware, vases, dishes, candlesticks, jewellery, figurines and florals etc.

'The shop for Wedgwood Group seconds is now in Fenton.'

In the countryside six miles south of Stoke.
   Full signposting from M6 exit 15 and from the A34 (also signs on other local roads). Keep following signs once you reach the Wedgwood Estate.

Open: All year Mon–Fri 9–4; Sat 10–5; Sun 10–4. Most Bank Holidays: phone to check.
Closed: Xmas,Box & NY Days.
Cards: Access,Amex,Diners,Visa
Cars: Large car and coach park.
Toilets: Yes, and for disabled.
Wheelchairs: Large Visitor Centre on one level.
Teas: Own restaurant.
Tours: Museum, cinema and demonstration area. £3.25 adults, £1.60 children, students, OAPs. £7.95 family ticket. Reduced for groups of 12+ (book in advance & mention this guide). Entrance to shop and refreshments free. Connoisseur Tour with own guide £7.25. Book in advance.
Transport: BR from Stafford or Stoke to Wedgwood Halt. Bus nos. 46, 47 from Hanley bus station. China Link stop 11.
Mail order: Yes incl. overseas. **Catalogue:** Free.

Crown Burslem Pottery
Unit C7, Sneyd Hill Ind Estate ST6 2EC
(01782) 839232

Planters, vases, lampbases, teapots, photo frames, money boxes.

'Seconds, perfects and chainstore items. Prices from 50p to £50; most items £1 to £5 (about 50% off retail prices).'

About 3/4 mile east of Burslem in Smallthorne.
From Burslem centre: at traffic lights near old town hall, turn east beside war memorial for Leek (B5051 leading to A53). Go along Moorland Road to roundabout at top of hill. Go right (BP station on right) then right at next two mini-roundabouts (Birchendale on right) into Sneyd Hill. After caravan centre, go right into industrial estate.*
From Hanley going north on A50: turn right at traffic lights at major junction on to A53. Pass Jet petrol on right; after 50 yds take left fork (opposite Focus Home Centre). Keep straight, go over traffic lights and uphill. Pass Rafferty Industrial Chimneys on left; go left into estate in front of 'A Plant' tool hire sign.*
*Clearly marked shop at back right.

Open: Mon–Thur 8.30–4.30; Fri 8.30–3.30; Sat 9–12.
Closed: Bank Holidays; one week at Easter; last week June and first week July; first week Sept; Christmas–New Year.
Cards: None.
Cars: Outside.
Toilets: Yes.
Wheelchairs: One step to small shop on ground floor.
Teas: Local cafés and pubs.
Groups: Shopping groups and free tours by arrangement with Mr Graham Jackson. Maximum 40 (but no children under 10).
Transport: Buses to Smallthorne then 5 minutes' walk. China Link stop 17 then 10 minutes' walk.
Mail order: No.
Catalogue: No.

W Moorcroft plc
Sandbach Road ST6 2DQ
(01782) 207943

Traditional *Moorcroft* designs: hand-made ornamental pottery, beautiful rich designs on vases, bowls, plates, table lamps etc.

NB This company does not sell tableware.

'Best quality and seconds. Prices to suit most budgets.'

Between Hanley and Burslem, just off the A53.
Via A50 coming north from Hanley or south from Burslem: at major junction with traffic lights, turn east on to the A53 towards Leek.*
Going north on A53 from A500/Newcastle towards Leek: cross major junction with A50 (traffic lights).*
*Pass Jet petrol on right. After 50 yds take left fork (opposite Focus Home Centre). After 150 yds turn left into well marked pottery with bottle kiln.

Open: Mon–Fri 10–5; Sat 9.30–4.30 including Bank Hols.
Closed: Christmas–New Year.
Cards: Access, Switch, Visa.
Cars: Own large car-park.
Toilets: Yes, and for disabled.
Wheelchairs: No step, wide door, spacious showroom.
Teas: In Hanley.
Groups: Welcome to wander round restored bottle oven to see how pottery was fired. Tours Mon, Wed, Thur at 11 & 2 and Fri at 11 by appointment only. Adults £1, children 50p. See the museum with beautiful examples of 'Old Moorcroft' – open daily, same times as shop. Coach parties welcome to shop.
Transport: Keele–Leek buses 218 and 24. Short walk from Hanley–Burslem bus routes. China Link stop 20.
Mail order: No.
Catalogue: Yes. £3.50

Moorland Pottery Ltd.

Chelsea Works, 72A Moorland Road ST6 1DY
(01782) 834631

Hand-decorated giftware, colourful spongeware with bold designs: jugs, dishes, egg cups, shaving mugs, large breakfast cups, jelly moulds etc. Also Staffordshire dogs and cats in traditional designs.

'Spongeware (decoration put on with sponge) is a revived 18th century Stoke speciality. 'Huntley Cottage' Art Deco tea set is the latest addition to our reproduction line. Most items are perfects; some seconds about 1/3 off perfects price. £2.50 for egg cup, £25 for pair of Staffordshire dogs. Design/modelling service.'

....

Go into Burslem centre on A50 (don't take new bypass). At traffic lights near the old town hall, turn east for Leek (towards A53) beside the war memorial. Go along Moorland Road for 200 yds to pottery on right. Drive through archway.

Coming into Burslem on B5051 from Leek: pass Burslem park on right, and the Enterprise Centre (by zebra crossing) on left; this former Royal Doulton pottery, with arch in centre, is 200 yds on left.

Open: Mon–Fri 10–4; Sat by appointment. Some Bank Holidays – please phone first.
Closed: Potters' Holidays; Christmas and New Year.
Cards: Access, Visa.
Cars: Drive in through arch to own car-park at rear.
Toilets: In Burslem.
Wheelchairs: No access: outside wooden staircase to attractive showroom on 1st floor.
Teas: Locally.
Groups: Shopping groups welcome; please telephone first. Unfortunately no tours of this pottery where Susie Cooper began her career.
Transport: Local buses; BR to Stoke or Longport. China Link stop 16 then 5 minutes' walk.
Mail order: Yes.
Catalogue: No.

Royal Doulton

Nile Street ST6 2AK
(01782) 292451

Royal Doulton figures, character jugs, giftware, nursery items. Also selection of seconds in tableware.

....

Close to Burslem centre, effectively behind large Solo supermarket on A50 on south side of Burslem.

Coming south on A50: go through Burslem, pass Solo supermarket on left. Go left at next mini-roundabout into Zion Street.*

Coming north on A50: go over first mini-roundabout in Burslem (left turn goes to M6/Newcastle); at second mini-roundabout go right into Zion Street.*

***At end, turn left into Nile Street – shop 200 yds on right.**

Open: Mon–Sat 9–5.30, Sun 10–4. Most Bank Holidays.
Closed: Phone to check Xmas.
Cards: Access, Amex, Diners, Visa, Switch.
Cars: Limited company parking. Car-park opposite.
Toilets: Yes, also for disabled.
Wheelchairs: Easy access.
Teas: Refreshments available.
Tours: Book in advance (Sandra Baddeley 01782 292434). 90 min. tours Mon–Thur at 10.30 & 2 . Adults £3; concessions £2.75; reductions for groups of 30+. Children must be 10+ (safety rules). Tours unsuitable for infirm. Sir Henry Doulton Gallery shows fascinating history of pottery: Mon–Fri 9–4.15. Free; no need to book.
Transport: 5 minutes' walk from bus station in Burslem centre. China Link stop 17.
Mail order: Items shipped.

Wade Ceramics

Greenhead Street ST6 4AF
(01782) 524218

Novelty tea pots, whimseys, lamps, figurines, money boxes, tea caddies, breakfast cups and saucers, casual dining ware. Range of collectable items.

'Mainly seconds but some firsts and discontinued lines. Collectable items. Teapots from £1.99. Overseas shipping service available.'

....

From the centre of Burslem: go north on the A50; pass Barratts Pottery on left, go left into Overhouse Street (in front of large car-wash) then left into Greenhead Street. Clearly visible shop is on right (go 40 yds further on to company car-park on right).

From the D-Road (A500): take A527 for Burslem. Go right at first roundabout, over next roundabout (Kwik Save on right) then turn left opposite Duke William and immediately after pelican crossing outside ornate NatWest bank on left into Westport Road. Take first right: after 100 yds turn left into Wade car-park.

Open: Mon–Fri 10–5.15; Sat 10–4.
Closed: Bank Holidays; Christmas–New Year.
Cards: Access, Amex, Eurocard, Visa.
Cars: Own car-park.
Toilets: Yes.
Wheelchairs: Five steps to sizeable shop on ground floor.
Teas: In Burslem.
Groups: Pre-booked shopping groups welcome.
Transport: Bus nos. 92, 94 from Newcastle; 22, 24 from Stoke. China Link stop 16.
Mail order: Yes.
Catalogue: Free. No restrictions. Regular limited editions directly from shop or by mail order.

Churchill Tableware

Crane Street ST1 6RC
(01782) 268870

Mugs, plates, cups, salt and pepper pots, dishes, meat platters, gravy boats, soup tureens, vegetable dishes, teapots and coffee pots in many patterns. Storage jars, soufflé dishes, glasses, cutlery, tablemats, foodsavers.

'Good quality seconds. Most prices 40-50% discounted from normal retail prices. Bargain basement items from 30p.'

....

North of Hanley, just off (east of) the A50 (Waterloo Road) near the large junction where the A50 crosses the A53.

Going north from Hanley on A50: go right about 100 yds before the traffic lights at this major junction, into small side road. *

Going south along the A50: at traffic lights, cross A53 then take the first little road left. *

From A500: come off dual carriageway at Etruria, follow A53 to Cobridge traffic lights and turn right on to A50 towards Hanley. Take first little road on left. *

*Follow large signs to shop just inside the large iron gates, to the left.

Open: Mon–Fri 9.30–4.30; Sat 9.30-4.
Closed: Bank Holidays; Christmas, Boxing and New Year's Days.
Cards: Access, Visa.
Cars: Own car-park.
Toilets: Nearest are in Hanley.
Wheelchairs: Easy access to large shop; four steps to bargain basement.
Teas: Hot drinks machine in shop.
Groups: Factory tours not available, but coach parties welcome to shop.
Transport: China Link stop 18. Main bus route to Hanley.
Mail order: Yes.
Catalogue: Yes. Only seconds quality by mail order.

Holland Studio Craft Ltd.
156 King Street ST4 3ER
(01782) 312113

Quality figurine manufacturer producing the world-famous *Enchantica* range of wizards and dragons, *Pigtails* novelty pigs, *Fables* unicorns and *Pegasus, Battlecry* warriors through the ages *Faeries, Sprogz,* whimsical frog characters, *E.J. Hog* (cute hedgehogs), *Littlegems* and *Dragongorge* all hand-made and hand-painted in adjacent factory.

'Best quality and seconds figurines always available at competitive prices. January and July sales.'

On the A50 between Fenton and Longton.

   Coming from Fenton towards Longton: pass the large Volvo car showroom on the right then turn left immediately after the pedestrian crossing and left again into company car-park.

   From Longton take the A50 north for Fenton/Hanley: pass The Miners Arms on right. After 150 yds, turn right before the pedestrian crossing and left into company car-park.

Open: Mon–Fri 9–5. Bank Holidays except Easter Monday.
Closed: Easter Week; last week in June and first week in July; late summer Bank Holiday week; Christmas–New Year period.
Cards: Access, Visa.
Cars: Own car-park.
Toilets: Yes.
Wheelchairs: Two steps to medium-sized shop.
Teas: In Hanley.
Groups: No factory tours. Groups welcome to shop; telephone call first appreciated.
Transport: Bus nos. 24, 28. China Link stop 6, then a few minutes' walk.
Mail order: No.

Royal Doulton
Victoria Road ST4 2PH
(01782) 291869

Wide selection of *Royal Doulton* figures, character jugs, dinner and tea services, giftware and nursery items. *Royal Albert* design a speciality.

'Good range of seconds tableware in Royal Doulton.'

Victoria Road is part of the A50 linking Hanley with Fenton/Longton.

   From Hanley: pass the Burmah petrol station on your right, then shop is 100 yds further along on the right, immediately after Audi showroom on right.

   From Longton: look out for the Audi showroom on left. The drive-in to this shop is immediately before Audi, opposite the Elf petrol station.

Open: Mon–Sat 9–5.30; Sun 10–4. Most Bank Holidays: phone to check.
Closed: Christmas and New Year.
Cards: Access, Amex, Diners, JCB, Switch, Visa.
Cars: Own car-park.
Toilets: No.
Wheelchairs: Three steps with handrail to fairly spacious shop.
Teas: In Hanley.
Groups: Groups of shoppers very welcome to this shop; prior phone call appreciated. For pottery tours, please see Royal Doulton entry under Stoke on Trent : Burslem.
Transport: Hanley/Longton buses.
Mail order: Items gladly shipped.

The Wedgwood Group Factory Shop

King Street ST4 3DQ
(01782) 316161

Large range of slightly sub-standard goods and ends of lines from *Wedgwood Group* companies, including *Coalport*, *Johnson Brothers* and *Masons*: fine china and glass tableware, vases, dishes, candlesticks, jewellery, figurines and florals etc. *Dartington Crystal* and *Arthur Price Cutlery* also available. *'All items at 25–50% off high street prices.'*

....

In the centre of Fenton.

From M6 exit 15: take the A500 towards Stoke. Turn right into City Road (A5007) to Fenton, joining the A50 at the traffic lights. The shop is about 1 mile on the right, opposite Elf petrol, next to The Potter pub.

From traffic lights in Longton: take A50 towards Fenton/Hanley; the shop is about 400 yds on the left.

Open: Mon–Sat 9–5; Sun 10–4. Most Bank Holidays – please phone to check.
Closed: Christmas and Boxing Days.
Cards: Access, Amex, Delta, Switch, Visa.
Cars: Large car-park.
Toilets: Yes.
Wheelchairs: No steps to huge shop.
Teas: Crown Hotel in Longton.
Groups: Groups of shoppers welcome – please ring shop to book in advance. For pottery demonstrations visit Wedgwood factory in Barlaston.
Transport: China Link stop 5.
Mail order: Yes.
Catalogue: Free. No seconds posted (seconds for personal customers only). Export.

Aynsley China

Unit N, Lewis's Arcade, The Potteries Shopping Centre
ST1 1PS
(01782) 204108

Fine bone china dinner and tea services; giftware, hand-made china flowers and hand-painted figurines; china-handled cutlery. Tablemats, textiles, trays and chopping boards to match best-selling designs. *Hammersley* giftware.

'We sell best quality and seconds in most items, plus bargains in perfect obsolete lines. Wedding gift service. Most patterns can be adapted for corporate use with initialling and company logo. Seconds at up to 50% off perfect price. Sales in January and July (phone for exact dates).'

....

In the large shopping precinct in the centre of Hanley (NOT Stoke).

From the M6 via the A500: aim for Stoke-on-Trent at first and then pick up signs to 'City Centre' and 'Potteries Shopping Centre'. You come to Hanley. Follow signs to the car-park. Shop is underneath Lewis's department store. Look for the Body Shop entrance: shop is on that level.

Open: Mon–Sat 9–5.30; *also Nov & Dec* late night Tues to 8. Bank Holidays.
Closed: Christmas, Boxing and New Year's Days.
Cards: Access, Visa.
Cars: Potteries Shopping Centre multi-storey car-park.
Toilets: In the Potteries Shopping Centre, including for disabled.
Wheelchairs: Easy access to Potteries Shopping Centre and this shop (no steps).
Teas: In the Potteries Shopping Centre.
Groups: Groups welcome to shop; no need to book.
Transport: BR to Stoke station, then any bus to Hanley. China Link stop 14.
Mail order: Yes.
Catalogue: Free. No restrictions.

Royal Worcester

Lewis's Arcade, Potteries Shopping Centre ST1 1PS
(01782) 204276

Porcelain, fine bone china and giftware. Also *Spode, Royal Brierley, Country Artists, Fo-Frame, Heredities, Cloverleaf* mats, *Pimpernel* mats, *Lakeland Studios, Paw Prints, Arthur Price Cutlery* and *Caithness Glass.*

'25% off high street prices.'

....

In the large shopping precinct in the centre of Hanley (NOT Stoke).

From M6 via the A500: aim for Stoke-on-Trent at first and then pick up signs to 'City Centre' and 'Potteries Shopping Centre'. You come to Hanley. Follow signs to the car-park. Shop is underneath Lewis's department store. Look for the Body Shop entrance: shop is on that level.

Open: Mon–Fri 9–5.30; Sat 9–6. Some Bank Holidays – please phone to check.
Closed: Christmas and Boxing Days.
Cards: All major cards.
Cars: Potteries Shopping Centre multi-storey car-park.
Toilets: In shopping centre.
Wheelchairs: No steps if you enter shop via Body Shop.
Teas: Café opposite, and various restaurants in shopping centre.
Groups: Shopping groups welcome.
Transport: Stoke-on-Trent BR station. All local buses stop outside shopping centre. China Link stop 14.
Mail order: Yes.
Catalogue: No. Any package, large or small, can be mailed world-wide.

St George's Fine Bone China Ltd.

77 Upper Huntbach Street ST1 2BV
(01782) 263709

Fine bone china: mugs, beakers, tankards, jugs, vases, plant pots, cachepots, loving cups, miniature cups and saucers, table lamps, thimbles, flower arrangements, even bone china greetings cards! Tea and dinner ware. Items can be personalised with names or messages.

'Prices from 50p–£30. Main store and mail order rejects available.'

....

In Hanley centre: easy to walk from the pedestrian area.

By car: go clockwise round Hanley to be on the correct side of the dual carriageway.

Coming south on A50 from Burslem: go to first major roundabout and turn left so that you go clockwise round Hanley; go uphill, underneath bridge and turn left after first and immediately before second pedestrian lights. Take first left (Garth Street) to company car-park.

Open: Mon–Fri 9–5.30; Sat 9–2; Most Bank Holidays, including Good Friday.
Closed: Easter Monday; Christmas–New Year.
Cards: Access, Visa.
Cars: Own car-park. If you make a purchase you may leave your car here while you do other shopping! (Ideal location for Hanley town centre.)
Toilets: In town centre.
Wheelchairs: One small step, fairly small compact shop.
Teas: In Hanley.
Tours: Pre-arranged for groups of at least 10. Please contact Mr Duncalf, mentioning this book. Shopping groups welcome too – phone first.
Transport: Close to Hanley bus station. China Link stop 19.
Mail order: Yes.
Catalogue: No. No restrictions on items sent.

Aynsley China

Sutherland Road ST3 1HR
(01782) 593536

Bests and seconds in fine bone china dinner and tea services.
Giftware – vases, hand-made china flowers, china-handled
cutlery. Hand-painted figurines and animal sculptures.
Textiles, trays, tablemats and chopping boards to match
best-selling patterns.

'Best quality and seconds in most items, plus bargains in perfect
obsolete lines. Wedding gift service. Most patterns can be
adapted for corporate use with initialling and company logo.
Seconds at up to 50% off perfect price. Sales in January and
July (phone for exact dates).'

....

In Sutherland Road, one street behind former location on A50.

Coming north into Longton on A50: go over pedestrian crossing,
turn right in front of Shire's Bathrooms into Meir Hay Road
(which becomes Sutherland Road). Clearly marked shop is 1/2
mile on right.

Coming south on A50 from Fenton: go under railway bridge
into the Longton one-way system; turn left at traffic lights in
front of Lloyds Bank then take first right (Sutherland Road).
Shop 250 yds on left.

Open: Mon–Sat 9–5.30.
Also Sundays 10–4 all year.
Bank Holidays.
Closed: Christmas, Boxing
and New Year's Days.
Cards: Access, Amex, Visa.
Cars: Own coach and car-park.
Toilets: Yes, and for disabled.
Wheelchairs: Ramp to
spacious shop.
Teas: Refreshments available.
Groups: Shopping groups
welcome.
Transport: Five minutes'
walk to Longton bus and train
stations. China Link stop.
Mail order: Yes.
Catalogue: Yes. Free.
Seconds and bests sent.

Ceramic World

31 Uttoxeter Road ST3 1NY
(01782) 593433

Decorative wall plaques (humourous, flowers, animals,
landscapes, works of art, Royal family, coal mining etc).
Special commissions – personalised china items, christening mugs, anniversary plates, etc. Plant pots, vases,
jardinières. Range of mugs, figures, military collectibles,
local souvenirs, some hand-painted.

'Factory shop representing "small" manufacturers. Limited
editions, exclusive designs unavailable elsewhere. £1–£300
price range with plaques at £2–£15. Best and second qualities.
Your own photos can be transfered on to china. January sale.'

....

Just south of Longton town centre, on Uttoxeter Road (A50)
opposite the Gladstone Pottery Museum.

From Longton: take A50 south for Uttoxeter, following signs to
Gladstone Museum. After you emerge from one-way system, the
shop (formerly Aynsley) is on left.

From Uttoxeter/Meir coming north on A50: pass the Burmah
petrol station on left and look for this shop on the right as you
go downhill into Longton.

Open: Mon–Fri 10–5;
Sat 10–4. Some Bank Holidays
– please phone to check.
Closed: Christmas–New Year.
Cards: Access, Amex,
Eurocard, Switch and other
debit cards, Visa.
Cars: In side streets and
Longton car-park.
Toilets: In Longton.
Wheelchairs: One step into
shop; one inside.
Teas: Crown Hotel; Gladstone
Museum in summer; oatcake
shop next door.
Groups: Phone call first to
Lynne Lockett appreciated.
Demonstrations in the shop
and factory.
Transport: China Link stop 7.
Mail order: Yes.
Catalogue: No. Mail order
service mainly for wall plaques.
UK only.

Gladstone Pottery Museum

Uttoxeter Road ST3 1PQ
(01782) 319232

Newly refurbished shop stocking unique *Master Potter Collection* by local manufacturers. Hand-thrown gardenware. Extensive range of local studio pottery. High class gifts and souvenirs in a wide price range. Books, greetings cards, posters and postcards.

'Complete Victorian museum with demonstrations giving vivid insight into local life – history of The Potteries, traditions, skills and conditions under which people worked and lived. Allow more than two hours.'

....

This museum, on the east side of Longton centre, is signposted from various directions.

If you leave the Longton one-way system on the A50 for Uttoxeter: you see the distinctive bottle ovens on the right after about 100 yards. Go right in front of museum for car-park on left.

If you come west from Uttoxeter towards Longton on A50: it is more difficult to see. Go downhill almost into Longton. Turn left after bottle ovens on left.

Open: 7 days a week 10–5.
Closed: Christmas, phone for details.
Cards: Access, Visa.
Cars: Coach and car-park.
Toilets: Yes, and for disabled.
Wheelchairs: Ramp; shop all on one level. Difficult for wheelchairs to tour all parts of museum.
Teas: Restaurant open to shop and museum visitors.
Tours: Museum: adults £3.75; concessions £2.90; children £2.25; family ticket £10. Reductions for parties booked in advance. One child free with each paying adult mentioning this book. Entrance to shop and restaurant is free.
Transport: 150 yds from Longton bus station. China Link stops 8, 10.
Mail order: No.

M R Hadida Ltd.

Old Foley Pottery, King Street ST4 3DG
(01782) 599544

Co-ordinating china bathroom accessories. Traditional jugs and bowls and wide selection of giftware. Some of the *Hadida* fabric collection.

'Seconds and best ware.'

....

On the A50, between Longton and Fenton.

From the Fenton direction: pass the Elf station on the left, then turn right after about 50 yds, immediately after the traffic island.

From Longton: take A50 for Fenton. Look for Evans Halshaw showroom on right. Continue for 50 yds, then turn left just before traffic island. Go in through large, green iron gates; park in front of shop.

Open: Mon–Sat 9–4.30.
Closed: Bank Holidays; Christmas–New Year.
Cards: Visa.
Cars: Factory car-park.
Toilets: Yes.
Wheelchairs: Two steps.
Teas: Local cafés and pubs.
Groups: No.
Transport: Five minutes from station; China Link stop 6.
Mail order: No.

Hudson & Middleton Ltd.

Sutherland Works, Normacot Road ST3 1PR
(01782) 319256

Beakers, tea and coffee cups and saucers; plaques; coasters, trays, giftware etc all in fine bone china. Specialise in fine decorative designs such as farm animals.

'Mostly seconds. Beakers from £1.25–£1.95, plaques £4.50 up, plates (5, 8, 10 inch) 75p–£1.25; "bargain basket" mugs 50p and plaques £2.25.'

....

A short way south-east of town centre.
  From Uttoxeter coming into Longton on A50: go downhill almost into Longton one-way system. Immediately after Gladstone Pottery Museum on left, go left into Chadwick Road. *
  From other directions: best to get on to Longton one-way system then exit on to A50 for Uttoxeter, following signs to Gladstone Pottery Museum. Go right in front of museum into Chadwick Street. *
  *Go left at next cross-roads; continue along Normacot Road. Clearly visible shop is several hundred yards on right, in large Victorian pottery (blue paintwork), opposite large stone church on left.

Open: Mon–Thur 9–5; Fri 9–1.
Closed: Bank Holidays; Potters' Holidays; Christmas–New Year.
Cards: Access, Eurocard, Mastercard, Visa.
Cars: Outside, and behind pottery.
Toilets: Yes.
Wheelchairs: One tiny step to small shop.
Teas: Hot drinks machine. Local cafés and pubs.
Groups: No pottery tours but coaches and shopping groups welcome – please phone receptionist first.
Transport: 5–10 minutes' walk from bus station. China Link stop 10.
Mail order: No.

John Beswick

Barford Street ST3 2JR
(01782) 291237

John Beswick animal sculptures. Also *Royal Doulton* figures, character jugs, nursery and giftware. Selection of seconds in tableware.

....

A small one-way street leading INTO The Strand, part of the one-way system encircling Longton. As there is no entry directly into Barford Street, continue around the one-way system (which you can't avoid once you are in Longton!) and take next left, Gold Street. Take two more left turns – you are in Barford Street, with shop clearly visible on right.

Open: Mon–Fri 9–4.30. Might open Sat before Xmas & Easter
Closed: Easter week, last week June (and previous Thur, Fri) and first week July; late Summer Bank Holiday week (and previous Thur, Fri); Christmas–New Year.
Cards: Access, Amex, Diners, Switch, Visa.
Cars: Company car-park in front of shop.
Toilets: In shopping precinct.
Wheelchairs: Five large steps, so access not really possible to medium sized shop.
Teas: Local pubs, cafés.
Groups: Arrange in advance mentioning this book. Tours (£2.50) last 1.5 hrs. Mon–Thur at 10.15 and 2. Fri 10.15 and 2.
Transport: 5 minutes' walk from Longton bus and train stations. China Link stop 12.
Mail order: Yes. Catalogue. Phone 01782 292292.

Portmeirion Potteries Ltd.
Sylvan Works, Normacot Road ST3 1PV
(01782) 326412

Large range of seconds at significantly reduced prices – tableware, cookware, vases, plant pots, porcelain jugs, trays, chopping boards and textiles. Small supply of first quality glassware, porcelain handled cutlery, porcelain on steel cookware, place mats.

'Please phone for exact dates of January and July sales.'

....

A short way south-east of the town centre.

From Longton: go along the A50 and turn right into Chadwick Street in front of Gladstone Pottery Museum.*

From Uttoxeter on A50: go north-west for Longton. As you go downhill into Longton pass the Gladstone Pottery Museum on the left then go left into Chadwick Street.*

From all other directions: aim for Longton, go clockwise round the one-way system – turn off for A50 to Uttoxeter following sign for Gladstone Pottery Museum; go right in front of it into Chadwick Street.*

*Turn left at cross-roads: shop is on right.

Open: Mon-Fri (incl. Good Friday) 9.30–5; Sat 9.30–3.
Closed: Bank Holidays; Christmas–New Year. Please ring to confirm exact dates.
Cards: Access, Amex, Visa, Switch.
Cars: Factory car-park.
Toilets: In Longton centre.
Wheelchairs: Ramp to sizeable shop.
Teas: Local hotels and cafés.
Groups: No pottery tours but parties welcome to shop – please contact Mrs Doreen Bath, mentioning this Guide.
Transport: Near Longton BR and bus stations. China Link stops 7 and 11.
Mail order: Yes.
Catalogue: No. No restrictions. Will post throughout the UK and overseas.

Queen's Fine Bone China Ltd.
Whieldon Road ST4 4ST
(01782) 745899

Fine bone china tableware and giftware. China mugs galore. Plaques, collectors' cups and saucers. *Dartington Crystal.* Also *Pimpernel* place mats, coasters and trays at reduced prices and *Cloverleaf* chopping boards.

'At least 40% savings. Perfect quality items available to order.'

....

NB This shop has moved from Longton to Stoke.
It is now just off (east of) the A500, a short way south-east of Stoke. It is reached from the southbound carriageway of A500.

Going south on the A500: go straight at the Stoke round-about (where City Road, A5007 goes left) and after a short distance take the left slip road (Whieldon Road).*

Going north on the A500: you need to double back at the Stoke roundabout then take the slip road for Whieldon Road.*

*The factory and shop are on the right at the end of the slip road: turn sharp right and enter through the security barrier.

If you come west along Whieldon Road: this is the last building on the left before you go under the A500.

Open: Mon–Sat 9.30–5. Bank Holidays (including Good Friday and Easter Mon) 10–4.
Closed: Few days at Christmas; New Year's Day.
Cards: Access, Amex, Switch, Visa.
Cars: In front of shop.
Toilets: Yes, including for the disabled.
Wheelchairs: No steps, new large shop.
Teas: In Stoke and Hanley.
Tours: No pottery tours but coaches welcome to shop if booked. Mention this guide.
Transport: 15 minutes'walk to train station. Bus nos. 45, 47.
Mail order: Yes.
Catalogue: Free leaflet when available. Mail seconds but do not accept returns.

Royal Grafton Fine Bone China

Marlborough Road ST3 1EE
(01782) 599667

English bone china tableware, giftware and collectors' items incuding wall plaques; dinner, tea and coffee sets; mugs, vases, trinket boxes etc.

'All goods are slight seconds or discontinued lines. All at excellent discounted prices.'

....

1/3 mile north-west of Longton centre, in quiet road parallel to (and north of) A50.

From Hanley coming south-east on the A50 into Longton: pass the Portland House Hotel on your left then immediately turn left into March Road.*

From the south and Longton town centre: because of one-way roads, probably easiest to go through Longton then head along King Street (A50) towards Fenton/Hanley for short distance. Turn right in front of the Portland House Hotel into March Road.*

*Follow the road round; at T-junction turn right into Marlborough Road. Pottery is on left, clearly signed.

Open: Mon–Fri 9–4.30; Sat 9–3. Good Friday; Bank Holidays and Potters' Holidays.
Closed: Christmas–New Year.
Cards: Access, Amex, Diners, Visa.
Cars: Easy parking in pottery grounds.
Toilets: Please ask.
Wheelchairs: No steps to sizeable shop.
Teas: Coke machine in shop. Hotels and coffee shops in Longton.
Groups: Groups welcome.
Transport: Near bus and train stations. China Link stop 7.
Mail order: Yes.
Catalogue: Free. Will send anywhere in the world by air or sea.

Salisbury China

Uttoxeter Road ST3 1DA
(01782) 319926/333466

Bone china dinner and tea ware, mugs, trinkets such as ginger jars, round boxes. Vases, jardinières. *Duchess* range of bone china tableware – plates, cereal bowls etc.

'Mostly seconds, but also some perfects.'

....

On the A50, a short way south of Longton centre.

From Longton: head for Uttoxeter on A50 and look for the Gladstone Pottery Museum on the right; this small shop is about 50 yds past, on the left.

Coming towards Longton on A50: pass the Burmah petrol station on the left, then look for this small shop in the parade of shops on the right.

Open: Mon–Sat 10.30–4. Good Friday and most Bank Holidays.
Closed: Potters' Holidays; Easter week; Christmas–New Year.
Cards: No.
Cars: In Chadwick Road, across the street.
Toilets: No.
Wheelchairs: One small step to fairly small compact shop.
Teas: Local cafés.
Groups: Parties welcome to shop – please telephone Jean Carnall first.
Transport: Easy walk to bus and BR stations. China Link stop 8.

Sovereign Ceramics

Sovereign House, Warren Street ST3 1QB
(01782) 324688

Hand-painted ceramics from Portugal and Italy including vases, wall plaques, jugs, bowls, baskets, cachepots, trays, umbrella stands, and many other functional and decorative gift lines.

'Seconds and discontinued lines as well as best quality. Prices from £2. We are a leading importer of these goods; we do not manufacture ourselves.'

South of Longton centre, just off the A50.

  From Longton centre: take A50 south towards Uttoxeter, pass Gladstone Museum. After another 600 yds pass Anglo petrol station on right then take first right. Shop in first building on left.

  Coming north into Longton on Uttoxeter Road (A50): pass Crownford China on right then take third left in front of WT Lighting. Shop is in first building on left.

Open: Mon–Fri 9.30–5.
Closed: Bank Holidays; week before Christmas–New Year, phone to check.
Cards: Access, Visa.
Cars: Own car-park.
Toilets: In shopping precinct.
Wheelchairs: No steps. Compact shop.
Teas: In Longton.
Groups: Groups welcome.
Transport: 10 minutes from Longton bus and BR stations.
Mail order: No.

Staffordshire Tableware
Uttoxeter Road ST3 7AB
(01782) 315251 [week] 311433 [Sat]

Large selection of mugs. 18, 20 and 30-piece earthenware dinner sets, plus open stock plates, cups, saucers, tea and coffee pots etc. Crystal glass. Porcelain gift items.

'Seconds with additional permanent special offers. January sale.'
....

Conspicuous well-signed shop in large factory premises in Whittle Road, just off A50 (Uttoxeter Road) about 2 miles south-east of Longton. New shop is on same factory site, 200 yds away.

From Longton: watch out for Little Chef on the left; the company is almost opposite, on the right. Continue to roundabout then double back and take first left, Whittle Road. Shop is on left.

From Uttoxeter: take A50, mostly dual carriageway. As you come towards Meir go over the roundabout, pass company on left. After pedestrian lights go left into Whittle Road. Shop on left.

Open: Mon–Fri 9.30–5; Sat 9.30–4.30. Some Bank Holidays including Good Friday, Easter Monday. Potters' Holidays.
Closed: Christmas–New Year.
Cards: Access, Visa.
Cars: Large customer car-park.
Toilets: Yes, and for disabled.
Wheelchairs: Ramp into new, larger shop.
Teas: Hot drinks machine; Little Chef opposite.
Groups: No pottery tours but coaches welcome to shop. Please book with Keith Wilshaw, Shop Manager.
Transport: Bus stop outside shop. Blythe/Bridge/ Uttoxeter/Cheadle service.
Mail order: No.
Catalogue: No. Customer Services Department where odd stock (no seconds) can be purchased.

Blakeney Pottery Ltd.
Wolfe Street ST4 4DA
(01782) 47244

Range of planters, jardinières and traditional decorative ware such as ewers and bowls in plain glazes and unique flow blue underglaze printed patterns.

'High quality seconds and discontinued lines at very reasonable prices.'
....

From M6 exit 15, Trent Vale, A34: take B5041 for Stoke. In Stoke, look for Minton on right by traffic lights. Blakeney is behind Minton. Either park here and walk; or go right round Stoke one-way system.*

From the A500: follow signs to Stoke.*

*Keep going clockwise round large one-way system. Pass classical town hall on right and large church with churchyard on left; go clockwise, over staggered crossing with lights. Pass another large churchyard on left, keep going clockwise, over pedestrian lights then take small road left, Wolfe Street – almost opposite Job Centre and Fleming Road pay-&-display car-park. (NB Company is on left before Minton.)

Open: Mon–Thur 9–4.30; Fri 9–3.30; late Spring Bank Holiday.
Closed: Bank Holidays; Potters' Holidays; Christmas–New Year.
Cards: None.
Cars: In factory yard.
Toilets: Nearest toilets 50 yds in the market square.
Wheelchairs: One small step to fairly small showroom.
Teas: In Stoke.
Groups: No pottery tours, but groups welcome to shop if they phone first.
Transport: Any bus to Stoke (NOT Hanley). Stoke station 20 minutes' walk. China Link stop 3.
Mail order: No.

Carlton House

Copeland Street ST4 1PU
(01782) 745464   *Closed*

Large range of *Royal Winton* seconds. *Hinchcliffe* and *Barber* tableware and giftware in spongeware by *Saville*. *Grindley Pottery* and *Hornsea Pottery* seconds. Wide selection of planters, vases, jardinières and hand-decorated giftware in earthenware; china beakers. Also lamps and shades, glassware etc.

'High-quality seconds, production trials, overruns and discontinued ranges. About 45% reduction on usual prices. Sales in January, Easter, August and November.'

Copeland Street is easily visible from, and parallel to, the A500.
   Going south on A500: turn right at the first roundabout for 'Stoke' and stay in the left lane*.
   Going north on the A500: at the second roundabout signposted 'Stoke' turn left; stay in left lane. *
   *Follow the curving road for 300 yds. Turn left at the first T-junction and follow the road round to the right. Clearly marked renovated pottery is on the right.

Open: Mon–Sat 10–5.
Closed: Christmas, Boxing and New Year's Days and Potters' Holidays.
Cards: Access, Visa, Switch.
Cars: In cul-de-sac just before large old pottery, or turn right into company's own car-park past shop.
Toilets: Yes.
Wheelchairs: Easy access to large shop.
Teas: Light refreshments available.
Groups: No pottery tours but groups welcome to shop. Please book with Mr Paul West.
Transport: BR to Stoke station then 10 minutes' walk; 5 minutes' walk from Stoke centre. China Link stop 4.
Mail order: Yes.
Catalogue: No.

Minton

London Road ST4 7QE
(01782) 292121

Minton bone china dinner and tea services (available as sets and tea services), best quality and seconds merchandise. Also best quality *Royal Doulton* figures, character jugs, nursery and giftware.

In the centre of Stoke.
   From M6 exit 15, Trent Vale, A34: take B5041 for Stoke. In Stoke, look for Minton on right by traffic lights. Either park here and walk across; or go right round Stoke one-way system. *
   From the A500: follow signs to Stoke.*
   *Keep going clockwise. Pass the classical town hall on the right and large church with churchyard on your left; keep going clockwise, and over the staggered crossing with lights. Pass another large churchyard on the left, go clockwise then over the pedestrian lights. Pass the Job Centre on right then this clearly marked pottery is on left, before the traffic lights.

Open: Mon–Sat 9–5.30. Good Friday.
Closed: Bank Holidays; Christmas, Boxing and New Year's Days.
Cards: Access, Diners, Visa.
Cars: Town car-parks & visitors' car-park in Fleming Road.
Toilets: No.
Wheelchairs: One step to medium sized shop.
Teas: A limited selection of cafés in Stoke.
Groups: Unique Minton Museum (free) open Mon–Fri 9–1 and 1.45–4.30. No need to book.
Transport: Any bus to Stoke (NOT Hanley). Stoke BR station 20 minutes' walk. China Link stop 3.
Mail order: Items gladly shipped.

Portmeirion Seconds Shop

London Road ST4 7QQ
(01782) 411756

Large range of seconds at significantly reduced prices – tableware, cookware, vases, plant pots, porcelain jugs, trays, chopping boards, and textiles. First quality glassware, porcelain handled cutlery, porcelain on steel cookware, place mats.

'Seconds pottery, first quality porcelain on steel cookware and place mats.'

....

About 1/4 mile outside Stoke centre in large converted red-brick chapel on B5041 (going south-west to Trent Vale, M6, Stafford).

From M6 exit 15, Trent Vale and A34: go along the B5041 towards Stoke. Shop is on left, opposite Elf services.

From Stoke: go round the one-way system! By Minton on left, turn left at T-junction traffic lights. After 1/4 mile, the shop is on right, just past Iceland on left and almost opposite Elf service garage.

Open: Mon–Fri 9.15–5.15; Sat 9.15–3.30. Good Friday; Potters' Holidays.
Closed: Bank Hols; Xmas–NY.
Cards: Amex, Mastercard, Switch, Visa.
Cars: Factory car-park (not Sat afternoon); otherwise nearby.
Toilets: Yes.
Wheelchairs: Small steps at entrance to very large shop.
Teas: In Stoke shopping centre.
Tours: No tours. Parties welcome to shop, 1 coach at a time. Phone Mrs Hobson in advance. Large shop and warehouse but allow extra time for a group.
Transport: 5 mins walk from Stoke. Bus 22 from Hanley stops outside; or bus opp. Stoke BR to Glebe St Stoke, then short walk. China Link 3 (Minton) or 4 (Spode) then 5 mins walk.
Mail order: UK & overseas. Leaflets. No restrictions. Mastercard & Visa taken.

Spode

Church Street ST4 1BX
(01782) 744011

Wide range of slightly imperfect fine bone china, and earthenware, in tableware (in sets or as individual pieces) and giftware.

'Firsts and seconds at bargain prices on sale. Sales in January and July. For special commissions contact Stephen Riley.'

....

In the centre of Stoke.

From the A500: follow signs to Stoke and keep going clock-wise, right round town. At T-junction traffic lights (Minton on left), go right into London Road; at far end, turn left into Church Street: well marked Spode entrance is shortly on the right, through large gates (take care in crossing the lane for buses which come from the opposite direction). Brown tourist signs make it easier to find.

From Newcastle: take A52 downhill into Stoke; you have to turn left into the one-way system. Shortly bear right into Elenora Street then turn right into Spode factory grounds.

Open: Mon–Sat 9–5; Sun 10–4. Bank Holidays.
Closed: Christmas, Boxing and New Year's Days.
Cards: Access, Amex, Visa.
Cars: Free parking on site.
Toilets: Yes.
Wheelchairs: Easy access.
Teas: Blue Italian restaurant on site for hot and cold snacks.
Groups: Tours by prior arrangement, weekdays only. Please book in advance with tours organiser (01782 744011). Admission includes visitor centre, factory tour and museum: adults £3.50; children 11+; concessions £1.75. Limited access for the disabled. Children 11+ only. Connoisseur's Tour by prior arrangement £6.
Transport: Short walk from main Stoke bus stop around corner. China Link stop 4.
Mail order: Yes, free catalogue.

Garden & Terracotta Products

As regular readers of *The Factory Shop Guide* will already be aware, garden pots (and dress fabrics) are the author's weakness. The regiment of terracotta lions' heads (from Rookes Pottery) which guard the patio has been augmented this year with two recruits. New acquisitions include giant strawberry pots from Henry Watson's Potteries, big tubs from Suffolk Potteries, a large urn from Haddonstone, wall planters from Weston Mill and various gardening accessories from LBS Polythene. Readers will now understand why we say that we have problems when faced with so many temptations in factory shops ... however, we have not yet succumbed to the impressive finials from Kemptown Terracotta or the large range of pots available at Brannams. Two interesting new shops are Wetheriggs Pottery near Penrith, the only steam-powered pottery in the country, and Blackwells in Swindon where you can buy house plant arrangements designed for high street stores at greatly reduced prices .

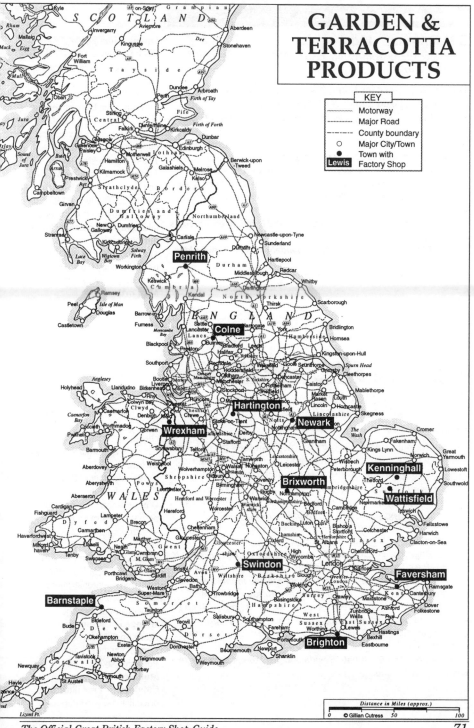

GARDEN & TERRACOTTA PRODUCTS

KEY

~~	Motorway
··········	Major Road
—·—·—	County boundary
○	Major City/Town
●	Town with
Lewis	Factory Shop

C H Brannam Ltd.
Roundswell Industrial Estate EX31 3NK
(01271) 43035

Terracotta pottery for home (kitchen and table) and garden in all sizes. Glazed and decorated stoneware.

'North Devon's oldest tourist attraction. Factory seconds shop with highly competitive prices.'

South of town off B3232 and new bypass.

From town centre, Braunton via A361 and Lynton via A39: follow signs to Bideford/Torrington. Pass large Sainsbury's, go left at next roundabout, following brown signs to Brannam's Pottery.

From the east on A361 and south on A377: follow brown signs to pottery as you reach bypass.

From Bideford on A39: go left at roundabout with brown signs to pottery.

Once in estate go right up to pottery.

Open: Mon–Sat 9–5; Bank Holidays.
Closed: Christmas–New Year.
Cards: Access, Visa.
Cars: Own large car-park.
Toilets: Yes; baby changing room.
Wheelchairs: Easy access including to restaurant.
Teas: Own restaurant.
Tours: Pottery tours Mon–Fri and Bank Holidays 9–4.15. £3 adults, £2.50 OAPs, £1.95 children. Throw your own pot to take away! Tour also includes museum visit.
Transport: Free bus service from Barnstaple town centre to Sainsburys then short walk.
Mail order: No.

Kemptown Terracotta
Unit 8, 5 Arundel Road BN2 5TF
(01273) 676603

Terracotta pots (up to 20" high), urns, 'chimney pots', tubs – some with green glazed rims – and saucers. Unusual ridge tiles with large flying dragons. Guaranteed frost-proof.

'Perfects and seconds at reduced prices – price depends on extent of flaw but often half price. Small personal business so please phone first if you are making special journey.'

1.5 miles east of Brighton central pier.

From Brighton: go east on cliff road (Marine Parade) almost to marina. Pass large Georgian crescent set back from road with overgrown private park in front; look for railings in middle of road (start of dual carriageway): go left here into Arundel Road.*

From Newhaven via Marine Drive: go left to 'Brighton Marina Village & Kemptown'; after underpass go right to Kemptown; after gasometer go left at lights; go left at next crossing into Arundel Road.*

*Park near The Bush pub. Beside pub go through archway to workshop at far end.

Open: Mon–Sat 9–6; *also April–end August* Sun 10–5; Bank Holidays. Always best to check.
Closed: Christmas–New Year.
Cards: No.
Cars: In Arundel Road.
Toilets: Locally.
Wheelchairs: No access: pottery upstairs on first floor; showroom up further (sturdy!) ladder.
Teas: Pub and café nearby. Lots of places in Brighton.
Groups: Demonstrations gladly given to groups of up to 12 people; but must be arranged in advance.
Transport: Buses to Kemptown, nos. 1 and 38C. Volksrailway on seafront.
Mail order: Yes.
Catalogue: Free illustrated price list. No seconds sent.

Haddonstone Ltd.

NN6 9BY
(01604) 882300

Top quality stone garden urns, statues, troughs, seats, sundials, fountains, bird baths, copings, columns etc. Items on sale vary from day to day.
'Seconds and slightly faulty items sold at reduced prices.'

Brixworth is about nine miles north of Northampton.
   The company is at northern end of village, just off A508 (Market Harborough–Northampton road).
   Going south on A508 from Market Harborough: at the first roundabout, go right for Brixworth. *
   Going north on A508 from Northampton: do not go left at first roundabout for Brixworth but go left at next roundabout. *
   ***Take second right, pass Burmah petrol station on left, go to far end and turn right into company. Seconds area is straight ahead.**

Open: Mon–Fri 7.30–4.30. Please see local press for occasional weekend sales.
Closed: Bank Holidays; Christmas–New Year.
Cards: Access, Visa.
Cars: Own car-park. Help with loading available.
Toilets: No.
Wheelchairs: Easy access to open air display area.
Teas: Local pubs.
Groups: No.
Transport: Difficult.
Mail order: Yes. No seconds. Delivery to any location in mainland UK by own transport (charge based on weight and distance).
Catalogue: Colour brochures: £5 complete (108-page); £3 garden ornaments.

LBS Polythene/Gardeners' Choice

Cottontree Lane BB8 7BW
(01282) 861816

Almost anything made of polythene in greatly expanded gardening department – seed trays, cloches, flower pots, gifts, compost, hanging baskets, artificial and dried flowers, heaters, hose pipes, incinerators, ornaments, patio and pond equipment, tools, troughs, waterbutts etc.
'We are the largest horticultural polythene products distributors in the country. 5% discount off brochure prices if you collect goods yourself.'

At the south-east end of town.
   From town centre, M65 and A561: aim for Keighley. Cross major roundabout; immediately after this, turn right on to B6250 to Trawden. *
   From Keighley: turn left on to B6250 just before big roundabout at beginning of town. *
   ***Go down to bottom of valley: you shortly see LBS straight ahead in right hand bend. Go through gates: shop is behind this building.**

Open: Mon–Fri 9–5; Sat 9–4; Sun and Bank Holidays 10–4.
Closed: Christmas and New Year's Days.
Cards: Access, Amex, Visa.
Cars: Own car-park.
Toilets: Yes, and for disabled.
Wheelchairs: No steps, easy access.
Teas: In town.
Groups: Groups and coaches welcome by appointment with Mr Wolfenden.
Transport: Bus no. 21 Colne/Trawden.
Mail order: Yes.
Catalogue: £1. No restrictions.

Rookes Pottery

SK17 0AN
(01298) 84650

Great range of terracotta garden pots and planters. All sizes and original shapes including heads (lions and humans!), cockerels, cats, dogs. Hanging wall pots. Bread crocks and mugs.

'Seconds always available. Items gladly made to order.'

In centre of this small attractive village with a duck pond, about 10 miles from Buxton, Ashbourne and Leek.

Coming into Hartington on B5054 from Warslow and the south: look for clearly marked pottery on right as you come into village.

From Buxton/Bakewell (A515) or Matlock (A5012): go into village then bear left on to B5054 for Warslow. Clearly marked pottery is shortly on left.

Open: Mon–Fri 8–5; Sat 10–5; Sun and Bank Holidays 11–5.
Closed: Christmas–New Year.
Cards: Access, Switch, Visa.
Cars: In front of pottery, and in village.
Toilets: Next to pottery, including for disabled.
Wheelchairs: Excellent access to sales area and workshop.
Teas: Several tea rooms in this attractive small village.
Tours: Individuals free to look round; parties welcome to shop, but must phone first if they wish to see potters.
Transport: Limited bus services from Buxton and Ashbourne.
Mail order: No.

Suffolk Potteries

Lopham Road NR16 2DT
(01379) 687424

Wide range of terracotta storage jars, wine coolers, bread and flour crocks, plant and parsley pots, insect-repellent garden candles, Suffolk Smellies (pots impregnated with aromatic oil) etc.

'From £2–£65. Some seconds. All pots hand-made on potter's wheel in workshop. Viewing usually possible. Commissions undertaken.'

One mile south of Kenninghall village centre, 2 miles north of South Lopham, 10 miles east of Thetford, 6 miles west of Diss.

From South Lopham (A1066): take B1113 north for Kenninghall; Suffolk Potteries well signposted on left (2 miles).

From Kenninghall market place (post office on left, White Horse on right): go straight for 1/4 mile then go south on to B1113 for N Lopham/Stowmarket; Suffolk Potteries well signposted on right (1 mile).

Open: Mon–Fri 9–5. Some weekends and Bank Holidays – phone to check.
Closed: Phone for Christmas closures.
Cards: Access, Visa.
Cars: Own car-park.
Toilets: Yes, including for disabled.
Wheelchairs: Easy access to small showroom.
Teas: Quidenham Tea Gardens about 2 miles north of shop. Swan House in Garboldisham about 4 miles south of shop.
Groups: Tours of pottery by arrangement – maximum 15 visitors. Contact Steve Harold. Groups welcome to shop if you phone first.
Transport: Sparse!
Mail order: Yes.
Catalogue: Free. Pots can be personalised and made to customers' specifications.

Weston Mill Pottery

Navigation Yard, Millgate NG24 4TV
(01636) 76835

Terracotta pottery for gardens and interiors – garden planters, patio pots, wall pots, parsley pots, and cookware such as chicken bricks, tandoori pots, casseroles, coffee sets, wine racks and coolers.

'Range of best items and some seconds at factory prices. Occasional discontinued lines at reduced prices.'

....

Close to centre of town, near river and castle.

Coming north on A46: at first roundabout, go right on to B6166 for Newark. Go over river by Newark Marina (on left). Take first left, in front of Spring House pub. After 500 yds go left into Navigation Yard: pottery, signposted here, is facing you, 20 yds ahead. (If you miss this little turning, best to park and walk back.)

From the market place: easiest to walk. Head for river and follow riverside walk in opposite direction from castle.

Open: Mon–Sat 9–5; Sun and Bank Holidays 11–5.
Closed: Christmas–New Year period.
Cards: None.
Cars: Adjacent car-park and town parks.
Toilets: Yes.
Wheelchairs: Two flights of stairs.
Teas: Great variety of places in Newark.
Groups: See the potters in action on weekdays. Booking essential for groups to shop or to see potters.
Transport: Any bus to Newark.
Mail order: Yes.
Catalogue: Free (leaflet and photographs). Only perfect stock items, ie cannot hand throw to specific requirements.

Wetheriggs Country Pottery

Clifton Dykes CA10 2DI
(01768) 899122

Traditional hand-thrown terracotta gardenware, earthenware and stoneware for casual dining, kitchen and table. 700 sq ft candle room.

'Museum and history trail of the historic pottery and original working steam machinery. Scheduled industrial monument and the only steam powered pottery in the UK.'

....

A few miles south south-east of Penrith.

From M6 exit 40: turn on to A66 towards Scotch Corner then take A6 towards Shap at next roundabout. *

From Penrith: go south on A6 and cross A66. *

***From this roundabout go for about 3 miles; turn left towards Cliburn. Follow signs to pottery about two miles on the right.**

Open: Seven days 10–5 (*summer* 9–8). Bank Holidays.
Closed: Christmas.
Cards: Mastercard, Switch, Visa.
Cars: Own car-park.
Toilets: Yes, including for disabled.
Wheelchairs: Excellent access; viewing ramps.
Teas: Own restaurant and coffee shop.
Groups: See this unique working Victorian country pottery, and make your own pot from local clay. Museum of pottery, industrial relics and artefacts. Pre-booked groups preferred.
Transport: None.
Mail order: Yes.
Catalogue: Phone 01768 899123 for catalogue and credit card orders.

Blackwell Bros. (International Plants) Ltd.

Stephenson Road, Groundwell Industrial Estate SN2 5AY
(01793) 706275

Company supplies major high street and DIY stores with house plants, patio plants, imported ceramics, house plant arrangements, terracotta patio pots, compost, basketware and a range of garden sundries.

'Most items, including house plant arrangements, are ends of lines at discounted prices (often about 30% off).'

....

On northern side of Swindon, off the A419 (M4–Cricklade Road).
   From M4 exit 15: go north on Swindon bypass (A419) for 6+ miles; turn left on to A4311 for Swindon centre. At first mini-roundabout, go left into Arkwright Road, then left into Stephenson Road.*
   From town centre going north: leave railway station on left. Go under railway bridge, follow signs to Gorse Hill, Penhill and Groundwell on A4311 (A345 on some maps!). Go under footbridge in Penhill; turn right at next roundabout into Arkwright Road, then left into Stephenson Road.*
   *Shop is at the end of the road on the right.

Open: Mon–Sat 10–4. Bank Holidays.
Closed: Christmas Eve–New Year's Eve.
Cards: Access, Delta, Switch, Visa.
Cars: Own car-park.
Toilets: No.
Wheelchairs: One step to shop – assistance available.
Teas: Happy Eater nearby.
Groups: Small shopping groups welcome to shop, but no coaches. No tours of the works.
Transport: Bus no. 16 to Penhill estate, 1/2 mile away.
Mail order: No.

HOW TO FIND OUT where you can ....

•• visit plant nurseries, garden centres and gardens open to the public
•• buy your plants direct
•• talk to expert plant growers
•• gather new ideas & products from garden centres
•• gain inspiration from gardens open to the public.

The Road Atlases for Gardeners feature ...

•• nurseries
•• gardens open to the public
•• garden centres
•• pick-your-own farms
•• giant scale, full colour road maps
•• clearly marked routes to all the places described
•• types of plants in which each nursery specialises
•• up-to-date opening days and hours
•• information for the disabled
•• and lots, lots more ...

The Road Atlases for Gardeners

for
Surrey, W Middlesex, SW London & West Middlesex

and
Derbyshire, Nottinghamshire & South Yorkshire

Our new easy to read, specially drawn road atlases are exactly what you need to plan outings to about 600 plant centres.
From good bookshops, or by mail (see form at end of book)

Household Linens, Towels & Bedding

You are spoilt for choice when it comes to towels, duvets, linens and bedding from the shops here.

When we looked at the history of bedding, we discovered that blanket weaving was a common industry in the middle ages. There was even a Company of Blanket Weavers. The trade gradually became polarised in two areas, Yorkshire and Oxfordshire.

Blanket weavers made coarse woollen broadloom cloth in different sizes and grades for distinct purposes: 'cuts' for sailor's hammocks; 'tilts' (left naturally greasy and waterproof) for gunroom floors, barge and wagon awnings; 'wednals' to line horse collars. Dark blue 'pilot cloth' was made into greatcoats and shaggy 'bearskins' became overcoats.

Traditionally, the weaver bought wool from fell-mongers (who acquired the skins from the butchers). Having sorted and mixed the wool into suitable grades, they distributed it to cottagers and their families for carding and spinning. A pack of wool (240 lbs) gave employment to about 60 people for a week.

To the outrage of cottagers, the spinning jenny replaced their services in the late 1700s. Such machines were, however, welcomed by weavers who had previously always found it difficult to obtain enough yarn. This was the decisive step towards industrialisation and the factory system.

Recent innovations have been cellular blankets (lightweight cotton blankets which can be sterilized), electric blankets and coloured blankets for people to co-ordinate their bedrooms and bedding. Duvets became a huge threat in the 1970s but many people (with whom the author shares a great bond) again prefer the luxury of a woollen blanket.

Over the centuries 'Witney blanket' became a world famous generic term for a quality blanket. Since the early 1900s only those made in the Witney area have been allowed to use this name. We thank Early's of Witney – the sole surviving blanket manufacturer in this area and therefore the only company still making Witney blankets – for the details above.

Hamilton McBride	92	**Accrington** Lancs
Northern Feather Home Furnishings	93	**Ashton-in-Makerfield** Gr Manchester
East Lancashire Towel Company	94	**Barrowford near Nelson** Lancs
Descamps	326*	**Bicester** Oxon
Hico	331*	**Bicester** Oxon
Sheltered Workshop for the Blind	95	**Blackburn** Lancs
McIntosh's Factory Shop	96	**Blaydon on Tyne** Tyne & Wear
Robin Hood Mill Shop (Sundour)	97	**Bolton** Gr Manchester
Tiviot Prints	98	**Broadbottom near Hyde** Gr Manchester
John Wilman	173*	**Burnley** Lancs
Factory Bedding and Fabrics Shop	99	**Carlisle** Cumbria
Hartleys (Mail Order) Shop	122*	**Colne** Lancs
Astbury Lighting	158*	**Congleton** Cheshire
Brooks Mill	376*	**Elland** W Yorks
Bedding Box, The	100	**Great Harwood** Lancs
Walton's Mill Shop	124*	**Harrogate** N Yorks
Slumberdown Enterprises	101	**Hawick** Borders
Den-Home Cushioning	126*	**Heckmondwike** W Yorks
Musbury Fabrics	102	**Helmshore** Lancs
Towel Mill Shop, The	103	**Horwich** Gr Manchester
Linen Mill Shop, The	104	**Huddersfield** W Yorks
Ashtons	105	**Hyde** Gr Manchester
Curtain Factory Shop, The	131*	**Lincoln** Lincs
Florentine Trading Co.	141*	**Nottingham : Sherwood** Notts
Oswaldtwistle Mills	443*	**Oswaldtwistle near Accrington** Lancs
Sherry's Towel Mill	106	**Padiham** Lancs
Burt Marshall, Lumsden	107	**Perth** Tayside
Joman Manufacturing Co.	142*	**Peterlee** Co. Durham
Coats Viyella	699*	**Somercotes** Derbys
Filigree	149*	**South Normanton** Derbys
LS & J Sussman	702*	**St Austell** Cornwall
Linen Cupboard, The	471*	**Street** Somerset
Bottoms Mill Co.	108	**Todmorden** Lancs
Beevers of Whitby	233*	**Whitby** N Yorks
Courtaulds Textiles Homeware	109	**Wigan** Gr Manchester
Early's of Witney	110	**Witney** Oxon
Vossen	111	**Wrexham** Clwyd
Factory Outlet Shopping Centre	491*	**York** N Yorks

* Please see full details in respective chapter

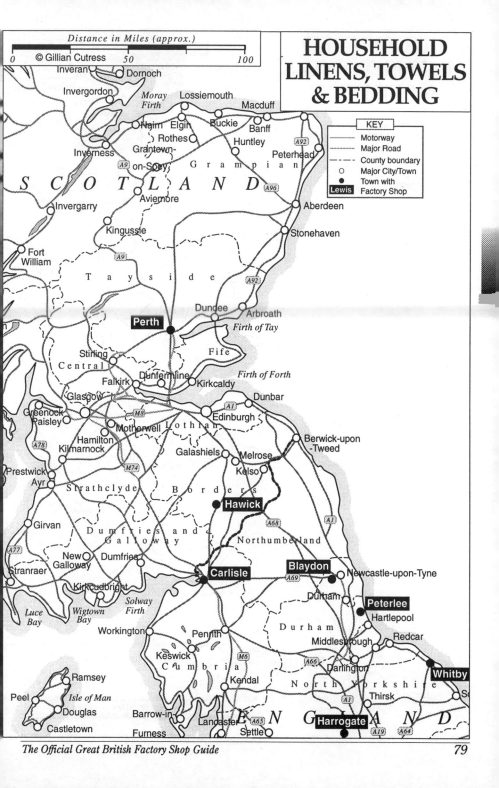

HOUSEHOLD LINENS, TOWELS & BEDDING

Distance in Miles (approx.)

© Gillian Cutress

0   50   100

KEY

——	Motorway
——	Major Road
—·—·	County boundary
○	Major City/Town
●	Town with
Lewis	Factory Shop

Inveran
Dornoch
Invergordon
Moray Firth
Lossiemouth
Macduff
Nairn Elgin Buckie Banff
Rothes Huntley
Inverness Grantown-on-Spey
A9
Peterhead
SCOTLAND
Grampian
A96
Invergarry
Aviemore
Aberdeen
Kingussie
Stonehaven
Fort William
A9
Tayside
A92
Dundee Arbroath
Perth
Firth of Tay
Stirling
Fife
Central
Dunfermline Kirkcaldy
Firth of Forth
Falkirk
Glasgow
A1
Dunbar
Greenock
Paisley
Edinburgh
Motherwell *Lothian*
Hamilton
Berwick-upon-Tweed
Kilmarnock
Galashiels
Prestwick
Melrose
Ayr
Strathclyde
Kelso
M74
Borders
Hawick
Girvan
Dumfries and Galloway
A68
A1
New Galloway
Dumfries
Northumberland
A77
Stranraer
Carlisle
Blaydon
Kirkcudbright
A69
Newcastle-upon-Tyne
Solway Firth
Durham
Peterlee
Luce Bay
Wigtown Bay
Workington
Hartlepool
Penrith
Durham
Middlesbrough Redcar
Ramsey
Keswick
M6
Cumbria
A66
Darlington
Peel *Isle of Man*
Kendal
Whitby
Douglas
North Yorkshire
Castletown
Thirsk
Barrow-in-Furness
Lancaster A65
ENGLAND
A1
Settle
Harrogate
A19 A64

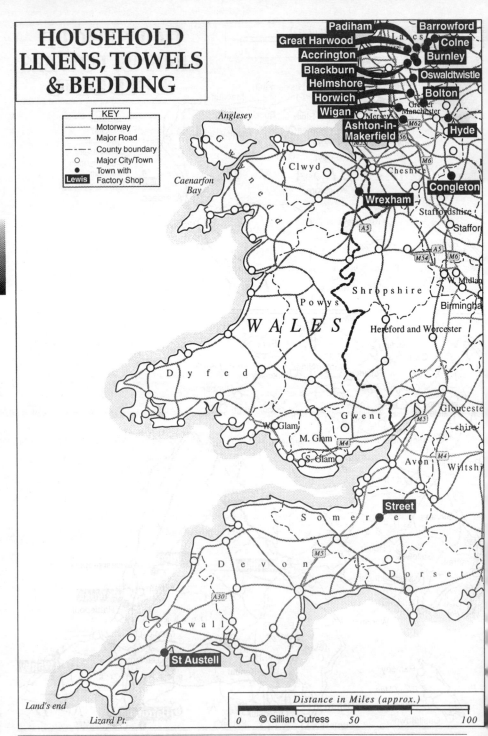

HOUSEHOLD LINENS, TOWELS & BEDDING

KEY
- ········· Motorway
- ———— Major Road
- – – – County boundary
- ○ Major City/Town
- ● Town with Factory Shop
- **Lewis** Factory Shop

Padiham
Barrowford
Great Harwood
Colne
Accrington
Burnley
Blackburn
Oswaldtwistle
Helmshore
Bolton
Horwich
Wigan
Ashton-in-Makerfield
Hyde
Wrexham
Congleton
Street
St Austell

Anglesey
Caenarfon Bay
Clwyd
Gwynedd
Cheshire
Staffordshire
Staffor
W. Midlan
Shropshire
Birmingha
WALES
Hereford and Worcester
Dyfed
Powys
Gwent
Glouceste
shire
W. Glam
M. Glam
Avon
Wiltshi
S. Glam
Somerset
Devon
Dorset
Cornwall
Land's end
Lizard Pt.

Distance in Miles (approx.)
0   © Gillian Cutress   50   100

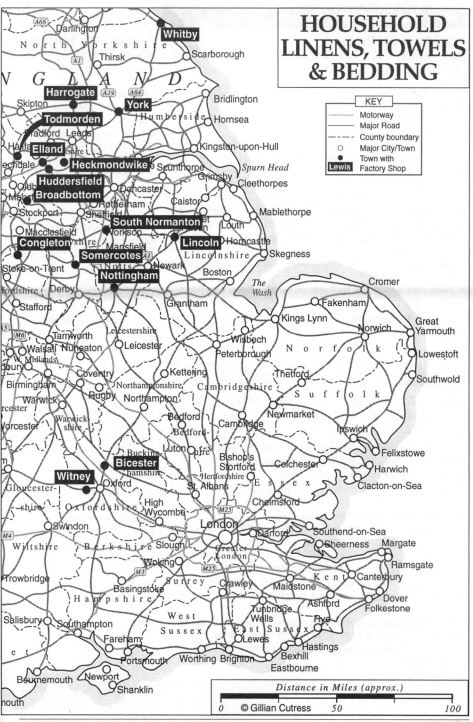

HOUSEHOLD LINENS, TOWELS & BEDDING

KEY

···········	Motorway
————	Major Road
— — —	County boundary
○	Major City/Town
●	Town with
Lewis	Factory Shop

Towns with factory shops: Whitby, Harrogate, York, Todmorden, Elland, Heckmondwike, Huddersfield, Broadbottom, South Normanton, Congleton, Lincoln, Somercotes, Nottingham, Bicester, Witney

Distance in Miles (approx.)

0   © Gillian Cutress   50   100

Hamilton McBride

Shorten Brook Drive, Altham Business Park BB5 5YR
(01282) 858206.

Co-ordinated fashion home textiles, featuring curtains, bed linen, table linen, table lamps and cushions.

'Perfect goods; discontinued lines; slight seconds and imperfects at about half price.'

NB Shop has moved to Altham Business Park on A678 (between Burnley and Accrington, north of M65).

From Accrington: take A680 north for Clayton-le-Moors/ Clitheroe. Go over motorway. At traffic lights, go right on to A678 for Padiham. Go through Altham village and keep straight, passing industrial estate on right. By Walton Arms on left, go right for Huncoat. Take second left into estate: company is 150 yds on right.

From Padiham: go west for Blackburn. At traffic lights, take A678 for Accrington.*

From M65 exit 8: aim for Padiham. At first lights turn left.*

*After 1/2 mile, opposite green/white Walton Arms pub on right, go left into estate. Take second left: company 150 yds on right.

Open: Wed, Thur, Fri 11.30–3 and 4–5.30; Sat 9–1; Sun 1–5. Most Bank Holidays: but please phone to check opening hours.
Closed: Monday, Tuesday; Christmas, Boxing and New Year's Days.
Cards: Access, Visa.
Cars: Factory car-park.
Toilets: Ask if desperate.
Wheelchairs: No steps to ground level shop.
Teas: In Accrington. Local pubs.
Groups: No mill tours but shopping groups always welcome with prior phone call.
Transport: No.
Mail order: Yes.
Catalogue: Photos sent on request if anyone has problems locating a product in stores. Perfects only.

Northern Feather Home Furnishings Ltd.

Lockett Road, South Lancs Industrial Estate WN4 8DK
(01942) 721771

Duvets and pillows with a variety of synthetic and natural fillings from hollow fibre to goosedown. Bedlinen and co-ordinates in wide range of designs.

'Perfects and seconds. Seconds in quilts from £7.50.'

North of town (Three Sisters area).

From Wigan (A49): turn left at lights on to B5207; take first left, Lockett Road. After 1/2 mile, brick and yellow offices/shop on right.

From M6 exit 23: take A49 into Ashton, join A58 from Liverpool to Bolton. Go through town centre on A58, pass Esso petrol station on right, take next left (B5207) then first right, Lockett Road.*

From Bolton (A58): enter Ashton; after Jet petrol station on left turn right on to B5207; next right is Lockett Road.*

*Pass Kwik Save depot on left: shop is clearly signed on right, in the factory.

Open: Tues–Sat 10–5.
Closed: Monday; Bank Holidays; Christmas week.
Cards: No.
Cars: Outside factory on road.
Toilets: No.
Wheelchairs: No steps.
Teas: In Ashton.
Groups: Groups of shoppers welcome; prior phone call appreciated.
Transport: Local buses to Bryn Road then 500 yds' walk down Lockett Road.
Mail order: No.
Catalogue: No.

East Lancashire Towel Company
Park Mill, Halstead Lane BB9 6HK
(01282) 612193

Jacquard woven hand towels, bath towels, bath sheets, babies' nappies, face cloths, tea towels, roller towels. Also cotton and poly/cotton sheets, pillowcases, handkerchiefs, dusters, dishcloths. Specialise in souvenir and promotional towels.

'Mail-order price list sent on request – please mention this Guide.'

....

On northern side of town, just off main road.

   From M65: take exit 13 for Nelson then follow signs into Barrowford. Go north along main road through Barrowford. Pass NatWest Bank on left; take first left just after 'Elderly People Crossing' sign.

   Coming south on A682: turn right into Halstead Lane soon after you reach Barrowford and 100 yds after 'Elderly People' sign. (After all these years, BT has at last replaced the red phone box with a non-descript glass one!)

   Coming west on B6247: pass left turn-off to Pendle Heritage Centre, go over river bridge, turn left, take the third right, Halstead Lane (phone box on the corner).

Open: Mon–Fri 8.30–5; Sat 10–12.30. Bank Holidays.
Closed: One week Easter; first three weeks July; one week Sept; two weeks at Christmas.
Cards: None.
Cars: Outside mill.
Toilets: Yes; also for disabled.
Wheelchairs: Easy access, ground floor shop.
Teas: Teas and traditional Lancashire meals served in 'Weaver's Loft' Kitchen.
Groups: To see towels made: please contact Mrs R Hobson beforehand. You will probably be shown round by leading British towel expert! Pre-booked coach parties welcome.
Transport: Regular local buses.
Mail order: Yes.
Catalogue: Free. Please mention this guide. No seconds.

Sheltered Workshop for the Blind & Disabled
Mill Hill Street BB2 2RA
(0254) 52666

Textiles, including curtains, bedding, household and table linens. Made-to-measure curtains. 95% of goods manufactured on premises by blind and disabled workforce.

'Some seconds and ends of lines available at factory shop prices.'

....

Near Mill Hill station, about 1.5 miles south-west of Blackburn centre.

   From Blackburn centre: take A674 for Chorley. Pass Citroën showroom on right with church opposite, go left at next traffic lights into Spring Lane.*

   From Preston (A677): pass Moat House Hotel at start of town, go over first traffic lights, take first right. At next lights go straight into Spring Lane.*

   From Chorley on A674: go right at traffic lights for Blackburn Royal Infirmary into Spring Lane.*

   *Take third right (to Mill Hill), pass Mill Hill pub on right, go straight at offset crossing. Take next left: shop at end of low building on left.

Open: Mon–Fri 9–12.30 and 1.30–4 (Fri 1.30–3); Sat 9–12.
Closed: Bank Holidays; last two weeks July; Christmas – New Year.
Cards: No.
Cars: Own large car-park.
Toilets: Ask if desperate; also disabled.
Wheelchairs: Easy access.
Teas: Tea available for booked parties.
Tours: By arrangement only. Please contact Ian Ainsworth.
Transport: Regular services from Blackburn centre.

McIntosh's Factory Shop

Tundry Way, Chainbridge Industrial Estate NE21 5SJ
(0191) 414 8598

Large selection of bedding including duvet covers, quilts, bedspreads, pillows, mattress covers, baby bedding; ready-made curtains, net curtains; cushion covers, towels, tea cosies, tablecloths, dusters, dishcloths etc.
'Wide range of perfects and slight seconds.'

....

Immediately south of the Tyne between the A1 and Scottswood bridge.

From A1 Western Bypass of Newcastle: turn on to A695 to Blaydon (south of river). Go under approach to old river bridge; take first left for 'Chainbridge Industrial Estate'. Factory Shop Centre is on left after you cross next bridge.

From Blaydon on A695: go under A1 Western Bypass, take first left into Chainbridge Industrial Estate. The Factory Shop Centre is on right just after left bend.

From Newcastle station: take A695 west. Pass long Vickers factory, go left over Scotswood bridge. After bridge, take first left, go under Scotswood bridge, take first left to Chainbridge Industrial Estate. The Factory Shop Centre is on left after you cross next bridge.

Open: Mon, Tues, Wed, Fri 10–5; Thur 10–7; Sat 9–5; Sun and Bank Holidays 10–4.
Closed: Good Friday, Christmas, Boxing and New Year's Days.
Cards: Access, Switch, Visa.
Cars: Own large car-park.
Toilets: Yes.
Wheelchairs: One step, but assistance given.
Teas: Own café.
Groups: Groups welcome to shop.
Transport: Many buses from Gateshead and Newcastle.

Robin Hood Mill Shop (Sundour) *Closed*

Lever Street BL5 6NV
(01204) 387802 x 263

Extensive range of quality curtains and furnishing fabrics; matching pelmets, tie backs, cushion covers. Face cloths, towels, towel gift sets, pillows, sheets, valances. Seconds in curtains, fabric, towels and bedding at further reduced prices.

'Amazingly low prices. Ready-made curtains from £6 (perfects), £4 (seconds); fabric from 99p per metre.'

....

About 1/3 mile south-west of Bolton station.

From the station: go south down Thynne Street, turn right into Lever Street, pass meat market and Edbro on left; conspicuous shop is on a corner on left.

Or take A579 (Bolton–Leigh road) for St Helens. Go to traffic lights at crossing with distinctive hexagonal Chinese restaurant China Garden on one corner, and Institute of Technology opposite. By the China Garden turn left into Fletcher Street. Go straight at next traffic lights. By Queen Elizabeth pub on right, go left (Lever Street). Shop, in large red-brick mill, on corner 200 yds on right.

Open: Tues–Fri 9.30–4; Sat 8.30–3.
Closed: Monday; Easter Fri–Mon; for Christmas period please phone.
Cards: Access, Visa.
Cars: In side road beside shop.
Toilets: Town centre.
Wheelchairs: Five steps to large shop.
Teas: Pubs, cafés nearby.
Groups: Shoppers welcome; please phone first.
Transport: Walk from town or local bus.
Mail order: No.

Tiviot Prints Ltd.
Lymefield Mill SK14 6AF
(01457) 763297

Printed cloth cut-outs of oven gloves, tea cosies, aprons, bags etc. Tablecloths, towels (hand, bath, sheet, children's and beach). Also made-up textiles, towel sets, bathrobes.

'New items and designs always on offer. Rummage boxes. 25p to £15. Ideal for charity fund raising.'

About three miles west of Glossop.

From Glossop: take A57 west for Manchester; after railway viaduct go left on to A626 for Marple. In Charlesworth take road for Broadbottom, go over very narrow bridge beneath railway viaduct, continue for 100 yds, turn left into Lymefield. Go left in mill yard.

From M67, Hyde or Stalybridge: turn south off A57(T) at Mottram in Longdendale to Broadbottom. Go through village, under railway arch, past The Cheshire Cheese on left and turn into track immediately on right. Turn left at mill. Shop in small detached stone building to left.

Open: Thur, Fri 10–4; Sat 10–3.30.
Closed: Bank Holidays; Christmas–New Year.
Cards: None.
Cars: Outside shop.
Toilets: Yes.
Wheelchairs: One step.
Teas: Local pubs. Tea rooms in Glossop.
Groups: Shopping groups please phone beforehand. No mill tours.
Transport: Trains from Manchester/Glossop to Broadbottom; buses from Hyde/Glossop.
Mail order: No.

The Factory Bedding and Fabrics Shop
Atlas House, Nelson Street, Denton Holme CA2 5NB
(01228) 514703

Large selection of ready-made bedding: duvet covers, quilts, bedspreads, pillows, mattress covers, baby bedding; ready-made curtains, net curtains; cushion covers, towels, tea cosies, tablecloths, dusters, dishcloths etc. Huge selection of sheeting, curtaining, upholstery fabrics. Make-up service.

'Wide range of perfects and slight seconds.'

On south-west side of town, off the road to Dalston.

From Dalston (going north on B5299): pass Caldew Hospital on left then turn right immediately before pedestrian lights into Nelson Street. Shop at end of four-storey mill, about 400 yds along.

From other directions: follow signs to station/Motorail terminal. Do not enter station but go into town between two arches like castle (The Citadel). From city centre, follow signs 'West'. Cross Victoria Viaduct to roundabout (baths on left). Take road to Workington; cross bridge, fork left, take fourth right (Nelson Street). Shop on corner of second turning on left.

Open: Mon–Fri 10–5.30; Sat 9–5. Bank Holidays 10–4.
Closed: Good Friday; Christmas, Boxing and New Year's Days.
Cards: Access, Connect, Switch, Visa.
Cars: Outside shop.
Toilets: No.
Wheelchairs: Easy access to spacious shop, but assistance given for first floor.
Teas: Own coffee shop.
Groups: Groups welcome to shop.
Transport: Buses from Woolworths to Morton/Denton Holme – get off by Co-op.
Mail order: No.

The Bedding Box
Vulcan Works, Back Clayton Street BB6 7AF
(01254) 888338

Continental quilts, pillows, duvet covers, pillowcases; curtains made to measure; tie backs, lampshades, mattress covers. Also fabrics by the yard.

'Perfects and seconds on sale. Chainstore items at very reasonable prices. Seven-day make-up service for curtains.'

See our display advertisement opposite.

....

Close to centre of town.

From M65 exit 7: take A680 (Accrington–Clitheroe road) then follow the first sign into Great Harwood. This road becomes Queen Street after gasometer on right. Turn left off Queen Street, the main shopping street, opposite the large classical building set back from road (swimming baths) into Clayton Street. At top of Clayton Street, look for The Merrie England pub on left: clearly marked large red brick shop is in small back street opposite.

Open: Mon–Fri 8.30–5; Sat 10–4.
Closed: Bank Holidays; Christmas–New Year.
Cards: Access, Connect, Mastercard, Switch, Visa.
Cars: In Clayton Street.
Toilets: Yes.
Wheelchairs: Short cobbled area then two steps to sizeable shop.
Teas: Cafés and pubs in Great Harwood.
Groups: You can see the action as you walk past. Groups welcome to shop (prior phone call please to Eric, mentioning this book).
Transport: Any bus to town.
Mail order: Yes.
Catalogue: Free.

Slumberdown Enterprises Ltd.
Burnfoot Industrial Estate TD9 8RW
(01450) 374500

Duvets and pillows in natural feather and down and in synthetic fibres; sleeping bags & other bedroom furnishings.

'Post Home service for bulky goods. First quality sold at factory shop prices; a few seconds.'

....

North-east of town centre.

From the south and town centre on A7: go over river and immediately turn right at traffic lights into Mansfield Road.*

From Selkirk and north on A7: go left at first traffic lights immediately before river bridge.*

*Continue for about 1/2 mile to roundabout and turn left into Hamilton Road. Slumberdown is second factory on left.

Open: Mon–Fri 12–4. Some Bank Holidays – please check.
Closed: Christmas and New Year.
Cards: Access, Visa.
Cars: Own car-park.
Toilets: Yes.
Teas: In Hawick.
Groups: Shopping groups welcome.
Transport: Local buses stop 300 yds from factory.
Mail order: Yes.
Catalogue: No.

102 Helmshore   Lancs

Musbury Fabrics

Park Mill, Holcombe Road BB4 4NQ
(01706) 221318

Co-ordinated household textiles, duvet covers, sheets,
valances etc from most top household names. Huge selection
of towels. Always remnants and sale lines.

'Firsts, seconds and ends of runs at keen factory prices. Special
emphasis on top brands in furnishing fabrics and sheeting.
Sewing service for quality furnishings and special size bedding.
Everything a mill shop should be!'

6 miles south of Accrington and 8 miles north of Bury.
In the red mill opposite Helmshore Textile Museum which is
well signposted. Follow brown road signs to this Museum from
area of Haslingden and Rawtenstall. Take care because signs on
A56 are at actual exits, with no advance warning.

Open: Seven days a week
9.30–4.30, including Bank
Holidays.
Closed: Christmas, Boxing
and New Year's Days.
Cards: Access, Switch, Visa.
Cars: In road, or public car
park opposite.
Toilets: Yes.
Wheelchairs: Easy access,
no steps, huge shop.
Teas: Helmshore Textile
Museum.
Groups: No mill tours but
shopping groups welcome:
prior phone call appreciated.
Charity events by arrangement.
Transport: Helmshore
Circular buses from
Rawtenstall and Haslingden
stop outside.
Mail order: Yes.
Catalogue: Free. Household
textiles only.

The Towel Mill Shop

Victoria Mill, Chorley New Road BL6 6ER
(01204) 695611

Towels of all colours and sizes. Bathrobes, skirts, blouses, knitwear, tops and men's shirts.

'Near-perfects and current stock sold here at discounted prices.'

....

A short way south of the town centre.

From Horwich town centre/Chorley: keep going south-east on A673 through town centre towards Bolton. Go over hump bridge, pass Texaco station on left, take second small road to right (in front of mill).*

From M61 exit 6: go north. This road meets A673 from Bolton at large roundabout. Continue north-west on A673 towards Horwich for about 1/2 mile; 200 yds after Elf petrol station take small turning left (past mill).*

*Shop 70 yds on left.

Open: Mon–Fri 9–4.30
(Thur late night to 7); Sat 10–3.
Closed: Bank Holidays;
Christmas–New Year.
Cards: Access, Switch, Visa.
Cars: Large car-park.
Toilets: No.
Wheelchairs: One step up then five steps down.
Changing rooms: Yes.
Teas: In Horwich.
Groups: Shopping groups welcome with prior phone call.
Transport: Local buses.
Mail order: No.

The Linen Mill Shop

Marsh Mills, Luck Lane HD3 4AB
(01484) 514463

Lace-trimmed bed, nursery and baby linens in poly/cotton and cotton, including blankets, sheets, towels etc. Co-ordinating gift ideas.

'Discontinued lines and seconds of goods which are usually supplied to top stores in London. Quality linens at greatly reduced prices all made in our adjoining factory. Please phone for details of our special sales.'

....

One mile north-west of town centre.

From town centre ring road: follow signs for M62 West (Manchester) and go uphill on A640 Trinity Street. After Leo's supermarket on left, immediately go left (Luck Lane): mill is on right.

From Manchester: take M62 exit 23: head for Huddersfield on A640 and go downhill to town. At the top end of Leo's supermarket on right, go right (Luck Lane): mill is on right.

From Leeds: take M62 exit 24: aim for Huddersfield. Go over traffic lights (Calverley Arms right) then take fourth right (Thornhill Road). At far end go left into Westbourne Road then right in front of Leo's supermarket: mill is on right.

Open: Mon–Sat 10–4.
Other times by appointment.
Closed: Bank Holidays;
Christmas, Boxing and New
Year's Days.
Cards: Access, Visa.
Cars: On site.
Toilets: Ask if required.
Wheelchairs: Ramp to shop.
Teas: Basic café in mill; good food pubs nearby.
Groups: No tours; large shopping groups please phone.
Transport: Bus stop 5 minutes' walk; Huddersfield BR station 15 minutes' walk.
Mail order: No.

Ashtons

Newton Street SK14 4NP
(0161) 368 1961

Towels: hand and bath sheet sizes, plain colours. Ashtons', and embroidered and embellished Christy brands. Bed linen. Baby products – nappies, baby nests, cotton pram quilts, cot duvet covers and matching curtains. Sheets and blankets.

....

In the huge mill just north of M67 exit 3.

Coming east from Manchester on M67: go left at top of slip road; coming west, turn right at end of the slip road. Turn right at second traffic lights and go straight uphill: mill is on right. *

Coming south from Ashton/Oldham via Dukinfield Road (A627): turn left at roundabout into Newton Street (B6170), go 100 yds uphill. *

*Shop is opposite stone church.

Open: Mon–Wed 9–4.30; Thurs 9–6.30; Fri 9–12.30.
Closed: Bank Holidays; Easter; Spring Bank Holiday week; second and third weeks in August; Christmas–New Year.
Cards: None.
Cars: In side roads or company parking facility (but not, please, within the site).
Toilets: Please ask if you need to!
Wheelchairs: Easy access to small shop. No steps.
Teas: In Hyde.
Groups: Unfortunately no factory tours any more.
Transport: Local trains and buses.
Mail order: No.

Sherry's Towel Mill

Stockbridge Mill BB12 7HA
(01282) 778416

Wide range of towels made here plus huge selection of household textiles: duvets, bedding, bathroom sets, flannelette sheet pieces and sets. Large range of ready-made curtains, perfumed candles and interesting gifts, silk flowers, bakeware, dressing gowns etc.

'Genuine factory shop, lots of bargains. Please browse without obligation.'

....

Close to centre of town.

From Burnley, or M65 exit 10: take main road (A671) to Padiham. Pass Gawthorpe Hall on right. As main road turns sharp right over river, go left round The Bridge Inn for Hapton. *

Coming east from Blackburn along Padiham main road (A671): go through town, pass Kwik Save on left, go sharp right over river. Main road then goes left but you go ahead for Hapton (Bridge Inn on left). *

*Go under railway: shop on left on corner of Stockbridge Road.

Open: Mon–Fri 9.30–5.30; Sat 10–5; Sun 10–4. Bank Holidays (usually incorporating an 'open weekend'.)
Closed: Christmas, Boxing and New Year's Days.
Cards: Access, Switch, Visa.
Cars: Ample parking for cars and coaches.
Toilets: Yes (but inaccessible for disabled visitors).
Wheelchairs: Easy access, no steps.
Teas: Free coffee and biscuits for pre-arranged groups.
Tours: Pre-booked groups (max 50) may see towels woven (phone Iris to arrange). Free. Individuals please ask at the time.
Transport: Buses from Burnley.
Mail order: Yes.
Catalogue: Leaflet.

Burt Marshall, Lumsden Ltd.

Luncarty Bleachfield PH1 3HE
(01738) 828382

Closed

Sheets, pillowcases, duvet covers, towels, tablecovers, curtaining and lining. Few printed fabrics such as curtaining.

'Company bleaches and dyes sheeting. Most items seconds. Sheets and pillow cases from £10.50 per set; curtain linings from £2 per m.'

....

In a small village 4 miles north of Perth.
   From Perth going north on A9: take slip road to Luncarty. Go into village; pass two bus shelters on right then go right into Marshall Way. *

   Coming south on B9099 and A9: go into village, turn left before bus shelter on left). *

   ***Turn left after 120 yds, go to end of lane then to far back left of mill yard (200 yds). Go in through green door (marked).**

Open: Mon–Fri 9–4;
also Easter–October: Sat 9–12.
Most Bank Holidays – please phone to check.
Closed: Christmas–New Year.
Cards: Access, Visa.
Cars: Own car-park.
Toilets: In Perth.
Wheelchairs: No steps to medium sized shop.
Teas: In Caithness Glass and Perth.
Groups: Small groups of shoppers welcome – should phone first.
Transport: None.
Mail order: No.
Catalogue: No.

Bottoms Mill Co. Ltd.

Rochdale Road, Walsden OL14 7UB
(01706) 812691

This company makes flannelette and cotton sheets with matching pillowcases; polycotton sheets; tea towels, dusters, chamois cloths, dishcloths, dust sheets, terry towels, counterpanes; cleaning rags and large cloth remnants.

'Small family company which weaves a range of cotton cloths. Perfects and seconds available.'

....

Walsden is about 7 miles north-east of Rochdale.
   From Burnley or Halifax: take the A646 to Todmorden. Then go nearly 2 miles south on the A6033 (towards Littleborough). The shop is on the right, opposite Gordon Rigg's garden centre. Walk through the arch and follow signs.

Open: Mon–Wed 9–4;
Thur 10–4; Fri 9–3.
Thur always open, other days please use intercom.
Closed: Christmas–New Year.
Cards: No.
Cars: Ample space.
Toilets: At the garden centre.
Wheelchairs: Easy access to medium sized shop on ground floor.
Teas: Drinks machine at garden centre. Pubs, and fish & chips nearby.
Groups: Groups welcome to shop. Small numbers can also visit weaving sheds. Please arrange in advance, mentioning this book.
Transport: Bus nos. 589 and 590 pass door from Rochdale to Halifax.
Mail order: Yes.
Catalogue: No. Goods gladly forwarded by post or carrier.

Courtaulds Textiles Homeware
Trencherfield Mill, The Pier WN3 4ES
(01942) 501331 (Mill Shop)

Duvet covers, pillowcases, sheets, bedspreads, valances, continental quilts, pillows. Curtains, towels, baby bedding (bumpers, cot and pram sheets), changing bags, nappies. Bathrobes, thread, ribbon, lace, fabric. Some leisurewear.

'Genuine mill seconds plus end of line bedding at factory shop prices (pillowcases from 50p; duvet covers from £5; sheets from £4).'

···

Half a mile from town centre. This magnificent brick mill is on banks of canal in the Wigan Pier tourist area.

As you come into Wigan from any direction follow signs 'Wigan Pier'. This mill shop, signposted, is on the ground floor of the huge mill on your left as you go round the one-way system; it is tucked away at back, next to staff car park and opposite the café.

Open: Mon–Fri 9.15–4.30; Sat, Sun and Bank Holidays 10–3.30.
Closed: Christmas–New Year.
Cards: Access, Visa.
Cars: In mill yard and all public car-parks at Wigan Pier.
Toilets: In cafeteria across yard.
Wheelchairs: No steps; easy access.
Teas: Cafeteria; Wigan Pier tea shop; George Orwell pub by canal.
Groups: Groups welcome to shop – please ring shop manager Mrs Gwen Roberts to arrange.
Transport: Close to both BR stations and town centre.

Recent history of towel manufacture in the UK

In the late 1970s, the previously flourishing British towel industry changed very rapidly. Whereas previous to this the 20 or more towel manufacturers in the UK had been able to cope with foreign competition, this country suddenly became flooded with cheap, artificially low priced towels from Portugal. Most of the UK towel mills were forced into closure very quickly and there are now only a handful remaining. Supermarkets and market traders were, and still are, selling these inferior products and 80% of towels now sold in the UK are imported from Portugal, India, Pakistan and China. It is now not necessary to label goods with the country of origin. Goods manufactured in the UK are clearly labelled.

The benefits of buying goods from a factory shop are that they are generally of better quality than can be purchased elsewhere at higher prices.

Thanks to Victor Hobson (Fellow of the Textile Institute; Chartered Textile Technologist) from East Lancashire Towel Co.

Caring for towels

Soak brightly coloured towels overnight in cold water then launder them separately for at least three washes. Don't use detergents with bleach in them. Towels shrink the first time they are washed but this makes the cloth firmer. If you pull a loop, cut it off with scissors. If you come across towels with linen loops in your travels, make the most of these unusual products. Although they are somewhat coarse at first, they are very absorbent and quickly soften. Treat yourself to some luxury!

110 Witney Oxon

Early's of Witney
Burford Road OX8 5EA
(01993) 703131

Wool, cotton and acrylic blankets; car rugs, hand-quilted bedspreads. Discontinued and job lines, offcuts of materials and woollens; bin ends.

'First quality goods and slight imperfects at very competitive prices.'

....

From town centre (old covered market cross with stone columns and clock): go north (Tourist office on right) along High Street. At second mini-roundabout, go left into Mill Street (to Faringdon A4095/4047) which becomes Burford Road. Mill is on right – after tall brick chimney go right through Gate 5.

From places west via A40: turn off to 'Witney, Abingdon A415'. At bottom of slip road, go left to 'Witney'.*

From Oxford on A40: don't take first exit to 'Witney East' but next exit to 'South & West Witney'. Go right at roundabout to 'Witney A415'.*

*At next roundabout go left to 'Bampton' & 'Industrial Estates'. Keep going round towards Minster Lovell (B4047); at T-junction traffic lights go right for Bicester (A4095). Continue to Early's chimney on left.

Open: Mon–Fri 10–4; Sat 9–2.
Closed: Public holidays; Christmas–New Year.
Cards: Access, Switch, Visa.
Cars: Free parking outside shop.
Toilets: In Witney.
Wheelchairs: Special ramp with hand-rail.
Teas: In Witney.
Groups: Shopping groups always welcome; a phone call first please. Factory tours gladly arranged – phone to organise.
Transport: Local buses pass the mill.
Mail order: Yes.
Catalogue: No.

111 Wrexham Clwyd

Vossen Ltd.
54 Clywedog Road South, Wrexham Industrial Estate
LL13 9XS   (01978) 661155

Wide range of quality towels and bathrobes in plain, patterned and printed designs including beach towels, gift sets, velours, bath mats and children's towels and bathrobes. Also pillows and quilts.

'Buy direct from Europe's largest manufacturer of towels and bathrobes and save 25–50% off high street prices.'

....

Three miles east of Wrexham in huge, well marked ind. estate.

From Wrexham: take A534 east for Holt/Nantwich/Wrexham Ind. Est. Keep straight. Go right into estate when you see signs.*

Going west to Wrexham on A534: go left into signposted estate.*

From Chester via A483: take slip road for Wrexham Industrial Estate (A534); at roundabout take first turn for estate. Follow road to end; at next roundabout go left. Turn right into estate.*

*At roundabout go right on to ring road for Clywedog Road. Pass Ash Road on left, go right to Clywedog Road (South). Take second right (Clywedog Road (South)). Vossen is 200 yds on right.

Coming north-west to Wrexham on A525: pass first entrance to estate on right; at mini-roundabout go right (for Information). Take first left [Clywedog Road (Sth)]. After 2/3 mile, go left to Vossen.

Open: Mon–Fri 9.30–4.
Closed: Bank Holidays; Christmas–New Year.
Cards: Access, Visa.
Cars: Own forecourt.
Toilets: In town.
Wheelchairs: One step to large shop.
Teas: In town.
Groups: No factory tours. Shopping groups always welcome – prior phone call appreciated.
Transport: None.

Blinds, Curtains, Curtaining & Furnishing Fabrics

Having struggled over the years (like most home curtain makers, we suspect) trying to work out how much fabric was needed to make various curtains, we had the bright idea of asking a curtain factory shop if professionals had a secret ready reckoner for making a rough calculation of the yardage required. No such luck – they too have to do individual sums, allowing for different width windows, different length repeats, shrinkage expected, etc. [Note: good opportunity for computer programmer.] So we asked if there was anything that customers could do to ease the process of buying yards of fabric. The reply was instant, heartfelt and emphatic: 'Make sure you know the dimensions of your windows before you come'. Apparently in the excitement of choosing new curtains, many shoppers totally overlook the necessity of measuring up first.

For those for whom the novelty of curtain making has palled, or who lack the skills or time required, this chapter features many companies who offer a making up service. In our experience the prices are most reasonable – and such a service is well worth the extra expense.

Blinds too are a very good buy from shops in this chapter. Moreover you do not even have to leave home, as some shops gladly send swatches and offer a mail order service.

One of our best buys was superb quality upholstery fabric from Yorkshire at £10 instead of £30 per yard. We took the fabric to a Nottinghamshire factory shop which did an excellent job re-upholstering our suite. In total we must have saved several hundred pounds.

Royal Aberdeen Workshops	201*	**Aberdeen**	Grampian
Hamilton McBride	92*	**Accrington**	Lancs
Red Rose Velvets	112	**Accrington**	Lancs
Fabric Shop, The	113	**Addingham**	W Yorks
Skopos Mill Shop	114	**Batley**	W Yorks
Boynett Fabrics	115	**Bedford**	Beds
Sheltered Workshop for the Blind	95*	**Blackburn**	Lancs
Factory Fabrics	116	**Blaydon on Tyne**	Tyne & Wear
McIntosh's Factory Shop	96*	**Blaydon on Tyne**	Tyne & Wear
Robin Hood Mill Shop (Sundour)	97*	**Bolton**	Gr Manchester
Warwick Fabrics	117	**Bourton-on-the-Water**	Gloucs
Ahmad Textiles	118	**Bradford**	W Yorks
Just Fabrics	119	**Burford**	Oxon
Color Blind	120	**Burnley**	Lancs
Factory Bedding and Fabrics Shop	99*	**Carlisle**	Cumbria
Curtain Choice	121	**Chorley**	Lancs
Hartleys (Mail Order) Shop	122	**Colne**	Lancs
Denholme Velvets	306*	**Denholme**	W Yorks
Bedding Box, The	100*	**Great Harwood**	Lancs
Carrington Curtains	123	**Harrogate**	N Yorks
Walton's Mill Shop	124	**Harrogate**	N Yorks
Fabric Factory, The	125	**Heanor**	Derbys
Den-Home Cushioning	126	**Heckmondwike**	W Yorks
Musbury Fabrics	102*	**Helmshore**	Lancs
GP & J Baker & Parkertex Fabrics	127	**High Wycombe**	Bucks
Mill Fabric Shop, The	128	**Hyde**	Gr Manchester
Paul Steiger	129	**Kirkby-in-Ashfield**	Notts
Standfast	130	**Lancaster**	Lancs
Factory Fabric Shop, The	309*	**Leeds**	W Yorks
Curtain Factory Shop, The	131	**Lincoln**	Lincs
Corcoran & May	132	**London : Ealing**	
Corcoran & May	133	**London : Putney**	
Barracks Fabrics	134	**Macclesfield**	Cheshire
Material Things	135	**Macclesfield**	Cheshire
Fabric Mill Shop, The	136	**Manchester**	
Homebirds	137	**Market Harborough**	Leics
Fabric Design	138	**Matlock Bath**	Derbys
Color Blind	139	**Middleton**	Gr Manchester
Abakhan Fabrics	140	**Mostyn**	Clwyd
Proud Fabrics	311*	**Nelson**	Lancs
Florentine Trading Co.	141	**Nottingham**	Notts
Oswaldtwistle Mills	443*	**Oswaldtwistle near Accrington**	Lancs
Sherry's Towel Mill	106*	**Padiham**	Lancs
Burt Marshall, Lumsden	107*	**Perth**	Tayside
Joman Manufacturing Co.	142	**Peterlee**	Co. Durham
P B A Mill Shop	143	**Rawtenstall**	Lancs
Ettrick Forest Interiors	144	**Selkirk**	Borders
Corcoran & May	145	**Sevenoaks**	Kent
Low Woods Furnishings	146	**Shepshed**	Leics
Skopos Mill Shop	147	**Shipley**	W Yorks
Fabric World	148	**South Croydon**	Surrey
Filigree	149	**South Normanton**	Derbys
Fabric World	150	**Sutton**	Surrey
John Heathcoat & Co (Sales)	315*	**Tiverton**	Devon
Yarnolds	151	**Wolverhampton**	W Mids
Carrington Curtains Ltd.	152	**York**	N Yorks

* Please see full details in respective chapter

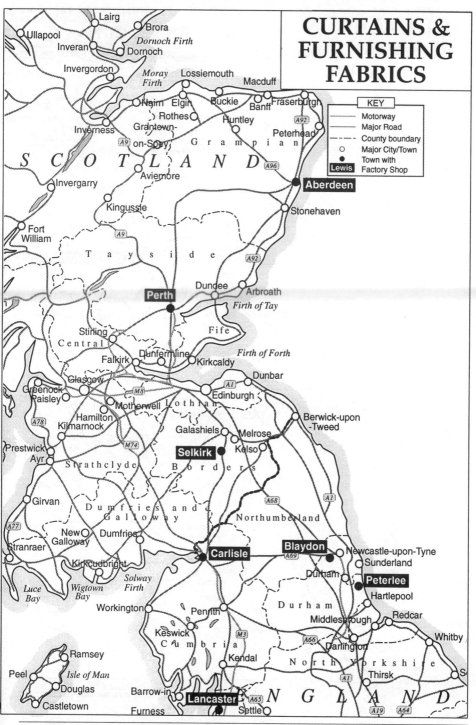

CURTAINS & FURNISHING FABRICS

KEY

————	Motorway
————	Major Road
—·—·—	County boundary
○	Major City/Town
● Lewis	Town with Factory Shop

Ullapool
Lairg
Brora
Inveran
Dornoch
Dornoch Firth
Invergordon
Moray Firth
Lossiemouth
Macduff
Nairn Elgin
Buckie
Banff
Fraserburgh
Rothes
Huntley
Inverness
Grantown-
on-Spey
Grampian
Peterhead
S C O T L A N D
Invergarry
Aviemore
Aberdeen
Kingussie
Stonehaven
Fort William
T a y s i d e
Perth
Dundee
Arbroath
Firth of Tay
Stirling
Fife
Central
Dunfermline
Firth of Forth
Falkirk
Kirkcaldy
Glasgow
Dunbar
Greenock
Paisley
Edinburgh
L o t h i a n
Berwick-upon-Tweed
Hamilton
Motherwell
Kilmarnock
Galashiels
Melrose
Prestwick
Ayr
Selkirk
Kelso
S t r a t h c l y d e
B o r d e r s
Girvan
*D u m f r i e s a n d
G a l l o w a y*
Northumberland
New Galloway
Dumfries
Stranraer
Carlisle
Blaydon
Newcastle-upon-Tyne
Kirkcudbright
Sunderland
Durham
Peterlee
Luce Bay
Wigtown Bay
Solway Firth
Hartlepool
Workington
Penrith
D u r h a m
Middlesbrough
Redcar
Keswick
C u m b r i a
Darlington
Whitby
Ramsey
Kendal
N o r t h   Y o r k s h i r e
Peel
Isle of Man
Thirsk
Douglas
Barrow-in-Furness
Lancaster
E N G L A N D
Castletown
Settle

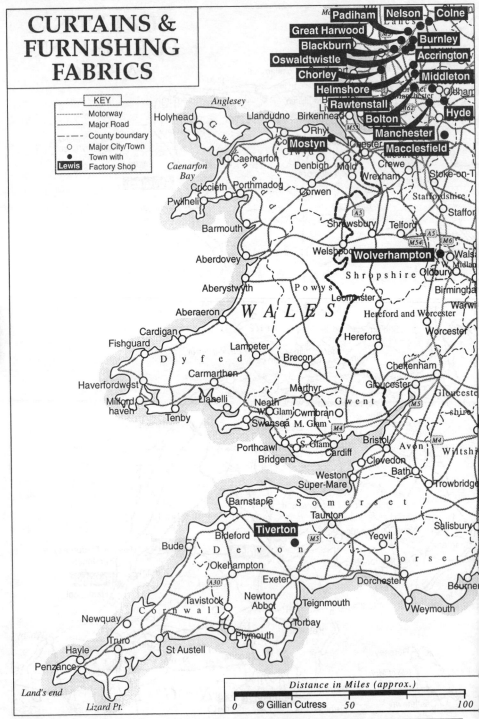

CURTAINS & FURNISHING FABRICS

KEY
- .... Motorway
- ———— Major Road
- – – – – County boundary
- ○ Major City/Town
- ● Town with
- Lewis | Factory Shop

Padiham · Nelson · Colne
Great Harwood · Burnley
Blackburn · Accrington
Oswaldtwistle · Middleton
Chorley · Oldham
Helmshore · Hyde
Rawtenstall
Bolton
Mostyn · Manchester
Macclesfield

Anglesey
Holyhead · Llandudno · Birkenhead · Rhyl
Caernarfon · Denbigh · Mold · Chester · Crewe · Stoke-on-Trent
Criccieth · Porthmadog · Corwen · Wrexham · Staffordshire
Pwllheli · Staffor
Barmouth · Shrewsbury · Telford
Welshpool · Wolverhampton · Walsall
Aberdovey · W. Midland
Shropshire · Oldbury · Birmingham
Aberystwyth · Powys · Leominster · Warwi
WALES · Hereford and Worcester · Worcester
Aberaeron · Hereford
Cardigan · Lampeter · Brecon · Cheltenham
Fishguard · Dyfed · Gloucester · Glouce
Carmarthen · Merthyr · Gwent · -shire
Haverfordwest · Neath · M5
Milford haven · Llanelli · W. Glam · Cwmbran
Tenby · Swansea · M. Glam · M4
Porthcawl · S. Glam · Bristol · Avon · Wiltsh
Bridgend · Cardiff · Clevedon · M4
Weston · Bath · Trowbridge
Super-Mare · Somerset
Barnstaple · Taunton
Bideford · Tiverton · M5 · Yeovil · Salisbury
Bude · Devon · Dorset
Okehampton · Exeter · Dorchester · Bour
Tavistock · Newton Abbot · Teignmouth · Weymouth
Newquay · Cornwall · Torbay
Truro · Plymouth
Hayle · St Austell
Penzance
Land's end
Lizard Pt.

Distance in Miles (approx.)

0   © Gillian Cutress   50   100

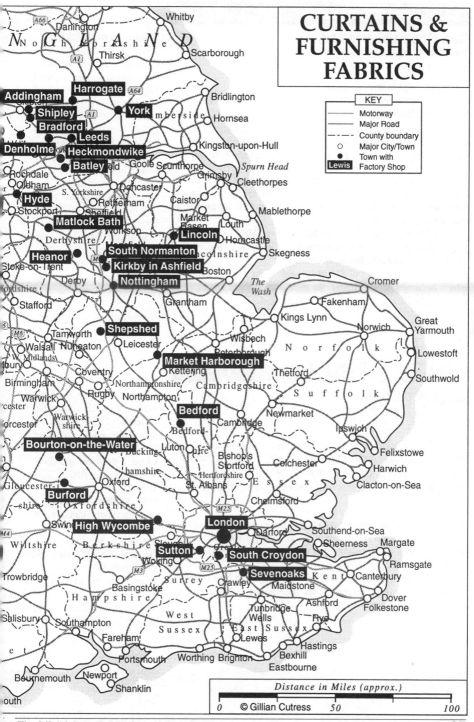

CURTAINS & FURNISHING FABRICS

KEY

....	Motorway
————	Major Road
—·—·—	County boundary
○	Major City/Town
●	Town with
Lewis	Factory Shop

Whitby
Darlington
Thirsk
Scarborough
N o G r t h   Y o r k s h i r e
A66
A1
Bridlington
Harrogate
A64
Addingham
Shipley
York
Bradford
A1
Hornsea
Leeds
Humberside
Kingston-upon-Hull
Denholme
Heckmondwike
Batley
Goole
Scunthorpe
Grimsby
Spurn Head
Rochdale
S. Yorkshire
Doncaster
Cleethorpes
Oldham
Rotherham
Caistor
Hyde
Stockport
Sheffield
Mablethorpe
Matlock Bath
Worksop
Market Rasen
Louth
Derbyshire
Lincoln
Horncastle
Heanor
South Normanton
Lincolnshire
Skegness
Staffordshire
Kirkby in Ashfield
Boston
Stoke-on-Trent
Derby
Nottingham
The Wash
Cromer
Stafford
Grantham
Fakenham
Kings Lynn
Great Yarmouth
Shepshed
Tamworth
Leicester
Wisbech
Norwich
M6
Walsall
Nuneaton
Peterborough
N o r f o l k
Lowestoft
W. Midlands
Coventry
Market Harborough
Kettering
Thetford
Southwold
Birmingham
Rugby
Northamptonshire
Cambridgeshire
S u f f o l k
Warwick
Northampton
Warwickshire
Bedford
Newmarket
orcester
Bedford
Cambridge
Ipswich
Bourton-on-the-Water
Luton
Felixstowe
Buckingham
Bishop's Stortford
Gloucester-shire
Oxford
Colchester
Harwich
Burford
St. Albans
E s s e x
Clacton-on-Sea
Oxfordshire
Hertfordshire
Chelmsford
M4
Swindon
High Wycombe
Slough
Southend-on-Sea
Wiltshire
B e r k s h i r e
London
Dartford
Sheerness
Margate
Sutton
Woking
Ramsgate
South Croydon
M3
M23
Canterbury
Trowbridge
S u r r e y
Sevenoaks
Maidstone
K e n t
Basingstoke
Crawley
Dover
H a m p s h i r e
West Sussex
Tunbridge Wells
Ashford
Folkestone
Salisbury
Southampton
E a s t   S u s s e x
Rye
Fareham
Lewes
Hastings
Portsmouth
Worthing
Brighton
Bexhill
Bournemouth
Newport
Eastbourne
Shanklin

Distance in Miles (approx.)

© Gillian Cutress

0   50   100

Red Rose Velvets Ltd.
Royal Mill, Victoria Street BB5 0PO
(01254) 392059

Curtain velvet fabric, clothing velvet fabric, velvet curtains
made-to-measure, all in cotton. Also cushions, curtain
linings, tie backs etc.

*'We only sell what we weave on the premises. Genuine low
prices. 48" wide curtain velvet in 30 colours from £4.95 per
yd; 60" wide dress velvet £6.50 per yd, 54" wide £5.50 per yd.'*

....

In town, on south-west side of main shopping area.

*From Baxenden/Haslingden/Rawtenstall (A680): in town,
pass fire station on left. After adjacent police station, go left
into Spring Gardens.**

*From Blackburn/Burnley via A679, or from M65 exit 7: turn on
to A680 in town centre for Haslingden. Pass Esso petrol station
(on left), go right into Spring Gardens.**

**Take third left, Nuttall Street (in large right hand bend),
which becomes Mount Street. Go right into Victoria Street;
company is 300 yds on right, clearly marked.*

Open: Mon–Fri 9.30–5;
also Sept–Dec Sat 10–1.
Closed: Easter three days;
last week May; last two weeks
July; third week September;
Christmas–New Year.
Cards: Access, Visa.
Cars: Outside shop in street.
Toilets: Ask if desperate.
Wheelchairs: One step only.
Teas: In town.
Groups: Small groups
welcome to shop; may also be
able to see round mill if visit is
arranged beforehand.
Transport: Not far to walk
from town centre.
Mail order: Yes.
Catalogue: No.

The Fabric Shop
82 Main Street LS29 0PL
(01943) 830982

Vast range of fabrics for furnishing, upholstery, loose
covers, curtains, linings etc. (No velvets, dralons or nets.)

*'This shop seems to stretch back for ever! Stock always
changing. Perfects, seconds and remnants on sale at much
reduced prices.'*

....

Easy to find on the main road (A65) in the centre of the village.

*From Ilkley via A65: come into the village, go over pedestrian
lights then this deceptively small village shop is 50 yds on the
right, on a corner.*

*From Skipton (A65) or Keighley (via A6034): go into village,
pass The Sailor Hotel on right. This shop about 150 yds on left,
opposite large square chimney.*

Open: Mon 10–6; Tues, Wed,
Fri 9–1; Thur 12–4; Sat 10–4.
Closed: Christmas and New
Year – phone for exact dates.
Cards: None.
Cars: Side street and short
stay parking 50 yds.
Toilets: Yes.
Wheelchairs: Unfortunately
no because of difficult stairs.
Teas: Tearooms 50 yds;
five local pubs.
Groups: Cannot accommodate
coach parties.
Transport: Hourly bus
services: no. 765 (Ilkley–
Keighley), 784 (Ilkley–Skipton).

Skopos Mill Shop

Cheapside Mills, Bradford Road WF17 6LY   *(01924) 475756*

Vast range seconds in printed 100% cotton furnishing fabrics suitable for all soft furnishing and upholstery. Sheer fabrics. Cushions, bedspreads etc. Remnants. Upholstered and discounted ex-display furniture. Wallpapers.

'Seconds fabrics from £1.50 per m, roll ends, remnants and quilt pieces. First quality from £7.95 per m. Curtain and blind-making service. January and July sales. In same mill: Pine Workshop, Sleepshop, Carpet Studio, Tansu antique Japanese furniture, Plant Shop and Lighting Gallery.'

See our display advertisement on p. 101

In an old mill, shop is clearly visible on A652, close to traffic lights where B6124 turns off.

From Batley market place: go downhill (Hick Lane) to traffic lights then go left.

From M62 exit 28: go south on A653 (for Dewsbury) then go right on to B6124 to Batley. At traffic lights, go right on to Bradford Road (A652). Large mill is shortly on right.

From Bradford: go south on A652. This huge mill is on the left shortly before the traffic lights where B6124 goes left.

Open: Mon–Sat 9.30–5.30; Sun 10–4.30; phone to check Bank Holidays.
Closed: Christmas Day; phone to check Boxing Day.
Cards: Access, Amex, Switch, Visa.
Cars: Own large car-park.
Toilets: Yes.
Wheelchairs: Access to large ground floor furniture show-room but not to first and second floor mill shops.
Teas: Hot-drink machine. Café 11–4 (except Mon). Pubs nearby.
Groups: Coach parties to shop very welcome.
Transport: Trains to Batley. Bradford–Dewsbury buses.
Mail order: Yes.
Catalogue: No.

Boynett Fabrics

2 Aston Road, off Cambridge Road MK42 0JM
(01234) 217788

Curtain and upholstery fabric by the metre. Curtain-making. New showroom for range of high quality upholstered furniture direct from own workshops. Protective table felt; lengths of PVC.

'Large selection of ends of ranges and slight seconds.'

Off the A5134 (Cambridge Road) south-east of Bedford centre.

From town centre: head south over river, go straight at traffic lights, take second exit at next roundabout (London Road). At second roundabout fork left, go straight at third roundabout; take second left, Aston Road.

From Luton on A6: go right at roundabout for Elstow (A5134). At next roundabout go straight (Mile Road). At next roundabout take second exit (Harrowden Road), go straight over next round-about into Cambridge Road. Take second left, Aston Road.

From A1, Sandy exit: take A603 for Bedford. After 5 miles go left at roundabout on to A5134 for Kempston. Take second right, Aston Road. Boynett 100 yds on left.

Open: Mon–Fri 9–5.30. Phone to check Saturdays.
Closed: Bank Holidays; Christmas–New Year.
Cards: Access, Eurocard, Mastercard, Visa.
Cars: On forecourt and street.
Toilets: Ask if desperate.
Wheelchairs: One small step to shop.
Teas: In local pub.
Groups: Groups welcome but must phone first.
Transport: Bus nos. 181, 182 to Hitchin; 176 to Biggleswade; 177 to Sandy.

Factory Fabrics

Tundry Way, Chainbridge Industrial Estate NE21 5SJ
(0191) 414 4515

Vast range of fabrics for curtains, furnishing, upholstery, loose covers etc, including leading designer names and department store clearance stock and over-runs. Curtain lining, tapes, and accessories. Curtain-making service.

'Perfects, seconds and remnants sold at discounted prices.'

Immediately south of the Tyne between the A1 and Scottswoood bridge

From A1 Western Bypass of Newcastle: turn on to A695 to Blaydon (south of river). Go under approach to old river bridge; take first left for 'Chainbridge Industrial Estate'. Factory Shop Centre is on left after you cross next bridge.

From Blaydon on A695: go under A1 Western Bypass, take first left into Chainbridge Industrial Estate. The Factory Shop Centre is on right just after left bend.

From Newcastle station: take A695 west. Pass the long Vickers factory, go left over Scotswood bridge. After bridge, take first left, go under Scotswood bridge, take first left to Chainbridge Industrial Estate. The Factory Shop Centre is on left after you cross next bridge.

Open: Mon–Fri 10–5 (Thur 10–7); Sat 9–5; Sun and Bank Holidays 10–4.
Closed: Christmas, Boxing and New Year's Days.
Cards: Access, Visa.
Cars: Own car-park.
Toilets: Yes.
Wheelchairs: One step; easy access.
Teas: Own café.
Groups: Groups of shoppers welcome.
Transport: Many buses from Gateshead and Newcastle.

Warwick Fabrics

Hackling House, Industrial Park GL54 2EN
(01451) 820772

Own-label furnishing fabrics: cotton satins, co-ordinating linen unions in patterns and plains plus woven jacquards. Linings, chintz, cushions, laptrays, muslins, moirés; heading tapes, fringes, cords, threads, tracks and poles.

'Perfect discontinued designs and some seconds. Discontinued designs from £2.95 per m for cottons (originally about £15). Current ranges also available. Most fabrics at 25–50% less than high street prices. Can recommend local seamstresses for curtain-making.'

On the northern side of the village, off the A429.

Coming south from Stow: just before you reach Bourton, follow sign left into Bourton Industrial Park. *

Coming north on A429: keep straight for Stow (don't go right into Bourton village); pass Coach and Horses Inn on right then take first right (for Bourton Industrial Park). *

***At first mini-roundabout go right; go over two speed humps, then company is on left. Shop is clearly visible.**

Open: Mon–Sat 10–5.
Closed: Bank Holidays; Christmas–New Year.
Cards: Access, Eurocard, Mastercard, Visa.
Cars: Car-park next to shop.
Toilets: In village.
Wheelchairs: No steps to ground floor but stairs to first floor.
Teas: Croft Cottage Restaurant in centre of village.
Groups: Groups always welcome to shop (larger groups please phone first).
Transport: None.
Mail order: Yes.
Catalogue: Samples of fabrics gladly sent.

SKOPOS MILL SHOP

FURNISHING FABRICS • WALLCOVERINGS
ROLL ENDS • REMNANTS • CUSHIONS
HUNDREDS OF NEWLY DISCONTINUED LINES
QUILTING • QUILTED PIECES • HABERDASHERY
CARPET SECONDS • CURTAIN TRACKS
ACCESSORIES • COFFEE SHOP

EX-DISPLAY FURNITURE WAREHOUSE

EX-DISPLAY & PROTOTYPE UPHOLSTERED
SOFAS • SOFA BEDS • CHAIRS

SKOPOS MILLS, BRADFORD ROAD BATLEY, WEST YORKSHIRE. WF17 6LZ
TEL: 01924 470489 FAX: 01924 472096

See our entries nos. 114, 147 and 228

Ahmad Textiles

348/350 Leeds Road BD3 9QY
(01274) 727069

Firsts, seconds, clearance and regular lines of furnishing, curtaining and dress fabrics and trimmings.

'Some of the cheapest fabrics in Yorkshire. Prices 30p–£4.50 per yard.

Special offer 10% discount to anyone who shows this book!'

....

On A647 east of Bradford, just inside the outer ring road.

From Bradford city centre on A647 towards Leeds: cross inner ring road A650; after about one mile, shop is on right, opposite Jet petrol.

From the end of M606: turn right on to A6177. Go over A650 and turn left on to A647 at traffic lights (Mr Value on far left corner). Pass Fina petrol on left; shop is shortly on the left opposite Jet petrol.

Open: Seven days a week 10–6.
Closed: Christmas Day.
Cards: No.
Cars: Car-park outside, parking for coaches nearby.
Toilets: In shop and in garage opposite.
Wheelchairs: No steps.
Teas: Sandwiches and drinks available from garage directly opposite; sandwiches from garage next door.
Groups: Shopping groups welcome, please telephone in advance.
Transport: Yorkshire Rider buses.
Mail order: No.

Just Fabrics

Burford Antiques Centre, Cheltenham Road OX18 4JA
(01993) 823391

Furnishing fabrics, own range of linen unions, weaves, chenilles, checks and stripes. Florals and chintzes, damasks, tapestries, jaquards, silks, moirés. Some designer clearance and seconds. Large stocks, all great value.

'Designer fabric clearance shop. Fabrics from £3.95 to £19.95 per yd.'

....

Clearly visible on the A40, south of Burford village and 50 yds from the major roundabout where A361 (Burford–Lechlade road) crosses A40. Shop is on south-west side of junction, diagonally opposite the Cotswold Gateway Hotel and beside Burford Antiques.

Open: Mon–Sat 9.30–5.30; Sun 2–5. Bank Holidays.
Closed: Christmas–New Year.
Cards: Access, Visa.
Cars: In forecourt.
Toilets: In Burford.
Wheelchairs: No steps to new large showroom.
Teas: Lots of hotels, old pubs and tea shops in Burford.
Groups: Shopping groups welcome if they phone first.
Transport: Buses from Oxford.
Mail order: Yes.
Catalogue: Swatches sent. Please describe what you are looking for.

120 Burnley Lancs

Color Blind

17 Farrington Court, Rossendale Road Industrial Estate
BB11 5ST   *(01282) 425504*

Blinds in large range of styles, colours, textures incl. washable.
Vertical, roller, pleated; conservatory roof blinds; Venetian
blinds in four slat widths. For DIY & commercial fitters.

*'Blinds also made to order. Fitting at nominal price within 30
miles. We only charge for width and believe our blinds are
cheapest in England. Vertical blinds £6 per ft width, any
length drop (eg patio door 6ft wide x 7ft for £36 + vat); roller
blinds trim and fit or made-to-measure £3 per ft width.'*

South-west of Burnley town centre.
   From town centre: take A679 west for Accrington.*
   **From M65 exit 10: aim for town centre. At large roundabout,
go right for Accrington (A679).***
   ***At traffic lights, go left into Rossendale Road (A646). After
1/2 mile, go right into Farrington Road. Shop 200 yds on left.**
   **From Rawtenstall on A56: at traffic lights, go left into
Rossendale Rd (A646). After 2/3 mile, go left into Farrington Rd.**
   **From Bacup on A671/Todmorden on A646: where these two
roads meet, south of town, go west on A646 for 2+ miles; go
left into Farrington Road.**

Open: Mon–Fri 10–5.30;
Sat 10–4.
Closed: Bank Holidays;
Christmas–New Year.
Cards: Access, Switch, Visa.
Cars: Outside shop.
Toilets: Yes.
Wheelchairs: Easy access
at rear.
Teas: Refreshment kiosk
nearby.
Groups: Max. 8 people –
phone Mr Donnelly in advance.
Transport: From town on
each half-hour: bus no. 1 to
Rose Grove/Whitegate; ask for
Farrington Road.
Mail order: Yes. Mail order
usual price plus carriage. No
seconds, fully guaranteed. Lots
of colourways and fabric sam-
ples for all types of blinds. Best
to phone first to clarify samples
and swatches required.

121 Chorley Lancs

Curtain Choice

Corporation Street PR6 0HK   *(01257) 272357*

Ready-made curtains including cotton velvets. Full range of
made-to-measure curtains and accessories. Nets, fabric by
the metre. Curtain poles, tracks. Bedding, quilts, towels etc.

*'Don't forget your window measurements! Clearance lines and
slight seconds. Perfects to order.'*

**A short way north-east of Chorley town centre and equidistant
from A6 (Park Road) and B6228 (Eaves Lane), which both run
north–south.**
   **Coming south on A6: go left to Highfield Ind. Estate; pass B&Q
on left; take second exit at double roundabout (Harpers Lane).***
   **From Chorley Town Hall (tall pointed clock tower): take A6 for
Preston. At first roundabout go right (B&Q on left); take second
exit (Harpers Lane).***
   ***Go over railway, take first right (Railway Road). Pass factory
on left, go left into Corporation Street. Shop is on right.**
   **From Eaves Lane (B6228): turn west into Geoffrey Street
opposite Halifax Building Society and beside Select Wine Co.; go
right at bottom (Doris Street), then first left (Corporation
Street). Shop is on corner. Take care – many small streets are
blocked off, others are one way!**

Open: Mon–Fri 10–4.30;
Sat 10–4.
Closed: Bank Holidays;
Spring Bank Holiday week;
last two weeks July (check);
Christmas–New Year.
Cards: Access, Visa.
Cars: In nearby streets.
Toilets: Town centre.
Wheelchairs: Access possible.
Teas: In Chorley centre.
Groups: Welcome small
groups of shoppers.
Transport: 15 minutes' walk
from town centre.
Mail order: No.

Hartleys (Mail Order) Shop

Regent House, Whitewalls Industrial Estate BB8 8LJ
(01282) 868587/861350

Large selection of quality silks, dress, curtain and sheeting fabrics; bedding (sheets, quilts, bedspreads, pillows), towels. Other textile bargains. Curtain-making service (don't forget your measurements). Wadding, patchwork squares, craft-work fabrics, remnants.

'An Aladdin's cave. Most fabrics and special offers way below high street prices. Savings galore, come and explore.'

....

Off the A56, between Nelson and Colne.
   From Colne: go south-west for Nelson, under railway bridge, follow signs to Whitewalls Industrial Estate.*
   From Nelson: take A56 for Colne; go left at sign to Whitewalls Industrial Estate.*
   From M65: follow signs to Whitewalls Industrial Estate.*
   ***Pass Asda on left then shop is 300 yds on right.**

Open: Mon–Fri 9.30–4.30; Sat 9.30–12.30.
Closed: Bank Holidays; Christmas–New Year.
Cards: Access, Visa.
Cars: Huge car-park outside.
Toilets: Ask if desperate.
Wheelchairs: No steps; large shop, one level.
Teas: Nearby pub for lunch.
Groups: No mill tours. Coaches welcome by appointment.
Transport: On main Nelson–Colne bus route, 3 minutes' walk from Asda bus stop.
Mail order: Yes.
Catalogue: Send 3 second class stamps for free mail-order catalogue and free samples – please mention this book. 95%+ are perfects. If imperfect or any doubts customers are advised accordingly in mail order.

Carrington Curtains Ltd.

23 Parliament Street HG1 2QV
(01423) 520198

Vast range of designer curtain and upholstery fabrics from most major manufacturers and designers. Full in-store making-up service for curtains, tie-backs, swags, tails, pelmets. Small selection of ready-made curtains.

Two floors with over 50,000 yds in stock. Perfects and seconds. Many fabrics reduced by 80%.'

....

Parliament Street is the main road (one-way, going north) through Harrogate centre.
   From the south/town centre: go through town for Ripon A61. Pass Betty's Tea Rooms on left. This huge shop, on a corner site, is further down the road on the left (opposite WH Smith on right and just uphill from Debenham's, also on right).
   From the north/Ripon: as you reach town, you come to traffic lights where you have to go left or right. This shop is in the road directly ahead, 100 yds on the right. However, as the road opposite is a one-way road coming towards you, you cannot enter. Park where you can and walk.

Open: Mon–Sat 9.30–5.30; Sun 11–4.30.
Closed: Christmas and New Year's Days.
Cards: Access, Switch, Visa.
Cars: One-hour blue-disc parking in Parliament Street. Public car-parks.
Toilets: In city centre.
Wheelchairs: Easy access to large ground floor but not to upstairs showroom.
Teas: Betty's Tea Rooms 50 yds uphill. Lots of places in town.
Groups: Shopping groups please book with shop manager.
Transport: Any bus or train to Harrogate.
Mail order: Postal service to forward customers' orders.

Walton's Mill Shop

41 Tower Street HG1 1HR
(01423) 520980

Wide range of household textiles, many commission-woven in Lancashire: table linen, bedding. Extensive range of international designer furnishing fabrics and furnishing braids/trimmings at clearance prices.

'Company set up in 1785 sells the more traditional textiles. Factory/clearance prices in Aladdin's cave of designer fabrics and mouthwatering braids and trimmings! Try our famous "Knaresborough" linen dish cloth and you'll never use anything else!'

Close to town centre, on southern side.
   Coming into town on A61 (from Leeds) or A658 (Otley/Bradford): cross roundabout at ring road (B6162) on to one-way system*
   From elsewhere: follow main road round town to roundabout with signs to 'Town Centre & Ripon A61'. Go to town on one-way system* (with park on left). Get into right lane. Turn right after Coach and Horses into Tower Street, at large car-park sign. Shop is 100 yds on left.

Open: Mon–Sat 10–5.
Closed: Bank Holidays; Christmas–New Year.
Cards: Access, Eurocard, Visa.
Cars: Two spaces by shop; nearby multi-storey car-park – first two hours free parking.
Toilets: By car-park.
Wheelchairs: One tiny step to medium-sized shop.
Teas: Cafés and tea rooms.
Groups: Please phone Mrs Jarratt to arrange shopping groups.
Transport: Trains and buses to Harrogate then 5–10 minutes' walk.
Mail order: Yes.
Catalogue: No.

The Fabric Factory

Navigation Garage Site, Loscoe Road, DE7 7FE
(01773) 718911

Large range of upholstery and furnishing fabrics and curtaining. Dress fabrics, fleece fabrics, T-shirting, lycra, cottons, linens, jerseys, bridal fabrics. Curtain making up service. Knitting wools and haberdashery department.

'Full range of Curtina curtain fabrics from £5.99 per m. Viscose prints from £1.99. Lowest possible prices on all fabrics. Patterns. Knitting wools (full range) plus haberdashery department. Children's play area with toys.'

See our display advertisement on p. 107

On the A6007 between Heanor and Codnor.
   From centre of Heanor: go north for Loscoe/Codnor/Ripley. Go downhill out of town and road bends to left: this conspicuous new building (brick with silver roof) is on right.
   From Ripley/Codnor: at traffic lights in Codnor, go south on A6007 for Heanor. Go through Loscoe then at start of Heanor pass Fina petrol station and Kwik-Fit on left. This new building is immediately past them.

Open: Mon–Fri 9.30–5.30; Sat 9.30–5; Sun 10–2. Some Bank Holidays.
Closed: Christmas and Boxing Days.
Cards: Access, Visa.
Cars: Own car-park.
Toilets: Yes.
Wheelchairs: One small step to large shop.
Teas: Self-service cafeteria with vending machines for tea/coffee, soft drinks and snacks. Also Sky TV lounge.
Groups: Groups of shoppers always welcome.
Transport: Buses from Ripley, Heanor and Alfreton.

Den-Home Cushioning

*Unit 2, Sycamore Industrial Estate, Walkley Lane WF16 0NL
(01924) 412188*

Ready-made and made-to-measure curtains, valances, tie
backs, swags and tails. Cotton satin and velvet cushion covers, cushion interiors and seat pads. Fabrics, bedding, table
covers and tea-towels. Curtain poles, tracks and accessories.
'We sell firsts and seconds.'

On the south side of Heckmondwike.

*From the centre of Heckmondwike: turn off main road (A638,
Bradford–Dewsbury Road) at clocktower into Market Street
(B6117 to Dewsbury Moor). NatWest is on your left. After 150
yds, this road becomes Walkley Lane. Pass the Exhaust Centre
on the right. Continue for 200 yds (Burma garage on left) and
shop is directly opposite on right in small industrial estate.*

Open: Mon–Thur 9–4;
Fri 9–3.30.
Closed: Bank Holidays;
Christmas–New Year.
Cards: No.
Cars: Customer car-park
outside shop.
Toilets: Ask in emergency.
Wheelchairs: Easy access.
Teas: Cafés in town centre.
Groups: Shopping groups
welcome by prior arrangement.
Transport: Bus nos. 254, 255,
256, 259 from Dewsbury to
other towns all stop at top of
yard.
Mail order: No.

GP & J Baker Ltd. & Parkertex Fabrics Ltd.

The Warehouse, Desborough Road HP11 2QE (01494) 467467

Wide range of curtain and upholstery fabrics: prints,
damasks, jacquards, selected range of naturals; also
wallpapers and borders.

*'Britain's leading suppliers of fine furnishing fabrics & wall-
papers. Large selection of near perfect & discontinued lines at
substantially reduced prices.'*

South of the town centre.

*From M40 exit 4: at roundabout take fifth exit (to Cressex
Ind. Est.). Go over mini roundabout; take next left by garage into
Desborough Ave. Go downhill past Kitchener Rd on left; take
second right (West End Rd) before mini-roundabout. Go to far
end; go right into clearly marked car-park.*

*From London via A40: go right towards town centre at triple
roundabout; with huge Buckinghamshire College on left and fire
station on right, go on to dual carriageway. Go left just after
college for Desborough Road Shopping Area. At T-junction go
left; keep straight to Bakers on left. Go left after company into
side road (West End Road).*

*From Oxford on A40: at traffic lights (Europcar on near right),
go right for Wycombe Gen. Hosp. At double mini-roundabout, go
left. Pass red-brick church on right; take next right (West End Rd).*

Open: Sat 9–1.
Closed: Christmas, New Year
and Easter weekend.
Cards: Access, Switch, Visa.
Cars: Yes.
Toilets: Yes.
Wheelchairs: Two steps
into shop.
Teas: Cafés in town.
Groups: Not really suitable
for shopping groups.
Transport: Local buses.
Mail order: No.

FABRIC
SUPER○STORE

MASSIVE STOCKS – LOW LOW PRICES

Simply the biggest, best, choice-quality-prices.
Located mid-way between Derby and Nottingham.

"Special treats" on dress-making fabrics

NEW LOOK Patterns-
STYLE
SIMPLICITY **BURDA**

BRIDAL FABRICS beautiful fabrics for low-budget brides

Fabrics for every occasion, every season & taste

Open to the public 7 days every week.
Mon – Sat 9.30 – 5.30
Sundays 10.00 – 2.00

CURTAIN FABRICS

POSSIBLY THE LARGEST STOCK IN THE AREA

1,000s & 1,000s of metres at embarrassingly low prices

Full measuring and making up service.

"END OF ROLLS" clearance curtain fabrics £1.99 always on offer.

LININGS, CHINTZ, MOIRE, ETC. complemented by large haberdashery department.

The FABRIC FACTORY

Loscoe Road Heanor, Derbys
Located on A6007 between Heanor & Codnor.
Telephone 01773 718911

See our entry no. 125

The Mill Fabric Shop

Cartwright Street, Newton SK14 4QU
(0161) 367 9337

Printed cotton and satin furnishing fabrics, curtain fabrics including plain dyed satin and chintz; curtain linings; ready-made and made-to-measure curtains. Scatter cushions, tablecloths, tea cosies, oven gloves, aprons and placemats.

'Perfects and seconds, most at half price or less, eg slightly imperfect fabric from £1.50 per yd.'

On the north-east side of Hyde.
    From Manchester/the west: take M67 exit 3 for Dukinfield/ Hyde town centre. Turn left for Duckinfield at sliproad traffic lights then right at next traffic lights into Clarendon Rd. *
    From Hyde centre: follow signs for Newton; continue as below when on Clarendon Road. *
    Going east on M67: exit for Hyde, go over motorway; at traffic lights go right into Clarendon Road. *
    **Keep straight, through next traffic lights into Victoria Street. After 1/2 mile fork left, Cartwright Street. Shop entrance is on right side opposite Park House, before junction with Talbot Rd.*

Open: Tues–Sat 9–5. Phone to check other days.
Closed: Bank Holidays; Easter; Christmas–New Year. Phone to confirm.
Cards: Access, Switch, Visa.
Cars: In nearby streets.
Toilets: No.
Wheelchairs: Ten steps to shop; entry through warehouse by arrangement with shop manager.
Teas: Pub on the corner.
Groups: Shopping groups by prior arrangement with Mr P Roberts.
Transport: BR Hyde Central station. Bus nos. 209 and 346 from bus station.
Mail order: No.

Paul Steiger

Byron Avenue, Lowmoor Industrial Estate NG17 7LB
(01623) 721628

Curtain lace, by the yard and all types of readymades; also enlarging range to cover a collection of roller blinds, shower curtains, display tables with table cloths and matching all lace window sets. All made on site.

'First quality at factory prices and good quality seconds.'

Between Kirkby and Sutton-in-Ashfield.
    From M1 exit 28: take A38 for Mansfield. Go right at fifth traffic lights (for Kirkby-in-Ashfield Industrial Estates); at next lights go right on to B6021 (Lowmoor Road); after 100 yds go left (Byron Avenue). *
    From traffic lights in centre of Kirkby (Nag's Head pub on left): take B6021 for 1 mile; pass Romo factory on left, go right off Lowmoor Road into Byron Avenue. *
    **Go left after Paul Steiger factory into Prospect Close: factory shop on left.*

Open: Tues–Fri 10–4; Sat 10–1. Some Bank Holidays – please phone.
Closed: Monday; Christmas–New Year.
Cards: Access, Visa.
Cars: Street parking and own car-park.
Toilets: In town.
Wheelchairs: Ramp to door.
Teas: In town.
Groups: Groups welcome; please phone Dorothy Adkin first.
Transport: Bus no. 120 to Lowmoor Road.
Mail order: No.

Standfast

Caton Road LA1 3PB
No phone in shop.

Seconds in printed fabrics, including many well known designer names for curtains and upholstery (cottons, linens, chintz and sateens). Also sell small pieces suitable for cushions or patchwork.

....

Nearly a mile north of the town.

From Lancaster: follow signs to the M6 (northbound). This takes you along the A683 (Caton Rd). Pass the clock-tower on the left, then the company is 100 yds on the left, with the name clearly displayed.

From M6 exit 34: follow the signs to Lancaster. Company is about a mile on your right, immediately past Shell petrol station.

Please do NOT park inside main gate – hinders emergency access.

Open: Mon–Fri 9.30–1;
Sat 10–12.30
Closed: Bank Holidays;
Christmas–New Year.
Cards: None.
Cars: Special car-park across the road.
Toilets: Yes.
Wheelchairs: Five steps into shop. You can arrange to go in via the warehouse for easier access.
Teas: In Lancaster.
Tours: No mill tours.
Transport: None.

The Curtain Factory Shop

279 High Street LN2 1JG
(01522) 522740

Full range of *Filigree* products. Lace and net curtains; ready made curtains; custom made voiles. Curtain rails and accessories also available.

'Filigree factory seconds at less than half perfect price.'
See our display advertisement on p. 119

....

The High Street (pedestrianised) is the main shopping street (running north–south) in Lincoln, on the south side of the cathedral hill. This shop is 20 yds north of Corporation Street, next to the Job Centre and 50 yds from Binns Department Store.

Open: Mon–Sat 9–5.30.
Closed: Bank Holidays;
Christmas, Boxing and New Year's Days.
Cards: Access, Switch, Visa.
Cars: Public car-park 200 yds away.
Toilets: Ask if desperate.
Wheelchairs: Easy access; no steps.
Teas: Many cafés in town.
Groups: Small shopping groups welcome.
Transport: Any bus or train to Lincoln, then walk.
Mail order: No.

Corcoran & May

11 Ealing Green, High Street W5 5DA
(0181) 567 4324

Fabrics for curtains and furnishing. Top designers such as
Parkertex, GP & J Baker, Colefax & Fowler, Monkwell and
Christian Fischbacher all use Corcoran & May to dispose of
seconds and overstocks. Thousands of metres available at
any one time. Curtains and blinds made-to-measure.

*'Many fabrics less than half recommended retail price.
Average price £9.95.'*

Near the Broadway Shopping Centre.
    From central London along Uxbridge Road (A4020): turn left
directly after Marks & Spencer into the High Street. Shop is just
before the mini-roundabout, on left-hand side.
    From M4 exit 2: at roundabout go north (right if you come
from London) into South Ealing Road. After 1 mile this road
becomes The Green: shop is on right-hand side.

Open: Mon–Sat 10–5.30.
Closed: Bank Holidays,
Christmas–New Year.
Cards: Access, Visa.
Cars: Many public car-parks
nearby.
Toilets: Yes.
Wheelchairs: No steps to
medium sized shop.
Teas: Local coffee shops
nearby.
Transport: Ealing Broadway
BR station and tube. Bus
no. 207.

Corcoran & May

157/161 Lower Richmond Road, Putney SW15 1HH
(0181) 788 9556

Fabrics for curtains and furnishing. Top designers such as
Parkertex, GP & J Baker, Colefax & Fowler, Monkwell and
Christian Fischbacher all use Corcoran & May to dispose of
seconds and overstocks. Thousands of metres available at
any one time. Curtains and blinds made to measure.

*'Many fabrics less than half recommended retail price.
Average price £9.95.'*

**Easy to see in the main road from Putney to Barnes. (NB Lower
Richmond Road is very long – you need the section nearer
Putney, not near Richmond and Mortlake cemetery.)**
    From the south side of Putney bridge: take the road leading
west along the Thames bank. Keep straight for 1/2 mile. Pass
Shell petrol on the left then this double-fronted shop is on the left.

Open: Mon–Sat 10–5.30.
Closed: Bank Holidays;
Christmas–New Year.
Cards: Access, Visa.
Cars: Side streets.
Toilets: Yes.
Wheelchairs: Two steps to
medium shop.
Teas: Coffee shops nearby.
Transport: Putney Bridge
tube; Putney BR station;
bus no. 22.

Barracks Fabrics

Black Lane SK10 2AZ
(01625) 423165

Closed - fabrics now sold at Standfast, see entry no. 130

Printers of fabrics: dress fabrics such as silks, wool challis, shawls and scarves; good range of furnishing fabrics for curtaining and upholstery.

....

From Macclesfield town centre: you need to aim for Whaley Bridge (A5002 Hurdsfield Road). Pass Tesco entrance on left. At traffic lights, go left (in front of Plumb Centre).*

From Manchester/Stockport, coming south into town on A523: passing Tesco on left, at roundabout go left for Whaley Bridge. Pass Tesco entrance. At traffic lights, go left (in front of Plumb Centre).*

From Whaley Bridge (A5002): as you come into town: go over two traffic lights then turn right after Plumb Centre into narrow Black Lane.*

*Keep straight along Black Lane, go through factory gates, past factory on right to car-park by shop at back left.

Open: Thur 10.30–3; Fri 10.30–5; Sat 10.30–3.30.
Closed: Bank Holidays; Christmas–New Year (phone to check).
Cards: None.
Cars: In factory yard.
Toilets: Yes.
Wheelchairs: No steps; easy access to medium sized shop.
Teas: Pubs and cafés in town. 5 minutes' walk to Arighi Bianchi store/coffee shop.
Transport: Easy walk from town centre/railway.
Mail order: No.

Material Things

38 Charlotte Street SK11 6JA   *(01625) 428923*

Curtain and upholstery fabrics by top designers; sheeting. Ends of lines and seconds.

'Cut lengths at quarter of usual retail price, rolls at half usual price.'

....

In the tangle of little streets in old town centre, facing and on downhill side of The Pickford Centre (Discount Giant) supermarket car-park.

From Stockport/Manchester via A523: at roundabout (Tesco on left) keep straight; follow new Silk Road; go right at lights, under railway lines, to station.*

From Buxton on A537: at traffic lights at bottom of hill, go straight under railway for station.*

*Pass station on your left; continue into Sunderland Street. Pass bus station and George & Dragon, both on right; go right after Animal World into Pickford Street.**

From Leek on A523 or Congleton on A536: from traffic lights where these road converge at bottom of main road through town (Mill Street), aim for station. Pass the Jolly Sailor on left then go left (Pickford Street).**

**Go right into Charlotte Street. Shop 50 yds on right.

Open: Mon, Tues 9.30–5; Wed 10–5; Thur–Sat 9–5.30.
Closed: Bank Holidays; Christmas, Boxing and New Year's Days.
Cards: Access, Visa.
Cars: Public car-park next door.
Toilets: In supermarket next door.
Wheelchairs: Access to ground floor showrooms; three small showrooms upstairs.
Teas: In supermarket next door.
Groups: Not suitable for groups.
Transport: Easy walk from bus and train stations.
Mail order: No.

The Fabric Mill Shop

21 North Street M8 8RF
(0161) 834 4920

Most famous brands of curtain fabrics by the yard; over 1200 rolls of plains and prints: damasks, brocades, chintz, jacquards and many more. Curtain linings: sateen, easy-care, thermal, black-out, bump interlining etc, and tapes. Made-to-measure curtain service.

'Only perfects; prices 25–50% lower than in high street on all branded fabrics. If any branded curtain fabric not in stock we will try to obtain it within 3–4 working days.'

....

Cheetham Hill is the area about 1.5 miles north of the city centre, just north of Victoria station.

From the city centre/Victoria station: take A665 north. This is Cheetham Hill Road (which becomes Bury Old Road). From Victoria station, keep straight for about 1/4 mile, then go sharp right (opposite Murco petrol) into Derby Street. At end of Derby Street go left into North Street. Shop is 50 yds on left.

Open: Mon–Fri 9.30–5.30; Sat 9–5; Sun 10–4. Bank Holidays please check.
Closed: 24 Dec–4 Jan.
Cards: Access, Switch, Visa.
Cars: Own customer car-park.
Toilets: Yes.
Wheelchairs: Level access to big shop.
Teas: Lots of places in city centre and in Cheetham Hill Road.
Groups: Shopping groups please phone for appointment.
Transport: Numerous buses from Manchester Piccadilly to Cheetham Hill.
Mail order: Yes. Anything under £250 carriage charge £10.
Catalogue: No.

Homebirds – The Fabric Trading Company

The Coach House, Langton Hall LE16 7TV   (01858) 545814

Top makes in furnishing fabrics including small specialised designers – fine chintz to upholstery weights at bargain prices. Complete making-up service, including curtains, cushions, loose covers, re-upholstery etc.

'Fabrics mostly seconds, from £2.95 per m. Perfect fabric & wallpaper to order (not discounted) including Osborne & Little, Hill & Knowles, Monkwell, Malabar Cotton Company, Nina Campbell, Brian Yates, Zoffany, Thomas Dare & Tabby Cat.'

....

West Langton (not on all maps!) is a small village 1/4 mile west of Church Langton and 4 miles north of Market Harborough.

Coming north on A6 from Market Harborough: take B6047 at roundabout, go under railway bridge, up hill for 1/4 mile, turn left at crossroads to West Langton. *

Coming south on B6047 (Melton/Market Harborough road): turn west for West Langton; *pass farms, houses then turn right into country estate.

Coming south on A6: after Kibworth Beauchamp; turn left immediately before railway bridge for The Langtons. After 1 1/3 miles, turn left through well marked gateway of Langton Hall (prominent sign for golfing hotel). Go straight for shop.

Open: Mon–Sat 9.30–5. Evenings and special events by appointment.
Closed: Bank Holidays; Christmas Day.
Cards: None.
Cars: Large car-park.
Toilets: Yes.
Wheelchairs: Short distance across gravel to medium-sized ground floor shop.
Teas: Tea available in Hall. Pub in Church Langton, tea room in Kibworth.
Groups: Happy to accommodate pre-booked groups.
Transport: None.
Mail order: No.

Fabric Design

10-12 North Parade DE4 3NS
(01629) 584747

Leading supplier of designer furnishing fabric seconds: linens, cottons, damasks, moirés and chintz.

'Phone for dates of special sales. Cottons from £3.75 yd, plain linen £5.99 yd. Majority of fabrics reduced up to 80%. Seconds and clearance lines.'

Easy to find in long parade of shops in Matlock Bath.
   From Matlock: as you reach Matlock Bath, look for detached, square stone Midland Hotel on left; shop is almost opposite.
   From Cromford/Derby on A6: go through Matlock Bath to far end of shops. Shop on left.

Open: Tues, Wed, Fri, Sat 10–5; Mon, Thur, Sun 1.30–5.
Closed: Bank Holidays; Christmas, Boxing and New Year's Days.
Cards: Access, Amex, Visa.
Cars: Limited parking outside; car-park across road near station.
Toilets: Opposite shop.
Wheelchairs: Two small steps; assistance if needed.
Teas: Lots of places in Matlock Bath.
Groups: Shopping groups welcome with prior notice.
Transport: Any bus or train to Matlock Bath.
Mail order: Yes.
Catalogue: Free brochure. No restrictions.

Color Blind

Unit 6, Middleton Central Industrial Estate, Oldham Road
M24 1AS   *(0161) 643 3800*

Blinds in large range of styles, colours, textures including washable. Vertical, roller, pleated; conservatory roof blinds; Venetian blinds in four slat widths. Ideal for DIY or commercial fitters.

'Blinds also made to order. Fitting at nominal price within 30 miles. Only charge for width and we believe our blinds are the cheapest in England. Vertical blinds £6 per ft width, any length drop (eg patio door 6ft wide x 7ft for £36 + vat); roller blinds trim and fit or made-to-measure £3 per ft width.'

Easy to find in the small industrial estate along road from huge Warwick mill on Oldham Rd, main road (A669) through Middleton.
   Going north on Manchester New Rd (A664): at first roundabout go right; double back at next roundabout. Pass huge mill on left.*
   Coming west from Oldham on A669: at first roundabout go straight; pass huge mill on left.*
   Via Manchester Old Rd (A576) going east: keep straight; pass Arndale Centre and bus station on left. At roundabout go straight; at next roundabout double back. Pass huge mill on left.*
   *Go left (by road sign) just before next roundabout, into estate.

Open: Mon–Fri 10–5.30; Sat 10-4.
Closed: Christmas holidays and Bank Holidays.
Cards: Access, Visa, Switch.
Cars: Outside shop.
Toilets: Nearest at bus station.
Wheelchairs: One step.
Teas: Café in Arndale Centre.
Groups: Max 8 people – phone Mr Donnelly prior to visit.
Transport: Bus nos. 17, 163, 59 from Manchester
Mail order: Yes.
Catalogue: Mail order usual price plus carriage. No seconds, fully guaranteed. Lots of colourways and fabric samples for all types of blinds. Best to phone first to clarify samples and swatches required.

Abakhan Fabrics

Coast Road, Llanerch-y-Mor CH8 9DX
(01745) 560312

One of the largest selections of fabrics, needlecrafts and knitting yarns in the North-West, housed in a carefully restored 100 ft main building on a 10-acre site.

'This former lead smelting shed was winner of the Prince of Wales Award 1988. Fabric and wool shops, crafts and gifts, children's play area, coffee shop and free parking. Company does not make anything but specialises in clearing lines, job lots etc. Special offer fabric rolls from 5p per m. Also in Liverpool, Manchester, Birkenhead.'

Large, conspicuous converted industrial building on the coast side of Coast Road (A548), 5 miles north of Flint and 2 miles south of Mostyn.

Open: Mon–Sun 9–5 (Thur 9–8). Bank Holidays.
Closed: Christmas Eve; Christmas, Boxing and New Year's Days.
Cards: Access, Connect, Switch, Visa.
Cars: Own large car-park.
Toilets: Yes; for disabled too.
Wheelchairs: Ramp to ground floor. Access to 60% of public areas.
Teas: Own coffee shop for snacks, light meals. Children's play area.
Groups: Pre-booked coach parties welcome, discounts given.
Transport: Trains to Flint and Rhyl stations. Bus nos. A8, A18, X1 to Llanerch-y-Mor (Mostyn).
Mail order: Yes.
Catalogue: No. Post specific orders only.

Florentine Trading Co. Ltd.

Sherwood Mills, 20 Victoria Road NG5 2NB
(0115) 960 5444

Make net curtains, jardinières, Austrian swags, Austrian blinds, café nets, macramé nets, lace tablecloths and mats, napery; also sell household linens.

'Some ends of lines and seconds usually available. Quick alteration service on non-standard size nets. Extra wide jardinières available. Made to measure service.'

On the north side of city centre.
From Nottingham: take Mansfield Road (A60) north. Go over first large roundabout and turn left at traffic lights (A611 for Hucknall). Pass Sunblest Bakery, go right at traffic lights into Haydn Road.*
From the ring road: turn south by City Hospital on to A611 (Hucknall Road) for city centre; at second traffic lights, go left (Haydn Road).*
***After 300 yds go left in front of pink glass building into Victoria Road. Shop in low white building on right.**

Open: Mon–Fri 9.15–4; Sat 9.15–1.
Closed: Bank Holidays; Christmas–New Year.
Cards: None.
Cars: In street.
Toilets: In Sherwood.
Wheelchairs: Four steep steps.
Teas: Café in Sherwood.
Groups: Not suitable for group visits.
Transport: Bus nos. 55–59 from Nottingham to Haydn Road.
Mail order: No.

Joman Manufacturing Co. Ltd.

1–3 Lister Road, North West Industrial Estate SR8 2RB
(0191) 518 1008

Large stocks of curtain material at factory prices, specialist manufacturers of curtains, stretch and loose covers. Mail order ends of lines – car seat covers, scatter cushions, underblankets etc; also caravan upholstery covers and curtains.

'Made-to-measure service. Firsts and seconds at factory prices.'

In large industrial estate west of the A19.

   From A19 exit for 'Peterlee/Horden' on B1320. From this exit roundabout, follow signs to North West Industrial Estate. Pass Dewhirst on right and take next left (into Lister Road). Joman is in first building on the left.

Open: Mon–Fri 9–5; Sat 10–4.
Closed: Bank Holidays; Christmas–New Year.
Cards: None.
Cars: Outside shop.
Toilets: Yes.
Wheelchairs: Easy access to large shop.
Teas: In town.
Groups: Pre-booked groups of shoppers welcome; please contact Mr Chapman or Mr Hall.
Transport: Sunderland, Hartlepool and Durham buses stop in vicinity.
Mail order: No.

P B A Mill Shop

Unit 5, New Hall Hey Road BB4 6HL
(01706) 222146

Big range of clearance lines and seconds from leading fabric manufacturers – *Romo, Crowson, Ametex, Sanderson* etc. Plain chintz, lining, wallpapers and brassware. All major names to order from pattern books at discounted prices. Making–up service.

'Roll ends from £1.95 per yd. Full rolls from £3.50 per yd. Perfects also available.

On the south-west side of Rawtenstall.

   From town centre and all directions: find huge roundabout with Asda on one corner and Shell on far side. With Asda on left, take Bury Road for Edenfield. Take first right (New Hall Hey Road), pass Kwik Save on right. Shop at far end on left before level crossing.

   If you miss above turn-off, take A682 for Bury/Manchester. After 400 yds go left on to slip road for New Hall Hey Industrial Estate. Go left in front of mill, over level crossing: shop in first building on right.

Open: Mon–Fri 10–5; Sat 10.30–4; Sun 11–4. Bank Holidays as normal.
Closed: Christmas and New Year's Days.
Cards: Access, Visa (2% extra).
Cars: Own yard.
Toilets: On first floor.
Wheelchairs: One step to large ground floor showroom; upstairs showroom.
Teas: Two minutes' walk, in Groundwork Trust.
Groups: Shoppers welcome if they phone first.
Transport: Any bus to town then 10 minutes' walk.
Mail order: Yes.
Catalogue: Customers can order by manufacturers' code any of the ranges. Seconds stock more difficult. Happy to supply cuttings by post. Linings, chintz, heading tape etc can all be sent.

Ettrick Forest Interiors
Forest Mill, Station Road TD7 5DK
(01750) 22519

Own range of cotton furnishing fabrics printed on premises. Designer seconds and discontinued ranges by *Sanderson, Monkwell* and many others. Remnants and fabrics for patchwork. *Ettrick Valley* own brand tea towels, PVC aprons and bags, oven gloves and tea cosies on Scottish and country themes.

'Fabrics from £3.95 per m. Seconds tea towels £1.75 each, seconds PVC aprons and bags £3.99 each. Postal service. Curtains and soft furnishings to order.'

From Peebles/Innerleithen on A707 and Moffat on A708: cross river, go left at once into Buccleuch Road. Take first left; shop straight ahead at T-junction.

From Hawick on A7: go through Selkirk, turn left after Exacta, before Selkirk Glass. *

From Edinburgh and Galashiels on A7: take first right after Selkirk Glass. *

*After 1 mile, go right to swimming baths. Shop is straight ahead at T-junction.

Open: Mon–Sat 10–5.
Closed: 3 April; 1 May; 15–17 June; 9 Oct; 22 Dec for two weeks.
Cards: Access, Visa.
Cars: Outside.
Toilets: Yes.
Wheelchairs: Two steps down into shop.
Teas: In Selkirk.
Groups: Groups welcome to shop; phone call first appreciated.
Transport: Bus from Galashiels or Hawick to Selkirk square, then 10 minutes' walk.

Corcoran & May
1 St Botolph's Road TN13 3AK
(01732) 741851

Fabrics for curtains and furnishing. Top designers such as *Parkertex, GP & J Baker, Colefax & Fowler, Monkwell* and *Christian Fischbacher* all use Corcoran & May to dispose of seconds and overstocks. Thousands of metres available at any one time. Curtains and blinds made to measure.

'Many fabrics less than half recommended retail price. Average price £9.95.'

Easy to find on the north side of town, 100 yds from the station.

From the M25/north: aim for Sevenoaks centre. Pass the station on your right. *

*From the station: go uphill; pass the Railway & Bicycle pub on right; shop is on next near left corner.

From the south/Hildenborough: go into town, pass Knowle House (NT) on right; fork left for Dunton Green/London/M25. Go through town and downhill. Pass Jaguar showroom on right then after several hundred yards, shop is clearly visible on far right corner.

Open: Mon–Sat 10–5.30.
Closed: Bank Holidays; Christmas–New Year.
Cards: Access, Visa.
Cars: Street parking nearby (double lines immediately outside).
Toilets: Yes.
Wheelchairs: No steps to medium sized shop.
Teas: Lots of tea shops in town.
Transport: Any train or bus to town.

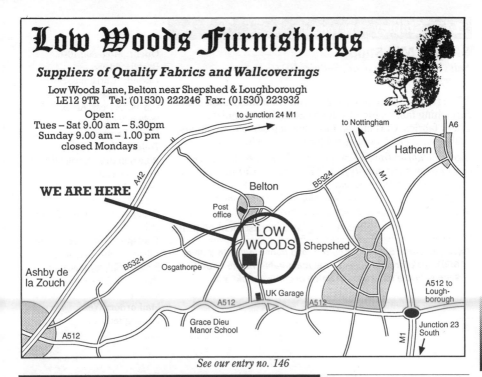

Low Woods Furnishings

Suppliers of Quality Fabrics and Wallcoverings

Low Woods Lane, Belton near Shepshed & Loughborough
LE12 9TR   Tel: (01530) 222246 Fax: (01530) 223932

Open:
Tues – Sat 9.00 am – 5.30pm
Sunday 9.00 am – 1.00 pm
closed Mondays

WE ARE HERE

See our entry no. 146

Low Woods Furnishings

Low Woods Lane, Belton LE12 9TP   *(01530) 222246*

30,000 metres of designer fabrics suitable for curtains and upholstery always in stock. Curtains, blinds and other soft furnishings made in our own workrooms.

'Extensive range of quality fabrics mostly off-shade seconds, discontinued lines etc. Fabrics from £2.95–£11 per yd. Most £6.99 per yd. Friendly staff always available to help with measurements or colour schemes. Children's play area.'

See our display advertisement above.

Low Woods is a small hamlet north of the A51 and west of M1.
    From M1 exit 23: aim west for Ashby on A512. After 4 miles, pass UK Garage on right; after 300 yds go right for Low Woods 1/2 mile.*
    From Ashby on A512: pass Grace Dieu Manor School on right; after 1/3 mile, go left for Low Woods. *Half a mile down this country lane go right (sign) to shop in first building on right.
    From A6 at Hathern: take B5324 to Belton (4 miles). From Belton sign 'Please go carefully through our village' stay on B5324. Go straight at two crossroads; at third crossroad (Belton Baptist Church far right corner), go left in front of pink cottage (far left corner) into Gracedieu Lane. After 200 yds take 1st left, Low Woods Lane. Shop 3/4 mile along lane (2nd building on left).

Open: Tues–Sat 9–5.30; Sun 9–1.
Closed: Mon; Christmas and New Year's Days; some Bank Holidays. Please phone to check.
Cards: Cash or cheque with bank card only.
Cars: Large car-park next to showroom.
Toilets: Yes.
Wheelchairs: Easy access.
Teas: Local pub serves refreshments all day.
Groups: Welcome everybody! Coach parties by prior phone call please.
Transport: None.
Mail order: No.

---

147 Shipley W Yorks

Skopos Mill Shop

Salt's Mill, Victoria Road, Saltaire BD18 3LA
(01274) 581121

Wide range of seconds and remnants in printed 100% cotton furnishing fabrics for all soft furnishing and upholstery. Sheer fabrics. Curtain and blind-making service. Cushions, bedspreads etc. Upholstered furniture. Wallpapers.

'Seconds fabrics from £1.50 per m, roll ends, remnants and quilt pieces. First quality from £7.95 per m. Curtain and blind-making service. January and July sales. Mill also houses Hockney Gallery, 1853 gallery bookshop, The Home for designer interiors and Skopos Furniture Gallery.'

See our display advertisement on p. 101

Once you are in Shipley, or on the road from Bingley to Shipley (A650), look for road signs to the remarkable village of Saltaire. Shop is in the basement of Salt's magnificent old mill.

Open: Mon–Sun 10–6. Bank Holidays.
Closed: Christmas, Boxing and New Year Days.
Cards: Access, Amex, Switch, Visa.
Cars: Large on-site car-park.
Toilets: Yes.
Wheelchairs: Small flight of steps, then lift.
Teas: American-style diner in the mill complex.
Groups: Welcome with phone call.
Transport: Few yards from Saltaire Metro station. Any Bingley–Shipley bus, then short walk. Canal buses in season.
Mail order: Yes.
Catalogue: No.

148 South Croydon Surrey

Fabric World

6–10 Brighton Road CR2 6AB
(0181) 688 6282

3,000 rolls of designer and branded curtain and upholstery fabrics sold by the metre.

'Most stock perfects (ends of ranges and repeatable designs), some seconds, at about 50% off normal high street price. From £3.30–£13 per metre. Interior design service – we visit your home (free, without obligation). Also make-up service for all types of curtains.'

About 1/4 mile south of Croydon on A235.
Going south from Croydon towards Purley: go straight at traffic lights (not left for Selsdon). Swan & Sugar Loaf pub is on left; Barclays Bank on far right corner. Shop is immediately after the bank. [To park, go right at these lights into Warham Road.]
Coming north from Purley: pass Whitgift School and sports field on left, then shop is shortly on left.

Open: Mon–Sat 9–5.30.
Closed: Most Bank Holidays. Christmas, Boxing and New Year's Days.
Cards: Access, Connect, Mastercard, Visa, Switch.
Cars: Meters in Warham Road.
Toilets: Yes.
Wheelchairs: No steps, large shop.
Teas: Tea made for weary customers; or in Croydon.
Groups: Shopping groups welcome – please phone Debbie Shinerock first.
Transport: Lots of buses from near East Croydon BR stop at Swan & Sugar Loaf pub opposite.
Mail order: No.

FILIGREE

Lace and Net Curtaining, Ready Made Curtains, Lace Tablecloths, Austrian Blinds, Roller Blinds, Duvets and other Bedding, Curtain Rails and Accessories

Filigree Factory Shop, Berristow Lane
South Normanton, Derbyshire DE55 2EG
Mon – Thur 9 – 4; Fri 9 – 6.30;
Sat 9 – 1.30; Bank Holidays 10 – 4.
Tel 01773 811630

The Curtain Factory Shop
279 High Street, Lincoln LN2 1JG
Mon – Sat 9 – 6.30;
Tel 01522 522740

See our entries nos. 131 & 149 (below)

149 South Normanton *Derbys*

Filigree
Berristow Lane DE55 2EF
(01773) 811630

Curtain lace, nets and other fabrics; ready-made curtains; Austrian blinds, roller blinds; duvets, pillows, other bedding. Also sell net rails, drape and valance rails. Household items, eg cushion covers.

'Special sales at various times of year: please see local press, or phone.'

See our display advertisement above

....

1/2 mile north-east of M1 exit 28.
   From Alfreton/M1 take A38 towards Mansfield (follow signs to 'South Normanton Industrial Estate', not 'South Normanton') for 1/2 mile, then go left into Berristow Lane (B6406).*
   From Sutton-in-Ashfield (on A38 towards M1): go straight at traffic lights (Huthwaite B6027 goes right) then take next right to 'South Normanton Industrial Estate'. You are in Berristow Lane.*
   *Filigree, clearly visible, is 50 yds ahead. Don't turn left – keep right of main building to clearly marked portakabin on left.

Open: Mon–Thur 9–4.;
Fri 9–6.30; Sat 9–1.30.
Bank Holidays 10–4.
Closed: Christmas, Boxing and New Year's Days.
Cards: Access, Switch, Visa.
Cars: Own large car-park.
Toilets: No.
Wheelchairs: Ramp.
Teas: Nearby hotel; Sutton, Alfreton and on motorway (going south). Area is not well endowed with refreshment places!
Groups: Groups of shoppers welcome. Prior phone call first please.
Transport: Trent Bus nos. 243 (Mansfield–Alfreton–Derby); no. 247 (Chesterfield–Alfreton –Mansfield); no. 130 (Mansfield– Normanton).
Mail order: No.

Fabric World

287/9 High Street SM1 1LM
(0181) 643 5127

3,000 rolls of designer and branded curtain and upholstery fabrics sold by the metre.

'Most stock perfects (ends of ranges and repeatable designs), some seconds, at about 50% off normal high street price. From £3.30–£13 per metre. Interior design service – we visit your home (free, without obligation). Also make-up service for all types of curtains.'

···

In Sutton centre near Tesco and opposite The Crown pub.

From the huge roundabout in Rosehill: go south along Rose Hill into Sutton. Pass Magnet Kitchens on right then this shop is shortly on right (immediately past car-park on right).

Coming north from Banstead/Epsom: because the High Street is partly pedestrianised, you have to bear left into one-way system. Pass Tesco and car-park on right. Fabric World car-park is straight ahead at T-junction. For shop go right into Crown Road then left into High Street.

Open: Mon–Sat 9–5.30.
Closed: Most Bank Holidays. Christmas, Boxing and New Year's Days.
Cards: Access, Connect, Mastercard, Visa, Switch.
Cars: Own car-park behind shop (on one-way system).
Toilets: Yes.
Wheelchairs: No steps into large shop.
Teas: Tea made for weary customers; or Sutton town centre.
Groups: Shopping groups welcome – please phone Debbie Shinerock first.
Transport: Any bus to Sutton. (Nearest tube Morden; BR Wimbledon.)
Mail order: No.

Yarnolds

106 Birmingham Road WV2 3NZ
(01902) 459321

Soft furnishings, various curtains including velvets, nets and blinds. All made to measure. Ends of rolls and discontinued lines.

'Firsts, slight seconds and remnants sold here.'

About 1/2 mile south of Wolverhampton along Birmingham Road (A4123) which leads off the ring road.

If you come south from Wolverhampton: the shop is on the right where the road bends slightly to the left. Huge signs on factory with flags on top.

Open: Mon–Sat 9–5.
Closed: Bank Holidays; Christmas–New Year.
Cards: Access, Eurocheque, Switch, Visa.
Cars: Outside factory.
Toilets: During week, not on Saturdays!
Wheelchairs: Easy access to huge spacious shop.
Teas: In Wolverhampton.
Groups: Shopping groups welcome. No need to book.
Transport: From Wolverhampton bus station bus nos. 581 (to Dudley) and 126 (to Birmingham) pass the door.
Mail order: No.

Carrington Curtains Ltd.

50 Goodramgate YO1 2LE
(01904) 635836 (fax 01904 635836)

Vast range of designer curtain and upholstery fabrics from most major manufacturers and designers. Full in-store making-up service for curtains, tie-backs, swags, tails, pelmets. Small selection of ready-made curtains.

'Three floors with over 50,000 yds in stock. Perfects and seconds. Many fabrics reduced by 80%. Postal service to forward customers' orders.'

Within the walls in the centre of the city, close to York Minster.

Open: Mon–Sat 9–5.30.
Closed: Christmas and New Year's Days only.
Cards: Visa, Mastercard, Switch.
Cars: Public car-parks.
Toilets: In town centre.
Wheelchairs: Easy access to ground floor only.
Teas: Many cafés in York.
Groups: Shopping groups please phone shop manager to book.
Transport: Local buses.
Mail order: No.

"This is how they used to spend their Saturday afternoons ...

until they tried Carr's Patent Ladder Tapes."

Electrical Goods & Lighting

Readers are sometimes wary of buying electrical items in factory shops, wondering if the word 'seconds' refers to the safety aspect. Nothing could be more wrong! All goods sold by these shops are electrically guaranteed to the highest standards. The term 'seconds' usually refers to scratches in the enamel, near-invisible marks on the paint, and scuffed packaging. Electrical items are more likely to be perfect items reduced in price because they are ends of ranges. Even designs in hair rollers and toasters are subject to fashion, and last season's range is this season's bargain.

The range of light fittings and lampshades available in British factory shops has expanded enormously in the last couple of years. The Midlands and North in particular offer a great variety of indoor and outdoor fittings – including normally expensive items such as garden, outdoor and security lights – at prices which make a special journey well worthwhile.

Look out too for power tools, cookers, dishwashers, microwaves, sewing machines (spare parts by post), Christmas tree lights, curling tongs, toasters, deep fryers, kettles, electric jugs and vital accessories like plugs and light bulbs.

* Please see full details in respective chapter

ELECTRICAL GOODS & LIGHTING

Pifco Salton Carmen Russell Hobbs Tower
Shefford Road B6 4PL
(0121) 359 8691 Closed

Small electrical appliances: kettles, toasters, irons, kitchen appliances, hairdryers and stylers, electrical housewares, Christmas tree lights, torches, cookware.

'Most items at factory prices.'

....

From Birmingham city centre: take the A38 towards Lichfield. Shortly turn left at Dartmouth Circus into Newtown Middleway.*

From M6 exit 6: take A38(M) for city centre. Take second exit (for ring road); go to Dartmouth Circus. Turn right into Newtown Middleway.*

*After 100 yds go right into Elkington Street; after 100 yds go right into Miller Street; at crossroads after 100 yds, go straight over into Shefford Road (main road) which kinks sharply left. Shop at far end on left.

Open: Mon–Thur 9–4.30; Fri 9–3.30. Some Bank Holidays.
Closed: Easter Friday–Tues; Spring Bank Holiday week; Christmas–New Year.
Cards: Access, Mastercard, Visa.
Cars: In road outside.
Toilets: Ask if desperate.
Wheelchairs: Access possible with assistance; no steps, medium sized shop.
Teas: Lots of places in town.
Groups: Groups of shoppers welcome by appointment.
Transport: Birmingham city centre bus nos. 65, 67, 102, 114, 115 via A38 stop at Dartmouth Circus, then 5 minutes' walk. Bus nos. 33, 51, 52, 107, 113 via A34 stop at Miller Street then 5 minutes' walk.
Mail order: No.

Moulinex Swan
see map on page 315
Pope Street B1 3DL
(0121) 200 1212

Electric jugs, kettles, toasters, slow cookers, pots and pans, teasmades, deep-fryers, blenders, microwave ovens etc.

'This company sells seconds, redundant stock and reconditioned items only.'

See our display advertisement opposite

....

One mile north of city centre in the Jewellery Quarter.

Take A457 going north to Smethwick. At roundabout with orange brick library with clocktower go right for Hockley/Handsworth. After 100 yds, take first left in front of Swan Housewares (despite sign pointing in other direction). Go up this one-way street, take next left and next left again: you are in correct direction for one-way Pope Street. Shop 100 yds on left, clearly signed.

From the clocktower in the middle of the Jewellery Quarter: go along Frederick Street (Barclays Bank on left). Take first right (Albion Street) then basically continue straight (road zigzags by old fire station) to Pope Street on right. Shop 100 yds down on left, clearly marked.

NB Do not confuse this shop with Swan Warehouse nearby.

Open: Mon–Fri 9–4; Sat 9–1.
Closed: Bank Holidays; Christmas–New Year.
Cards: None.
Cars: Outside shop.
Toilets: Yes.
Wheelchairs: Two steps to spacious shop.
Teas: In Hockley and Jewellery Quarter.
Groups: No tours of the works but groups welcome. Please phone first.
Transport: Short bus ride from city centre.
Mail order: No.

155 Cannock W Mids

Lighting Bug

173 Walsall Road, Bridgtown WS11 3JB
(01543) 577776

Huge range of domestic lighting: soft shades and table lamps made here; full ranges of polished solid brass light fittings; crystal, wood and panel glass ceiling fittings. Wall lamps to complement ceiling fittings. Outdoor lighting, spot lights, downlighters, low voltage and fluorescent lighting. Light switches, bulbs, doorbells etc.

'Perfects and seconds at discounts of 25–50%. Always special offers on discontinued lines. Gladly pack and post (at cost) if you can't carry purchases home. We are a happy-go-lucky company (biggest lighting shop in the West Midlands) and will do anything to take your money!'

....

Bridgtown is on the southern side of Cannock, between Cannock town centre and A5.

   This conspicuous shop is on the A34, on a far left corner if you come south from Cannock.

   Coming north from A5: the conspicuous shop is on the right before the island in the road.

Open: Mon–Sat 9.30–5.30. Bank Holidays.
Closed: Few days during Christmas–New Year period.
Cards: Access, Delta, Eurocard, Mastercard, Visa.
Cars: Free large car-park.
Toilets: Town centre.
Wheelchairs: No steps to large shop.
Teas: Pubs, cafés and McDonald's nearby.
Groups: No factory tours but shopping groups welcome.
Transport: Cannock–Walsall buses stop outside.
Mail order: No.

Vectase Lighting plc

Unit 4B Gorrels Way, Transpennine Trading Estate
OL11 9XY
(01706) 341636

Light fittings: wall, ceiling and picture lights; lamp bases, lampshades, Christmas lights, security lights, bulbs etc.
'Both perfects and seconds on sale at wholesale prices.'

Open: Mon–Fri 11–3.
Closed: Bank Holidays; Christmas–New Year period.
Cards: No.
Cars: In front of shop.
Toilets: Yes.
Wheelchairs: One step to medium sized shop.
Teas: In Castleton.
Tours: No tours.
Transport: None.
Mail order: No.

A short distance north of M62 exit 20 and two miles south of Rochdale centre.

From M62 exit 20: take A627M north for Rochdale. At first roundabout, go right; at next roundabout go right for Middleton.*

Coming south on A58 from Rochdale: at a large roundabout, turn left on to A664. Go over next roundabout and right at third on to Queensway (A664) for Middleton.*

*Go right, before Honda garage and overpass, into Gorrels Way.**

From Middleton via A664: follow signs to Rochdale, bear right in Castleton towards estate, go under the overpass, past Honda garage and turn left.**

**Once on estate, keep left. Company is on right and shop on far side of it.

Gorse Mill Lighting

Gorse Mill, Gorse Street, Broadway OL9 9RK
(0161) 628 4202

Modern and traditional light fittings, lamps, shades, spots, glass panel pendants, wall washers, track 12v halogen and recess lighting, crystal chandeliers, security & outdoor lighting.
'Europe's largest decorative lighting disposal centre. 220,000 sq ft with £1 million stock! Perfects unless otherwise marked. Average saving 50% off normal retail prices. Lighting displayed amongst reproduction artefacts, furniture and clothing, which are also for sale.'

Open: Mon–Fri 9–4.30; Sat, Sun 10–4; Bank Holidays.
Closed: Christmas, Boxing and New Year's Days.
Cards: Access, Switch, Visa.
Cars: Own car-park for 300 cars.
Toilets: Yes.
Wheelchairs: Six steps or ramp to very large shop.
Teas: Own café opening soon.
Tours: Four tours a year – ask for details. Shopping groups welcome.
Transport: Buses from Oldham and from Manchester to Chadderton.
Mail order: No.

Between Middleton and Oldham off the A663.

From M62 exit 20: go south on A627(M) for Oldham. This road becomes the A663; keep straight (do not take slip road for Oldham). Continue until you cross B6189 at traffic lights; take first right after pedestrian lights. Go to far corner of Gorse Mill following signs.

From Manchester: take A62 towards Oldham then turn left at traffic lights on to A663 for Rochdale. At end of dual carriageway, cross A6104 at lights, pass Boat and Horses pub on left and take next left. Gorse Mill factory shop is at end of mill on right.

Astbury Lighting Ltd. (Lampshade & Table Lamp Manufacturers)

Victoria Mill, Foundry Bank CW12 1DT
(01260) 298176

Wide selection of traditional and pleated lampshades (all sizes); lamp bases, chandeliers, wall lights, standard lamps, oriental bases etc. Also in mill: bedding, curtain and clothing centre; upholstered furniture and beds.

'Prices second to none. Most items well below typical retail prices. Seconds and perfects.'

On north-east side of Congleton, 1/4 mile from town centre.
   From Macclesfield/Buxton/Leek on A54: as you reach Congleton, pass BFL petrol then large stone St Stephen's church on right, and Berisford Ribbons on left; take first right (where road bends sharp left). Shop is a few yards down steep hill on right.
   From all other directions: aim out of town on A54 Buxton/Macclesfield. From the roundabout continue 100 yds then bear left down steep hill where main road goes right. Shop is down steep hill on right.

Open: Mon–Sat 10–5.
Closed: Bank Holidays; Christmas–New Year.
Cards: None.
Cars: Ample space outside shop or by Leisure Centre.
Toilets: Yes.
Wheelchairs: Six steps, but access available through alternative door.
Teas: The Antelope Hotel, 100 yds (snacks, coffee etc).
Groups: Welcome, but phone to book first.
Transport: 10 minutes' walk from the town centre.
Mail order: No.

Pifco Salton Carmen Russell Hobbs Tower

Princess Street M35 0HS
(0161) 681 8321

Small electrical goods – hairdryers, tongs, electric kettles, irons, toasters; kitchen appliances; Christmas tree lights; torches; pans.

'Most of our goods are at factory prices.'

In a side road off the A62 Manchester–Oldham road.
   From Manchester: take A62 east for Oldham; pass A663 turn-off (Broadway) on left. *
   From M62 exit 20: follow signs to Oldham (A627M); continue down A627M on to A663. Turn left on to A62. Stay on A62 for 1/4 mile. After traffic lights and *just before Shell station on left (look for Pifco Tower on right) go right into Princess Street.
   From Oldham via A62: go through Hollinwood, pass Failsworth Town Hall on left; immediately after Shell petrol on right, go left into small Princess Street to large Pifco tower. Shop 50 yds on left.

Open: Mon, Wed–Fri 9–5.30; Sat 9–1.
Closed: Tuesday; Bank Holidays; Christmas–New Year.
Cards: Access, Visa.
Cars: Car-park behind shop.
Toilets: Ask if desperate.
Wheelchairs: No steps; easy access.
Teas: In Failsworth.
Groups: No tours, but pre-booked groups of shoppers welcome.
Transport: Three minutes' walk from Failsworth BR station. Oldham–Manchester buses stop nearby.
Mail order: No.

Rutland Lighting
10–12 Watergate NG31 6PP
(01476) 591049

Full range of lampshades in many different styles and fabrics; table lamps, standard lamps, chandeliers, pendants, exterior lights; accessories.

'Items made by this company. Also chainstore returns and ends of lines.'

On the main road through town.
   From the High Street, with the ancient Angel & Royal Hotel on right: go 200 yds along High Street/Watergate; clearly marked shop is on right, 100 yds before Gateway on left.
   Coming south into Grantham from A1: take old A1 into town centre. This brings you into Grantham in southerly direction, past Gateway on right; clearly marked shop 100 yds on left.

Open: Mon–Sat 9–5.30.
Closed: Christmas and Boxing Days.
Cards: Access, Switch, Visa.
Cars: 25 yds from shop.
Toilets: No.
Wheelchairs: Access easy, one small step.
Teas: In town.
Groups: No guided tours; coach parties of shoppers welcome but please phone first.
Transport: Regular buses from outlying towns & villages.
Mail order: No.

Appliance Centre
87 Lothair Road, Aylestone Park LE2 7QE   (0116) 244 0150

Fully reconditioned gas & electric cookers, freestanding and built-in. All types of new appliances at discount prices: cookers, washing machines, dishwashers, fridges, freezers, gas fires, etc.

'Reconditioning done on premises. Full 12 months' guarantee on parts and labour (distance limitation on labour guarantee). About half new prices. New perfects and seconds (graded) appliances with full manufacturer's guarantee.'

On south side of Leicester. From Leicester centre: go south on A50, follow signs to A426 Rugby. After one-way system take Aylestone Road (A426); after 1/4 mile take left fork in front of Toyota Garage into Saffron Lane (B5366). Opposite Saffron Lane Sports Centre, go right into Lothair Road. Shop 150 yds on left.
   From M1 exit 21: take A46. At roundabout go left on to A46; continue for 1 mile. At traffic lights go right into Braunstone Lane East (becomes Middleton St), over Grand Union Canal. At traffic lights go left on to A426 (Aylestone Rd). After 1.25 miles, after pedestrian lights, go right (Hughenden Drive), right again (Brooksby St) then left (Lothair Rd). Shop 50 yds on right.
   Coming north from Oadby/Wigston along Saffron Lane (B5366): after 1.25 miles (near sports centre on right), go left into Lothair Road. Shop 150 yds on left.

Open: Mon–Fri 7.45–5.45.
Closed: Some Bank Holidays: please phone to check.
Cards: None.
Cars: Own car-park.
Toilets: In Knighton Lane East 1/3 mile from shop.
Wheelchairs: Easy access.
Teas: Two or three cafés within 5 minutes' walk.
Groups: No.
Transport: Bus no. 37 from Charles Street: alight on Aylestone Road at Lothair Road. Bus nos. 25, 35, 38 alight on Saffron Lane at end of Lothair Road. Walk 200 yds.

Singer Factory Services

Unit F5, Hilltop Road LE5 1TL   (0116) 274 2681/2764969

New and reconditioned (guaranteed) sewing machines (including industrial machines), presses, knitting machines, domestic overlockers. Spare parts.

'Trade-in allowance. Reconditioned guaranteed sewing machines from £30; new slight imperfects at considerable savings. Delivery in UK £7.'

....

On the north-east side of Leicester. From central Leicester: follow A47 for Uppingham. Cross traffic lights (where A6030 ring road goes right for General Hospital). Over pedestrian lights, then left for Troon Industrial Area (A667 Humberstone Drive).*

Via A6030 (outer ring road): go round till you reach A47, east of city. At these traffic lights, go on to A47 for Uppingham. Go left for Troon Industrial Area (A667).*

From east (Peterborough/Uppingham) on A47: pass Shell on right/public park on left. Turn right (signs to Troon Ind. Area.).*

From Thurmaston on A667: pass Marshall's Garage on left; continue to large roundabout.**

*Follow signs round Humberstone Golf Course to large roundabout.**

**At roundabout go into Waterside Rd; after 200 yds go right before Cyril John Painting Contractors. Singer is third unit on right.

Open: Mon–Fri 10-4; Sat 10–2.
Closed: Christmas, Boxing and New Year's Days. Some Bank Holidays, please phone to check.
Cards: Access, Visa.
Cars: Free parking outside warehouse.
Toilets: Yes, including for disabled.
Wheelchairs: Ramp to large warehouse; one level inside.
Teas: Local pubs and cafés.
Groups: No.
Transport: Not available.
Mail order: Yes. Spare parts sent.
Catalogue: No.

Rutland Lighting

Thistleton Road Industrial Estate LE15 7PP
(01572) 767587

Full range of lampshades in many different styles and fabrics; table lamps, standard lamps, chandeliers, pendants, exterior lights; accessories.

'Many items about half retail price. Genuine factory shop with most goods made on the premises.'

....

Market Overton is between Oakham and the A1, 6 miles north-east of Oakham and 11 miles east of Melton Mowbray.

From Oakham: take B668 to Cottesmore, go left for Market Overton.*

From A1: turn off at Stretton on to B668 for Cottesmore; go right for Market Overton.*

*In the village, turn right at T-junction into Thistleton Road towards Thistleton. Take first left into industrial estate (signposted). Company is last building on the estate on right.

Open: Mon–Fri 9-4; Sat 10-4.
Closed: Bank Holidays; Christmas–New Year.
Cards: Access, Mastercard, Visa.
Cars: Own car-park.
Toilets: Yes.
Wheelchairs: One step.
Teas: Good pubs in village.
Groups: Welcome to shop; please telephone first, mentioning this book. Regret no factory tours.
Transport: None.
Mail order: No.

Helix Lighting Ltd.

Helix House, Wellingborough Road NN10 9AG
(01933) 318522

Closed

Large selection of decorative and domestic
table lamps, soft and hard quality shades including pleats
for the home. Spotlights, ceiling fittings, uplighters, floor
standards and lighting accessories.

*'All shades and table lamps made on the premises. Mainly
perfects including discontinued and sample lines at competitive
prices.'*

....

About 1.5 miles north-west of Rushden.

*From Rushden: go round the one-way system to sign for
Wellingborough. Keep going straight along Wellingborough Road
(only one sign!) for a mile and a half almost to the T-junction;
well marked company is on right, 50 yds before this junction.*

*From A45 (either direction): turn off at roundabout for
Rushden (A5001). Keep going to Rushden. Clearly marked
company is shortly on left at a roundabout.*

*From the north (Market Harborough) via the A6: turn right
before you get to Rushden on to the A45 for Wellingborough and
Northampton then turn left for Rushden (A5001) as above.*

Open: Tues–Fri 11–5;
Sat 10–5.
Closed: Monday; phone to
check Easter and Christmas–
New Year openings.
Cards: No.
Cars: Car-park in front of shop.
Toilets: Duck Street car-park
in Rushden.
Wheelchairs: Easy access (no
step) to medium sized shop.
Teas: Cafés in Rushden.
Groups: Groups of shoppers
welcome by appointment with
Dawn Durkin.
Transport: X94 from Rushden
and Northampton/Welling-
borough stops 3 minutes' walk
from shop.
Mail order: No.

A E Clutterbuck Ltd.

Cranmore Drive, Shirley Trading Estate B90 4PG
(0121) 704 3134

Domestic light fittings; variety of brass wall and ceiling
lights with glass shades; table lamps; outside lighting etc.

*'Genuine opportunity to purchase quality domestic lighting at
half to two thirds normal prices. Wide selection of styles from £5.'*

....

On the south-west side of Solihull.

*From M42 exit 4: take A34 north for Birmingham (on M42
southbound, first sign says 'Henley in Arden A3400'). Turn right
off A34 at first roundabout (signs to Cranmore Industrial
Estate). At roundabout, go left (Highlands Road); at T-junction
at far end go right into Cranmore Boulevard. Go right in front of
Bryants Builders office block into Cranmore Drive. Shop is in end
building on left.*

*From Birmingham coming south on A34: cross B4102 then
shortly turn left into Cranmore Boulevard. Take third right,
Cranmore Drive (in front of Bryants Builders office block on
right). Shop is in end building on left.*

Open: Mon–Fri 8–12.30 and
1–4; Sat 9–12; Good Friday.
Closed: Most Bank Holidays;
Christmas Eve, Christmas,
Boxing and New Year's Days.
Cards: No.
Cars: In road outside.
Toilets: Yes.
Wheelchairs: Easy access to
medium-sized sales area within
factory.
Teas: In Solihull or Shirley.
Groups: Groups of shoppers
welcome; please telephone first.
Transport: Bus nos. 5 and 6
from Birmingham centre to
Highlands Road.
Mail order: No.

Goodson Lighting Ltd.

Church Lane, Hixon ST18 OPS
(01889) 270752 Closed

Lampshades, table lamps and ceiling fittings manufactured here. Many end of line fabrics. Customer fabric make-up service available.

'We sell seconds, design samples, returns and ends of lines.'

Open: Mon–Sat 9–5.
Closed: Bank Holidays; Christmas–New Year.
Cards: Yes.
Cars: Own large parking area.
Toilets: Yes.
Wheelchairs: Easy access; no steps.
Teas: Own coffee shop.
Groups: Factory tours by prior arrangement.
Transport: None.
Mail order: No.

A small villlage just east of A51 (Rugeley–Stone road), about five miles north-east of Stafford.

From M6 exit 14: take Stone/Uttoxeter Road then take A513 at island, pass RAF MIUI Stafford to next island. Take A518 past County Showground to dual carriageway. Go right on to A51 (road from Stone to Rugeley/Lichfield). After 1.5 miles go under low bridge; after 100 yds go left down Church Lane, Hixon.*

From Rugeley: take A51 north for Stone. In a long left bend, go right into Church Lane for Hixon.*

*Factory is first large building on left - use second gateway.

From Stone: take A51 south. Pass Anglo petrol station on right, then first left for Hixon. Go over railway crossing, pass airfield and industrial estate on left. At cross roads, go right for Great Haywood; pass school. Hixon Ind. Est. on right; use first gate.

Pifco Salton Carmen Russell Hobbs Tower

Heath Mill Road, Wombourne Ind Estate WV5 8AO
(01902) 324123

Small electrical appliances: kettles, toasters, irons, kitchen appliances, hairdryers and stylers, electrical housewares, Christmas tree lights, torches, cookware.

'Most items at factory prices.'

Open: Tues–Fri 9–4.30; Sat 9–12.30.
Closed: Monday; Bank Holidays; Christmas–New Year.
Cards: No.
Cars: In factory yard.
Toilets: Yes.
Wheelchairs: One step to shop.
Teas: Local pubs.
Groups: Groups of shoppers welcome by appointment. No factory tours.
Transport: Not easy.
Mail order: No.

West of Wombourne.

Wombourne Industrial Estate is signposted at traffic lights at the crossing of A449 (Stourbridge–Wolverhampton road) and B4176 (Dudley–Bridgnorth road). Take the B4176 for Bridgnorth. Pass the Waggon and Horses on the right, then turn left into industrial estate. Company is first on left: shop is inside the gates on the left, clearly marked.

From Bridgnorth on B4176: pass Wombourne Ford on right; keep going till you see industrial estate on right; turn right into it. Company is first on left: shop is inside the gates on the left, clearly marked.

Floor & Wall Coverings

If you plan to *spend* several hundred pounds, then you can also *save* hundreds of pounds by buying wall tiles, quarry tiles, clay pavers for patios, reproduction Victorian tiles, carpet and wallpaper at factory shop prices. Such significant savings make all the difference between being able to afford a standard kitchen, bathroom, conservatory or garden or a remarkable one. You are also likely to find carpet overmakes from hotel and cruise liner commissions – heavy contract carpet in unusual designs at normal domestic price.

Delivery of these large, heavy items is easily arranged at low cost throughout the UK so you need not worry whether you can actually get your purchases home.

Despite the large number of advertisements for *Axminster* and *Wilton* carpets, few people seem to appreciate the differences between them – or understand what a *tufted* carpet is.

The answer lies in the weaving techniques.

Axminsters and *Wiltons* are *woven* carpets: the pile and backing are woven together simultaneously. The pile of *tufted* carpet is inserted into a ready-made backing by needles.

In *Axminster* carpets, the tufts are cut in the form of a U and are held in place by the weft backing threads. They are usually multi-coloured; but the popular trend for plain carpeting has made one-colour Axminster more readily available.

The weaving of *Wilton* is costlier as the yarn is continuous and buried into the backing threads. This 'dead' yarn, gives Wilton its extra weight and strength. A sculptured texture can be achieved with differing pile heights.

In *tufting*, density of pile is determined by the number of times the needles are inserted per inch into the backing, and by the weight of yarn used. Latex holds the tufts, then a final backing gives the carpet extra body. Tufting is speedy, highly automated and generally cheaper than weaving.

At one time carpet width was restricted to three feet, but sophisticated looms have allowed the production of much wider carpets, hence the expression 'broadloom'. Twelve feet is the common width although wider carpets are available, eliminating the need for seaming in larger rooms.

Some manufacturers will produce to your own width requirements and some will make up your own design at very reasonable prices. You can also have carpet made to your own colour at no extra price.

Jorgus Carpets	168	**Anderton** Lancs	
Shaw Carpets	169	**Barnsley** S Yorks	
Graham & Brown	170	**Blackburn** Lancs	
Weavers Shop, The	171	**Bloxham** Oxon	
Bristol Carpets	172	**Bristol** Avon	
John Wilman	173	**Burnley** Lancs	
Marlborough Tiles	174	**Cheltenham** Gloucs	
Shireburn Carpets	175	**Clitheroe** Lancs	
Crucial Trading	176	**Craven Arms** Shropshire	
S. Lyles, Son & Co.	177	**Dewsbury** W Yorks	
Glenpatrick Mill Shop	178	**Elderslie near Johnstone** Strathclyde	
Creative Carpets	179	**Enderby near Leicester** Leics	
Grandford Carpet Mills	180	**Fareham** Hampshire	
Red Rose Carpet Manufacturers	181	**Fleetwood** Lancs	
Custom Carpets	182	**Frome** Somerset	
GP & J Baker & Parkertex Fabrics	127*	**High Wycombe** Bucks	
Fred Lawton & Son	183	**Huddersfield** W Yorks	
Rowe Carpets	184	**Kidderminster** Worcs	
Victoria Carpet Weavers Shop	185	**Kidderminster** Worcs	
Weavers Shop, The	186	**Kidderminster** Worcs	
Phoenix Carpets	187	**Little Horwood** Bucks	
Crucial Trading	188	**London : Bermondsey**	
Marlborough Tiles	189	**Marlborough** Wilts	
Candy & Co	190	**Newton Abbot** Devon	
Pilkington's Tiles	191	**Poole** Dorset	
Marlborough Tiles	192	**Salisbury** Wilts	
Wilton Carpet Factory	193	**Salisbury** Wilts	
Johnson, H & R Tiles	194	**Stoke-on-Trent : Tunstall** Staffs	
Carpets of Worth	195	**Stourport-on-Severn** Worcs	
Carpet Shop (Carpets of Worth)	196	**Stroud** Gloucs	
Homemaker Edging Services	197	**Wakefield** W Yorks	
Carpet Company, The	198	**Westhoughton nr Bolton** Gr Manchester	
Rowe Carpets	199	**Worcester** Worcs	
Dennis of Ruabon	200	**Wrexham** Clwyd	
Factory Outlet Shopping Centre	491*	**York** N Yorks	

* Please see full details in respective chapter

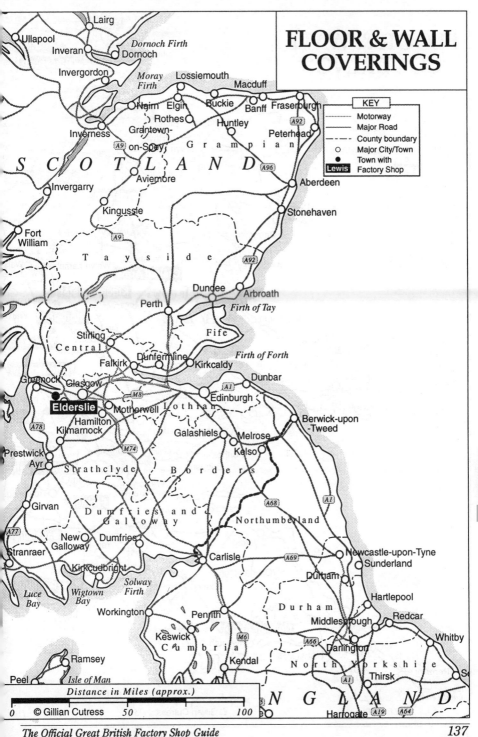

KEY

- .... Motorway
- —————— Major Road
- — · — · — County boundary
- ○ Major City/Town
- ● Town with
- **Lewis** Factory Shop

Distance in Miles (approx.)

0   © Gillian Cutress   50   100

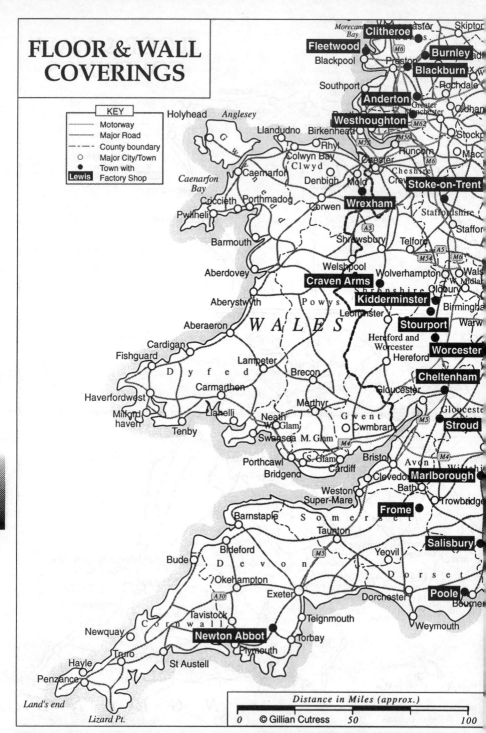

FLOOR & WALL COVERINGS

KEY
- .... Motorway
- ——— Major Road
- ---- County boundary
- O Major City/Town
- ● Town with Factory Shop
- Lewis

Distance in Miles (approx.)

0   © Gillian Cutress   50   100

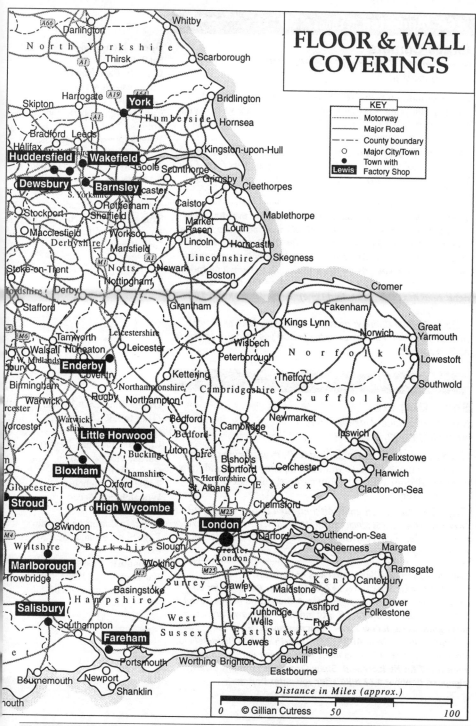

FLOOR & WALL COVERINGS

KEY

········· Motorway
———— Major Road
—·—·— County boundary
○ Major City/Town
Lewis Town with Factory Shop

Distance in Miles (approx.)

0 © Gillian Cutress 50 100

Jorgus Carpets
Grimeford Mill, Grimeford Lane PR6 9HK
(01257) 482636

Carpets made on premises. Special colours gladly made to order. Twist piles, saxonies, velvets etc. 80/20% wool/nylon mixtures in 12' to 13'6" and 15' widths. Carpet with small design in 8 colourways.

'Genuine mill shop (3,000 sq ft) with everything made here. Twist piles and velvets, 80/20% plains and berbers from £7.50 per sq yd. Reduced price roll ends. Fitting service. 80–100 rolls displayed in shop.'

Short distance south of Adlington and almost in the shadow of M61; between A6 and A673 (Grimeford Lane links these 2 roads).

Going north on A6 to Chorley: look for The Pavilion on left – immediately go right (Grimeford Lane). Keep going; pass under motorway; after 100 yds go left into complex of small factories.

Coming north on A673 from Horwich: pass The Millstone on right; take next left (Grimeford Lane): factory complex is 100 yds on right.

Via A673 from Chorley: go under motorway, take next right (Grimeford Lane). Factory complex is 100 yds on right; Jorgus is at far back left.

Open: Mon–Fri 8–12 and 1–5; Sat 9–12.
Closed: Bank Holidays; Christmas–New Year.
Cards: None.
Cars: Large car-park in yard.
Toilets: Yes.
Wheelchairs: Easy access, ground floor sales area.
Teas: Nearby pubs; cafés and tea shops in Chorley.
Tours: No tours but you can see carpets being made.
Transport: Horwich–Chorley buses stop near the end of Grimeford Lane.

Shaw Carpets
Huddersfield Road, Darton S75 5NH
(01226) 390133

Huge range of carpets including 80/20% wool-rich patterned and plain ranges; 50/50% wool twists; cut pile, cut and loop; cords; bedroom and bathroom carpets; contract carpets, rugs, underlay.

'Slight imperfects, roll ends, discontinued carpet ranges, all at bargain prices. Most stock manufactured here. Delivery service plus list of local carpet fitters. Special privilege card for purchasers for future discount offers.'

Darton is about 3 miles north-west of Barnsley.

From M1 exit 38: take A637 for Barnsley. Continue for one mile, go over motorway, pass Rose & Crown and Murco petrol station on right; then go left into entrance of Shaw Carpets; pass gatehouse, follow signs to factory shop.

From Barnsley: take A635 (A637) north-west to Huddersfield. Once out of town, at roundabout with Citroen garage on right, take A637 for Huddersfield. Shaw Carpets is on right, clearly signposted, about 1/2 mile after you enter Darton.

Open: Mon–Sat 9.30–4.45 (Thur to 7.30). Some Bank Holidays.
Closed: Christmas–New Year.
Cards: Access, Switch, Visa.
Cars: Own car-park.
Toilets: At gatehouse.
Wheelchairs: Access from side door.
Teas: In Darton, and Wooley Edge Service Station near M1 exit 38.
Transport: Buses from Barnsley, Leeds, Wakefield etc; BR Darton station nearby.

Graham & Brown Ltd.

Daveyfield Road, Roman Road Industrial Estate BB1 2NR
(01254) 582229

Wide selection of wallpapers, including ready-pasted vinyls
and blown vinyls (with raised designs) and borders; decorating
accessories including paints and brushes.

*'Ends of lines and seconds in current ranges at significantly
reduced prices.'*

....

About 1.5 miles south of Blackburn.

**From Blackburn: take road for Haslingden. Pass Blackburn
Arena, retail park and Asda on left. Keep straight at two mini-
roundabouts. At traffic lights, go straight (Blackamoor pub on
far right corner). At sign to Davyfield Ind. Est. go right. Take first
right.**

**Coming north to Blackburn from Edgeworth: pass right turn-off
to Waterside village and papermill; continue for 1/2 mile. Go left
at sign to Davyfield Ind. Est. Take first right.**

Open: Wed, Thur, Fri 10–6;
Sat 9.30–5; Sun 10–4.
Closed: Monday and Tuesday.
Cards: Access, Switch, Visa.
Cars: Own large car-park.
Toilets: No.
Wheelchairs: Three steps at
front; gentle ramp at side.
Teas: Local pubs and in
Blackburn.
Groups: No factory tours.
Transport: Bus service.

The Weavers Shop

Barford Road OX15 4HB
(01295) 721225

Wilton, broadloom and tufted carpets. Wools for weaving,
knitting and tapestry work. Rugs, canvas, carpet-fitting
accessories.

*'Expert advice willingly given, together with accessories and
delivery service. List of recommended fitters.'*

....

Bloxham is on the A361 (Chipping Norton–Banbury road.)

**Coming north from Chipping Norton: as you reach village, pass
Esso station on right then take next right (Barford Road)
towards Adderbury; keep going straight till you see Steele's
Carpets on left. Shop clearly marked at back.**

**From Banbury: go through village, pass church and Old School
House Hotel on left, then go left for Adderbury. Then as above.**

**From the Barfords: as you reach village outskirts, Steele's are
on right.**

Open: Mon–Sat 9–5.
Closed: Bank Holidays;
Christmas–New Year.
Cards: None.
Cars: Large car-park.
Toilets: Yes.
Wheelchairs: Easy access;
large shop.
Teas: Pubs in the village and
locally.
Tours: Factory tours by
appointment. Groups of
shoppers welcome but prefer-
ably book first.
Transport: Local buses from
Banbury.

Bristol Carpets

Weavers Mill, Crew's Hole Road BS5 8AV
(0117) 954 1011

Own range of Axminster carpets designed and woven here in 80/20% wool/nylon in most widths. Special widths without joins made. Also supply full range of other carpets.
'All carpets at big savings on shop prices. Ends of rolls, remnants, sub-standard stock. Free quotations for fitting throughout UK. £5 delivery charge in 10 mile radius.

On east side of Bristol, halfway towards Kingswood.
   From centre of Bristol: take A420 east for Chippenham. *
   From M4 exit19: take M32 for Bristol. At large roundabout, exit 3, turn south, Easton Way. At next roundabout go left on to A420 for Chippenham. *
   ***At St George's Park traffic lights, go right into Blackswarth Road, pass the Three Crowns on right then turn left into Crew's Hole Road. Company entrance is shortly visible on left.**

Open: Mon–Sat 9–5 (Fri to 6). Most Bank Holidays 10–4, please phone to check.
Closed: Christmas and Boxing Days.
Cards: Access, Amex, Visa.
Cars: Own large car-park.
Toilets: No,
Wheelchairs: Easy access to large showroom.
Teas: Local pubs.
Tours: Please contact Mrs Ford for organised tours of factory. Individuals can view carpets being manufactured from showroom.
Transport: Local buses stop in St George's Park then 5 minute walk.
Mail order: Yes.
Catalogue: No.

John Wilman Ltd.

Culshaw Street BB10 4PO
(01282) 427008

Wide range of co-ordinated wallpapers, furnishing fabrics, lampshades, paint, textiles. Curtaining from £3.50 per metre.
'Vinyl wallcoverings from £2.99 per roll, papers from £1.99.'

At south-eastern end of town.
   From A56: turn east for Brunshaw at roundabout (Sainsbury's on left). Go under canal and straight at traffic lights. *
   Coming north on A671 from Bacup: at second traffic lights go right, Brunshaw Road (The Wellington on near right corner); *pass Burnley football club on left. **
   From M65 exit 10: take A671 to Town Centre (Happy Eater on right). Get in right lane for 'Through traffic'. At lights, go straight (The Mitre on right) into Trafalgar Street. At roundabout, take second exit (Centenary Way to Nelson A682). At next round-about take third exit, in front of Sainsbury's; go over traffic lights, pass football ground on left. **
   ***Take second right (Mitella Street). Go straight to company on right – shop is beyond blue building, and signposted.**

Open: Mon–Fri 9–5; Sat 9–12.
Closed: Bank Holidays.
Cards: Access, Switch, Visa.
Cars: Large car-park.
Toilets: Yes.
Wheelchairs: Easy access, wide door, huge shop.
Teas: In Burnley.
Groups: No factory tours. Shopping groups welcome, no need to book.
Transport: Bus to Burnley football club then walk.

Marlborough Tiles
14 Montpellier Street GL50 1SX
(01242) 224870

Wall tiles made by *Marlborough Tiles;* floor tiles imported from elsewhere.

'In the Montpellier area of Cheltenham where individual boutiques mix happily with antique and craft shops. Prices from £3.24 per sq yd for seconds. Wall tiles are seconds and discontinued lines (may be perfect); floor tiles mostly perfects at reduced prices.'

In a small street of interesting shops in the town centre. You can park in any town centre car-park and walk.

From all directions: take A46 into town centre following signs to town hall. Turn left into The Promenade; pass Queen's Hotel on left. At roundabout take third exit and double back at small island just past pedestrian crossing. Take second left and immediately turn right into Montpellier Street. Shop is on left half way along.

Open: Mon–Sat 9.30–5.
Closed: Bank Holidays; please phone for Christmas times.
Cards: Access, Mastercard, Visa.
Cars: 1 1/2 hours' free parking outside.
Toilets: In Montpellier Gardens on Montpellier Walk (1–2 minutes away).
Wheelchairs: Factory shop is on lower ground floor; access by stairs.
Teas: Many restaurants and street cafés nearby.
Tours: No tours (factory at different site). Groups welcome to shop.
Transport: Bus nos. 46, 46B, 50. Bus station nearby. Easy walk from all parts of town centre.
Mail order: Yes.
Catalogue: No.

Shireburn Carpets Ltd.
Primrose Works, Primrose Road BB7 1BS
(01200) 29066

Large range of quality tufted carpets in all yarns and mixes. Large selection of room-sized roll ends, many at less than trade prices. Patterned Axminsters and Wiltons; Wilton persian rugs.

'Genuine mill shop with almost everything made on premises. Free measuring service and expert fitting available. Seconds generally on sale. Annual sale last Saturday and Sunday in January.'

On the southern edge of town.

Leave town for 'Preston and Whalley' (turn out of main street, Market Place, beside NatWest bank); at T-junction go right and follow signs for Whalley. Pass Shell petrol and Barkers Garden Centre, on left, then take second right, immediately before bridge at bottom of hill.*

From Padiham via A671: Primrose Road is on left as you reach Clitheroe, just after bridge and immediately before town sign.*

*Mill is 100 yds on left. Park near clearly visible shop.

Open: Mon, Tues 9–5; Thur 9–8; Fri 9–4.30; Sat 10–4. Bank Holidays.
Closed: Wednesday; Easter; Christmas–New Year.
Cards: None.
Cars: In front of main showroom.
Toilets: Ask if desperate.
Wheelchairs: Access possible.
Teas: In Clitheroe.
Tours: You can see work in progress in the mill (no tours or coach parties).
Transport: Buses from Clitheroe – get off at Primrose Bridge.

Crucial Trading Ltd.
The Market Hall, Market Street
SY7 9NY
(01588) 673666

Large selection of conveniently sized natural fibre floor coverings including sisal, seagrass, coir, jute, wool etc at discount prices.

'Many ends of rolls, returned orders, discontinued lines etc at half-price. Also list of larger pieces up to whole roll (30 x 4 m) held at factory can be purchased at large discount through this shop. Free measuring service. Fitting can be arranged for most parts of mainland Britain. Complete collection of over 120 natural floorcoverings available for inspection and/or order.'

....

On A49, seven miles south of Church Stretton and seven miles north of Ludlow.

  Coming north from Ludlow on A49: go right on to B4368 in Craven Arms. Market Street is first right and shop is on left.

  Coming south from Church Stretton: turn left on to B4368. Market Street is first right.

Open: Mon–Fri 10–4.
Closed: Bank Holidays; Christmas–New Year.
Cards: Access, Amex, Switch, Visa.
Cars: Easy street parking.
Toilets: By the Craven Arms.
Wheelchairs: Two steps.
Teas: Local cafés and pubs.
Groups: No tours; unsuitable for group visits.
Transport: BR and buses from Ludlow and Shrewsbury.
Mail order: Yes.
Catalogue: Free. No seconds or factory shop merchandise posted.

S. Lyles, Son & Co. Ltd.
Calder Bank Mills, Calder Bank Road WF12 9QV
(01924) 466441

Large range of carpets: suitable for domestic and contract use: 80/20% wool/nylon; rugs and carpet tiles; plain in stock, patterned to order.

'First and seconds quality in plain carpets from £7.50 per sq yd. Rugs from £10.'

....

Off the B6117 south-east of Dewsbury.

  From Dewsbury/the east: take A644 for Brighouse and Huddersfield. Go up dual carriageway, under railway, pass tall church on right and Lookers garage then The Shepherd's Boy pub on left; take next sharp left (Fall Lane).**

  From M62 exit 25: take A644 south; cross A62; take A644.*

  From Huddersfield/Brighouse on A644: *enter Dewsbury; look for fire station on right then go right on to B6117 to Horbury.**

  **Go down hill, under railway; take next left (opposite The Gate pub). Shop in main building on left at end of drive.

Open: Mon–Fri 9–5; Sat 9–4. Some Bank Holidays – please phone.
Closed: Easter Bank Holidays; Christmas–New Year.
Cards: Access, Switch, Visa.
Cars: Large private car-park.
Toilets: Yes.
Wheelchairs: One shallow step to ground floor showroom.
Teas: Several tea places and pubs in Dewsbury.
Tours: Free tours of the mill can be arranged with Timothy Lyles – please phone. Groups to shop also welcome – prior phone call also appreciated.
Transport: Five minutes' walk from bus and train stations.

178 Elderslie near Johnstone Strathclyde

Glenpatrick Mill Shop

Glenpatrick Road PA5 9UK
(01505) 321121

Wide range of ends of rolls in carpets, mostly 80/20% wool/nylon in a range of patterns and plain colours. Axminster, Wilton, bonded and tufted. Underfelt.

'Offcuts, remnants, discontinued lines, ends of contract orders and imperfects at prices significantly lower than elsewhere. Reasonably priced delivery arranged in UK.'

Easy to find, between Johnstone and Paisley.
 From Johnstone: turn right off B789 at traffic lights with Citroën garage facing turnoff, The Cabin on one corner.*
 From M8 exit 29: take A737 towards Irvine. At next exit turn left onto A761 towards Paisley and Elderslie. Pass Asda on left, then go under railway and at roundabout turn right for B789 Johnstone. In Elderslie turn left at traffic lights opposite Citroën garage.*
 *Continue along Glenpatrick Road. Pass large carpet mill on left and follow signs to Mill Shop. Car-park at far end.

Open: Tues, Wed, Thur, Sun 9–4.30.
Closed: Monday, Friday, Saturday; Christmas–New Year period.
Cards: Access, Mastercard, Switch, Visa.
Cars: Large car-park.
Toilets: Yes.
Wheelchairs: One small step to large shop.
Teas: Not in immediate vicinity. Pubs in area.
Tours: No mill tours.
Transport: Difficult.

---

179 Enderby near Leicester Leics

Creative Carpets Ltd.

Unit 8, Mill Hill Ind. Estate, Quarry Lane LE9 5AV
(0116) 284 1455

Quality carpets in 80/20% wool/nylon. Many colours, including plain dyed berbers and heather tweeds.

'Real factory shop; all carpets made here. Genuine savings of about 50%. Unusual colours. First quality from about £8.75 per sq yd; seconds from £5.85. Fax (0116) 275 2550.'

Enderby lies in the triangle south of where the M1 and M69 join. Company is north of village, just off B582 (Blaby–Desford road).
 From Leicester go south (Narborough Road, A46): cross outer ring road, take next right (small sign to Enderby). In village go right, take third left.*
 From M1 exit 21: go towards Leicester; follow signs 'Outer ring road and Narborough/Enderby'. Go towards Narborough; at roundabout with Foxhunter pub on left, go right to Enderby/Desford. Go over motorway, through village and go left after Plough into Quarry Lane.*
 *Continue to back of estate; company on right.

Open: Sat 9–3. Weekday visits gladly arranged if you phone.
Closed: First two weeks in July; Christmas–New Year.
Cards: No.
Cars: Plenty of space outside company.
Toilets: Yes.
Wheelchairs: Easy access via loading bay; large ground floor sales area.
Teas: Local pubs serve food.
Tours: You can see the tufting machines beyond the sales area but no tours as such.
Transport: Midland Fox bus no. 50 from Leicester.

Grandford Carpet Mills
Unit 11, Bridge Industries, Broadcut
 PO16 8ST
(01329) 289612

Carpets tufted here: 4 metre wide heavy duty domestic range in various qualities from 100% synthetic fibre to 80/20% wool/nylon. Specialise in 80/20% heather mixtures. Also rubber underlay and accessories.

'Small family business also offering dye-to-order service (minimum 50 sq yds). Seconds sometimes available. Prices from £7.95–£15.95, about half usual retail prices.'

On the north-eastern side of Fareham, about 1 mile from town centre.
   From M27 exit 11: go towards Fareham; follow signs to Fareham Industrial Park at two roundabouts. You come into Broadcut.*
   From town centre: go towards A32; at huge roundabout, go left before Roundabout pub; at next roundabout go right into Broadcut.*
   ***Unit 11 is one of the brown buildings 400 yds on right, near new Sainsbury store.**

Open: Mon–Fri 9–5; Sat 10–4. Some Bank Holidays, please phone to check.
Closed: Christmas–New Year; Easter (open Easter Sat).
Cards: Access, Visa.
Cars: In own forecourt.
Toilets: Ask if you are desperate.
Wheelchairs: Easy access, ramp to shop.
Teas: In Fareham.
Tours: Free tours for groups of up to 12; please phone Mr Copplestone first.
Transport: None.
Mail order: No.

Red Rose Carpet Manufacturers Ltd.
Kilbane Street FY7 7PE
(01253) 878888   *Closed*

Carpets made from wool-rich yarns; mainly 4 metres wide, some 3.66 m (12 ft). Patterned and regular ranges. All accessories including underlay.

'Bespoke manufacturing service. Free measuring/estimating. Firsts and seconds. Annual sale first week January.'

In industrial estate just south of Fleetwood.
   From M55 exit 3: take A585 to Fleetwood. As you reach town at roundabout with large warehouse Fisherman's Friend on left, turn left; take second left.*
   From Fleetwood: take A585 for Preston. At roundabout with sign 'To docks' go straight on. At the next roundabout turn right into industrial estate then take next left.*
   ***Go along the Blackpool tram lines: company is 1/2 mile on left in corner with Kilbane Street.**

Open: Mon–Fri 9–5; Sat 9–1.
Closed: Bank Holidays; Christmas & New Year's Days.
Cards: None.
Cars: Outside shop.
Toilets: Yes.
Wheelchairs: Easy access.
Teas: Lots of cafés and fish & chip shops in town.
Tours: Customers welcome to see carpets being manufactured in the factory. All welcome but large groups arrange first with Christine Roberts.
Transport: Trams from Blackpool.
Mail order: Yes.
Catalogue: Carpet samples posted direct to customers for selection. Colour matching service.

Custom Carpets Factory Shop

Unit 11 Manor Road, Marston Trading Estate BA11 4BC
(01373) 472430

Tufted carpets to order from standard range of colours in different widths/weights. New 80/20% twist pile carpet in two weights (32 oz, 37 oz) in plain & Berber colours. Standard 12' wide, 4 m wide to order. Also 40 oz sq yd. Polypropylene bedroom carpet in 32 oz hessian-backed. *Duralay* underlay. Remnants.

'Dyed to order service. First quality goods at £5–£10.30 (about half retail price). Some seconds and slight imperfects. Recommended local fitters. Delivery in south-west and M4 area. NB This company is NOT Custom Carpets Warehouse.'

....

In trading estate south of Frome centre.

From Radstock/Warminster via A362: go into Frome centre, turn towards Glastonbury (A361); go over top of hill; go left into Marston Trading Estate at next roundabout.

From Shepton Mallett on A361: go straight on to B3090 at roundabout for Frome. *

From Trowbridge & Bath: stay on A361 bypass to south of Frome; at roundabout go right on to B3090 for Frome. *

*Go straight at 1st roundabout (Sainsbury's on right); go sharp right at 2nd roundabout into Marston Tr. Est. Take 1st right: shop at end of drive.

Open: Mon–Fri 9–5.30; Sat 9–4.30. Phone to check Bank Holidays.
Closed: Easter; Spring Bank Holiday week; last week *July*, first week *August;* Christmas–New Year.
Cards: No.
Cars: Outside shop.
Toilets: Yes.
Wheelchairs: No access to first floor showroom.
Teas: In Frome.
Tours: Individuals welcome to see round factory; please phone Keith Berry to arrange.
Transport: None.
Mail order: No.

Fred Lawton & Son Ltd.

Meltham Mills HD7 3AV
(01484) 852138

Carpets: plain dyed, tweeds, berbers, twist pile, saxony and velvet. 100% wool and 80/20% wool/nylon. Various widths – 12', 13'1", 15' broadloom. Some plain dyed rugs.

'Stock made from yarn spun in our mill. Most carpets half shop price.'

....

About 4 miles south-west of Huddersfield.

From Huddersfield ring road: take A616 for Sheffield; at third traffic lights, go straight to Meltham (B6108). Large mill is on left as you come downhill into Meltham.

From Holmfirth: take A6024 for Huddersfield. Shortly turn left on to B6107 for Netherthong. Keep going on this road into Meltham; go right opposite The Swan on to B6108. *

From Meltham: take road for Huddersfield (B6108). *After 1/2 mile, you see Lawton's red brick mill ahead.

From Honley: aim for Meltham. Go downhill into Meltham, keep right, passing old mill on right. At T-junction go right. Lawtons in large mill on right.

Open: Mon–Fri 9–5.30; Sat 9–12.30. Phone for Bank Holiday openings.
Closed: Christmas–New Year.
Cards: None.
Cars: Huge car-park.
Toilets: Yes.
Wheelchairs: No access yet – 8 steps to large, spacious shop.
Teas: Cafés and pubs in Meltham and Huddersfield.
Groups: No mill tours but groups of shoppers welcome – contact Malcolm Walker.
Transport: Huddersfield–Meltham buses stop outside.
Mail order: Yes.
Catalogue: Free swatches available on request.

Rowe Carpets

Green Street DY10 1HM
(01562) 820821

Wide selection of Axminster carpets made by this company. Large range of plain colours. Also all types of woven and tufted carpets. Large selection of rugs.

'Factory seconds, roll ends, remnants, perfects. Shop offers a fitting service for local area and a nationwide delivery service (free in Kidderminster, about £10 for Birmingham area, up to about £35 throughout the UK).'

Green Street is in the centre of town.

This shop is at the southern end near the ring road roundabout where the Stourport Road (A451) meets the Worcester Road (A449). From this roundabout take the exit marked 'Town Centre' then first right and next left. The shop, clearly visible, is 50 yds on the right.
[Near Victoria Carpets, see next entry.]

Open: Mon–Sat 8.30–5.30.
Closed: Bank Holidays; Christmas, New Year's Days.
Cards: Access, Amex, Connect, Visa.
Cars: Behind shop (entrance to the left of the shop).
Toilets: Yes.
Wheelchairs: Two steps to huge, spacious shop.
Teas: Plenty of places in Kidderminster.
Tours: No factory tours.
Transport: Easy walking distance from town centre bus station; 10 minutes from the BR station.

Victoria Carpet Weavers Shop

Green Street DY10 1HL
(01562) 754055

Wide range of Axminsters, Wilton and non-woven carpets, all manufactured in own factories. Excellent selection of colours/designs in variety of qualities and widths for immediate delivery. Also underlays, gripper etc.

'Gladly arrange delivery within West Midlands for £10–£20. List of recommended fitters in the local area.'

This shop is at the southern end of town near the ring road roundabout where the Stourport Road (A451) meets the Worcester Road (A449). From this roundabout take the exit marked 'Town Centre' then go first right and next left. The shop, clearly visible, is 150 yds on the right.
[Near Rowe Carpets, see previous entry.]

Open: Mon–Fri 10–5.30; Sat 9–5; Bank Holidays.
Closed: Four days at Christmas.
Cards: Access, Visa.
Cars: Own car-park at back, with the drive-in to the right of the shop.
Toilets: Yes.
Wheelchairs: Wide doors, no steps to spacious shop.
Teas: Café opposite shop. Plenty of places in town.
Tours: Unfortunately no tours of the works.
Transport: Within easy walking distance of town centre bus station and 10 minutes' walk from BR station.

The Weavers Shop

Duke Place, Churchfields DY10 2JP
(01562) 820680

Wide selection of Axminster carpets and tufted roll ends, discontinued lines and slight rejects. Also rugs and mats.

'Expert advice available, together with accessories and nation-wide delivery service – about £10 within 20 miles, with rate varying for elsewhere according to amount of carpet bought but always very reasonable. Recommended fitters' list for West Midlands.'

....

Just outside the northern section of the ring road.

Going south from Wolverhampton & Kinver (A449) and Stourbridge (A451): after these roads merge (Broadwaters pub on right), continue towards town centre on Stourbridge Road; with Murco petrol on right go right for town centre. Keep straight for 1/2 mile. Pass Mobil petrol then The Horsefair pub on right; go right, keep straight (over crossing) to shop on right.

From other directions: get on to ring road, take Stourbridge exit (A451). Go left at traffic lights then go immediately left again to Churchfields. Shop 250 yds on right.

Open: Mon–Fri 8.30–5; Sat 9–12.30.
Closed: Bank Holidays; Christmas–New Year.
Cards: No.
Cars: Own car-park in front of shop.
Toilets: Yes.
Wheelchairs: Ramp through double door to spacious shop.
Teas: In Kidderminster.
Groups: No.
Transport: Short walk from the town centre.

Phoenix Carpets

Unit 17, Bacon House Farm MK17 0PS
(01908) 501019

Wool twist plain and heather tufted carpets in wide range of colours and widths in 80/20% wool/nylon and 50/50% wool/nylon or polypropylene mix. From 38 oz (general domestic weight) up to 50 oz (industrial use). Carpets can be made to exact colour requirements.

'Special service for making carpet in any shade and width (50 cm–5 m) you wish at no extra charge for minimum order of 20 sq yds (15 x 12 ft). Prices usually a few pounds below normal retail, eg 38 oz about £14. Can organise complete fitting service.'

....

North of Little Horwood just off the A421.

From M1 exit 13: follow A421 towards Buckingham. Go through Milton Keynes and Bletchley. Shortly after roundabout with sign to Mursley (left) and Whaddon (right) turn left (sign-posted to Little Horwood). After 400 yds take first left, between the first house and a pink bungalow, then follow signs.

From Buckingham on A421: turn right towards Little Horwood at first sign. At T-junction turn left and after about 1/2 mile turn right immediately after the pink bungalow. Then follow signs.

Open: Mon–Sat 9–5.30.
Closed: Bank Holidays; Christmas Eve–New Year.
Cards: Eurocard, Mastercard, Visa.
Cars: Ample parking.
Toilets: Yes.
Wheelchairs: Easy access, no steps.
Teas: Can supply hot drinks on request.
Groups: Groups welcome by prior arrangement.
Transport: None available.
Mail order: No.

Crucial Trading Ltd.
174 Tower Bridge Road SE1 3LS
(0171) 234 0000

Large selection of conveniently sized natural fibre floor coverings including sisal, seagrass, coir, jute, wool etc at discount prices. May also inspect and order complete collection of over 120 natural floor coverings.

'Many ends of rolls, returned orders, discontinued lines etc at half-price. Also list of larger pieces up to whole roll (30 x 4 m) held at factory can be purchased at large discount through this shop. Free measuring service. Fitting can be arranged for most parts of mainland Britain.'

Easy to find on the main road leading south from Tower Bridge.
   Going south across Tower Bridge: keep straight. Go under the railway bridge. The clearly marked company is 100 yds on the left.
   Going north along Tower Bridge Road: look for the large railway bridge ahead. The shop is on the right, just before the bridge.

Open: Mon–Fri 10–6; Sat 10–5; Sun 12–5.
Closed: Bank Holidays; Christmas–New Year.
Cards: Access, Amex, Switch, Visa.
Cars: Easy street parking.
Toilets: Yes.
Wheelchairs: Difficult access: shop is in basement. However, there are usually two strong men on premises to help!
Teas: Café on third floor for food to eat in or take away.
Tours: No tours; unsuitable for group visits.
Transport: London Bridge BR station and tube; Tower Hill tube, Bus nos. 42, 78 and 188.
Mail order: Yes.
Catalogue: Free. No seconds or factory shop merchandise posted.

Marlborough Tiles
16 High Street SN8 1AA
(01672) 515287

Wall tiles (seconds and discontinued lines) made by *Marlborough Tiles.* Imported floor tiles.

'Prices from £3.24 per sq yd for seconds. Wall tiles are seconds and discontinued lines (may be perfect). Floor tiles mostly perfects at reduced prices.'

In town centre, on south side of High Street, next to Waitrose and opposite Lloyds Bank (large black and white building).
   From east or west: enter town on A4.
   From M4 exit 15: take A345 south. Keep going downhill into town; at roundabout, go right into New Road (town hall on right after 100 yds) then go straight into High Street – shop on left.

Open: Mon–Sat 9.30–5.
Closed: Bank Holidays. Please phone for Christmas times.
Cards: Access, Mastercard, Visa.
Cars: In High Street or behind Waitrose.
Toilets: Behind Town Hall in High Street.
Wheelchairs: Not possible; shop on lower ground floor.
Teas: Several super tea shops; local hotels and pubs.
Tours: No tours, small shop on different site from factory.
Transport: Bus no. 48 Swindon to Marlborough via Hungerford. Bus stop in High Street.
Mail order: Yes. Payment, including cost of mailing, has to be received before goods are despatched.

Candy & Co. Ltd.

Great Western Potteries TQ12 6RF
(01626) 832641 x 244

Wall and floor tiles; adhesives, grout, bathroom accessories, tiling tools, fireplaces and surrounds.

'A vast range of firsts, slight seconds and clearance lines at reduced prices.'

....

Actually on the A38 (north side of dual-carriageway) near exit for A382/Newton Abbot.

From Plymouth going north on A38: pass the roundabout/exit to Newton Abbot A383; go under next large roundabout (A382 junction) then go slowly for 1/2 mile. Entrance is on left, 400 yds after slipway.

From Exeter going south on A38: at large roundabout, exit for A382 to Newton Abbot but continue round and backtrack about 400 yds on other side of dual-carriageway to factory entrance.

Open: Mon–Sat 8.30–5. Bank Holidays 10–4.
Closed: Christmas–New Year please phone for opening times.
Cards: Access, Eurocard, Mastercard, Switch, Visa.
Cars: Own car-park.
Toilets: Yes.
Wheelchairs: Small step to shop.
Teas: Canteen and hot drinks machine.
Groups: Not suitable for groups.
Transport: Newton Abbot–Bovey Tracey buses stop 100 yds away in Battle Road.
Mail order: No.
Catalogue: Free brochure.

Pilkington's Tiles Ltd.

Blandford Road, Hamworthy BH15 4AP
(01202) 672741

Wide selection of seconds quality wall and floor tiles; also adhesives, grouts and fixing aids.

'Tiles ideal for hotels, catering trade kitchens, bathrooms, patios, conservatories. All seconds or discontinued lines at affordable prices.'

....

Hamworthy is on A350, just west of Poole.

From north and east: follow signs to Old Quay from where you cross over Poole Bridge to Hamworthy; go right into Blandford Road just before pedestrian traffic lights. Works well signposted.

From Wareham on A351: in Upton turn right on to A350.*
From Blandford and A31: go south on A350.*

*At large roundabout go towards Upton; go over two small roundabouts at Upton into Blandford Road; continue to just before Poole Bridge. Go left into factory premises: car-park by shop on left.

Open: Mon–Sat 8.30–4.30 (Thur to 8); Sun 10–3. Bank Holidays.
Closed: Easter Friday; Christmas Day.
Cards: Most major cards.
Cars: Large car-park.
Toilets: Ask here if required – or toilets on quayside.
Wheelchairs: One step to showroom; then collect purchases from large warehouse next door.
Teas: On quayside.
Groups: No factory tours.
Transport: Hamworthy bus stop 'Potters Arms' outside the factory from Poole bus station.

Marlborough Tiles

13 Milford Street SP1 2AJ
(01722) 328010

Wall tiles made by *Marlborough Tiles:* seconds and discontinued lines. Imported floor tiles.

'Prices from £3.24 sq yd for seconds. Wall tiles are seconds & discontinued lines (may be perfect); floor tiles mostly perfects at reduced prices.'

In the centre of Salisbury, opposite the Red Lion Hotel in Milford Street, just off the Market Place.

Open: Mon–Sat 9.30–5.00.
Closed: Bank Holidays; please phone for Christmas times.
Cards: Access, Mastercard, Visa.
Cars: Limited parking outside; car-parks nearby.
Toilets: In Market Square.
Wheelchairs: No; factory shop is on first floor (ground floor is first quality shop).
Teas: Numerous tea shops.
Groups: No tours, factory at different site. Groups welcome to shop.
Transport: Railway station is 10/15 minutes' walk.
Mail order: Yes. Payment, including cost of mailing, has to be received before goods are despatched.

Wilton Carpet Factory

King Street, Wilton SP2 0AV
(01722) 744919/742733

Downstairs carpet shop: first grade carpets, discontinued ranges, remnants and seconds. Upstairs clothes shop: branded ladies', men's and children's clothing; household linens, rug yarns and canvasses.

See our display advertisement opposite.

From Salisbury on the A36: go over roundabout as you enter Wilton; company is clearly marked on left.

From Bath/Warminster on A36: factory is clearly marked on right. Slow down on bend into Wilton (The Wheatsheaf on right) – concealed entrance.

Open: Mon–Sat 9–5; Sun 11–5.
Closed: Ten days over Christmas and New Year: please phone to check.
Cards: Access, Switch, Visa.
Cars: Large car-park.
Toilets: Yes.
Wheelchairs: Up 17 steps to first floor over carpet shop.
Teas: Coffee shop for hot drinks, light snacks and cream teas.
Tours: Four tours a day; Mon–Sat: 10.15,11.45, 2 and 3.30; Sun 11.15, 12.45, 2.30 and 3.45. Please phone in advance.
Transport: Bus nos. 60, 61 from Salisbury at the new canal every 10 minutes. From Salisbury BR station: turn left under bridge to bus stop for buses to Wilton.
Mail order: Yes.
Catalogue: No. Mail order service for rug making yarns and canvasses. Please phone 01722 744183.

194   Stoke-on-Trent : Tunstall   Staffs

H & R Johnson Tiles Ltd.
Harewood Street ST6 4JY
(01782) 575575

Slight seconds in wall and floor tiles and ends of range tiles. Ceramic giftware, mirrors, tiled trays, clocks. Also some chainstore giftware such as trays, lamps, vases, pictures, candlesticks. Tile adhesives, grouts etc.

'Seconds and discontinued firsts. Most prices reduced by 50% off normal retail price. 6" x 6" tiles @ £11.83 per 2 sq yd carton, 8" x 6" tiles @ £10.29 per 1 1/2 sq yd carton, flooring tiles at £8.23 per carton. Prices might vary.'

....

Situated west of Tunstall town centre.

   From south (Burslem) on A50: in front of 'Dewhirst Ladieswear' fork left at the roundabout. After 400 yds (where the main road goes left) turn right for Tunstall District Centre then immediately left into Connaught Street. *

   From A500: take A527 for Tunstall. Pass Price & Kensington on left; at next roundabout follow signs left to Tunstall. Go underneath H & R Johnson overpass and take first left to Tunstall District Centre; go immediately left again into Connaught Street (Office Stationery on corner, Lloyds Bank opposite). *

   *At far end turn left then follow signs to car-park and shop.

Open: Mon–Wed and Fri–Sat 9–4.
Closed: Thursday; Bank Holidays. Ten days at Christmas.
Cards: No.
Cars: Own adjacent car-park.
Toilets: Public toilets in Tunstall near Town Hall.
Wheelchairs: Two bays for the disabled outside factory door; 7 steps from car-park to shop.
Teas: At Three Cooks in High Street, Tunstall.
Groups: Shopping groups welcome, no need to book.
Transport: Buses to centre of town, shop 5 minute walk.

Carpets of Worth Ltd.
Severn Valley Mills DY13 9HB
(01299) 827222 x 210

Wide range of woven Axminster carpets in good variety of colours and patterns and in different widths; few Axminster rugs; picture rugs; tufted carpets. Mainly wool/nylon.

'All items are seconds, imperfects, overmakes or discontinued lines. Also ends of contract rolls. Regret that children under 14 not allowed into shop. Delivery can be arranged throughout UK; price quoted at time of purchase.'

....

Stourport has rather complicated one-way systems!

From Bewdley (B4195), Kidderminster (A451), Hartlebury (B4193) and Worcester (A4025): don't go right into the town centre but keep going clockwise round the one-way system; in Mitton Street look for sign (on left in a right-hand bend) pointing left to Carpets of Worth and go left*.

From Great Witley: go through town for 'All other routes' or 'Kidderminster'. Pass the adjacent Repsol, Esso and Texaco petrol stations then keep clockwise until you see the sign on the left to the carpet shop. Turn left.*

*The mill is on the left with a clearly marked shop entrance.

Open: Mon–Fri 9–5; Sat 8–12.
Closed: Bank Holidays; Christmas–New Year.
Cards: None.
Cars: Visitors' car-park.
Toilets: Factory toilets available.
Wheelchairs: Easy access.
Teas: In attractive town of Stourport.
Groups: No.
Transport: 5 minutes from town centre.

Carpet Shop (Carpets of Worth Ltd.)
Ham Mills, Thrupp GL5 2BE
(01453) 882421

Wide range of woven Axminster carpets in good variety of colours and patterns and in different widths; few Axminster rugs; picture rugs; tufted carpets. Mainly wool/nylon.

'Seconds, imperfects, overmakes or discontinued lines. Don't forget to take room measurements! Free delivery if company's carpet fitter used.'

....

On the A419 (Stroud–Cirencester road), 1.5 miles east of Stroud.

From Cirencester direction: pass Thrupp post office on right then after 200 yds look for factory shop sign on left; take next left turning into mill.

From Stroud: look for this clearly marked mill on right with the large sign 'Carpet bargains'. Keep going on main road – take next entrance into mill yard.

Open: Mon–Fri 9–5; Sat 9–1.
Closed: Bank Holidays; Easter; Spring Bank Holiday week; last week July/first week Aug; 2 days mid-Sept; Christmas–New Year.
Cards: None.
Cars: Outside shop.
Toilets: In Stroud.
Wheelchairs: Easy access, large display area.
Teas: In Stroud; lots of attractive local pubs.
Groups: Groups welcome to shop; please book in advance with Pauline Goddard.
Transport: Buses from Stroud to Thrupp every half hour.

Homemaker Edging Services

2A Avondale Street WF2 8DP
(01924) 376021

Overlocking service and fringing for carpet and rug edges; runners and stair carpets also. Turn your carpet remnants into matching rugs and mats to coordinate with your home. Renovation service for worn edges on carpets and rugs (except Chinese). All colours and types of yarn available.

'One of the few carpet overlocking companies which offers this useful service directly to the public as well as to carpet fitters. About 25p per foot for short lengths. Now you can restore the rug that your dog chewed!'

....

South of town off dual carriageway section of A636.

From town centre: take the A636 for Denby Dale/M1. Go over the large roundbout (B&Q on far right corner). Enter the dual carriageway section and take first left (Avondale Street).*

From M1 exit 39: take the A636 to Wakefield. This becomes a dual carriageway. Go over river Calder; go over the huge bridge and continue to large new roundabout (B&Q on near left corner). Double back at this roundabout and take first left (Avondale St).*

*Company is 200 yds on left (sign says 'White Knight Services').

Open: Mon–Fri 9.15–3.30.
Closed: Bank Holidays; Christmas–New Year period.
Cards: None.
Cars: In street.
Toilets: Please ask if necessary.
Wheelchairs: No steps into factory area.
Teas: In Wakefield, 3 minutes away.
Tours: This is a small factory, but customers (no children) can see work being done if time allows.
Transport: Bus nos. 443 or 484 from town centre.
Mail order: Yes. Service available by post, but please phone first and explain what work is required and on which type of product.

The Carpet Company

Perseverance Mill, Bolton Road BL5 3DZ
(01942) 815532

Quality carpets all made here: plain tufted and berbers 80/20% wool/nylon; also vinyl and some patterns available. Underlays, door trims, roll ends etc. Fitting service.

'All carpets at factory prices. Oriental rug service, please ring first.'

....

Fifteen miles north-west of Manchester city centre, 5 miles south-west of Bolton.

From M61 exit 5: follow signs to Westhoughton A58. Go to roundabout, go right (A6, signposted 'Chorley'). After 1/2 mile, go left at traffic lights (White Horse pub on far left); pass the Grey Mare on left (about 400 yds) and clearly marked mill is 1/4 mile on right (look for yellow sign).

Open: Wed–Fri 11.30–5; Sat and Sun 11.30–4. Worth phoning first.
Closed: Monday, Tuesday; Bank Holidays; Christmas–New Year.
Cards: No.
Cars: Large yard at the front.
Toilets: Yes.
Wheelchairs: No steps to large showroom and factory.
Teas: In Westhoughton.
Groups: Not suitable for groups. You can see carpets being made from the showroom.
Transport: Buses from Bolton, Wigan and Manchester 100 yds.

Rowe Carpets

Castle Street WR1 3AV
(01905) 619515

Wide selection of Axminster carpets made by this company. Large range of plain colours. Also all types of woven and tufted carpets. Large selection of rugs. Three-piece suites, beds and mattresses from well known manufacturers.

'Factory seconds, 700 roll ends, remnants, perfects. Expert fitting service for local area and a nationwide fitting and delivery service (local deliveries free, up to about £35 throughout UK).'

To the north side of the town centre, opposite the Royal Infirmary.
  Coming south from M5 exit 6 on A449, and on A38 from Droitwich: go towards town along first Barbourne Road then The Tything. Pass Grammar School on left; at traffic lights go right into Castle Street. Shop is 200 yds on right directly opposite Royal Infirmary.
  From the west: go over River Severn; go left into one-way system. Keep straight, with river on left. Go under railway. Pass race-course on left: shop is 50 yds on left.
  From town centre: go north along Foregate Street and under multi-coloured railway bridge; pass the Odeon on left; after 150 yds, go left at traffic lights into Castle Street. Shop is 200 yds right.

Open: Mon–Sat 9–5.30.
Closed: Bank Holidays; Christmas, Boxing and New Year's Days.
Cards: Access, Amex, Connect, Visa.
Cars: Own large car-park to front and side of shop.
Toilets: Yes (but not for disabled).
Wheelchairs: No step, huge shop (19,000 sq ft).
Teas: Tea or coffee made on request by customers!
Tours: No factory tours.
Transport: 5 minutes' walk from bus station; 5 minutes' walk from BR station.

Dennis of Ruabon

Hafod Tileries, Ruabon LL14 6ET
(01978) 840233

First and second quality traditional Welsh quarry unglazed clay tiles in a variety of colours, shapes and sizes (including traditional border tiles etc); clay pavers suitable for drives and patios; *Keope* Italian porcelain floor tiles in a large and varied selection of sizes and colours. Grouts, adhesives and cutters are also available; garden pots and wall tiles.

'Tiles and pavers made from local clay. Prices for own tiles from about £12 + vat per square yard. Please telephone or call in for full details.'

About 4 miles south-west of Wrexham.
  From Wrexham: take A483 dual carriageway south for Oswestry. Take exit signposted B5426 Bangor-On-Dee/The Plassey. At top of slip road go right, then over bypass to crossroad: turn right (B5605). Shop 500 yds on left, after offices.
  From Oswestry go north on A483. Take slip road to Johnstown (B5426). After 50 yds turn right. Shop is 500 yds on left, after offices.

Open: Mon–Fri 8–4; Sat 8–1 and 1.30–3.30.
Closed: Christmas–New Year. Most Bank Holidays but phone to check.
Cards: Access, Visa.
Cars: At front of shop.
Toilets: Yes.
Wheelchairs: Three steps, no ramp.
Teas: Facilities and pubs nearby.
Tours: Tours of the factory by prior arrangement only.
Transport: None.
Mail order: Yes.
Catalogue: Free. Will send items by post (carriage paid by customer).

Furniture

Glossy home magazines always advise readers to buy well made furniture but they never tell you how to *identify* it. Buying an upholstered three piece suite is somewhat akin to having your teeth fixed or roof mended. You never know how good your craftsman was until it is too late. Nor can you know, unless you ask the correct questions, what life-span your chairs are likely to have. The beautiful surface appearance can belie a poor interior construction.

We asked PF Collections of Long Eaton, a manufacturer of upholstered suites in Nottinghamshire, for a list of questions to ask before you buy.

1. Is the frame made of particle board or more substantial hard wood?

2. Is the frame stapled together of does it have a stronger construction with glue and dowels?

3. Is there a protective layer between the frame and covering fabric? *Without this protective layer, your upholstery fabric will wear out more quickly. You can tell if there is a protective layer by feeling the frame.*

4. Which springing system is used? *A no-sag springing system gives a firmer seat (not for use with feathers). Mesh-topped coil springs give a softer overall feel. Remember that the springing system and cushion have to work together to give the feel you want.*

5. Is there a choice of cushion filling? *Comfort is subjective and only you can choose from feathers, foam, fibre or feather/fibre mix.*

6. Is the upholstery fabric cut by hand to ensure a high degree of pattern matching? *A sign of quality is that the fabric matches all the way over the piece, ie bottom border, platform, inside and outside back, and cushions.*

7. What is the wearability of the upholstery fabric? *Choose from careful domestic through to heavy contract quality.*

In addition to upholstered furniture (and re-upholstery services), this book leads you to a wide range of pine, mahogany, yew and walnut furniture, fine period style pieces, farmhouse tables, kitchen and bathroom fittings, office and computer desks, beds, conservatory chairs and even luxurious swing hammocks.

You also have the opportunity to have a item made to fit your room, stained to match your other furniture or covered in your own fabric. And all the shops arrange very reasonably priced delivery around the country.

Royal Aberdeen Workshops for the Blind	201	**Aberdeen**	Grampian
End of the Line Furniture	202	**Ambergate**	Derbys
Croydex	203	**Andover**	Hants
Blindcraft	204	**Ayr**	Strathclyde
Croydex	205	**Barnstaple**	Devon
Skopos Mill Shop	114*	**Batley**	W Yorks
Boynett Fabrics	115*	**Bedford**	Beds
Heyford's Upholstery	206	**Bicester**	Oxon
Treetops Pine Furniture	207	**Birmingham**	W Mids
Frenni Furniture	208	**Crymych**	Dyfed
Croydex	209	**Dartford**	Kent
Dovetail Enterprises	210	**Dundee**	Tayside
Blindcraft Edinburgh	211	**Edinburgh**	Lothian
Nova Garden Furniture	212	**Faversham**	Kent
Table Place, The	213	**Fenstanton near St Ives**	Cambs
Royal Strathclyde Blindcraft Industries	214	**Glasgow**	Strathclyde
Collins and Hayes	215	**Hastings**	E Sussex
Langley Furniture	216	**Heanor**	Derbys
Furniture Direct	217	**High Wycombe**	Bucks
Providence Reproductions	218	**Hyde**	Gr Manchester
Frank Knighton & Sons	219	**Ilkeston**	Derbys
Highland Society for the Blind	220	**Inverness**	Highlands and Islands
Table Place, The	221	**Kenilworth**	Warks
P F Collections	222	**Long Eaton**	Notts
Palatine Products	223	**Newcastle upon Tyne**	Tyne & Wear
Table Place, The	224	**Oakham**	Leics
Chelsee Design	225	**Ripley**	Derbys
Hubbinet Reproductions	226	**Romford**	Essex
Sheban Furniture	227	**Seaford**	E Sussex
Skopos Furniture Gallery	228	**Shipley**	W Yorks
Lincoln House Home Furnishings	229	**Somercotes**	Derbys
Sunelm Products Sheltered Workshops	230	**Sunderland**	Tyne & Wear
Marden Furniture	231	**Sutton-in-Ashfield**	Notts
Brunel (By Testall) Upholstery	232	**Westhoughton, Bolton**	Gr Manchester
Beevers of Whitby	233	**Whitby**	N Yorks

* Please see full details in respective chapter

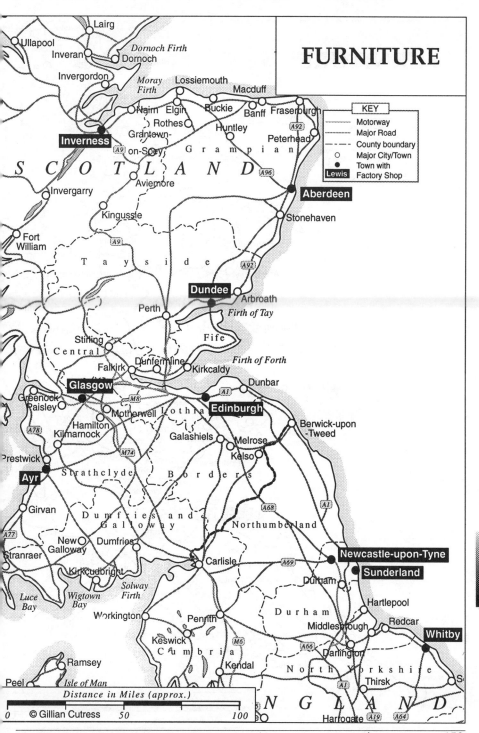

FURNITURE

KEY
- Motorway
- Major Road
- County boundary
- ○ Major City/Town
- ● Town with Factory Shop Lewis

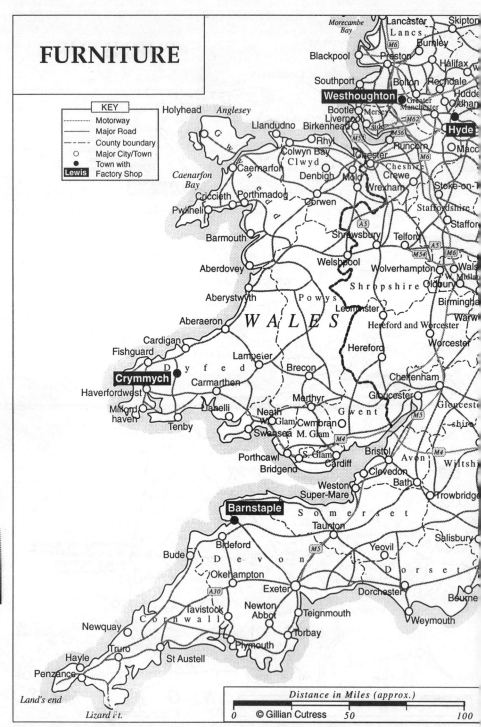

FURNITURE

KEY
.... Motorway
──────── Major Road
── ─ ── County boundary
○ Major City/Town
● Town with
Lewis Factory Shop

Holyhead *Anglesey*

Morecambe Bay Lancaster Skipton

Blackpool L a n c s Burnley

Southport Bolton Rochdale Halifax

Westhoughton Greater Manchester Oldham Hudde

Bootle Mersey **Hyde**

Birkenhead Liverpool Macc

Llandudno Rhyl Runcorn

Colwyn Bay Chester Ches h i r e

Caernarfon C l w y d Denbigh Mold Crewe Stoke-on-T

Caenarfon Bay Wrexham Staffordshire Staffo

Criccieth Porthmadog Corwen Shrewsbury Telford

Pwllheli Welshpool Wolverhampton Wals

Barmouth W. Midla

Aberdovey S h r o p s h i r e Oldbury Birmingha

Aberystwyth P o w y s Leominster Warw

Aberaeron W A L E S Hereford and Worcester Worcester

Cardigan Hereford

Fishguard D y f e d Lampeter Brecon Cheltenham

Crymmych Carmarthen Merthyr Gloucester Gloucest

Haverfordwest Neath Cwmbran -shire

Milford haven W. Glam G w e n t

Llanelli Swansea M. Glam Bristol A v o n

Tenby Porthcawl S. Glam Cardiff M4 W i l t s h i

Bridgend Clevedon Bath

Weston-Super-Mare Trowbridge

Barnstaple S o m e r s e t

Bideford Taunton Salisbury

Bude D e v o n Yeovil

Okehampton D o r s e t

Exeter Dorchester Bourne

Newquay Tavistock Newton Abbot Teignmouth Weymouth

C o r n w a l l Torbay

Hayle Truro Plymouth

Penzance St Austell

Land's end

Lizard Pt.

Distance in Miles (approx.)
© Gillian Cutress
0 ——— 50 ——— 100

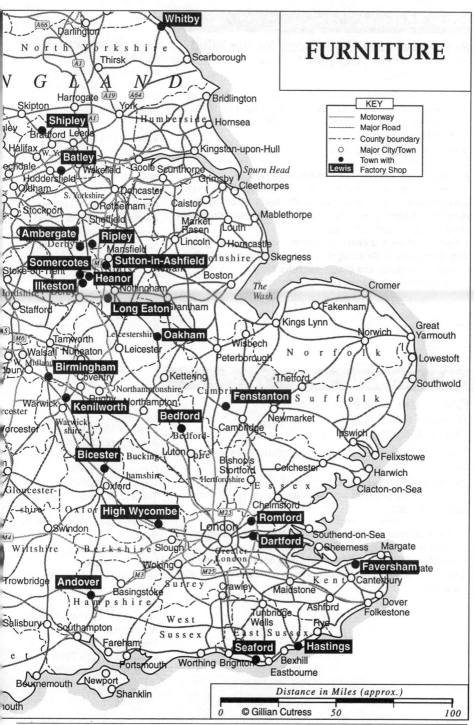

FURTURE

KEY

	Motorway
	Major Road
	County boundary
○	Major City/Town
●	Town with
Lewis	Factory Shop

Royal Aberdeen Workshops for the Blind

132 Wellington Road, West Tullos Industrial Estate AB9 1LO
(01224) 873366

All sizes of beds and divans, matching mattresses; three-piece suites, range of armchairs with high backs and firm upholstery; bedding, curtains, curtain-making service, re-upholstery service.

'Established since 1843. All products hand-made.'

In Tullos, south of River Dee and Aberdeen town.
 From town centre: follow signs to Tullos/A956. Cross river, pass prison on left, go straight at traffic lights (Gateway on right). Go straight at next traffic lights; go right into Craigshaw Drive at next (third) traffic lights. *
 From south on A92 dual carriageway: turn on to A956 to Aberdeen Harbour. Go straight at first roundabout, then left at first traffic lights into Craigshaw Drive. *
 *Take first right: entrance 100 yds on right.

Open: Mon–Fri 8.30–4.30; Sat 10–4.
Closed: Bank Holidays; Christmas and Boxing Days.
Cards: Access, Visa.
Cars: Private parking outside shop.
Toilets: Yes, and for the disabled.
Wheelchairs: Easy access.
Teas: In Aberdeen.
Groups: Gladly show you round the works but please telephone first to arrange.
Transport: Bus no. 13 from town centre to Cove. Ask for Craigshaw Drive.

End of the Line Furniture

32 Derby Road DE56 2GF
(01773) 856082

Top quality upholstered, sprung furniture: sofas, armchairs etc.

'Perfect quality items which are cancelled orders. Fully guaranteed. At prices at least 40% lower than rrp. Fabric samples available.'

On the main road (A6) through Ambergate, a short distance south of the traffic lights where the A610 turns off for Nottingham. The shop is in the old Co-Op beside the pedestrian lights, almost opposite the White House pub (black and white building).

Open: Thur, Fri, Sat 10–5; Sun 12–5.
Closed: Monday, Tuesday, Wednesday. Christmas, Boxing and New Year's Days.
Cards: Access, Visa.
Cars: On forecourt.
Toilets: In pub across the road.
Wheelchairs: Three shallow steps.
Teas: Little Chef and pub meals along road.
Groups: No tours; large shopping groups please phone first.
Transport: Any bus through Ambergate.
Mail order: Yes.
Catalogue: Free. Photos and fabric samples available.

Croydex

Unit 27, Chantry Centre SP10 1LS
(01264) 336018

Large range of bathroom and household accessories including bath panels, cabinets, mirrors, toilet seats, towel rings and rails, soap dishes, bath mats, shower and window curtains, Austrian blinds, trays, chopping boards, place mats and coasters, wine coolers, ice buckets, pillows etc.

'Goods made for well known chainstores: at least 40% off normal retail prices. Firsts, seconds, samples and ends of ranges.'

....

From all directions aim for town centre.
   The Chantry Centre is a pedestrianised shopping precinct in the town centre. Shop is close to the multi-storey car-park, opposite Le Café and by Boots.

Open: Mon–Sat 9–5.30.
Closed: Most Bank Holidays; Christmas, Boxing and New Year's Days.
Cards: Access, Mastercard, Visa.
Cars: Multi-storey car-park.
Toilets: Outside the shopping mall.
Wheelchairs: No steps.
Teas: Café opposite shop.
Groups: Groups welcome.
Transport: Any bus or train to Andover.
Mail order: No.

Blindcraft

105 Main Street KA8 8BV
(01292) 263986

Beds, chairs, suites. Canetex furniture.

'All first quality.'

....

In the centre of town (now partly pedestrianised).
   From Prestwick: go straight over roundabout into Main Street. Shop is on the right, opposite the post office.

Open: Mon–Sat 9–5.30.
Closed: Glasgow holidays; Christmas, Boxing and New Year's Days.
Cards: Access, Visa.
Cars: Local car-parks.
Toilets: In local superstores.
Wheelchairs: Easy access.
Teas: Local cafés.
Groups: No.
Transport: Any bus to Ayr.
Mail order: No.

Croydex

Gratton Way, Roundswell Industrial Estate EX31 3NK
(01271) 78555

Wide range of bathroom accessories in natural, antique pine and mahogany finish, including bath panels, cabinets, mirrors, towel rings and rails. Shower and window curtains, Austrian blinds, chopping boards, place mats and coasters, wine coolers, ice buckets, bath mats and pillows.

'Goods made here for well known chainstores: at least 40% off normal retail prices. Firsts, seconds, samples, ends of ranges etc.'

....

South of town off B3232 and new bypass.

From town centre, Braunton via A361 and Lynton via A39: follow signs to Bideford and Torrington. Pass large Sainsbury's, go left at next roundabout following brown signs to Brannam's Pottery.

From the east on A361 and south on A377: follow brown signs to pottery as you reach bypass.

From Bideford on A39: go left at roundabout with brown signs to pottery.

Once in estate go straight to end: shop on right.

Open: Mon–Sat 10–5.
Closed: Bank Holidays; Christmas, Boxing and New Year's Days.
Cards: Access, Mastercard, Visa.
Cars: Opposite factory shop.
Toilets: No.
Wheelchairs: Access not possible.
Teas: At Brannams Pottery or Sainsbury's.
Groups: Groups welcome but no factory tours.
Transport: Bus no. 12 either to Sainsbury's or Roundswell Estate. Barnstaple BR station.
Mail order: No.

Heyford's Upholstery

Units 7 & 8, Launton Road OX6 0US   (01869) 323244

Hand-made sofas, chairs, sofabeds and footstools in modern and traditional designs. Choice of over 2,000 fabric designs . Customers can select own seating grade from soft, medium & hard, foam, fibre and feathers. Stock clearance lines also on display in 2,500 sq ft showroom at special clearance prices. Also curtain fabric, arm caps and curtain make-up service.

'Up to 50% reductions; chairs from £150–£450, three seat sofas from £290–£700, two seat sofas from £250–£650. Clearance suites from £499. Free delivery in UK.'

....

Close to the town centre and Bicester Outlet Shopping Village.

From M40 exit 9: head towards Bicester; go right on to Boundary Way (A41) for Aylesbury, passing Tesco and Bicester Village complex on left. At next roundabout go left into London Road (for Bicester B4100); go over level-crossing; at mini roundabout go right (Launton Road).*

From Bicester centre: from one-way system around square, exit to left of King's Arms. After 100 yds, go left at mini roundabout for Launton/car park.*

*Pass Esso on left. Go under railway bridge, pass first left turnoff: factory and shop are immediately on left.

Open: Mon–Sat 10–4. Bank Holidays: phone to check.
Closed: Sunday; Christmas –New Year period.
Cards: No.
Cars: Car-park for 60 cars.
Toilets: Yes.
Wheelchairs: 10 steps; help available.
Teas: Coffee and tea.
Groups: Weekdays only; no more than 10 people. Please phone sales office, giving minimum 48 hours' notice.
Transport: Bicester North BR station less than 1/4 mile. Nearest bus stop, in Market Square, five minutes' walk to factory.

Treetops Pine Furniture

Grange Road B14 7RJ
(0121) 444 8475

Pine furniture, fitted bedrooms and kitchens.
'Seconds and ends of ranges on sale.'

....

In King's Heath a short distance off the High Street.

From Birmingham on the A435 towards Redditch: pass the town name sign just after roundabout and take the third right with Argos on the near right corner.

From the south on the A435: go through King's Heath High Street, pass the Crossed Guns on the left and take the next left with Argos on corner. The shop is about 250 yds on the right in a white building.

Open: Mon–Fri 9–5; Sat 10–4.
Closed: Christmas and Boxing Days.
Cards: Access, Amex, Delta, Switch, Visa.
Cars: Easy parking in road outside factory.
Toilets: Yes.
Wheelchairs: One step.
Teas: In High Street.
Tours: Happy to show pre-booked groups over factory. Please phone in advance.
Transport: Various local bus routes.
Mail order: No.

Frenni Furniture

Tenby Road SA4 3QG
(01239) 831557

Solid mahogany furniture, such as tables, cabinets, bookcases, chairs, bureaux, desks, bedside cabinets etc all made on the premises.
'All products are seconds, and are sold at around 30–40% less than high street prices. Special commissions undertaken. Orders by post or telephone accepted. Delivery can be arranged, £10 anywhere within the UK.'

....

Crymych is on the A478 about eight miles south of Cardigan.

Coming south from Cardigan: stay on this road into the village; the shop is on the right, opposite the pharmacy.

Coming north towards Cardigan: go into village, pass petrol station, then butcher on left, then this shop is shortly on the left.

Open: Mon–Thur 8–5; Fri 8–2.
Closed: Some Bank Holidays, please phone to check; Christmas–New Year.
Cards: Access, Eurocard, Mastercard, Visa.
Cars: Large car-park at rear.
Toilets: Across the road.
Wheelchairs: One step to shop.
Teas: Café and pub meals within 50 yds.
Tours: Guided tours of factory, for small groups only, must be booked in advance.
Transport: Daily bus service from Cardigan.
Mail order: No.

Croydex

41 The Priory Centre DA1 2HP
(01322) 294642

Large range of bathroom and household accessories
including bath panels, cabinets, mirrors, toilet seats, towel
rings and rails, soap dishes, bath mats, shower and window
curtains, Austrian blinds, trays, chopping boards, place mats
and coasters, wine coolers, ice buckets, pillows etc.

'Goods made for well known chainstores: at least 40% off
normal retail prices. Firsts, seconds, samples and ends of
ranges etc.'

From all directions head for the town centre.
   The Priory Centre is a pedestrianised shopping precinct in the
town centre.

Open: Mon–Sat 9–5.30.
Closed: Bank Holidays;
Christmas, Boxing and New
Year's Days.
Cards: Access, Mastercard,
Visa.
Cars: Multi-storey car-park in
shopping centre.
Toilets: In Centre.
Wheelchairs: Ground level;
lifts to car-park.
Teas: In Centre.
Groups: Groups of shoppers
welcome.
Transport: 5 minutes' walk
from Dartford BR station and
Dartford bus terminus.
Mail order: No.

Dovetail Enterprises
(formerly Royal Dundee Blindcraft)

51 Nethergate DD1 4DO
(01382) 224761

Willow baskets, dog baskets, hampers, laundry baskets;
beds and mattresses, high back chairs. Also cane furniture.

'Standard size beds – delivery from stock. Special sizes made to
order.'

In the city centre, underneath the Angus Hotel.

Open: Mon–Sat 9–5.30.
Closed: Bank Holidays;
Christmas, Boxing and New
Year's Days.
Cards: Access, Delta,
Mastercard, Switch, Visa.
Cars: Outside but restricted.
Toilets: In town.
Wheelchairs: One step to
medium sized shop.
Teas: In town.
Groups: No.
Transport: Buses stop in
Nethergate.
Mail order: No.

Blindcraft Edinburgh

Peffer Place EH16 4BA
(0131) 659 6473

Beds and bedding for hotels, contract and domestic use; special sizes to order. Pine bunks and headboards; pocket and interior sprung mattresses; pillows and quilts; ottoman and bedroom stools and chairs. Pine furniture.

'Direct from factory prices. Delivery service within the UK – ask for quotation (price usually varies with weight).'

On south-east side of Edinburgh.
   From A68 (Dalkeith–Edinburgh road): take A6095 at roundabout for Craigmillar. Pass brewery on left, go left at next traffic lights.*
   From east/Musselburgh: take A6095. Go under A1; continue until you pass Shoprite on right. Go right at next traffic lights.*
   ***Take next right (Peffer Place): factory is first on right. Follow signs to shop.**

Open: Mon–Sat 9.30–5; Sun 11–4.
Closed: Public holidays. 1, 2 Jan; 14–17 April; 1, 8, 22 May; 16–18 Sept; 25, 26 Dec.
Cards: Access, Switch, Visa.
Cars: Outside shop.
Toilets: If desperate.
Wheelchairs: Easy access, no step.
Teas: In nearby Carmeron Toll shopping centre.
Groups: No factory tours.
Transport: Bus no. 21 from Princes Street; C3 and 14 from North Bridge.
Mail order: Yes.
Catalogue: Brochure available on request.

Nova Garden Furniture

Graveney Road ME13 8UM   *(01795) 535321*

Luxurious couch swing hammocks, synthetic resin patio sets, reclining resin chairs; tubular folding frames, parasols, sunbeds, other accessories. All frames with wide selection of cushion designs. Also a large selection of cast aluminium and timber furniture.

'One of Britain's leading manufacturers of attractive luxury upholstered garden furniture. Seconds, discontinued lines; many items half-price or less.'

East of Faversham, 2 minutes from M2 exit 7.
   From M2 exit 7 and A299 (Thanet Way, main Faversham–Whitstable road): take B2040 for Faversham. As you come into town go right for Graveney.*
   From Faversham town centre: with station on right, follow road round to left. At traffic lights go right (B2040 for Whitstable). Cross railway; take first left, for Graveney.*
   From Sittingbourne via A2: stay on A2 to Shell petrol on left – go left for Graveney. Go right for Graveney Ind. Est.*
   ***Pass Nova factory on left: shop 150 yds on left.**
   From east via A2: take first turn-off to Faversham; keep going towards Faversham – company is on right.

Open: *March–September only;* Mon, Wed, Fri 10.30–2; Sat 9.30–3; Bank Holidays except Good Friday.
Closed: *October–February;* Good Friday.
Cards: No.
Cars: Outside shop.
Toilets: In Faversham (1.5m).
Wheelchairs: Wide double doors, huge shop, no steps.
Teas: In Faversham.
Groups: Groups welcome to shop, please phone first, mentioning this guide.
Transport: No.

The Table Place

13–15 High Street PE18 9LQ
(01480) 460321

Extensive selection of Regency reproduction furniture in mahogany, yew and walnut for dining, sitting and bedrooms. Also Tudor/Jacobean reproduction furniture in oak and a fine range of solid pine furniture. Desk chairs, desk lamps, chaises longues, pictures and mirrors etc.

'Showcase for a dedicated company of cabinet makers and french polishers from the heart of Rutland. The quality has to be seen and touched to be appreciated. Individual design commissions welcome. Also colour match to own furniture. Some items not up to high standard sold as seconds. Other showrooms in Oakham, Rutland and Kenilworth, Warks.'

....

In middle of the village – well marked.

  From Huntingdon on A14 (old A604): turn off for Fenstanton/ Dairy Site.*

  From Cambridge on A14 (old A604): turn off for Fenstanton/ Dairy Site.*

  ***Shop near The George (on same side) and near the Crown & Pipes (across the road).**

Open: Thur, Fri 10–5;
Sat 10–4; Sun 11–4; Mon 10–5.
Bank Holidays.
Closed: Tuesday, Wednesday; few days over Christmas (please phone to check).
Cards: Access, Delta, Switch, Visa.
Cars: In High Street.
Toilets: Yes.
Wheelchairs: Easy access to ground floor, but unfortunately not to upstairs showroom.
Teas: Free coffee or tea on request.
Transport: Many buses from Cambridge or Huntingdon and St Ives.
Mail order: No.
Catalogue: Relevant photocopy pages gladly supplied.

Royal Strathclyde Blindcraft Industries

Atlas Industrial Estate G21 1BR
(0141) 558 1485

Office furniture, beds, school furniture, residential furniture and computer furniture.

....

In Springburn, north/north-east of the city centre.

  From city centre/other directions: get on M8, go to exit 15; take A803 for Kirkintilloch and Springburn (A8 also gets to this junction). At traffic lights turn right, pass Barnhill BR station; immediately go left into Edgefauld Road. Atlas Industrial Estate is next on left; Blindcraft straight ahead.

Open: Mon–Thur 9–4;
Fri 9–12.30.
Closed: Bank Holidays.
Cards: Access, Visa.
Cars: Own car-park.
Toilets: In shopping centre.
Wheelchairs: Easy access to limited showroom.
Teas: In town.
Groups: No.
Transport: Bus nos. 11, 12, 37 pass nearby.
Mail order: No.

Collins and Hayes Ltd.

Menzies Road, Ponswood Industrial Estate TN34 1XE
(01424) 443834

Upholstered furniture: three-piece suites, sofas, chairs and some sofa beds. Upholstery/furnishing fabrics by the metre.

'All top quality upholstered furniture made in our factories on site. Most items perfect ends of lines and cancelled orders at about half high street price or less. Furniture delivered free within the UK.'

....

On the north-west side of Hastings.
From Hastings: go along seafront towards Bexhill. Pass the pier on left and White Rock Theatre on right. At traffic lights go right (London Road) and keep straight. At next traffic lights, in Silverhill, go straight for Battle. A short way down the hill (fish & chip shop on far left corner), take first left (Menzies Road). Company is shortly on left.

From Battle: take A2100 south-east for Hastings. Pass Beauport Park Hotel on left. At mini-roundabout follow sign to Hastings/Ponswood. Go under bridge, downhill, over lights then zebra. Pass the Tivoli Tavern on right. Take first right (Menzies Road) signed Ponswood. Company is shortly on left.

Open: Mon–Sat 9–5.
Closed: Bank Holidays; Christmas–New Year period.
Cards: Access, Visa.
Cars: In factory car-park.
Toilets: Yes.
Wheelchairs: No steps to large shop.
Teas: Local cafés and pubs in St Leonards and Hastings.
Groups: No factory tours, but groups welcome to shop.
Transport: St Leonards Warrior Square BR, then taxi.
Mail order: No.

Langley Furniture

Delves Road, Heanor Gate Industrial Estate DE75 7SJ
(01773) 765544

Reproduction pine furniture made here: bedside cupboards, chests of drawers, kitchen and dressing tables, kitchen units, welsh dressers, wardrobes, chairs, bathroom accessories, bookcases, cabinets, mirrors etc; also manufacture and install windows.

'Furniture can be designed to customer's own specifications – free quotations. Fax a sketch with dimensions to 01773 531322. Free delivery within 20 miles of Heanor on orders over £150. Occasional seconds. Also in Digby Street, Ilkeston Junction (0115) 930 9641.'

....

On industrial estate west of Heanor: enter from Derby Rd (A608).
Coming east along Derby Road (A608) to Heanor: go right after Heanor Gate school into Heanor Gate Road. Langley is first factory on the right.
From Heanor: take A608 for Smalley/Derby. Pass Nottingham House pub on left, take first left (to Shipley Country Park). After UK petrol on right, go right into Heanor Gate Road. Shop is 1/3 mile on left, just after Delves Road on left.

Open: Mon–Fri 8–6; Sat 8–5; Sun & Bank Holidays 10.30–4.
Closed: Christmas, Boxing and New Year's Days.
Cards: Access, Delta, Switch, Visa.
Cars: Own car-park.
Toilets: Yes.
Wheelchairs: Ramp to medium sized shop.
Teas: Coffee and biscuits. Shipley Country Park cafeteria nearby.
Groups: Small groups welcome to shop (but not to factory itself).
Transport: Nottingham and Derby buses stop nearby; two miles from BR station at Langley Mill.
Mail order: Yes.
Catalogue: Telephone for free brochure and price list.

Furniture Direct

Riverside Business Centre, Victoria Street HP11 2LS
(01494) 462233

Quality upholstered furniture: sofas, upholstered chairs and
sofa beds. Choose your own fabric from thousands available.
'All furniture made here. Also curtain-making service.'

....

**One mile west of High Wycombe centre, just off West Wycombe
Road (A40, High Wycombe–Oxford road).**

  **From High Wycombe: take A40; go over traffic lights with
Europcar Rental on far left corner; after 100 yds go left into
Victoria Street.***

  **From Oxford via A40: as you reach High Wycombe, pass BP on
right then The White Horse then Bird in Hand on right; take next
right, Victoria Street.***

  ***Riverside Business Centre clearly visible on left with large
off-road car-park in front.**

Open: Mon–Sat 9.30–5;
Sun 10–4; Bank Holidays.
Closed: Christmas and
Boxing Days.
Cards: Access, Visa.
Cars: Own car-park.
Toilets: Yes.
Wheelchairs: One tiny step,
large showroom.
Teas: In High Wycombe.
Groups: No tours.
Transport: Local buses go
along the A40.

Providence Reproductions

Providence Mill, Alexandra Street SK14 1DX (0161) 366 6184

Vast selection of period style furniture for bedrooms, dining
and living rooms in mahogany, yew and oak finishes.
Specialists in solid mahogany dining tables and chairs.
*'Special service to stain/polish pieces to your own requirements
in workshop on premises. Repair and re-polishing services.'*

....

West side of Hyde, south of M67 exit 3, near Hyde Central station.

  **Via A627 from south and A57 from east: go into town centre.
From Market Street (main shopping area) in central Hyde go left
into small Croft Street at sign to this company. At far end, go
left into Alexandra Street.**

  Via M67 from east: exit for Hyde and turn right over motorway.*
  From Manchester: exit for Hyde and turn left.*

  ***Go round long left bend, go through two traffic lights and
over motorway again. At next lights go straight; by station turn
left (Gt Norbury St).****

  **Via A57 from Denton/Manchester: go right (sign to station)
immediately before railway bridge into Gt Norbury Street.****

  ****Take first right (Railway Street), go right (Croft Street) and
left (Alexandra Street). Go right for huge red-brick mill. Entrance
on left side.**

Open: Mon–Sat 9–5;
Sun 10–4; Bank Holidays 10–4.
Closed: Christmas and
Boxing Days.
Cards: Access, Visa.
Cars: In mill yard.
Toilets: Yes.
Wheelchairs: Huge shop on
first floor up stone staircase.
Lift (enquire at office).
Teas: In Hyde.
Transport: 10 minutes' walk
from town centre.

219 Ilkeston   Derbys

Frank Knighton & Sons

Critchley Court, Wood Street DE7 8GF
(0115) 930 6567

Wide selection of leather chairs and suites, and also upholstered suites.

'Leather suites from £999 to £2,500. Coil sprung dralon suites from £1,175. Also at Castle Boulevard, Nottingham (0115 950 9440).'

See our display advertisement above.

....

From M1 exit 26: follow signs to Ilkeston. Stay on A6096 into town. You come into Station Road; Wood Street is second to last turning on right before roundabout.*

From Nottingham/Derby: go uphill in town; at roundabout, take fourth exit, on to new Ilkeston bypass. At next roundabout go right for M1 north/Kimberley/Awsworth; take first left, Wood Street.*

From Heanor: come downhill into town; at roundabout, take second exit on to Ilkeston bypass. At next roundabout, go left for M1 north/Kimberley/Awsworth. Take first left, Wood Street.*

*Shop is in old large red-brick building 50 yds on left.

Open: Mon–Sat 9–6; Sun 11–1 (viewing only). Bank Holidays.
Closed: Christmas, Boxing and New Year's Days.
Cards: Access.
Cars: Space for 100.
Toilets: Yes.
Wheelchairs: Two steps; help gladly given. Large shop.
Teas: In Ilkeston.
Groups: You can always ask to see your suite being made. Group visits to shop welcome – no need to book.
Transport: Easy walking distance from town centre.

Highland Society for the Blind
(Northern Counties Institute for the Blind)
39 Ardconell Street IV1 3HA
(01463) 233662

Beds and accessories, mattresses and fireside chairs.
'Gladly make odd size mattresses to order.'

....

Close to town centre, on south side.
   **From A9: get on to A96 (Nairn–Inverness road). Follow signs
to A82 Fort William; you come parallel to river. At traffic lights
where the A82 turns right over river, go left.***
   **Via A862 from Beauly and A82 from Fort William: follow signs
to town centre. At traffic light immediately after river, go straight.***
   ***Go up Bridge Street (museum and Tourist Information Centre
on right), follow road right into Castle Street, pass castle on
right, go over next traffic lights. Take next left (Old Edinburgh
Road), first left (Mitchells Lane), then left again and finally right.
Clearly marked shop on left.**

Open: Mon–Fri 9–5; Sat 9–4.
Closed: 17 April; 1 May; 8
May; 3 Sept; 2 Oct; two weeks
at Christmas–New Year.
Cards: Access, Visa.
Cars: Own small car-park.
Toilets: 250 yds half-way
down the steps to town centre.
Wheelchairs: Easy access.
Teas: In town.
Groups: Factory tours by
appointment please (max.
number 12).
Transport: Bus to town. From
Marks & Spencer in High
Street walk up steps opposite
main entrance; go right at top.
Shop 250 yds on right.
Mail order: No.

The Table Place
30–32 Warwick Road CV8 1HE   *(01926) 863488*

Extensive selection of Regency reproduction furniture in
mahogany, yew and walnut for dining, sitting and bedrooms.
Also Tudor/Jacobean reproduction furniture in oak and a
fine range of solid pine furniture. Desk chairs, desk lamps,
chaises longues, pictures and mirrors etc.

*'Showcase for a dedicated company of cabinet makers and
french polishers from the heart of Rutland. The quality has to
be seen and touched to be appreciated. Individual design
commissions welcome. Also colour match to own furniture.
Some items not up to high standard sold as seconds. Other
showrooms in Oakham, Rutland and Fenstanton, Cambs.'*

....

In the middle of town opposite the Fells & Firkin.
   **From M40 exit 15 then A46 (Warwick–Coventry road): go north
into town centre; you come into Warwick Road. Pass Motor World
on far left corner of Randall Road: this shop is two shops on left.**
   **Coming south on A452 from Birmingham into town: follow
signs for Leamington/Warwick, passing the memorial clocktower on your right. Continue for several hundred yards along
Warwick Road. Go over pedestrian lights – this shop is on right
(entry to car-park is on left, between the building societies).**

Open: Thur, Fri 10–5;
Sat 10–4; Sun 11–4; Mon 10–5.
Bank Holidays.
Closed: Tuesday, Wednesday;
few days over Christmas
(please phone to check).
Cards: Access, Delta, Switch,
Visa.
Cars: 150 spaces behind
the White Hart; cheap (free
Sunday).
Toilets: Yes.
Wheelchairs: No steps,
sizeable shop.
Teas: Free coffee or tea on
request.
Transport: Many buses from
Warwick and Birmingham.
Mail order: No.
Catalogue: Relevant photo-
copy pages gladly sent.

LOOK THREE TIMES BEFORE YOU BUY LUXURY SOFAS AND CHAIRS DIRECT FROM OUR FACTORY

P.f. COLLECTIONS LIMITED

Firstly........ Visit our factory showroom and look at the beautiful furniture and exciting fabrics you can buy at direct factory prices.

Secondly.... Look in the shops and check if their furniture is as beautiful or as well made.

Thirdly...... Look at the shop prices and compare them with ours, so that you can see the large savings you can make by buying direct from our factory.

So take the first look at the following times: Mon – Fri 10 – 4; Sat 10 – 1. Ample parking.
P.F. Collections are specialist manufacturers of high quality furniture for some of the leading furniture retailers in Europe. Frames are built with seasoned European or American hardwoods. A variety of seat and back support systems are offered to produce the correct degree of comfort and durability. Each sofa and chair is individually cut, sewn and upholstered by craftsmen using traditional methods to ensure a very high standard of pattern matching and finish.

The choice of fabrics is endless and our suppliers include some of the best known names in Europe: Ametex, GP&J Baker, Crowsons, Designers Guild, Monkwell, Osborne and Little, Parkertex, Romo, Sanderson and Warners.

For further details see our entry below

---

222 Long Eaton Notts

P F Collections Ltd.
Oakleaf House, Acton Road NG10 1FY
(0115) 946 1282

Luxury upholstered traditional country house sofas and chairs in a large selection of fabrics.

'Large savings, eg chairs from £200–£500; sofas from £300–£800.'

See our display advertisement above.

....

On the southern side of town.

From M1 exit 25 and places west: take A6005 (Derby Road) to mini-roundabout in town centre (superstore on left). Go straight; take first right (Waverley Street).*

From Nottingham on A6005: go over railway, take first left (Waverley Street).*

*Keep straight, pass Co-op and The Old Stillage on left; at roundabout with The Tapper's Harker go straight on to Field Farm Road. After 1/2 mile (road bends left), company is on right on far corner of Acton Road.

From south on A6540: at roundabout at Long Eaton station go right into Field Farm Road. Continue for one mile. Factory is on left.

Open: Mon–Fri 10–4; Sat 10–1.
Closed: Most Bank Holidays; last week July plus first two weeks August; Christmas and Boxing Days.
Cards: None.
Cars: Car-park at front.
Toilets: Yes.
Wheelchairs: One step. Large shop.
Teas: Vending machine. Cafés in town.
Groups: 3–4 visitors can see around at a time. Please phone J. Campbell.
Transport: 10 minutes' walk from town centre. 1 mile from station.
Mail order: No.

Palatine Products

Whickham View NE15 6UM
(0191) 241 0170

Wide range of beds in all price ranges: from cheaper firm-top bases to top quality sprung-edge, pocketed sprung bases. Range of mattresses. Three-piece suites. Household furnishing accessories, eg headboards, pillows.

'All items first quality. Genuine manufacturer selling at "unbeatable" trade prices.'

About 2 miles due west of Newcastle city centre.

From western bypass (A1): at large junction with A69 (Carlisle turn-off), take A69/A6115 towards Newcastle. At first roundabout, go right into Denton Road (A191).*

From central Newcastle: take A6115 for Carlisle. After about 2 miles, at roundabout where A696 crosses, go left into Denton Road (A191).*

*At next roundabout go left, Whickham View (B1311). Shop in huge factory, half a mile on left.

Open: Mon, Wed, Sat 9–5; Thur–Fri 9–5.30.
Closed: Please phone about Bank Holidays; Christmas–New Year.
Cards: Access, Visa. Credit facilities.
Cars: Own car-park.
Toilets: No.
Wheelchairs: Ramp to front door.
Teas: Coffee available.
Groups: Groups welcome to free factory tour if arranged in advance – please contact Mike Hughes.
Transport: Bus nos. 30, 31, 38, 38B from outside Odeon in city centre.

The Table Place

74 Station Road LE15 6QV
(01572) 722166

Extensive selection of Regency reproduction furniture in mahogany, yew and walnut for dining, sitting and bedrooms. Also Tudor/Jacobean reproduction furniture in oak and a fine range of solid pine furniture. Desk chairs, desk lamps, chaises longues, pictures and mirrors etc.

'Showcase for a dedicated company of cabinet makers and french polishers from the heart of Rutland. The quality has to be seen and touched to be appreciated. Individual design commissions welcome. Also colour match to own furniture. Some items not up to high standard sold as seconds. Other showrooms at Fenstanton, Cambs and Kenilworth, Warks.'

This shop is close to the railway station.

Turn off the main road (A606) through Oakham at the level crossing (on the town side) signposted 'Cottesmore, Grantham'. Pass the station on left, follow the road round sharp right bend; clearly marked showroom is about 200 yds along road on right.

Open: Mon–Fri 10–5; Sat 10–4; Sun 11–4. Bank Holidays.
Closed: Few days over Christmas (phone to check).
Cards: Access, Delta, Switch, Visa.
Cars: In forecourt and Station Road.
Toilets: Yes.
Wheelchairs: Access to ground floor but unfortunately not to showroom upstairs.
Teas: Self-service coffee and tea at weekends only. Tea shops, cafés/pubs in Oakham.
Transport: Two minutes from Oakham station and a few minutes' walk from the town centre.
Mail order: No.
Catalogue: Relevant photocopy pages available.

225 Ripley Derbys

Chelsee Design

Prospect Court, 194 Nottingham Road DE5 3AY
(01773) 570057

Pine chests of drawers, wardrobes, bookcases, farmhouse tables, coffee tables, bedside cupboards. Shelves, display racks, plate racks, dressing tables, desks, dressers, bathroom cabinets etc. Also linen and soft furnishings, mirrors, pictures, bric-a-brac, teddies.

'All items perfect, at prices considerably up to 50% less than street shops. Items can be made to size and colour matched.'

On the south-east side of Ripley, a few yards off the A610.

Going north on A610 (Nottingham Road): pass Moss Cottage pub on left; after 1/4 mile, go sharp left into track into small industrial estate. *

From Ripley town centre: follow signs to M1 (south)/Nottingham A610. Go right at roundabout (Sainsbury's on left). After 150 yds go right into track. *

From A38: take A610 for Nottingham. Continue round bypass. At roundabout (Sainsbury's on right), go left for Nottingham. After 150 yds go right under tall arch into track. *

*Company is 150 yds at back left.

Open: Mon, Tues, Thur, Fri 10–5; Sat, Sun 10–4.
Closed: Wednesday; some Bank Holidays.
Cards: Access, Eurocard, Mastercard, Visa.
Cars: Beyond shop.
Toilets: Ask if desperate.
Wheelchairs: No steps. Easy access.
Teas: In town (5 minutes' walk).
Groups: No factory tours, but shopping groups welcome. Please phone Carol Free or Jackie Sheehan.
Transport: Bus no. R11 (Derby–Nottingham).
Mail order: No.

226 Romford Essex

Hubbinet Reproductions

Unit 7, Hubbinet Industrial Estate, Eastern Avenue West RM7 7NV
(01708) 762212

Maker of quality traditional and reproduction furniture in hand finished mahogany and yew wood veneer. Over 100 models of bookcases (from £80), library bookcases (from £500), dining sets (from £600), desks, bureaux, TV, hi-fi and video units (from £200), occasional tables.

'Factory seconds and export rejects at up to 50% off. Special sales January, April and November. Advice on furnishings; also modify and colour to customer's requirements.'

Off the A12 north of Romford.

From London on A12: cross A1112 at traffic lights. After a mile cross another set of traffic lights, then pass Mercedes garage and take first left. *

From M25 exit 28: aim for London on A12. At Gallows Corner (flyover/big roundabout) stay on A12. After 2 miles pass MFI and BAC on left then make U-turn at next traffic lights. After Mercedes garage take first left. *

*Pass Falconcraft on left then go into next industrial estate on left. Inside, turn left and follow signs.

Open: Mon–Fri 9–5; Sat 10–4; Sun phone for information.
Closed: 24 Dec–10 Jan.
Cards: Visa, Access.
Cars: Easy, outside shop.
Toilets: Yes.
Wheelchairs: No steps to shop.
Teas: Sandwiches and cold drinks at nearby garage.
Transport: Romford BR station then bus to Eastern Avenue; Newbury Park underground station on Central Line. Then no. 66 or Eastern National bus to Parkside, Romford.

Sheban Furniture Ltd.   *Closed*

Cradle Hill Ind Est BN25 3JF
(01323) 891710

Fine reproduction furniture in mahogany, yew and burr elm wood veneer finishes. All pieces are hand-finished. Models available are bookcases, bureaux, desks, dining suites, bedroom furniture and occasional pieces.

'Save up to 40% on high street prices when buying directly from this manufacturer. Delivery service available: for small items, a charge of £25 is made; for larger purchases, 6% of the value of the purchase.'

....

In industrial estate at north-east edge of town.

From Brighton and town centre on A259: go towards Eastbourne on the A259. About half a mile from town centre turn left following sign to Alfriston.*

From Eastbourne on A259: pass Esso petrol station on left; after about 30 yds go right towards Alfriston, also Drusilla's Zoo Park (brown sign).*

*After nearly half a mile turn left immediately before the cemetery on left. Shop is about 300 yds on right.

Open: Mon–Fri 10–5; some Sats 10–1, phone to check.
Closed: 23 Dec–8 Jan.
Cards: Access, Visa.
Cars: Own car-park.
Toilets: Yes.
Wheelchairs: No steps to shop.
Teas: In Seaford; attractive country pubs in area.
Groups: Welcome with phone call.
Transport: Short taxi ride from Seaford BR station.
Mail order: No.
Catalogue: Brochure on request.

Skopos Furniture Gallery

Salt's Mill, Victoria Road, Saltaire BD18 3LA
(01274) 531731

The latest in upholstered furniture design from Skopos and many other leading furniture manufacturers in 10,000 sq ft showroom. Wallpapers and accessories.

'Ex display furniture available at excellent prices. Mill also houses Hockney Gallery, 1853 gallery bookshop, The Home for designer interiors and the Skopos Mill Shop.'

See our display advertisement on p. 101

....

Once you are in Shipley, or on the road from Bingley to Shipley (A650), look for road signs to the remarkable village of Saltaire.

Shop is on the second floor of Salt's magnificent old mill.

Open: Mon–Sun 10–6. Bank Holidays.
Closed: Christmas and Boxing Days.
Cards: Access, Amex, Switch, Visa.
Cars: Large on-site car-park.
Toilets: Yes.
Wheelchairs: Three steps, then lift.
Teas: American-style diner in mill complex.
Groups: Welcome with phone call.
Transport: Few yards from Saltaire Metro station. Any Bingley–Shipley bus, then short walk. Canal buses in season.
Mail order: Yes.
Catalogue: No.

Lincoln House Home Furnishings

Birchwood Way
DE55 4QO
(01773) 604241 x 201

Full range of domestic upholstered furniture, wallcoverings and fabrics.
'Full delivery service available.'

···

On an industrial estate on the east side of Nottingham Road (B600, Alfreton–Leabrooks).

   Coming from Leabrooks north towards Alfreton: take right turn immediately before Cotes Park Inn (West Way). *

   From Alfreton going south on B600: turn left immediately after Cotes Park Inn into West Way. *

   *At far end, go right at T-junction (Birchwood Way), take the first right (Ashfield Avenue). Shop is in the first building on left.

Open: Mon–Fri 8.30–4.30 (Wed 8.30–1); Sat 9–4.
Closed: Bank Holidays; please phone to check Christmas times.
Cards: Access, Visa.
Cars: Own car-park.
Toilets: No.
Wheelchairs: Easy access to large shop; one step.
Teas: In Alfreton. Nearby pubs.
Groups: Groups welcome to shop; please book in advance, mentioning this guide.
Transport: Bus nos. 242/3, 245, 330, 332/3 from Alfreton, Derby, Nottingham.
Mail order: No.

Sunelm Products Sheltered Workshops

Leechmere Industrial Estate SR2 9TO
(091) 521 1721

Beds and mattresses in all standard sizes. Occasional furniture including coffee tables and nests of tables. Pine bedroom furniture.
'Seconds and ends of lines always available.'

···

At the back of Asda.

   From A1(M): take A183 or A690 for Sunderland, cross A19(T), turn right at signs for Grangetown. At roundabout with signs to 'Leechmere Industrial Estate EAST' fork right and take next left. *

   From Teeside on A19: turn on to A1018 for Sunderland. Go through to Ryhope and turn left at first roundabout, straight over next roundabout, then first right. *

   From Sunderland centre: take A1018 south. When dual-carriage section ends, pass Fina petrol station on left and turn right at second roundabout, then first right. *

   *In industrial estate go first left then first right. Car-park is immediately on left.

Open: Mon–Thur 9–4; Fri 9–3.
Closed: Bank Holidays; Christmas–New Year.
Cards: No.
Cars: Own car-park.
Toilets: Yes.
Wheelchairs: Easy access.
Teas: In Sunderland.
Groups: Groups please telephone sales office first.
Transport: Buses from Sunderland to Asda.

Marden Furniture Ltd.

Unit 12, Hamilton Road (Coxmoor Road) NG17 5LD
(01623) 512828

Solid pine furniture in natural or antique finishes: wardrobes, chests, beds, bunk beds, dressers, tables and chairs etc. Also solid pine kitchens and fitted bedrooms.

'Seconds available; perfects usually to order. Prices well below retail. Will deliver anywhere in UK. Fax (01623) 441195.'

....

Just off the new section of the A38, on Mansfield/Sutton border.
   From Mansfield: take A38; at roundabout go left; after reservoir go left at first traffic lights (Coxmoor Rd).*
   From M1 exit 28: take A38 for Mansfield. Go through six sets of traffic lights, and turn right at seventh set (Coxmoor Rd).*
   From Sutton: aim for Mansfield (old A38, now B6023); turn right in front of Citroen showroom into Eastfield Side (B6021). Keep straight, cross A38 into Coxmoor Road.*
   *Go over railway and through first gate on right.

Open: Mon–Fri 9–5; Sat 10–1.
Closed: Bank Holidays; Easter Tues; Spring Bank Holiday week; last week July and first week August; Christmas–New Year.
Cards: None.
Cars: Large car-park at side of factory.
Toilets: Yes.
Wheelchairs: Flight of outside stairs or long ramp.
Teas: In Sutton.
Groups: No tours but can see furniture being made through glass.
Transport: None.
Mail order: No.
Catalogue: Free, but please send SAE.

Brunel (By Testall) Upholstery

Perseverance Mill, Bolton Road BL5 3DZ
(01942) 814461

Showroom for three piece suites; settees and chairs in any combination. Two, three and four-seater settees and chairs all made to order on site. Wide choice of fabrics. Curtains made to match; customers' own fabrics made up in any design.

'Curiosity does pay off. Come and visit us today. Genuine factory shop. See your own suite being made. Friendly and helpful staff.'

....

15 miles north-west of Manchester city centre, 5 miles from Bolton.
   From M61 exit 5: follow signs to Westhoughton A58. Go to roundabout, go right (A6, signposted 'Chorley'). After 1/2 mile, go left at traffic lights (White Horse pub on far left); pass the Grey Mare on left (about 400 yds) and clearly marked mill is 1/4 mile on right (look for yellow sign).

Open: Mon–Fri 9–4.30; Sat 10–4; Sun 11–3; Bank Holidays.
Closed: Christmas–New Year.
Cards: No.
Cars: Large yard at front.
Toilets: Yes.
Wheelchairs: Easy access to ground floor showroom.
Teas: In Westhoughton.
Groups: Customers welcome to see furniture being made; unsuitable for groups.
Transport: Buses from Bolton, Wigan and Manchester 100 yds.
Mail order: No.

233   Whitby   N Yorks

Beevers of Whitby

Stakesby Vale YO21 1JY
(01947) 604351

Hand made open coil and pocketed sprung beds to any size; electric adjustable beds, water resistant beds; contract beds all made here; bases and mattresses sold separately. Huge showroom with carpets, pine and upholstered furniture, vinyls, pine chairs, curtains; linens first and second quality.

'Always mix/match, seconds available. Finest hand-made beds made to any size for bad back sufferers. Up to 2500 pocketed springs in the queen luxury size. Factory prices. Delivery anywhere on UK mainland.'

See our display advertisement above

....

Quarter mile west of Whitby station.

From railway station: leave Whitby on A171 Guisborough road. After 400 yds go right up A174 Sandsend/Saltburn road. After only 10 yds go left at side of Arundel Hotel (signposted to Beevers).*

From Saltburn on A174: go into town and 10 yds before T-junction go sharp right into track before Arundel Hotel.*

***Go under tunnel: showrooms on left.**

Open: Mon–Sat 9–5.30 (Fri–8). Sunday by appointment. Some Bank Holidays – please phone.
Closed: Christmas, Boxing and New Year's Days.
Cards: Access, Visa.
Cars: Own car-park.
Toilets: Yes.
Wheelchairs: Three floors accessible with ramps; help available for access to top floor.
Teas: Tea and coffee available. Cafés and pubs in Whitby.
Tours: Groups welcome to look round factory (2 miles from shop) for talk & demonstration; phone Debbie or Gordon first. No coach park at shop.
Transport: From station take Sleights & Castle Park bus, alight at Arundel Hotel.

Carry out an MOT
(Mattress Obsolescence Test)

Poor posture is the cause of many back problems; yet how many people consider their posture when they are lying down? We spend about a third of our lives in bed and while we are asleep we have no control over our muscles and ligaments which can relax completely, leaving the bed to support our bodies.

When you lie on your side, your spine should be straight; when on your back, it should retain its natural 'S' curve. But the bed should also have top layers which mould to the contours of your body for evenly distributed support.

Do the bed test! Lie on the bed on your back, slip your hand (palm down) between the mattress and the small of your back. If you can do this easily, and there is a gap, your mattress is harder than you need. If that is difficult, and it is an effort to turn from side to side, then the bed is probably too soft.

If you are wondering whether to buy a new bed because a back problem has developed, consider your existing bed. Is it more than 8–10 years old. Is the mattress or base sagging or lumpy? Has the mattress gone floppy? Can you feel the springs easily? All these are signs that your bed is past its best and that you need a new one.

Mattresses and bases are designed to work as a unit. Always try out a mattress with the correct base. A solid base is firmest. A sprung base prolongs the life of the mattress as it absorbs some of the wear and tear. Bases with flexible slats are quite firm but have a degree of bounce. If you buy a mattress on its own, make sure it is suitable for your own base, especially if it is slatted. Putting a mattress together with a base not designed for it could invalidate your guarantee.

The term 'orthopaedic' bed (along with a variety of derivative brand names) is used to describe beds which are firmer than normal. But there is no standard specification: manufacturers make their own permutation (usually the firmest bed in their range), through a varying combination of springs, filling materials and base construction. It is therefore vital to look at several kinds. Firmness is a very individual assessment, dependent on your weight and build, size and age, the way you sleep, the sort of aches and pains you might have, or just personal perception.

With thanks to the bed manufacturer Beevers of Whitby.

Extraordinary Variety of Other Tempting Items for the Home

How many of us ever dare sit down and add up the cost of presents we bought during a whole year, for birthdays, weddings, thank-you gifts, and, not least, for Christmas – even the (not-so-humble in cash terms) Christmas stocking? The total outlay would probably astonish us, so it makes sense to stock up on presents you know you will need to give from factory shops.

You may not be aware that you can buy – at far less than the usual high street prices – items as diverse as high quality soap, bathroom accessories, art materials, hand-made paper for artists and stationery, stainless steel table and kitchen ware, and beautiful candles of all kinds. More unusually, for that special present, you will find hand-chased silverware; shoe horns and other horn goods, such as salad servers, from the oldest working horn works in the country; hand-painted enamel snuff and pill boxes, and so on. And how about desk accessories with covers and spines made to resemble authentic old leather bound books? You can also have pictures framed at factory shop prices. The list of shops is long, and many of the manufacturers are household names.

These pages will point you in the right direction, but please do not blame us if you end up by keeping some of these things for yourselves! After all, it is merely our job to bring the shops to your attention!

* Please see full details in respective chapter

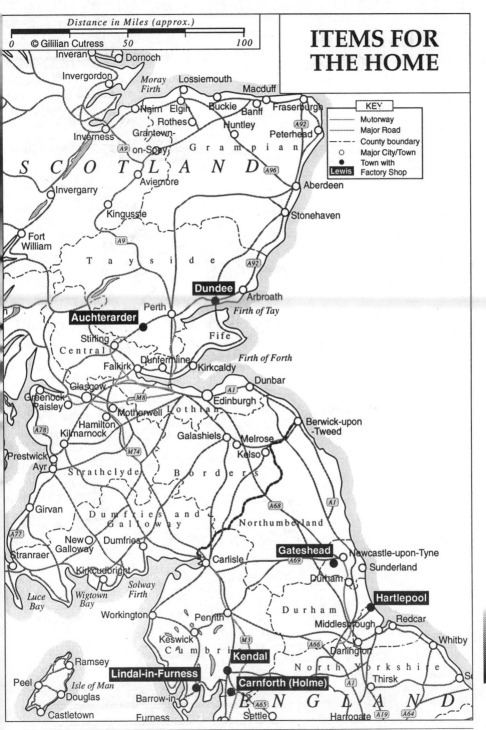

ITEMS FOR THE HOME

KEY

- Motorway
- Major Road
- County boundary
- ○ Major City/Town
- ● Town with Factory Shop

Lewis

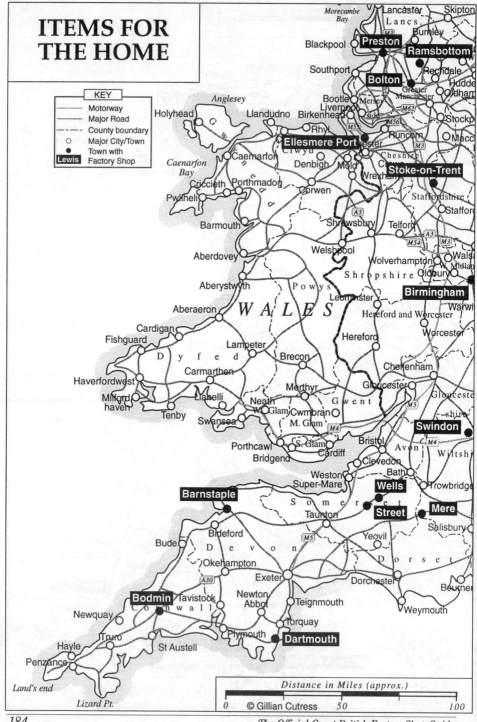

ITEMS FOR THE HOME

KEY
- Motorway
- Major Road
- County boundary
- ○ Major City/Town
- ● Town with
- **Lewis** Factory Shop

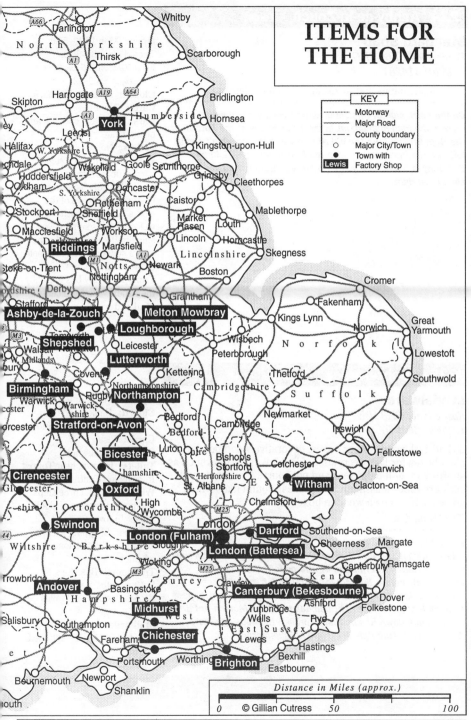

ITEMS FOR THE HOME

KEY

··········	Motorway
———	Major Road
– – –	County boundary
○	Major City/Town
●	Town with
Lewis	Factory Shop

Distance in Miles (approx.)

0   © Gillian Cutress   50   100

Standard Soap

Derby Road LE65 2HG
(01530) 414281

Soap in all shapes and forms and various toiletries.

On the north side of this small, attractive market town.
From the mini-roundabout in the town centre at the bottom of the High Street: take the old A50 towards Burton. Don't swing left but continue straight into the B5006 towards Ticknall. Company is about 100 yds on right: go through the gate and shop is on right.

Open: Mon 10.30–5.30;
Tues–Thur 9.30–5.30;
Fri 9.30–3. *Also 6 weeks before*
Christmas Sat 9–12.
Closed: All Bank Holidays.
Cards: None.
Cars: Company car-park and outside gate.
Toilets: No.
Wheelchairs: Two steps, narrow doors to small shop.
Teas: Lots of places in town.
Groups: No tours of the works but coach parties are welcome. This small (sweet-smelling!) shop cannot cope with a sudden influx of people so please phone first.
Transport: Any bus to Ashby then short walk from centre.
Mail order: No.

Lyndalware

Rossie Place PH3 IBE
(01764) 662966

Cylindrical wood veneer boxes, decorative wood boxes, plain boxes for DIY decoration, filled boxes for gifts such as shortbread, golf balls, teas and pot-pourri. Place mats and coasters (not melamine). Specialise in round mats which are available in own wooden boxes.
'Simply the best.'

At southern edge of town.
From A9(T): exit into Auchterarder via A824; go through town, pass the Tourist Information Centre on left, then turn left immediately before the Morven Hotel on left.*
From Stirling and Crieff (west): go towards town centre, pass Esso on left, take next right immediately after Morven Hotel.*
***Continue down Rossie Place through the housing estate.**
At the bottom turn right for the light blue factory.

Open: Mon–Thur 9–4; Fri 9–1.
Closed: Bank Holidays; Christmas–New Year period.
Cards: Visa.
Cars: Outside shop.
Toilets: In town, near Tourist Information Centre.
Wheelchairs: Three steps, a ramp and extra-wide doors.
Teas: In town.
Groups: Shopping groups welcome. Please phone in advance.
Transport: Bus stops, 5–10 minutes' walk, in town. Gleneagles station 2 miles out of town.
Mail order: Yes.
Catalogue: No. Telephone for a form.

Brass and Copper Shop
(Hassall & Hughes Hand-Chasing)
64 Warstone Lane B18 6NG
(0121) 236 3012

Brass and copper table-lamps, photograph frames, ornaments, planters, fire-side companion sets (brushes, poker) etc plus silverplated wares. Also hand-chased trays, punch-bowls, trophies, sterling silver pens etc. Individual commissions welcomed. New line in cast-iron house name plates, £18–£44 (about third off usual prices).

'Chasing is decorative work similar to engraving which is hammered into the metal with an amazing variety of hammer-like chisels. This is one of the few companies left in Birmingham that still does hand-chasing of silverware on the premises.'

....

From the clocktower: go downhill for 100 yds (Midland Bank on your right). The clearly marked shop is on the left, immediately opposite dilapidated (and rather impressive) old cemetery gate.

Open: Mon–Fri 8–5.30; Sat 10–3.30.
Closed: Bank Holiday Mondays.
Cards: None.
Cars: Limited street parking; multi-storey car-park in Vyse Street.
Toilets: No.
Wheelchairs: Difficult access for the less-than-agile: several steps to shop on raised ground floor.
Teas: Bistro and local pubs.
Tours: Please ask if you would like to see how chasing is done.
Transport: Bus no. 101 from city centre.
Mail order: No.

For more details and map, see pages 312 & 315

F W Needham
84 Great Hampton Street B18 6ER   *(0121) 554 5453*

Wide range of clocks: grandfather, cuckoo, brass carriage and wooden mantel clocks. Italian ormulu sets (clock with two matching candlesticks) and wall regulators (3–4 ft long wooden and glass cased pendulum wall clocks). Barometers. Range of 9 ct gold ladies' & men's bracelet and strap watches.

'Seconds, ends of lines and ex-display samples all at much reduced prices starting at £5. This family business also repairs quality clocks and watches.'

....

Close to the city centre, on the northern side. Great Hampton Street (A41) is the main road bordering the Jewellery Quarter.

   Coming north out of city centre on A41: cross traffic lights (Hockley Street on left) then look for large clock hanging up on wall of this company on left. [At next traffic lights go left into Vyse Street to park.]

   Coming south on A41 to city centre: go over Hockley flyover and company is a few yards on right. Look for large clock. [To park, go right at previous traffic lights.]

   From Jewellery Quarter: from clocktower, go down Vyse Street. At far end, go right. Shop is a few yards on right.

Open: Mon–Fri 9–5; phone to check Sat.
Closed: Good Friday and most Bank Holidays – please phone to check. Some days in Christmas–New Year period.
Cards: Access, Visa.
Cars: Car-parks in Jewellery Quarter.
Toilets: Yes.
Wheelchairs: On first floor but staff very willing to help people who find stairs difficult.
Teas: In Jewellery Quarter.
Groups: No factory tours.
Transport: Lots of buses along Great Hampton Street. Bus stop outside.

For more details and map, see pages 312 & 315

Art Candles

Dunmere Road PL31 2QM
(01208) 73258

Large range of candles in variety of colours and sizes; candleholders and pottery. Also joss sticks, candle-making materials.

'We have become known as "The Candle Shop" and sell some seconds at reduced prices.'

....

West of town centre, on A389 (Bodmin–Wadebridge road).

From town centre: go west to three mini-roundabouts and turn right for Wadebridge then continue for about 800 yds. As you pass hospital on left, shop is in single-storey building on right, set back from road behind car-park.

Coming into town on A389 from Wadebridge: look for shop on left.

Open: All year Mon–Fri 10–6; *also Easter–Sept:* Sat 10–5; Sun 11–6. *Sept–Xmas:* Sat 10–3.30.
Closed: Christmas-New Year.
Cards: Access, Visa.
Cars: Large car & coach park.
Toilets: Yes.
Wheelchairs: Easy access to medium sized shop.
Teas: In Bodmin.
Groups: Unfortunately you cannot see candles made (safety regulations) but groups of shoppers welcome. Prior phone call appreciated.
Transport: Any bus to Bodmin then 10 minutes' walk along Wadebridge Road.
Mail order: Yes.
Catalogue: Free but please send s.a.e. Only candle-making materials by mail order.

Modec Fine Arts Ltd.

Cobden Mill, Draycott Street, off Blackburn Road BL1 8HV
(01204) 525610

Ready framed pictures. Large selection of plain and bevelled mirrors. Pictures and framing undertaken at factory prices to customers' requirements.

'Framed pictures as supplied to chainstores, DIY shops. Perfects and seconds. Prices reduced by 40–50%. Stock always changing. Special area for sale items.'

....

On north side of Bolton town centre.

From north side of A58 (which skirts town): go south at traffic lights on to A666 (Blackburn Road) for Bolton. After 2/3 mile, Kwik Save is on left; go right before pedestrian crossing into Draycott Street. Factory and shop on right.

From Bolton town centre: follow signs for Blackburn. Go along Higher Bridge Street. Go over traffic lights (crossing A6099); after pedestrian crossing go left, Draycott Street.

Via A666 going north: at end of A666 (St Peter's Way), keep straight on, over several traffic lights. Where main road forks, take right fork (Warburtons on right). After pedestrian crossing, go left (Draycott Street).

Open: Mon–Fri 9–4.30; Sat 10–1.30.
Closed: Bank Holidays; Easter weekend; maybe last week June & first week July; end Aug/beginning Sept; Christmas–New Year. Please phone first.
Cards: Access, Visa.
Cars: Car-park opposite.
Toilets: Yes.
Wheelchairs: Unfortunately no access.
Teas: Coffee on premises. Many small cafés in town.
Groups: Always welcome (maximum 40) – phone first please.
Transport: Bus nos. 525, 526, 528, 530, 531, 534, 535, B4 from Bolton Interchange. Bus stops opposite the Iron Church Antique Centre.
Mail order: No.

Essentially Hops
Chalkpit Farm, Adisham CT4 5ER
(01227) 830666

Wide variety of home grown dried flowers. Arrangements ready made and made to order. Dried hop bines (traditional Kentish garland 8ft long) for sale all year; fresh bines in September if ordered in advance.

....

Two miles east of Canterbury, near Howletts Zoo.
   From London on A2: after Canterbury exit, take slip road to Howletts Zoo/Bekesbourne.*
   From Canterbury: head for Dover/A2. Follow signs to Howletts Zoo/Bekesbourne.*
   From Dover via A2: take slip road to Bekesbourne/Bridge and Howletts Zoo. Keep following signs to Bridge village. Go through Bridge, then right to Bekesbourne. Go to mini-roundabout then to Howletts Zoo/Bekesbourne.*
   *In Bekesbourne, before railway bridge, go right into School Lane, following brown 'Hop Farm' signs – farm entrance 1/2 mile on right. (If you get to Howletts Zoo, you've gone too far!)

Open: Mon–Fri 12.30–5; Sat 9–5; Sun 12.30–4.30. Always phone first to check. Bank Holidays.
Closed: For two weeks following Christmas Day.
Cards: Access, Mastercard, Visa.
Cars: Ample parking in field.
Toilets: Ask if desperate.
Wheelchairs: Access to ground floor.
Teas: Bring your own picnic; or local pubs.
Groups: Tours £1.75 per head (tea & biscuits can be provided). Please phone to book. Individuals free to look round.
Transport: BR from Victoria to Canterbury East .
Mail order: Yes.
Catalogue: Free. Mail order hops available – orders by Sept. Dried flowers & mixed dried flower boxes available.

Abbey Horn of Lakeland
Units 6a & 6b Holme Mills, Holme LA6 1RD
(01524) 782387

Shoe horns, spoons, spatulas, salad servers, soldiers' mugs, paperweights, bottle openers, corkscrews, walking sticks, all made of ox horn. Also horn ships, brushes, combs.
'All items perfect with prices reduced by 1/3.'

....

Holme is 6 miles north of Carnforth, just west of M6, between M6 exits 35 and 36. Company in industrial estate south of Holme.
   From M6 exit 36: go towards Kirkby Londsale; after 150 yds go right for Holme on A6070. After 2 miles go right for Holme over motorway. In Holme, go left opposite The Smithy pub.*
   From Milnthorpe on A6: turn towards Holme at traffic lights; once out of Milnthorpe, fork right for Holme. In Holme turn right opposite The Smithy.*
   *Continue until you pass mill pond on left and first entrance to industrial estate. Take second entrance after about 200 yds. Park on right in marked spaces. Walk down 80 yds between the units: units 6A and B on right.

Open: Mon–Fri 9–4.
Closed: Bank Holidays; Christmas–New Year.
Cards: None.
Cars: Small area in front of factory.
Toilets: No.
Wheelchairs: Access to factory tour but not to shop (16 steps).
Teas: Local pub.
Tours: Abbey Horn, established in 1749, is the oldest working horn works and the only one open to public. Factory tours £1 per head. Groups welcome – please call Heather McKellar first.
Transport: Bus no. 55 from Kendal.
Mail order: No.

Goodwood MetalCraft Ltd.

Terminus Road Industrial Estate   Closed
 PO19 2UI
(01243) 537956

Wide range of *Chichester* stainless steel tableware (teapots, carving dishes etc), saucepans and stainless steel cookware; glass, china, porcelain, Russian dolls, wooden boxes, gifts.
'All at exceptional prices. Seconds and ends of ranges.'

....

On the south side of Chichester.
   From the north: follow Chichester ring road; turn off to 'The Witterings' and keep following signs. After crossing railway, pass The Richmond Arms on left; take next right (Terminus Road) to 'Industrial Estate'. Company 1/2 mile on left.*
   From Portsmouth via A27: at first roundabout south-west of Chichester turn off for 'Terminus Ind. Estate'. Company on right.*
   From Arundel on A27: stay on A27 (Chichester bypass), going round town; at 4th roundabout go right; go left for Terminus Ind. Estate. Company 1/2 mile on left.*
   *Park at front; walk down drive on left to rear entrance.

Open: Mon–Fri 10–3; Sat 10–1.
Closed: Bank Holidays; Christmas–New Year; one week late May and one week late August – phone for dates.
Cards: Access, Visa.
Cars: In front of company, then walk 100 yds to rear of factory.
Toilets: Please ask.
Wheelchairs: Sizeable shop on 1st floor up metal staircase (no lift).
Teas: Tea, coffee available. Lots of places in Chichester.
Groups: No factory tours. Pre-booked shopping groups always welcome.
Transport: 1/2 mile from BR station and bus depot.
Mail order: No.

The Original Book Works

1 Wilkinson Road, Love Lane Industrial Estate GL7 1YT
(01285) 641664

Desk accessories with covers and spines resembling authentic old leather-bound books – box files, ledger boxes, video cases, telephone directory holders, magazine tidies, book-ends, paperweights, storage boxes, umbrella stands etc. Painted furniture, eg bedside tables, hand-painted lamps.
'Special commissions welcome: please phone for details.'

....

On the southern side of town, just off a roundabout on the ring rd.
   Coming north into town from Swindon on A419: at roundabout as you reach Cirencester, go left; at next roundabout go left again (Midland Road) for industrial estate.*
   From Stroud and directions south-west: at roundabout as you reach town, go right on to dual carriageway around town. At first roundabout, go right*
   Coming south on A417: stay on town centre bypass to round-about where the A419 goes off to Swindon – but at this round-about go right. At next roundabout go left (Midland Road) for industrial estate.*
   *At T-junction go left for Wilkinson Road; at mini-roundabout go right to company on corner site.

Open: Wed–Sat 10–4.
Closed: Monday; Tuesday; Bank Holidays; Christmas–New Year period.
Cards: Access, Visa.
Cars: Some visitors' spaces by shop; free street parking adjacent to factory.
Toilets: Yes.
Wheelchairs: No steps to shop.
Teas: Lots of teashops in town; Little Chef by roundabout.
Groups: Small shopping groups welcome with phone call; no factory tours yet.
Transport: 15 minutes' walk from town centre.
Mail order: Yes.
Catalogue: Please telephone for free brochure.

See our entry 242 (opposite)

244 Gateshead Tyne & Wear

Ward Art & Crafty Warehouse

Halifax Road, Dunston Industrial Estate NE11 9HV
(0191) 460 5915

Art materials; craft products; stationery; children's art and drawing products; pens and markers; paper; school stationery; paints and brushes; art cases; drawing boards; airbrushes; drawing, sketching and painting sundries.

'Many special offers up to 50% off retail price, eg watercolour sets half-price; free videos with drawing sets; briefcases from £9.95; drawing pads from 85p each; artists' brushes from 58p for six etc.'

From the A1 (Western Bypass) going north: pass A692 turn-off into Newcastle but take next exit to Dunston. *

From the A1 going south: pass 'Metro Centre' exit; take next exit to Dunston. *

*Turn downhill towards Dunston. Pass Burmah petrol station on left, go under railway bridge, take first left (Lancaster Road) then take first left again. Shop is 100 yds on left, clearly signed.

From Metro Centre: follow signs to Dunston, pass brewery on right and take next right (Lancaster Road) then take first left. Shop is 100 yds on left, clearly signed.

Open: Mon–Sat 9–5.
Closed: Bank Holidays; Christmas & New Year's Days.
Cards: Access, Switch, Visa.
Cars: In street.
Toilets: By request.
Wheelchairs: Nine steps. Access at rear on request .
Teas: In Dunston or Metro Centre and from take-away van. Sweets and chocolates in shop.
Groups: Shopping groups book with Karen Carpenter or Carole Creed. Free factory visits for groups of up to 15. Contact John Moreels or Miriam Wright. Sometimes art and craft demonstrations/ exhibitions.
Transport: Metro Centre railway station. Bus nos. 745, M8, M7 stop nearby.
Mail order: No.

Colony Country Store

LA12 0LK
(01229) 465099

All kinds of candles: tapers, pillars, decorated, scented, novelty. Many different colours and fragrances. Floral rings, candlesticks, holders, lamps. Textiles, ceramics, placemats, napkins, tablecloths, kitchen accessories (co-ordinating designs/colours). Christmas shop open all year.

'Unrivalled for colour & scent. From 10p–£60 with substantial discounts on firsts and seconds.'

....

On the A590, 2.5 miles south-west of Ulverston on road to Barrow. Look for 'Candle Workshop' signs.

From Ulverston via A590: pass The Anchor on right then go left opposite post office into London Road, just after pedestrian crossing. *

From Barrow on A590: go through Dalton-in-Furness and pass sign 'Lindal' on left. After 400 yds go right into London Road before the pedestrian crossing, opposite post office (at start of town). *

*Go over railway bridge. Shop is on left.

Open: Mon–Sat 9–5; Sun 12–5.
Closed: Christmas and Boxing Days.
Cards: Access, Visa.
Cars: Parking by factory; space for two coaches.
Toilets: Yes, and for disabled.
Wheelchairs: No steps; easy access.
Teas: Chandlers café on site for snacks/full lunch Mon–Sat 10–4.45, Sun 12–4.45.
Groups: See traditional candle-making through shop viewing gallery. Visit grotto where Santa tells fairy tales to animated woodland friends. Groups welcome: prior phone call appreciated.
Transport: Ulverston–Barrow buses each 1/2 hour.
Mail order: No.

Price's Patent Candle Co. Ltd.

100 York Road SW11 3RV
(0171) 801 2030

Large selection of candles, holders and accessories suitable for every occasion: Christmas candles, novelties, dinner candles, church, decorative, catering, party, floating, scented, patterned and garden. Brassware, silverware, wrought iron, coloured glassware, napkins, flower rings etc.

'Bargains always available – discontinued lines, damaged stock and lots more! Please phone for sale dates and to check shop opening hours (often seasonal) before arriving. Huge discounts. New shop in Bicester Village.'

....

Immediately south of the Thames, between Wandsworth and Battersea bridges.

Going east along York Road from Wandsworth Bridge: pass Texas Homecare on left, go over traffic lights (shop was formerly on left in York Place, but this is now the trade counter) and shop is 50 yds further along the main road on the left.

Going west along York Road towards Wandsworth: go over traffic lights (Latchmere theatre pub on far left); go under railway, straight at lights. Immediately after Dovercourt/Audi garage on the right, shop is on right, just before traffic lights (York Place).

Open: Mon–Fri 9.30–5.30; Sat 10–5.30; (Sun 10–5.30 during summer and Christmas sales).
Closed: Bank Holidays; Christmas Eve (pm)–New Year.
Cards: Access, Connect, Switch, Visa.
Cars: Own parking spaces off road.
Toilets: No.
Wheelchairs: Seven shallow steps to medium sized shop.
Teas: Wide selection of cafés, restaurants and pubs in Battersea Park Road.
Tours: Factory tours for up to 12 people. Please phone first.
Transport: Local buses.

Roger Lascelles Clocks

29 Carnwath Road SW6 3HR
(0171) 731 0072

Highly distinctive award-winning range of traditionally inspired quartz clocks featuring dial designs taken from antique clocks of the last century. Available in all major departments and leading gift shops.

'Seconds and previous year's lines at half price; regular lines at competitive retail prices. "The ideal gift". Family business.'

Immediately north of Wandsworth Bridge.
  From Chelsea/Fulham/Central London: go along King's Road until it becomes New King's Road. Go left down Wandsworth Bridge Road. Carnwath Road is last right turn before bridge.*
  From south London: go over Wandsworth Bridge; take first left (Carnwath Road).*
  *After 200 yds, pass Fulham Kitchen Centre on left; go in through gates. Company is at back right.

Open: Mon–Fri 9–4.30.
Closed: Bank Holidays; Christmas Eve–New Year.
Cards: Access, Visa.
Cars: Off-street directly outside factory.
Toilets: Yes.
Wheelchairs: Easy access, no steps to small shop.
Teas: Lots of places in locality. Easy walk to excellent riverside pub.
Tours: Phone Mrs Winship about free tours. Maximum 15 adults. Flexible times.
Transport: District Line tube to Fulham Broadway, then 28 or 295 bus to Wandsworth Bridge.
Mail order: Yes. No seconds.
Catalogue: Free. Mail order service to anywhere in the world – mention this guide when requesting catalogue.

Lady Clare Ltd.

Leicester Road LE17 4HF
(01455) 552101

Top quality hand-finished table mats, trays, wastepaper bins, home accessories. Lacquer-finished or melamine mats. Also sell complementary giftware. Henry Ling greeting cards; Caspari and Alan Hutchinson stationery; full range of Factory Shop Guides.

'Wide variety of prices. Can produce individual items. No chainstore items. Perfects and seconds (only small blemishes).'

Lutterworth is just off the M1, about a mile north-west of exit 20.
  From the centre of this small, busy market town: go north towards Leicester on the A426. The clearly marked shop is on the right almost at the end of town, just where the No Stopping area begins.
  If you come south into Lutterworth from Leicester on A426: shop is in the first factory on the left, after the garage.

Open: Mon–Thur 9–1 and 1.30–4.45; Fri 9–1 &1.30–3.45; *also during March, August* and *Nov* sales: Sat 9.30–1 . These months could alter – phone to check sales dates.)
Closed: Bank Holidays; Christmas–New Year.
Cards: Access, Mastercard, Visa.
Cars: In front of shop.
Toilets: Yes.
Wheelchairs: One shallow step to medium sized shop.
Teas: Cafés and pubs in town.
Groups: Groups welcome to shop if they phone first, but no factory tours.
Transport: Bus stop nearby but not many buses! 10 minutes' walk from centre of town.
Mail order: No.

Ethos Candles Ltd.

Quarry Fields Industrial Estate BA12 6LB
(01747) 860960

A wide range of candles in varying sizes, colours and perfumes: for dining, decoration, church, garden etc. Also large variety of china, glass and metal candle holders.

'Probably the leading maker of church candles in the UK. Most items slight seconds with prices from 10p. Almost all candles made on site. Discounts around 50% – more on certain items. Firsts and seconds sold. Any colour matched.'

....

Mere is just south of A303, about 7 miles east of Wincanton. This company is on the west side of the village.

From the east on A303: turn left on to B3095 for Mere. Go through town following signs to Quarry Ind Est. This estate is on the right just as you leave town. Shop is at the end of the first drive on the left.

From the west: turn off the A303 on to B3092 for Mere. After the right turn-off to Gillingham (B3095), go left into Quarry Industrial estate. Take next left: shop is at the end, facing you.

Open: Mon–Fri 9–5.
Closed: Bank Holidays; Christmas–New Year period.
Cards: Access, Visa.
Cars: Own forecourt by shop.
Toilets: In main car-park in Mere.
Wheelchairs: No steps to small shop.
Teas: Several pubs and teashops locally. Don't forget to visit the famous wine shipper in same village!
Groups: Small shopping groups welcome. No factory tours.
Transport: Nearest BR station in Gillingham (Dorset).
Mail order: No

Dexam International Ltd.

Holmbush Way Industrial Estate GU29 9HX
(01730) 814188

Wide range of cookware, glass, china, porcelain, giftware, greetings cards etc.

'Seconds and ends of ranges. All at exceptional prices.'

See our display advertisement on p. 191

....

On the south side of Midhurst.

From the centre of Midhurst: go south for Chichester. Go over mini-roundabout; keep going. After long left bend, go right before the fire station (Holmbush Way).*

Coming north from Chichester (A286): as you reach Midhurst, look for fire station on left. Go left just after it into Holmbush Way.*

*Follow signs to Industrial Estate: bear left at mini roundabout, take second left at end of pine trees. Warehouse is at back left of cul-de-sac.

Open: Mon–Fri 10–3; Sat 10–1.
Closed: Bank Holidays; Christmas–New Year.
Cards: Access, Switch, Visa.
Cars: Plenty of space.
Toilets: Yes.
Wheelchairs: Large shop on ground floor.
Teas: Cafés and pubs in Midhurst.
Groups: Shopping groups welcome if pre-arranged. Please phone.
Transport: 20 minutes' walk from town; bus no. 260 stops at fire station.
Mail order: No.

Nimbus

Lower Farm Road, Moulton Park NN3 6XF
(01604) 646411

Soaps, shampoos, conditioners, toothpaste, hand creams, novelty soaps and pre-packed baskets.

'Nimbus is a Sheltered Workshop for the Blind, and a registered charity. It manufactures quality toiletry items for major UK retailers and overseas customers. All goods at factory shop prices, and include ends of runs and redundant stocks.'

··

Moulton Park Industrial Estate is north of Northampton.
   Go north from Northampton on A508 towards Market Harborough. In Kingsthorpe pass Safeway on left, go over traffic lights, pass shopping parade then the Frog & Fiddler on left and turn right in front of The Prince of Wales (sign 'Weight limit 7.5 tonnes'). Pass Nene College and at roundabout take third exit.*
   Coming south on A508 towards Northampton: pass cemetery on left then go left at traffic lights into Holly Lodge Drive for Nene Campus Kettering. At roundabout take second exit. *At next roundabout take first exit (Lower Farm Road): Nimbus is just over 1/2 mile on left. Shop in portakabin in car-park.

Open: Mon–Thur 8–2; Fri 8–1.
Closed: Bank Holidays; Christmas–New Year.
Cards: None.
Cars: On site.
Toilets: No.
Wheelchairs: One step to portakabin.
Teas: None locally.
Tours: By appointment.
Transport: None.
Mail order: No.

History Craft

Gloucester Green OX1 2BV
(01865) 200029

Wide range of History Craft giftware – decorative clocks, men's gifts, walking sticks, scrimshaw (carved reproduction whalebone), board games etc. Also pottery, stationery, imported china and hand-crafted wooden pieces.

'Most goods slight seconds, ends of runs, discontinued lines etc at factory prices.'

··

In the pedestrianised city centre, a few yards from the bus station and tourist office and facing the market place.
   Probably easiest to orientate from the bus station: go through the arch towards city centre. This shop is a short distance on the left, in a row of shops on the ground floor of a new building of flats.

Open: Seven days a week 10–6. *April–Oct*: longer hours (Wed, Thur, Sat 9–6).
Closed: Christmas, Boxing and New Year's Days.
Cards: Access, Amex, Connect, Switch, Visa.
Cars: Car-park underneath Gloucester Green.
Toilets: At bus station.
Wheelchairs: No steps to large shop.
Teas: Lots of places locally.
Groups: Shopping groups welcome, please phone in advance.
Transport: Local buses and BR station; several park and ride services to Oxford.
Mail order: Yes.
Catalogue: No.

Maitland Enterprises

Paul Catterall Mill, Maitland Street PR1 1QF
(01772) 703169

Picture framing to your own requirements; screen-printing including T-shirts. Indoor & outdoor signs; badges; packing and collating (of special interest to businesses, hotels etc).
'Unit in Essex Street (0772 556036) just round corner from old Infirmary specialises in wooden items – rocking horses (from £53), dolls houses, bird tables, picnic tables. Some items on display and for sale; others gladly made to order. Furniture restoration service.'

Open: Mon–Fri 8.30–4.30.
Closed: Bank Holidays; Christmas–New Year.
Cards: None.
Cars: In street.
Toilets: No.
Wheelchairs: No access (first floor).
Teas: In town.
Transport: Local buses along New Hall Lane.

Maitland Street is on east side of town centre, a small road on north side of and parallel to New Hall Lane, the busy road linking town centre to M6 exit 31.
　From town: follow signs to M6. Go left at first traffic lights then right. Shop on left.
　From M6 exit 31: go towards town. Do not go right for ring road but go right at first lights after roundabout.

Standard Soap Co. Ltd.

Greenhill Industrial Estate DE4 4LA
(01773) 604063

Soaps, talc powder, gift sets, dusting powders, bath grains, bath cubes. Also splash-on deodorants, hand cream, powder puffs, flannels, bath foam, bath pearls and face powder.
'We mainly sell end-of-line toiletries plus a selection of soap especially produced for sale direct to the public.'

Open: Mon–Thur 9.30–4.00; Fri 9.30–2.45.
Closed: Bank Holidays; Whitsun week; Christmas–New Year.
Cards: None.
Cars: In road.
Toilets: No.
Wheelchairs: Not possible.
Teas: Several places within a mile.
Groups: No fctory tours. Groups welcome to small shop: please contact Mrs Chris Carr in advance.
Transport: Trent bus nos. 148 (Ripley–Mansfield), 330 (Heanor–Alfreton), 333 (Alfreton – Nottingham) pass through Riddings.
Mail order: No.

Clearly marked entrance to this industrial estate is in Greenhill Lane, the main road going uphill through Riddings.
　Go into estate, then after 400 yds the shop, easily visible, is on right.

Staffordshire Enamels Ltd.

Cinderhill Estate, Weston Coyney Road ST3 5JT
(01782) 599948

Extensive collection of fine hand-painted enamels including traditional snuff and pill boxes, musical boxes and travel alarm clocks.

'This company has revived the 18th century English art of enamelling on copper. Perfects and seconds on sale.'

....

Longton is on the east side of the Stoke-on-Trent area. The shop is about a mile east of Longton, not far from junction of A50 and A520.

From Longton: take A50 east towards Uttoxeter; after about 1 mile turn left between Shire's Bathrooms/fire station and follow brown signs to shop.

From Uttoxeter on A50 or Stone on A520 : at the traffic lights at the junction of these two roads in Meir, take A520 north for Leek. After 3/4 mile, go left opposite Lautrec's pub.*

From Leek: take A520 south for Stone. In Weston Coyney look for brown signs: go right opposite Lautrec's pub.*

***Follow brown signs to shop.**

For more details see page 52

Open: Mon–Fri 9–5; Sat 10–4. Some Bank Holidays.
Closed: Christmas and New Year: please check.
Cards: All major cards.
Cars: Outside shop.
Toilets: Yes.
Wheelchairs: Ramp access; double door.
Teas: Drinks machine.
Tours: Groups to shop welcome although advance notice recommended. Tours may also be booked but please note safety regulations (up to 10 per tour). Due to proximity of other factory shops, large groups can be split.
Transport: China Link bus service, stop No. 9.
Mail order: Firsts only.
Catalogue: Yes.

History Craft

32 Sheep Street CV37 6EE
(01789) 293066

History Craft giftware – clocks, men's gifts, walking sticks, scrimshaw (carved reproduction whalebone), board games etc. Also pottery, stationery, imported china and hand-crafted wooden pieces.

'Most goods slight seconds, ends of runs, discontinued lines etc at factory prices.'

....

Easy to find in the centre of town.

Coming north from Oxford, London or Banbury: go over river into Stratford; go left into Waterside.*

From M40 exit 15: go into town, cross main road (Bridge Street) into Waterside.*

***Take first right, Sheep Street: shop on right.**

From Evesham, Worcester, Birmingham: follow signs right into town centre. At roundabout go right into High Street, then take first left, Sheep Street.

Open: Seven days a week 10-6.
Closed: Christmas, Boxing and New Year's Days.
Cards: Access, Amex, Eurocard, Switch, Visa.
Cars: In nearby car-parks. Very limited street parking.
Toilets: By river.
Wheelchairs: Several steps inside shop.
Teas: Lots of places locally.
Groups: Too small for large shopping groups.
Transport: Local buses and BR station.
Mail order: Yes.
Catalogue: No.

Clover Leaf Giftware Ltd.

Arkwright Road, Groundwell SN2 5BA
(01793) 724556

Large selection of table mats, trays, coasters, moulded goods, kitchen accessories, oven-to-tableware, pottery etc. Many co-ordinated lines. Wooden bathroom and kitchen accessories.

'Perfects, seconds and many ends of lines at reduced prices.'

....

On northern side of Swindon, off A419 (M4–Cricklade road).
   From M4 exit 15: go north on Swindon bypass (A419) for 6+ miles. Go left on to A4311 for Swindon centre. At first mini-roundabout go left into Arkwright Road. Entrance on right (past Triumph).
   From town centre going north: leave railway station on left. Go under railway bridge, follow signs to Gorse Hill, Penhill & Groundwell on A4311 (A345 on some maps!). Go under footbridge in Penhill; go right at next roundabout (Arkwright Road).

Open: Mon–Sat 9.30–4.30.
Closed: Bank Holidays; phone to check Christmas dates.
Cards: Access, Visa, Switch.
Cars: Own car-park.
Toilets: Yes.
Wheelchairs: Four shallow steps, large shop. Ask for special access.
Teas: Tea and coffee available from vending machine.
Tours: Free 3/4 hour tours by appointment only, Tuesday evenings. Coach parties welcome. Shop is open – and cup of tea!
Transport: Bus no. 16 to Penhill Estate 1/2 mile away.
Mail order: Yes. No seconds posted.
Catalogue: No.

Wookey Hole Caves & Papermill

Wookey Hole BA5 1BB
(01749) 672243

Hand-made paper by the sheet and in pads – wide range of weights, sizes and textures (polished and unpolished) for writing and painting. Papers for calligraphers & watercolour artists plus accessories, eg pens, inks etc. Unusual papers made from hemp and denim (with old – unused!– jeans). Presentation packs, line drawings, cards, stationery etc.

'Shop is part of tour so it is not possible to buy paper without going on this fascinating tour.'

....

Wookey Hole is a small village north-west of Wells.
   From Wells town centre: follow one-way system south. Go right along A371, following sign to Cheddar & Weston-super-Mare. Leave town; at Haybridge, take right lane to Wookey Hole.*
   Going north to Wells from Glastonbury: take A371 as above just past hospital on left.*
   *Mill complex is to right of large car-park.

Open: Seven days: *summer* 9.30–5.30; *winter* 10.30–4.30.
Closed: 17–25 December; open again Boxing Day.
Cards: Access, Visa.
Cars: Large car-park.
Toilets: Yes, including for the disabled.
Wheelchairs: Level access to all parts of tour including shop, but not to caves.
Teas: Self-service restaurant.
Groups: 2-hour tours of caves, paper-making, video and exhibitions. Adults £6, OAPs £5, children (4–16) £3.50; reduced rates for visitors in wheelchairs. Groups book in advance by ringing party organiser; individuals can join tours without prior booking.
Transport: Regular bus service from Wells bus station.
Mail order: Yes.
Catalogue: Free price list.

Hole Farm Dried Flowers
Rivenhall CM8 3HC
(01376) 570434

Pick-your-own flowers for drying. Large range of reasonably priced dried flowers and also some arrangements, ready made and to order. Accessories such as baskets etc. In season, sell pick-your-own strawberries, sweetcorn etc.

'All flowers at lower than usual prices. Buy £30 worth of flowers and get 15% discount.'

Just off the A12, about mid-way between Chelmsford and Colchester.

   From London/Chelmsford on A12: take the Kelvedon exit; after 300 yds go sharp right and under the A12; the clearly marked farm is on the left.

   Coming south-east from Colchester on A12: look for 'Dried Flowers 1 mile' sign; drive slowly in left lane then take left slip road, also signposted. Farm is on left.

Open: Seven days a week, 9–5.
Closed: Please phone to check Christmas openings.
Cards: None.
Cars: Ample parking.
Toilets: Yes.
Wheelchairs: Two shallow steps to small shop.
Teas: Bring your own picnic. Little Chef 1/2 mile.
Groups: Please wander round the farm. Family groups always welcome.
Transport: None.
Mail order: No.

History Craft
Barnby Way, Stonegate Walk YO1 2QQ
(01904) 638707

History Craft giftware – clocks, men's gifts, walking sticks, scrimshaw (carved reproduction whalebone), board games etc. Also pottery, stationery, imported china and hand-crafted wooden pieces.

'Most goods slight seconds, ends of runs, discontinued lines etc at factory prices.'

In York City Centre.

   From York Minster: go straight down Stonegate, turn right into Stonegate Walk.

Open: Seven days a week 10–6.
Closed: Christmas, Boxing and New Year's Days.
Cards: Access, Amex, Eurocard, Switch, Visa.
Cars: Multi-storey car-parks in city.
Toilets: Near Tourist Information Centre.
Wheelchairs: No steps to large shop.
Teas: Lots of places locally.
Groups: Welcome. Please phone in advance.
Transport: Local buses and BR station. Park and ride services available.
Mail order: Yes.
Catalogue: No.

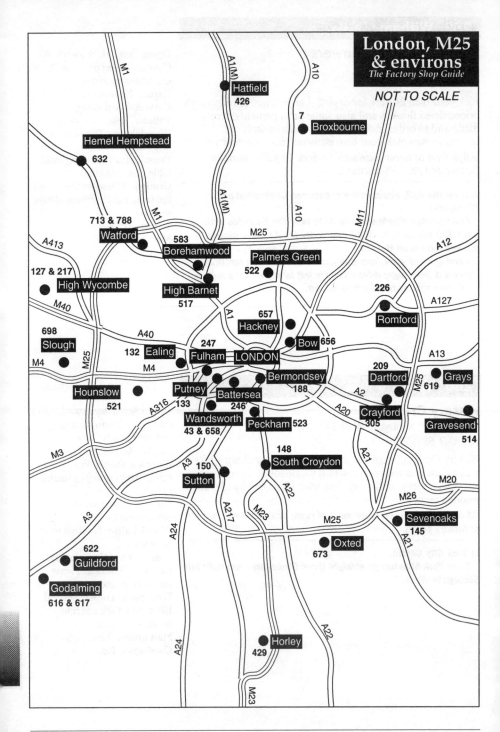

London, M25 & environs
The Factory Shop Guide

NOT TO SCALE

Hatfield
426

Broxbourne
7

Hemel Hempstead
632

713 & 788
Watford

583
Borehamwood

Palmers Green
522

127 & 217
High Wycombe

High Barnet
517

226
Romford

698
Slough

132 Ealing

247
Fulham

657
Hackney

Bow 656

LONDON

Bermondsey

188

209
Dartford

Grays

619

Hounslow
521

Putney

Battersea

246

Crayford
305

Gravesend
514

Wandsworth
43 & 658

Peckham 523

148
South Croydon

150
Sutton

Sevenoaks
145

622
Guildford

Oxted
673

Godalming
616 & 617

Horley
429

Food & Drink

Can there be anything better to satisfy the needs of the inner man – and woman – than buying traditional British foods and beverages superbly fresh or correctly matured as the case may be, direct from those who make or process it?

In this chapter are dairies which specialise in Stilton, for many the undisputed king of cheeses. (Did you know that seventeen gallons of milk, many years of experience and up to four months' careful attention go into each prime Stilton?)

Also included is the oldest known smokery in Sussex and several companies who smoke fish, chicken, mussels, venison etc. If you want to shop for smoked food without moving from the proverbial armchair, there are postal services, so you need never go without such a delicacy for lack of opportunity to travel. One of the Grimsby fish suppliers has pioneered modern methods of processing shellfish. A fish smoker, also from Grimsby, occupies a building where fish has been smoked for 70 years; the building has been altered to comply with new hygiene regulations but the smoking process remains unchanged.

Here you will find a manufacturer who makes chocolate for diabetics. And also a world famous shortbread maker, winner of several awards, from whom you can buy factory reject shortbread and oatcakes.

Let us not forget our traditional British drinks. The chapter includes whisky and cider manufacturers, and a brewery that also sells beer-related specialities – beer and mustard cheeses, Old Ale chutney and barley wine cakes.

Some companies have intriguing visitor centres and interesting factory tours and tastings. Goods are often cheaper than in normal shops, but remember that in many cases prices are seasonal.

Please see full details in respective chapter

FOOD & DRINK

KEY

~~	Motorway
————	Major Road
--------	County boundary
○	Major City/Town
●	Town with
Lewis	Factory Shop

Walkers Shortbread Ltd.
AB38 9PD
(01340) 871555

Shortbread, cake, biscuits, meringues, oatcakes.
'Rejects at factory prices.'

....

**On many maps, this town is called Charlestown of Aberlour.
Company is at the eastern end of town on the main road.**

Open: Mon–Fri 8.30–5; *also*
Sat in summer. Bank Holidays.
Closed: Christmas, Boxing
and New Year's Days; 2 Jan.
Cards: Access, Mastercard,
Switch, Visa.
Cars: Limited space for visitors'
parking.
Toilets: No.
Wheelchairs: Ramp.
Teas: In Aberlour village.
Tours: No factory tours.
Mail order: No.
Catalogue: Price list on
request.

The Chiltern Brewery
Nash Lee Road, Terrick HP17 0TQ
(01296) 613647

Beer brewed here including de-luxe Old Ale (pint bottles)
and barley wine (1/2 pints). Unique range of beer-related
items – beer and mustard cheeses, mild and strong beer
mustards, Old Ale chutney, malt marmalade, barley wine
cake, onions pickled in hop vinegar, pickled eggs and some
pickled customers! New range of beer, malt and hop-based
toiletries, eg shampoo. Books, beer recipes. Hampers; fruit
wines, speciality ciders.

*'Most people regard the brewery as an experience to visit, not
just a shopping excursion. Ask for leaflet, mentioning this book.'*

....

**Tiny village 4 miles south of Aylesbury, 2.5 miles west of Wendover.
From A413 (Aylesbury–Wendover road): go west on to B4009
for Princes Risborough/High Wycombe. Keep going for just
under a mile; brewery well signposted on left, in farm building.
From Princes Risborough: take A4010 north for Aylesbury.
After Great Kimble go right at next roundabout, following signs
to Wendover (B4009). Keep straight; brewery is short distance
on right.**

Open: Mon–Sat 9–5;
Bank Holidays.
Closed: Christmas, Boxing
and New Year's Days.
Cards: No.
Cars: Own yard.
Toilets: Yes.
Wheelchairs: No steps.
Teas: In Aylesbury and
Wendover.
Tours: Group tours for 12–50
people by arrangement during
the day: Tippler's tour, £5.50,
includes a free drink, as does
the Drayman's at £9.95 (includ-
ing substantial buffet). Also
self-conducted tours, £1 per
head, and regular Saturday
tours, £2.50 each, at 12 noon
conducted by Head Brewer.
England's first small brewery
museum now included in tours.
Transport: Aylesbury–High
Wycombe buses stop 1/4 mile
away.
Mail order: No.

The Welsh Whisky Co. Ltd.
2 Parc Menter, Warren Road LD3 1XY
(01874) 622926/625007

Whisky, gin, vodka and liqueurs plus ceramics, gifts and confectionery.
'Daily tasting sessions.'

Two miles west of town, off main west-bound roundabout on A470/A40.

From Brecon town centre: go over main Usk bridge, then keep straight through Llanfaes to end of town, to main west-bound roundabout. Take third exit (signs to Welsh Whisky).

Coming north into Brecon on A470: as you reach A40 take first exit off roundabout, then first left into Parc Menter.

Open: Mon–Sat 9–5; Sun 12–5; Bank Holidays.
Closed: Christmas and New Year's Days.
Cards: Access, Amex, Visa.
Cars: Own car-park.
Toilets: Yes.
Wheelchairs: Easy access, no steps.
Teas: In Visitor Centre.
Tours: Visitor Centre: 'The World and History of Welsh Whisky'. Adults £2.50; OAPs and groups £2pp; children free. Free entry to shop. Tours welcome in evening by appointment.
Transport: Silver Line coaches from town centre or taxi (two miles from town, about £1.50). Coaches to Brecon from Abergavenny station (20 miles)
Mail order: Yes.
Catalogue: Colour packshots, not catalogue.

Colston Bassett & District Dairy Ltd.
Harby Lane NG12 3FN
(01949) 81322

Stilton cheese. Usually pre-cut cheese available from cheese sales shop to the right of the dairy.
'Traditionally-made Blue Stilton cheeses for sale.'

On the south side of this very small village about 10 miles north of Melton Mowbray.

From the south (Hose or Harby direction) you will see this dairy on your left as you reach the outskirts of village.

From Colston Bassett: follow signs to Hose and Harby. The dairy, easy to see, is on your right just as you leave the village.

Open: Mon–Fri 9.30–12.30 and 1.30–4; Sat 9.30–11.30.
Closed: Christmas, Boxing and New Year's Days; Bank Holidays.
Cards: None.
Cars: In yard frontage.
Toilets: No.
Wheelchairs: No steps; easy access to sales shop.
Teas: Excellent local pubs.
Tours: No.
Transport: None.
Mail order: Yes.

The Weald Smokery

Mount Farm, The Smokery, The Mount TN5 7QL
(01580) 879601

Foods traditionally smoked here over oak logs and chippings: salmon, trout, haddock, eel, gravad lax, mussels; chicken and duck breasts, venison, Toulouse sausages. Also British and Continental farmhouse cheeses, wines, gourmet foods.

'Smoked chicken breasts £3.95 for two; smoked Scottish trout £4.10 per lb; smoked Scottish salmon sides £20 per 2 lb sides; smoked Scottish salmon sliced £6.75 per 1/2 lb; smoked duck breasts £5.75 per breast.'

Just off A21, on A268 eastwards towards Hawkhurst.
   Going east towards Hawkhurst: the smokery is on the left.
   From Hawkhurst: take A268 west for Flimwell. Look for Sunnybank Garage then smokery is 200 yds on right at top of hill (after Bird Park on left).

Open: Mon–Sat 9–5.30; *also* Sunday in summer; Bank Holidays.
Closed: Easter Sunday; Christmas and Boxing Days.
Cards: Access, Visa.
Cars: Own car-park.
Toilets: No.
Wheelchairs: No steps.
Teas: In Ticehurst.
Tours: Tours by appointment.
Transport: Bus stop outside. From south: go to Etchingham BR station; from north: go to Stonegate or Wadhurst BR station.
Mail order: Yes.
Catalogue: Yes. Free. Everything despatched by 1st class post. Phone orders with credit card.

Baxters Visitor Centre

IV32 7LD
(01343) 820666

Full range of own world-famous speciality foods – soups, chutneys, jams. Victorian Kitchen with unusual quality gift items and cookery utensils. The George Baxter Cellar is stocked with the complete range of Baxter speciality food products and the Best of Scotland.

'Visit and share in the Baxter story.'

One mile west of Fochabers and 8 miles east of Elgin on A96 (main Aberdeen/Inverness road).
   From Fochabers: go west for Elgin/Inverness. Baxters are about 1 mile out of town on right, just after you cross river.
   From Inverness/Elgin direction on A96: the Visitor Centre is clearly marked on left before you enter Fochabers.

Open: Mon–Fri 9.30–5; Sat, Sun 10–5.
Closed: Christmas and Boxing Days; 1–2 Jan.
Cards: Access, Visa.
Cars: Large car-park for cars and coaches.
Toilets: Yes, and for disabled.
Wheelchairs: Easy access to large Visitor Centre (but not on factory tour).
Teas: Self-service restaurant, picnic area.
Tours: Free factory tours 9.30–11.30 and 12.30–4. Last tour on Friday at 2. Parties please book in advance. No tours weekends and during factory holidays.
Transport: Local bus from Elgin (town) about every hour.
Mail order: Yes.
Catalogue: Free. Mail order freephone 0800 186800.

Springs Postal Service

Cannonberries
Fulking near Henfield BN5 9NB
(01273) 857452

Open: Service available all year round.

Springs Postal Service is a mailing service for all occasions supplying traditionally oak smoked wild and farmed scotch salmon and a small selection of other smoked goods from Springs Smoked Salmon in Edburton, the oldest known smokery in Sussex.

Please remember that fish prices may fluctuate according to season.

Grimsby

The following four shops are close to one another.

Coming south from M18 on A180 into Grimsby: go straight at the three roundabouts; at the traffic lights, take left slip road for 'Fish Docks 1 & 2' (NatWest on far left corner). After 20 yds, take second left (for 'Docks'), in front of the large red warehouse. Then see individual directions.

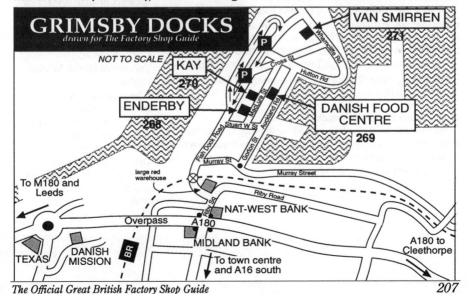

268 Grimsby Humberside

Alfred Enderby Ltd.
Fish Docks Road, Fish Docks DN31 3NF
(01472) 342984

7-lb boxes of freshly smoked haddock, cod and salmon direct from specialist fish smokers. Smoked Scottish salmon sliced and vacuum packed in 8 oz packs and whole 2–3 lb sides. Fresh haddock, cod and salmon. Irregularly sized pieces of freshly smoked fish at reduced prices usually available to callers too.

'Family business with two generations' experience. All fish processed in 80-year old traditional smoke houses ensuring a unique flavour and aroma. Mail order service - please mention this guide when making enquiries.'

In the clearly marked fish docks.
Go over the level-crossing and follow the road round (Fish Docks Road). Where the road becomes one-way, look for large building on the right with seven chimneys and the black/yellow Enderby company sign. Park here or double back round the one-way system to park beside the company.

Open: Mon–Fri 8–4; some Sats 8–11 (please phone).
Closed: Bank Holidays; Christmas–New Year fortnight.
Cards: None.
Cars: Adjacent car-park by newsagent kiosk.
Toilets: Yes.
Wheelchairs: 20 steps.
Teas: Several cafés on docks. Also the Danish Mission, Lock Hill roundabout.
Tours: Please contact Richard Enderby about tours to see the smoking process (for groups, max 20 adults or 30 children, between 10 am–2 pm). Small groups welcome to shop.
Transport: Most local buses stop at Riby Square Docks station.
Mail order: Yes. 3lb sides of smoked salmon, sliced or unsliced. £6 per lb + carriage. Please mention this Guide when making enquiries.

269 Grimsby Humberside

Danish Food Centre
Auckland Road, Fish Docks DN1 3RD
(01472) 342080

Probably the widest range of Danish foods in the UK, including some unavailable elsewhere in this country. Huge selection of herrings marinated in sweet vinegars, curry and other sauces etc. Other Danish everyday and speciality foods including cheese, rye breads, pickles, coffee, pastries.

'Company supplies Danish fishing/commercial boats – hence the huge selection of foods available.'

In the clearly marked fish docks.
Go over the level-crossing and follow the road down (Fish Docks Road). Take second turning on right into Stuart Wortley Street; then at end turn left into Auckland Road; the shop is in the middle of the block on the left.

Open: Mon–Fri 8am–5.30; Sat 8–12.
Closed: Bank Holidays; may open in Christmas–New Year period – please phone to check times.
Cards: None.
Cars: In street.
Toilets: At Danish Mission Centre.
Wheelchairs: Easy access to medium sized shop.
Teas: Several cafés on Docks. Also the Danish Mission, Lock Hill roundabout.
Groups: Not suitable.
Transport: Most local buses stop at Riby Square Docks station.
Mail order: No.

Kay & Son, Prime Fish Merchants

Maclure Street, Fish Docks DN31
(01472) 355974

Prime wet fish straight from the fish auction – such as halibut, plaice, sole, turbot, brill, salmon, cod and trout. Prices vary slightly daily: cod fillets £2 lb; haddock fillets £1.80 lb; plaice fillets £2.30 lb; salmon 4–7 lb size £2 lb; halibut fillet £2.50–3 lb; whole halibut £1.80–2.30 lb.

'Callers welcome (even better with prior phone call).'

....

In the clearly marked fish docks.
   Go over the level-crossing and follow the road round (Fish Docks Road). Where the road becomes one-way, look for large building on the right with seven chimneys and the black/yellow sign for Enderby's. Park here or double back round the one-way system to park between Enderby's and the kiosk. Walk the few yards along narrow Maclure Street to Kay's on the left.

Open: Mon–Fri 9–3.30.
Closed: Bank Holidays; Christmas–New Year fortnight.
Cards: None.
Cars: Adjacent car-park by newsagent kiosk.
Toilets: Yes, upstairs.
Wheelchairs: Sales area is downstairs.
Teas: Several cafés on Docks. Also the Danish Mission, Lock Hill roundabout.
Transport: Most local buses stop at Riby Square Docks station.
Mail order: No.

Van Smirren Seafoods

30 Wharncliffe Road, Fish Docks DN31 3QE
(01472) 350551

Huge range of fresh and frozen seafoods, especially shellfish. Most items available in small quantities, eg selection of prawns, scampi, langoustines, crabs and crab products, lobsters, whelks, cockles, kippers, mackerel, squid, whitebait, fresh trout, haddock and cod fillets etc. Extra large greenland prawns about £3.20 lb; dressed crab £3.30 lb; whitebait 95p lb according to market fluctuation. Always special offers.

'Over 100 years old, this company has pioneered virtually every modern method of shellfish production, such as commercial processing of scallops, crab canning and mussel jarring. Discounts on larger orders. Ask about direct delivery service.'

....

In the clearly marked fish docks.
   Go over the level-crossing and follow the road round (Fish Docks Road). Keep going when the road becomes one way, passing the car-park on the right. At the far end go right then straight (where the new dock is being constructed). Van Smirren's shop is easy to see in the row of buildings on the right.

Open: Mon–Fri 6 am–4 pm (best times Tues–Fri pm).
Closed: Bank Holidays; may open in Christmas–New Year period.
Cards: None.
Cars: In street.
Toilets: Nearby car-park.
Wheelchairs: Easy access to small shop.
Teas: Several cafés on Docks. Also the Danish Mission, Lock Hill roundabout.
Groups: Groups of shoppers welcome but no tours of processing plant.
Transport: Most local buses stop at Riby Square Docks station.
Mail order: Yes. Please mention this Guide when making enquiries.

W W Wales Ltd./Burns Country Foods

Unit 4, Glencairn Industrial Estate KA1 4AV
(01563) 535689 (fax 01563 536126)

Beef, pork and poultry from own farm, various savoury pies from own bakery, also frozen vegetables and meat. Haggis, black pudding and traditional recipes.
'Best Scotch Beef from Wales.'

....

In industrial estate south of the town centre.

From one-way system round town centre: pass the Palace Theatre on left and Marks & Spencer on right, then follow signs to 'Local' at lights. Pass McDonald's on right then go left at lights (Clydesdale Bank on near left corner, Safeway on far right). At mini-roundabout go right: company is clearly visible on left.

From outside town: go to the interchange of the A71 (Irvine–Edinburgh road) and A77 (Glasgow–Prestwick). From this junction take the A735 for Kilmarnock. Just after the river bridge turn left at roundabout (Lawson Street). Follow road round to left. At mini-roundabout go straight: company is clearly visible on left.

Open: Mon–Sat 7–5.
Closed: Christmas and New Year's Days.
Cards: No.
Cars: Outside shop.
Toilets: In town.
Wheelchairs: Easy access to sizeable shop. No steps.
Teas: In town.
Tours: No tours.
Mail order: No.

Long Clawson Dairy Ltd.

West End LE14 4PJ
(01664) 822332

Blue and white Stilton plus a selection of speciality cheeses pre-cut; help yourself from the cooling cabinet inside front door and pay the receptionist. Whole Stiltons on request.
'Only top quality cheeses are sold here. An assortment of cheeses can be purchased by mail order. Please phone to enquire.'

....

Long Clawson is a long village, lying east–west, and this conspicuous dairy is at the west end.

From the A6, Kettleby or Nether Broughton: turn towards Hose and Harby. Dairy is 50 yds on left.

From other directions: follow the sign to Nether Broughton and keep going through the village until you see the dairy on your right.

Open: Mon–Fri 8.30–5 all year.
Closed: Bank Holidays.
Cards: No.
Cars: In front of dairy.
Toilets: Yes.
Wheelchairs: One tiny step inside foyer.
Teas: Nearby pubs.
Tours: Unfortunately tours no longer available.
Transport: None.
Mail order: Yes.
Catalogue: Retail price list available on request.

O P Chocolate Ltd.

Dowlais CF48 3TC
(01685) 723291

Cream filled wafers, chocolate covered wafers, mallow products, eg Snowballs, diabetic chocolate bars and wafers, chocolate covered fudge bars.

'Subject to availability. Some goods misshapen.'

On A4102 on north-eastern edge of Merthyr Tydfil.

Via Heads of the Valley road (A465): at roundabout (Asda, large BP garage) take second exit to Dowlais downhill for about 1 mile. Go left just before next roundabout.

From town centre: take A4102 for Abergavenny. Go uphill for about a mile: look for conspicuous OP Chocolate on right above roundabout.

From the south: stay on A470 dual carriageway to Merthyr to far end. Take third turning at roundabout (A4060 to Abergavenny). Go uphill for 1 mile, go left at roundabout into Goatmill Road. After 1/2 mile take third exit off roundabout. OP Chocolate is on right. Go past Reception: small, well sign-posted, shop on right.

Open: Mon–Fri 9–4.30.
Closed: Bank Holidays; Spring Bank Holiday week; Christmas–New Year.
Cards: None.
Cars: Factory car-park.
Toilets: In town.
Wheelchairs: Not really suitable – shop is small. One step.
Teas: In Merthyr.
Groups: Unfortunately you cannot see chocolate being made. Coach parties welcome to shop but please book first, mentioning this Guide.
Transport: Local buses stop outside factory.
Mail order: No.

Putting chocolate creams into boxes in 1884

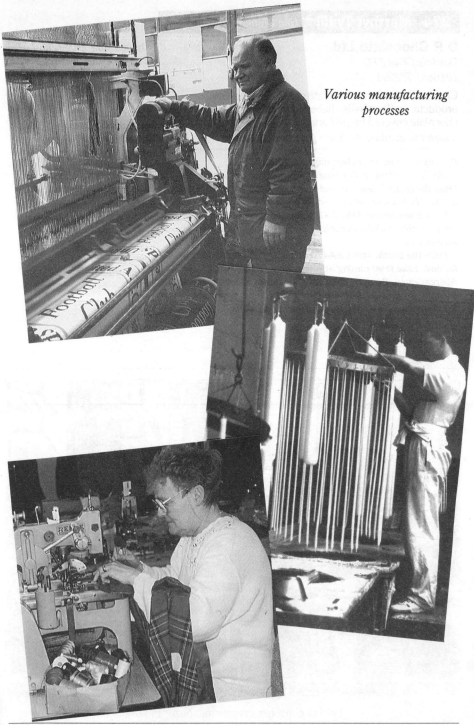

Various manufacturing processes

Sports, Leisure & Toys

There is little we can tell readers with children, or those keen on sport, how expensive it is to buy toys, games and sports equipment. We can say, however, that buying such items from the shops listed in this chapter should improve the feel-good factor.

The choice of toys available to today's children is overwhelming. One game, however, played by children around the world, goes back thousands of years: marbles.

The ancient Greeks and Romans played with nuts, and children playing marble games appear on Roman murals in Bath. Shakespeare referred to marble games too.

Early marbles were made of local stone, in some cases real marble, and clay. Coloured glass marbles are known to have been made in Venice and Bohemia as early as the fifteenth century – probably by glass workers for their own children. China marbles began to be made around 1800. Various tools and processes perfected over the years made the manufacture of glass marbles possible on a commercial basis, and machines were first introduced in the 1890s. Marbles are, however, still hand-crafted. Those made in pure ground marble (in one or two mills in Europe and India) are regarded as most accurate for shooting; the most intricate and beautiful hand-made glass marbles are the most expensive.

With thanks to House of Marbles, who display the largest collection of marbles in the world.

Karrimor International	560*	**Accrington**	Lancs
Shark Group	275	**Amble**	Northumberland
Kids Playfactory	343*	**Bicester**	Oxon
House of Marbles/Teign Valley Glass	276	**Bovey Tracey**	Devon
Peaklander Footwear	731*	**Calver**	Derbys
John Chapman	282*	**Carlisle**	Cumbria
Galt Toys	277	**Cheadle**	Cheshire
Hawk Cycles	278	**Cradley Heath**	W Mids
Nike	396*	**Ellesmere Port**	Cheshire
Toyworld	422*	**Hartlepool**	Cleveland
K Shoes Factory Shop, Sports Factory & Baggage Factory	755*	**Kendal**	Cumbria
New Balance Athletic Shoes (UK)	760*	**Maryport**	Cumbria
Charterhouse Holdings	449*	**Shepshed**	Leics
Playdri Products	279	**Stanton, Bury St Edmunds**	Suffolk
T P Activity Toys	280	**Stourport-on-Severn**	Worcs
Fred Perry	465*	**Street**	Somerset
Sports Factory	479*	**Street**	Somerset
S R Leisure	712*	**Washington**	Tyne and Wear

* Please see full details in respective chapter

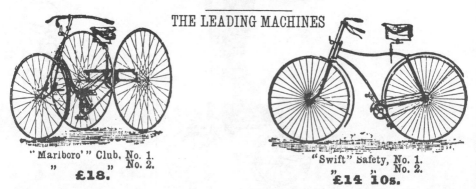

COVENTRY MACHINISTS' COMPANY, LIMITED.

By Special Appointment to H.R.H. THE PRINCE OF WALES.

"CLUB" CYCLES.

THE LEADING MACHINES

" Marlboro' " Club, No. 1.
" " No. 2.
£18.

"Swift" Safety, No. 1.
" No. 2.
£14 10s.

KEY

....	Motorway
....	Major Road
---------	County boundary
○	Major City/Town
● Lewis	Town with Factory Shop

SCOTLAND

Kyle
Mallaig
Rhum
Eigg
Mull
Oban
Jura
Sound of Jura
Bute
Arran
Campbeltown

Invergarry
Fort William
Kingussie
Aviemore
on-Spey
Grampian

Aberdeen
Dee
Stonehaven

Tayside
Perth
Dundee
Arbroath
Firth of Tay

Stirling
Central
Fife
Dunfermline
Kirkcaldy
Dunbar
Falkirk
Firth of Forth
Edinburgh
Lothian
Berwick-upon-Tweed

Glasgow
Greenock
Paisley
Motherwell
Hamilton
Kilmarnock
Melrose
Galashiels
Kelso

Prestwick
Ayr
Strathclyde
Borders

Girvan
Dumfries and Galloway
Northumberland
Amble

Stranraer
New Galloway
Dumfries
Kirkcudbright
Carlisle
Newcastle-upon-Tyne
Sunderland
Washington
Hartlepool

Luce Bay
Wigtown Bay
Solway Firth
Workington
Penrith
Durham
Middlesbrough
Redcar

Maryport
Keswick
Cumbria
Darlington
Whitby

Peel
Isle of Man
Douglas
Ramsey
Kendal
North Yorkshire
Thirsk

Castletown
Barrow-in-Furness
Morecambe
Lancaster
Settle
Skipton
Harrogate
York
Bridlington
Homsea

Accrington
Blackpool
Preston
Burnley
Bradford
Leeds
Humberside
Kingston-upon-Hull

Southport
Rochdale
Halifax
Huddersfield
Wakefield
Goole
Scunthorpe
Grimsby
Cleethorpes
Spurn Head

Holyhead
Anglesey
Llandudno
Bootle
Liverpool
Birkenhead
Cheadle
Stockport
Sheffield
Doncaster
Caistor
Mablethorpe

Ellesmere Port
Chester
Runcorn
Macclesfield
Calver
Market Rasen
Lincoln
Horncastle
Skegness

Caernarfon Bay
Caernarfon
Porthmadog
Denbigh
Crewe
Stoke-on-Trent
Mansfield
Newark
Lincolnshire
Boston

Pwllheli
Wrexham
Staffordshire
Derby
Nottingham
The Wash

Barmouth
Shrewsbury
Telford
Stafford
Grantham
Kings Lynn
Norwich
Cromer
Fakenham
Great Yarmouth

Aberdovey
Welshpool
Wolverhampton
Walsall
Tamworth
Nuneaton
Leicester
Peterborough
Norfolk
Lowestoft

Aberystwyth
Powys
Shepshed
Coventry
Kettering
Cambridgeshire
Thetford
Suffolk
Southwold

WALES
Stourport
Hereford and Worcester
Birmingham
Cradley Heath
Northamptonshire
Bedford
Cambridge
Newmarket
Ipswich
Stanton

Cardigan
Lampeter
Brecon
Hereford
Worcester
Warwickshire
Bedfordshire
Hertfordshire
Essex
Harwich

Fishguard
Dyfed
Cheltenham
Gloucester
Bicester
Luton
Bishop's Stortford
Colchester
Clacton-on-Sea

Haverfordwest
Carmarthen
Merthyr
Gwent
Oxford
St Albans
Chelmsford

Milford Haven
Llanelli
Neath
Cwmbran
Swindon
Oxfordshire
High Wycombe
London
Southend-on-Sea
Margate

Tenby
Swansea
Cardiff
Bristol
Avon
Wiltshire
Berkshire
Slough
Sheerness
Ramsgate

Porthcawl
Bridgend
Weston-Super-Mare
Bath
Trowbridge
Woking
Surrey
Crawley
Maidstone
Canterbury
Dover
Folkestone

Barnstaple
Somerset
Taunton
Street
Basingstoke
Hampshire
Tunbridge Wells
Ashford
Rye

Bude
Bideford
Devon
Yeovil
Salisbury
Southampton
West Sussex
East Sussex
Hastings
Bexhill
Eastbourne

Okehampton
Dorset
Fareham
Portsmouth
Worthing
Brighton

Bovey Tracey
Exeter
Teignmouth
Dorchester
Bournemouth
Newport
Shanklin

Newquay
Cornwall
Newton Abbot
Torbay
Weymouth

Hayle
Truro
St Austell
Plymouth

Lizard Pt.

Distance in Miles (approx.)

0   © Gillian Cutress   50   100

Shark Group

Nordstrom House, North Broomhill NE65 9UJ
(01670) 760365

Wetsuits, drysuits, buoyancy aids, inflatable life jackets and accessories for all watersports.

'We sell slight seconds at very competitive prices.'

....

Three miles south of Amble, at the southern end of North Broomhill.
   Follow the sign to the Radar pub (on your left if you come from Amble); go behind the pub to the factory.

Open: Mon–Fri 10–4 throughout the year; *also early April–mid Dec* Sat 9.30–12.
Closed: Three weeks in late July/early Aug; one week late Oct; three weeks at Christmas; Bank Holiday weekends.
Cards: Access, Visa.
Cars: Outside factory.
Toilets: No.
Wheelchairs: One large step so not suitable.
Changing rooms: Yes.
Teas: Meals, morning coffee etc in pub next door.
Groups: No tours but groups of shoppers welcome any time if they arrange in advance.
Transport: Regular bus services to North Broomhill.
Mail order: Yes.
Catalogue: Free on request.

House of Marbles and Teign Valley Glass

The Old Pottery, Pottery Road TQ13 9DR
(01626) 835358

Decorative glass gifts, vases, glasses, scent bottles etc. Traditional games and toys; the largest collection of marbles in the world. Also men's gifts, kitchen ideas, hundreds of toys and games, many from local craftsmen and others from all over world.

'Firsts and seconds in glass, including one-off practice pieces, at discounted prices.'

See our display advertisement opposite

....

At the southern end of Bovey Tracey.
   From A38: turn on to A382 towards Bovey Tracey. After about 2 miles fork left at roundabout with sign to Pottery Road. Shop about 100 yds on right.
   From town centre: follow signs to Newton Abbot; at roundabout at southern end of town, follow signs to Pottery Road.

Open: All year Mon–Sat 9–5; *also Easter–Sept:* Sun 9–5. Some Bank Holidays.
Closed: Christmas–New Year.
Cards: Access, Visa.
Cars: Own large car-park.
Toilets: Yes.
Wheelchairs: Easy access, no steps.
Teas: Own coffee shop/ restaurant.
Groups: Self guided tours with free leaflets.
Transport: Bovey Tracey–Newton Abbot buses pass by.
Mail order: No.

277 Cheadle   Cheshire

Galt Toys Ltd.

Brookfield Road, off Councillor Lane SK8 2PM
(0161) 428 7893

Quality educational toys, plus large range of other toys, children's books, party presents, pocket money toys. Mint products at full retail price.

'Largest toy shop in North-West (7000 sq ft on ground floor alone). Playroom (soft play area, slides). Creche Mon–Fri (9.30–4): £1 for 30 mins. Two-week sales (including seconds) mid-Feb and mid-Sept. Arrange birthday parties on these premises!'

From M63 eastbound take exit 11; from westbound, exit 12; get on to A560 for Cheadle. After large roundabout with railway line over it, go left at next traffic lights into Councillor Lane, then right into Demmings Road (after school on right). Brookfield Road is next right; shop, clearly signed, is 150 yds on left.

Coming south on A34: go left at traffic lights on to A560 to Cheadle/Stockport. Go straight at next two road traffic lights, then right (in front of police station) into Oak Road; at T-junction go left; shop 1/3 mile on right.

Open: Mon–Sat 9–5.30.
Closed: Bank Holidays.
Cards: Access, Amex, Diners, Switch, Visa.
Cars: In front of shop.
Toilets: Yes. Baby changing facilities.
Wheelchairs: Easy access to ground floor but not to toilets; coffee and toilets on request.
Teas: Own coffee shop.
Groups: Shopping groups welcome – please book. Gladly open specially for 25+.
Transport: Local buses from Cheadle to top of Brookfield Road, then 5 minutes' walk.
Mail order: Yes.
Catalogue: Free.

Hawk Cycles

Forge Lane B64 5AM
(01384) 636535

Cycles for all ages: ATB, sports, unisex, BMX, kiddies. Accessories, spares and repairs.

'New 4,000 sq ft shop. Large range of cycles made in own factory and sold at factory prices plus others from leading UK manufacturers, many at trade prices. Frames guaranteed for life. Prompt after-sales service, all spares available.'

From Merry Hill Shopping Centre: take A4036 south (to Bromsgrove (A491)). At large staggered crossing, turn left at traffic lights on to A4100 for Cradley Heath. Go downhill, pass the right turn to Cradley (B4174); the white building is 400 yds uphill on the left.

From traffic lights in Cradley Heath High Street: take the A4100 downhill (west) for Merry Hill and Brierley Hill. Look for the railway and bus stations on the left, then this white building is on the right.

Open: Mon–Sat 9–6; Sun and Bank Holidays 9–4.30.
Closed: Christmas Day. Please phone to check for Boxing and New Year's Days.
Cards: Access, Delta, JCB, Switch, Visa.
Cars: Ample free parking at factory.
Toilets: Public toilets 50 yds.
Wheelchairs: No steps to large shop.
Teas: In Cradley Heath.
Transport: Trains from all areas. Buses from Brierley Hill, Stourbridge and Dudley.

Playdri Products Ltd.
Shepherd's Grove Industrial Estate IP31 2AP
(01359) 251420

Waterproof suits, windcheaters, casual jackets. Golf shoes, bags, balls, golf trollies, travel bags, clubs etc.
'Sales at Easter and in November. Phone for exact dates.'

....

Eleven miles north-east of Bury St Edmunds, 12 miles south-west of Diss.

From Bury: take A143 north-east. In Stanton, just after Mobil garage on left, go right into Stanton village. Pass church and war memorial on right. After 150 yds go right for industrial estate. *

From Diss: go south on A143. Turn left for Shepherd's Grove Ind. Est. West. Keep following signs to this estate, turning left. *

Pass school on right and windmill on left. Go left into Grove Lane. Continue round road for 2/3 mile; go right to estate; take first left; at end of lane go right. Clearly visible factory 300 yds on right, set back.

Open: Mon–Fri 9–4.30.
Closed: Bank Holidays, and near a sale (ie, closed week before Easter and week in November).
Cards: Access, Visa.
Cars: Outside factory.
Toilets: Yes.
Wheelchairs: Rather restricted movement within shop.
Changing rooms: No.
Teas: 1/2 mile up Grove Lane.
Groups: Groups of shoppers welcome, but please telephone first.
Transport: None.
Mail order: No.

T P Activity Toys Ltd.
Severnside Works, Severn Road DY13 9EY
(01299) 827300

Quality garden toys, climbing frames, slides, trampolines, large swings, netball sets etc. Also large selection of unusual party bag and stocking fillers, and extensive range of *Lego, Playmobil, Galt, Brio* and other brands.
'Play area available. Seconds and ends of ranges of our own products available at greatly reduced prices.'

....

On the south side of town centre, beside the river Severn. Stourport has rather complicated one-way systems!

From Bewdley (B4195), Kidderminster (A451), Hartlebury (B4193) and Worcester (A4025): don't go right into town centre but keep going clockwise round the one-way system; in Mitton Street look for the sign (on the left in a right-hand bend) pointing left to Carpets of Worth and turn left. *

From Great Witley: go through town for 'All directions' and Kidderminster. Pass adjacent Repsol, Esso & Texaco petrol stations; go clockwise until sign on left pointing left to carpet shop. *

Pass the carpet factory and keep going to the end of Severn Road (long cul-de-sac leading down to the river). T P Activity Toys are straight ahead.

Open: Mon–Fri 9–5; Sat 9.30–4.30.
Closed: Bank Holidays.
Cards: Access, Visa.
Cars: Private car-park across road.
Toilets: Yes.
Wheelchairs: All at ground level.
Teas: In Stourport.
Groups: Groups of shoppers please phone first.
Transport: Easy walking distance of the bus station.
Mail order: No.
Catalogue: Free.

*Factory Shops
around Britain*

DEWHIRST
FACTORY SHOP
Value Clothing

SECONDS

Luggage & Handbags

At the beginning of the 19th century the leather industry in England enjoyed a boom. The network of roads around Britain improved and expanded rapidly, more people took to travelling and transporting goods, and there was an increased demand for horses. This in turn led to an increase in demand for their tack – saddles, bridles, harnesses, saddle bags and so on. As the loriners who made the metal bits and fittings for horse tack were already based in Walsall the leather workers were attracted to the town because it made economic sense to set up business in the same area.

Today Walsall is still the leather capital of Britain. The industry has adapted to keep pace with the times and this area is the centre for the manufacture of light leather goods as well as equestrian equipment.

Leather is used in a huge variety of products and there are as many different kinds of leather as there are uses for it: hard or soft, stretchy or rigid, thick or thin, flexible or stiff. For use not only in bridles, saddles and tack but in boats, industrial belts and bellows, tents, stretchers, surgical supports and trusses, clothing and clothing accessories, armour, weaponry, parts for musical instruments, bats and balls, footwear and furniture. To name but a few!

Look out for leather goods and a great range of good value luggage, briefcases, travel bags etc as you visit these shops.

With thanks to the Leather Museum in Walsall

Equator	328*	**Bicester**	Oxon
Jane Shilton	335*	**Bicester**	Oxon
Carpet Bags	281	**Bury St Edmunds**	Suffolk
John Chapman	282	**Carlisle**	Cumbria
Equator	386*	**Ellesmere Port**	Cheshire
Richard Draper	746*	**Glastonbury**	Somerset
Equator	414*	**Hartlepool**	Cleveland
K Shoes Factory Shop, Sports Factory & Baggage Factory	437*	**Kendal**	Cumbria
Potterton Cases	283	**Leicester**	Leics
Regent Belt Co.	284	**Long Buckby**	Northants
Ashlie Craft	285	**Long Eaton**	Notts
Bargain Baggage	286	**North Shields**	Tyne & Wear
K & M (Leather Clothing)	669*	**Nottingham**	Notts
Papworth Travel Goods	287	**Papworth Everard**	Cambs
Baggage Factory	455*	**Street**	Somerset
Harvergrange & Spartan Luggage	288	**Tibshelf**	Derbys
Walsall Leather Museum	289	**Walsall**	W Mids

* Please see full details in respective chapter

FULL SIZE BRIAR PIPE, Finest Amber Mouthpiece, Massive 15-ct. Gold Mount, Pigskin Case, 30s.

LADY'S PURSE, DREWS' OWN MAKE, Green Crocodile, Silver Mounts, 4½ in. long, 12s. 6d.

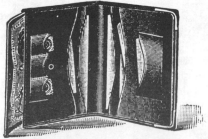

DREWS' NEW PATTERN LETTER-CASE, With Secret Pocket for Bank Notes, &c. In Polished Gold Brown Crocodile, with 4 Silver Corners, 30s.

LADY'S CARD-CASE, Hand-Chased Silver Mounts, and Polished Pigskin, 36s. 6d.

LUGGAGE, HANDBAGS & LEATHER ITEMS

North Shields

Carlisle

Hartlepool

Kendal

Ellesmere Port

Tibshelf

Nottingham

Long Eaton

Wallsall

Leicester

Papworth Everard

Long Buckby

Bury St Edmunds

Bicester

Street

Glastonbury

Distance in Miles (approx.)

0   © Gillian Cutress   50   100

Carpet Bags

2000 St John's Street, IP33 1SP
(01284) 700170

Unique range of carpet, tapestry and fabric products: luggage, holdalls, gladstones, shoulder bags, totebags, handbags, pouches, purses, spectacle cases. Clothing includes men's and ladies' waistcoats and topcoats, ladies' jackets, boleros, trousers, hats and accessories, many in matching fabrics.

'Shop sales and mail order at less than usual retail prices. Further reductions on ends of lines and prototypes. Custom design and fabric selection by appointment only.'

....

In town centre.

   From A14 (the old A45): turn off for Bury St Edmunds Central A134. Go under railway, straight at two roundabouts and turn left at mini-roundabout by the gasometer.*

   From other directions and town centre: follow signs to Thetford (A134). Pass Burmah petrol and Honda garage on left then go right at the mini-roundabout by the gasometer.*

   *Take first possible left: the shop is at the end on the near left corner (one-way street).

Open: Mon–Sat 9–6.
Closed: Christmas–New Year.
Cards: Access, Visa.
Cars: One-hour parking outside shop; all day parking 4 minutes' walk.
Toilets: In town.
Wheelchairs: Front of showroom is on ground floor, rear part down two wide steps.
Changing rooms: Yes.
Teas: Pubs, cafés, restaurants and fish & chips locally.
Groups: Small shopping groups welcome; no factory tours.
Transport: 3 minutes' walk from bus terminal (library); 5 minutes from BR station.
Mail order: Yes.
Catalogue: £2, refundable against first order.

John Chapman Ltd.

Gallery House, Harraby Green Business Park CA1 2SS
(01228) 514514

Huge collection of award winning fishing bags, shooting and hunting bags, travel and shoulder bags, in multi-layered canvas, tweeds and tartans with leather trim and solid brass fittings.

'These bags are found in only the finest department stores and speciality shops worldwide. Bags of classic British design and rugged construction, built from all British raw materials to last a very long time. First quality, test models, some seconds and used bags available.'

....

In beautiful old mill at southern edge of Carlisle, close to British Telecom tower.

   From town centre: take A6 south. By BT tower (large transmitting aerial with satellite dishes), go right (20 yds before Esso station on left) to Harraby Green Business Park (signposted).*

   From M6 exit 42: take A6 into Carlisle. By BT tower, take first left after Esso petrol station (on right).*

   *Immediately go sharp left betwen two rows of terraced houses to Gallery House (signposted).

Open: Mon–Thur 9–5; Fri 9–3.
Closed: Bank Holidays; Christmas–New Year. Please check spring/summer holidays (usually Spring Bank Holiday week; last week July, first week Aug).
Cards: No.
Cars: Outside.
Toilets: Yes.
Wheelchairs: Two small steps to shop.
Teas: Local pubs; teas in town.
Groups: Suitable for small shopping groups only.
Transport: Bus nos. 61, 62 south from town. Get off at Harraby Green/BT tower.
Mail order: Yes.
Catalogue: Please phone or write for free catalogue.

Potterton Cases

80 Coleman Road LE5 4LE
(0116) 276 7562

Executive briefcases (ABS, leather and vinyl), art portfolios, clipboards and presenters. Steamer trunks by *Mossman*. Luggage, suit carriers, overnight cases, travel bags by *Delsey, Carlton, Samsonite, Antler, Skyflite* and *Globetrotter*. Also *Potterton* tool cases and computer cases.

'Occasional special sales. Some seconds available. Too many other items to list here! Discounts always given.'

In North Evington, about 1.5 miles east of the city centre.

From central Leicester: follow the A47 towards Uppingham. At the crossing with A6030 (traffic lights, sign to General Hospital) go right for M1/M69. The clearly marked factory shop is 300 yds on left.

NB The A6030 is not well marked; it is the outer ring road not the inner ring road. Get on to the outer ring road from any direction coming into Leicester; keep going round until you find this shop, which will be on your left if you are going clockwise.

Open: Mon–Fri 9–5; Sat 9.30–12.30.
Closed: All Bank Holidays.
Cards: Access, Visa.
Cars: To sides and front of factory.
Toilets: Yes.
Wheelchairs: No steps to medium sized shop.
Teas: Lots of places in city centre.
Groups: No factory tours, but shopping groups welcome if they phone first.
Transport: Take bus no. 52 Fox Cub for Scraptoft Campus from outside Littlewoods and ask for Coleman Road.
Mail order: Yes.
Catalogue: Yes.

Regent Belt Co.

85 Station Road NN6 7QB
(01327) 842434

Wide selection of quality leather items: men's and ladies' belts; silk braces with leather attachments; wallets, purses, organisers; travel bags, tie cases, garment bags, holdalls; handbags and shoulder bags; gift items such as golf ball cases and insulated champagne bottle holders.

'Leather belts at £5. Other items (all ends of lines or slightly substandard) about 30–50% off retail prices for perfect goods.'

On the south edge of this large village.

From A5: follow signs into Long Buckby. Pass railway station on right. Go uphill. Clearly marked factory is on left, behind phone box. Shop entrance at far end, at side.

From small square in centre of Long Buckby: follow sign for Long Buckby castle. Keep straight. Pass Long Buckby Rugby Football Club on left. Factory is immediately on right. Shop entrance at near end of building.

Open: Thur, Fri 12.30–3.30; Sat 10–2.
Closed: Bank Holidays.
Cards: Mastercard, Visa.
Cars: Car-park at rear.
Toilets: Public toilets in village square, or ask if desperate.
Wheelchairs: Unfortunately not suitable for wheelchairs.
Teas: Local pubs and tea rooms.
Groups: Shopping groups maximum 20 people welcome. No factory tours.
Transport: BR station in village, then 1/4 mile walk to shop.
Mail order: No.

Ashlie Craft

The Bakehouse, 55 Canal Street NG10 1GA
(0115) 972 9233

Soft leather handbags, patchwork shoppers, fabric bags with co-ordinating leather trim purses, wallets and bum bags. Also repairs on leather coats and bags. Plus footstools and hinged lid pouffes in flatweave fabric, dralon prints or leather.

'Everything made on premises. Also repairs on leather coats and bags. Prices from £20 for small leather patchwork shoppers, £25 footstools and hinged lid pouffes from £35.'

....

On the north-west side of town.

From M1 exit 25: follow signs to Long Eaton. Pass Novotel and SleepInn. At mini-island go left into Longmoor Road (B6002). Take second right (Fina petrol on far right corner) then continue down Curzon Street. After 1/2 mile go left into Canal Street. Ashlie Craft is immediately on right.

From town (roundabout with superstore): go west along Derby Road (A6005). Pass church on right then go right (Bredon Street). Take first left (Canal Street): company on left.

Open: Mon–Thur 8–5; Fri 8–1.
Closed: Bank Holidays; Christmas–New Year.
Cards: Access, Visa.
Cars: Directly outside shop.
Toilets: Yes.
Wheelchairs: Easy access to ground floor shop.
Teas: Cafés in Long Eaton.
Groups: Groups welcome to shop.
Transport: Few minutes' walk from main Derby/ Nottingham bus route.
Mail order: Yes.
Catalogue: Free.

Bargain Baggage Factory Shop

Bugatti House, Norham Road NE29 7HB
(0191) 258 4451

Branded luggage by *Pierre Cardin, Gino Ferrari;* business accessories and attaché cases in quality leather and man-made fibres. Wide range of small leather goods and handbags. Shopping bags, beach bags.

'Perfects, seconds and ends of lines at well below high street prices.'

On the north-east side of North Shields.
   From A19 (formerly A1): turn on to A193 for North Shields. At next roundabout go left for Tynemouth (A1058). After 0.4 miles turn left immediately after Bugatti House. Shop is about 80 yds on left.
   On A1058 from Newcastle: cross over A19 and take next exit; turn right at the top and company is 1/2 mile on right. Turn right immediately before Bugatti House: shop is 80 yds on left.

Open: Tues 10–2; Wed–Fri 10–3. *Also Sat, Sun in December:* phone for details.
Closed: Monday; Christmas–New Year.
Cards: Access, Diners, Visa.
Cars: Outside shop.
Toilets: No.
Wheelchairs: Easy access, no steps.
Teas: In North Shields and Tynemouth.
Groups: Shopping groups please write to Christine Quinn to book.
Transport: Percy Main metro station. Buses for Newcastle and Whitley Bay. Bus nos. 42 and 55 from North Shields go past; 305 and 308 coast road buses stop outside Formica factory, then 3 minutes' walk.
Mail order: No.

Papworth Travel Goods

CB3 8RC
(01480) 830345

Range of top quality leather travel goods, briefcases and suitcases.

'Seconds and discontinued lines only.'

Easy to find, on the A1198 (Huntingdon–Royston road) about 6 miles south of Huntingdon and 11 miles west of Cambridge.
   There is only one road through this village. Shop is next to the park and beside the pedestrian lights. Follow signs to car-park. Shop entrance is through reception.

Open: Mon–Thur 8.30–12.30 and 1.30–5; Fri 8.30–11.30.
Closed: Bank Holidays; Spring Bank Holiday week; first two weeks in August; Christmas–New Year.
Cards: Access, Amex, Visa.
Cars: Outside reception.
Toilets: Yes.
Wheelchairs: No access to upstairs showroom.
Teas: Local pubs or Little Chef.
Groups: No factory tours. Groups of shoppers welcome.
Transport: Hourly buses from Cambridge and St Ives.
Mail order: Yes.
Catalogue: Free. Seconds and discontinued lines only.

Harvergrange plc & Spartan Luggage

Saw Pit Industrial Estate DE5 5NH
(01773) 875393

Luggage, travel bags, suitcases, pilot boxes, leather executive cases, vanity cases etc. Stoneware and porcelain dinner and tea sets. Oven-to-tableware, knife sets, cookie jars, whole range of kitchen gadgets.

'Executive cases: leather £20–£35, PVC £6–£15. Suitcases £12-£40. Tea sets (12-piece) from £3.95; dinner sets: 20-piece from £5.99; 45-piece from £24.99. Also oddments, discontinued lines and seconds.'

From Tibshelf centre: go to north end of village, branch right on to B6014, cross the M1 and this estate is on right.

From M1 exit 28: take A38 towards Mansfield. At first traffic lights, go left. Continue to Huthwaite. At first junction, go straight; at second, turn left (sign to Tibshelf). After 1.5 miles, turn left at T-junction. Estate is 500 yds on left. Company is first on right.

Open: Tues, Thur 10–5; Wed, Fri, Sat 10–4.
Closed: Monday; Bank Holidays; Christmas–New Year.
Cards: Access, Visa.
Cars: Own large forecourt.
Toilets: Yes.
Wheelchairs: Easy access: one small step.
Teas: Alfreton and local pubs.
Groups: No factory tours but groups to shop welcome. Please book with Mr J Doe, mentioning this Guide.
Transport: Difficult! Train to Alfreton then taxi.
Mail order: No.

Walsall Leather Museum

Wisemore WS2 8EQ   *(01922) 721153*

Leather items made by Walsall factories: belts, purses, wallets, personal organisers etc. Leather jewellery, horse brasses. Also 'designer' leather goods. Firsts and seconds on sale from £3.

'Walsall is Britain's leather goods' capital specialising in the manufacture of saddlery and small leather items. The museum tells the story of Walsall's leather history and acts as a show-case for the best of the industry today.'

On the north side of Walsall, this museum is on the ring road (where the A34 turns off for Cannock and Stafford).

Museum is signposted from M6 exits 7, 9, 10. From M6 exits 9 and 10, Wolverhampton or Wednesbury: get on to the ring road A4148 and go clockwise. When you reach a public car-park in the middle of a one-way system turn right into it opposite the large Renault garage. The Leather Museum is opposite.

From Cannock on the A34: you join the ring road just before the Renault garage.

From Birmingham via A34 or Aldridge via A454: get on to ring road anti-clockwise. Half a mile after large roundabout by the arboretum go right into car-park with brown sign 'Leather Centre'.

Open: Tues–Sat 10–5; Sun 12–5 (*Nov–March* closes at 4); Bank Holiday Mondays.
Closed: Most Mondays; Christmas and New Year.
Cards: No.
Cars: Public car-park. Limited street parking in Lord's Drive behind museum.
Toilets: Yes, including for disabled.
Wheelchairs: Ramps and special lifts.
Teas: Own café.
Tours: Demonstrations in museum most days. Group tours welcome at no charge, but please book first.
Transport: 5 minutes' walk from town centre. Short walk from station.
Mail order: No.

Knitting Yarns, Haberdashery & Crafts Materials

One of the great bonuses of researching factory shops around the country is that we have the chance to glimpse British manufacturing at work. From time to time we come across important industries which we had never thought of (or heard of). One of these is fabric pleating; another is carpet edging; a third is thread making. Thread serves a huge variety of functions in many industries. It needs to be of the correct thickness, made of the correct materials, of suitable strength, to have the correct tension, to be sufficiently slippery and to withstand heat generated during rapid sewing processes. A company specialising in thread manufacture in Colne sells a selection in its shop, particularly lace makers' supplies. Other shops in this chapter sell spectacular selections of knitting yarns, many of which you can obtain by post, wonderful choices of embroidery materials, and extraordinary ranges of haberdashery and toy making materials.

British Mohair Spinners	290	**Bradford**	W Yorks
Texere Yarns	291	**Bradford**	W Yorks
Yorkshire Mohair Mill, The	292	**Bradford**	W Yorks
Empress Mills (1927)	293	**Colne**	Lancs
R L & C M Bond	294	**Farsley**	W Yorks
Skep Mill Shop, The	295	**Farsley**	W Yorks
Craft Collection Mill Shop	296	**Horbury**	W Yorks
Fent Shop, The	297	**Macclesfield**	Cheshire
Abakhan Fabrics	140*	**Mostyn**	Clwyd
Gardiner of Selkirk	693*	**Selkirk**	Borders
Jamieson & Smith	298	**Shetland**	
British Mohair Spinners	299	**Shipley**	W Yorks
Embsay Mills Needlecraft Centre	300	**Skipton**	N Yorks
John Heathcoat & Co (Sales)	315*	**Tiverton**	Devon
Dainty Supplies	301	**Washington**	Tyne & Wear

Please see full details in respective chapter

KNITTING YARNS, HABERDASHERY & CRAFTS MATERIALS

KEY
- Motorway
- Major Road
- County boundary
- ○ Major City/Town
- ● Town with Factory Shop
- Lewis

Distance in Miles (approx.)

0   © Gillian Cutress   50   100

British Mohair Spinners

Corner of Valley Road and Cape Street BD1 4RJ
(01274) 728456

Big selection of brushed mohair knitting wools plus other yarns. Some sweaters and other clothing for all the family.
'Luxury mohair at mill prices.'

Just over 1/4 mile north of central Bradford.
    From central Bradford: pass main post office on Canal Road. After 1/4 mile, go left at traffic lights by Do It All into Valley Road Trading Estate. Follow road round towards Hamm Strasse (large dual carriageway). Cape Street is on left, 25 yds before traffic lights at Hamm Strasse; signposted shop in huge mill.

Open: Mon–Fri 9–4.
Closed: Bank Holidays; Christmas–New Year.
Cards: Access, Visa.
Cars: One-hour parking in Cape Street.
Toilets: Yes.
Wheelchairs: Access difficult (three steps at front door). Another door with easier access gladly opened on request.
Changing rooms: Yes.
Teas: Many places in town.
Groups: No mill tours but coach parties welcome to shop. Prior phone call appreciated.
Transport: 5–10 minutes' walk from city centre.
Mail order: Yes.
Catalogue: Shade cards £2 a set, including price list.

Texere Yarns

Barkerend Road BD3 9AO
(01274) 722191

Vast range of yarns for hand and machine knitting, hand-loom weaving and embroidery: from high quality silks, mohair and fancy yarns etc to conventional wools and acrylics. Also embroidery yarns in wool, cotton and silk.
'10–15,000 kg of yarns, set out in bins, spread over two floors (10,000 square feet).'

Close to, and slightly north-east of, Bradford centre.
    From Forster Square in city centre: go up Church Bank (steep hill) which leads into Barkerend Road. Texere is on right, before first traffic lights.
    Coming west into Bradford on B6381: go straight at huge Barkerend roundabout, cross new inner ring road (A650) at next traffic lights: company is immediately on left.
    Going north or south on inner ring road (A650): go towards city centre at traffic lights with B6381 (to Cathedral). Company clearly visible on left.

Open: Mon–Fri 9–5; Sat am (check first); Sun by arrangement with Robin Smith.
Closed: Good Friday–Easter Tues; Spring Bank Holiday Mon and Tues; May Day; August Bank Holiday; Christmas–New Year.
Cards: Access, Switch, Visa.
Cars: Upper Park Gate (downhill from company) and car-park by traffic lights.
Toilets: Yes.
Wheelchairs: Access tricky.
Teas: Hot drinks available.
Groups: For group visits please contact Chris or Robin Smith, mentioning this Guide. Machine-knitters are especially welcome.
Transport: 15 minutes' walk from Bradford Interchange; also taxis from there.
Mail order: Yes.
Catalogue: £2.90 for shade card.

The Yorkshire Mohair Mill
Gibson Street BD3 9TS
(01274) 668686

Hand and machine-knitting yarns both on cone and balled in packs. Chunky Aran double knitting and 4 ply. 430 shades in 28 different ranges. Mohair (11 ranges), wool (5), cotton (3), acrylic (2), chenille (1). Luxury yarns: pure silk, pure and mixed angora and alpaca. Patterns, mohair brushes, labels.

'Clearance bargains from £1.99 per cone. Mohair from 1p per gramme.'

....

About 1 mile east of Bradford centre, just off Leeds Road (A647) near the inner ring road (A650). Turn south off Leeds Road beside The Lemon Tree pub (Wilsons); go to end of Laurel Street, turn left. Shop is shortly on right.

Open: Mon–Thur 9–5; Fri 9–4; *also* Sat *Sept–April* 9–2.
Closed: Bank Holidays; first two weeks August; Christmas–New Year.
Cards: Access, Visa.
Cars: Outside shop.
Toilets: Yes.
Wheelchairs: Easy access.
Teas: Nearby.
Groups: Please book with Christine Willis, mentioning this Guide. Welcome Mon–Fri 9–5 all year plus Sat (*Sept–April*) 9–2.
Transport: Bus nos. 14, 15, 72, 610–613 from Bradford Interchange.
Mail order: Yes.
Catalogue: Yes. £2.99. No restrictions on mail order.

Empress Mills (1927) Ltd.
Hollin Hall Sewing Centre, Hollin Hall Mill BB8 8SS
(01282) 863181

Wide range of sewing threads in nearly 100 colours for all types of hand and machine sewing – overlocking, embroidery and quilting. Also gift boxes and a range of sewing accessories.

'Contact us for calendar of workshops for beginners and advanced sewing enthusiasts. Regular exhibitions held.'

....

This company has moved from Colne centre to Trawden on the south-east side of Colne.

Arriving in Colne from Lancashire (via M65) or Yorkshire (via A56 or A6068): follow 'Trawden B6250' signs. Follow road through Trawden village until you reach a fork (St Mary's church straight ahead). Bear left (signposted Hollin Hall). Go along Lane House Lane until you see the Sewing Centre on your left.

From Colne town centre: follow signs to Keighley. Immediately after large roundabout, go right for Trawden B6250. Follow road through Trawden village, fork left in front of St Mary's Church and look for Sewing Centre on left.

Open: Mon–Thur 9–5; Fri 9–4. Sat 10–4.
Closed: Easter Friday and Monday; two weeks at Christmas.
Cards: Access, Visa.
Cars: Own car-park.
Toilets: Yes.
Wheelchairs: Easy access; lift to workshop room.
Teas: Tea & coffee available. Can cater if booked in advance.
Groups: Groups to shop welcome any time. Demonstrations and workshops by arrangement.
Transport: Colne–Trawden buses.
Mail order: Yes. Fax 01282 870935 for details.
Catalogue: Free.

R L & C M Bond Ltd.
93 Town Street LS28 5HY
(0113) 257 4905

An amazing range of haberdashery! Includes huge selection of buttons, zips, fringes, trimmings, thread, appliqués, shoulder pads – and everything else you can think of!

'Our prices are unbeatable! Allow yourself plenty of time to browse round this shop brimming with goodies.'

....

Please see the map in the display advertisement opposite.
   Town Street is the main road through Farsley and shop is at the bottom left (opposite The Fleece) if you go down the hill.

Open: Wed–Sat 9–4.30.
Closed: Bank Holidays; Christmas, Boxing and New Year's Days.
Cards: None.
Cars: In street or to the side/rear of the shop.
Toilets: Yes.
Wheelchairs: Unfortunately no access as there are stairs.
Teas: Nearby pubs.
Groups: Coach parties to the shop very welcome. Please book, mentioning this guide. Sunday morning openings can also be arranged.
Transport: Buses from Bradford and Leeds pass the door.
Mail order: No.

The Skep Mill Shop
Reuben Grants, Coal Hill Lane LS28 7US
(0113) 255 6769

Classical all-wool fabrics made for some of the top designer houses, including *Jean Muir, Daks Simpson & Aquascutum.* Now stock American craft fabrics, furnishing fabrics, wool coatings, wool crêpes etc. Large range of knitting yarns to complement the fabrics in mohair, cotton, double knitting and aran.

'A favourite hunting ground for interesting and unusual fabrics. Most of these fabrics only seen in garments costing hundreds of pounds. Ideal chance to buy high quality designer fabrics at reasonable prices.'

....

Please see the map in the display advertisement opposite.
   Coal Hill Lane leads south off Rodley Lane/Town Street, the A657 (Leeds–Calverley–Shipley road).
   From Farsley centre: turn out of Town Street at bottom of hill into Bagley Lane and go straight over into Coal Hill Lane where Bagley Lane turns sharp left. The shop, lying back from the road, beneath the tall chimney, is clearly visible on right, half way up the hill.

Open: Mon–Sat 9.30–4.30; Sunday by appointment.
Closed: Bank Holidays; Christmas–New Year.
Cards: None.
Cars: Large car-park.
Toilets: Yes.
Wheelchairs: One step.
Changing rooms: No.
Teas: Attractive local pubs with good food.
Groups: Coach parties to the shop very welcome.Contact Mr Horrocks, mentioning this guide when you book.
Transport: Buses from Bradford and Leeds.
Mail order: Yes.
Catalogue: No.

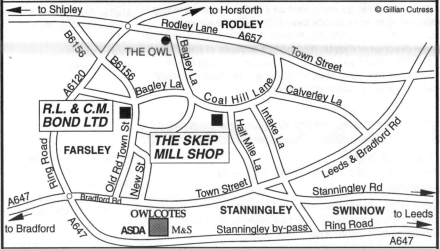

Craft Collection Ltd. Mill Shop

Terry Mills, Westfield Road WF4 6HE
(01924) 811908

Craft bargains including our own screen-printed tapestry kits, hand stencilled rug kits, hand-knitting yarns, cross-stitch and embroidery kits. Full range of *Paterna* Persian tapestry yarns.

'An absolute must for the craft enthusiast! Visit our Doll House and miniatures department, where we have an extensive range of 1/12th scale miniatures plus a delightful selection of porcelain dolls, accessories and doll making kits.'

Horbury is about 2.5 miles south-west of Wakefield. This company is easy to find on the west side Horbury town centre, on the road to Ossett (B6128).

From Wakefield: go south-west on A642; go under motorway then fork right on to B6128 through Horbury. Clearly visible company in a large detached building is just over a mile on right in the direction of Ossett. Well marked entrance at back.

From Dewsbury: you come to a T-junction in the middle of Horbury. Go left. Keep straight till you see this large detached building a short distance on the right.

Open: Mon–Fri 10–4; Sat 10–3.
Closed: Bank Holidays; Christmas–New Year.
Cards: Access, Visa.
Cars: Large car-park.
Toilets: No.
Wheelchairs: Ramp into large shop.
Teas: Local cafés.
Groups: Coach parties very welcome. Please book in advance.
Transport: Wakefield BR station 3 miles. Bus nos. 126, 127 (Wakefield-Dewsbury).
Mail order: Yes.
Catalogue: Yes. Write to Craft Collection or phone (01924) 810811 (not the shop number).

The Fent Shop

Pickford Street Mill, Pickford Street SK11 6HY
No telephone in shop.

Huge range of haberdashery, crafts items and fabrics for dresses, clothing, curtains and upholstery. Some toys, sheeting and evening wear.

'Large range of rolls and remnants at vastly reduced prices.'

In the tangle of little streets in old town centre, facing & on downhill side of Pickford Centre (Discount Giant) supermarket car-park.

From Stockport/Manchester via A523: at roundabout (Tesco on left) keep straight; follow new Silk Road; go right at lights, under railway lines, to station.*

From Buxton on A537: at traffic lights at bottom of hill, go straight under railway for station.*

***Pass station on your left; continue into Sunderland Street. Pass bus station and George & Dragon, both on right, then go right after Animal World into Pickford Street. Shop immediately on left.**

From Leek on A523 or Congleton on A536: from traffic lights where these road converge at bottom of main road through town (Mill Street), aim for station. Pass the Jolly Sailor on left then go left (Pickford Street). Shop immediately on left.

Open: Mon, Tues, Thur 9.30–4.30; Wed 9.30–12.30; Fri 9.30–3.30; Sat 9–1.
Closed: Bank Holidays; Christmas, Boxing and New Year's Days.
Cards: None.
Cars: Public car-park 20 yds.
Toilets: In supermarket next door.
Wheelchairs: No steps. Easy access to ground floor show-rooms crammed with items.
Teas: In supermarket next door.
Groups: Shopping groups welcome.
Transport: Easy walk from bus and train stations.
Mail order: No.

Jamieson & Smith (Shetland Wool Brokers)
90 North Road
(01595) 693579

Knitting yarns in 230 shades (156 coned for machine knitting).

....

Situated on the south side of the Shetland Hotel.

Open: Mon–Fri 9–1 & 2–5; Sat 9–1.
Closed: Bank Holidays.
Cards: Access, Eurocard, Mastercard, Visa.
Cars: On road.
Toilets: Ask if desperate.
Wheelchairs: Difficult access, several steps to shop.
Teas: In Lerwick.
Groups: Shopping groups welcome, please phone in advance.
Transport: Regular bus services on the island.
Mail order: Yes.
Catalogue: £2.00 for shade card.

British Mohair Spinners
Otley Road BD17 7EV
(01274) 583111

Colourful selection of brushed mohair knitting wools plus other yarns. Some sweaters and other clothing for all the family.

'Luxury mohair at mill prices.'

....

Nearly 1/2 mile north-east of Shipley on A6038.
   From Shipley: go north-east on A6038 for Otley. Go over river, through first traffic lights, past the DIY centre on right, then shop is clearly visible in old mill on right.
   From Otley (A6038) or Baildon (B6151): this mill is on left beside traffic lights where these two roads join. Shop is at far end of building.

Open: Mon–Fri 9–4.
Closed: Bank Holidays; third week September (please ring to check); Christmas–New Year.
Cards: Access, Visa.
Cars: Own car-park outside shop.
Toilets: Yes.
Wheelchairs: Ramp to shop.
Changing rooms: Yes.
Teas: In Shipley and Saltaire.
Groups: No mill tours but group visits and coach parties welcome to shop. No need to book.
Transport: Buses from Bradford: 650 to Ilkley; 653, 654 to Harrogate; 655, 755 to Leeds.
Mail order: Yes.
Catalogue: Contact shop in Bradford for shade cards.

Embsay Mills Needlecraft Centre

Embsay BD23 6QE
(01756) 700946

Everything for needlecraft, cross stitch, embroidery, tapestry; patchwork and quilting fabrics, patterns and accessories; wadding, charts and books. *Coats, DMC, Tootal, Kinetic, Paterna* and many more. Own range of cross stitch kits, printed samplers, tapestry kits, quilted cushion kits.

'Perfects and seconds. A good choice of specials always on sale, which can be as much as 50% off.'

Nearly 2 miles north-east of Skipton, in the centre of Embsay village.

From Skipton town centre and Skipton castle: follow the sign to A59 (Harrogate–Settle road). Go left at signs 'Embsay 1 mile' and 'The Steam Railway'. Look for the Cavendish Arms on right; drive to shop is immediately on left.

From A65 (Harrogate–Settle road), Skipton by-pass: follow signs to 'Embsay Steam Railway'. Mill entrance is on the left directly opposite the Cavendish Arms.

Open: Seven days a week, 10–5.
Closed: Christmas Eve, Christmas, Boxing and New Year's Days.
Cards: Access, Visa.
Cars: Own coach and car-park.
Toilets: Yes.
Wheelchairs: Welcome – one small step with ramp to ground floor; stairs to upper showroom.
Teas: Own coffee shop for sandwiches, snacks, cakes, fresh tea and coffee.
Groups: Shopping groups welcome; please book with manager.
Transport: Trains from Skipton. Bus no. 214 from Skipton.
Mail order: Yes.
Catalogue: No. Gladly accept telephone orders.

Dainty Supplies Ltd.

Unit 35, Phoenix Road, Crowther Industrial Estate, District 3
NE38 0AA *(0191) 416 7886/417 6277*

Huge range of craft materials, dress fabrics, ribbons, lace, fur fabric, teddybear noses and components, plastic eyes for soft toys, toy and cushion fillings. Range of decoupage frames and craft frames. Huge selection of miniature items. *Frame Craft* items. Aida fabric for cross stitch, embroidery silks, tapestry wool, canvas. Bridal fabrics, flowers and accessories. Bridal shoes, veils and sequinned motifs.

'We are a craft person's/sewer's paradise. Garment/toy labelling services. Gladly help with new European Toy Safety Standards.'

On north-west edge of town, near junction of A1(M) and A1.

From A194(M) south or northbound: exit on to A182 to Washington; go right on to A1231. Take next exit; at roundabout go into Crowther Industrial Estate. *

From A1 Western Bypass southbound: go left on to A1231 for Washington. Go right at first roundabout and turn off at next exit into Crowther Industrial Estate. *

*Go to end of Crowther Road, go right and follow road around to left, going uphill. Take next left – Unit 35 is shortly on right.

Open: Mon–Sat 9–5.
Closed: Bank Holidays; Christmas and Boxing Days.
Cards: Access, Switch, Visa.
Cars: Outside shop.
Toilets: Yes.
Wheelchairs: Easy access.
Teas: In town centre.
Groups: Groups of shoppers and club visits welcome – please phone first.
Transport: Very difficult!
Mail order: Yes.
Catalogue: Free price list and samples (mention this guide).

Dress Fabrics

Those who can sew are doubly blessed. They can not only save huge amounts of money but have that rare opportunity of indulging their creative impulse, of making their imagination a reality. There is nothing more intoxicating for dressmakers than that moment when, scissors poised, they prepare for that first snip.

The following pages will take you from Scottish cashmere to fine worsted cloth from Yorkshire; from silks in Derbyshire, Kent and Suffolk to the only remaining British velvet maker; from mohair and cloth from the largest tartan manufacturer in the world to couture fabrics from Yorkshire and the Scottish borders. And if you are about to make the dress for a bride – and her retinue – we promise you will not be disapointed in your search for just the right stunning fabric at a price which will not spoil the occasion.

But be warned! These shops with their gorgeous fabrics are highly addictive, as the author, a hopeless addict herself, happily confirms.

Red Rose Velvets	112*	**Accrington**	Lancs
Ahmad Textiles	118*	**Bradford**	W Yorks
Bateman, Ogden & Co.	302	**Bradford**	W Yorks
C & R Barnett	303	**Bradford**	W Yorks
Liberty	304	**Burnley**	Lancs
Hartleys (Mail Order) Shop	122*	**Colne**	Lancs
David Evans and Co.	305	**Crayford**	Kent
Denholme Velvets	306	**Denholme**	W Yorks
Fine Fabrics	307	**Derby**	Derbys
Skep Mill Shop, The	295*	**Farsley**	W Yorks
Peter MacArthur & Co.	308	**Hamilton**	Strathclyde
Fabric Factory, The	125*	**Heanor**	Derbys
Shop at the Mill	636*	**Huddersfield**	W Yorks
Factory Fabric Shop, The	309	**Leeds**	W Yorks
Nottingham Laces & Trimmings	310	**Long Eaton**	Notts
Barracks Fabrics	134*	**Macclesfield**	Cheshire
Fent Shop, The	297*	**Macclesfield**	Cheshire
Abakhan Fabrics	140*	**Mostyn**	Clwyd
Proud Fabrics	311	**Nelson**	Lancs
Black Dyke Mill Shop	312	**Queensbury near Bradford**	W Yorks
Claridge Mills	313	**Selkirk**	Borders
D C Dalgliesh	556*	**Selkirk**	Borders
Gardiner of Selkirk	693*	**Selkirk**	Borders
Vanners Mill Shop	314	**Sudbury**	Suffolk
John Heathcoat & Co (Sales)	315	**Tiverton**	Devon
Dainty Supplies	301*	**Washington**	Tyne & Wear
BTM Fabrics	316	**Wigston**	Leics

* Please see full details in respective chapter

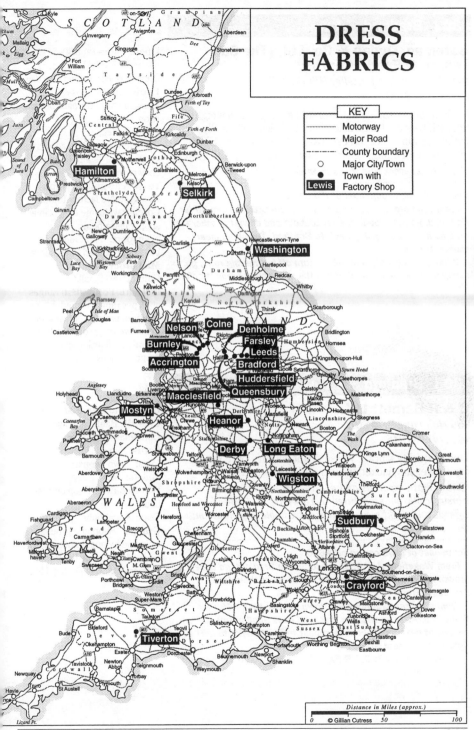

DRESS FABRICS

KEY

.... Motorway
———— Major Road
— · — · — County boundary
○ Major City/Town
● Town with
| Lewis | Factory Shop

Bateman, Ogden & Co. Ltd. (The Suit Length & Fabric Centre)

918 Wakefield Road, Dudley Hill BD4 7QO
(01274) 729103

Huddersfield and Scottish worsted suitings of all weights. Scottish tweeds. Large selection of fabrics specifically for ladies. Coating in cashmere/wool, all wool fabrics. Skirt lengths, satin linings, gents' knitwear, caps, ties and gloves.
'Annual two-week sale starts in mid-November.'

About 1.5 miles south-east of the city centre.
   From Bradford: follow signs to Wakefield (A650). Turn off for ring road, go right round the roundabout and down the other slip road as if you were going back to Bradford. The shop, clearly visible, is on left.
   Coming into Bradford on A650: turn off for the ring road, go straight at the roundabout, down the slip road towards Bradford. The shop is on left.

Open: Mon–Sat 8.30–5.
Closed: Bank Holidays; Christmas, Boxing and next day.
Cards: Access, Visa.
Cars: Private car-park behind shop.
Toilets: Yes.
Wheelchairs: Easy access to ground floor (stairs to upper showroom).
Teas: 'Pub grub' close by.
Groups: No factory tours. Coaches welcome to spacious shop. Please book.
Transport: Any Dudley Hill bus from Bradford Interchange.
Mail order: Yes.
Catalogue: Small free brochure. Post pattern ranges at £3 per range, refundable on return of patterns. In view of extensive range of fabrics, can operate mail order on certain ranges only. No seconds.

C & R Barnett Ltd.

136 Hall Lane BD4 7DH
(01274) 737046

Luxury quality fabrics; worsted suit lengths, pure wools, cashmere; suit, jacket, trouser and skirt lengths.
'One of main exporters and distributors of woollen and worsted cloths manufactured in Yorkshire or Scotland. Off-cuts and slight seconds always available at genuine mill shop prices.'

South-east of town centre off A650.
   From Wakefield via A650: descend into Bradford, go under brown/red railway bridge and go left at roundabout into Prospect Street.*
   From all other directions and town centre: take A650 for Wakefield. After leaving the ring road pass Shell petrol station on left; at next roundabout (signpost to Laisterdyke to left) go right into Prospect Street.*
   ***Take second left: C & R Barnett are about 300 yds on right.**

Open: Mon–Fri 9.30–5.30.
Closed: Bank Holidays; Christmas–New Year.
Cards: No.
Cars: Own car-park.
Toilets: Yes.
Wheelchairs: Shop on first floor.
Teas: Local pubs.
Groups: Shopping groups welcome by appointment with Howard Cantor or Ian Barnett.
Transport: Any Dudley Hill bus.

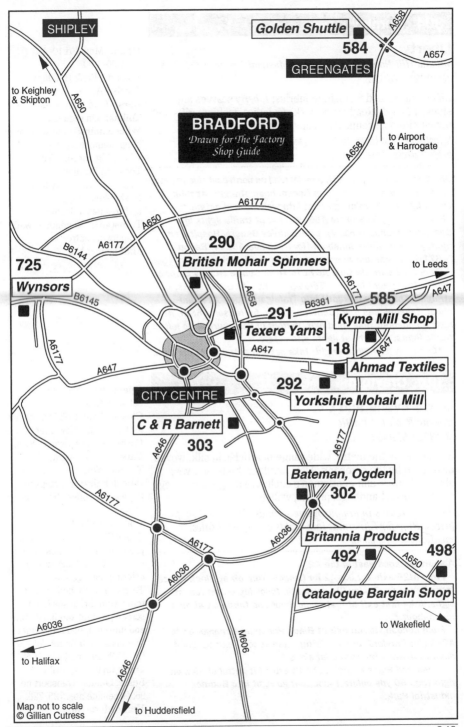

SHIPLEY

to Keighley & Skipton

Golden Shuttle 584

GREENGATES

A657

A658

A658

to Airport & Harrogate

BRADFORD
Drawn for The Factory Shop Guide

A6177

A650

A6177

A6177

B6144

725

Wynsors

B6145

A6177

A647

290
British Mohair Spinners

A658

B6381

585
Kyme Mill Shop

to Leeds

A647

291
Texere Yarns

A647

118
Ahmad Textiles

CITY CENTRE

292
Yorkshire Mohair Mill

A6177

C & R Barnett
303

A646

A6177

A6177

Bateman, Ogden
302

A6036

Britannia Products
492

498
Catalogue Bargain Shop

A650

to Wakefield

A6036

A6036

M606

to Halifax

A646

to Huddersfield

Map not to scale
© Gillian Cutress

The Official Great British Factory Shop Guide

243

Liberty

Widow Hill Road, Heasandford Industrial Estate BB10 2TK
(01282) 424600

Liberty dress and furnishing fabrics; *Liberty* scarves and shawls; *Liberty* Ready-to-Sew skirts; ladies' fashion; gifts and novelty items; scents and soaps; fashion jewellery.

'Mostly ends of lines and imperfects. Some reduced price perfect dress fabrics.'

Off Eastern Avenue (A6114), a major road on north-east side of town.
   Coming north on A671 from Bacup: keep straight. At third traffic lights in Burnley, go right into well marked estate. *
   From Burnley/Nelson via A56: go east at traffic lights into Casterton Avenue (A6114); pass Burnley General Hospital on right; go over mini-roundabout [for Rochdale A6114/Bacup (A671)] into Eastern Avenue; go left at traffic lights. *
   From M65 exit 10: take A671 to Town Centre (Happy Eater on right). Get in right lane for 'Through traffic'. At traffic lights, go straight (The Mitre on right) into Trafalgar Street. At roundabout, take second exit (Centenary Way, for Nelson A682). At next roundabout take third exit, in front of Sainsbury's; go left at traffic lights; go right at lights into estate. *
   *Company 150 yds on right; take second entrance to car-park.

Open: Mon–Fri 10–4; Sat 9.30–1.00.
Closed: Bank Holidays.
Cards: Access, Amex, Visa.
Cars: Own forecourt.
Toilets: On request.
Wheelchairs: One step, large shop. Ramp available.
Changing rooms: Yes.
Teas: In Burnley.
Groups: No factory tours. Pre-booked shopping groups and coaches welcome.
Transport: 30 minutes' walk from town centre.
Mail order: No.

David Evans and Co.

Bourne Road DA1 4BR
(01322) 559401

Silk fabric by the metre; wide range of articles in silk, woven or printed by the company. Ties, handkerchiefs, scarves, shawls. Ladies' and gentlemen's exclusive range of gifts, eg boxer shorts, handbags, purses, wallets.

'Lots of bargains in famous name seconds. All at mill shop prices. Ring for Christmas late nights and special sales, mentioning this book.'

A short distance east of the A2.
   From M25 exit 2: take A2 for London. Turn off at Black Prince Interchange for Bexley/Bexleyheath; following brown tourist signs, take first exit at first roundabout and third exit at next roundabout. *
   From London via A2: exit at Black Prince Interchange on to A223 (for Crayford, Bexley, Erith), take second exit at roundabout, following brown tourist signs. *
   *Pass Hall Place on right; shortly after Jet petrol station on right (and 50 yds before T-junction) go right into Bourne Industrial Park.

Open: Mon–Fri 9.30–5; Sat 9.30–4.30.
Closed: Bank Holidays; check for Christmas–New Year.
Cards: Access, Switch, Visa,
Cars: Own car-park.
Toilets: Yes.
Wheelchairs: No steps to large shop, coffee shop, craft centre.
Teas: Own Mulberry Tree Coffee Shop for home baked produce, light lunches, cream teas etc. (01322) 529198 for catering manageress.
Tours: Pre-booked guided tours Mon–Fri to see hand-screen printing and finishing, and museum. Including video tour lasts 1 1/4 hours. Adults £2, OAPs and students £1.50.
Transport: Crayford BR. Buses: London Transport no. 96; Greenline nos. 725, 726.
Mail order: No.

Denholme Velvets Ltd.
Halifax Road BD13 4EY
(01274) 832185

Cotton and rayon dress velvets, some with interesting textures. Plastic-backed velvets for lining boxes etc. Curtain velvets. Low cost fents and remnants.

'This is the only British firm still making dress velvet. Samples and mail order catalogue available.'

....

Nearly 1.5 miles south of Denholme on the road to Halifax (A629).

   From Denholme village going south for Halifax: clearly visible mill is on right with shop at the far end.

   From Bradford: take B6145 (Thornton Road). At the T-junction with the A629 (Keighley–Halifax Road) go right: this conspicuous mill is 100 yds on left.

Open: Mon–Fri 1–5; Sat 9–5. Some Bank Holidays – please phone.
Closed: Christmas–New Year.
Cards: Access, Visa.
Cars: Outside shop.
Toilets: No.
Wheelchairs: Several wooden steps.
Changing rooms: No.
Teas: Several attractive local pubs.
Groups: No factory tours but groups welcome to shop; please phone first.
Transport: Bradford–Keighley buses pass the door.
Mail order: Yes.
Catalogue: Yes.

Fine Fabrics (*formerly* Courtaulds Textiles Fabric Shop)
Alfreton Road DE2 4AE
(01332) 243631

Dress and nightwear fabrics, including pure cotton, wide range of pure silk, polycottons, polyester. Shower curtain and curtain fabrics.

'Huge range of fabrics and other items at factory prices. Constantly changing stock.'

....

One mile north of city centre.

   From Derby area and Derby ring road: take A52 for Nottingham. *

   From Nottingham & M1 exit 25: take A52 for Derby. *

   ***Turn off A52 for A61 to Chesterfield (Sir Frank Whittle Way) at County Cricket Ground island. At first roundabout go left, then left again. Go over bridge then right at mini-roundabout to Alfreton Road Industrial Estate. Company 300 yds on right.**

   From A38 north and south: leave ring road for Derby city centre (A61) at Abbey Hill island. At next roundabout (Nurdin & Peacock on right) go right for Alfreton Road Industrial Estate. Continue until you see company on left.

Open: Mon–Fri 9–4.30; Sat 9–2.30.
Closed: Bank Holiday Mondays; Christmas–New Year.
Cards: Most credit cards.
Cars: Company car-park in front of shop.
Toilets: Ask if necessary.
Wheelchairs: Ramp to large, spacious shop.
Changing rooms: Yes.
Teas: New bakery for filled rolls, cakes etc close by. Teas in Derby.
Groups: Coach parties welcome at any time. Prior phone call appreciated.
Transport: Buses from Derby. You can also take train to Derby then bus.
Mail order: No.

Peter MacArthur & Co. Ltd.

Woodside Walk ML3 7HZ
(01698) 282544

Woollen cloths, woollen and mohair travel rugs, knee rugs and stoles; skirts and scarves in wool, mohair and cashmere. All natural fibres.

'Largest tartan manufacturers in the world. Mostly perfects, fabrics from £5 per metre, skirts from about £20. Often special offers.'

Close to town centre (south of railway line) in a one-way street.
   From all directions except Strathaven: get on to town centre one-way system. Follow signs to A723 Strathaven. After leaving one-way system for Strathaven, go over railway bridge. At next roundabout go left then sharp left into one-way road.*
   From Strathaven on A723: go downhill towards town centre. After Shell petrol station at roundabout go right, then take first sharp left into one-way street.*
   *After next bend shop is 120 yds on left.

Open: Mon–Fri 9–5. Bank Holidays.
Closed: Possibly week before Easter. Worth phoning if travelling far in mid-summer; Christmas–New Year.
Cards: No.
Cars: Car-park past shop on left.
Toilets: On request.
Wheelchairs: Three steps to medium sized shop.
Changing rooms: Yes.
Teas: In town.
Groups: No.
Transport: From bus/railway station go to railway bridge, turn right in front of it. Take second left; shop 80 yds on right.
Mail order: Yes.
Catalogue: Will post specific items by special request.

The Factory Fabric Shop

55 Cardigan Lane LS4 2LF
(0113) 275 9621

Interesting range of dress fabrics and sample lengths from design and production departments of large ladies' wear manufacturer. Polycotton sheeting in plains and prints. Complementary haberdashery and linings. Pleating service (including mail order).

'All items perfects, no seconds. January and July sales. First week each month is "Remnant Time". Ask for free leaflet on having your own fabric pleated (mention this Guide).'

About 1.5 miles north-west of Leeds centre.
   From the inner ring road: go along Kirkstall Road (A65), under the viaduct, over pedestrian lights; just after Cardigan Arms go right into Greenhow Road.*
   Coming into Leeds on A65: go over pedestrian lights with pillar box to left, then turn left in front of Cardigan Arms.*
   *Go to top, turn right, take next left: shop is 200 yds on left.

Open: Mon–Fri 10–1 and 2–5.
Closed: Bank Holidays; Spring Bank Holiday week; Christmas–New Year.
Cards: Access, Visa.
Cars: Outside.
Toilets: No
Wheelchairs: No – four steps.
Teas: Leeds and Headingley.
Groups: Group visits welcome to fairly small shop; please book first. Expert, friendly advice from manageress Alice Boyle.
Transport: Burley Metro station (Leeds–Harrogate line) 300 yds; local buses along Burley and Cardigan Roads.
Mail order: No.

Nottingham Laces & Trimmings Ltd.

Turret E Harrington Mills, Leopold Street NG10 4QE
(0115) 946 0766

Bridal fabrics, laces and applique motifs. Silk dupion, satin, Thai silk, taffeta etc. Beaded and sequinned laces, corded and ribbon laces. Veiling, dress net, ribbons, beads and sequins; lace frillings and lace collars.

'Prices below usual retail eg pure silk dupion from £5.39 + vat per metre. Please telephone for catalogue and samples.'

....

Off the A6005, Derby Road, west of town centre. (Phone for free easy map.)

From M1 exit 25: follow signs to Long Eaton (not Nottingham).*

From Nottingham: take A52 Derby Road to M1 exit 25; follow signs to Long Eaton.*

*At large roundabout turn into A6005 Derby Road. Pass Trent College on right. After about 1/3 mile go right into Leopold Street, immediately before Harrington Arms on right. Showroom entrance 200 yds to the right.

From town centre: take A6005 towards Derby. Go over canal and go left into Leopold Street immediately after Harrington Arms on left. Showroom entrance about 200 yds on right.

Open: Mon–Sat 9–5.
Closed: Most Bank Holidays (phone previous week); Christmas–New Year.
Cards: Access, Eurocard, Mastercard, Visa.
Cars: Free car-park on opposite side of road.
Toilets: Yes.
Wheelchairs: Regret access too difficult.
Teas: Many places in nearby town centre.
Groups: No tours or large shopping groups.
Transport: Long Eaton BR station. Buses to The Green, Long Eaton.
Mail order: Yes.
Catalogue: £3.95 Samples available.

Proud Fabrics

Bowling Mill, Lonsdale Street BB9 9HF   (01282) 699138

Huge selection of high-class curtaining, bridal and dress fabrics from leading companies. Many leading brand fabrics to order. Special bridal room. New craft section. Curtains and soft furnishings made to requirements.

'Very low prices. Perfects and seconds from £2 per yd. January and July sales. Discount floor all year with prices up to 50% off rrp.'

....

On the east side of town centre, south of the A56 (main Nelson –Colne road).

From Colne coming south on A56: pass Burmah petrol on left then immediately go left (in front of the New Inn) into Barkerhouse Road.*

From Nelson going north on A56 towards Colne: go right immediately before Burmah petrol on right (after the New Inn) into Barkerhouse Road.*

From M65 exit 13: aim for Nelson town centre then (Food Giant on left) go left on to A56 (Leeds Road) for Colne. Go right immediately before Burmah petrol on right (after the New Inn) into Barkerhouse Road.*

*Go uphill, over level-crossing; go left into Wren Street which becomes Lonsdale Street. Shop is in well marked mill on left.

Open: Mon–Fri 9–5; Sat 10–3. Bank Holidays.
Closed: Christmas–New Year.
Cards: Access, Visa.
Cars: In street in front of shop.
Toilets: Yes.
Wheelchairs: One step to ground floor. Assistants gladly bring goods from huge display area upstairs on first floor.
Teas: Nelson town centre.
Groups: Shopping groups welcome, including coach parties. Phone Susan Proud to book if more than 10 people. Carpeted play area for children.
Transport: 15 minutes' walk from town centre.
Mail order: No.

Black Dyke Mill Shop

Black Dyke Mill Complex BD13 1QB
(01274) 882271 x 308 Closed

Large selection of wool, wool/mohair suit lengths, trouser lengths, skirt lengths. Small selection of own ladies' skirts and men's trousers.

'All cloth manufactured on premises in world famous Victorian mill. Mill shop prices for perfects, slight seconds, oddments, ends of lines. Skirt lengths from £2.50, trouser lengths from £6, suits lengths from £10. Buy British!'

Midway between Bradford and Halifax.

Shop is near the traffic lights in the centre of Queensbury, in a large clearly marked mill on the A644 (Brighouse–Denholme road).

From Shelf/Brighouse going north on A644: as you come into Queensbury, mill is on left before traffic lights.

From Denholme coming south on A644: at traffic lights in Queensbury, go straight; mill is 100 yds on right.

From Bradford coming west on A647: go left at the lights; mill is 100 yds on right.

From Halifax coming east on A647: go right at lights; mill is on right.

Open: Mon, Tues, Thur, Fri 9–5; Wed 9–12.
Closed: Saturday; mill and Bank Hols (phone to check).
Cards: Access, Visa.
Cars: Large customer car-park opposite entrance to mill.
Toilets: Yes.
Wheelchairs: Four large steps.
Changing rooms: Yes.
Teas: Nearby coffee shop/pubs.
Groups: Interesting to seamsters; phone manager for groups (Sat/Sun by arrangement).
Transport: On the Bradford–Halifax bus route.
Mail order: Yes.
Catalogue: Swatches of cloth sent. Exclusive for mail order customers: gift wrap (small charge) cloth sent to choice of address. 'Ideal Christmas or birthday present for the man who appreciates the best cloth in the world.' Can recommend local tailors.

Claridge Mills Ltd.

Riverside Industrial Estate TD7 5DV
(01750) 20300

Cashmere, silk and fine wool accessories, and couture quality fabrics.

'Perfects and seconds direct from the mill.'

To north of town.

From Peebles/Innerleithen on A707 and Moffat on A708: cross river and turn left immediately into Buccleuch Road. After nearly 1.25 miles go left into Level Crossing Road; shop 120 yds on right.

From Hawick on A7: go through Selkirk and turn left after Exacta and before Selkirk Glass. *

From Edinburgh and Galashiels on A7: take first right immediately after Selkirk Glass, signposted to Moffat. *

*After 300 yds take first right (Level Crossing Road).

Open: Mon–Fri 9–5.
Closed: Christmas, Boxing, New Year's Days and 2 Jan.
Cards: Most major cards.
Cars: Outside shop.
Toilets: No.
Wheelchairs: Easy access to medium sized shop.
Teas: In Selkirk Glass at end of estate.
Groups: No factory tours but special openings by appointment.
Transport: Bus from Galashiels or Hawick to Selkirk Square, then 10 minutes' walk.
Mail order: Yes.
Catalogue: No.

Vanners Mill Shop

Gregory Street CO10 6BC
(01787) 313933

Silk fabric by the metre. Wide range of articles in silk, woven here or printed at company's Crayford mill – scarves, boxer shorts, ties, handkerchiefs, purses, wallets etc.

'Most items perfect but some fabric slightly substandard. All at mill shop prices. Many bargains in firsts and "famous name" seconds. From £2.50 per metre for pure silk. For special sale dates, ring (01322) 559401, mentioning this book.'

....

Easy to find in middle of town (large one-way system).
   From Market Square: go clockwise (Midland Bank on left).*
   From other directions: follow road round for Bury St Edmunds (A134).*
   *After junction where A131 goes left to Chelmsford, keep clockwise on A131 (A134) for Bury. Clearly marked mill 100 yds on right (before fire station on left).
   From Chelmsford on A131: you must go left on to one-way system as you reach town. Shop 100 yds on right.
   From Bury St Edmunds on A134: go into town, take first turn for Chelmsford (A131) then A134 back towards Bury as above.

Open: Mon–Fri 9–5; Sat 9–12.
Closed: Bank Holidays; Christmas–New Year.
Cards: Access, Visa.
Cars: Car-park opposite, beside fire station.
Toilets: In factory – ask if desperate!
Wheelchairs: No steps to expanded showroom.
Teas: Lots of places in town.
Groups: No mill tours. Shopping groups always welcome – prior phone call, please.
Transport: Any bus to town then short walk.
Mail order: No.

Tips on caring for silk

Use very fine pins and, if you are sewing by hand, a fine sewing needle too. Use a fine ball point sewing maching needle. Before cutting out, use a warm dry iron on the wrong side of the fabric (cool iron for chiffon). Use silk thread because this has a natural elasticity. If the silk is very fine, tack the fabric on to tissue paper and sew through two layers. A lightweight sew-in interfacing is best. Do not spray water on to silk fabrics as they become water marked and stained. Press carefully with a cool iron. Wash by hand in luke warm water with a gentle liquid detergent. Rinse well, roll in a towel to squeeze out surplus moisture and hang to dry away from direct sunlight or heat. While it is slightly damp, press the wrong side with a warm iron.

Thanks to Courtaulds Shamash for these hints.
Their silks are available at Fine Fabrics in Derby.

John Heathcoat & Co (Sales) Ltd.

West Exe EX16 5LL
(01884) 252816/254949

Extensive range of furnishing and fashion fabrics (many made here) – cottons, polycottons, polyester, satin, silk, crêpe-de-chine, wools, suiting, cords, fishermen's and garden nets, ripstop for kites and hot air balloons. All you require for dressmaking – haberdashery, patterns etc. Craft and toy-making fabrics.

'Home furnishing studio with curtain-making service. Perfects and seconds at factory shop prices.'

Close to town centre.
 From all directions: follow A361 bypass to large cultivated island then follow 'town centre' signs on A396. Pass East Devon Technical College on right; go right at next mini-roundabout, pass Safeways; go over bridge, go left past Heathcoats. Stay in middle lane of one-way system; pass stone wall on left which becomes metal fence. Here make sharp left turn into factory entrance. Shop on right.
NB Some road atlases show present A361 as A373.

Open: Mon–Fri and Bank Holidays 9–4.30; Sat 9–1.
Closed: Christmas–New Year.
Cards: Access, Switch, Visa.
Cars: Own car-park.
Toilets: Yes.
Wheelchairs: Ramp to large three-roomed shop.
Teas: Machine in canteen; lots of places in town.
Groups: Shopping groups welcome.
Transport: Bus station in town – no buses pass mill.
Mail order: Yes.
Catalogue: No.

BTM Fabrics Ltd.

Unit 2, St George's House, Moat Street LE18 2NH
(0116) 281 2383

Wide range of knitted fleece fabrics in 40 different colours; also stripes and prints. Ideal for T-shirts, leisurewear, pyjamas etc. Also ribbed collars, cuffs and welts in same wide colour range.

'Plain fleece from £2.70 per metre; stripes and printed slightly more.'

On the south side of Wigston, just off the A50.
 Coming south from Leicester on A50: at traffic lights (Texaco on right), turn right for S Wigston/Blaby.*
 From Northampton on A50: at traffic lights, turn left for S Wigston/Blaby.*
 *After 300 yds look for long, low brick factory on left. Entrance to yard at far end; go through to back left.
 From South Wigston on B582: aim for Wigston. Pass The Plough on left, go over mini-roundabout (large stone church on right).**
 From Wigston centre: aim for South Wigston (B582). At mini-roundabout (stone church facing), go left.**
 **Pass the Old Crown on left; after pedestrian crossing turn right at start of long, low brick factory into yard.

Open: Mon, Wed 12–3; Tues, Fri 11–3; Sat 10–12.
Closed: Bank Holidays; two weeks at Christmas.
Cards: None.
Cars: In factory yard.
Toilets: Yes,
Wheelchairs: Easy access to medium-sized shop.
Teas: In Wigston shopping centre.
Groups: Shopping and sewing groups welcome – please contact Jane Measures first.
Transport: Local buses from town centre stop near factory.
Mail order: Yes.
Catalogue: £2 for set of swatches. Mention this book when requesting.

Factory Outlet Centres & Shops for Wide Product Ranges

What a change has taken place in the evolution of factory shopping in Britain! A couple of years ago there were a few places where factory shops were gathered together on one site. Clarks Shopping Village – the first purpose built shopping village – had just started to trade in Somerset. Several million visitors have visited Street since then, proving the popularity of this type of shopping. Now there are several specially designed factory shopping centres around the country, with plans for more.

Factory shop 'villages' or 'malls' take the travel out of factory shopping. On one site you can find as many as sixty factory shops selling a huge range of products of interest to the entire family. Moreover, the coffee shops and restaurants offer sustenance to those members of your family who flag first. Facilities for people with prams, for the elderly and the disabled are excellent, with special toilets, convenient car parking and easy access to all the shops.

Perhaps it is too easy to spend money too!

The shops on these sites are run by a mixture of manufacturers and well known brand name companies with a sprinkling of supporting shops such as book and toy shops. You will find some French and American brands not normally available in the UK. Most of these malls have contractual agreements to sell their ranges at a minimum of 25% off the normal retail price so you should find good things to buy.

Tenants within the shopping villages change quite often. You might find, unfortunately, that a shop has closed. You are more likely to find that new shops have opened up. Most villages have plans to extend; and they are adding shops and brand names from month to month.

Over the past couple of years also, an increasing number of large factory shops around the country have opened, selling an extremely wide range of products under one roof. They, too, offer cafés, children's play areas, toilets and car-parks.

Good value shopping has never been easier!

FACTORY OUTLET CENTRES & SHOPS WITH WIDE PRODUCT RANGES

Factory Shop, The	317	**Basildon** Essex	
De Bradelei Mill Shops Ltd.	318	**Belper** Derbys	
Bicester Outlet Shopping Village	319	**Bicester** Oxon	
Merchants Quay	363	**Brighton** E Sussex	
The Factory Shop Ltd.	371	**Bristol** Avon	
The Factory Shop Ltd.	372	**Bury St Edmunds** Suffolk	
Boundary Mill Shop	373	**Colne** Lancs	
The Factory Shop Ltd.	374	**East Dereham** Norfolk	
The Factory Shop Ltd.	375	**Egremont** Cumbria	
Brooks Mill	376	**Elland** W Yorks	
McArthur Glen, Designer Outlet Village	377	**Ellesmere Port** Cheshire	
Darley Mill Centre	407	**Harrogate** N Yorks	
Jackson's Landing	408	**Hartlepool** Cleveland	
Winfields	425	**Haslingden near Rossendale** Lancs	
The Galleria	426	**Hatfield** Herts	
Ponden Mill	427	**Haworth** W Yorks	
The Factory Shop Ltd.	428	**Holbeach** Lincolnshire	
The Factory Shop Ltd.	429	**Horley** Surrey	
Hornsea Freeport	430	**Hornsea** Humberside	
The Factory Shop Ltd.	431	**Keighley** W Yorks	
K Village	432	**Kendal** Cumbria	
The Factory Shop Ltd.	439	**Lancaster** Lancs	
The Factory Shop Ltd.	440	**Liverpool** Merseyside	
The Factory Shop Ltd.	441	**Minehead** Somerset	
The Factory Shop Ltd.	442	**Morley** W Yorks	
Oswaldtwistle Mills	443	**Oswaldtwistle near Accrington** Lancs	
The Factory Shop Ltd.	444	**Pershore** Worcs	
Peel Mill	445	**Ramsbottom** Gr Manchester	
The Factory Shop Ltd.	446	**Ripon** N Yorks	
Lightwater Village Factory Outlets	447	**Ripon** N Yorks	
The Factory Shop Ltd.	448	**Rugby** Warks	
Charterhouse Holdings plc	449	**Shepshed** Leics	
The Factory Shop Ltd.	450	**Sileby** Leics	
Skipton Mill Shop Ltd.	697*	**Skipton** N Yorks	
Famous Fashion Discounts	451	**Stockton-on-Tees** Cleveland	
The Factory Shop Ltd.	452	**Stoke-on-Trent : Newcastle-u-Lyme** Staffs	
Clarks Village	453	**Street** Somerset	
The Factory Shop Ltd.	487	**Stroud** Gloucs	
The Factory Shop Ltd.	488	**Tiptree** Essex	
The Factory Shop Ltd.	489	**Trowbridge** Wilts	
The Factory Shop Ltd.	490	**Warminster** Wilts	
Factory Outlet Shopping Centre	491	**York** N Yorks	
The Yorkshire Outlet		**Doncaster** S Yorks	
		(late entry, see page 286)	

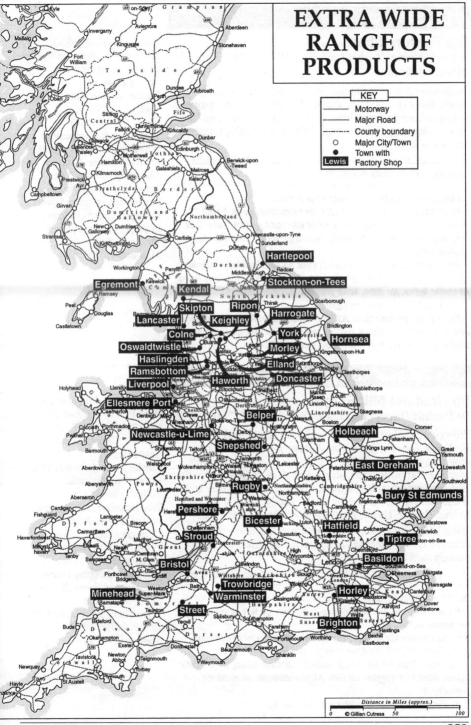

EXTRA WIDE RANGE OF PRODUCTS

KEY

- ‥‥‥‥ Motorway
- ‥‥‥‥ Major Road
- —·—·— County boundary
- ○ Major City/Town
- ● Town with
- Lewis Factory Shop

Hartlepool
Stockton-on-Tees
Egremont
Kendal
Skipton   Ripon   Harrogate
Lancaster   Keighley
Colne   York   Hornsea
Oswaldtwistle   Morley
Haslingden   Elland
Ramsbottom   Doncaster
Liverpool   Haworth
Ellesmere Port
Belper
Newcastle-u-Lime   Holbeach
Shepshed
East Dereham
Rugby   Bury St Edmunds
Pershore
Bicester   Hatfield
Stroud   Tiptree
Bristol   Basildon
Minehead   Trowbridge   Horley
Warminster
Street   Brighton

Distance in Miles (approx.)

0   © Gillian Cutress   50   100

The Factory Shop

4c The Gloucesters, Luckyn Lane, Pipps Hill Ind. Estate SS14 3AY
(01268) 520446

Large selection of melamine, household lines, china, glass, linens, fancy goods, toys, garden furniture and accessories, seasonal lines and novelties, greetings and Christmas cards, paper, stationery. Underwear, clothes, tracksuits, trainers and some food.

'Specialise in ends of ranges: brand name stock clearances, seconds, rejects, ends of line etc.'

Open: Mon–Sat 9–5.30; Sun and Bank Holidays 10–5.
Closed: Christmas and Boxing Days.
Cards: Access, Amex, Switch, Visa.
Cars: Outside shop.
Toilets: Ask if desperate.
Wheelchairs: Easy access, no steps to huge shop.
Changing rooms: Yes.
Teas: Cold drinks, prepacked sandwiches, crisps and sweets.
Groups: Groups welcome to shop, but please phone Mr Cantor first.
Mail order: No.

On industrial estate north-east of Basildon.

From M25 exit 29: take A127 for Southend. Look for A176 Basildon/Billericay exit – at end of slip road go left; take first left, Miles Gray Road. At traffic lights go right; take first left, Luckyn Lane.*

Going towards London on A127: take A176 (Basildon/ Billericay exit). At end of slip road, go straight across on to Miles Gray Road. At traffic lights, go right. Take first left (Luckyn Lane).*

*Shop clearly signed on right.

From town centre: take A176 for Billericay. At large round-about, go right for Pipps Hill; at next roundabout go left; take first left, Luckyn Lane; shop 200 yds on left.

De Bradelei Mill Shops

De Bradelei House, Chapel St DE56 1AP   *(01773) 829830*

Women's clothing: *Jaeger, Windsmoor, Planet, Precis, Berkertex, Genesis, Leslie Fay, Kasper, Liz Claiborne* and other top designers. Children's: *Jeffrey Ohrenstein, Jo Kids.* Men's: *HOM* underwear, shirts, sweaters, swimming trunks; *Wolsey* sweaters, shirts, shorts, casual trousers, *Farah* and *Whitbread* ranges. Shoes for all the family: *Lilley & Skinner, Roland Cartier, Gabor, Hush Puppies, Pierre Cardin* etc.

'Ends of lines and many bargains for all the family. Up to 70% discount in four shops in courtyard setting. Excellent service, friendly staff.'

See our display advertisement inside back cover

Open: Mon–Fri (including Bank Holidays) 9.30–5.30; Sat 9.30–6; Sun 11–5.
Closed: Christmas and New Year's Days.
Cards: Access, Switch, Visa.
Cars: Own car-park.
Toilets: Yes.
Wheelchairs: Easy access, no steps, large shops.
Changing rooms: Yes.
Teas: Safeways coffee shop, tea shop in town.
Groups: Shopping groups welcome, but if over 25 people please phone first.
Transport: Bus nos. R30, 31, 32. Belper BR station.
Mail order: No.

On A6 on southern side of town centre.

From Derby via A6: as you reach Belper, go left at roundabout for Safeway.*

From Heanor via A609: stay on this road downhill to round-about with A6. Go straight over for Safeway.*

From Matlock on A6: keep straight through town, over traffic lights, past bus station on left. At roundabout, go right for Safeway.*

*Pass Shell petrol on right: shop is on right.

BOND STREET COMES TO BICESTER

*Enjoy the opportunity to shop for end-of-season designer
fashions, mens and childrenswear, tableware, shoes and
more, **all on permanent sale at prices reduced from
25%-50%**. Find 48 shops owned by famous British and
International brands, who will be bringing Bond Street style to Bicester Village.
Just off the M40 at Junction 9. For further information call 01869 323200.*

**BICESTER
VILLAGE**

Opening Times: 10am to 6pm Monday to Saturday and Bank Holidays. 11am to 5pm Sunday.

For full details see next page

Bicester Outlet Shopping Village

OX6 2WD
(01869) 323200

End-of-season designer fashions, men's and children's wear, tableware, shoes and much more.

'A wide range of shops owned by famous British and International brands, bringing Bond Street style to Bicester Village. Discounts of 25–50% off retail prices.'

See our display advertisement on previous page

Easy to find on the outskirts of Bicester.
From M40 exit 9: take A41 two miles towards Bicester. At the first roundabout follow signs to Village Retail Park, clearly visible past the superstore.

Open: Mon–Sun (including Bank Holidays) 10–6 (late night Thur to 8).
Closed: Christmas Day.
Cards: All shops accept major credit cards.
Cars: Free parking for 675 cars and 12 coaches.
Toilets: Yes.
Wheelchairs: Easy access to all shops.
Changing rooms: Where applicable.
Teas: Brioche d'Orée.
Groups: Coach parties always welcome.
Transport: Bicester North BR station 15 minutes' walk.

Included in this village are:

320 Aquascutum
(01869) 325943
Men's and women's ready-to-wear.

321 Benetton
(01869) 320030
Full range of Benetton merchandise at discounts from 30%.

322 Big Dog
(01869) 323280
Californian casualwear.

323 Cerruti 1881 Femme
(01869) 325519
Women's ready-to-wear.

324 Clarks
(01869) 325646
Discounted footwear for all the family.

325 Converse
(01869) 325070
Sports shoes and sportswear.

326 Descamps
(01869) 323636
Fine linens and bathroom accessories.

327 Edinburgh Crystal
(01869) 324209
Cut crystal tumblers, decanters, gifts etc.

328 Equator
(01869) 240444
Luggage, bags and leather goods.

329 Fred Perry
(01869) 325504
Men's, women's and children's casual and sportswear.

330 Helly Hansen
(01869) 325944
Men's and women's outdoor clothing.

331 Hico
(01869) 325650
Wide range of bedding: duvets, sheets, pillow cases, cushions etc

332 Hobbs
(01869) 325660
Women's shoes, contemporary ready-to-wear.

333 Hom
(01869) 325400
Men's underwear and swimwear.

334 Jaeger
Men's and women's fashions. Opening November 1995.

335 Jane Shilton
(01869) 325387
Handbags and women's shoes.
336 Jeffrey Rogers
(01869) 323567
Women's fashions.
337 Jigsaw
(01869) 325621
Women's contemporary ready-to-wear.
338 Joan & David
(01869) 323387
Women's and men's designer shoes and ready-to-wear.
339 John Jenkins
(01869) 324300
Crystal and china.
340 John Partridge
(01869) 325332
Country clothing.
341 JoKids
(01869) 324477
Children's clothing (0–10 years).
342 Karen Millen
(01869) 325932
Women's contemporary ready-to-wear.
343 Kids Playfactory
(01869) 323434
Toys and games.
344 Kurt Geiger
(01869) 325410
Women's and men's shoes.
345 Monsoon
(01869) 323286
Ladies' clothing.
346 Museum Merchandise
(01869) 324432
Gifts and cards.
347 Oneida
(01869) 324789
Cutlery and silverware.
348 Osh Kosh B'Gosh
(01869) 322855
Children's wear.
349 Pepe Jeans
(01869) 325378
Casualwear.

350 Price's Candles
(01869) 325520
Candles and gifts.
351 Principles
(01869) 325300
Men's and women's fashions.
352 Racing Green
(01869) 325434
Casualwear.
353 Red/Green
(01869) 323324
Men's and women's ready-to-wear.
354 Sapphire Books
(01869) 325417
Books.
355 Suit Company/Moss Bros
(01869) 324321
Men's wear.
356 The Scotch House
(01869) 323522
Men's and women's classic fashions.
357 TOG 24
(01869) 323278
Golf, outdoor and leisure wear.
358 Triumph
(01869) 325400
Lingerie and swimwear.
359 Villeroy & Boch
(01869) 324646
China and crystal.
360 Warners
(01869) 324401
Ladies' lingerie.
361 Woods of Windsor
(01869) 325307
Fragrances and soaps.
362 Wrangler
(01869) 325225
Jeans, shirts, jackets and T-shirts for all the family.

Merchants Quay

Brighton Marina Village BN2 5UE
(01273) 693636

Over 30 brand names in clothing, shoes, bedding, toiletries, cosmetics, ceramics, housewares, lighting, crystal and luggage.

'The relaxed atmosphere of a Marina is combined with discount retail shopping. Facilities include a variety of pubs and restaurants, a superstore and an eight screen cinema. Many products are at heavily discounted prices.'

See our display advertisement opposite

....

Brighton Marina is on the east side of town, below the high chalk cliffs.

   From Brighton town centre: go east on cliff road (Marine Parade), following signs to Marina.

   From Newhaven via Marine Drive: go left at sign to 'Brighton Marina Village'.

Open: Seven days a week. Shops may vary but most open 10–5 at least.
Closed: Christmas amd Boxing Days.
Cards: All major credit cards.
Cars: Free multi-storey car-park for 2000 cars.
Toilets: Yes.
Wheelchairs: Easy access within the complex.
Changing rooms: Yes, in clothing shops.
Teas: Two pubs and three restaurants.
Groups: Shopping groups very welcome.
Transport: Regular bus services from Brighton BR station.

Included in Merchants Quay are:

364 Bookscene
   (01273) 818719
Discounted books, stationery, jigsaws and posters.

365 Edinburgh Crystal
   (01273) 818702
Cut crystal tumblers, decanters, wine glasses, giftware etc.

366 The Factory Shop Ltd.
   (01273) 818590
Over 30 famous brands of clothing for all the family at discount prices, including *Selfridges, Bruna Cavvalini, Little Levis* and *Dannimac*. Chainstore items include footwear, toiletries, kitchen and tableware.

367 Giovanna
   (01273) 818918
Ladies' fashion clothing and jewellery.

368 Hornsea Pottery
   (01273) 818444
Tableware and giftware at up to 50% off first quality high street prices.

369 TOG 24
   (01273) 818759
Golf, outdoor and leisure wear.

370 Tom Sayers
   (01273) 818705
Designer men's wear.

A GREAT DAY OUT
& SOME GREAT
SAVINGS

M ERCHANTS QUAY AT
BRIGHTON MARINA.
FACTORY OUTLET SHOPPING
INCLUDING CLOTHING,
HOUSEWARES, SHOES,
LUGGAGE, TOILETRIES,

MAJOR SAVINGS ON A WIDE RANGE OF BRANDED GOODS

COSMETICS, TABLEWARE,
CRYSTAL, BEDDING, ARTS,
GIFTWARE, JEWELLERY,
BOOKS AND LOTS, LOTS
MORE.

FREE PARKING FOR OVER 2000 CARS

The Factory Shop
A SALE EVERY DAY

·OPTIONS·
SHOPPING MALL WITH 18 BRAND NAMES

BRAND NAME SALE
SALE SHOPS

ARTS, JEWELLERY, GIFTS

ASDA

PUBS & RESTAURANTS

MGM CINEMAS
8 SCREEN CINEMA

CHANDELRY

OPEN 7 DAYS

MERCHANTS Quay

Factory Outlet Shopping
Brighton Marina

Something for everyone and savings for all

MERCHANTS QUAY, BRIGHTON MARINA VILLAGE, BRIGHTON, EAST SUSSEX BN2 5UF TEL: (01273) 693636

The Factory Shop Ltd.

Straight Street, Broad Plane BS99 7DN   *(0117) 929 7055*

Men's, ladies' and children's clothing, footwear, luggage, toiletries, toys, music, books and new fashion concessions department with famous brand names for ladies, men and children.

'Large stock of chainstore items, all at greatly reduced prices. Deliveries of new stock every week to give an ever changing selection.'

Off the dual carriageway (Temple Way) on the east side of the city centre, by the huge Evening Post building.

Coming into the city with Temple Meads station on your right: at major intersection, go under overpass then right on to dual carriageway, Temple Way. At next intersection go up to round-about (Hilton Hotel on left) and double back. *

Coming south into the city on M32: in city centre, go left into dual carriageway Bond Street (which becomes Temple Way). At intersection, go to roundabout. *

*Pass Evening Post building, go left into Unity Street. Enter Gardiner Haskins car-park. The Factory Shop is part of this complex.

Open: Mon–Sat 9–6; Sun 10–4. Bank Holidays 9–6.
Closed: Christmas Eve, Christmas, Boxing and New Year's Days.
Cards: Access, Switch, Visa.
Cars: In Gardiner Haskins DIY shop car-park (three hours free).
Toilets: In Gardiner Haskins.
Wheelchairs: Ramps for easy access through the Pine Shop.
Changing rooms: Yes.
Teas: In Gardiner Haskins.
Groups: Shopping groups welcome. For organiser/driver incentives please phone.
Transport: Ten minutes' walk from Broadmead Centre.
Mail order: No.

The Factory Shop Ltd.

Barton Business Centre, Barton Road IP32 7BO (01284) 701578

Men's, ladies' and children's clothing, footwear, luggage, toiletries, hardware, household textiles, gifts, bedding, lighting, and new fashion concessions department with famous brand names.

'Large stock of chainstore items, all at greatly reduced prices. Deliveries of new stock every week to give an ever changing selection.'

On the east side of Bury St Edmunds.

From A14 (the old A45T): exit at signs to Bury St Edmunds East and turn towards Moreton Hall Estate. Go straight at first roundabout (Sainsbury's on your right). *

From town centre: follow signs to Ipswich (A14) via A1302 ring road. Go underneath A14 (old A45) and straight at first roundabout with Sainsbury's on right. *

*Go left at second roundabout, then straight at the third and fourth roundabouts. Go downhill and turn left just before the railway bridge. Shop is in second building on right.

Open: Mon–Fri 9.30–5.30; Sat 9–5.30; Sun 11–5.
Closed: Easter Sunday; Christmas, Boxing and New Year's Days.
Cards: Access, Switch, Visa.
Cars: Own large car-park.
Toilets: In town.
Wheelchairs: No steps to large shop.
Changing rooms: Yes.
Teas: Cafés and pubs in town.
Groups: Shopping groups welcome. For organiser/driver incentives please phone.
Transport: 20 minutes' walk from station; 15 minutes from town centre.
Mail order: No.

Boundary Mill Shop – Libra Textiles Ltd.

Burnley Road BB8 8LS   *(01282) 865229*

Vast range of ladies' and men's quality garments from all over Europe. Over 100 brands including *Alexon, Austin Reed, Christian Dior, Dannimac, Dash, Double Two, Farah, Laura Ashley, Lyle & Scott, Polo Ralph Lauren, Timberland, Windsmoor, Wolsey, Wrangler.* Shoes and boots by *Bally. Warners, Charnos* and *Gossard* lingerie. Home furnishings from *Coloroll, Dorma* and *Laura Ashley.*

'One of the largest mill stores of its kind in the country.'

A few yards off the A56, between Colne and Nelson, and beside Asda.

From Colne: go south-west towards Nelson, under railway bridge and follow signs to Whitewalls Industrial Estate/Superstores. Turn left in front of Asda.

From Nelson coming north-east on A56: pass Jet petrol then Golden Ball Inn on left; at mini-roundabout, go left into Corporation Street. Boundary Mill is on left.

From the end of M65: follow signs to Whitewalls Industrial Estate/Superstores. Turn left in front of Asda; Boundary Mill is beside Asda.

Open: Mon–Fri 10-6; Sat and Bank Holidays 10–5; Sunday 11–5.
Closed: Christmas Day.
Cards: Access, Mastercard, Switch, Visa.
Cars: Large car-park on all sides; reserved coach area.
Toilets: Yes.
Wheelchairs: Easy access to vast shop with lift to first floor.
Changing rooms: Yes.
Teas: BB's coffee shop within main shop; Bannisters Restaurant at rear for meals.
Groups: Welcome to shop.
Transport: Main Nelson–Colne bus route, two minutes' walk from Asda bus stop.
Mail order: No.

The Factory Shop Ltd.

South Green NR19 1PP   *(01362) 691868*

Wide selection of clothing and footwear for all the family. Good range of branded bedding, towels, toiletries and fancy goods. Also shoes and pottery.

'Large stock of chainstore items, all at greatly reduced prices. Deliveries of new stock every week to give an ever changing selection.'

About 15 minutes' walking distance from the town centre.

From the centre: follow the 'A47 bypass' sign along London Road. At the traffic lights with Texas DIY on the near right, turn right towards 'A1075 Watton' then right again to 'South Green Industrial Estate'. The shop is 150 yds on the right.

Open: Mon–Sat 9–5.
Closed: Bank Holidays (but phone to check). Christmas, Boxing and New Year's Days.
Cards: Access, Delta, Switch, Visa.
Cars: Own car-park.
Toilets: In town centre.
Wheelchairs: Easy access, no steps, but not advisable on busy Saturdays.
Changing rooms: Yes.
Teas: In town centre.
Groups: Shopping groups welcome. For organiser/driver incentives please phone.
Transport: Bus no. 794 to town centre, then 15 minutes' walk.
Mail order: No.

The Factory Shop Ltd.
Empire Buildings, Main Street CA22 2BD
(01946) 820434

Clothing and footwear for all the family. Good range of branded bedding, towels, toiletries, pottery, lighting and fancy goods. *Lee Cooper* concession. New fashion concessions department with famous brand names for women.

'Large stock of chainstore items, all at greatly reduced prices. Deliveries of new stock every week to give an ever changing selection.'

....

In the town centre beside Wyndham School (signposted).

Turn into the side road immediately beside the town hall (with magnificent clocktower) and almost opposite tourist information centre. Go to end of that road and shop is clearly signposted.

Open: Mon–Sat 9–5;
also in December: Sunday.
Closed: Bank Holidays;
Christmas, Boxing and
New Year's Days.
Cards: Access, Switch, Visa.
Cars: In factory car-park.
Toilets: Ask if desperate.
Wheelchairs: Easy access
to large shop.
Changing rooms: Yes.
Teas: In town.
Groups: Shopping groups
welcome. For organiser/driver
incentives please phone.
Transport: Buses from
Whitehaven.
Mail order: No.

Brooks Mill
South Lane HX5 0HO
(01422) 377337

Direct from manufacturers: large range of quality ladies' and men's fashions, footwear and branded household linens, all at discount prices.

'Toddlers' play area and baby change facilities.'

....

On the uphill side of town centre.

From all directions: go into town centre. From roundabout with Leo's supermarket, exit for M62/Aynley's Industrial Estate. Turn right (opposite Esso petrol on left) in front of Kwik Save. Huge mill is clearly marked, 50 yds on left.

Open: Mon–Sat 9.30–5.30;
Sun 10–5.30.
Closed: Christmas and
Boxing Days only.
Cards: Access, Switch, Visa.
Cars: Own car-park.
Toilets: Yes.
Wheelchairs: Easy access to
huge shop.
Changing rooms: Yes.
Teas: Coffee shop serving
meals, snacks, teas and cakes.
Seats 50.
Groups: Shopping groups
welcome. Please contact general
manager Vanessa Towne.
Transport: Local buses.

With such tempting prices on so many top brands, you'll be glad the car park's so handy.

At Designer Outlet Village, Cheshire Oaks you'll find around 30 individual stores selling shoes to glassware, sportswear to electrical goods. Together with a great choice of women's, men's and children's fashions.

They're all top brands. And all at unbelievably good prices. So come along soon. It's a shopping experience you simply can't afford to miss.

McArthur Glen
DESIGNER OUTLET VILLAGE™
CHESHIRE OAKS

The brand new way of shopping.

OPENING TIMES:
10am-6pm Mon-Wed and Sat. 10am-8pm Thurs and Fri. 11am-5pm, Sunday and Bank Holidays.
Cheshire Oaks is located at Junction 10 off the M53, a mile from the intersection with the M56.
FOR MORE INFORMATION CALL 0345 140 140.

For full details see next page

McArthur Glen, Designer Outlet Village

Cheshire Oaks Business Park, Kinsey Road L65 9JJ
(0345) 140140

Over 60 individual stores selling top brand names like *Paul Costelloe, Viyella, Nike, Timberland* and *Levi's*. Women's, men's and children's fashions, casualwear, sportswear, footwear, glassware, electrical goods and books.

'Discounts of 30% or more off retail prices.'

See our display advertisement on previous page

....

Easy to find, 6 miles north of Chester city centre and a short distance south of Ellesmere Port.

From M53 exit 10: follow signs to Cheshire Oaks Business Park. This huge new development is next to Sainsbury's, with the entrance on the roundabout.

From Runcorn/Liverpool direction on the M56, follows signs to North Wales (this brings you to M53 exit 10), then as above.

Open: Mon–Sat 10–6; Sun and Bank Holidays 1–4.
Closed: Christmas Day.
Cards: All shops accept major credit cards.
Cars: Free parking for over 800 cars, and coaches.
Toilets: Yes.
Wheelchairs: Easy access to entire shopping area.
Changing rooms: In clothes shops.
Teas: Site includes Garfunkel's and McDonald's restaurants and coffee bar.
Groups: Coach parties always welcome. For group bookings please phone (0151) 356 7932 for details.
Transport: Buses from Ellesmere Port.

Included in this village are:

378 Acced
(0151) 357 1579
Men's and women's fashions.

379 Benetton
(0151) 357 3131
Full range of Benetton merchandise at discounts from 30%.

380 Big L
(0151) 356 8484
Levi's jeans and casualwear.

381 Catamini
(0151) 357 1521
Children's wear.

382 Collective
(0151) 357 3249
Women's fashions.

383 Dim
(0151) 357 2585
Ladies' hosiery, lingerie and accessories.

384 Edinburgh Crystal
(0151) 357 3661
Cut crystal tumblers, decanters, wine glasses, giftware etc.

385 Eminence
(0151) 357 1562
Lingerie.

386 Equator
(0151) 357 3248
Luggage, bags and leather goods.

387 Famous Footwear
(0151) 357 1512
Footwear.

388 Fred Perry
(0151) 357 1383
Men's, women's and children's casual and sportswear.

389 Fruit of the Loom
(0151) 355 6169
Casualwear.

390 James Barry
(0151) 357 1416
Quality men's suits, jackets, trousers and accessories.

391 Jeffrey Rogers
(0151) 355 6797
Women's fashions.

392 John Partridge
(0151) 357 1729
Country clothing.

393 JoKids
(0151) 357 1404
Children's clothing (0–10 years).

394 Kurt Geiger
(0151) 357 1793
Women's and men's shoes.

395 Liz Claiborne
(0151) 357 3271
Women's wear, separates and accessories.

396 Nike
(0151) 357 1252
Sportswear.

397 Paco
(0151) 357 1383
Casualwear.

398 Paul Costelloe
(0151) 357 1681
Women's fashions.

399 Principles
(0151) 357 1033
Men's and women's fashions.

400 Remington
(0151) 357 2477
Table cutlery, scissors, kitchen and pocket knives and small electrical appliances.

401 Sapphire Books
(0151) 357 3889
Books.

402 Scotch House
(0151) 357 3203
Men's and women's classic fashions.

403 Suits You
(0151) 355 6701
Men's wear.

404 Tie Rack
(0151) 355 6166
Fashion accessories.

405 Timberland
(0151) 357 1359
Casualwear.

406 Viyella
(0151) 357 2627
Ladies' clothing in classic styles and fashions made up with end-of-line fabrics.

Darley Mill Centre
Darley HG3 2Q0
(01423) 780857

Huge range of bedding, household linens and soft furnishings. Gifts, crafts and books. Country clothing. Pine and cane furniture. Shop on three large floors.

'This former corn mill, with existing water-wheel, has been converted into a huge mill shop.'

Nine miles west of Harrogate, just north of the A59 (Harrogate–Skipton road), well signposted from this main road.

Turn north off the A59 and follow signs. As you go downhill into Darley, this large, well marked mill is on the left.

Open: Mon–Sat 9.30–5.30; Sun 10–5.30.
Closed: Christmas and Boxing Day only.
Cards: Access, Switch, Visa.
Cars: Own car-park at rear.
Toilets: Yes.
Wheelchairs: Access to restaurant only.
Changing rooms: Yes.
Teas: Own restaurant for coffees, teas, snacks and lunches.
Groups: Welcome any time. If you require a meal, please book with Christine Clunes, general manager.
Transport: Buses run from Harrogate town centre.

For full details see next page

Jackson's Landing

Hartlepool Marina TS24 0XM
(01429) 866989

Jackson's Landing is the north-east's only purpose-built factory outlet mall. Well known designer label fashions and household goods within their units.

'Perfect surplus stock and discounted lines. Plus factory seconds all at unbelievably low prices direct from the manufacturers. Up to 60% off normal retail prices on quality brand name goods.'

See our display advertisement on previous page

In dock area north of town centre.

From A179 southbound: follow signs for town centre and Hartlepool Marina. Jackson's Landing is on the left as you pass the docks.

From the A689 northbound: go through town centre following signs to Hartlepool Marina, go over the railway bridge and Jackson's Landing is on the right past the Heritage Centre.

Open: Mon–Sat 10–6; Sun 11–5.
Closed: Christmas Day.
Cards: Major credit and debit cards.
Cars: Free parking for 2500 cars and 10 coaches.
Toilets: Yes.
Wheelchairs: Automatic doors, lifts, toilets; wheelchairs available.
Changing rooms: Yes.
Teas: Full catering facilities on site.
Groups: Shopping groups always welcome, incentives available; contact centre manager.
Transport: Hartlepool BR station 10 minutes' walk.

Included in Jackson's Landing are:

409 Benetton
(01429) 862123
Benetton merchandise at discounts from 30%.

410 Bookscene
(01429) 861223
Discounted books, stationery, jigsaws, posters.

411 Charles Clinkards
(01429) 866939
Discounted quality footwear.

412 Chas N Whillans
(01429) 273994
Knitwear including lambswool & cashmere.

413 Edinburgh Crystal
(01429) 234335
Cut crystal tumblers, decanters, gifts etc.

414 Equator
(01429) 235998
Luggage, bags and leather goods.

415 Hallmark
(01429) 275680
Cards and gifts at half normal price.

416 Honey
(01429) 260488
Knitwear, T-shirts and leggings including sizes up to 24.

417 James Barry
(01429) 260364
Quality men's suits, jackets and accessories.

418 JoKids
(01429) 862638
Children's clothing (0–10 years).

419 Royal Brierley
(01429) 865600
Hand-made crystal, eg bowls, vases, gifts etc.

420 TOG 24
(01429) 866103
Outdoor and leisure wear, Mileta golfwear.

421 Tom Sayers
(01429) 861439
Designer men's wear.

422 Toyworld
(01429) 866606
Major branded toys at low prices.

423 Treasure Island
(01429) 263000
Collectable teapots, lighters, pens, T-shirts, polo and sweat shirts with local designs.

424 Wrangler
(01429) 273488
Jeans, shirts, jackets. T-shirts for the family.

Winfields

Hazel Mill, Blackburn Road BB4 5DB
(01706) 227916

A vast range of discounted footwear and clothing for men, women and children, accessories and ex-catalogue goods. Manufacturers and retailers of slippers.

'Perfects, seconds and clearance lines in a wide variety of quality goods at value-for-money prices; many items are at half the usual high street price.'

....

About a mile north of Haslingden, on the A680.

From the roundabout where the A680 and A56 (extension of the M66 from Manchester) join: turn south towards Haslingden. After a few yards, Winfield's entrance is clearly marked on left.

From Haslingden: take A680 north for Accrington. As you leave town, look for Winfields clearly marked on your right. The drive entrance is further on right, just before roundabout.

Open: Mon–Fri 10–5.30 (Thur late night to 8); Sat 9–5.30; Sun 11–5.
Closed: Christmas Day.
Cards: Access, Switch, Visa.
Cars: Free parking for over 400 cars and coaches.
Toilets: Yes, with baby changing facilities.
Wheelchairs: Easy access to all departments, special parking.
Changing rooms: Yes.
Teas: 174 seater cafeteria with high chair facilities and a children's menu. Also takeaway service and a weekend B-B-Q.
Groups: Shopping groups welcome at all times. No need to book.
Transport: Bus nos. 4 (Accrington–Bacup), 464 (Accrington–Rochdale), 701 (Clitheroe–Manchester).

The Galleria

Comet Way AL10 0XR
(01707) 278301

Wide range of clothing for all the family, jeans, high fashion wear, children's wear, outdoor wear, footwear, household items and china. Names include *TK Maxx, Major Oak* men's wear, *B52* jeans, *Jacadi, Stefanel, Shelfstore* and many more over coming months.

'This newly redesigned off price shopping mall contains a mixture of factory shops and retailers offering significant savings on full price. Please phone for complete list of shops. Other facilities include 9-screen cinema, dry-ice skating rink and toddlers' activity centre.'

....

Easy to see, this purpose built shopping centre spans the A1 at Hatfield.

Driving north or south on A1: turn off at signs to Hatfield then follow signs to The Galleria.

Open: Mon–Fri 10–8; Sat 10–6; Sun and Bank Holidays 11–5.
Closed: Christmas and Boxing Days.
Cards: Most shops accept credit cards.
Cars: Free surface and multi-storey car-park.
Toilets: Yes, including for disabled. Parent & baby facilities.
Wheelchairs: Easy access, and lifts, to all areas. Wheelchairs (from Shopmobility) on loan.
Changing rooms: Yes.
Teas: McDonald's, Mama Amalfi, Deep Pan Pizza, self-service café.
Groups: Coach parties welcome. Please phone in advance.
Transport: Trains (King's Cross to Hatfield BR station). Local buses from Hatfield centre.

Ponden Mill

Colne Road, Stanbury BD22 0HR
(01535) 643500

Huge range of bedding, household linens and soft furnishings. Gifts, crafts and books. Wide range of country clothing.

'Both perfects and seconds are available from this large converted mill.'

Nearly 2 miles west of Haworth, on the B6144 to Colne.
From Haworth: go through the village of Stanbury, then continue for nearly 1/2 mile, passing the Old Silent Inn on the left. The mill is very conspicuous, down the hill on the left.
From the Colne direction: continue along the road towards Haworth for about 5 miles after you have turned off the A6068 (Colne–Gisburn road). This large mill is easily visible on right.

Open: Mon–Sat 9–5.30; Sun 10–5.30. Bank Holidays.
Closed: Christmas and Boxing Days only.
Cards: Access, Switch, Visa.
Cars: Ample space in own car-park.
Toilets: Yes.
Wheelchairs: Easy access to large ground floor (for bedding) but not upstairs.
Changing rooms: Yes.
Teas: Own restaurant on first floor seats 60.
Groups: Shopping groups welcome. To book please write to or phone Mrs Margaret Hodgson, general manager.
Transport: Daily buses to Stanbury village then 1/2 mile walk. Buses pass the mill on Saturdays only.

The Factory Shop Ltd.

51 Fleet Street PE12 7AU
(01406) 422180

Clothing and footwear for all the family. Toiletries, cosmetics, luggage and bags. Good range of branded bedding and towels, housewares, kitchenware and toys. Several concessions selling quality merchandise.

'Large stock of chainstore items, all at greatly reduced prices. Deliveries of new stock every week to give an ever changing selection.'

On the east side of town, about half a mile from the town centre on the site of the old bus garage.
From the north on A17 and the west on A151 follow signs into Holbeach. At the only traffic lights in town take the B1515 towards Fleet Hargate and Kings Lynn. The shop is about half a mile on the left, set back from the road 10 yds after the sign pointing to the right to Holbeach Community Centre.
From Kings Lynn on A17 turn on to B1515 for Holbeach. Pass the Burmah petrol station on left and the shop is about 500 yards on the right, set back from the road.

Open: Mon–Sat 10–5; Sun 10–4.
Closed: Christmas and Boxing Days.
Cards: Access, Switch, Visa.
Cars: Ample free car-parking.
Toilets: No.
Wheelchairs: Good access into and around shop.
Changing rooms: Yes.
Teas: Cafés and restaurants in Holbeach.
Groups: Shopping groups welcome. For organiser/driver incentives please phone.
Transport: Buses from King's Lynn, Boston, and Spalding.
Mail order: No.

The Factory Shop Ltd.
Old Engine Shed, Consort Way East RH6 7AV
(01293) 823883

Men's, ladies' and children's clothing, footwear, luggage, toiletries, hardware, household textiles, gifts, bedding, lighting and new fashion concessions department with famous brand names for ladies and men.

'Large stock of chainstore items, all at greatly reduced prices. Deliveries of new stock every week to give an ever changing selection.'

....

Close to the town centre.
   Find the station. With the station on your left: go over railway line into High Street; take first right, Consort Way East. The shop is 200 yds on the right (after Do-It-All) in a converted engine shed.

Open: Mon–Sat 9–5.30; Sun 10–4.
Closed: Christmas, Boxing and New Year's Days.
Cards: Access, Switch, Visa.
Cars: Own car-park.
Toilets: In town centre.
Wheelchairs: Easy access – ramps and lifts to both floors of huge shop.
Changing rooms: Yes.
Teas: In town centre.
Groups: Shopping groups welcome. For organiser/driver incentives please phone.
Transport: Two minutes' walk from Horley town centre.
Mail order: No.

Hornsea Freeport
Rolston Road HU18 1UT
(01964) 534211

Over 20 top high street names for a wide selection of men's, women's and children's clothes (including suits, trousers, dresses, blouses, coats, knitwear, jeans and leisure wear), crystal, jewellery, books etc. Names include *Aquascutum, The Factory Shop, Simpson, Edinburgh Crystal, Claude Gill, Damart, Hornsea Pottery, Wrangler, Alexon, Laura Ashley, Jumpers, Windsmoor, Warners, Jersey Pearl* and *Dartington.*

'These shops are located in a large leisure park which also includes Freeport car collection, Butterfly World, Birds of Prey, model village, outdoor adventure playground, Bee World and Neptune's Kingdom. Free admission to site and shops. Other attractions charged separately or Day/Family ticket.'

....

Find your way to the small town of Hornsea. This large retail and leisure complex is well signposted, on the B1242 which runs south along the coast.

Open: Mon–Sun 10–5 (10–6 school holidays).
Closed: Christmas Eve, Christmas and Boxing Days.
Cards: Access, Switch, Visa.
Cars: Extensive free parking for cars and coaches.
Toilets: Yes.
Wheelchairs: Easy access to grounds and each shop.
Changing rooms: Yes.
Teas: Restaurant for meals and light refreshments, snack facilities, ice-cream parlours.
Groups: Shopping groups welcome. Coaches please book in on arrival – incentive scheme for 20+.
Transport: Buses from Hull, Beverley and Bridlington to Hornsea.

The Factory Shop Ltd.
Lawkholme Lane BD21 3JR
(01535) 611703

Men's, ladies' and children's clothing, footwear, luggage, toiletries, hardware, household textiles, gifts, bedding, lighting, and new fashion concessions department with famous brand names for ladies.

'Large stock of chainstore items, all at greatly reduced prices. Deliveries of new stock every week to give an ever changing selection.'

Close to the town centre.

From the north (Skipton/Addingham): follow 'Town centre' signs, go over pedestrian lights, keep going. Go left (Alice Street), 50 yds before the traffic lights.*

From Halifax: go towards town centre, through first lights, right at roundabout, left at the lights into town centre. Go over next lights, take next right (in front of Keighley News), Alice Street.*

*Shop is at far end on left.

From Bingley: stay on A650, do not turn left for 'Town centre A6035' at roundabout but go straight for Skipton A650. Go left opposite Shell petrol station into Lawkholme Lane. Pass Peter Black factory on right. Shop entrance is on right, round the corner in Alice St.

Open: Mon–Sat 9.30–5; Bank Holidays 10–4.
Closed: Christmas, Boxing and New Year's Days.
Cards: Access, Switch, Visa.
Cars: In street; company car–park.
Toilets: In town.
Wheelchairs: Huge shop, easy access.
Changing rooms: Yes.
Teas: In town.
Groups: Shopping groups welcome. For organiser/driver incentives please phone.
Transport: 2 minutes' walk from the centre of Keighley.
Mail order: No.

K Village

Netherfield LA9 7DA
(01539) 721892

Under-cover mall with factory shop units operated by *Jumpers, Crabtree & Evelyn, Dartington Crystal, Denby Pottery, K Shoes Full Price Shop, K Shoes Factory Shop, The Sports Factory, The Baggage Factory and the Village Gift Shop.*

'Shop at your leisure in undercover shopping mall and visit our unique Heritage Centre.'

See our display advertisement inside front cover

....

On the A65 on south-east side of town.

From town centre: take A6 south to M6. When you see signs to A65, follow these until you see K Village on right. Entrance at far end of complex.

From south via A65: as you come into Kendal, clearly sign-posted complex is on left shortly after you reach river (on left).

From A591(T) northbound (Kendal bypass): take A6 for Kendal and turn right at first traffic lights signpost to K Factories. Take first left after bridge then first left into car-park. (This is quickest way from M6 exit 36.)

Open: Mon–Fri 9.30–6; Sat 9–6; Sun 11–5; Bank Holidays 9–6.
Closed: Christmas Day.
Cards: Access, Switch, Visa.
Cars: Large free car and coach park outside shop; spaces for disabled drivers.
Toilets: Yes, including for disabled; baby changing facilities.
Wheelchairs: Most entrances and exits have ramps for wheelchairs and shopping aisles are wide enough for easy access.
Teas: Leith's at Food Factory Restaurant. Sandwich bar.
Groups: Coach parties welcome, concessions for drivers and organisers. £1 voucher per passenger towards purchases in K Shoes Factory Shop. Play area for children.
Transport: Ten minutes' walk from town centre or bus route 41/41A.

Included in this village are:

433 Crabtree and Evelyn
(01539) 735595
Luxury foods, toiletries and gifts.

434 Dartington Crystal
(01539) 734263
Hand made crystal.

435 Denby Pottery
(01539) 735418
Pottery products from lamps to dinner services.

436 Jumpers
(01539) 723990/732482
Knitwear and casual clothing for men and women.

437 K Shoes Factory Shop, Sports Factory and Baggage Factory
(01539) 721892
Extensive range of quality shoes, sandals, boots, walking boots, slippers, trainers, handbags, luggage, sports clothing, sports equipment, outdoor clothing, accessories and gifts.

438 K Shoes Full Price
(01539) 724041
Huge selection of the latest K Shoes. All items here at full price.

The Factory Shop Ltd.
Lancaster Leisure Park, Wyresdale Road LA1 3LB
(01524) 846079

Clothing and footwear for all the family. Toiletries, cosmetics, luggage and bags. Good range of branded bedding and towels. Housewares and kitchenware. Posters and toys. Full range of *Hornsea* pottery and giftware. New fashion concessions department with famous brand names including *J.J. Sloane*.

'Deliveries of new stock every week to give an ever changing selection. Antique centre, animals, children's attractions and ride a train. Golf driving range and club house. Indoor children's play area. Site shops and restaurant areas free – other attractions charged individually.'

On the east side of town.
  From the A6: go into town and follow signs to the Ashton Memorial; turn right when you see sign for 'Cattle Market'. Pass the abattoir and this Leisure Park is on the right.
  From the M6: go into the city centre; from here follow signs to 'Ashton Memorial', pass it and take next left downhill.

Open: Mon–Sat 10–5; Sun 11–5.
Closed: Christmas and Boxing Days.
Cards: Access, Eurocard, Switch, Visa.
Cars: Ample free car and coach parking.
Toilets: On the leisure site.
Wheelchairs: Good access into and around the shop.
Changing rooms: Yes.
Teas: Café and restaurant on leisure site.
Groups: Shopping groups welcome. For organiser/driver incentives please phone.
Transport: Bus no. 253 bus from Lancaster bus station.
Mail order: No.

The Factory Shop Ltd.
Unit 22, Britannia Pavilion, Albert Dock
(0151) 709 3316

Men's, ladies' and children's clothing, footwear, luggage, toiletries, hardware, household textiles, gifts, bedding, lighting, and new fashion concessions department with famous brand names for ladies.

'Large stock of chainstore items, all at greatly reduced prices. Deliveries of new stock every week to give an ever changing selection.'

Easy to find in the centre of Liverpool.
  From all directions: follow signs to Albert dock. This shop is on the left side of the dock.

Open: Mon–Sat 10–5.30; Sun 11.30–5.30. Bank Holidays.
Closed: Christmas Day.
Cards: Access, Switch, Visa.
Cars: Huge car-park in Albert Dock.
Toilets: In Albert Dock.
Wheelchairs: No step to ground floor; stairs to upper floor.
Changing rooms: Yes, including large cubicles for disabled.
Teas: In Albert Dock.
Groups: Shopping groups welcome. For organiser/driver incentives please phone.
Transport: Buses every twenty minutes from city centre, or 10 minute walk from city centre.
Mail order: No.

The Factory Shop Ltd.
Mart Road TA24 5BJ
(01643) 705911

Large selection of men's, ladies' and children's clothing and footwear. Luggage, toiletries, hardware, household textiles, gifts, bedding, lighting and new fashion concessions department with famous brand names. Books and greetings cards. Leather jackets for men and women.

'Large stock of chainstore items, all at greatly reduced prices. Deliveries of new stock every week to give an ever changing selection.'

....

A short walk off the seafront, at the back of the station.
  From all directions: probably easiest to follow signs to station. With station on your left, go along Warren Street which becomes The Avenue. *

  From the seafront: go into The Avenue. *

  ***After a few yards go left into Glenmore Road; take third left (Mark Road): shop is on right, opposite Jewsons.**

Open: Mon-Sat 9.30–5.30; Sun 11–5.
Closed: Easter Sunday, Christmas, Boxing and New Year's Days.
Cards: Access, Delta, Switch, Visa.
Cars: Own large car-park.
Toilets: Yes.
Wheelchairs: No steps to large shop. Wide aisles.
Changing rooms: Yes.
Teas: In town.
Groups: Shopping groups welcome. For organiser/driver incentives please phone.
Transport: Any bus to Minehead; West Somerset Railway along coast from Watchet and inland towards Taunton.
Mail order: No.

The Factory Shop Ltd.
Commercial Street LS1 6EY
(0113) 253 1024

Men's, and ladies' clothing, footwear, luggage, toiletries, hardware, household textiles, gifts, lighting and new fashion concessions department with famous brand names. Good range of branded bedding.

'Large stock of chainstore items, all at greatly reduced prices. Deliveries of new stock every week to give an ever changing selection.'

....

Easy to find in the centre of Morley, in a small street parallel to the main road through town. Turn off this main road opposite the Town Hall and then take the first left. The shop is 50 yards on the left.

Open: Mon–Fri 9.30–5; Sat 9–5.
Closed: Bank Holidays; Christmas, Boxing and New Year's Days. Easter Tuesday.
Cards: Access, Switch, Visa.
Cars: Free car-park few yards away.
Toilets: In town.
Wheelchairs: Unfortunately no access: four steps to ground floor and flight of stairs to upper floor.
Changing rooms: Yes.
Teas: Cafés and pubs in town.
Groups: Shopping groups welcome. For organiser/driver incentives please phone.
Transport: Couple of minutes' walk from town centre.
Mail order: No.

Oswaldtwistle Mills

Moscow Mill, Collier Street BB5 3DF
(01254) 871025

Two adjacent shops for wide range of pottery; full range of domestic cleaning products; books, stationery, giftware, curios. Wide range of textiles including exclusive range of fabrics woven on premises – Egyptian cotton, household textiles; also crafts, curios, antiques.

'Perfects and seconds on sale.'

....

On the north-east side of Oswaldtwistle.
  From Blackburn Road (A679, main Accrington–Blackburn road): go south at traffic lights in Church into Market Street (B6231) to Oswaldtwistle.*
  From Accrington: go west on A679 for Blackburn. In Church, go over first traffic lights then left at second lights into Market Street (B6231) for Oswaldtwistle.*
  *This becomes Union Road. Go under railway; opposite Total garage on right, go left (Collier Street). Shop clearly visible 100 yds ahead.
  From southerly end of town (Union Street): keep straight along main road. Opposite Total petrol on left, go right. Shop clearly visible 100 yds ahead.

Open: Mon–Sat 9–5; Sun 10-5; Bank Holidays as normal.
Closed: Christmas and Boxing Days.
Cards: Access, Visa.
Cars: In own car-park, Moscow Mill Street.
Toilets: Yes; for disabled too.
Wheelchairs: Easy access, no steps, huge warehouse. Wheelchairs available.
Teas: Own Pavilion Coffee Shop open 7 days a week.
Tours: Shopping groups and coaches welcome by prior arrangement. Weaving shed tours by appointment. New Stockley's Visitor Centre - see traditional sweets made. Soon - Textile Time Tunnel.
Transport: Hyndburn circular bus stops across road.
Mail order: Yes.
Catalogue: Swatches of fabrics woven in this mill.

The Factory Shop Ltd.

New Road WR10 1BV
(01386) 556467

Huge range of pottery, footwear, houseware, bedding, lighting, clothing, toiletries, luggage, basketware and leisurewear. New fashion concessions department with famous brand names on first floor.

'Large stock of chainstore items, all at greatly reduced prices. Deliveries of new stock every week to give an ever changing selection.'

....

By the old Infants School close to town centre.
  From Upton-on-Severn via A4140: pass Esso petrol station on right then take second right (New Road).
  From Worcester on A44: shortly after you enter town, go right on to A4104 for Upton.*
  From Evesham and town centre: follow A44 towards Worcester; go left on to A4104 towards Upton.*
  *Pass BP petrol station on left then take second left (New Road).
  Shop is on right just before New Road bends sharp left.

Open: Mon–Sat 9–5; Sun 10.30–4.30.
Closed: Christmas and Boxing Days.
Cards: Access, Visa.
Cars: Own free car-parks in front and rear of shop.
Toilets: Yes.
Wheelchairs: Easy access to spacious shop on ground floor. Steps to first floor.
Changing rooms: Yes.
Teas: Own coffee shop; cafés in Pershore.
Groups: Shopping groups welcome. For organiser/driver incentives please phone.
Transport: Under 5 minutes' walk from town centre.
Mail order: No.

Peel Mill

Prince Street BL0 9BB
(01706) 822800

Linens, country clothing, outdoor jackets, knitwear, sleeping bags, clothing for outdoor pursuits, books, candles, unusual crafts and gifts, greeting cards and wrapping paper, coffee beans, preserves and biscuits in cookshop area.

....

About 250 yds from the station.

From the only traffics light in town: go downhill towards East Lancs Railway (brown sign). At the bottom of the hill turn right past The Railway Hotel, just before level crossing.*

From M66 exit 1: aim for Ramsbottom and East Lancs Railway. On slip road go left at first traffic lights; proceed into town, go over level crossing, take first left.*

*Take first right and the mill is on the left hand corner of the T-junction.

Open: Mon–Sat 9.30–5.30; Sun 11–5.
Closed: Christmas and Boxing Days.
Cards: Access, Switch, Visa.
Cars: Alongside building.
Toilets: Yes, including for disabled.
Wheelchairs: No steps.
Changing rooms: Yes.
Teas: 70 seat restaurant.
Groups: No factory tours. Coach parties please book in advance with Jo Terry.
Transport: Steam train at weekends, main bus stop at all times.
Mail order: No.

The Factory Shop Ltd.

5 North Street HG4 1JV
(01765) 601156

Men's and ladies' clothing, footwear, handbags, holdalls, purses, toiletries, hardware, household textiles, gifts, bedding and lighting. Assorted hardback books.

'The manageress, Mrs Pandora Heap, is happy to open the shop out of hours for shopping groups. Please phone her to arrange. Wide range of goods at significantly reduced prices. Deliveries of new stock every week to give an ever changing selection.'

....

Close to the centre of town.

From Harrogate going north via the A61: keep going straight to T-junction with traffic lights in town; turn right, then left into Market Square and again go straight into Fishergate, which becomes North Street. Cearly visible shop is shortly on right.

From Thirsk or Masham: go south towards the town centre on the A61. After the pedestrian lights, this shop is 150 yds on the left, just before the start of the one-way system.

Open: Mon–Sat 9–5; Bank Holidays 11–4.
Closed: Christmas, Boxing and New Year's Days.
Cards: Access, Switch, Visa.
Cars: Market Square and town car-parks nearby.
Toilets: In market square.
Wheelchairs: Easy access.
Changing rooms: Yes.
Teas: Nearby cafés and pubs in town.
Groups: Shopping groups welcome. For organiser/driver incentives please phone.
Transport: Bus no. 36 from Harrogate.
Mail order: No.

Lightwater Village Factory Outlets

North Stainley HG4 3HT
(01765) 635321

Large complex of retail and factory outlets with wide range of branded ladies' wear including blouses, skirts, suits, dresses, lingerie, outerwear, shoes and accessories: *Country Vogue, Windsmoor, Planet, Precis*. Men's wear from *Lee Cooper* jeans to *James Barry* formal wear. Shoes, jewellery, perfumery, home furnishings, *Edinburgh Crystal* glass, *Hornsea* pottery, seasonal shop; toys and bookshop. Garden centre.

'Next to Lightwater Valley Theme Park, the north's action attraction, home to many record breaking rollercoasters – the Ultimate and The Rat; over 100 rides and attractions and a great day out.'

Three miles north of Ripon in North Yorkshire on the A6108. The park is well signposted and clearly visible.

Open: 10–5 (up to 6.30 depending on time of year). Please phone to check closing time.
Closed: Christmas Day only.
Cards: Access, Connect, Switch, Visa.
Cars: Ample free parking for 4,000 cars and 120 coaches.
Toilets: Yes.
Wheelchairs: Easy access.
Changing rooms: Yes.
Teas: Own restaurant, coffee shop and many snack bars. The Yorkshire Larder sells wholesome country foods, freshly baked bread, confectionery, wine, meat. Also huge cheese shop and delicatessen.
Groups: All welcome.
Transport: No.
Mail order: Yes.
Catalogue: Christmas hampers only.

The Factory Shop Ltd.

The Fashion Wearhouse, Corporation Street CV21 2DM
(01788) 542253

Men's, ladies' and children's clothing, footwear, luggage, handbags and accessories, toiletries, hardware, household textiles, gifts, bedding, lighting, and new fashion concessions department with famous brand names.

'Large stock of chainstore items, all at greatly reduced prices. Deliveries of new stock every week to give an ever changing selection.'

Not far from town centre.
From M6 exit 1: take A426 south for Rugby town centre. Follow A426 into town centre, passing Tesco on left and retail park on right. At next roundabout go left, follow signs for Town Centre. At next roundabout take third exit, continuing on dual carriageway until you reach the NCP: you see the Fashion Wearhouse on right. Follow one-way system and double back down dual carriageway.
From town centre on foot: pass the Co-op towards the dual carriageway. As you approach pedestrian crossing, you see the Fashion Wearhouse on right.

Open: Mon–Sat 10–6; Sunday and Bank Holidays 11–5.
Closed: Easter Day, Christmas and Boxing Days.
Cards: Access, Switch, Visa.
Cars: Large on-site car-park.
Toilets: No.
Wheelchairs: No steps into huge shop on ground floor. Ramps to first level. Steps to second level. Checkout and changing rooms suitable for wheelchairs.
Changing rooms: Yes.
Teas: Tea shops, cafés in Rugby.
Groups: Shopping groups welcome. For organiser/driver incentives please phone.
Transport: Buses from town centre. Railway station 15 minutes' walk.
Mail order: No.

Charterhouse has quality clothing and footwear for all the family with genuine savings on regular store prices. We have substantial investments in manufacturing units both in the UK and overseas and a successful record of importing from across the world for the past 25 years.

Coupled with excellent facilities its no wonder we recieve hundreds of customer comments:

"On my first visit to Charterhouse I was so impressed by the unique childrens play area. There was everything I needed, toilets, refreshments and friendly staff. Not even the best chainstores provide such amenities."

MRS P A QUORN

Our facilities include,Kids cartoon theatre, Mother & Baby Room, No quibble exchange, Refund guarantee, Dog Park, Private changing facilities, Large customer car park, Convenient parking for the disabled, Toilets, Bottle bank, Fully equiped and supervised childrens play room.

Coach parties welcome, please call 01509 505050 Ext 140

173 CHARNWOOD ROAD, SHEPSHED, TEL 01509 505050

Discover The Real Thing

A Genuine Factory Shop

ACCESS SWITCH VISA

WE ARE HERE * CHARNWOOD RD LEICESTER RD M NORTH
A512 ASHBY RD JNC 23
JUST TWO MINUTES FROM THE M1 JUNCTION

Tues, Wed & Sat 10am – 5.30pm
Thurs & Fri 10am – 8pm
Sun 11am – 5pm
AND ALL BANK HOLIDAYS
JUNCTION 23 OFF THE M1

Please see following page

Charterhouse Holdings plc

173 Charnwood Road LE12 9NN
(01509) 505050

Huge range of quality family clothing, sportswear, accessories and 'market place' (toiletries, books, towels etc). Many branded and licensed products including footwear.

'Probably the finest manufacturing retail outlet in UK. Free kids' cartoon theatre. Fully equipped playroom. Bottle bank. Public phones. No-quibble exchange/refund guarantee.'

See our display advertisement on previous page

From Loughborough and M1 exit 23: take A512 to Ashby-de-la-Zouch. Go right at second traffic lights (B588 to Hathern).*

From Ashby via A512: go left at first traffic lights (sign to Hathern).*

*Follow road downhill to clearly marked shop on left.

From Hathern: pass The Crown then Red Lion on left; go left for Loughborough, Coalville, Cropston. At mini-roundabout (Bull Ring) with NatWest on left and Halifax on right: take Charnwood Road (B588 to Coalville/Ashby). Go uphill to conspicuous company on right.

Open: Tues, Wed 10–5.30; Thur, Fri 10–8; Sat and Bank Holidays 10–5.30; Sun 11–5.
Closed: Monday; Christmas and Boxing Days.
Cards: Access, Switch, Visa.
Cars: Large car-park across road. 'Dog park' by shop!
Toilets: Yes, including mother and baby room.
Wheelchairs: Easy access to huge shop. Parking for disabled by shop.
Changing rooms: Yes – extensive and private.
Teas: Own Corner Café in store.
Groups: Coach parties particularly welcome and well catered for. Please book in advance with shop manager on (01509) 505050, ext. 140, mentioning this guide.
Transport: Buses from Loughborough and Coalville stop outside.

The Factory Shop Ltd.

Newbold Premises, Brook Street LE12 7RE
(01509) 813514

Shoes, bags, toiletries, pottery, silk flowers, pictures, melamine and luggage. Also sell family clothing and a wide range of flight and sports bags.

'Large stock of chainstore items, all at greatly reduced prices. Deliveries of new stock every week to give an ever changing selection.'

If you go down the High Street (B5328): turn left before river into Brook Street (B674). Go under railway arch. Turn left into the main factory gate. Continue for 100 yds to the shop.

Coming into Sileby on B674 from A46 (Fosse Way) or Seagrave: go right into shop car-park just before railway arch.

Coming into Sileby on B5328 from south (Cossington/Rothley direction): pass the thatched Free Trade Inn on right, cross over river, turn right into Brook Street for Seagrave (B674). Go under railway arch; shop on left.

Open: Mon–Sat 9–5.
Closed: Bank Holidays; Christmas, Boxing and New Year's Days.
Cards: Access, Switch, Visa.
Cars: Own free car-park.
Toilets: No. Nearest in village.
Wheelchairs: Easy access to huge shop.
Changing rooms: Yes.
Teas: Tea shop and café in Sileby High Street.
Groups: Shopping groups welcome. For organiser/driver incentives please phone.
Transport: Frequent buses from Leicester and Loughborough.
Mail order: No.

Famous Fashion Discounts

Chandlers Wharf, Bridge Road TS18 3BA   *(01642) 608205*

Huge selection of top brands including ladies' fashions, men's suits, men's casual wear, children's wear, lingerie, baggage, shoes, gifts and linens. Brands include *Windsmoor, Planet, Gossard, Centaur, Hush Puppies, Lilley & Skinner, Lee Cooper, Dannimac, Farah, Falmer, Joe Bloggs, Fruit of the Loom, Michael de Leon, Accord* and *Coloroll.*

'A bargain-hunter's paradise. Current and end of season ranges, overstocks etc, all at factory prices. Blouses from £12, suits from £75. Large reductions from high street prices.'

....

On south side of town centre, next to Netto.

From A19 going south: take A1046 at Haverton Hill for Stockton. Turn right at large roundabout keeping Wickes DIY on your left. Continue straight along Portrack Lane and bear left with Reg Vardy on right. At small roundabout go left towards Thornaby, follow the river and turn left at large roundabout with Famous Fashions on left. Turn left at next lights in front of Thrust petrol station into car-park.

From Darlington or Middlesbrough on A66: exit for A1130 for Stockton centre. At lights turn right, then left at roundabout onto A1045 (one way), straight over mini roundabout. Follow round to lights, go straight at next lights and over Victoria bridge and "SCS" on left. At lights with Thrust petrol station on right turn right.

Open: Mon–Fri 9.30–5.30 (Tues 10–5.30); Sat 9–6; Sun 11–5. Bank Holidays 10–5.
Closed: Christmas Day.
Cards: Access, Joplings Storecard, Visa.
Cars: Large free car-park.
Toilets: Yes (gents up steps).
Wheelchairs: Store on one level.
Changing rooms: Yes.
Teas: In-store café – hot & cold drinks, wide range of snacks.
Groups: Shopping groups welcome but prior phone call to store manager appreciated. Two coach–parking bays at rear.
Transport: Bus stop outside. Transit bus nos. 37, 52, 54, 58, 63, 64, 75, 80, 84, 181, 113, 114; TMS 37, 116, 598; Tees United bus nos. 235, 268, 269, 272; Express bus nos. X68, X73.

The Factory Shop Ltd.

115 High Street ST5 1PR
(01782) 717364

Wide range of family clothing including outsizes. Shoes, bags, bedding, toiletries, pottery, melamine, luggage and lampbases with shades. Cosmetics. Health products.

'Large stock of chainstore items, all at greatly reduced prices. Deliveries of new stock every week to give an ever changing selection.'

....

The High Street is the wide pedestrian area where the market stalls are set up. This shop is at the end near the ring road.

When you drive to Newcastle, you cannot avoid the ring road! Go round clockwise or anti-clockwise, looking for signs to 'Service Area C' (and drive in for car-park); shop is just past the two café/restaurants on the right corner.

Open: Mon–Sat 9–5.30. Good Friday.
Closed: Bank Holidays; Christmas, Boxing and New Year's Days.
Cards: Access, Switch, Visa.
Cars: In multi-storey car-park: follow signs to Service Area C.
Toilets: In town.
Wheelchairs: One low step into shop; four steps in middle of large shop.
Changing rooms: Yes.
Teas: Nearby cafés and pubs in town.
Groups: Shopping groups welcome. For organiser/driver incentives please phone.
Transport: Any bus to Newcastle then short walk.
Mail order: No.

Clarks Village
Farm Road BA16 0BB
(01458) 443131

A wide range of manufacturers' shops selling quality branded merchandise, including shoes, tableware, clothing, home furnishings etc. at factory prices.

'On Clarks Shoes' original manufacturing site, a new shopping and leisure development in an attractive landscaped setting.'

See our display advertisement inside front cover

....

Easy to find and clearly marked off the Street by-pass.

Open: Summer: Mon–Sat 9–6; Sun 11–5; Bank Holidays 9–6.Winter: Mon–Sat 9–5.30; Sun 11–5; Bank Holidays 9–5.30.
Closed: Christmas Day.
Cards: Access, Delta, Switch, Visa.
Cars: Large park for cars and coaches adjoining town centre car-park.
Toilets: Yes, plus baby changing facilities.
Wheelchairs: Easy access plus wheelchairs available on request.
Changing rooms: Yes.
Teas: Leith's at the Food Factory Restaurant, Burger King takeaway, plus sandwich and pizza kiosks. Picnic area.
Groups: Groups welcome. Please contact ext. 2746 for details of special events. Free entry to Shoe Museum.
Transport: Any bus to Street.

Included in Clarks Village are:

454 Alexon/Eastex/Dash
(01458) 841831
Quality ends of lines in fashion and casual wear for women.

455 Baggage Factory
(01458) 443131, ext. 3163
Antler, Samsonite luggage, designer handbags, leather goods at discounts of 10–60%.

456 Benetton
(01458) 841692
Full range of Benetton merchandise at discounts from 30%.

457 Black & Decker
(01458) 840205
Factory-reconditioned products and accessories with damaged packing.

458 Clarks Factory Shop
(01458) 443131
Discounted footwear for all the family.

459 Clarks Shop, The
(01458) 443131, ext. 3150
Huge selection of the latest Clarks top quality products. All items here at full price.

460 Claude Gill Books
(01458) 841323
Books on all subjects in perfect condition. Remaindered stock.

461 Crabtree & Evelyn
(01458) 841440
Luxury foods, toiletries and gifts.

462 Dartington Crystal
(01458) 841618
Hand made crystal.

463 Denby Pottery
(01458) 443131
Pottery products from lamps to dinner services.

464 Esprit
(01458) 446627
High quality designer clothing and accessories for men, women and children.

465 Fred Perry
(01458) 841730
Men's, women's and children's casual and sportswear.

466 Hallmark
(01458) 447005
Cards and gifts at half normal price.

467 Jaeger/Jaeger Man
(01458) 447215
Men's and women's fashions.

468 James Barry
(01458) 840478
Quality men's suits, jackets, trousers and accessories.

469 JoKids
(01458) 841909
Children's clothing (0–10 years).

470 Jumpers
(01458) 840320
Knitwear and casual clothing for men and women.

471 Linen Cupboard
(01458) 447447
Dorma, Christy, Fogarty, Polywarm, Vantona and chainstore household textiles.

472 Liz Claiborne
(01458) 447311
Women's wear, separates and accessories.

473 Monsoon/Accessorize
(01458) 840890
Ladies' clothing and accessories from scarves to jewellery.

474 The Pier
(01458) 840190
Unusual furnishings and gifts from around the world.

475 Remington
(01458) 840209
Table cutlery, scissors, kitchen and pocket knives and small electrical appliances.

476 Rohan
(01458) 841849
Clothing for travellers, adventurers and everyday use.

477 Royal Brierley
(01458) 840039
Hand-made crystal including bowls, vases, decanters and glasses. Poole Pottery and Cardew Design.

478 Royal Worcester
(01458) 840554
Range of fine china, from gifts to complete dinner services.

479 Sports Factory
(01458) 443131 ext. 3156
Sports shoes, clothing and equipment from brands including Avia, Puma and Mizuno.

480 Thorntons Chocolates
(01458) 841553
Quality confectionery mis-shapes and unselected lines. Full price current stock also available.

481 Triumph/Hom
(01458) 840700
Ladies' and men's underwear, nightwear and swimwear.

482 Village Gift Shop
(01458) 443131, ext. 2436
Gifts, postcards and souvenirs from the local area.

483 Viyella
(01458) 840647
Ladies' clothing in classic styles and fashions made up with end-of-line fabrics.

484 Windsmoor
(01458) 840888
Windsmoor, Planet, Precis and Genesis women's wear. Centaur, Pin Stripe, Jeff Banks and Van Gils men's wear.

485 Woolea
(01458) 841378
Ends of lines in suede, leather, lambskin and wool for men, women and children.

486 Wrangler
(01458) 841799
Jeans, shirts, jackets and T-shirts for all the family.

The Factory Shop Ltd.
Westward Road, Cainscross GL5 4JF
(01453) 756655

Clothing and footwear for all the family. Good range of branded bedding, towels, toiletries and fancy goods; pottery; toys; wicker.

'Large stock of chainstore items, all at greatly reduced prices. Deliveries of new stock every week to give an ever changing selection.'

....

On A419 (Stroud–Bristol road) on western outskirts of Stroud.
   From the town centre: follow signs to Bristol (A419), go over the large roundabout in Cainscross.*
   From Nailsworth/Bath: turn left off A46 south of Stroud into Dudbridge Road for Cheltenham, Gloucester, M5; go to roundabout with A419; turn left for Bristol, *turn right after 100 yds in front of White Horse Inn, turn first left :shop is at back left.
   Coming into Stroud on A419 from Bristol: turn left for 'Cashe's Green & Randwick' 100 yds before large roundabout on outskirts of town.

Open: Mon–Sat 9–5; Fri 9–6; Sun 11–5. Open Bank Holidays.
Closed: Christmas, Boxing & New Year's Days.
Cards: Access, Switch, Visa.
Cars: Free, large car park.
Toilets: Locally.
Wheelchairs: Yes.
Changing rooms: Yes.
Teas: Pubs locally.
Groups: Shopping groups welcome. For organiser/driver incentives please phone.
Transport: Local buses; 30 minutes' walk from town centre.
Mail order: No.

The Factory Shop Ltd.
The Crossroads CO5 7VW
(01621) 817662

Large selection of men's, ladies' and children's clothing, footwear, luggage, toiletries, hardware, household textiles, gifts, bedding, lighting and new fashion concessions department with famous brand names.

'Large stock of chainstore items, all at greatly reduced prices. Deliveries of new stock every week to give an ever changing selection.'

....

In the middle of Tiptree by the crossing of the B1022 and the B1023.
   From the north (on B1023): the shop is on the right just by the crossing with B1022.
   From the south: pass the windmill (no sails) and Burmah petrol station on right, and the shop is on far left corner of the crossing.

Open: Mon–Sat 9–5.30; Sun 11–5.
Closed: Easter Sunday; Christmas, Boxing and New Year's Days.
Cards: Access, Switch, Visa.
Cars: Own large car-park.
Toilets: Public toilet facilities opposite.
Wheelchairs: No steps.
Changing rooms: Yes.
Teas: Cafés and pubs in town.
Groups: Shopping groups welcome. For organiser/driver incentives please phone.
Transport: Bus service from Clacton to Maldon. Bus stop outside.
Mail order: No.

The Factory Shop Ltd.

36/37 Roundstone Street BA14 8DF
(01225) 751399

Clothing and footwear for men and women. Good range of towels, toiletries and fancy goods; lighting; luggage. New fashion concessions department with famous brand names for men and women.

'Large stock of chainstore items, all at greatly reduced prices. Deliveries of new stock every week to give an ever changing selection.'

....

Almost opposite the main post office, in town centre.

  From the Shires Shopping Centre: enter the shopping mall and follow signs to Market Street; Roundstone Street is a continuation of Market Street.

  From Devizes on A361: pass fire station and ambulance station on left. At next roundabout go straight (signposted to police station) and shop is 300 yards on the right.

  From Frome on A361: stay on A361 until you pass huge Tesco on right. At second roundabout after Tesco turn left (signposted to police station) and shop is 300 yards on the right.

Open: Mon–Sat 9–5.30.
Closed: Bank Holidays; Christmas, Boxing and New Year's Days.
Cards: Access, Visa, Switch.
Cars: Lowmead car park 30 yds from shop.
Toilets: In market hall and car park.
Wheelchairs: Access to ground floor only. Steps to first floor.
Changing rooms: Yes.
Teas: Local cafés and restaurants.
Groups: Shopping groups welcome. For organiser/driver incentives please phone.
Transport: Any bus to Trowbridge.
Mail order: No.

The Factory Shop Ltd.

24 Market Place BA12 9AN
(01985) 217532

Clothes and shoes for men and women. Toiletries, household linen, *Coloroll* bedding. Christmas gifts and decorations (November and December only).

'Large stock of chainstore items, all at greatly reduced prices. Deliveries of new stock every week to give an ever changing selection.'

....

Warminster is on the A36, 19 miles south-east of Bath and 19 miles north-west of Salisbury.

  This shop is in the centre of town, opposite Boots and Lloyds Bank and next to Currys. It is 100 yds from the traffic lights in the main shopping street (A36) at the T-junction of the A350 to Blandford and Shaftesbury.

Open: Mon–Sat 9–5.30. Some Bank Holidays. Also Sundays during Dec.
Closed: Christmas, Boxing and New Year's Days.
Cards: Access, Switch, Visa.
Cars: Large, free, town car-park; behind Safeways, parallel to main street.
Toilets: Safeways.
Wheelchairs: Easy access to medium sized shop.
Changing rooms: Yes.
Teas: In the High Street.
Groups: Shopping groups welcome. For organiser/driver incentives please phone.
Transport: 10 minutes walk from Warminster BR station.
Mail order: No.

Factory Outlet Shopping Centre (FOSC)
Hull Road YO1 3JA
(01904) 430481

Ladies', men's, and children's clothing, both smart and casual. Sportswear, jeans, suits, footwear, housewares, books, bedding, textiles, rugs. Cards and gifts.

'The UK's first factory outlet shopping centre with a variety of shops run by manufacturers. All prices reduced by up to 70%. Mainly first quality items, only very few seconds. Some chain-store items.'

Near the A64 ring road, east of York.

From city centre: take A1079 for Market Weighton/Hull. Shortly after the road becomes a dual carriageway, go left (immediately after MFI) for Osbaldwick. FOSC is the first building after MFI on left.

From other directions: go around the ring road (to the A64 section, south and east of town). Turn on to the A1079 for York. Take first right, for Osbaldwick, immediately before MFI; FOSC is first on left (same car-park entrance as MFI).

Open: Mon–Sat 10–6; Sun 11–5.
Closed: Christmas Day only.
Cards: Mastercard, Switch, Visa.
Cars: 300 spaces.
Toilets: Yes, including for disabled.
Wheelchairs: Easy access to spacious shops, all on ground floor.
Changing rooms: Yes.
Teas: Own coffee shop.
Groups: Welcome. No appointment necessary.
Transport: From York take the Grimston Bar park-and-ride bus.

Late entry! Doncaster S Yorks

The Yorkshire Outlet
Doncaster Lakeside
(01302) 366444

High quality national and international branded merchandise at factory prices. Over 40 manufacturers' shops, including fashion and sports clothing, shoes, tableware and home furnishings. Brands such as *Lee Jeans, Levis, Jeffrey Rogers, Windsmoor, Moss Bros, Ciro Citterio, Black & Decker, Remington* etc.

'A brand new, purpose-built factory outlet centre, situated at the southern gateway to Doncaster Lakeside. The development includes the Dome leisure centre, a multiplex cinema, a bowls centre, a range of restaurants and pubs and many other leisure attractions.'

Situated near M18 exit 3.

From M18 exit 3: follow brown signs to Doncaster Lakeside (formerly Doncaster Business and Leisure Park). The Yorkshire Outlet is easily found at the southern entrance to Lakeside.

Open: Mon–Sun 9.30–6.30 including Bank Holidays.
Closed: Christmas Day.
Cards: All major cards.
Cars: Extensive free car-park.
Toilets: Yes. Facilities for the disabled.
Wheelchairs: Easy access to all shops.
Changing rooms: Yes, in clothing shops.
Teas: On-site restaurant. Several pubs and restaurants in the Doncaster Lakeside area.
Groups: Shopping groups and coach parties welcome. Please contact the Centre Manager about special events.
Transport: Local buses.

Mail Order Catalogue Shops

If there is one place where we are guaranteed to find something we need, it is one of these extraordinary shops where catalogue surplus items or factory seconds are sold.

Mail order is huge business. The range of items sold, and the number of companies which offer this service, have both expanded greatly in recent years. Designer label clothes and internationally recognised brands are now available through the post. Readers will be pleased to find that Lands' End now have a shop in Leicestershire for their fashionable leisurewear where they sell perfect goods and seconds.

We have bought Christmas cards in April and a special folding clothes dryer. We have bought cassettes at under £2; kitted out children in a playgroup with serviceable T-shirts; succumbed to tracksuits originally sold by a top national newpaper as a readers' special offer; a much reduced price radio, a cordless coffee maker, a set of garden chairs, and more. We even acquired a set of pencils, pre-embossed with a boy's name, as a present for a friend's son with the same name. It is amazing how one can be tempted by useful items one did not realise one needed.

It is worth pointing out that electrical goods are fully guaranteed.

Prices in these shops are significantly less than in the catalogues. Allow yourself to be intrigued by the selection.

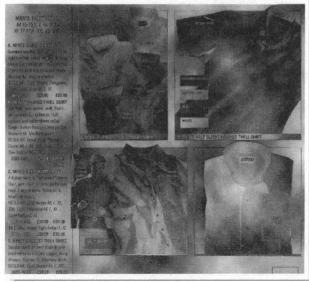

Britannia Products	492	**Bradford**	W Yorks
Webb Ivory	493	**Burton-on-Trent**	Staffs
Selective Marketplace	494	**Loughborough**	Leics
Lands' End Direct Merchants	495	**Oakham**	Leics
Town & Country Manner	674*	**Penrith**	Cumbria
Webb Ivory	496	**Swadlincote**	Derbys

* Please see full details in respective chapter

Catalogue Bargain Shop	497	**Bilston**	W Mids
	498	**Bradford**	W Yorks
	499	**Bridgnorth**	Shrops
	500	**Burnley**	Lancs
	501	**Caerphilly**	Mid Glamorgan
	502	**Chorley**	Lancs
	503	**Cowdenbeath**	Fife
	504	**Doncaster**	S Yorks
	505	**Droitwich**	Worcs
	506	**Ebbw Vale**	Glamorgan
	507	**Eccles**	Gr Manchester
	508	**Farnworth**	Gr Manchester
	509	**Faversham**	Kent
	510	**Gainsborough**	Lincs
	511	**Glasgow**	Strathclyde
	512	**Glasgow**	Strathclyde
	513	**Gloucester**	Gloucs
	514	**Gravesend**	Kent
	515	**Hamilton**	Strathclyde
	516	**Heckmondwike**	W Yorks
	517	**High Barnet**	Herts
	518	**Huddersfield**	W Yorks
	519	**Lincoln**	Lincs
	520	**Llandudno**	Gwynedd
	521	**London : Hounslow**	
	522	**London : Palmers Green**	
	523	**London : Peckham**	
	524	**Malvern**	Worcs
	525	**Manchester : Central**	
	526	**Mansfield**	Notts
	527	**Merthyr Tydfil**	Mid Glamorgan

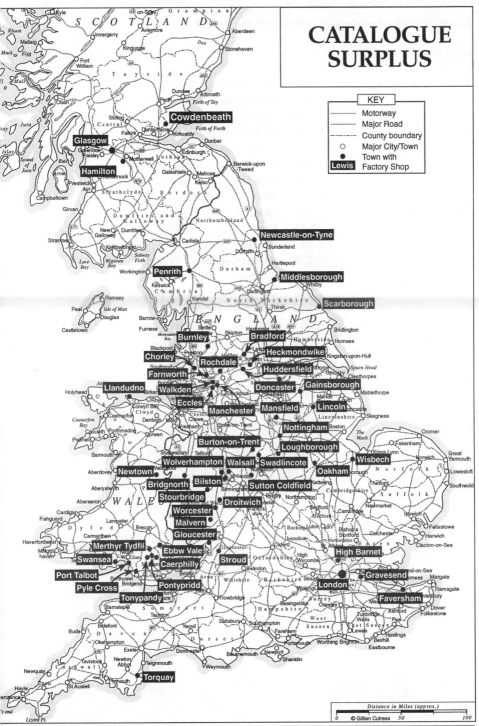

CATALOGUE SURPLUS

Distance in Miles (approx.)

0   © Gillian Cutress   50   100

contd. from p. 288

Catalogue Bargain Shop	528	**Middlesbrough** Cleveland
	529	**Newcastle** Tyne & Wear
	530	**Newtown** Powys
	531	**Nottingham : Bulwell** Notts
	532	**Pontypridd** Mid Glamorgan
	533	**Port Talbot** West Glamorgan
	534	**Pyle Cross** Mid Glamorgan
	535	**Rochdale** Lancs
	536	**Scarborough** N Yorks
	537	**Stourbridge** W Mids
	538	**Stroud** Gloucs
	539	**Sutton Coldfield** W Mids
	540	**Swansea** West Glamorgan
	541	**Tonypandy** Mid Glamorgan
	542	**Torquay** Devon
	543	**Walkden** Gr Manchester
	544	**Walsall** W Mids
	545	**Wisbech** Cambs
	546	**Wolverhampton** W Mids
	547	**Worcester** Worcs

Britannia Products Ltd.
Dawson Lane, Dudley Hill BD4 6HV
(01274) 784364

Huge range of all types of greeting cards, wrap and trim, gifts, toys, household items and mail order surplus.
'At least half off normal retail and catalogue prices.'

About 1.75 miles south-east of Bradford.
  Leave Bradford on Wakefield Road (A650). Cross ring road (Dudley Hill roundabout) and pass Asda on left. Continue straight (Tong Street). Go over traffic lights. After 200 yds go right (fourth turning) down Dawson Lane. *
  Coming into Bradford from Wakefield (A650) or Dewsbury (A651): after traffic lights where these two roads merge, go over second set of lights towards Bradford. After Bramall Ford garage (about 1 mile) go left down Dawson Lane. *
  *Look for security gates and factory shop on left after 100 yds.

Open: Mon–Fri 10–4.30; Sat 9.30–12.30.
Closed: Bank Holidays; Christmas, Boxing and New Year's Days.
Cards: None.
Cars: Ample parking and turning for coaches and cars.
Toilets: No.
Wheelchairs: 4 low steps down to shop.
Teas: In Asda; local pubs. Don't forget the famous fish & chip shops around Bradford.
Groups: Coaches welcome – please book first.
Transport: Regular local services.
Mail order: No.

Webb Ivory
Queensbridge Works, Queen Street DE14 3LP
(01283) 506371

Fascinating variety of surplus catalogue stocks of greetings cards, wrapping papers, household goods, toys, small gifts and clothing.
'50% off catalogue prices.'

Close to the centre of town, on the south-west side.
  From Tutbury: go into town, proceed along Guild Street and Union Street. At traffic lights (Comet on near left corner) go right into New Street. *
  From shopping precinct with W H Smith car-park: turn left; at traffic lights go right (New Street). *
  *At next lights, go left (Uxbridge Street); cross next lights (Evershed Way); take third left (Queen Street). Company 100 yds on left.
  From other places in town centre: find Safeway and pass it on left; at roundabout go right into Evershed Way; at traffic lights turn left into Uxbridge Street (Keepmere Engineering on far left corner). Go left at Queen Street. Company is 100 yds on left.

Open: Mon–Thur 9.30–5.30; Fri 9.30–5; *also Oct–Dec* Sat 9.30–12.
Closed: Bank Holidays; Christmas–New Year.
Cards: None.
Cars: Own car-park.
Toilets: Yes.
Wheelchairs: Yes; ground level shopping, no steps.
Teas: In Burton.
Groups: Pre-booked shopping groups welcome.
Transport: 15 minutes' walk from town centre.
Mail order: No.

Selective Marketplace Ltd.

Belton Road West LE11 0XK
(01509) 239471

Large selection of ladies' fashions and accessories – including ex-catalogue stock and rails of factory seconds. Sizes 12–24. Gifts such as crockery, cutlery, electrical and household wares.

'Bargain prices. Ladies' fashions from £2 to £50. Special offers, end of season clearance sales. Trade enquiries welcome if you mention this book.'

....

3/4 mile north-west of town, on a large industrial estate.

Lots of one-way streets so from town aim for A6 north (Derby Road). Go right at traffic lights into Belton Road (B6004) then first left opposite Mercedes garage and beside B&Q to Industrial Estate. Keep going, over canal; shop on left.

Going south on A6 from Derby/Midlands Airport: turn off at large roundabout to Bishop Meadow/Derby Road Estates. Take first right (Belton Road West) opposite Do-it-All; company is 1/4 mile on right.

From M1 exit 23: take A512 for town. At first roundabout turn left on to ring road (Epinal Way); go to roundabout mentioned below.

Open: Tues–Sat 9–4.
Closed: Monday; Bank Holidays.
Cards: Access, Visa.
Cars: Own large car-park beside shop.
Toilets: Please ask.
Wheelchairs: Large, spacious shop. One step to side door. Ramp to double doors at front – gladly opened on request.
Changing rooms: Yes.
Teas: In town.
Groups: Coach parties welcome. No need to book but phone call appreciated.
Transport: None.
Mail order: Yes.
Catalogue: Free.

Lands' End Direct Merchants

Pillings Road LE15 6NY
(01572) 722553

Quality casual clothing for men, women and children, including trousers, shorts, shirts, ties, belts, accessories, swimwear, tailored items, sweaters, outerwear, dresses and skirts.

'Mainly firsts, with a few items not quite perfect (further reduced). 30–70% off catalogue prices. All products carry our famous unconditional guarantee. If not entirely satisfied, customers can return any item at any time for full refund or exchange.'

....

On west side of the town centre.

From the town centre: go west along the main street, over the level-crossing towards Melton Mowbray on A606. Keep right into Pillings Road (Rutland Sixth Form College on left).*

From Melton Mowbray/west on A606: as you reach town turn left into Pillings Road after Rutland Sixth Form College.*

*Shop and car-park are shortly on the right.

Open: Mon–Sat 9–6; Sun, Bank Holidays 10–4.
Closed: Christmas Day.
Cards: Access, Amex, Connect, Delta, Switch, Visa.
Cars: Ample free parking on site or at overflow car-park opposite.
Toilets: Yes.
Wheelchairs: Access ramp to big shop.
Changing rooms: Yes.
Teas: Wide selection of cafés, pubs and restaurants in town.
Groups: Welcome. For tours, please phone PR department.
Transport: Oakham station 1/3 mile (on Leicester–Peterborough main line).
Mail order: Yes.
Catalogue: Free monthly catalogue. Phone 0800 220 106. Features quality casual wear for all the family.

Webb Ivory

Unit 10, The Rink Shopping Centre DE11 8JL
(01283) 226700

Fascinating variety of surplus catalogue stocks of greetings cards, wrapping papers, household goods, toys and small gifts.

'50% off catalogue prices.'

Situated in town centre pedestrian area 2 minutes' walk from shops and market hall.

Open: Mon–Sat 9.30–5 (Wed 9.30–1).
Closed: Bank Holidays; Christmas–New Year.
Cards: No.
Cars: Free public car-park.
Toilets: Yes.
Wheelchairs: Easy access, no steps.
Teas: In Swadlincote.
Groups: No.
Transport: Two minutes' walk from central bus station.
Mail order: No.

Catalogue Bargain Shops

The 51 shops listed in the following pages sell a huge range of mail order surplus goods: clothing, fashions, household, footwear, hardware, electrical items, toys and gifts. With the exception of those at Cowdenbeath, Glasgow (Parkhead), Gravesend, High Barnet, London (Hounslow), London (Palmers Green) and Walkden, the shops all sell items of furniture. For other details, please contact the individual shops directly.

Catalogue Bargain Shops offer both firsts and seconds at large savings from original catalogue prices, and all the usual guarantees apply.

Changing rooms: Yes (except Nottingham, Bulwell).
Cards: Access, Delta, Switch, Visa. **Mail order:** No.

497 Bilston W Mids

95 Church Street WV14 0BJ   *(01902) 353624*

In Bilston centre, near the town hall.
   From Wolverhampton on A41: as you reach Bilston, you must fork right at traffic lights; go left at roundabout into High Street (which becomes pedestrianised Church Street). Go left (Broad Street) then park on right. Walk through alley to shop.
   From M6 exit 10: take A454 dual carriageway for Wolverhampton/ Bilston. At roundabout with signs to Bilston to the right, go right. At lights in front of town hall, fork left. You have to turn right in front of pedestrianised area. Park then walk up pedestrianised Church Street: shop is 250 yds on right.

Open: Mon-Sat 9–5.30. Bank Holidays.
Closed: Christmas and Boxing Days.
Cars: Public car-park at rear of shop.
Toilets: No.
Wheelchairs: No step to ground floor; stairs to first floor.
Teas: Taylors Cake Shop directly opposite.
Transport: Bus station near market; no BR station.

498 Bradford W Yorks

Holme Lane BD4 6NB   *(01274) 681711*

Just over two miles south-east of the city centre.
   From Bradford: take Wakefield Road (A650). Cross over the ring road and keep going. Look for large conspicuous stone pub 'The Holme Lane' on right with pedestrian lights in front. At next traffic lights, go left into Holme Lane. *
   Coming into Bradford from Wakefield (A650) or Dewsbury (A651): after traffic lights where these two roads merge, go right at second traffic lights into Holme Lane. *
   *Shop is 150 yds on the right; follow signs.

Open: Mon–Sat 9.30–5.30 (Thur to 7); Sun 10.30–4.30. Bank Holidays.
Closed: Christmas and Boxing Days.
Cars: Large car-park adjacent.
Toilets: Yes.
Wheelchairs: 3 steps to huge shop; also ramp available.
Teas: Local pubs; lots of places in town centre.
Transport: Frequent buses from Bradford Interchange.

499 Bridgnorth Shrops

59 High Street WV16 4DX
(01746) 763282

From all directions go into town centre. The High Street is one-way. This shop is on the left by the town hall arch.

Open: Mon–Sat 9–5.30; Sun 10.30–4.30. Bank Holidays.
Closed: Christmas and Boxing Days.
Cars: Car–parks in centre.
Toilets: No.
Wheelchairs: Two steps to ground floor; stairs to upstairs showroom.
Teas: Several cafés in town.
Transport: Wolverhampton BR station then bus no. 890.

500 Burnley Lancs

Kingsway BB11 1AE *(01282) 420202*

In a large, well marked building in the town centre.
   From M65 exit 10: follow signs to town centre. Go left immediately after Do It All. At the roundabout by the railway viaduct stay on inner ring road, Rochdale A679; pass Halfords Superstore on left and take next right at the lights.*
   From Nelson on A56: go over canal hump bridge, past Prestige Group on right; follow signs to Central Station at the lights (bearing right). At next lights go left.*
   *Shop is at far end of huge GUS building on right.

Open: Mon–Sat 9–5.15 (Thur late night to 7); Sun 10.30–4.30. Bank Holidays.
Closed: Christmas Day.
Cars: Car-park across road.
Toilets: No.
Wheelchairs: 25 steps; entrance for disabled via reception.
Teas: At least four cafés in Standish St or Burnley Mkt Hall approximately 100 yds away.
Transport: Burnley bus station within walking distance.

501 Caerphilly Mid Glamorgan

81 Cardiff Road CF83 1FQ
(01222) 852699

In the town centre. Cardiff Road is a one-way street leading towards the castle and tourist information centre.
   From Cardiff: take A469 north to Caerphilly. Go over railway bridge, passing station on right. Shop is 200 yds on left after Kwiksave.

Open: Mon–Sat Mon–Sat 9–5.30. Sundays before Christmas. Bank Holidays.
Closed: Christmas Day.
Cars: Car-parks in town.
Toilets: No.
Wheelchairs: No steps; ramp to one floor shop.
Teas: Cafés in town.
Transport: Bus and BR station 400 yds away.

502 Chorley Lancs

40–42 Market Street PR7 2SF
(01257) 268325

In the centre of town, on Market Street (A6).
   From all directions and M61: take A6 into town centre. This shop (between NatWest and Midland banks) is five shops away from the traffic lights beside the impressive town hall.

Open: Mon–Sat 9–5.15; Sun 10.30–4.30. Bank Holidays.
Closed: Christmas Day.
Cars: Town centre car-parks.
Toilets: No.
Wheelchairs: No steps; easy access to spacious shop.
Teas: Muffins across the road.
Transport: Two minutes' walk from bus station; 5 minutes' walk from BR station.

503 Cowdenbeath Fife

315–317 High Street KY4 9QK *(01383) 611054*

In the main road in the town centre, between Woolworths and Iceland and a few yards from the railway station.
   From M90 exit 3: take A92 for Kirkcaldy. Follow signs to Cowdenbeath/Burntisland and go into town. At the mini-round-about, go straight (Cowdenbeath Business Centre on left) into High Street. Pass Woolworths and Boots on right: shop is 100 yds further on.
   Coming south into town: continue into main shopping street. Go under railway: shop is 100 yds on left.

Open: Mon–Fri 9–5.30; Sat 9–5. Bank Holidays.
Closed: Christmas Day.
Cars: Public car-parks.
Toilets: Across the road.
Wheelchairs: No steps.
Teas: Pub (Partners) across the road.
Transport: Bus no. 19 stops outside door. Cowdenbeath BR station.

504 Doncaster S Yorks

40–44 Silver Street DN1 1JL
(01302) 329933

In the centre of Doncaster, just off the High Street.

Coming into Doncaster: probably easiest to follow signs to the Frenchgate Shopping Centre (park there) then walk down the High Street. At first traffic lights go left: shop is on right, half way down Silver Street.

Open: Mon–Sat 9–5. Some Bank Holidays.
Closed: Christmas Day. Please phone to check exact days.
Cars: NCP car-park in Frances Street behind store.
Toilets: Across road in market place.
Wheelchairs: No steps to ground floor, steps to other levels.
Teas: Several cafés opposite.
Transport: Any bus or train then short walk.

505 Droitwich Worcs

West Bank, Berryhill Ind. Est. WR9 9AX   (01905) 779850

North-west of Droitwich, just off roundabout where A38 (Droitwich bypass) meets A442 (Kidderminster–Droitwich road).

From Kidderminster: take A442 for Droitwich; at roundabout with A38 turn off for Berryhill Industrial Estate (signposted). *

From town centre: take A442 for Kidderminster; at roundabout with A38 aim for Berryhill Industrial Estate (signposted). *

From A38 at roundabout with A442: turn off for Berryhill Industrial Estate (signposted). *

**This is a one-way road. Go all the way around to the first left turn-off (West Bank); shop clearly signed on right.*

Open: Mon–Fri 9–8; Sat 9–5.30; Sun 10.30–4.30.
Closed: Easter Sunday; Christmas Day.
Cars: On the road before 4.30 pm; on site after 4.30 and all day Sat and Sun.
Toilets: No.
Wheelchairs: Access via back door.
Teas: In town centre.
Transport: Bus to Westlands from town centre; walk to industrial estate; turn left.

506 Ebbw Vale Glamorgan

Bryn-Ferth Road, Rhyd-Y-Blew NP3 5YD
(01495) 309297

About a mile north of Ebbw Vale.

From Heads of the Valley road (A465): at roundabout aim south (downhill) for Ebbw. Take second right: pass Pioneer supermarket on right then double-back at roundabout. Shop is in same building as Pioneer.

From Ebbw Vale: take road north, following signs for Tredegar. Pass technical college on right. At roundabout take third exit for Pioneer store. Shop is in same building as Pioneer.

Open: Mon–Sat 9–8 (late night Fri to 9); Sun 10–4. Bank Holidays.
Closed: Easter Sunday and Christmas.
Cars: Own large free car-park.
Toilets: On site, at Pioneer next door. Also for disabled.
Wheelchairs: No steps; easy access.
Teas: Pioneer canteen on site.
Transport: Ebbw Vale bus station (free bus Thur and Fri).

507 Eccles Gr Manchester

Worsley Road, Patricroft M30 8NP   (0161) 787 7726

On the west side of Eccles, a short distance south-east of the huge junction where M62 meets M602 (Eccles bypass) and M63.

Take M62 exit 13. At the roundabout almost underneath it, pass the turnoff for Swinton (A572) then take next exit, Barton Road (B5211 for Eccles). Keep straight for nearly 1.5 miles south, passing under M602. Bear left after pedestrian lights; pass The Withies old persons' home on right. Entrance to huge GUS building is on left, just before railway bridge. Park in car-park and walk to shop at back.

Open: Mon–Fri 10–5.30 (Thur late night to 8); Sat 9–5.15. Bank Holidays.
Closed: Christmas Day.
Cars: Car-park on site. Disabled park outside shop.
Toilets: No.
Wheelchairs: Four steps, but assistance in carrying if required.
Teas: A number of small cafés within 10 minutes of shop.
Transport: Eccles BR station; bus nos. 10, 11, 67.

508 Farnworth Gr Manchester

Lorne Street BL4 7LT   *(01204) 73511 x 146*

From Little Hulton on A5082, or Worsley on A575: go along A575 until you pass The Shakespeare on left; take 5th left, Cawdor St.*
   From M61: aim for Bolton but take the first exit on to A6053 to Farnworth. After the traffic lights (Jaguar garage and Texaco petrol on right) take second left, Francis Street which is one way. Cawdor Street is the continuation of this road.*
   From Bolton on A6053: go over traffic lights at Moses Gate station, take 2nd right (Francis St: continue straight into Cawdor St.*
   *Take 3rd turn on right then next left, Lorne St. Mill is on right.

Open: Mon–Fri 10–4.30 (Thur late night to 7); Sat 9–4.30. Bank Holidays.
Closed: Christmas Day.
Cars: Public car-park in Lorne Street.
Toilets: No.
Wheelchairs: Three steps; please ask staff for assistance.
Teas: In town.
Transport: Moses Gate BR station; bus no. 22 from Farnworth or Bolton.

509 Faversham Kent

19A Preston Street ME13 8NY   *(01795) 591203*

In the town centre opposite Safeways.
   From M2 exit 6: take A251 (Ashford Road) for Faversham; pass fire station on left. At T-junction go left on to A2 then first right (The Mall). Follow road round under railway bridge, go left by garage to shoppers' car-park. With The Railway Hotel on your right, walk into Preston Street. Shop is on right, opposite Safeways.
   On foot from the station: turn left out of station, take first right (Preston Street): shop is about 30 shops on right.

Open: Mon–Sat 9–5.30; Sun–10–4. Bank Holidays.
Closed: Christmas and Boxing Days.
Cars: Several car-parks within a few minutes; disabled park outside shop.
Toilets: Near Safeways.
Wheelchairs: No steps into large shop, stairs to 1st floor area.
Teas: Cartons, Preston Street; Shelly's, High Street; & others.
Transport: BR station 200 yds; bus stop 3 minutes' walk.

510 Gainsborough Lincs

12–14 Silver Street DN21 2DP
(01427) 810604

A pedestrian road in the centre of town.
   Silver Street leads out of Market Place through to Ropery Road (main road through town). Shop is on right, half way down, next to Lloyds Bank.

Open: Mon–Sat 9–5.30; Sun 10.30–4.30. Bank Hols 9–5.30.
Closed: Easter Sun.; Xmas Day.
Cars: Car-park nearby (off Ropery Rd, behind Woolworths).
Toilets: In the Lindsey Centre.
Wheelchairs: One step into big shop; stairs to upper floor, but will gladly bring items down.
Teas: Lindsey Shopping Centre; Curtis Walk tearooms 200 yds.
Transport: Bus station 3 minutes' walk; Lea Road BR station 25 minutes' walk.

511 Glasgow : City Centre Strathclyde

36 Queen Street G1 3DY
(0141) 552 2886

In the centre of Glasgow. Best to find a public car-park and walk!
   From St Enoch shopping centre (huge glass-covered centre): cross Argyle Street and go up Queen Street. The shop is 60 yds on the right.
   From Queen Street station entrance: you look straight down Queen Street. Shop is 400 yds on the left, just before Argyle Street. Look for narrow doorway on to the street.

Open: Mon–Sat 9–5; Sun 12–5. Bank Holidays.
Closed: Christmas Day.
Cars: Public car-parks (St Enoch Centre best).
Toilets: In St Enoch Centre.
Wheelchairs: Lift to first floor shop.
Teas: Pizzaland and Littlewoods next door.
Transport: Queen Street BR station; most buses heading for city.

512 Glasgow : Parkhead Strathclyde

Units 51–55, The Forge Shopping Centre G31 4EE
(0141) 556 5352

About two miles east of Glasgow city centre, in a well marked shopping centre.
   From the city centre: take Gallowgate (A89) or Duke Street eastwards. Turn off into this shopping centre where you see it marked.
   From M8 exit 13: you need to go about a mile south of here, aiming for Parkhead Cross. Enter the shopping centre from Duke Street.

Open: Mon–Wed 9–6; Thur 9–7; Fri, Sat 9–6; Sun 11–5. Bank Holidays.
Closed: Christmas Day.
Cars: Shopping centre car-park.
Toilets: In shopping centre.
Wheelchairs: Lift to shop.
Teas: Food court within shopping centre.
Transport: Bus nos. 1, 8, 46, 56, 61, 62, 63.

513 Gloucester Gloucs

1–6 Grosvenor House, Station Road GL5 3DA
(01452) 308779

In the centre of town.
   Shop is next to bus station and in front of BR station.
From all directions, follow signs to station.

Open: Mon–Sat 9–5.30; Sun 10.30–4.30. Bank Holidays.
Closed: Christmas and Boxing Days.
Cars: At bus station; can park outside shop to pick up.
Toilets: No; nearest at bus station.
Wheelchairs: One small step.
Teas: Café next door.
Transport: Bus station and taxi rank outside shop.

514 Gravesend Kent

24 High Street DA11 0AZ
(01474) 564860

In the town centre beside the entrance to the market.
   Go along the pedestrianised High Street; pass Woolworths on a right corner then this shop is a short distance further along on right nearly opposite the Buffalo's Head pub.

Open: Mon–Sat 9.30–5.30. Bank Holidays.
Closed: Christmas Day.
Cars: Market and Lord Street car-parks.
Toilets: No.
Wheelchairs: No steps into shop but two steps to back area Assistance easily given. .
Teas: Town centre.
Transport: Gravesend station 5 minutes' walk; local buses.

515 Hamilton Strathclyde

12–16 Cadzow Street ML3 6DF
(01698) 421112

In the centre of town, Cadzow Street is part of the clockwise one-way system. Shop is on left just before traffic lights.
   From all directions: get on to one-way system around town.
   Best to park in Duke Street multi-storey car-park (below Wyler tower block on your left as you go round one-way system) or Somerfield car-park (clearly marked on your right as you go round). From either, walk down through the pedestrianised area to the shop.

Open: Mon–Sat 9–5.30; Sun 12–4. Bank Holidays.
Closed: Christmas Day.
Cars: Duke Street multi-storey car-park.
Toilets: Locally.
Wheelchairs: No steps. Lift to furniture department on first floor.
Teas: Tea room 100 yds away.
Transport: Hamilton central bus and train stations.

516 Heckmondwike   W Yorks

57–59 Market Place WF16 0EZ
(01924) 402674

In the town centre, virtually on the main road (A638, Bradford–Dewsbury Road) through town and facing the clocktower.

From Bradford direction: go into town centre; turn right off main road at clocktower into Market Street (B6117 to Dewsbury Moor). This shop is on your right and NatWest is on your left.

Open: Mon–Sat 9–5.15; Sun 10.30–4.30. Bank Holidays.
Closed: Easter Sunday; Christmas Day.
Cars: Car-park at back of shop; also front (except Tues & Sat).
Toilets: In supermarket.
Wheelchairs: 1 step to ground floor; stairs to other levels.
Teas: Watson's coffee shop opposite; Morrison's supermarket café at rear.
Transport: Bus stops in town centre.

517 High Barnet   Herts

101 High Street EN5 5UZ   *(0181) 364 9654*

In the centre of High Barnet.

Going north from Whetstone/Finchley on A1000: go up Barnet Hill; at traffic lights in High Barnet fork right (church on left). Look for Halifax building society on a far left corner: this shop is immediately past it. [To park, pass the shop, bear left at traffic lights into St Albans Road (A1081), go left into Stapylton Road for open car-park on right or Spires Centre on left.]

Coming south into High Barnet: go over traffic lights, shop is shortly on right, beside the Halifax. Multi-storey car-park (Spires Centre) behind this shop in Stapylton Road.

Open: Mon–Sat 9–5.30. Bank Holidays.
Closed: Christmas Day.
Cars: Spires Centre; metres in High Street.
Toilets: Spires Centre.
Wheelchairs: No steps, large ground floor shop.
Teas: McDonald's or Moon under Water pub.
Transport: High Barnet tube station; bus stop 100 yds away.

518 Huddersfield   W Yorks

Lion Chambers, John William Street HD1 1EP
(01484) 535112

In the town centre, virtually facing the station

John William Street is a one-way street leading into the town centre from the east side of town/railway station.

From the ring road: drive round till you see signs to the station. With the station on your left/behind you: look straight ahead to the building with the big lion on the top. The shop is beneath the lion.

Open: Mon–Sat 9–5; Sun 10.30–4.30. Bank Holidays.
Closed: Easter Sun; Xmas Day.
Cars: Limited street parking; public car-parks at rear (all day parking); at station (one-hour).
Toilets: 300 yds away.
Wheelchairs: 19 steps in front, 10 at rear: assistance gladly given. 5000 sq ft on two floors (stairs between them).
Teas: Café/sandwich bar nearby.
Transport: BR station facing shop; many bus stops facing and adjacent.

519 Lincoln   Lincs

29–31 The Strait LN1 1JD
(01522) 527276

In the town centre, on the pedestrianised street which links the High Street and Steep Hill (which leads to the cathedral).

If you walk towards the cathedral, this shop is on the right, a few yards after the road forks to the right at the end of the High Street.

Open: Mon–Sat and Bank Hols 9–5.30; Sun 10.30–4.30.
Closed: Easter Sunday; Christmas Day.
Cars: Grantham St & Danesgate car-parks behind shop.
Toilets: Nearby public toilets.
Wheelchairs: Two sets of two steps so no wheelchair access. Large shop.
Teas: Numerous local cafés. Wine bar across street.
Transport: Bus and BR stations within 400 yds.

520 Llandudno Gwynedd

6–8 Madoc Street LL30 2TT
(01492) 877561

Madoc Street is parallel to the main street in town (Mostyn St).
From Mostyn Street: between Midland and NatWest banks, go into Lloyd Street. Opposite the fish and chip restaurant on right, go left into Madoc Street. Shop is a short distance on right.
From the railway station: go left along Augustus Street. At the traffic lights, go straight over into Madoc Street. Shop is at far end on left.

Open: Mon–Sat 9–5; Sun 10–4. Bank Holidays.
Closed: Christmas Day.
Cars: Limited parking in street; multi-storey car-park nearby.
Toilets: Nearby.
Wheelchairs: One step; Please ask for assistance.
Teas: Café opposite; other cafés and pubs for lunches nearby.
Transport: Central to both BR and bus station.

521 London : Hounslow

261 High Street TW3 1EE
(0181) 570 3118

Hounslow High Street is the A315 (Chiswick–Staines road) but is now pedestrianised. The shop is next to Woolworths.
Because of the pedestrianisation, best to park in the Treaty Shopping Centre (clearly marked) then walk through to High Street.

Open: Mon–Sat 9–5.30; Sun 10.30–4.30. Bank Holidays.
Closed: Christmas Day.
Cars: Treaty Centre multi-storey car-park. Other public car-parks nearby.
Toilets: Treaty Centre.
Wheelchairs: No steps; easy access to medium sized ground floor shop.
Teas: Lots of places nearby.
Transport: Hounslow Central tube (Piccadilly line).

522 London : Palmers Green

252 Green Lanes N13 5TU   *(0181) 886 9532*

Half mile north of the North Circular.
From the North Circular: at traffic lights go north into Green Lanes (A105) for Winchmore Hill. Cross traffic lights (Aldermans Hill leading to Palmers Green station to left); shop is opposite triangle island in road near Woolworths, Cyprus Bank and Superdrug on right.
Coming south from Winchmore Hill along Green Lanes (A105): cross traffic lights (Bourne Hill to right, Hedge Lane to left); pass post office on left. Shop is on left, immediately before Superdrug.

Open: Mon–Sat 9–5.30; Sun 10–4. Bank Holidays.
Closed: Christmas Day.
Cars: In supermarket opposite Palmers Green station.
Toilets: On triangle (island in middle of road near traffic lights).
Wheelchairs: No steps; easy access to medium sized ground floor shop.
Teas: Ice cream shop; burger bar; Inn on the Green pub.
Transport: Bus nos. W2, W3, 221, 329; Southgate tube station.

523 London : Peckham

103–113 Rye Lane SE15 4ST
(0171) 358 1308

Rye Lane is a busy main road; shop is across the road from Peckham Rye station.
If you come out of the station, go left: the shop is across the road, opposite McDonald's. If you drive down Rye Lane, pass the station on your left then the shop is on your right. Parking is not possible in Rye Lane itself.

Open: Mon–Sat 9–5.30; Sun 10.30–4.30.
Closed: Christmas Day.
Cars: Safeway car-park.
Toilets: No.
Wheelchairs: No steps to ground floor; stairs to upper floor.
Teas: McDonald's and cafés.
Transport: BR station 50 yds; bus nos. 12, 36, 63, 78, 171, P3.

524 Malvern Worcs

233 Worcester Road, Malvern Link WR14 1SY
(01684) 893062

Malvern Link is on the north side of Great Malvern. Worcester Road (A449) is the main road through town.
   From Great Malvern go north; pass Malvern Link station of left then Brooklyn petrol; shop is shortly on left, before traffic lights.
   Coming south from Worcester: go over traffic lights; shop is shortly on right.

Open: Mon–Sat 9–5.30; Sun 10.30–4.30. Bank Holidays.
Closed: Xmas & Boxing Days.
Cars: Half-hour parking outside; pay-&-display car-park nearby.
Toilets: No.
Wheelchairs: One step into ground floor shop.
Teas: Take-aways, pubs and tea rooms opposite.
Transport: Bus nos. 42A, 44A, 44D, 45 200 yds stop down road, outside Co-Op.

525 Manchester : Central

3 Dale Street M1 1JA
(0161) 236 0005

In the city centre, on the north side of Piccadilly station .
   From the station: go down the approach road and right into Ducie Street. Cross over. Take first left (Dale Street) and continue almost to far end. Shop is on far right corner with Spear Street.

Open: Mon–Fri 9–5; Sat 9.15–5; Sun 10.30–4.30. Bank Holidays.
Closed: Christmas Day.
Cars: Dale Street car-park 300 yds away.
Toilets: City centre.
Wheelchairs: Three steps; ask staff for assistance.
Teas: Coffee shop 50 yds; Central Sandwich shop 50 yds.
Transport: Piccadilly BR station; Stevenson Square bus stop.

526 Mansfield Notts

24–26 Leeming Street NG18 1NE
(01623) 23353

In the centre of town, Leeming Street is a small one-way street leading into the pedestrianised area from the museum/art gallery. If you walk downhill, the shop is on the left next to the Imperial Bar.
   Best to park in Clumber Street car-park (or any other car-park) and walk.

Open: Mon–Sat and Bank Holidays 9–5.30.
Closed: Christmas Day.
Cars: Three nearby car-parks; disabled badge holders park in street.
Toilets: Clumber Street car-park.
Wheelchairs: One step to ground floor; stairs to upper sales area. Large shop.
Teas: Three cafés in Leeming Street.
Transport: Any bus to town.

527 Merthyr Tydfil Mid Glamorgan

61 High Street CF47 8DE
(01685) 385653

In the town centre, nearly opposite WH Smith, with BR station behind. This street is pedestrianised.

Open: Mon–Sat 9–5.30. Bank Holidays.
Closed: Christmas Day.
Cars: Two major open air free car-parks in town.
Toilets: Bus station.
Wheelchairs: No steps into shop, but 1st floor not accessible.
Teas: Burger Master next door.
Transport: BR and bus station 100 metres.

528 Middlesbrough Cleveland

51 Acklam Road TS5 5HA   *(01642) 825925*

On A1032 south-west of town centre & south of West Lane Hosp.
From Darlington on A66: turn right on to A19 south.*
*From Middlesbrough: easiest to take A66 west then turn on
to A19 south.**
From the north on A19 cross the river Tees and A66.*
   **Pass race course on right; exit for A1130. At the top, go left
and immediatley left again (Levick Crescent). At the end
(church on right), go left into Acklam Road A1032. Shop is on
right shortly after second turn-off to right.*

Open: Mon–Sat 9–5;
Sun 10.30–4.30; Bank Holidays.
Closed: Christmas Day.
Cars: In side roads.
Toilets: No.
Wheelchairs: No steps;
easy access.
Teas: None nearby.
Transport: Bus nos. 21, 22,
24; most Middlesbrough
Corporation buses.

529 Newcastle upon Tyne Tyne & Wear

51 Shields Road, Byker NE6 1DJ   *(0191) 265 6033*

About 1.25 miles east of city centre, off the A193.
   *From the south on A167: go over Tyne bridge, pass exit to city
but take next exit to A193 signed Byker/Walker.**
   *From the north on A167(M): turn on to A193 signed
Byker/Walker (large Warner Bros cinema on left).**
   *From city centre: follow signs to Byker/Walker/North Shields
via A193 and cross the A167(M).**
   **Go over three traffic lights, then the high Byker bridge; go
left at first roundabout. Shields Road swings to the right: the
shop is on near left corner by next traffic lights.*

Open: Mon–Sat 9–5;
Sun 10.30–4.30; Bank Holidays.
Closed: Easter Sunday;
Christmas Day.
Cars: In Roger Street at rear.
Toilets: No.
Wheelchairs: One step.
Teas: Several snack bars in
Shields Road.
Transport: Bus nos. 12, 39,
40 to Shields Road, or Metro
to Byker Station.

530 Newtown Powys

Old Kerry Road SY16 1BJ   *(01686) 628283*

On the east side of this small town.
   *From Welshpool coming south on A483: as you come into
Newtown, at roundabout go left for Kerry. After 100 yds (before
railway bridge) go right into Old Kerry Road. After 100 yds go
left into Station Road: car-park is opposite station and shop
entrance is in car-park.*
   *From town centre: park in car-park opposite post office, go left
on to pavement and walk up to traffic lights, cross over into Old
Kerry Road. Shop car-park is 100 yds on right: shop entrance
through car-park.*

Open: Mon–Sat 9–5; Sun
10.30–4.30. Bank Holidays.
Closed: Easter Sunday;
Christmas Day.
Cars: Large car-park outside.
Toilets: In car-park; also on
floor above (lift).
Wheelchairs: No steps; 5000
sq ft on ground floor.
Teas: On next floor (lift
available).
Transport: BR opposite; no
regular bus service but stop is
5 minutes away.

531 Nottingham : Bulwell Notts

50 Main Street NG6 8EY   *(0115) 927 8373*

On the north-west side of Nottingham, near M1 exit 26.
   *From M1 exit 26: take A610 for Nottingham. At next round-
about, keep straight on A610. At next roundabout, go left
(Cinderhill Road).**
   *From Nottingham: take A610 north-west towards M1 exit 26.
Cross ring road and keep straight along Nuthall Road. At round-
about go right for Bulwell into Cinderhill Road.**
   **Main Street is a continuation of Cinderhill Road but is now
pedestrianised, so go left at traffic lights on to ring road, park
and walk through. Shop is next to Co-op Superstore.*

Open: Mon–Sat 9–5.30; Sun
10.30–4.30. Bank Hols. 9–5.30.
Closed: Easter Sunday;
Christmas Day.
Cars: Free parking in Coventry
Road then walk through to
Main Street.
Toilets: At bus station.
Wheelchairs: No steps into
shop; staircase to upper floor.
Large shop.
Teas: Small café round corner.
Transport: Buses and trains
(Robin Hood line) to Bulwell.

532 Pontypridd Mid Glamorgan

5 High Street CF37 1QJ
(01443) 486156

....

In the town centre at the end of the High Street.
From Cardiff on A470: go into town. Pass Marks & Spencer
on left then this shop is on left.

Open: Mon–Sat 9–5; Sun
10.30–4.30. Bank Holidays 9–5.
Closed: Easter Day; Xmas Day.
Cars: Various car-parks in
town.
Toilets: Nearest in High St.
Wheelchairs: One step at
entrance, several steps inside.
Teas: Cafés either side of
store.
Transport: BR station two
minutes' away; bus stops bottom
end of town.

533 Port Talbot West Glamorgan

31 Station Road SA12 1NN
(01639) 899419

....

Near the station (but on the other side of the roundabout).
From M4 exit 40: head for Port Talbot (A48), going right at
traffic lights. At large roundabout (BR station on left, hotel on
right) bear right into Station Road: shop is shortly on left.
(For car-park, pass shop then go right [not Tues or Sat].)

Open: Mon–Sat 9–5.
Bank Holidays.
Closed: Christmas Day.
Cars: Car-parks at rear of shop.
Toilets: No.
Wheelchairs: No steps; easy
access.
Teas: Wimpy Bar next door.
Transport: BR station a few
yards away; bus station in
precinct a little further.

534 Pyle Cross Mid Glamorgan

Ffald Road CF33 6BH
(01656) 746426

....

Pyle is just north of M4 between Bridgend and Port Talbot. Shop
is near the traffic lights.
From M4 exit 37: go north into Pyle. Pass Pyle garden centre
on right. At traffic lights go right; take first right into Pioneer
car-park. Shop clearly visible.

Open: Mon–Sat 9–8 (Fri to 9);
Sun 10.30–4.30. Bank Holidays.
Closed: Easter Sunday;
Christmas Day.
Cars: Own free car-park.
Toilets: In Pioneer.
Wheelchairs: No steps;
easy access.
Teas: In adjacent Pioneer
building; at petrol station.
Transport: Bus stop outside
car-park; BR station.

535 Rochdale Lancs

87–89 Yorkshire Street OL16 1DV   *(01706) 710600*

....

In a small street just off A58 (which skirts north side of town).
From Halifax on A58: go into Rochdale. At huge roundabout
with church in centre, go straight. *
From Whitworth on A671: go into Rochdale. At huge round-
about with church in centre, go right round – exit on to A58. *
From M62 exit 20: stay on A58 into Rochdale. At huge round-
about (Texas Homecare on left, huge church in middle), double
back on far side of dual carriageway. *
***Take first left (Whithall Street), take second right (Yorkshire**
Street). Shop is shortly on right.

Open: Mon–Sat 9–5;
Sun 10–4. Bank Holidays.
Closed: Christmas Day.
Cars: One hour pay-&-display
outside; Wheatsheaf car-park.
Toilets: No.
Wheelchairs: One step.
Teas: Cafés in Wheatsheaf
centre. Local pubs for lunch.
Transport: 10 minutes' walk
from bus station.

536 Scarborough N Yorks

20 St Thomas Street YO11 1DP
(01723) 371733

Close to the town centre, just north of the pedestrianised shopping centre.
  St Thomas Street is a one-way street leading from the town hall to opera house. Because Scarborough has so many one-way streets, probably easiest to park in the Brunswick Centre, North Street or St Thomas Street car-parks then walk. Shop is next to Kwik Save.

Open: Mon–Sat 9–5.30; Sun 10.30–4.30. Bank Holidays.
Closed: Easter Day; Xmas Day.
Cars: Car-parks in Brunswick Centre and North Street (at back of shop).
Toilets: Car-park opposite.
Wheelchairs: No steps; easy access; large shop.
Teas: Lots of bakeries, cafés and restaurants in town.
Transport: Many buses stop outside; BR station 10 minutes' walk.

537 Stourbridge W Mids

77-78 High Street DY8 1DX
(01384) 374544

Stourbridge is a small town totally enclosed by the ring road; the High Street is a one-way street. Keep going clockwise round the ring road; pass Mercedes showroom on left, then exit right into the town centre. Shop is several hundred yards on right, opposite McDonald's.

Open: Mon–Sat 9–5.30; Sun 10.30–4.30.
Closed: Easter Sun.; Xmas Day.
Cars: Multi-storey car-park at Crown Centre.
Toilets: In the Rye Market.
Wheelchairs: Two steps into large ground floor; assistance given.
Teas: Several cafés in town centre.
Transport: Buses and BR station nearby connected by subway.

538 Stroud Gloucs

47 King Street GL5 3DA
(01453) 766344

In the town centre near the multi-storey car-park.
  Shop is on corner of King Street/Gloucester Street. Entrance is in King Street (frontage in Gloucester Street).

Open: Mon–Sat 9–5. Bank Holidays.
Closed: Christmas Day.
Cars: Multi-storey at Merrywalks shopping centre.
Toilets: No.
Wheelchairs: No steps into shop; steps to ladies' fashions; stairs to first floor.
Teas: The Gorge at Merrywalks shopping centre.
Transport: Bus stop outside Woolworths, 300 yds.

539 Sutton Coldfield W Mids

Gracechurch Centre, The Parade B72 1PA
(0121) 321 3889

Gracechurch Centre is in the town centre. This shop is near British Home Stores.

Open: Mon–Sat 9–5.30. Bank Holidays.
Closed: Christmas Day.
Cars: Pay-&-display Grace-church car-park behind shop.
Toilets: In the centre.
Wheelchairs: No steps into shop; stairs to upper showroom.
Teas: At British Home Stores.
Transport: Local buses and trains.

540 Swansea West Glamorgan

229–230 High Street SA1 1NY
(01792) 456748

In the town centre, the High Street (B4489) is the main road running beside the railway station.
  Going south along the High Street: pass the station on your left then this shop is further along on the same side.

Open: Mon–Sat 9–5.30.
Bank Holidays.
Closed: Christmas Day.
Cars: Behind the store,
The Strand.
Toilets: No.
Wheelchairs: No steps
to medium sized shop on
ground floor.
Teas: Eynons café opposite.
Transport: Bus stop nearby.
BR station 200 yds.

541 Tonypandy Mid Glamorgan

113–115 Dunraven Street CF40 1AS
(01443) 441408

On south side of town centre on A4119.
  From M4 exit 34 & Tonyrefail: take A4119 north into Tonypandy. Continue towards town centre.*
  From Tonypandy bypass (A4058): follow sign into town centre. You come into Dunraven Street.*
  *Pass Woolworths then shop is shortly on left.

Open: Mon–Sat 9–5.
Bank Holidays.
Closed: Xmas & Boxing Days.
Cars: Town car-park,
Dunraven street market.
Toilets: No.
Wheelchairs: Access
difficult inside: shop narrow
and has steps.
Teas: Local fish-and-chip shop.
Transport: BR and bus
station at Tonypandy Square
15 minutes' away.

542 Torquay Devon

62 Union Street TQ2 5PS   Closed
(01803) 215757

In town centre, Union Street is the main shopping street. Shop is close to (on same side as) Boots.

Open: Mon–Sat 9–5.30;
Sun 10.30–4.30. Bank Holidays.
Closed: Christmas Day.
Cars: Car-parks in town
centre.
Toilets: No.
Wheelchairs: No steps at
entrance, but narrow steps to
basement and halfway along
shop.
Teas: In Littlewoods nearby
and other cafés.
Transport: Local buses.

543 Walkden Gr Manchester

Units 82–83 Egerton Walk, Ellesmere Centre M28 3ZD
(0161) 703 9311

In Walkden/Worsley, in a shopping precinct off the A575 (Bolton Road).
  From Farnworth going south on A575: go over M61, keep straight, pass Kwik Save on right then go right before pelican crossing into Tesco car-park.
  From Manchester Road (A6): at traffic lights, go north on to Bolton Road (A575) direction of Farnworth. This conspicuous shopping centre is a short distance on the left.

Open: Mon–Sat 9–5.30.
Bank Holidays.
Closed: Christmas Day.
Cars: In Tesco car-park
nearby.
Toilets: In Centre.
Wheelchairs Acess to ground
floor only; seven steps to 1st
floor entrance.
Teas: In Tesco and cafés in
precinct.
Transport: Bus stop outside
Ellesmere Centre.

544 Walsall W Mids

17 Bradford Street WS1 1PD *(01922) 722286*

Bradford Street is a major road in town centre.
  From M6 exit 9: aim for Walsall on A461. At first lights fork left (filter lane) on to ring road. At next lights go right (Wednesbury Road, A4038). Go over railway, pass Jet petrol on left, go straight at next lights.This road eventually becomes Bradford Street (far end pedestrianised). At lights where pedestrianised area starts (only buses may go straight), go right in front of Cantors' furniture shop to park. Walk back to lights, go right into pedestrianised area: shop is 100 yds on right.

Open: Mon–Sat 9–5.30; Sun 10.30–4.30. Bank Holidays.
Closed: Christmas Day.
Cars: Car-parks in town.
Toilets: No.
Wheelchairs: One small step to ground floor, stairs to upper floor. 8000 sq ft.
Teas: Local pubs and cafés.
Transport: Bus outside shop; BR station 1/2 m.

545 Wisbech Cambs

51 West Street PE13 2LV *(01945) 584327*

Not far from town centre.
  On foot from Market Square: exit into Church Terrace (Andrews china shop on right); take right fork (St Peter's car-park on right).*
  Coming north on A47: follow signs into town. At roundabout, take first exit; keep straight, cross traffic lights (Maxey estate agents on right). At roundabout go right on to dual carriageway (petrol station on left); at next lights (Mervyn hairdresser on right), go right (right filter). Follow road round to left; go right into St Peter's car-park. Walk into West Street.*
  ***Pass Harlequin pub; shop is short distance further on, set back.**

Open: Mon–Sat 9–4.30; Sun 10.30–4.30. Some Bank Hols.
Closed: Christmas Day.
Cars: St Peter's car-park, 5 minutes.
Toilets: No.
Wheelchairs: No step to ground floor; stairs to first floor (ladies' and children's wear).
Teas: The Bread Bin or Honey Pot in Norfolk Street, or Westgate Restaurant.
Transport: Bus station 10 minutes.

546 Wolverhampton W Mids

59–60 Dudley Street WV1 3EN
(01902) 714309

In the city centre, Dudley Street is pedestrianised.
  Park in any city centre car-park then walk to Queen's Square (bronze monument of man on horse, on pillar!). Walk down Dudley Street: shop is 100 yds on right, opposite Lloyds Bank.

Open: Mon–Sat 9–5.30; Sun 10.30–4.30. Bank Holidays.
Closed: Christmas Day.
Cars: Car-parks in town.
Toilets: No.
Wheelchairs: No steps to sizeable ground floor but stairs to other two floors.
Teas: At Druckers and Littlewoods.
Transport: Many local buses.

547 Worcester Worcs

15 Pump Street WR1 2QX
(01905) 617211

In the pedestrianised city centre off the High Street.
  Easiest to aim for St Martin's Gate car-park or Lychgate car-park then walk. Shop is opposite the Lychgate Centre.

Open: Mon–Sat 9–5.30; Sun 10.30–4.30. Bank Holidays.
Closed: Christmas Day.
Cars: Local car-parks.
Toilets: Nearest in Crowngate Shopping Centre.
Wheelchairs: Steps inside.
Teas: Cafés in town.
Transport: Local bus and BR station.

Jewellery, Accessories, Gloves, Hats, Scarves, Belts, Spectacles

Not often would the author like to live in the past, but how enjoyable it must have been in times when the wearing of a large, splendid hat was de rigeur ... hats are such fun or can give such a feeling of elegance ... no wonder a woman would go out and treat herself to a new hat when she felt depressed. If only hats were to become fashionable (or obligatory) for everyday wear once again!

A trip to Atherstone to try on the hats at the factory shop there relives some of that experience, and the items are so reasonable in price that few customers can come away without a hat for that special occasion – or even a bowler or top hat for a man. The hats can be complemented with a leather belt from Long Buckby or a pair of dashing silk and leather braces. The final touch could be a pair of top value leather gloves from Warminster, where you will find a large and colourful range. In fact so many colours confront you that it is vital to remember to take with you whatever item you want to match.

This chapter also leads you to excellent value jewellery (which you can have made to your own design), silk, cashmere and lambswool scarves, shawls, sashes and serapes. For the first time too we include a couple of shops run by lens makers who not only offer reduced price spectacles but also provide cheaper (but totally professional) eye tests.

JEWELLERY, ACCESSORIES, SCARVES, HATS, GLOVES, BELTS & SPECTACLES

* Please see full details in respective chapter

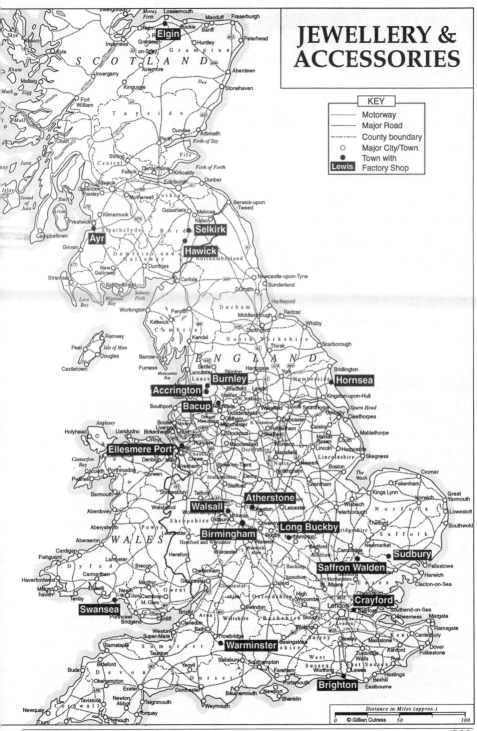

JEWELLERY & ACCESSORIES

KEY	
··········	Motorway
----------	Major Road
-·-·-·-·-	County boundary
○	Major City/Town
●	Town with
Lewis	Factory Shop

Optical Direct (C-L-M) Ltd.

5 Cunliffe Court off Petre Road, Clayton Enterprise Park,
Clayton-le-Moors BB5 5JF
(01254) 395725

Over 1300 budget and designer frames. From £14.95 including
s/v lenses. Designer styles at reduced prices. Contact lenses
from £35. Free spectacles/eye tests for children and people on
income support or family credit; choose from special collection.
*'Professional advice on all types of lenses, single vision to
complicated bifocals and varifocals. Save up to 50%.
Registered family health service authority practice. Half price
eye tests for senior citizens. Tests by appointment or bring own
prescription. **Free tints with this advertisement.**'*

Clayton-le-Moors is on north-west side of Accrington.
*From Accrington: follow signs to M65 and Rishton. Cross
under M65 at exit 7. Turn right at traffic lights opposite GEC
Industrial Estate; Petre Road is first left. Cunliffe Court is on
right: Unit 5 clearly visible on right.*
*From M65 exit 7: follow signs to Clitheroe (A6185). Go right
at traffic lights opposite GEC Industrial Estate; Petre Road is
first on left.*

Open: Mon–Sat 9–5.
Closed: Christmas, Boxing
and New Year's Days. Please
check for Bank Holidays.
Cards: Access, Switch, Visa.
Cars: Car-park.
Toilets: Yes.
Wheelchairs: Easy access,
no steps.
Teas: Tea and coffee free on
request. Cafés and pubs.
Groups: Groups welcome to
the shop. Contact Stuart
Robinson for eye-test appoint-
ments. Please phone for
groups over 20.
Transport: None.
Mail order: No.

The Hat Shop

Coleshill Road CV9 2AA
(01827) 717941

Wide variety of ladies' and men's hats and caps in all
colours, shapes and sizes for all seasons, occasions,
weddings, Ascot, etc.

*'A genuine factory shop with everything manufactured on the
premises. Mostly perfects with some seconds. Prices in the
range £7–£18.'*

South-west of Atherstone, near the canal.
*From Tamworth via A5: follow signs to Atherstone town cen-
tre. Follow the one-way system through the town. Pass the
public car-park/bus station on left and The White Lion on right;
at the mini-island turn right (Coleshill Road B4116).**
*From Hinckley and Nuneaton on A5: follow signs to
Atherstone. Pass Total petrol on left, go left at mini-island, and
right at next mini-island. Turn left after 200 yds (mini-island)
into Coleshill Rd.**
**Pass Jet petrol, cross the canal hump bridge: the shop is
40 yds on left.*

Open: Mon–Fri 10–4; *also first
Sat Mar–last Sat Sept* 10–2.
Closed: Last week July and
first week Aug; Bank Holidays;
Christmas–New Year.
Cards: Access, Switch, Visa.
Cars: In street outside.
Toilets: In town.
Wheelchairs: One step to
medium-sized shop.
Teas: In town.
Groups: Shoppers welcome
by prior arrangement. No
factory tours.
Transport: Walk from town
centre.
Mail order: No.

Optical Direct Ltd.

1A Toll Bar Business Park, Newchurch Road OL3 ONB
(01706) 870524

Prescription spectacles – bifocals, varifocals, sunglasses, lenses for all purposes. Contact lenses. Tints for shooting, golf, driving, cosmetic purposes, dyslexia etc. Accessories. Repairs a speciality. All products first quality. Comprehensive eye tests.

'Any lens for any application; specialise in the thinnest lenses for strong prescriptions. All year offers on designer frames. Prices reduced by 25–60%. Complete spectacles from: single vision, £14.95; varifocals, £74.95; bifocals £39.95.'

....

In Stacksteads, easy to find on the A681, 1.25 miles west of Bacup centre.

From Bacup: go west for Waterfoot/Rawtenstall. Shop is in old stone mill on the left beside the only mini-roundabout along this road (where Booth Road goes right, uphill). Go left into the car-park before the mini-roundabout.

From Rawtenstall/Waterfoot: aim for Bacup. In Stacksteads, go straight at mini-roundabout and immediately right into car-park at back. Shop entrance at front of building.

Open: Mon–Sat 9–5.30. Some Bank Holidays and late nights: please ring.
Closed: Christmas and New Year's Days.
Cards: Access, Visa.
Cars: Behind mill or across road.
Toilets: Yes.
Wheelchairs: Ramp at back entrance.
Teas: Free coffee/tea; Rose & Bowl restaurant/pub (smart and reasonable) 20 yds.
Groups: Shopping groups welcome, but please telephone first. Factory tours (up to 6) by appointment.
Transport: Bacup–Rawtenstall bus stops outside door.
Mail order: No.

Some hints for choosing lenses

If you want a thinner lens:
choose a frame with a smaller eye size because a smaller lens is thinner than a large lens;

ask for aspheric lenses (most lenses are spheric, like a slice off a football, but aspheric lenses are like a slice off a rugby ball);

ask for hi-index plastic – more expensive, it is denser than other plastics so you need less of it to bend the light rays.

Photochromatic lenses darken in bright light.

Anti-reflection coatings improve cosmetic appearance, preventing rings in short-sight lenses and reflections in all lenses. They improve night-driving vision by eliminating distracting reflection images.

Lenses can be tinted for cosmetic effects, for sports use, VDU use, UV protection, scratch resistance (not needed for glass lenses) and sun protection. Any colour or shade is possible on plastic lenses and colours may be combined in rainbow tints.

With thanks to Robin Standen of Optical Direct Ltd.

Less than a mile north-west of the city centre, beckons the fascinating small conservation area known as the Jewellery Quarter, or Hockley. About 15 minutes' walk from New Street station, it is home to a myriad of small workshops and jewellery shops with glittering windows. If you do not have the energy to go on foot, take bus no. 101 or the new train line to Vyse Street where you will see the colourful clocktower.

This clocktower is an excellent landmark for finding the jewellers in this section (also *Moulinex Swan* for electrical items, *FW Needham* for clocks, and *The Brass & Copper Shop*). Walking is by far the best way to explore the area.

Birmingham was the most important city in the world for manufacturing jewellers and still retains great importance, as proved by its assay office, the bullion dealers and ancillary trades. Because security is tight in the area you usually have to ring the bell before you can enter a shop, but don't let that deter you. You can buy gems, brooches, necklaces, rings, both new and antique gold pieces; have stones set, pearls threaded, gold polished, and cuff links commissioned; heirlooms valued, one-off designs made up and frail jewellery reworked. Buy copper and brass items, silver hip flasks, trophies, watches, badges ... the wonderful thing is that prices are extremely reasonable, and the crafts people very helpful if you wish to discuss (without obligation) an idea for a design or gift. We have received several reports from people who have bought jewellery at these shops for under half their usual price.

Who wouldn't want something original for less than the price you would pay for a mass produced item in a high street shop?

551 Birmingham : Jewellery Quarter

Consortium Jewellery Ltd.

39 Vyse Street B18 6JV

(0121) 554 9297

Specialise in diamond rings and sell whole range of gold items including bracelets and chains. Jewellery for ladies and men (such as cuff links, tie tacks, bracelets, neck chains and rings).

'Family business which buys and sells all types of jewellery. One-off pieces and commissions welcomed. Prices from £10–£2000. Happy to carry out repairs and give valuations.'

From clocktower: go down the left side of Vyse Street; go over the railway, with a brick wall on the left, and this is the third shop on the left.

Open: Mon–Sat 9–4.
Also Nov–Dec Sun 10–3.
Closed: Bank Holidays; Christmas, Boxing and New Year's Days.
Cards: Access, Amex, Transax (for clearing cheques), Visa .
Cars: Pay-&-display in street and multi-storey car-park.
Toilets: At car-park.
Wheelchairs: Two steps to medium sized shop.
Teas: Local cafés and pubs.
Groups: You are welcome to look into the workshop.
Transport: Bus from city centre. Jewellery train line station few yards away.
Mail order: No.

Jeff & Annabel's Diamond Gallery

35 Warstone Lane B18 6JQ
(0121) 236 5799

A small family business specialising in 18 and 9 carat gold hand-crafted quality jewellery, particularly engagement and diamond dress rings, all types of wedding rings etc. Exclusive range of English hand-made chain and bracelets, lockets, earrings, etc.

'Personal, friendly service. The only member of the National Association of Goldsmiths in the Jewellery Quarter. Rings bought here altered to size within one hour. Also repair modern and antique jewellery on the premises. Factory Shop Guide readers receive discount on any purchase.'

....

From the clocktower: go along Warstone Lane (Rose Villa pub on left). Stay on right side. Cross over Vittoria Street then this shop is few yards on right.

Open: Mon–Sat 9–5; most Sundays 10–2 and Bank Holidays (phone first, please).
Closed: Christmas and Boxing Days; Easter Sunday.
Cards: Access, Amex, Switch, Visa. Interest free credit (subject to status; details on request).
Cars: Pay-&-display in street and multi-storey car-park.
Toilets: At car-park.
Wheelchairs: One step to medium sized shop.
Teas: Bistro and restaurant three shops along.
Groups:
Transport: Bus no. 101 from Birmingham centre. New 'Jewellery' train line. Station few yards away.
Mail order: No.

Jewellery Quarter Discovery Centre

77–79 Vyse Street B18 6HB
(0121) 554 3598

Jewellery Quarter products made in this factory and selection of contemporary jewellery from Birmingham's talented young designer jewellers. Jewellery books and wide selection of beads and minerals.

'Visit the "time capsule" workshop of Messrs Smith and Pepper, a unique jewellery factory which has hardly changed since the turn of the century. Like the 'Marie Celeste' everything was left untouched when it closed down – from the contents of drawers to tea cups and jewellery tools – all in a state of suspended animation. '

....

From the clocktower: go down Vyse Street. This original workshop is towards the bottom on the right, past Spencer Street.

Open: Mon–Fri 10–4; Sat 11–5. Some Bank Holidays – please check.
Closed: Sunday; Christmas, Boxing and New Year's Days.
Cards: Access, Visa.
Toilets: Yes.
Wheelchairs: Good access.
Teas: Tea room now open.
Tours: Guided tours round this award winning museum built around the original jewellery workshop. Audio guides in French, Spanish, Hindi, German, Italian, Japanese. Individuals need not book, groups phone first. £2 adults; £1.50 concessions. Discounts for groups of 10+. Evening openings arranged. Meet a jeweller at work at the factory's benches and see the displays.
Transport: Jewellery Quarter train station a few yards away.

P J Gold Depot Ltd.

37 Vyse Street B18 6JY
(0121) 554 6165

Diamond, wedding and signet rings, pendants and necklets, all made on the premises. Specialist in eternity rings. Hand-made chains; cameos with hand-made gold mountings – which can be worn as either pendants or brooches. Jewellery made to customers' own designs. Wide range of imported chains too.

'This company produced the first ever eternity ring, set in yellow gold with white stones! Immediate re-sizing of rings. VIVAT tax free shopping.'

From the clocktower: go down the left side of Vyse Street; go over the railway, with a brick wall on the left, and this double-fronted shop with white columns is the second company on the left.

Open: Mon–Sat 9–4; *also Nov and Dec* Sun 9–4.
Closed: Bank Holidays, Christmas, Boxing and New Year's Days.
Cards: Access, Amex, Diners, Visa.
Cars: Pay-&-display in street and multi-storey car-park.
Wheelchairs: two steps – help willingly given – to spacious shop. Disabled (including groups) also welcome to go behind the scenes and see jewellery made.
Teas: Local cafés and pubs.
Transport: Bus no. 101 from city centre. Jewellery train line station a few yards up road .
Tours: You can see diamond cutter and gemstone mounter at work. Coach parties welcome (also in evening) – please phone Mr Hamlington first.
Mail order: No.

V & F Parker Ltd. (Arden Jewellery)

51 Vyse Street (off Gt Hampton Street) B18 6HS
(0121) 554 3587

Ring-making and gem-stone setting. Choose both your own stone and mounting from the wide selections of unmounted stones and settings available here. Price range of £10–£4,000 in stock. Company designs to order, undertake commissions such as gold company cuff-links and specialise in remaking old gold rings which have become frail with wear.

From the clocktower: go along the left hand side of Vyse Street for 300 yards. Cross over both ends of Hylton Street, then this is the second shop from the corner.

Open: Mon–Fri 9–5; Sat 9–3; *also Dec* Sunday mornings. Usually open Bank Holidays–please check.
Cards: Access, Amex, Diners, Visa.
Cars: Pay-&-display in street and multi-storey car-park.
Wheelchairs: Rather difficult – three steps to small shop.
Teas: Local cafés and pubs.
Transport: Bus no. 101 from city centre. Jewellery train line station 100 yds away.

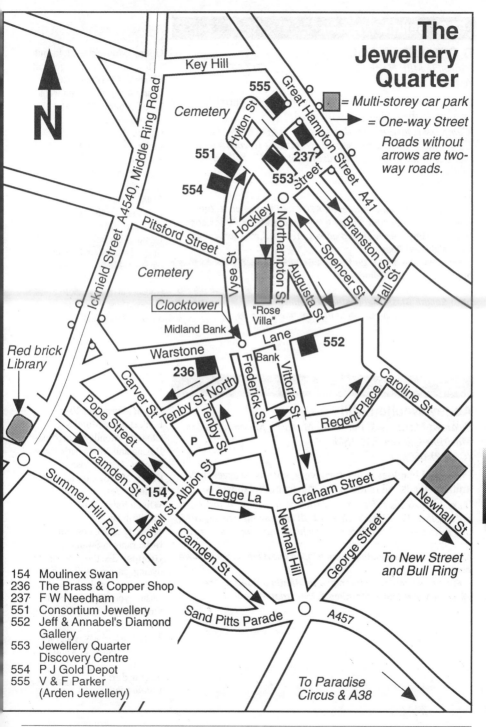

The Jewellery Quarter

■ = Multi-storey car park

→ = One-way Street

Roads without arrows are two-way roads.

Key Hill

555

Cemetery

Great Hampton Street A41

Hylton St

551

237

553

554

Hockley

Street

Branston St

Pitsford Street

Vyse St

Northampton St

Spencer St

Hall St

Cemetery

Augusta St

Clocktower

"Rose Villa"

Midland Bank

Lane

552

Warstone

Bank

Carver St

236

Frederick St

Vittoria St

Regent Place

Caroline St

Red brick Library

Pope Street

Tenby St North

Tenby St

P

Camden St

154

Powell St

Albion St

Legge La

Graham Street

Newhall St

Summer Hill Rd

Camden St

Newhall Hill

George Street

To New Street and Bull Ring

Sand Pitts Parade

A457

To Paradise Circus & A38

Icknield Street A4540, Middle Ring Road

154 Moulinex Swan
236 The Brass & Copper Shop
237 F W Needham
551 Consortium Jewellery
552 Jeff & Annabel's Diamond
     Gallery
553 Jewellery Quarter
     Discovery Centre
554 P J Gold Depot
555 V & F Parker
     (Arden Jewellery)

D C Dalgliesh Ltd.

Dunsdale Mill, North Riverside Ind. Area TD7 5EC
(01750) 20781

Headsquares in pure new wool and pure silk. Pure silk
evening sashes. Also tartan material.

*'Company is tartan specialist supplier to the Queen. Feature
"Reproduction Tartans", soft muted tartans resembling those
made with natural vegetable dyes before 1745. Sell perfects
and seconds.'*

....

To north of town.
  **From Peebles/Innerleithen on A707 and Moffat on A708:
cross river into Selkirk and go left immediately into Buccleuch
Road. Factory clearly signed on left after 1/2 mile, on corner
with Whinfield Road.**
  **From Hawick on A7: go through Selkirk, turn left after Exacta
on left and before Selkirk Glass.***
  **From Edinburgh/Galashiels on A7: take first right immediately
after Selkirk Glass, signposted to Moffat.***
  ***Shop clearly marked on right after nearly a mile.**

Open: Mon–Fri 9–11.45 and
1.15–4.15; Sat by arrangement.
Closed: Christmas–New
Year; 2–3 April; second week
June (Common Riding);
last two weeks July.
Cards: No.
Cars: Outside factory.
Toilets: No.
Wheelchairs: Easy access to
small shop.
Teas: In town.
Groups: Parties wanting to
shop should book with Mrs
Kemp. Also free tours round
the mill – must be booked in
advance. Max 40.
Transport: Bus from
Galashiels or Hawick to Selkirk
square, then 10 minutes' walk.
Mail order: Yes.

Abbey Woollen Mill

*Swansea Maritime & Industrial Museum, Museum Square,
Maritime Quarter SA1 1SM*
(01792) 650351

Pure wool blankets, rugs, turnovers, shawls, scarves and
knitting wools. All made in the mill from Welsh wools.

*'Very competitive prices, good value. Mill originally located in
Port Talbot, then Neath. In 1974 all equipment was rebuilt in
this museum and continues to produce traditional patterns.'*

....

**Museum is on fascinating, redeveloped quayside, close to town
centre.**
  **From town centre: follow signs to Maritime Quarter. The
Woollen Mill is inside Maritime & Industrial Museum.**

Open: Tues–Sun 10–5.
Bank Holiday Mondays.
Closed: Monday; Christmas,
Boxing and New Year's Days.
Cards: Access, Visa.
Cars: Nearby car-parks.
Toilets: Yes.
Wheelchairs: Full access for
the disabled.
Teas: Lots of cafés and
restaurants in Swansea.
Groups: See the processes of
dyeing, carding, spinning and
weaving on original machinery.
Ensure you allow sufficient
time to enjoy the whole of this
museum.
Transport: Easy walking
from city centre, bus and train
stations.
Mail order:
Catalogue:

Dents.
A
glove
for all
reasons

DENTS

THE
ESSENTIAL
ACCESSORY
ESTABLISHED
—1777—

For full details see our entry below

Dent's Factory Shop
Fairfield Road BA12 9DL
(01985) 212291

Extensive range of handbags, gloves in leather, suede and wool for ladies and men; sports gloves (ie shooting, equestrian). Leather goods, wallets, belts, purses, gifts, umbrellas etc.

'Discontinued or imperfect ranges, many at less than half retail price.'

See our display advertisement above

....

Warminster is off A36, halfway between Salisbury and Bath.
In the centre of the town: aim for main car-park, library, station and tourist information. Turn off the A36 at mini-roundabout by post office towards station, library and tourist information. Fairfield Road is first turning on right just after Warminster police station on the left. From Trowbridge on reaching town centre turn left at mini-roundabout, go over lights where A350 goes off to Shaftesbury and turn left in front of post office. From Shaftesbury turn right onto A36 at lights in town centre, then left in front of post office at mini-roundabout.

Open: *1 Sept–end May:*
Wed–Sat 10–4.
Closed: *June–August;*
Christmas and Boxing Days.
Cards: No.
Cars: Own car-park.
Toilets: No.
Wheelchairs: Easy access.
Teas: In Warminster.
Groups: Shoppers welcome.
Visit Dent's Museum, by prior appointment only.
Transport: Local buses.
400 yds from Warminster BR station.
Mail order: No.

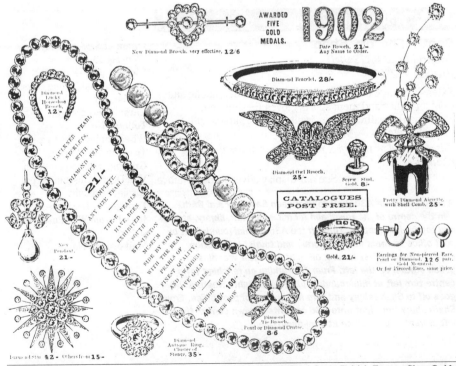

New Diamond Brooch, very effective, **12/6**

AWARDED
FIVE
GOLD
MEDALS.

1902

Date Brooch, **21/-**
Any Name to Order.

Diamond Lucky Horseshoe Brooch, **12/-**

FAULKNER PEARL SERLETS, WITH DIAMOND ESAP.
PRICE **21/-**
COMPLETE.
ANY SIZE PEARL.

THESE PEARLS HAVE BEEN EXHIBITED IN SOUTH KENSINGTON MUSEUM SIDE BY SIDE WITH THE REAL PEARLS OF FINEST QUALITY AND AWARDED FIVE GOLD MEDALS.

SUPERIOR QUALITY. **40/- 60/- 100/-** PER ROW.

New Pendant, **21/-**

Diamond Star, **42/-** Others from **15/-**

Diamond Antique Ring, Cluster of Stones, **35/-**

Diamond Bracelet, **28/-**

Diamond Owl Brooch, **25/-**

Screw Stud, Gold, **8/-**

Pretty Diamond Aigrette, with Shell Comb, **25/-**

CATALOGUES POST FREE.

Gold, **21/-**

Earrings for Non-pierced Ears, Pearl or Diamond, **12/6** pair, Gold Mounted.
Or for Pierced Ears, same price.

Diamond Tie Brooch, Pearl or Diamond Centre, **8/6**

Clothing

This is our largest chapter, and one which affords the greatest variety. The shops here will enable you not just to equip every member of the family (of any age, sex or size) with essential clothes at much reduced prices, but to indulge in the kind of luxury purchase which may have, so far, seemed beyond your means (or conscience!). From the humblest pair of shorts for a little boy to famous name garments, the finest lingerie or Scottish cashmeres for yourself, they are all there.

Many manufacturers find that they are holding perfect stock which cannot be disposed of through normal high street outlets. Products may be overmakes, cancelled orders, ends of line or, quite simply, last year's stock. None of these factors detract from the overall quality.

Other products, known as 'seconds', may be slightly less than perfect, but each manufacturer's idea of 'less than perfect' varies from that of the next; a damaged wrapping can, in some cases, make an item a 'second'. Slightly incorrect seams, a missing button, colour variations or a pulled thread will also make a garment a 'second'. If the flaw is not apparent (and, often, it may be minute) it is worth asking what it is before you buy, if only to satisfy your curiosity.

Velmore Fashions	610	**Ellesmere Port**	Cheshire
Viyella	406*	**Ellesmere Port**	Cheshire
Balmoral Mill Shop	611	**Galston**	Strathclyde
Jockey	612	**Gateshead**	Tyne & Wear
Mister Mackenzie	613	**Glasgow**	Strathclyde
Claremont Garments	614	**Glasgow**	Strathclyde
Morlands	745*	**Glastonbury**	Somerset
Richard Draper	746*	**Glastonbury**	Somerset
Keela International	615	**Glenrothes**	Fife
Alan Paine Knitwear	616	**Godalming**	Surrey
Kent & Curwen	617	**Godalming**	Surrey
Witham Contours	618	**Grantham**	Lincs
Choice Discount Stores	619	**Grays**	Essex
Guernsey Woollens	620	**Guernsey**	Channel Islands
Le Tricoteur	621	**Guernsey**	Channel Islands
Susan Walker Classics	622	**Guildford**	Surrey
Choice Discount Stores	623	**Hadleigh**	Essex
Katie Gray Factory Frock Shop	624	**Halifax**	W Yorks
Darley Mill Centre	407*	**Harrogate**	N Yorks
Benetton	409*	**Hartlepool**	Cleveland
Chas N Whillans	412*	**Hartlepool**	Cleveland
Honey	416*	**Hartlepool**	Cleveland
James Barry	417*	**Hartlepool**	Cleveland
JoKids	418*	**Hartlepool**	Cleveland
TOG 24	420*	**Hartlepool**	Cleveland
Tom Sayers	421*	**Hartlepool**	Cleveland
Wrangler	424*	**Hartlepool**	Cleveland
Winfields	425*	**Haslingden**	Lancs
Thistle Trading Co.	625	**Haverfordwest**	Dyfed
Hawick Cashmere Company	626	**Hawick**	Borders
Peter Scott & Co.	627	**Hawick**	Borders
Short & Robertson Knitwear	628	**Hawick**	Borders
Valerie Louthan and Country Store	629	**Hawick**	Borders
Wrights of Trowmill	630	**Hawick**	Borders
Ponden Mill	427*	**Haworth**	W Yorks
Abrovian Factory Shop	631	**Hebden Bridge**	W Yorks
Aquascutum	632	**Hemel Hempstead**	Herts
M & G Designer Fashions	633	**Hickstead Village**	W Sussex
Factory Shop Ltd., The	428*	**Holbeach**	Lincolnshire
Factory Shop Ltd., The	429*	**Horley**	Surrey
Hornsea Freeport	430*	**Hornsea**	Humberside
Claremont Garments	634	**Howdon, Wallsend-on-Tyne**	Tyne & Wear
Jaeger	635	**Hucknall**	Notts
Shop at the Mill	636	**Huddersfield : Lockwood**	W Yorks
Dewhirst	637	**Hull**	Humberside
Charnos	638	**Ilkeston**	Derbys
J B Armstrong & Co.	639	**Ilkeston**	Derbys
Match Leisurewear Manufacturers	640	**Ilkeston**	Derbys
R S Sports & Leisurewear	641	**Ilkeston**	Derbys
Daleswear Factory Shop	642	**Ingleton**	N Yorks
Lambourne Clothing	643	**Ipswich**	Suffolk
Barbour	644	**Jarrow**	Tyne & Wear
Warner's	645	**Keady**	Co. Armagh, Northern Ireland
Factory Shop Ltd., The	431*	**Keighley**	W Yorks
Jumpers	436*	**Kendal**	Cumbria

Glen Alva	689	**Sauchie by Alloa**	Central
Hide Park Leather Co.	690	**Scunthorpe**	Humberside
Farfield Clothing	691	**Sedbergh**	Cumbria
Brenire	692	**Selkirk**	Borders
Gardiner of Selkirk	693	**Selkirk**	Borders
Charterhouse Holdings	449*	**Shepshed**	Leics
Mulberry	694	**Shepton Mallet**	Somerset
Durham Clothing Co.	695	**Shildon**	Co. Durham
Claremont Garments	696	**Shoreham-by-Sea**	W Sussex
Factory Shop Ltd., The	450*	**Sileby**	Leics
Skipton Mill Shop	697	**Skipton**	N Yorks
Mexx Factory Outlet	698	**Slough**	Berks
Coats Viyella	699	**Somercotes**	Derbys
Claremont Garments	700	**South Shields**	Tyne & Wear
Tweedmill	701	**St Asaph**	Clwyd
LS & J Sussman	702	**St Austell**	Cornwall
Playdri Products	279*	**Stanton, Bury St Edmunds**	Suffolk
Factory Shop Ltd., The	452*	**Stoke-on-Trent : Newcastle**	Staffs
Alexon/Eastex/Dash	454*	**Street**	Somerset
Benetton	456*	**Street**	Somerset
Esprit	464*	**Street**	Somerset
Fred Perry	465*	**Street**	Somerset
Jaeger/Jaeger Man	467*	**Street**	Somerset
James Barry	468*	**Street**	Somerset
JoKids	469*	**Street**	Somerset
Jumpers	470*	**Street**	Somerset
Liz Claiborne	472*	**Street**	Somerset
Monsoon/Accessorize	473*	**Street**	Somerset
Rohan	476*	**Street**	Somerset
Triumph/Hom	481*	**Street**	Somerset
Viyella	483*	**Street**	Somerset
Windsmoor	484*	**Street**	Somerset
Woolea	485*	**Street**	Somerset
Wrangler	486*	**Street**	Somerset
Factory Shop Ltd., The	487*	**Stroud**	Gloucs
Dewhirst	703	**Sunderland**	Tyne & Wear
Claremont Garments	704	**Sutton-in-Ashfield**	Notts
Cooper & Roe	705	**Sutton-in-Ashfield**	Notts
Dewhirst	706	**Swansea**	West Glamorgan
Triumph International	707	**Swindon**	Wilts
Jaeger Sale Shop	708	**Tamworth**	Staffs
Fruit of the Loom	709	**Telford**	Salop
Callant of Scotland (Knitwear)	710	**Tillicoultry**	Central
Lindsay Allan Designs	711	**Tillicoultry**	Central
Factory Shop Ltd., The	488*	**Tiptree**	Essex
Factory Shop Ltd., The	489*	**Trowbridge**	Wilts
Factory Shop Ltd., The	490*	**Warminster**	Wilts
S R Leisure	712	**Washington**	Tyne and Wear
Next 2 Choice	713	**Watford**	Herts
Fashion Factory	714	**Wellington**	Shropshire
East Quay Knitwear	715	**Wells-next-the-Sea**	Norfolk
Claremont Garments	716	**West Auckland**	Co. Durham
Next 2 Choice	717	**Wickford**	Essex
Benco Hosiery	718	**Wirksworth**	Derbys
Velmore Fashions	719	**Wrexham**	Clwyd
Bridge of York	720	**York**	N Yorks
Factory Outlet Shopping Centre (FOSC)	491*	**York**	N Yorks

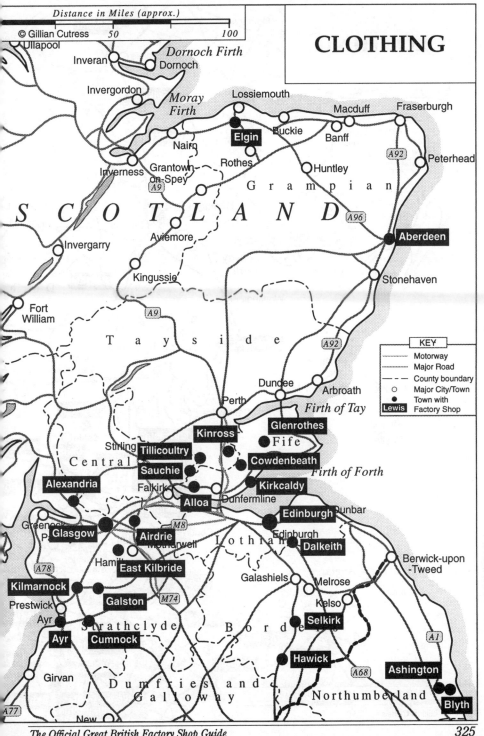

CLOTHING

Distance in Miles (approx.)

© Gillian Cutress   50   100

KEY
.... Motorway
.... Major Road
– – – County boundary
○ Major City/Town
● Town with
Lewis Factory Shop

Ullapool
Inveran
Dornoch Firth
Dornoch
Invergordon
Moray Firth
Lossiemouth
Macduff
Fraserburgh
Nairn
Elgin
Buckie
Banff
A92
Peterhead
Inverness
Grantown-on-Spey
Rothes
Huntley
A9
G r a m p i a n
Invergarry
Aviemore
Aberdeen
A96
Kingussie
Stonehaven
Fort William
A9
T a y s i d e
A92
Dundee
Arbroath
Perth
Firth of Tay
Glenrothes
Kinross
Fife
Stirling
Tillicoultry
Cowdenbeath
Central
Sauchie
Kirkcaldy
Firth of Forth
Alexandria
Falkirk
Alloa
Dunfermline
Greenock
M8
Edinburgh
Dunbar
Glasgow
Airdrie
Edinburgh
Motherwell
L o t h i a n
Dalkeith
Hamilton
Berwick-upon-Tweed
East Kilbride
Galashiels
Melrose
A78
Kilmarnock
Prestwick
Galston
M74
Kelso
A1
Ayr
S t r a t h c l y d e
Selkirk
Ayr
Cumnock
B o r d e r s
Hawick
Girvan
A68
Ashington
D u m f r i e s   a n d
G a l l o w a y
Northumberland
A77
New
Blyth

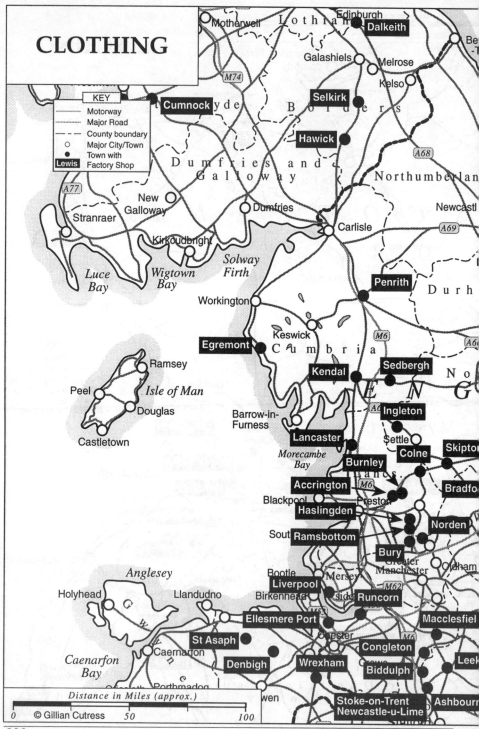

CLOTHING

KEY
——	Motorway
....	Major Road
— —	County boundary
○	Major City/Town
●	Town with
Lewis	Factory Shop

M74

Motherwell *L o t h i a n* Edinburgh **Dalkeith** Be-T

Galashiels Melrose

Kelso

Cumnock yde Selkirk

B   o   r   d   e   r   s

Hawick

A68

D u m f r i e s a n d
G a l l o w a y *Northumberlan*

A77

New Galloway Dumfries Newcastl

Stranraer A69

Kirkcudbright Carlisle

Solway Firth

Luce Bay *Wigtown Bay*

Penrith *D u r h*

Workington

C u m b r i a A6

Keswick

Egremont **Sedbergh** *N o*

Ramsey **Kendal**

Peel *Isle of Man* E N G

Douglas A6 **Ingleton**

Castletown Barrow-in-Furness

Lancaster Settle

Morecambe Bay **Colne** **Skipto**

Accrington M6 **Bradfo**

Blackpool Preston

Haslingden **Norden**

Sout **Ramsbottom**

Bury Oldham
Greater
Manchester

Anglesey Bootle Mersey M62

Holyhead Llandudno **Liverpool** **Runcorn**

Birkenhead side

Ellesmere Port **Macclesfiel**

Chester

St Asaph **Congleton**

Caenarfon Bay Caernarfon **Leek**

Denbigh **Wrexham** **Biddulph**

Porthmadog

Distance in Miles (approx.)

wen **Stoke-on-Trent** **Ashbourn**
Newcastle-u-Lime

0 © Gillian Cutress 50 100

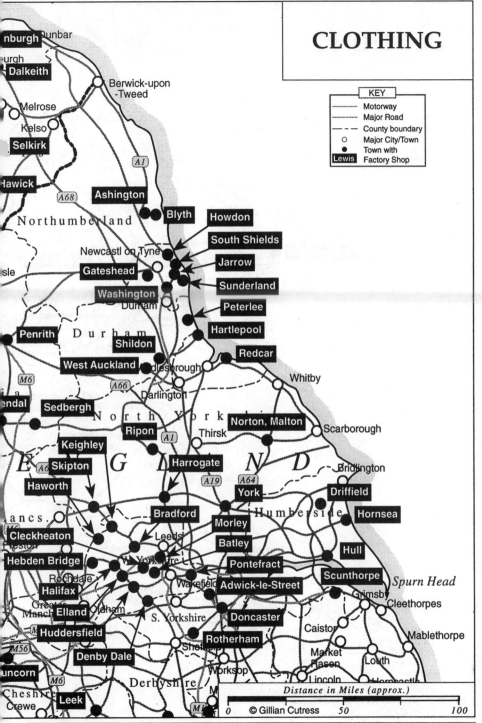

CLOTHING

KEY
- Motorway
- Major Road
- County boundary
- ○ Major City/Town
- ● Town with Factory Shop
- Lewis Factory Shop

nburgh · Dunbar
urgh
Dalkeith
Melrose
Kelso
Selkirk
Hawick
Berwick-upon-Tweed
A1
A68
Ashington
Northumberland
Blyth
Howdon
Newcastl on Tyne
South Shields
Gateshead
Jarrow
Sunderland
Washington
Durham
Peterlee
sle
Penrith
Durham
Hartlepool
Shildon
West Auckland
Middlesbrough
Redcar
M6
A66
Darlington
Whitby
endal
Sedbergh
North York...
Kendal
Ripon
Thirsk
Norton, Malton
Scarborough
Keighley
A1
E   N   G   L   A   N   D
Skipton
Harrogate
Bridlington
A6
Haworth
A19   A64
York
Driffield
Lancs.
Bradford
Humberside
Hornsea
Cleckheaton
Morley
Leeds
Preston
Batley
Hebden Bridge
W. Yorkshire
Hull
Rochdale
Pontefract
Scunthorpe
Spurn Head
Halifax
Wakefield
Adwick-le-Street
Grimsby
Great
Manch
Elland
Oldham
Cleethorpes
Huddersfield
S. Yorkshire
Doncaster
Caistor
Mablethorpe
M56
Denby Dale
Rotherham
uncorn
M6
Worksop
Sheffield
Market Rasen
Louth
Hornc...
Cheshire
Derbyshire
Lincoln
Crewe
Leek

Distance in Miles (approx.)

0   © Gillian Cutress   50   100

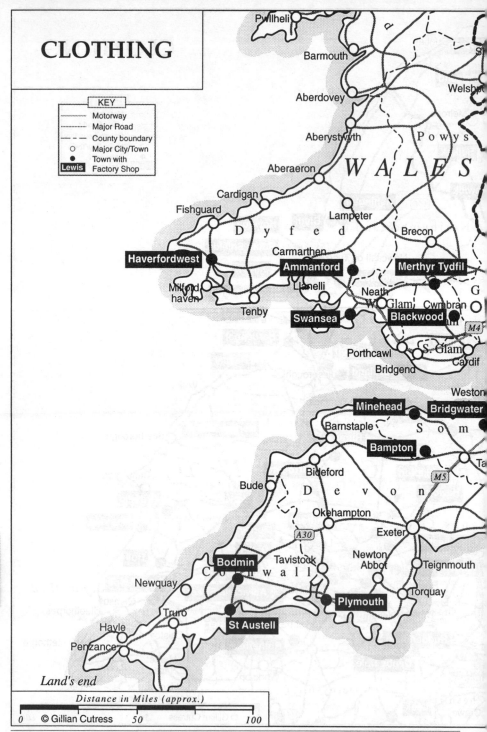

CLOTHING

KEY
- Motorway
- Major Road
- County boundary
- ○ Major City/Town
- ● Town with Factory Shop
- Lewis

Pwllheli
Barmouth
Aberdovey
Welshp
Aberystwyth
P o w y s
Aberaeron
W A L E S
Cardigan
Fishguard
Lampeter
D y f e d
Brecon
Carmarthen
Haverfordwest
Ammanford
Merthyr Tydfil
Milford haven
Llanelli
Neath
G
Tenby
W
Glam
Cwmbran
Swansea
Blackwood
M4
Porthcawl
S. Glam
Bridgend
Cardif

Weston
Minehead
Bridgwater
Barnstaple
S o m
Bampton
Ta
Bideford
M5
Bude
D e v o n
Okehampton
A30
Exeter
Bodmin
Tavistock
Newton Abbot
Teignmouth
Newquay
C o r n w a l l
Plymouth
Torquay
Truro
St Austell
Hayle
Penzance

Land's end

Distance in Miles (approx.)

0   © Gillian Cutress   50   100

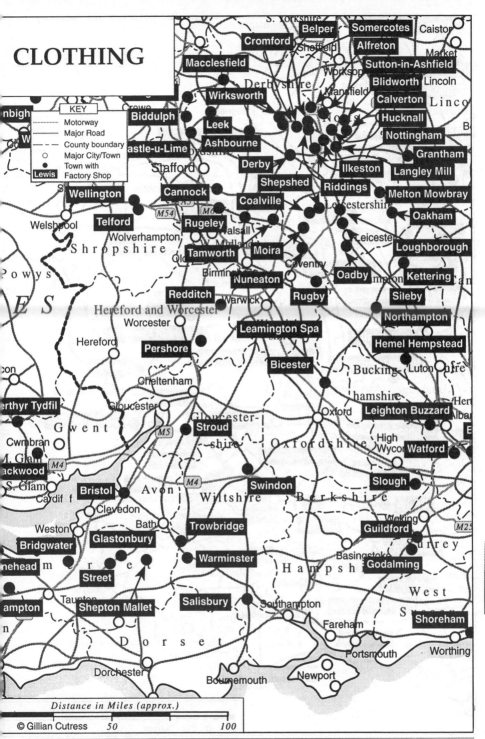

CLOTHING

KEY
- ┈┈┈┈ Motorway
- ──── Major Road
- ─ ─ ─ County boundary
- ○ Major City/Town
- ● Town with
- Lewis Factory Shop

Belper
Somercotes
Caistor
Cromford
Sheffield
Alfreton
Macclesfield
Market
Sutton-in-Ashfield
Wirksworth
Derbyshire
Mansfield
Blidworth
Lincoln
Worksop
Calverton
Linco
Biddulph
Leek
Hucknall
Notts
Nottingham
astle-u-Lime
Ashbourne
Crewe
Stafford
Derby
Ilkeston
Grantham
Langley Mill
Shepshed
Riddings
Melton Mowbray
Cannock
Coalville
Leicestershire
Oakham
Wellington
Telford
Rugeley
Walsall
Oadby
Loughborough
Wolverhampton
W. Midlands
Leicester
Tamworth
Moira
Coventry
Shropshire
Old
Birmingham
Nuneaton
Oadby
ington
Kettering
Redditch
Warwick
Rugby
Sileby
Hereford and Worcester
Northampton
Worcester
Leamington Spa
Hemel Hempstead
Hereford
Pershore
Bicester
Buckingham
Luton
Cheltenham
hamshire
Her
erthyr Tydfil
Gloucester
Oxford
Leighton Buzzard
Albe
Gwent
Stroud
Gloucester-shire
Oxfordshire
High Wycombe
Watford
Cwmbran
M5
M. Glam
ackwood
M4
M4
Swindon
Slough
S. Glam
Bristol
Avon
Wiltshire
Berkshire
Cardiff
Clevedon
Woking
M25
Weston
Bath
Trowbridge
Guildford
Surrey
Bridgwater
Glastonbury
Basingstoke
Godalming
nehead
more
Warminster
Hampshire
Street
West
ampton
Taunton
Shepton Mallet
Salisbury
Southampton
Sussex
Shoreham
Fareham
Worthing
Dorset
Portsmouth
Dorchester
Bournemouth
Newport

Distance in Miles (approx.)

© Gillian Cutress   50   100

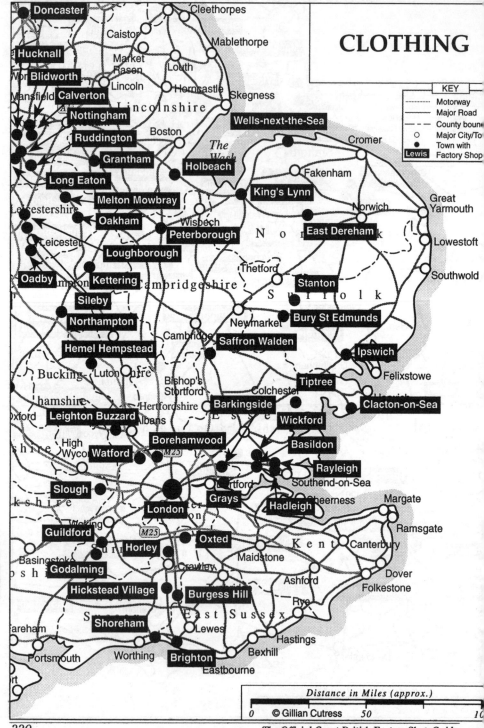

CLOTHING

KEY
- .... Motorway
- ───── Major Road
- ─ ─ ─ County boundary
- ○ Major City/Town
- ● Town with
- Lewis Factory Shop

Doncaster
Cleethorpes
Caistor
Mablethorpe
Hucknall
Market Rasen
Louth
Blidworth
Lincoln
Horncastle
Skegness
Mansfield Calverton
Lincolnshire
Nottingham
Wells-next-the-Sea
Cromer
Ruddington
Boston
Grantham
Holbeach
Fakenham
The Wash
Long Eaton
King's Lynn
Great Yarmouth
Melton Mowbray
Leicestershire
Norwich
Oakham
Wisbech
East Dereham
Lowestoft
Leicester
Peterborough
Norfolk
Loughborough
Southwold
Thetford
Oadby
Kettering
Cambridgeshire
Stanton
Suffolk
Sileby
Northampton
Bury St Edmunds
Hemel Hempstead
Newmarket
Saffron Walden
Ipswich
Bucking-hamshire
Luton
Cambridge
Felixstowe
Bishop's Stortford
Colchester
Tiptree
Oxford
Leighton Buzzard
Hertfordshire
Barkingside
Clacton-on-Sea
St Albans
Essex
Wickford
High Wycombe
Watford
Borehamwood
Basildon
M25
Rayleigh
Slough
Southend-on-Sea
London
Grays
Sheerness
Margate
Woking
Hadleigh
Guildford
M25
Oxted
Ramsgate
Basingstoke
Horley
Kent
Canterbury
Godalming
Maidstone
Dover
Hickstead Village
Burgess Hill
Ashford
Folkestone
Shoreham
Rye
Fareham
East Sussex
Lewes
Hastings
Portsmouth
Worthing
Brighton
Bexhill
Eastbourne

Distance in Miles (approx.)

0   © Gillian Cutress   50   100

330

The Official Great British Factory Shop Guide

Wirksworth Factory Shop

HOT AND COLD DRINKS CHILDREN'S PLAY AREA

OPEN SEVEN DAYS A WEEK
9.00 am – 5.00pm
LATE NIGHT THURSDAYS UNTIL 8.30pm

AS SEEN ON THE BBC CLOTHES SHOW

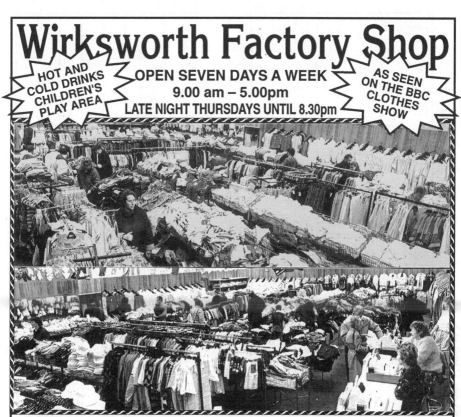

OUR PRICES ARE SO LOW IT'S SCANDALOUS
..........and it's not just our socks..........

MENSWEAR
Trousers & Jeans
Jackets & Coats
Boilersuits & Bodywarmers
Workshirts & Sportshirts
Pullovers & Sweatshirts
Pyjamas & Jog trousers
Vests, Briefs & Hankies
Boxershorts & Swimtrunks
HOUSEHOLD LINENS
Towels & Teatowels
Velour & Beach towels

LADIESWEAR
Dresses & Skirts
Lycra leggings & Shorts
Blouses & T-shirts
Bras, Briefs & Slips
Jogging suits & Slacks
Nighties & Dressing gowns
Socks, Tights & Stockings
Pantaloons & Spencers
Cardigans & Waistcoats
Hats, Gloves & Shawls

CHILDRENSWEAR
Sportswear & Swimwear
Trousers & Jeans
Leggings & Skirts
Vests, Briefs & Crop sets
Socks & Tights
Dresses & Jumpers
T-shirts & Shorts
BABYWEAR
Dresses & Rompers
Anoraks & Jackets
Cardigans & Jumpers
Bibs & Padders
Nappies & Towels
Blankets & Sheets

ONE OF THE
LARGEST FACTORY SHOPS
IN THE COUNTRY

BENCO HOSIERY, NORTH END MILLS,
CEMETERY LANE, WIRKSWORTH, DERBYS
(01629) 824731

Fire station — Lime Kiln Pub
WIRKSWORTH — MATLOCK
WE ARE HERE
School
Car park

See our entry no. 718

SIZE CHART

With this chart you have no excuse for not knowing the sizes of your family or your home!

NAME	Ring size										
	Shoes										
	Socks										
	Tights Stockings										
	Pants										
	Bra										
	Shirt collar										
	Jacket										
	Trouser leg										
	Trouser waist										
	Trousers										
	Sweater										
	Skirt										
	Dress Blouse										
	Bust Waist Hip										

ROOM	Bed size					
	Yds fabric upholstery					
	Rolls wallpaper					
	Yds fabric needed 2					
	Curtain length 2					
	Window width 2					
	Yds fabric needed 1					
	Curtain length 1					
	Window width 1					
	Room Size					

The Mill Shop
Grandholm Mill, Woodside AB9 2SB
(01224) 483201

Ladies' skirts, jackets, blazers, trousers, coats. Gents' blazers, sports jackets, suits, trousers, overcoats. Ladies' and gents' knitwear.
'Ends of lines, seconds or last season's models. Special sales twice a year.'

....

By the river Don north of town.
From the town centre: take A96 for Inverness; at traffic lights with a right turn to Fraserburgh, Peterhead and Old Aberdeen, go straight; go right at next lights.*
From the south, south-west and west: go into town as far as the A947 (signposted (A96) Inverness) and turn towards Inverness. When you reach the A96 at the large roundabout (Texaco on corner), go right for city centre then left at next traffic lights.*
From Inverness via A96: pass the airport and go straight at the roundabout with large Fiat garage at corner. Turn left at next traffic lights.*
*Take second left; at bottom go left again into Gordon's Mill Road, go over river bridge and turn right; follow signs.

Open: Mon–Sat 9–4.30; Sun 12–4.30.
Closed: Christmas and Boxing Days; 1, 2 and 3 Jan.
Cards: Access, Amex, Eurocard, Switch, Visa.
Cars: Own large car-park.
Toilets: Yes.
Wheelchairs: Easy access; no steps.
Changing rooms: Yes.
Teas: Own restaurant and coffee shop. Also picnic area.
Groups: Museum and audio-visual display. Coach parties and large shopping groups please phone 01224 483201. You can also enjoy riverside walks, fishing.
Transport: Bus no. 25 (Tillydrone).
Mail order: No.

Karrimor International Ltd.
Petre Road, Clayton-le-Moors BB5 5JR
(01254) 385911 and 388466

Rucksacks, child carriers, cycle bags, outdoor garments including waterproofs. *Trangia* stoves, *Karrimats*. Footwear for outdoor activities.
'Seconds, ex-display, samples and ends of lines. Gore-Tex new and seconds; cycle clothing range; Phoenix mountain and ski clothing.'

....

Clayton-le-Moors is on north-west side of Accrington.
From Accrington: follow signs to M65/Rishton. Cross under M65 at exit 7.*
From M65 exit 7: follow signs to Clitheroe (A6185).
*Turn right at traffic lights opposite GEC Industrial Estate; Petre Road is first on left. Karrimor is at end of road.

Open: Mon 2–7.30; Tues and Wed 12–5; Thur 12–7.30.
Closed: Friday; Saturday; Bank Holidays; Christmas–New Year.
Cards: Access, Switch, Visa.
Cars: Own car-park.
Toilets: Yes.
Wheelchairs: Yes.
Changing rooms: Yes.
Teas: In Accrington.
Groups: Small shop, so unsuitable for large groups.
Transport: None.
Mail order: Yes.
Catalogue: Free. Catalogue only has items which cannot be found in outdoor specialist shops. Sent by Securicor, except small items.

Stagslax Menswear Ltd.

Church Lane DN6 7AV
(01302) 727550

Make top quality middle-weight trousers for men in worsteds, corduroy and some lighter fabrics.
'Mostly firsts, a few seconds, all at factory prices.'

Easy to see on the B1220, on the north-eastern side of Adwick.
From both the north (A1 or Wakefield) and the south (Doncaster): take A638 to Woodlands. Then ...
from the south: go right at the Broad Highway pub, go through the village, over the railway bridge then this company, in the converted red-brick cinema, is 300 yds on the right.
from the north: turn left off the A638 at the gearbox shop, go to the fork in the road, over the railway bridge, then this company, in the converted red-brick cinema, is 300 yds on the right.

Open: Mon–Fri 10–4; Sat 10–3.
Closed: Bank Holidays; Christmas–New Year.
Cards: None.
Cars: Two large car-parks.
Toilets: No.
Wheelchairs: One small step to medium-sized shop.
Changing rooms: Yes.
Teas: Local cafés and pubs.
Groups: Not suitable for shopping groups.
Transport: Doncaster–Carcroft buses.

Unique Fashions

Unit 13/14, Stirling Road Industrial Estate ML6 7UD
(01236) 762684

Huge range of ladies', gents' and children's quality sheepskin, suede and leather garments – jackets, coats, waistcoats, sheepskin jackets etc. Also large range of skins in different textures and colours. Accessories such as purses, wallets, gloves and bags.
'Repair and alteration service. Made-to-measure from extra small to oversize. Large choice in stock.'

On the north side of Airdrie, just off the A73 (road to Cumbernauld).
Coming south on the A73: as you get to the edge of town, go under pylons and take next left, signposted Stirling Road Ind. Est.*
From town: aim for Cumbernauld/Stirling (A73). Pass Jet petrol on the right, then take next right (Dykehead Road) signposted Stirling Road Ind. Est.*
***Turn right into estate (Dalmacoulter Road) then turn left (Laverock Road) and continue to shop at far back right (well signed).**

Open: Mon 9–4.30; Tues–Fri 9–5.30; Sat 10–5; Sun 11–5.
Closed: Spring Bank Holidays; Christmas, Boxing and New Year's Days; 2 Jan.
Cards: Access, Amex, Switch, Visa.
Cars: Own large car-park.
Toilets: Yes.
Wheelchairs: Two steps to large shop; assistance can be given.
Changing rooms: Yes.
Teas: Many cafés and hotels nearby.
Groups: No.
Transport: Bus no. 47 from Airdrie bus station.
Mail order: No.
Catalogue: Yes.

Cocoon Coats

Lomond Trade Centre, Lomond Industrial Estate G83 0TK
(01389) 755511

Top quality lightweight crease-resistant ladies' rainwear with carrying pouches, plus some coats for men. Cotton and wax look; waterproofed; optional warm lining. Made-to-order service.

'Also shops at 28 Victoria Street, Edinburgh (0131 226 2327) and 110 Kensington Church Street, London W8 (0171 221 7000).'

....

Lomond Industrial Estate is at northern end of Alexandria.

From town centre: aim for Balloch and the north, pass huge red derelict building, go right immediately after it.*

From A82 going north or south: turn off at signs to Lomond Industrial Estate. Go right at roundabout then left, opposite hospital, towards estate.*

*At far end of road, turn right on to estate. This shop is in third unit in first building on right after you get on to estate.

Open: Mon–Fri 8.30–5.30; Sat, Sun 11–5.
Closed: Christmas–2 Jan.
Cards: Access, Amex, Visa.
Cars: Outside shop.
Toilets: Yes.
Wheelchairs: Easy access to medium sized shop.
Changing rooms: No.
Teas: In building.
Groups: No factory tours. Groups (maximum 15) welcome to shop; phone first.
Transport: Balloch railway station; local bus to hospital at top of road.
Mail order: Yes.
Catalogue: Yes. £1.50.

David Nieper Ltd.

Orange Street, Nottingham Road DE55 7LE
(01773) 833335

Finest quality designer lingerie, nightwear and leisurewear, dressing gowns and bed jackets, full slips, slippers, swimwear and high class daywear. Fabrics and laces. Design room samples; discontinued lines and slight imperfects.

'An Aladdin's cave – unlike any other factory shop.'

....

About 1/3 mile east of Alfreton on B600 and 5 minutes from M1 exit 28.

From M1 exit 28: take A38 west, signposted Matlock. Take first main exit to Alfreton (B600); at top of slip road, turn right then go straight for Alfreton. Pass petrol station on right: take next left (Orange Street).*

From Alfreton town centre: go towards Somercotes on Nottingham Road. Take the right fork, signposted Selston (not B6019 to Pinxton). Turn into the third right (Orange Street) opposite Watson's paint shop.*

*Shop at bottom right of car-park.

Open: Mon–Sat and Bank Holidays 10–4.
Closed: Christmas and New Year's Days.
Cards: All major cards.
Cars: Own large car-park.
Toilets: Yes.
Wheelchairs: One step.
Changing rooms: Yes, spacious.
Teas: Tea, coffee, light refreshments usually available in canteen.
Groups: Welcome to shop, but please telephone first.
Transport: Alfreton/Somercotes buses stop at factory entrance.
Mail order: Yes.
Catalogue: Free. No seconds, but the entire perfect range. Ring (01773) 836000.

Jaeger

Tullibody Road, Lornshill FK10 2EY
(01259) 218985

Large range of ladies' wear: knitwear, blouses, skirts, trousers, jackets, suits. Men's suits, trousers, jackets, shirts and ties. Towels, bedding.
'Quality merchandise at reduced prices.'

....

On the B9096 at Tullibody end of Alloa.
   From Stirling on A907: go left on to B9096 into Tullibody.
Go through town; factory is first building on right after large
Lornshill School on left.
   From A907 through Alloa: turn on to B9096 towards Tullibody
at large roundabout with impressive stone town hall on one
corner and modern police station on other corner. Factory is
one mile from here, on left.

Open: Seven days a week, 10–4.
Closed: Please telephone for Christmas and Bank Holiday closures.
Cards: Access, Switch, Visa.
Cars: Visitors' car-park.
Toilets: In Tullibody.
Wheelchairs: Three steps to huge shop.
Changing rooms: Yes.
Teas: Cafés in Alloa.
Groups: No factory tours. Shopping groups welcome – prior phone call please.
Transport: Local buses from Alloa and Stirling.
Mail order: No.

Scottish Knitwear

Scotland is one of the most exciting areas for mill and factory shops. The number of shops is considerable, the selection wide, and the quality of goods outstanding.

Scottish knitwear is quite justly world famous. The choice of lambswool and cashmere products is stunning. Designs are exciting. You can buy from companies using modern knitting machines or from small enterprises using hand knitters. Fair Isle designs originate in Shetland. From the finest silk and cashmere jumper to rugged pullovers designed to withstand hard weather, they are all here.

A great deal of knitwear is on sale in Scotland. However, many companies have latched on to the phrase 'mill shop' and are using it regardless of whether they themselves manufacture anything. Be aware that many knitwear shops, including vast Scottish theme shops aimed at tourists, claim to be mill shops. Drive round the towns in the Borders or visit the obligatory 'mill shop' in any town that receives its share of visitors and you will quickly see what we mean. There is plenty of excellent knitwear available at good prices. However, we ourselves cannot see any difference between these shops and any normal high street shop so we do not list them.

In contrast, this book tells you where you can derive satisfaction of buying directly from the maker. It is very possible that you too will find yourself unable to leave the shops described here without a 'souvenir'. Or two.

Alan Paine Knitwear Ltd.

New Road SA18 3ET
(01269) 592316

Luxury knitwear in natural fibres including cashmere, camelhair, lambswool and cotton (sweaters, cardigans, slipovers). Brushed cotton shirts and polo shirts.

'Knitwear made here for sale worldwide. All stock at factory shop prices, mostly perfects, some seconds. Stock approximately half-price, always some seconds. Lambswool from £20, cashmere from £75. Special offers from time to time. Genuine factory shop!'

....

Easy to find, about 1/2 mile south-west of traffic lights in town centre. From these lights start on the A483 (Pontardulais/Swansea M4 road). Take left fork to 'New Road Industrial Estate/Pantyffnon 1'. Alan Paine is third factory, about 350 yds on left, after Corgi.

    From M4 on A483: go right about 1/2 mile after 'Welcome to Ammanford' sign, signposted to 'New Road Industrial Estate'. Company about 300 yds on left.

Open: Mon–Sat 9–4.
Closed: Bank Holidays; Christmas, Boxing and New Year's Days.
Cards: Mastercard, Switch, Visa.
Cars: Outside shop, within factory complex.
Toilets: No.
Wheelchairs: No, three steps to shop.
Changing rooms: No.
Teas: In Ammanford.
Groups: Shopping groups welcome provided they phone first. No factory tours.
Transport: 1/2 mile walk from Pantyffynnon station.
Mail order: No.

Corgi Hosiery Ltd.

New Road SA18 3DR
(01269) 592104/593147

Superb hand-framed knitwear and hosiery in cashmere, wool and other natural fibres. Most items perfects at factory prices.

'The only Welsh company to hold a Royal Warrant for HRH The Prince of Wales for knitwear and hosiery.'

....

Easy to find, about 1/2 mile south-west of traffic lights in town centre on A483 (Pontardulais/Swansea/M4 road). Take left fork to 'New Road Industrial Estate/Pantyffnon 1'. factory 300 yds on left.

    From M4 via A483: go right about 1/2 mile after 'Welcome to Ammanford' sign (sign to 'New Road Industrial Estate').

BY APPOINTMENT TO H.R.H. THE
PRINCE OF WALES KNITWEAR
AND HOSIERY MANUFACTURERS

Open: Mon–Thur 9–4.30; Fri 9–1.
Closed: Bank Holidays; last week July/first week Aug; Christmas–New Year.
Cards: Access, Visa.
Cars: Own car-park.
Toilets: Yes.
Wheelchairs: Easy access, small ground floor display area.
Changing rooms: You are welcome to try on sweaters.
Teas: In Ammanford.
Tours: You can see knitters in action as you go through to sales area. Interesting factory – hosiery machines are over 100 years old and all garments individually made on hand-operated intarsia knitting machines.
Transport: 10 minutes' walk from the town centre.
Mail order: No.

The Elite Factory Clothes Shop
Elite Buildings, Market Place DE6 1ES
(01335) 344065

Many branded names in a large and varied selection of clothing and shoes for ladies, men and children; chainstore garments; designer knitwear; underwear etc.
'Mainly perfects, some seconds and clearance lines.'

Clearly marked in the centre of Ashbourne on the market square, 50 yds down from the town hall.
 Much of Ashbourne is on a one-way system. Go clockwise until you see the market square sloping uphill on the left then take the next left.

Open: Mon–Sat 9–5; Sun 11–5.
Closed: Christmas, Boxing and New Year's Days.
Cards: Access, Delta, Visa.
Cars: Opposite shop on market square.
Toilets: 200 yds away.
Wheelchairs: One small step to large shop.
Changing rooms: Yes.
Teas: Several attractive cafés in town.
Groups: No tours, but groups welcome; please phone to arrange.
Transport: Any bus to Ashbourne.
Mail order: No.

Dewhirst Ltd.
Newbiggin Road, North Seaton Industrial Estate NE63 04B
(01670) 813493

Men's wear: quality suits, sports jackets and blazers, trousers, formal and casual shirts, casual jackets, coats. Ladies' wear: blouses, skirts, trousers, dresses, fashion jackets & blazers, suits, casual jackets, coats, handbags, shoes. Children's wear: shirts, blouses, trousers, skirts, dresses, jackets, coats, schoolwear.
'Products are high quality famous chainstore slight seconds. Men's suits from £80.'

South-east of Ashington, not far from the Spine Road (A189).
 North Seaton Industrial Estate is well signposted from the centre of town and all approach roads. Enter the estate by the large Focus DIY centre and take the first right behind it. The shop is at the far end of the drive, on the right, well signposted.

Open: Mon–Fri 9–5.30; Sat 9–5; Sun 10.30–4.30. Bank Holidays.
Closed: Easter Sunday; Christmas, Boxing and New Year's Days.
Cards: Access, Connect, Switch, Visa.
Cars: On site, outside shop.
Toilets: No.
Wheelchairs: Ramp, easy access.
Changing rooms: Yes.
Teas: In town.
Groups: No factory tours, but shopping groups welcome, please phone first.
Transport: Ashington town mini service bus stops at factory on request. Bus no. 435 (Morpeth–Newbiggin) and 434 (Newcastle–Newbiggin) stop 100 yds away.
Mail order: No.

See our entry no. 571

570 Ayr   Strathclyde

Begg of Ayr
Viewfield Road KA8 8HK
(01292) 267615

High quality cashmere and lambswool: scarves, stoles,
plaids, travel rugs etc, plain and tartan. Knitted garments
in natural fibres from other companies.

'Fabrics woven on the site. Modest prices: perfects & seconds.'

....

*At the northern end of Ayr, which is now pedestrianised. From
Ayr you must aim for Prestwick.*

*From Prestwick going south on A79: go over railway bridge,
turn left at roundabout into Viewfield Road*.*

*From Ayr town centre: aim north for Prestwick. Go north over
river. Go right after Texaco on left (do not enter one-way street
straight ahead); go straight at roundabout into Viewfield Road.**

*From Ayr/Prestwick bypass (A77): turn into A719 for Ayr
(north) [B743 leads off same roundabout]. Go straight at traffic
lights. Pass Tesco on left then racecourse. At next two
roundabouts go right.**

*If you go north across river: at fire station, go left (ring road
north). At next roundabout go straight (for Prestwick) then
right at second roundabout into Viewfield Road.**

*Shop 100 yds on left.

Open: Mon–Fri 1–4.
Bank Holidays.
Closed: Christmas–New Year.
Cards: Access, Amex, Visa.
Cars: In yard.
Toilets: Ask if desperate.
Also by roundabout.
Wheelchairs: One step to
medium sized shop.
Changing Rooms: n/a
Teas: In Ayr.
Groups: Groups by special
arrangement. Weaving can be
viewed from shop.
Transport: Buses from Ayr
to Prestwick: ask to be let off
at Viewfield Road.
Mail order: No.

Origin
Station Road Trading Estate EX16 9NF
(01398) 331704/331792

Ladies' dresses, soft suits, blouses, shirts and skirts in
Liberty of London, Viyella and *Rose & Hubble* fabrics.
'First quality garments only, extremely well priced.'
See our display advertisement on previous page.

....

West of town centre near public car-park.
From town centre crossroads: take B3277 towards South
Molton. Go left at sign to trading estate, take first left and
first right. Factory to right.

Open: Mon–Fri 9–5.
Closed: Bank Holidays;
Christmas–New Year.
Cards: None.
Cars: Outside factory and
public car-park.
Toilets: Yes.
Wheelchairs: No steps.
Changing rooms: Yes.
Teas: In town.
Groups: Coaches welcome.
Transport: None.
Mail order: No.

Choice Discount Stores Ltd.
26–28 High Street IG6 2DO
(0181) 551 2125

Surplus stocks including men's, women's and children's
fashions from *Next plc, Next Directory* and other high street
fashions. *Next Interiors* and footwear.
'Save up to 50% of normal Next first quality prices; seconds sold
from 1/3 of normal retail price. Special sales Jan and Sept.'

....

In modern dark brown building in the High Street.
From the south on A123 from Gants Hill roundabout: pass the
Barkingside police station and McDonald's on left and Chequers
pub on right. The shop is about 100 yds on right in the only
brown building.
From the north and Fullwell Cross on A123: pass the Fullwell
Cross swimming pool and recreation centre on left, go across
pedestrian lights and the shop is 100 yds on left after the next
street traffic lights.

Open: Mon–Sat 9–5.30;
Sun 10–4.
Closed: Easter Sunday;
Christmas and Boxing Days.
Cards: Access, Amex,
Switch, Visa.
Cars: In street or in
Sainsbury's large car-park.
Toilets: No.
Wheelchairs: No steps to
large shop.
Changing rooms: No, but
refund for goods returned in
perfect condition within 28 days.
Teas: In town centre.
Groups: Shopping groups
welcome! Book with store
manager.
Transport: Gants Hill tube
station, then bus nos. 129, 150
or 167. Barkingside tube sta-
tion, then a short walk.

Choice Discount Stores Ltd.

Unit 6a, Mayflower Retail Park, Gardiners Link SS14 3AR
(01268) 288331

Surplus stocks including men's, women's and children's fashions from *Next plc, Next Directory* and other high street fashions. *Next Interiors* and footwear.

'Save up to 50% of normal Next first quality prices; seconds sold from 1/3 off normal retail price. Special sales Jan and Sept.'

North-east of Basildon, next to huge Tesco and Pizza Hut.
  From London on A127: don't turn off onto A176 but take next exit for A132 and turn back on yourself towards London on A127. *
  From the east on A127: pass over exit for A132, continuing straight. *
  From Basildon centre: follow signs to Wickford A132. Pass the huge Watermill pub on right, then GEC Marconi Avionics on left and then turn onto A127 towards London. *
  ***After 800 yds take slip road signposted to Mayflower Retail Park. Pass McDonald's on left and shop is near the end next to Pizza Hut.**

Open: Mon–Wed 9–6; Thur, Fri 9–7; Sat 9–5.30; Sun 11–5.
Closed: Easter Sunday; Christmas and Boxing Days.
Cards: Access, Amex, Switch, Visa.
Cars: Large free car-park in front of store.
Toilets: At Tesco, on same site.
Wheelchairs: Easy access. No steps.
Changing rooms: No, but refund for goods returned in perfect condition within 28 days.
Teas: On-site Tesco, McDonald's, Kentucky.
Groups: Shopping groups welcome! Book with store manager.
Transport: Wickford or Basildon BR stations.

Tor Outdoor Products

Skopos Mills, Bradford Road WF17 6LZ
(01924) 478481

Specialised clothing – waterproof clothing for climbers and ramblers. Active leisurewear in polycotton, fleece and microfibres for all seasons.

'Perfects direct from factory, near perfects and discontinued lines.'

This shop is in the Skopos complex, an old mill clearly visible on the A652, close to traffic lights where the B6124 turns off.
  From Batley market place: go downhill (Hick Lane) to traffic lights then go left.
  From M62 exit 28: go south on A653 (for Dewsbury) then go right on to B6124 to Batley. At traffic lights, go right on to Bradford Road (A652). Large mill is shortly on right.
  From Bradford: go south on the A652. This huge mill is on the left shortly before the traffic lights where the B6124 goes left.

Open: Mon–Fri 10–5; Sat 9–4; Sun 10–4. Please check for New Year's Day and other Bank Holidays.
Closed: Christmas and Boxing Days, Dec 27.
Cards: All credit cards (except Amex).
Cars: Ample parking.
Toilets: In complex.
Wheelchairs: Difficult, but assistance given.
Changing rooms: Yes.
Teas: Two coffee shops in complex.
Groups: No factory tours. Groups of shoppers from eg walking clubs welcome. Please phone first.
Transport: Bus and BR stations 1/4 mile away.
Mail order: Yes.
Catalogue: Free. No restrictions on mail order.

Warner's

Church Street
(00353) 978 2026

Ladies' lingerie: bras in all sizes, briefs, body suits and cami tops. Ladies' blouses, skirts, jackets and nightwear. Children's clothing, including nightwear, baby to toddlers. Gentleman's shirts, boxer shorts, vests, T-shirts and socks. *'End of range perfects. Seconds at 40% discount. Specialist fitting available. Please phone for details of special weekend sales. Make the most of the beautiful Mullet peninsula, local golfing and surfing while you are in the area!'*

On the west coast of Southern Ireland, at the north-west tip of Co. Mayo, 40 miles west of Ballina.
From all directions: aim west for Belmullet. As you approach the town, look for road on left to the industrial estate. Turn left in front of Texaco petrol. Warners is the last factory on estate, on the left. Well marked.

Open: Tues and Thur 11.30–4; Fri 9.30–1.30.
Closed: Monday, Wednesday; two weeks mid-August; Christmas week.
Cards: No.
Cars: Own car-park.
Toilets: Ask if required.
Wheelchairs: One step, access with help.
Changing rooms: Yes.
Teas: Coffee shops and cafés in town centre.
Groups: Groups of shoppers welcome.
Transport: From Galway and Ballina.
Mail order: Yes.

George Brettle and Co.

Chapel Street DE56 1AR
(01773) 821532

Ladies', men's and children's wear; many well known high street brands in a large variety of sizes, including hosiery, socks. Comprehensive range of household textiles. Own manufacture and from other factories.

'Very competitive prices. Seconds and perfects. Many miscellaneous items make regular visits well worthwhile.'

On A6 close to town centre.
From Derby via A6: go straight at roundabout (Safeway on left).*
From Heanor via A609: stay on this road downhill to roundabout with A6 (Safeway opposite). Go right.*
***Shop 50 yds on right, before bus station.**
From Matlock on A6: keep straight through town, over traffic lights, past bus station on left. Clearly marked shop a few yards on left.
On foot from main shopping street: go downhill to bottom, turn left into Chapel Street; shop 100 yds on left.

Open: Mon–Fri 9–4; Sat 9–2.30.
Closed: Bank Holidays; Christmas, Boxing and New Year's Days.
Cards: Access, Visa.
Cars: Own car-park behind shop. Coaches please phone first.
Toilets: Locally.
Wheelchairs: No steps, easy access to medium-sized shop.
Changing rooms: Yes.
Teas: Tearoom/restaurant opposite with wheelchair access.
Groups: No factory tours but glad to have coaches and shopping groups. Please phone first.
Transport: Almost next to bus station.
Mail order: No.

Jaeger

De Bradelei Mill, Chapel Street DE56 1AP
(01773) 829830

High quality ladies' and men's knitwear together with
ladies' blouses, skirts and dresses etc; men's suits, jackets
and trousers etc.

'Ladies' wear and men's wear at greatly reduced prices.
Perfects and imperfects.'

....

This shop has moved around the corner into De Bradelei Mill.
For full directions, please see entry no. 318 on p. 254.

Open: Mon–Fri (including
Bank Holidays) 9.30–5.30;
Sat 9.30–6; Sun 11–5.
Closed: Christmas and New
Year's Days.
Cards: Access, Switch, Visa.
Cars: Own car-park.
Toilets: Yes.
Wheelchairs: Easy access.
Changing rooms: Yes.
Teas: Several teashops in
Belper.
Groups: Shopping groups
please phone Mrs Betty
Morley.
Transport: Any bus or train
to Belper.
Mail order: No.

Charnos *Closed*

Old School, Outclough Road, Brindley Ford ST8 7QE
(01782) 523485

Large range of ladies' lingerie, hosiery, underwear and
knitwear. Also children's wear, dresses, skirts, blouses;
men's wear; sportswear.

'Prices are normally reduced by 40%. Sell perfects, end of
season lines, slight seconds and samples.'

See our display advertisement on inside back cover

....

In a small village on the A527 between Tunstall and Biddulph.
From Biddulph: take the A527 south for Burslem/Stoke.
Brindley Ford is at bottom of the shallow valley shortly after you
leave Biddulph. Shop is at beginning of village on left, almost
opposite the New Black Bull.

From Stoke/Hanley: take A50 north; fork on to the A527 in
Tunstall. Pass Chatterley Whitfield Mining Museum on your
right; the shop is at the end of Brindley Ford on right.

Open: Tues–Fri 10–4;
Sat 9.30–1.
Closed: Monday;
Christmas–New Year.
Cards: Access, Amex,
Mastercard, Visa.
Cars: Car-park.
Toilets: No.
Wheelchairs: Easy access.
No steps to large shop.
Changing rooms: Yes.
Teas: Two local pubs for
coffee.
Groups: No factory tours but
coaches welcome; contact
Louise Stephen on (01602)
322191, mentioning this book.
Transport: Biddulph–Hanley
bus nos. 6a, 6b every 10
minutes; Biddulph–Newcastle
bus no. 98 each half hour. Stop
outside shop.
Mail order: No.

Gossard

Penmaen Road, Pontllanfraith NP2 2DK
(01495) 228171

Gossard and Berlei ranges of bras and co-ordinates.
'Discontinued items and slight seconds. 25–70% off high street prices.'

···

Just south of Blackwood, towards Pontllanfraith on B4251 (Oakdale–Ystrad Mynach road).

   From this road: go west into small Industrial Estate marked 'Penmaen Industrial Estate'. Gossard, clearly marked, is first factory on right. Shop, clearly signed, is behind factory.

Open: Mon–Sat 9.30–5.30.
Closed: Phone to check dates.
Cards: No.
Cars: Own car-park.
Toilets: In Blackwood.
Wheelchairs: No steps, easy access.
Teas: In Blackwood.
Groups: Larger groups please phone first.
Transport: Local buses, two minutes' walk away.
Mail order: No.

The Major Oak Clothing Company

Dale Lane NG21 0SB
(01623) 793073

Quality men's wear manufactured for high street multiple shops: suits, jackets, trousers, waistcoats, shirts, socks, ties.
'Prices 30–50% less than high street on ends of lines, and a very few seconds.'

···

Clearly visible near the centre of town.

   From A620 (main Blidworth–Kirkby road): turn off between Fina petrol and Forest Folk pub towards Sherwood Forest (brown sign) into Dale Lane. Clearly marked shop is 150 yds on left in converted chapel.

Open: Mon–Thur 10–4; Fri, Sat 9–12.
Closed: Bank Holidays; Christmas–New Year.
Cards: Access, Visa.
Cars: Easy, by shop.
Toilets: Yes.
Wheelchairs: Unsuitable, 11 stairs.
Changing rooms: Yes.
Teas: Pubs in village.
Groups: Most welcome. Phone call to notify appreciated.
Transport: Regular bus route.
Mail order: No.

581 Blyth   Northumberland

Claremont Garments

*Ennerdale Road, Kitty Brewster Trading Estate NE24 4RF
(01670) 351195*

Ladies' wear: lingerie, swimwear, casualwear (bodies, leggings etc), dresses, blouses, skirts, trousers, and tailored suits, coats and jackets. Schoolwear: boys' trousers and shirts; girls' skirts and shirts. Boys' wear: a limited range of casual shirts and trousers.

'All garments are leading chainstore perfects, seconds or ends of lines, and are offered at greatly reduced prices.'

See our display advertisement on p. 347

On the west side of Blyth.

From the A189 (Spine Road): turn on to A193 for Blyth. After two pedestrian lights turn left at mini-roundabout, following sign to Kitty Brewster Trading Estate.*

From Blyth town centre: follow signs to A193, Ashington & North. As you leave town, turn right into the Kitty Brewster Trading Estate. at mini-roundabout.*

*Take first left: shop 200 yds on right.

Open: Mon–Fri 9–4.30; Sat 9.30–2.30.
Closed: Bank Holidays.
Cards: Most major credit cards.
Cars: Own car-park.
Toilets: In Asda.
Wheelchairs: One small step to medium-sized shop; assistance given.
Changing rooms: Yes.
Teas: In Asda.
Groups: Shopping groups welcome, but large groups please phone first.
Transport: Local buses from Ashington, Blyth, Morpeth, Newcastle.
Mail order: No.

⁊n Ladder Factory Outlet
Vu. ⁊ria Square, Roche PL26 8LY
(01726) 891092

Huge range of ladies' blouses and tops. Also skirts, sets and nightwear. Cotton, polyester, polycotton, silk etc. Pretty hand embroidery, exquisite cutwork and plain everyday designs in wide price range. Accessories – tights, pants, earrings, men's ties, shirts etc. Remnants.
'Line ends, samples, seconds and "experiments" at good reductions. Blouses from £5.95. Current range at full price from £14–£120. Many lines at bargain prices. Prima Donna range up to size 30. Supply groups including choirs, restaurants, hotels and tour guides. Extended shop accommodates more Silken Ladder and La Scala Di Seta goods, Kinloch Anderson skirts, Début and Tessa Sandison leisure wear, lingerie by Arabella. Enlarged section for large sizes up to 30.'

On the A30 about 6 miles west of Bodmin and 6 miles north of St Austell. Shop is next to BP petrol station, on north side of the road opposite Victoria Inn.

Open: Mon–Sat and Bank Holidays 10–5. Also Summer Sundays 12.30–5.
Closed: Good Friday, Easter, Christmas and Boxing Days.
Cards: Access, Diners, JCB, Switch, Visa.
Cars: Plenty of parking in front and behind. Please don't block filling station access.
Toilets: No, but nearby.
Wheelchairs: Easy access.
Changing rooms: Yes.
Teas: Little Chef 400 yds away and Victoria Inn opposite.
Groups: Shopping groups welcome; please book an evening appointment with Hilary or Brian Spong.
Transport: None.
Mail order: No.
Catalogue: No.

---

583   Borehamwood   Herts

Rubert of London
Unit 7, Stirling Industrial Centre, Stirling Way WD6 2BS
(0181) 207 2620

Vast range of quality ladies' fashions at least 20–40% off retail prices. Coats and jackets in wool and cashmere, knitwear, suits, skirts and blouses, raincoats. Complete summer wardrobe. No seconds.
'Offer a friendly personal service to our customers. Sundays very busy, so advise first visit on a weekday. Clearance sales in January and July/August.'

A few yards off the A1.
   Going north or south on A1: at Stirling Corner (roundabout, with Shell garage and TJ restaurant, where the A411 crosses the A1) take small slip road in front of Curry's into industrial estate.*
   From M25 exit 23: take the A1 south for 3 miles; at first roundabout (Stirling Corner, with Shell garage on near left and TJ restaurant on far left corner) take small slip road in front of Curry's into industrial estate.*
   *Pass BonusPrint on the left, then Stirling Industrial Centre on left and immediately go left into alley. Rubert is 50 yds on left.

Open: Mon–Fri 10–4; Sun 10–2.
Closed: Saturday; most Bank Holidays, but phone to enquire; Christmas–New Year period – please phone for exact dates.
Cards: Access, Delta, Switch, Visa.
Cars: Outside shop or in nearby car-park.
Toilets: Yes.
Wheelchairs: Main show-room upstairs but items gladly brought down.
Changing rooms: Yes.
Teas: TJ's at Stirling Corner; also in Borehamwood.
Groups: Shopping groups always welcome: please phone first.
Transport: Edgware tube station then taxi. Can provide transport if you phone first (weekdays only).

Golden Shuttle

Albion Road, Greengates BD10 9TO
(01274) 623450

Gents', ladies' and children's wear of British and continental make. Ladies' sizes 10–24; men's 34–48" chest. Children's clothes 0–10 years. Worsted/wool and wool/terylene cloth by the metre. Department selling unusual gifts. Handbags and luggage.

'95% items perfect. Sometimes designer labels of seconds quality (usually just a minor flaw, eg wrong shade).'

....

About 3.5 miles north-east of Bradford.
  Near the junction of A658 (Bradford/Yeadon/Harrogate road) and A657 (Shipley/Calverley/Leeds road). From traffic lights at this junction: go west along A657 for Shipley, turn left into Albion Road at large Parkland mill. Clearly marked shop 100 yds uphill on left.

Open: Mon–Sat 9.30–5. Please phone about Bank Holidays.
Closed: Christmas, Boxing and New Year's Days.
Cards: Access, Eurocard, Switch, Visa.
Cars: In nearby street.
Toilets: Yes.
Wheelchairs: No – access is up nine steps.
Changing rooms: Five.
Teas: Nearby supermarket; local pubs with good bar meals.
Groups: Coach parties welcome. Please book with Manager, mentioning this guide.
Transport: Buses 648 from Interchange, Bradford; 670 and 760 (Leeds–Keighley).
Mail order: No.

Kyme Mill Shop *Closed*

Kyme Mills, Napier Terrace, Laisterdyke BD3 8DE
(01274) 669205

Men's suits, jackets, trousers. Wide selection of men's coats, knitwear, leisurewear, shirts, underwear, socks, accessories. Also wide range of ladies' wear: suits, skirts, blouses, underwear, nightwear, knitwear. Towels and tea towels.

'Perfects and seconds. Men's slight seconds suits from £39.99.'

....

This mill is about 1.3 miles east of Bradford, outside the old ring road and situated behind Alba Tyres.
  From Bradford: take A647 (Leeds Road); cross new ring road; go over next traffic lights (Manorgrove shop on left). After 150 yds this mill is on left, behind Alba Tyres.
  From Leeds: go to Thornbury roundabout, take A647 towards Bradford. Large mill will be on right, opposite The White Bear and just before old ring road traffic lights. The large shop is in the basement of the mill.

Open: Mon Sat 9.30–5.
Closed: Bank Holidays (please phone to check); Christmas, Boxing and New Year's Days.
Cards: Access, Visa.
Cars: Free car-park at right hand side of mill.
Toilets: No.
Wheelchairs: Several stone steps down to large spacious shop in basement.
Changing rooms: Yes.
Teas: In town.
Groups: Coach parties very welcome. Please book with shop manageress, mentioning this Guide.
Transport: Bradford–Leeds buses pass the shop.
Mail order: No.

Jaeger Factory Sale Shop

208 London Road RH15 9RD
(01444) 871123

Ladies' blouses, skirts, jackets and knitwear etc. Men's jackets, trousers, ties, socks and knitwear. Household goods including towels, linen etc.
'Perfect ends of lines etc.'

....

1/4 mile west of town centre, on the A273 (old main London–Brighton road).

Coming south from A23 into town: keep straight on A273, follow signs to Brighton. Look for huge Do-It-All on right; turn left at second roundabout into Queen Elizabeth Avenue.*

Coming north into town on A273: follow signs to town centre, turn right at first roundabout into Queen Elizabeth Avenue.*

*Go immediately left into School Close, pass a block of flats, then go immediately left into gateway signposted Jaeger Factory Sale Shop.

Open: Mon 12.30–4; Tues–Fri 9.30–4; Sat 9.30–3.30.
Closed: Bank Holidays; Christmas and New Year.
Cards: Access, Amex, Diners, Switch, Visa.
Cars: Limited parking in car-park or on the road.
Toilets: In town.
Wheelchairs: Easy access, no steps.
Changing rooms: Yes.
Teas: In town.
Groups: Pre-booked shopping groups welcome.
Transport: 5 minutes' walk from town centre.
Mail order: No.

Barden Mill Shop

Barden Lane BB12 0DY
(01282) 420333

Full range of discounted clothing. Specialise in outerwear, rainwear, coats, anoraks and jackets for all the family. Very wide range of men's suits. Soft furnishings – ready made or made to measure curtains, cushions etc. Jewellery and handbags.
'Perfects and overmakes all at substantial savings, eg ladies' raincoats at £12.95. Over 2000 men's suits – all at £39. Monthly sales: first Friday of every month for three days.'

....

North of town between canal and railway.

From M65 exit 12: go through Brierfield. After Oaks Hotel on left, go right at traffic lights down Windermere Avenue. At end go right, Barden Lane. Shop on right immediately after railway bridge.

From town centre and all southern/western directions: take A56 for Nelson. In small one-way system about half mile north of canal hump bridge, fork left for Fence just after Derby Arms on left. Shop in large mill, 1/2 mile on right immediately after railway bridge.

Open: Mon–Sat 10–5 (*April–Oct*: Thur late evening to 7); Sun 11–5. Bank Holidays 10–5.
Closed: Christmas Eve and Christmas Day.
Cards: Access, Visa.
Cars: Large car-park by shop.
Toilets: Yes.
Wheelchairs: Easy access, no steps. Huge shop.
Changing rooms: Yes.
Teas: Tea room.
Groups: Coach trips welcome.
Transport: Wizzard bus no. 5 to Reedley Hallows.
Mail order: Not yet.

The Wrangler Factory Outlet

Pepper Road NG14 6GC
(0115) 965 4043

Large selection of men's, ladies' and youths' jeans. Also sweatshirts, jackets, T-shirts and shirts.

'Stock is slightly substandard or ends of lines at reduced prices.'

....

A large village a couple of miles north of Arnold and mid-way between the A60 (Nottingham–Mansfield road) and A6097 (Lowdham–Ollerton road). Shop is in centre of village (near Co-Op) but can be tricky to find. Please use the landmarks below to orientate yourself.

Coming north from Arnold: cross the B684 and continue into village. At junction in village, go right (Main Street) for Epperstone. Immediately go left, opposite Happy Shopper general stores into Mews Lane. At far end (Cherry Tree pub on left), go right (Collyer Road) then left (Co-Op on left) into Flatts Lane. By William Lee School Annexe on right, take first left (Pepper Road). Shop is 50 yds on left.

Open: Mon–Sat 9–5; Bank Holidays 10–4.
Closed: Christmas, Boxing and New Year's Days.
Cards: All major credit cards.
Cars: Outside shop.
Toilets: No.
Wheelchairs: Ramp to sizeable shop on ground floor.
Changing rooms: Yes.
Teas: Local pubs.
Groups: Groups of shoppers welcome but please phone beforehand.
Transport: Bartons buses from Nottingham.
Mail order: No.

Fashion Factory

Unit 5, Wyrley Brook Park, Vine Lane, Bridgetown
WS11 3XE
(01543) 466000

Huge selection of quality branded ladies' and mens' wear and shoes.

'Personal shoppers only. Internationally famous brand names at savings of 40–70% off high street prices. 30–40,000 garments of constantly changing merchandise. No chainstore items. Summer and winter sales.'

....

Across the A5 from Cannock, near B&Q on the south side of this major road.

Going north-west on A5 from Tamworth: at traffic lights at Cannock turn-off go left (not right for Cannock). *

From M6 exit 12: turn east on to A5 towards Cannock/Tamworth. Cross the junction with the A460; at traffic lights at Cannock turn-off on left, go right. *

*Shortly turn right into Vine Lane: shop is short distance on right.

Open: Mon–Sat 9.30–5.30; Sun 11–5.
Closed: Easter Sunday; Christmas Day.
Cards: Access, Visa.
Cars: Ample.
Toilets: Yes.
Wheelchairs: Easy access, no steps to large shop on one floor.
Changing rooms: Yes.
Teas: Drinks machine and seating. Coffee shop opening soon.
Groups: Shopping groups welcome, but please phone first.
Transport: Regular bus route via Vine Lane bus stop.
Mail order: No.

Mascot Clothing

401 Old Road CO15 3RK
(01255) 432773

Ends of ranges and seconds of quality waxed cotton; breathable waterproof clothing for men, ladies and children. Tweed shooting jackets; quilted garments and hats, caps. Materials.

'Savings of up to 40%.'

North of town.
From Colchester on A133: turn left on to B1027 to Frinton and Walton at roundabout with fire station on far right. Go past Queen's Head Hotel then turn sharp right 20 yds after pedestrian lights: shop is first on right.
From town centre: follow signs to A133 Colchester. At crossing with Esso on far left, follow signs to B1369 Great Clacton. You are now in Old Road. Shop is on left in last building by T-junction.

Open: Wed 12–4; Fri 12–6; first Sat in every month 10–1.
Closed: Bank Holidays; Christmas; New Year's Day.
Cards: Access, Visa.
Cars: Large car-park.
Toilets: Public toilets across the road.
Wheelchairs: Stone staircase to shop on second floor.
Teas: Several tea shops and pubs in village.
Groups: Coach parties welcome by prior arrangement. Please phone.
Transport: Local bus 50 yds; station 10 minutes' walk.

Jaeger

Gomersal Mills BD19 4LV
(01274) 852303

Large range of high quality ladies' and men's wear. Household goods.

On A643 between Cleckheaton and Gomersal.
From crossroads in centre of Gomersal: take A643. Shop is 200 yds on right in conspicuous mill with 'Burnley' on tall chimney.
From Cleckheaton: take A643 for Leeds. Go uphill. Red-brick mill is on left, opposite church, just before you reach Gomersal. Go in through gates; shop clearly marked on the left. Follow signs.

Open: Mon 12.30–4.30; Tues–Fri 9.30–4.30; Sat 9.30–3.30.
Closed: Please phone for holiday closures.
Cards: Access, Switch, Visa, Jaeger account card.
Cars: In forecourt and side road.
Toilets: Yes, at entrance to shop.
Wheelchairs: Easy access to much enlarged shop.
Changing rooms: Yes.
Teas: Public may use the coffee bar on site.
Groups: Shopping groups welcome to shop. Please book in advance.
Transport: On bus route from Leeds/Bradford/Huddersfield.
Mail order: No.

Jaeger Factory Shop

Wolsey Road LE6 4ES
(01530) 835506

High quality ladies' blouses, skirts, dresses and knitwear etc. Men's suits, jackets, trousers and knitwear.

....

In the town centre, 150 yards from the clocktower/war memorial. From A50 (main road through town): take B585 for Whitwick. Pass clocktower.*

From Snibston Park: go into town; at traffic lights go left for Whitwick B585 then left again at the clocktower/war memorial.*

*Pass the first little road left then veer left, beside East Midlands Housing Association on your left, into Wolsey Road (do not go down the railway underpass!): shop is 40 yds on left.

Open: Tues–Fri 10–5; Sat 10–3.
Closed: Christmas Eve–New Year; Bank Holidays.
Cards: Access, Switch, Visa.
Cars: In street.
Toilets: In town.
Wheelchairs: One large step.
Changing rooms: Yes.
Teas: In town and at new Snibston Park.
Groups: By prior arrangement with Mrs Coral Wells.
Transport: Short walk from town centre.
Mail order: No.

R H Lowe plc

The Roldane Mills, Mill Green CW12 1JO
(01260) 277911

Children's wear, ladies' and men's fashions; footwear; luggage and leather goods. Gifts. Homewear including towels and bedding. Chainstore ends of lines and seconds.
'Great reductions from original chainstore prices.'

....

On north side of Congleton, 1/4 mile from town centre.

From Congleton centre: go towards A34 on A54 signposted 'Nantwich and M6'; cross cast-iron bridge over river, then turn sharp right (sign to Congleton Park).*

Via A34: at traffic lights go towards town. Go down Rood Hill for 200 yds: Mill Green leads off left immediately before cast-iron bridge over river (look for magnificent copper beech tree).*

*Company drive is 20 yds on right: shop at back.

Open: Mon–Sat 9.30–4.30; Sun 12–4.30; Bank Holidays 9.30–4.30.
Closed: Christmas, Boxing and New Year's Days.
Cards: Switch, Visa.
Cars: In road or car-park.
Toilets: Yes.
Wheelchairs: Easy access; ramp to large ground floor shop.
Changing rooms: Yes, six.
Teas: In town.
Groups: Parties of shoppers welcome – please telephone in advance.
Transport: Easy walk from town centre.
Mail order: No.

Babygro

Old Perth Road KY4 9EA
(01383) 511105

Good range of baby clothes.

'Range of seconds starting at £2.99 for a sleepsuit.'

....

North-east of town.
   From A92: follow signs into town and continue along main shopping street. Go under railway. About 100 yds uphill, take first left (signposted 'Police Station') into Stenhouse Street; go to top of this road (3/4 mile) past police station. *
   From the north on A909: go downhill into town, pass the post office on the right, go over the pedestrian lights and turn right (for police station) into Stenhouse Street. *
   ***Turn right at T-junction. Take next left, backtrack along first building to shop entrance at end.**

Open: Mon 12–4.30; Tues–Thur 9.30–1.30 and 2.30–4.30; Fri 9.30–1.
Closed: Bank Holidays; Christmas–New Year; three weeks July/Aug.
Cards: All major credit cards.
Cars: In access road.
Toilets: In main shopping area.
Wheelchairs: Three steps.
Changing rooms: No.
Teas: In town.
Groups: Shopping groups welcome. Please phone first.
Transport: No buses pass this way.
Mail order: No.

John Smedley

Lea Mills, Lea Bridge DE4 5AG
(01629) 534571

High quality knitwear for men and women. Sea Island cotton casual shirts, day shirts, socks (own yarn), handkerchiefs, tights, ties etc.

'Knitwear and cotton shirts made by this company.'

....

Lea Bridge is a small village south-east of Matlock.
   Turn off A6 (Derby–Matlock road) to Cromford Mill and continue for about 2 miles towards Holloway. At junction in Lea Bridge, go left. You see the large mill ahead; shop on left.
   From Crich: pass Tramway Museum to Holloway. Go straight for 1/2 mile to Lea Bridge. Large mill is on right; park downhill; then shop is few yards up on left.
NB Lea Bridge is about a mile south-west of Lea.

Open: Seven days a week 10–4.
Closed: Christmas, Boxing and New Year's Days.
Cards: Access, Visa.
Cars: Own car-park downhill from shop.
Toilets: No.
Wheelchairs: One step. Large shop.
Changing rooms: No.
Teas: Teas in Lea, Matlock, Wirksworth.
Tours: For 12–20 persons by prior arrangement with Meg Hatton; no charge. Tours all year on Wed and Thur at 1.30. Group visits welcome to sizeable shop: please book as above.
Transport: Matlock–Crich bus passes through Lea Bridge.
Mail order: No, but willing to post orders to customers.

Falmer Jeans Ltd.
Caponacre Industrial Estate KA18 1SH
(01290) 421577

Jeans and casualwear: dungarees, sweatshirts, cords, jumpers etc.

'All items ends of lines, previous year's ranges or slightly sub-standard stock at reduced prices.'

In the industrial estate south of Cumnock.

From the A70, A76 southbound and town centre: head south for Dumfries for about 1/2 mile. Pass fire station on left, go downhill and at bottom go right into estate.*

From Dumfries coming north on A76: enter town; as you get to bottom of hill, pass Thistle Inn on left then go left into estate.*

***Follow road round to right: factory is on left at next T-junction.**

Open: Mon–Thur 9.30–3.30; Fri 9.30–12.30; Sat 9–11.45. Some Bank Holidays – please phone to check.
Closed: Christmas–New Year; one week April; three weeks July; a few days mid Sept ; please phone to check.
Cards: Access, Visa.
Cars: Outside factory.
Toilets: In Cumnock.
Wheelchairs: Easy access to very large shop.
Changing rooms: Yes.
Teas: In Cumnock.
Groups: Pre-booked shopping groups welcome.
Transport: Local buses.

Dalkeith Mill Shop & Wool Centre
Thornybank Industrial Site EH22 2NE
(0131) 663 4502

Ladies' and men's knitwear in lambswool, shetland, and angora. Hand knitting and machine knitting yarns. Housecoats, nightdresses, dressing-gowns, pyjamas and slippers; children's clothing and babywear.

'High-quality seconds on sale. Stock changes frequently.'

Easy to find on north-east side of Dalkeith.

From the Edinburgh bypass (A720): turn off for Dalkeith (A68). At T-junction in town, go left for Musselburgh (A6094).*

From other directions: go into town and take the A6094 for Musselburgh.*

***Follow the road round; at the roundabout go straight towards Thornybank Industrial Site and Tranent. Take the first left: the shop is 200 yds on the right.**

From Tranent, coming into Dalkeith on B6414: look for shop on the left as you reach town.

Open: Mon–Thur 9–4.30; Fri 9–3.30.
Closed: Christmas–New Year.
Cards: Access, Visa.
Cars: In road outside.
Toilets: Yes.
Wheelchairs: One step to small shop.
Changing rooms: Yes.
Teas: In Dalkeith.
Groups: Shopping groups welcome – please contact shop supervisor in advance.
Transport: Ten minute walk from town centre.

Wetherall
Love Lane LL16 3LF
(01745) 815592

Top quality ladies' wear, especially reversible garments in pure wool: long coats, short jackets, rainwear, suits, capes, waistcoats. Sizes 8–28. Co-ordinated accessories such as berets, travel rugs.

'Will gladly make garments to your own size, including mail order. Significant price reductions – all items at factory prices.'

....

Easy to find in a one-way street which leads off the main road through town.
   From Ruthin on A525 or St Asaph on A525: follow signs to town centre. Go uphill to centre of town, passing library/museum on left. Go over pedestrian lights. Go round Halifax Building Society on left into Highgate, which becomes Love Lane.*
   From the west on the A543: go into Denbigh and uphill. Pass The Plough pub on the left then go right opposite Woolworths into Highgate, which becomes Love Lane.*
   ***Shop is 50 yds on right.**

Open: Mon–Sat 9–5.
Bank Holidays.
Closed: Christmas–New Year.
Cards: Access, Visa.
Cars: In street nearby; local car-parks.
Toilets: Yes.
Wheelchairs: Access into medium sized ground floor shop.
Changing rooms: Yes.
Teas: Several places in town.
Groups: Shopping groups welcome with prior phone call.
Transport: Any bus to Denbigh.
Mail order: Yes.
Catalogue: Free if you write or phone. All first class, no seconds.

The Mill Shop
Springfield Mills, Norman Road HD8 8TH
(01484) 865082

Women's wear, men's wear and children's wear from major chainstores and selected lines.

'Firsts and some slight seconds, ends of lines and over-runs; prices reduced by 50%.'

See our display advertisement on p. 357

....

Go into the village on the A636 and turn off the main road beside the Midland Bank (and very close to the PO) into Norman Road, and go down the hill. The converted old mill is shortly on the left, as the road bends left. Look for 'Mill Shop' signs.

Open: Mon–Sat 9–5 (Thur, Fri until 8); Sun 10–5. Bank Holiday.
Closed: Christmas and New Year's Days.
Cards: Access, Delta, Eurocard, Mastercard, Switch, Visa.
Cars: Own car-park.
Toilets: Yes, including facilities for disabled.
Wheelchairs: Level access.
Changing rooms: Yes.
Teas: Coffee shop/café for snacks, light meals and teas.
Groups: Welcome, but no guided tours. Contact Mr or Mrs May, or any staff member.
Transport: Buses from Huddersfield, Barnsley, Sheffield, Holmfirth, Wakefield. Also Denby Dale BR station on main Huddersfield–Wakefield line.
Mail order: No.

Claremont Garments

399 Boulton Lane, Allenton DE21 9TB
(01332) 691909

Ladies' wear: lingerie, swimwear, casualwear (bodies, leggings etc), dresses, blouses, skirts, trousers, and tailored suits, coats and jackets. Schoolwear: boys' trousers and shirts; girls' skirts and shirts. Boys' wear: a limited range of casual shirts and trousers.

'All garments are leading chainstore perfects, seconds or ends of lines, and are offered at greatly reduced prices.'

See our display advertisement on p. 347

About 3 miles south-east of Derby city centre.
Take the A514 (Osmaston Road) from the inner ring road sign-posted to 'Melbourne'. Go straight at the major roundabout into Chellaston Road; after 1/3 mile turn left at traffic lights into Boulton Lane: factory is on right, just past Jubilee Road (first turning on right).
From M1 exit 24: take the A6 for Derby. At the major round-about in Alvaston (where Shardlow Road joins London Road), turn sharp left into Boulton Lane. Shop is at far end on left, almost opposite park.

Open: Mon–Fri 9–4.30; Sat 9–3.
Closed: Some Bank Holidays.
Cards: All major credit cards.
Cars: On site.
Toilets: No.
Wheelchairs: Ramp to ground floor, steps to first floor.
Changing rooms: Yes.
Teas: Lots of places in Derby.
Groups: Shopping groups welcome, but large groups please phone first.
Transport: Regular buses from Derby to Melbourne and Shelton Lock go down Chellaston Road and stop at Boulton Lane.
Mail order: No.

The Factory Shop

44 Market Place
(01302) 364545/344118

Large range of nightwear, underwear and dressing gowns. Clothing for all the family. Sizes up to 32 (XXXOS).

'All garments sold in this huge shop are leading chainstore overmakes.'

In pedestrianised town centre.
From all directions follow sign into town centre and Frenchgate Centre. Park here or one of the other town centre car-parks and walk.

Open: Mon–Sat 9–5.30. Some Bank Holidays (please phone to check).
Closed: Christmas, Boxing and New Year's Days.
Cards: Access, Amex, Diners, Switch, Visa.
Cars: Multi-storey car-park in Frenchgate Centre. Then 10 minutes' walk.
Toilets: 2 minutes' walk from shop.
Wheelchairs: Easy access to large shop.
Changing rooms: Yes.
Teas: Café next door, and numerous pubs and cafés in Doncaster.
Groups: Shopping groups welcome.
Transport: Doncaster BR station 10 minutes' walk.
Mail order: No.

SPRINGFIELD MILL

SHOPPING COMPLEX

Norman Road, Denby Dale nr Huddersfield, Tel: 01484 865082

THE MILL SHOP

Fashions from the major chain stores and specially selected lines for ladies, children and men.

OTHER ATTRACTIONS WITHIN THE COMPLEX

"YOUR NUTS" for healthy eating

Stationery

Furniture

Carpets & Rugs

Records & Music

Party hire

THE COFFEE MILL
for tea & stickies

ANTIQUES

GOLF SHOP

DRIED FLOWERS
and arrangements

WINE CELLAR

Books

A CRECHE
for the kids

Materials

Wools

Bedding

Haberdashery

Shoes

Beauty & health

Opening times		All major credit cards accepted
Monday to Saturday	9am to 5pm	(Mill Shop only).
Thursday & Friday		Large free car-park.
(late night Mill Shop only)	9am to 8pm	Access for the disabled.
Sunday	10 am to 5pm	Groups & coach parties welcome

See our entry no. 599

602 Doncaster S Yorks

John Smedley
Rands Lane, Armthorpe DN3 3DV
(01302) 832346

High quality knitwear for men and women in lambswool.
Sea Island cotton sports and casualwear. Wool and Sea
Island cotton underwear. Also some men's shirts, ties,
handkerchiefs.
*'Everything at very reasonable prices. Seconds and perfect
ends of ranges.'*

....

Just over 4 miles north-east of Doncaster centre.
**Leave town along Wheatley Hall Road (A630) or Leger Way
(A18). Continue on A630 (towards M18) and at roundabout go
right at sign to Armthorpe.***
**From M18 exit 4: take A630 towards Doncaster. At first
roundabout, go left to Armthorpe.***
***Take first left (Mercel Avenue) and go right at end; Smedleys
are a few yards along on the left.**

Open: Mon–Fri 11–3.30;
Sat 10–3.
Closed: Easter Fri–Tues;
Spring Bank Holiday week
(+ previous two days); last
week July + first week Aug
(+ previous two days); First
week Sept (+ previous two
days); Christmas–New Year;
Bank Holidays.
Cards: Access, Visa.
Cars: Own car-park.
Toilets: Yes.
Wheelchairs: One step.
Changing rooms: No.
Teas: Locally.
Groups: No factory tours but
coach parties welcome. Please
book with Mr J Sutherland.
Transport: Bus no. 181 from
Doncaster to Armthorpe.
Mail order: No mail order,
but willing to post orders to
customers.
Catalogue: No.

603 Doncaster S Yorks

Topping Howard Enterprises *Closed*
Unit 2, Shaw Lane Industrial Estate
Ogden Road DN2 4SO   *(01302) 369212*

Men's quality suits, jackets, and trousers; sports trousers.
*'Suits from £40; sports jackets from £30; trousers from £10.
Many items in pure wool. Discounts on purchases of more
than one suit.'*

....

On the north-east side of town.
**Easiest from M18 exit 4: take A630 west for Doncaster. Go
over first roundabout; continue for one mile. At 2nd roundabout
go left. After 500 yds, at 3rd roundabout, go left into Shaw Lane
Ind. Est. Take 1st left. Company clearly visible shortly on left.**
**From M18 exit 3: take A630 (mainly dual carriageway) north
for Doncaster. Pass Fina petrol on left, fork right for A18,
Scunthorpe. Go straight at 1st roundabout; at 2nd roundabout
take 2nd exit (for Royal Infirmary). Pass race course on right.***
**From Doncaster town: aim for race course; go left on to A18;
pass race course on right.***
***Go over next roundabout, continue along Leger Way. At next
roundabout take 2nd exit (A18/Scunthorpe). Pass Rover on
right. At next roundabout, go right for Shaw Lane Industrial
Estate. Take 1st road left. Company clearly visible on left.**

Open: Be certain to phone
before visiting.
Mon, Tues, Wed, Thur 7.30–5.
Closed: Bank Holidays; Sept
5–11; Christmas and New Year.
Cards: None.
Cars: Ample parking at
Unit 4.
Toilets: Yes.
Wheelchairs: Medium sized
shop on first floor up staircase.
Changing rooms: Yes.
Teas: Sandall Park Café
2 minutes from factory.
Groups: All welcome with
prior phone call.
Transport: Doncaster station.
Buses for Wheatley Hills and
Hatfield from St Sepulchre
Gate in Doncaster.

Dewhirst Ltd.

42 Middle Street, North YO25 7TI
(01377) 256209

Men's quality suits, sports jackets and blazers, trousers, formal and casual shirts, casual jackets, coats. Ladies' blouses, skirts, trousers, jeans dresses, fashion jackets, blazers, suits, coats. Children's shirts, blouses, skirts, trousers, dresses, jackets, coats, schoolwear.

'Wide selection of famous name high quality seconds and perfects for all the family. Bargain prices. Men's suits from £80.'

....

On the main road through town, almost opposite Driffield Post Office.

Open: Mon–Fri 9–5.30; Sat 9–5; Sun 10-4.
Closed: Some Bank Holidays; Easter Sunday, Christmas, Boxing and New Year's Days.
Cards: Access, Switch, Visa.
Cars: Local streets and town car-parks. Company car-park on Saturdays ONLY.
Toilets: In town.
Wheelchairs: One large step to medium-sized shop. Help gladly given.
Changing rooms: Yes.
Teas: In town.
Groups: For group visits to the shop please book in advance.
Transport: Any bus or train to Driffield (Scarborough–Hull route).
Mail order: No.

Warner's

Mount Street BT25 1AT
(01846) 692466

Ladies' lingerie; bras in all sizes, briefs, body suits and cami tops. Ladies' blouses, skirts, jackets and nightwear. Children's clothing, including nightwear, baby to toddlers. Gentleman's shirts, boxer shorts, vests, T-shirts and socks. All at discount prices.

'End of range perfects. Seconds at 40% discount. Specialist fitting available. Please phone for details of special weekend sales.'

....

Dromore is about 18 miles south-west of Belfast.
From Belfast/Lisburn: go south on M1/A1. Take the first exit for Dromore. After about 1/2 mile the road goes straight into Dromore Square. The shop is in the factory on left.
Coming north from Newry/Banbridge on A1: take the first right turn for Dromore. The shop is in Mount Street, opposite the war memorial in the square.

Open: Tues, Wed, Fri and Sat 11–4; Thur 1–7. Please phone for Christmas shopping hours.
Closed: Two weeks July and Christmas week.
Cards: Most major cards.
Cars: Own car-park.
Toilets: Ask if required.
Wheelchairs: Ramp access available.
Changing rooms: Two.
Teas: Coffee shop and cafés in Town Square.
Groups: Groups of shoppers welcome.
Transport: Bus no 38 from town centre. Bus stop 200 yds away from shop.
Mail order: Yes.

Big L
Unit 7B, Kingsgate Retail Park G74 4UN
(013552) 41413

Massive range of jeans, T-shirts, sweatshirts, shirts and jackets.

'Irregulars and discontinued styles. Jeans from £19.99.'

North of East Kilbride off A749.
 From M74 exit 5: take A725 to East Kilbride. At the V-junction (left to town centre) fork right following sign to Nerston. At roundabout turn right towards Glasgow; at next roundabout exit for retail park.*
 From East Kilbride: take A749 for Glasgow. As you leave town on A749, exit for retail park at roundabout with Sainsbury's petrol on left.*
 From Glasgow and Rutherglen on A749: pass Nerston Village on left. At first roundabout, turn right for retail park.*
 *Shop is near top right hand corner.

Open: Mon–Fri 10–8; Sat 10–6; Sun 10–5.
Closed: Christmas and New Year's Days.
Cards: Access, Amex, Diners, Switch, Visa.
Cars: Own large car-park.
Toilets: In Sainsbury's.
Wheelchairs: Easy access, no steps, large shop.
Changing rooms: Yes.
Teas: In Sainsbury's.
Groups: No tours. Shopping groups welcome. Large groups should phone in advance.
Transport: Bus nos. 14, 14a, 14b, 66, 66a, 66b.

Fruit of the Loom
Unit 7B, Kingsgate Retail Park G74 4UM
(013552) 45452

Huge range of leisurewear including sweatshirts, T-shirts, jogging pants for all the family.

'Firsts, irregulars and discontinued lines. Sweatshirts from £4.99, T-shirts from £1.'

North of East Kilbride off A749.
 From M74 exit 5, and Hamilton: take A725 to East Kilbride. At the V-junction (left to town centre) fork right following sign to Nerston and Glasgow. At roundabout turn right towards Glasgow; at next roundabout exit for retail park.*
 From East Kilbride: take A749 for Glasgow. As you leave town on A749, exit for retail park at roundabout with Sainsbury's petrol on left.*
 From Glasgow and Rutherglen on A749: pass Nerston Village on left. At first roundabout, turn right for retail park.*
 *Shop is near top right hand corner.

Open: Mon–Fri 10–8; Sat 10–6; Sun 10–5.
Closed: Christmas and New Year's Day.
Cards: Access, Visa.
Cars: Own large car-park.
Toilets: In Sainsbury's.
Wheelchairs: Easy access, no steps, large shop.
Changing rooms: Yes.
Teas: In Sainsbury's.
Groups: No tours. Shopping groups welcome.
Transport: Bus nos. 14, 14a, 14b, 66, 66a, 66b.

Belinda Robertson Cashmere
22 Palmerston Place EH12 7AM
(0131) 225 1057

Ladies' and men's knitwear in cashmere.

'Showroom with current collections plus discounted lines, cancelled orders and overruns at greatly reduced prices.'

....

In the west end of Edinburgh.
   From town centre, ie Princes Street: go towards Glasgow. This takes you to the one-way system by Haymarket station. Go around one-way system until you face back to Princes Street again but take first left after the Bank of Scotland (lights and signpost to Forth Road Bridge). Shop is 100 yds on left.
   From the west and south-west on A70, A71 or A8: join the Haymarket one-way system. Follow sign to Forth Road Bridge at lights with Bank of Scotland on your near left and Royal Bank of Scotland on far left. The shop is 100 yds on left.

Open: Mon–Fri 9–5.30; Sat 10–4.
Closed: Christmas and Boxing Days; 1–2 January.
Cards: Access, Amex, JCB, Visa.
Cars: A few pay-&-display spaces outside shop. Car-parks in town.
Toilets: Yes.
Wheelchairs: Four steps.
Changing rooms: Yes.
Teas: If requested. Cafés nearby.
Groups: Shopping groups should phone in advance.
Transport: Any of numerous buses that go to Haymarket. Edinburgh Haymarket BR station.
Mail order: Yes. Please phone or write. No seconds sent.
Catalogue: Yes.

The Mill Shop (Johnstons of Elgin)
Newmill IV30 2AE
(01343) 554099

Cashmeres and woollen knitwear, cloth and classic tailored clothes, scarves, rugs, serapes etc.

'Perfects and occasionally seconds on sale.'

....

Across the river Lossie from the cathedral ruin.
   From town centre: go east towards Aberdeen; at roundabout with signpost to cathedral, go towards cathedral.*
   From Aberdeen on A96: go right at roundabout to cathedral.*
   From Inverness: the A96 goes north around town centre.*
   From Rothes on A941: go right at roundabout after railway bridge.*
   *At roundabout with signs to cathedral, follow them: pass cathedral ruin. Shop is clearly marked on right. Follow Cashmere Visitor Centre signs.

Open: *Oct–June:* Mon–Sat 9–5.30. *July–Sept:* Mon–Fri 9–6; Sat 9–5.30; Sun 11–4. Bank Holidays.
Closed: Christmas, Boxing, New Year's Days and 2 Jan for a week.
Cards: Access, Amex, Diners, Switch, Visa.
Cars: Own car-park.
Toilets: Yes.
Wheelchairs: Easy access (lift) to large shop.
Changing rooms: Yes.
Teas: Own coffee shop for light snacks etc.
Tours: Free access to Visitor Centre. Audio-visual presentation in 6 languages. Free mill tours on working days by prior appointment (no max number but large parties make arrangements in advance).
Transport: Town bus service.
Mail order: Yes.
Catalogue: Free.

Velmore Fashions Ltd.
Thornton Road Industrial Estate L65 5ER
(0151) 357 1212

Ladies' wear: dresses, skirts, jackets, trousers, suits, shorts.

'Leading chainstore seconds only sold here, at factory shop prices.'

....

About 3/4 mile east of town centre.
  From M53 exit 9: go south into town centre along Station Road; go over railway bridge; go left at traffic lights for stadium. Keep following signs to stadium.*
  From Council Offices in town centre: go east along Stanney Lane (B5132); take fourth left (Wolverham Road). Go towards motorway until you can turn right into Thornton Road.*
  *Turn left into Telford Road between Evason's and Wolverham Social Club. Shop is the fourth unit on the right.

Open: Tues–Thur 10.30–3; Fri 10.30–2; Sat 9–1.
Closed: Monday; Bank Holidays; Christmas–New Year.
Cards: Access, Switch, Visa.
Cars: In streets outside factory.
Toilets: In town.
Wheelchairs: One step to small shop.
Changing rooms: No.
Teas: In town.
Groups: Welcome to shop but must telephone first.
Transport: Local buses; Ellesmere Port BR station.

Balmoral Mill Shop
16 Church Lane KA4 8HE
(01563) 820213

Classics in cashmere, plain lambswool, kilted skirts, blouses, embroidered knitwear. Fashionable branded knitwear including *Farah, Lyle & Scott, Alice Collins, Acorn Designs.* Leisurewear including polo shirts, sweatshirts, golf shirts, pullovers and anoraks. Ladies' and gents', children's and babies' wear.

'Many seconds (some from £4.95) including own brand plus chainstore items.'

....

On the A719, the main road heading through Galston, by the river bridge.
  From town centre: follow A719 towards A71 for Edinburgh. As road begins to rise over river you see shop on left.
  From Kilmarnock or Edinburgh on A71: at roundabout take A719 for Galston. Cross the river: clearly marked shop is in first building on right.

Open: Mon–Sat (including Bank Holidays) 9–5; Sun 11–4.30.
Closed: Christmas, Boxing and New Year's Days.
Cards: Access, Switch, Visa.
Cars: Ample space at rear of shop.
Toilets: Yes.
Wheelchairs: Ramp from car-park entrance; front entrance five steps.
Changing rooms: Yes.
Teas: Own coffee shop with home baking.
Groups: Coaches welcome by arrangement.
Transport: Buses from Kilmarnock, Glasgow, Ayr etc stop outside.
Mail order: Yes.
Catalogue: Club brochure. Minimum order 8 garments with standard embroidery design, or 24 with club's own design.

Jockey

Eastern Avenue, Team Valley Trading Estate NE11 0PB
(0191) 491 0088

Wide selection of men's and ladies' underwear, T-shirts, knitwear, tights, socks; towels, bedding, baby accessories, swim/sportswear (in season).
'Perfects and seconds.'

The Team Valley Trading Estate is just off the A1 Western Bypass. Exit from the A1 to 'Team Valley', NOT 'Team Valley and A692 Consett' (the northern end of the estate). Continue down this dual carriageway to a roundabout signposted to Low Fell (right) and turn right into Eastern Avenue. Shop is on the right in the first building after the first turn-off to the right.

Open: Mon, Tues, Thur 10–4; Fri 10–2.30.
Closed: Please check with company.
Cards: No.
Cars: Own car-park outside shop.
Toilets: No.
Wheelchairs: Easy access to large shop.
Changing rooms: Yes.
Teas: In Low Fell.
Groups: No factory tours. Groups of shoppers welcome but please phone first.
Transport: Bus from Gateshead to Team Valley.
Mail order: No.

Mister Mackenzie Ltd.

30 Bell Street G1 1LC
(0141) 552 0855

Wide selection of ladies' rainwear: shiny fashion raincoats, gaberdine coats, nylon raincoats, school raincoats. Bowling and golfing waterproofs; rain hats. Baby anoraks and suits; toddlers' coats and jackets. Capes, bodywarmers. Sizes XS to XXL.
'Ladies' shiny PVC raincoats from approx £39 (£139 in shops).'

Right in the heart of Glasgow's 'Merchant City' opposite Candleriggs Market. Candleriggs leads north off Trongate (opposite the Tron Theatre), one of the major shopping streets in Glasgow.
From Trongate: turn into Candleriggs; take first right, Bell Street: entrance to number 30 is 50 yds on right, facing Candleriggs Market Hall.

Open: Mon–Sat 9.30–4.30; Sun 11–4.
Closed: Bank Holidays; Christmas, Boxing and New Year's Days.
Cards: Access, Style, Visa.
Cars: City centre car-parks; meters in Bell Street.
Toilets: No.
Wheelchairs: Lift to sizeable shop on 2nd floor.
Teas: Local cafés and good wine bars.
Groups: You can see the garments being made from the shop.
Transport: Buses and trains to Glasgow City.
Mail order: No.

Claremont Garments

2 Coustonholm Road G43 1VF   *(0141) 649 7080*

Huge shop selling ladies' wear: jackets, separates, trousers, blouses, skirts, coats and lingerie.

'Ends of lines, slightly substandard stock etc at considerably reduced prices. Newly refurbished shop.'

See our display advertisement on p. 347

Close to Pollokshaws East BR station.

Going north from Kilmarnock via A77: go under orange railway bridge marked Pollokshaws East. Take next left (Coustonholm Road). After railway bridge, shop is 150 yds on left.

From Glasgow Central station: go down Jamaica Street, cross Glasgow Bridge on to A77; pass Queens Park on left, go straight at lights at far end of park; go straight at next lights, take third street right (Coustonholm Road). After railway bridge, shop is 150 yds on left.

From M8 westbound: at exit 22 turn on to M77; at the end, go left and fork left at lights. At lights after Safeway on right, go right over railway, then right again (signs to Kilmarnock Rd). In Kilmarnock Road go right after 350 yds, after pedestrian lights in front of Bank of Scotland. After railway bridge, shop is 150 yds on left.

Open: Mon–Sat 9.45–4.45.
Closed: Easter Monday; Christmas, Boxing and New Year's Days; 2 Jan; Glasgow holidays.
Cards: Access, Visa.
Cars: In street.
Toilets: No.
Wheelchairs: No lift to upstairs shop.
Changing rooms: Yes.
Teas: Café near station.
Groups: No factory tours but groups to shop welcome. Prior phone call please.
Transport: Trains to Pollokshaws East then short walk.
Mail order: No.

Keela International Ltd.

Nasmyth Road, Southfield Industrial Estate KY6 2SB
(01592) 771241

High performance waterproof, breathable jackets, fleece jackets, waterproof overtrousers, golf suits, waterproof padded jackets, ventile garments, high visibility reflective clothing.

'Ends of lines, slight substandard items at reduced prices.'

South-west of Glenrothes.

From A92 northbound: at first roundabout coming to Glenrothes turn left for B921 to Kinglassie.*

From A92 southbound and from town centre: stay or get onto A92 towards Kirkcaldy. At roundabout crossing the B921 turn right for Kinglassie.*

*Go straight at next two roundabouts (Stenton and Southfield roundabouts) [disregard sign to Southfield at second roundabout] and exit for Leslie and Glenrothes West at next exit. At end of slip road turn right. Take second right (Cavendish Way), then first right into Ramsden Road. Shop is in second unit left after left bend.

Open: Mon–Thur 9–4.30; Fri, Sat 9–11.30.
Closed: Christmas and New Year.
Cards: Access, Visa.
Cars: Outside shop and in street.
Toilets: Yes.
Wheelchairs: One step to small shop.
Changing rooms: No.
Teas: In town.
Groups: No tours of factory but shopping groups welcome.
Transport: None.
Mail order: Yes.
Catalogue: Yes.

Alan Paine Knitwear Ltd.

Scats Country Store, Brighton Road GU7 1NS
(01483) 419962

Luxury knitwear in natural fibres including cashmere, camelhair, lambswool and cotton (sweaters, cardigans, slipovers). Brushed cotton shirts and polo shirts.

'Stock about half price; always some seconds. Lambswool from £20, cashmere from £75. Knitwear made here for sale world-wide. Mostly perfects, some seconds. Special offers from time to time. Genuine factory shop!'

In Scats Country Store complex on B2130 on eastern side of town.

From A3100, main road through town: turn on to B2130 to Cranleigh at traffic lights. After 50 yds go left into the Scats Country Store yard. Shop is on left as you go into complex.

Open: Mon–Fri 9
Sat 8.30–4.30.
Closed: Bank Holida
Christmas, Boxing and
New Year's Days.
Cards: Access, Switch,
Visa.
Cars: Outside shop.
Toilets: In town centre.
Wheelchairs: Easy access
to shop.
Changing rooms: Yes.
Teas: In Godalming.
Groups: Shopping groups
welcome provided they phone
first. No factory tours.
Transport: 10 minutes'
walk from railway station
Mail order: No.

Kent & Curwen Ltd.

21 Farncombe Street, Farncombe GU7 3AY
(01483) 426917

Top quality men's wear – suits, jackets, shirts, ties, trousers, knitwear and sportswear including cricket sweaters. Large selection of top quality golf wear. Silk ties made to order for colleges, clubs etc.

'Many perfect items at full price. Ends of line, samples and seconds at reduced prices in this genuine factory shop.'

Farncombe is a village a short distance north-east of Godalming.

From Godalming: take A3100 north towards Guildford. Look for the conservatory company on left then The Three Lions pub on left. Turn left into Hare Road. *

Coming south from Guildford on A3100: pass Burmah petrol on right, then take third right (Hare Road) in front of The Three Lions. *

*Keep going uphill to the T-junction; turn left. Shop is on right, just before the level crossing.

Open: Fri–Sat 10–5.
Closed: Bank Holidays;
Christmas–New Year.
Cards: Access, Amex, Visa.
Cars: Far side of the railway.
Toilets: Across the railway.
Wheelchairs: One very small
step to medium sized shop.
Changing rooms: Yes.
Teas: Local pubs in
Godalming.
Groups: Shopping groups
welcome but only by prior
arrangement.
Transport: Next to
Farncombe BR station
(direct service from London,
Waterloo).
Mail order: No.

Witham Contours

Harlaxton Road NG31 7SA
(01476) 65268

Ladies' high fashion underwear, night and swimwear for the young at heart.
'Won Designer of Year Award 1990.'

....

Short distance from town centre towards A1.
From town centre: follow A607 towards Melton Mowbray. Go under railway to the end of a long row of terraced houses. Pass Eddison factory on left and go to end of tree-lined section of this road: Witham Contours is on left.
From A1: turn towards Grantham at junction with A607 (second turn-off from south or third from north). Go over traffic lights; Witham Contours is on right.

Open: Mon–Thur 10–5; Fri 10–3; Sat 10–4.
Closed: Bank Holidays; Christmas–New Year.
Cards: No.
Cars: Outside shop.
Toilets: Yes.
Wheelchairs: Two steps to medium-sized shop.
Changing rooms: Yes.
Teas: Pub next door (open all day) and in town.
Groups: By arrangement please. Small charge but 100% goes to charity.
Transport: Buses every 20 minutes to Earle's Field. About 15 minutes' walk from station.
Mail order: No.

---

619 Grays Essex

Choice Discount Stores Ltd.

14–16 High Street RM17 6LV
(01375) 385780

Surplus stocks including men's, women's and children's fashions from *Next plc, Next Directory* and other high street fashions.
'Save up to 50% of normal Next first quality prices; seconds sold from 1/3 of normal retail price. Special sales Jan and Sept.'

....

In the pedestrianised High Street in the centre of town.
From all directions aim for town centre. This gets you to the ring road around the centre. Park in any car-park and then walk. The shop is near the war memorial at the northern end of the pedestrian area, on the left as you go north.

Open: Mon–Sat 9–5.30.
Closed: Christmas and Boxing Days.
Cards: Access, Amex, Switch, Visa.
Cars: Town centre car-park.
Toilets: No.
Wheelchairs: No steps to large shop.
Changing rooms: No, but refund for goods returned in perfect condition within 28 days.
Teas: In town centre.
Groups: Shopping groups welcome! Book with store manager.
Transport: Grays BR station.

Guernsey Woollens
Pitronnerie Road
St Peter Port GY1 2RH
(01481) 727176

Guernseys in wool and cotton in various designs and colours; cardigans, jackets and gilets.

'Seconds as well as firsts sold here.'

....

20 minutes walk, to the north-east of St Peter Port.

Coming from Town Church: go left and walk east towards St Sampson along sea front for 10 minutes, then go left (by supermarket) into road called Bouet, go over traffic lights, then right into Pitronnerie Road Industrial Estate. Turn left again, and shop is at end on left.

Open: Mon–Fri 9–5.
Closed: Bank Holidays;
9 May; Christmas–New Year.
Cards: Access, Visa.
Cars: Outside factory.
Toilets: Yes.
Wheelchairs: One step, medium-sized shop.
Changing rooms: No.
Teas: In St Peter Port.
Groups: Yes; please book in advance with Philip Walker.
Transport: Bus to Bouet, then 100 yds walk.
Mail order: Yes.
Catalogue: Free.

Le Tricoteur
Perelle Bay
St Saviours GY7 9QE
(01481) 64040

Traditional Guernsey sweaters; jackets; cotton guernseys; hats and scarves. Indigo denim, cotton knitwear.

'Seconds sometimes available. Goods at retail prices.'

....

200 yds off the coast road.

Open: Mon–Fri 8–5.
Closed: Bank Holidays, including 9 May.
Christmas–New Year.
Cards: Yes.
Cars: Large car-park.
Toilets: Ask if desperate.
Wheelchairs: One step to small shop.
Changing rooms: Yes.
Teas: In St Saviours.
Groups: Groups welcome to shop.
Transport: Bus to St Saviours.
Mail order: Yes.
Catalogue: Free brochure.

Susan Walker Classics Ltd.

12 High Street, Bramley GU5 0HF
(01483) 893602

Top quality perfect Scottish knitwear in cotton, silk, lambs-wool, merino and cashmere (*N Peal & Co.* label) for men and women.

'Perfect quality at about a third of London prices – ladies' cashmere cardigans from £80 with occasional seconds.'

··

This shop has moved from Peasmarsh.

Bramley is about three miles south of Guildford on the A281.
If you come south from Guildford: go into the High Street. This shop is at the far end on the left, just before the traffic lights.
Coming north into Bramley: the shop is on the right, just before the traffic lights.

Open: Mon–Sat 9–5.
Closed: Please check Bank Holidays and Christmas–New Year opening.
Cards: Amex, Mastercard, Switch, Visa.
Cars: Free car-park by library; free parking spaces beside shop.
Toilets: Nearby side street.
Wheelchairs: Easy access, medium sized shop.
Changing rooms: Yes.
Teas: Local pubs.
Groups: Larger groups please phone first.
Transport: Any bus to Bramley.

Choice Discount Stores Ltd.

14–20 Rectory Road SS7 2ND
(01702) 555245

Surplus stock including men's, women's and children's fashions from *Next plc, Next Directory* and other high street fashions. *Next Interiors* and footwear.

'Save up to 50% off normal Next first quality prices; seconds from 1/3 of normal retail price. Special sales Jan and Sept.'

···

In town centre near Iceland.

From the west on A13: as you pass Safeway and Elf petrol on left, enter one-way system. *

From the east on A13: enter one way system with church on right. Take next right, following one way system, and pass Safeway and Elf petrol on left. *

***At next traffic lights go left (Bradford & Bingley on left): shop is 50 yds on right.**

Open: Mon–Sat 9–5.30.
Closed: Christmas, Boxing and New Year's Days.
Cards: Access, Amex, Switch, Visa.
Cars: Car-park opposite shop.
Toilets: Public toilet facing store.
Wheelchairs: Easy access. No steps.
Changing rooms: No, but refund if goods returned in perfect condition within 28 days.
Teas: Tea shops in Hadleigh town.
Groups: Shopping groups welcome! Book with store manager.
Transport: Hadleigh bus stop on A13; Rayleigh BR station.

Katie Gray Factory Frock Shop

10 Westgate HX1 1DJ
(01422) 320313

Superb range of children's famous chainstore clothing, from babies to teenagers. Girls' and boys' outerwear including dresses, blouses, skirts, culottes, jog suits, stretch lycra, co-ordinating sets. Boys' trousers, shirts, shorts and jumpers. *'Ends of lines and seconds plus one-off designer samples.'*

In the centre of Halifax near the Piece Hall.
From Huddersfield and M62 exit 24: take A629 for Halifax. Fork right at lights with sign to 'Town centre east and station'. At next lights, by station on right, go left; take first right (Union Street) then first left into Westgate
From other directions: follow signs to Huddersfield A629. This takes you close around the town centre. At traffic lights with Civic Theatre on left, go straight (A629 turns right here). Take second left (Union Street) then first left into Westgate.

Open: Mon–Sat 10–5.
Closed: Mondays; Bank Holidays; Christmas–New Year.
Cards: No.
Cars: Outside shop and public car-park.
Toilets: In the Piece Hall.
Wheelchairs: One step to small shop.
Changing rooms: Two.
Teas: Across the street.
Groups: Not suitable for groups.
Transport: Buses pass close by; 5 minutes' walk from station.
Mail order: No.

Thistle Trading Co.

Withybush Industrial Estate SA62 4BV
(01437) 763080

Wide range of clothing with something for all the family. Famous chainstore items at very reasonable prices, especially men's and boys' underwear; polo, rugby and sweat shirts.

'Genuine factory shop with many goods made by this company. The range is expanded by buying in from other manufacturers and clearance outlets.'

Just off the A40 on the north side of town.
From Fishguard coming south on A40: as you reach town, pass Ridgeway service station on right; at first roundabout, go left into the industrial estate.*
From town centre: aim north on A40 for Fishguard. At large roundabout exit for Withybush industrial estate.*
From Carmarthen on A40: do not go into town centre, but at two roundabouts stay on A40 around town. At third roundabout exit for industrial estate. Follow signs for Sunday market.*
*Go right in front of Bookers: the shop is behind it.

Open: Mon–Sat 9–5; Sun 10–4. Phone about Bank Holidays.
Closed: Christmas–New Year.
Cards: Access, Visa.
Cars: Own car-park.
Toilets: In showground across the road.
Wheelchairs: Ramp to spacious shop.
Changing rooms: Yes.
Teas: Café in garden centre 1/2 a mile away.
Groups: Shopping groups welcome. Please phone Mrs Gillian Richards to arrange.
Transport: Haverfordwest BR station then taxi (about £3).
Mail order: No.

Hawick Cashmere Company Ltd.

Trinity Mills, Duke Street TD9 9QB
(01450) 372510

High quality ladies' and men's knitwear. Specialise in cashmere and cashmere/silk fashion styles and accessories, including skirts, trousers, capes and gloves. Range includes geelong and merino. Wholesale pieces of designer cashmere, also silk and silk/cashmere blends.

'Good selection at competitive prices.'

....

By the river Teviot north-east of town centre.
From Selkirk on A7: take first left after first traffic lights and river bridge.*
From Carlisle: continue on A7 through town towards Selkirk, pass Shell petrol station on right and turn right immediately before the river bridge.*
*Shop is on the corner of second road to the right. Entrance from side road.
From Kelso on A698: go to the first roundabout and turn right. At the end turn right again: the shop is on corner of the next right turn. Entrance from side road.

Open: Mon–Fri 10–5.
Closed: Some Bank Holidays; possibly Easter week; Christmas–New Year.
Cards: Access, Diners, Visa.
Cars: In street outside shop.
Toilets: Yes.
Wheelchairs: Easy access to spacious shop.
Changing rooms: Yes.
Teas: In Safeways nearby.
Groups: Shopping groups should telephone in advance. No mill tours.
Transport: Bus to Hawick then short walk.
Mail order: No.

Peter Scott & Co. Ltd.

11 Buccleuch Street TD9 0HK
(01450) 372311

Top quality knitwear in cotton, lambswool and cashmere for men and women. Unusual designs.

'Founded 1878. Ladies' cashmere sweater £99. Fine cotton sweater £26. All perfects, probably 20% less than comparable quality in high street.'

....

Easy to find in town centre.
Coming into Hawick on A7 from Langholm/Carlisle: pass Hawick High School on left and look for this mill and shop on right, just before junction in town.
From other directions: follow signs to A7 Carlisle, turning into Buccleuch Street at mini-roundabout. Shop is fourth on left.

Open: Mon–Fri 9–12.30 and 1.30–5; Sat 9–12.30 and 1.30–4; Bank Holidays.
Closed: 8–15 April; Christmas–New Year.
Cards: Access, Amex, Diners, Visa.
Cars: 30 minute parking outside.
Toilets: Yes.
Wheelchairs: Four steps to spacious medium sized shop. Also ramp at rear.
Changing rooms: Yes.
Teas: Next door to coffee shop.
Tours: Tuesday and Thursday at 2 pm prompt. Please contact Mr N Thomson or Mr N Roddan.
Transport: Any bus to town.
Mail order: Yes.

Short & Robertson Knitwear
Ladylaw Centre TD9 7DR
(01450) 377648

Ladies' and men's knitwear in cashmere.

'Current collections plus discounted lines, cancelled orders and overruns at greatly reduced prices.'

....

From Selkirk on the A7: turn right at first traffic lights just before river. Then turn right immediately after Texaco petrol station, then right again after Chas N Whillans.*

From Carlisle: turn left at first roundabout, cross bridge and turn left in front of and right just after Chas N Whillans.*

From Jedburgh and Newcastle: go through town centre, turn right at roundabout to go over the river, then turn left in front of and right just after Chas N Whillans.*

***Shop is 100 yds down the alley to the right of the Job Club. Sign says Trust Training.**

Open: Mon–Fri 9–4.30.
Closed: 25 Dec–8 Jan.
Cards: Access, Visa.
Cars: In street or car-park in front of Ladylaw Centre.
Toilets: In public car-park.
Wheelchairs: This is a smallish shop upstairs.
Changing rooms: Yes.
Teas: In town.
Groups: No mill tours. Shopping groups should phone first.
Transport: Close to centre of town.
Mail order: No.

Valerie Louthan and Country Store
Wiltonburn Farm TD9 7LM
(01450) 372414 mobile (0374) 192 551

Top of the market dresses, camisoles, trousers, jackets, capes, sweaters for men and women in cashmere and silk, by internationally famous designer. Matching skirts, trousers, capes, gloves. Sometimes lambswool and cottons. Other top quality products, eg costume jewellery.

'Subtle colours, witty designs. Mixture of cancelled orders, samples, slight seconds. Men's and women's sweaters costing £400 in London and Paris couture houses from £80.'

....

On the Carlisle side of town, about 1.5 miles south-west of town.

Take the A7 south from Hawick: turn right on to the B711 to Roberton then go sharp right again along the riverside. Keep left, go round left corner and go into lane marked 'No through road' to far end. Wiltonburn is a white house on the right at the end of the road.

Open: Mon–Fri 10–6, or by appointment.
Closed: 31 Aug; Common Riding 9, 10 June; 24 June; Christmas and New Year period – phone for dates.
Cards: Access, Visa.
Cars: By sales area.
Toilets: Ask if desperate.
Wheelchairs: No access.
Changing rooms: Yes.
Teas: Lots of places in town.
Groups: No factory tours but groups welcome to shop, please book with Sheila Shell. B & B accomodation is also available.
Transport: None, 1 mile walk from town.
Mail order: Yes.

Wrights of Trowmill Ltd.

Trowmill TD9 8SV
(01450) 372555

Shetland and lambswool; sportscoats; ties and caps, scarves, travel rugs, skirts and tweed lengths. Locally made knitwear. *'70% of goods are exported. Perfects and seconds available.'*

On A698 (Hawick–Jedburgh road), 2.5 miles north-east of Hawick.

From Hawick via A698: pass A6088 turn-off on right; mill is clearly signed about a mile further on left.

From Newcastle on A6088: go right on to A698: mill about a mile on left.

From Kelso/Jedburgh: on A698 go through Denholm; shop is 3 miles on right.

Open: Mon–Fri 9–5; Sat, Sun 10–5. Bank Holidays.
Closed: Christmas–New Year.
Cards: Access, Visa.
Cars: Outside shop.
Toilets: Yes.
Wheelchairs: Easy access to big shop.
Changing rooms: Yes.
Teas: Cold drinks and confectionery. Picnic tables on front lawn.
Tours: Self-guided tours of yarn preparation, warping and weaving in factory hours.
Transport: No local transport.
Mail order: No.

Abrovian Factory Shop

Croft Yard, off Albert Street HX7 8AV
(01422) 842258

Make men's trousers (bottoms turned up while you wait) and men's knitwear. Also sell ladies' separates, short coats, knitwear.

'Good quality garments at reasonable prices. Men's trousers made here, ladies' items from many sources. Most perfects, some seconds. From briefs at £1 to winter jackets at £40. Men's trousers average £27.'

In the town centre.

Albert Street is a one-way street leading from town towards the A646 (main road to Halifax).

From Halifax: go right into Commercial Street as you come into Hebden Bridge, then take first left. Albert Street bears left out of this little square. Croft Yard (no sign) is a turning off to the left at the bottom, just past the Chapel of Rest; the shop is in a corner of the car-park.

Open: Wed and Fri 11–4.30; Thur 10–4.30; Sat 10.30–4.30. Bank Holidays 11–4.30.
Closed: Monday and Tuesday; Christmas and New Year's Days.
Cards: None.
Cars: In car-park outside shop.
Toilets: In town.
Wheelchairs: One step.
Changing rooms: Two.
Teas: Lots of teashops nearby.
Groups: Coaches welcome to shop. Please book with Mrs Greenwood or Miss Allen.
Transport: Halifax–Todmorden buses. Railway station (on Calder Valley Line, Manchester–Leeds) 5 minutes' walk.
Mail order: Yes. No restrictions on items sent.
Catalogue: Free.

Aquascutum

Cleveland Road, Maylands Wood Estate HP2 7EV
(01442) 248333

Wide selection of men's and women's suits, jackets, trousers, coats, knitwear. Men's shirts. Ladies' blouses, skirts, raincoats. Few scarves.

'Last season's stock, returned items, rejects, factory clearance lines. Occasional sales. Ask to go on mailing list.'

....

On the east side of town.

From M1 exit 8: take A414 for Hemel Hempstead; go over first roundabout, right at second (to 'Industrial Area') into Maylands Avenue (A4147).*

From town centre: take St Alban's Road (A414) for M1 exit 8. At large roundabout, go left into Maylands Avenue (A4147).*

*Go straight at traffic lights; take first road to left (Cleveland Road). Shop on right, clearly signed.

Open: Mon–Sat 10–4. Please check times before visit.
Closed: Please check with company.
Cards: Yes.
Cars: Large car-park in front of shop.
Toilets: No.
Wheelchairs: One step to large shop.
Changing rooms: Yes.
Teas: In town.
Groups: Shopping groups should check with the shop beforehand.

M & G Designer Fashions

Old London Road (A23) RH17 5RK
(01444) 881511

Wide range of upmarket designer label clothing for men and women at least 20%–70% less than normal retail prices. Sizes 10–26. Daywear, separates, cocktail wear, ballgowns, ladies' shoes.

'Some prices up to 50% less than retail, eg black pleated chiffon evening skirt reduced from £69.95 to £33.'

....

On A23 (old London–Brighton road), on north-bound side of dual carriageway.

Going south on A23: shop is on far side of dual carriageway, so you must cross A23 and double back: take left slip-road for Hickstead Village/Twineham; cross A23 and go back north (following signs to Ricebridge) to warehouse 1/2 mile on left.

Going north: take slip-road to Hickstead Village/Twineham. Go up to roundabout then straight ahead (following signs to Ricebridge) to warehouse 1/2 mile on left.

Open: Mon–Sat 10–5.
Closed: Please phone for Christmas and Bank Holiday closures.
Cards: Access, Amex, Switch, Visa.
Cars: Free large car-park outside warehouse.
Toilets: Yes.
Wheelchairs: One step; ramp available to sizeable shop.
Changing rooms: Yes.
Teas: Everyone offered free tea or coffee. Pub and café nearby.
Groups: Shopping groups welcome – please phone first. Coach parties can be accommodated.
Transport: None.
Mail order: No.

Claremont Garments

Howdon Green Industrial Estate, Willington Quay NE28 6SY
(0191) 263 1690

Ladies' wear: lingerie, swimwear, casualwear (bodies, leggings etc), dresses, blouses, skirts, trousers, and tailored suits, coats and jackets. Schoolwear: boys' trousers and shirts; girls' skirts and shirts. Boys' wear: a limited range of casual shirts and trousers.

'All garments are leading chainstore perfects, seconds or ends of lines, and are offered at greatly reduced prices.'

See our display advertisement on p. 347

In an ind. est. east of Wallsend, near Howdon Metro Station.
From Wallsend: take the A193 to Howdon and North Shields. In Howdon go straight at the traffic lights, then take the fourth right into Howdon Lane. (Fish & chip shop on the corner and large pub 'Bewick Park' opposite).*
From the A19 just north of the Tyne tunnel: take the A193 towards Howdon & Wallsend. After A19/A193 interchange, turn left into Howdon Lane (immediately after first pedestrian crossing).*
*Continue across the level crossing at Howdon Metro Station, take the first left and next left again. Shop is 50 yds on your left through the last door of that building.

Open: Mon–Fri 9–4.30; Sat 9.30–2.30.
Closed: Some Bank Holidays; Christmas, Boxing and New Year's Days.
Cards: Most major credit cards.
Cars: Own car-park.
Toilets: No; nearest in town centre.
Wheelchairs: No steps; easy access to large shop.
Changing rooms: Yes.
Teas: In town centre.
Groups: Shopping groups welcome, but large groups please phone first.
Transport: Howdon Metro station about 300 yds; various bus routes.
Mail order: No.

Jaeger

39 Watnall Road NG15 7JR
(0115) 963 9334

High quality ladies' and men's knitwear together with ladies' blouses, skirts and dresses etc; men's suits, jackets and trousers etc.

'Ends of lines and slight substandards.'

From Hucknall High Street (A611): at traffic lights near Boots, turn off towards Watnall B6009 and 'Police'. Shop is 300 yds on left, on corner of Watnall Road and Beardall Street.
From Watnall: take B6009 for Hucknall. Pass the Flying Bedstead pub on right; after 1/4 mile, Police Headquarters is on left; shop (with broad white fascia) is on right, on corner of Watnall Road and Beardall Street.

Open: Tues–Fri 9.45–4.45; Sat 10–1.
Closed: Monday; Bank Holidays; Christmas–New Year.
Cards: Access, Connect, Switch, Visa.
Cars: Local side streets.
Toilets: In town centre.
Wheelchairs: Four steps to sizeable shop.
Changing rooms: Yes.
Teas: Locally.
Groups: Shoppers please phone Mrs Dorothy Hill.
Transport: Any bus to Hucknall.
Mail order: No.

Shop at the Mill

Park Valley Mills, Meltham Road HD4 7BI
(01484) 664418

Extensive range of top quality ladies' and men's fashions for all occasions. Pure wool and poly/wool fashion fabrics, direct from the mill.

'Classic seconds – about half normal retail price. Top quality merchandise all at less than rrp.'

....

1.5 miles south-west of Huddersfield. From M62 take exit 24.
From Huddersfield ring road: take A616 to Holmfirth; at third traffic lights go straight towards Meltham (B6108). Clearly signed mill is on left, 500 yds after you go under railway viaduct.
From Holmfirth: turn left off A6024 (main Huddersfield road) on to B6110 to Meltham. After 1/2 mile, at T-junction go right to Huddersfield. Entrance to long private drive is on right, as road winds right (before railway viaduct); you must turn sharp right, almost doubling back.

Open: Mon–Sat 9.30–5. Please phone for all Bank Holiday openings.
Closed: Christmas Day, Easter Monday.
Cards: Access, Switch, Visa.
Cars: Own car-park.
Toilets: Yes.
Wheelchairs: Two steps to medium sized shop.
Changing rooms: Yes.
Teas: In Holmfirth and Huddersfield. Nearby pubs with good bar meals.
Groups: Coach parties welcome to shop. Please make appointment with manageress.
Transport: Bus nos. 320, 321, 322 from Huddersfield centre.
Mail order: No.

Dewhirst Ltd.

Amsterdam Road, Sutton Fields Ind Estate HU8 0XE
(01482) 820166

Men's quality suits, sports jackets and blazers, trousers, formal and casual shirts, casual jackets, coats. Ladies' blouses, skirts, trousers, jeans dresses, fashion jackets, blazers, suits, coats. Children's shirts, blouses, skirts, trousers, dresses, jackets, coats, schoolwear.

'Wide selection of famous name high quality seconds and perfects for all the family. Bargain prices. Men's suits from £80.'

....

About 3.5 miles north of city centre.
Going north or south along Beverley Road (A1079): go east at traffic lights when you see signs to Outer Ring Road. Go over roundabout to next roundabout and turn right. Take the first left, in front of Humberside County Council, and keep going left until you see shop on left.
[This shop is near The Shoe Factory Shop.]

Open: Mon–Fri 9–5.30; Sat 9–5; Sun 10–4.
Closed: Some Bank Holidays; Easter Sunday, Christmas, Boxing and New Year's Days.
Cards: Access, Switch, Visa.
Cars: Own large car-park by shop.
Toilets: Yes.
Wheelchairs: Tiny step to spacious shop on ground floor.
Changing rooms: Yes.
Teas: Nearby pubs.
Groups: Group visits welcome to shop. Please book first.
Transport: Bus no. 10 (to Bransholme) from town centre.
Mail order: No.

Charnos

Corporation Road DE7 4BR
(0115) 944 0301

Wide range of ladies' lingerie, hosiery, underwear, knitwear, dresses, skirts and blouses; children's wear; men's wear; sportswear; household linens.

See our display advertisement inside back cover

....

At the southern end of Ilkeston on A609.
From Nottingham/Trowell: On A609 cross railway and canal.
After Rutland Windows showroom take first left (Thurman Street)
which leads to Corporation Road. Charnos at far end on left.*
From Derby/Spondon via A6096: turn right to Little Hallam half
way up Little Hallam Hill. This is Quarry Hill Road. Take first left
(Longfield Lane) then seventh left, Corporation Road. Charnos is
large building on right.*
*Follow signs to shop at rear.

Open: Tues–Fri 10–4; Sat 9.30–1.
Closed: Monday; Christmas–New Year.
Cards: Access, Visa.
Cars: In factory yard and Corporation Road.
Toilets: No.
Wheelchairs: Easy access to large shop.
Changing rooms: Yes.
Teas: Cafés in Ilkeston.
Groups: Tours of factory for organised groups – please contact Louise Robinson (0115) 932 2191 to arrange. Shopping groups welcome, prior phone call appreciated.
Transport: Trent bus no. 235 from Nottingham; Trent bus nos. 253 and 254 from Ilkeston Market Place – stop on Corporation Road.
Mail order: No.

J B Armstrong & Co. Ltd.

Armstrong's Mill, Middleton Street, off Station Road DE7 5TT
(0115) 932 4913

Men's suits, jackets, trousers and accessories. Ladies' suits, jackets, skirts, blouses and accessories.

'Perfects and seconds at very competitive prices.'

....

Close to town centre.
From Nottingham M1 exit 26: take A610, follow signs for
Ilkeston, leave at first intersection (A6096); enter Ilkeston over
railway bridge; turn immediately sharp left. Armstrong's Mill is
on right.
From Nottingham/Trowell on A609: straight over large round-
about at top of town centre on to dual carriageway; turn right at
next island into Station Road for Kimberley/M1.*
From Derby on A609: turn left at large roundabout at top of
town centre into dual carriageway, then right at next island into
Station Road for Kimberley/M1.*
From Heanor on A6007: as you enter Ilkeston, at first island
follow sign to Nottingham, then turn left at next roundabout into
Station Road for Kimberley/M1.*
*Pass Vauxhall dealership on left then veer right before going
over railway bridge. Armstrong's Mill is straight ahead on right.

Open: Mon–Sat 9–5; Sun and Bank Holidays 10–4.
Closed: Christmas, Boxing and New Year's Days.
Cards: Access, Switch, Visa.
Cars: Own large free car-park.
Toilets: Yes.
Wheelchairs: Difficult but assistance gladly given.
Changing rooms: Yes.
Teas: Cafés and pubs in town.
Groups: Groups including coaches welcome to shop. Please phone first.
Transport: Any bus to Ilkeston.

International clothing sizes

MEN   Suits and coats

British	36	38	40	42	44	46
USA	36	38	40	42	44	46
Europe	46	48	50	52	54	56

Shirts

British	14	14 1/2	15	15 1/2	16	16 1/2
USA	14	14 1/2	15	15 1/2	16	16 1/2
Europe	36	37	38	39/40	41	42

Shoes

British	7	7 1/2	8 1/2	9 1/2	10 1/2	11
USA	8	8 1/2	9 1/2	10 1/2	11 1/2	12
Europe	41	42	43	44	45	46

LADIES   Dresses and suits

British	8	10	12	14	16	18
USA	6	8	10	12	14	16
Europe		36	38	40	42	44

Shoes

British	4 1/2	5	5 1/2	6	6 1/2	7
USA	6	6 1/2	7	7 1/2	8	8 1/2
Europe	38	38	39	39	40	41

640 Ilkeston   Derbys

Match Leisurewear Manufacturers

Norton Buildings, 10 Heanor Road DE7 8EP
(0115) 944 4554

Top quality clothing: jackets, trousers, skirts, lingerie; schoolwear, leisurewear, sportswear, including golf, gym, bowls, football strips; reversible school rugby tops. Also fleece cardigans, jumpers and tracksuits.

'Sizes from 1 yr to 60" chest. Most things made on premises. Orders taken. Embroidery service and screen printing. School orders.'

On the northern edge of Ilkeston.
   From Ilkeston: take A6007 north for Heanor. *
   From M1 and directions south: at roundabout in town, get on to new bypass. Go over three roundabouts, exiting for Heanor A6007 and American Adventure. *
   ***Shop is 50 yds on right, on second floor of Norton Buildings opposite Wileda.**
   From Heanor: take A6007 south to Ilkeston. Pass Texaco then Rutland Cottage, both on left. After red brick church on left, continue on down Heanor Road about half mile. Shop is on left on second floor of Norton Buildings (big sign 'Norton Plastics'), opposite Wileda.

Open: Mon–Sat 9–5. Bank Holidays 10–4.
Closed: Christmas, Boxing and New Year's Days. Phone Mrs Smedley to confirm times.
Cards: Access, Visa.
Cars: At front of shop on main road.
Toilets: Yes.
Wheelchairs: Shop on second floor.
Changing rooms: Yes.
Teas: Local cafés.
Groups: Coach parties welcome any time.
Transport: Buses from Heanor and Ripley.
Mail order: Yes.
Catalogue: No.

R S Sports & Leisurewear

194 Norman Street, Cotmanhay DE7 8NR   *(0115) 932 3865*

Sports and leisurewear for all the family: jogging suits, sweatshirts, bottoms, cardigans, ski pants and leggings; school wear. Wide range of exclusive styles all made on premises in choice of over 15 colours from stock or made-to-measure. All sizes from 1–2 years to 596XL (54" chest, 60" waist). No size too big! Customers' own designs.

'Small family business welcoming party planners and traders. Best local prices since 1984. Sweatshirts from £3; jog suits from £6; cardigans from £3.75; jog bottoms from £3.'

....

On the northern edge of Ilkeston.

From Ilkeston: take A6007 north for Heanor. Cross brick railway bridge, look for Apricot Nursing Home on left & school on right: take next right, before red brick church on right (Charlotte St.).*

From Heanor: take A6007 south to Ilkeston. Pass Texaco then Rutland Cottage, both on left. After red brick church on left, go left (Charlotte Street).*

*Turn left again (Norman Street); go almost to far end. Well marked entrance through archway on right; follow signs to back.

Open: Mon– Fri 9–4; Sat 10–2 (phone to confirm). **Closed:** Bank Holidays; Christmas–New Year. Ring to check. **Cards:** None, but school vouchers accepted. **Cars:** In street. **Toilets:** Ask if desperate! **Wheelchairs:** One small step, small shop. **Changing rooms:** Yes. **Teas:** Local cafés. **Groups:** Not really able to cope with groups. **Transport:** Ilkeston/Heanor bus: get off at nursing home then 10 minutes' walk. **Mail order:** Yes. **Catalogue:** Phone for free price list, mentioning this guide.

Daleswear Factory Shop

High Street LA6 3AB
(015242) 42373

High quality outdoor and leisurewear. Fleece jackets, pullovers, pants, accessories etc for adults and children, including *Polartec 200* fleece. Aquatex waterproof mountain jackets, overtrousers and salopettes. *Kingsdale* caving over-suits and undersuits, *Gold Flash* tackle, *SRT* bags etc.

'Mostly firsts, competing in standard and design with market leaders, at much lower prices. Also prototypes, seconds, clearance and bargain lines. Discount 10% (off non-sale items) to anyone showing this guide.'

....

Ingleton Village is on the A65 between 28 miles north-west of Skipton and six miles south-east of Kirkby Lonsdale.

Follow one-way system up through the village centre. The High Street is up from the square and the shop is next to the Wheatsheaf pub.

Factory Shop may move to Laundry Lane at edge of village, with own car-park, in late 95.

Open: Mon–Sat 9–5 (including Bank Holidays); Sun 9.30–5. **Closed:** Christmas, Boxing and New Year's Days. **Cards:** Access, Switch, Visa. **Cars:** Limited High Street parking; main parking at Community Centre. **Toilets:** Ask if desperate. **Wheelchairs:** Three steps; large shop. **Changing rooms:** Yes. **Teas:** In Ingleton. **Groups:** Shopping groups welcome; group factory tours by arrangement. **Transport:** None. **Mail order:** Yes. We sell everything by mail order. **Catalogue:** Free.

Lambourne Clothing

Tudor Place, off Woodbridge Road IP4 2DR
(01473) 250404

Skirts, blouses, trousers, jackets; men's jackets, trousers, suits; waistcoats; knitwear and shirts; small range of T-shirts and knitwear, depending on season; tights. Some towels, bedding.

'Overmakes, seconds, ends of ranges, some samples of own label & well known high street labels. 10% discount for senior citizens.'
....

Few hundred yards north-east of city centre.
From Colchester: follow signs to town centre. At roundabout with Civic Hall straight ahead, go left; go right at next roundabout on to A1156 eastbound. *
From south and east: follow 'Through Traffic' signs; at roundabout with Civic Hall on right, go straight; at next roundabout go right on to A1156 (Crown Street). *
*Pass bus station on right, swimming pool on left. Pass Odeon on right; after 50 yds turn left into car-park.
From Norwich/Stowmarket: go left on to A1156 for Ipswich; stay on it to Odeon on right. After 50 yds turn left into car-park.

Open: Tues and Wed 10–4; Thur and Fri 12–4; Sat 10–1.
Closed: Monday Bank Holidays; last week July and first week August; Christmas; New Year's Day.
Cards: Access, Diners, Visa.
Cars: One-hour parking 100 yds up road. Multi-storey car-park nearby.
Toilets: Yes.
Wheelchairs: No steps.
Changing rooms: Yes.
Teas: Local pubs, cafés.
Groups: No factory tours; shopping groups welcome with prior phone call.
Transport: Short walk from town centre and bus station.

Barbour

Monksway, Bede Industrial Estate NE34 2HF
(0191) 428 4707

Oiled cotton jackets, trousers, moleskin shirts and trousers; warm pile linings; corduroy trousers; all made by this company. Also sell sweaters, shirts, hats, bags, quilted jackets and waistcoats.

'All items are factory seconds plus some discontinued lines.'
....

Next to Bede Metro station and half a mile from south entrance of Tyne Tunnel.
From roundabout at south entrance of tunnel: take A185 dual carriageway towards South Shields; after about 600 yds take first right (soon after dual carriageway ends). Turn left at T-junction, then take first right and right again before second factory. Shop is at the end of this building.

Open: Tues–Fri 10–5; Sat 9–12.
Closed: Mondays. Bank Holidays; first week June; last week July; first two weeks August; two weeks at Christmas. Please phone for exact dates.
Cards: Access, Switch, Visa.
Cars: Own car-park outside.
Toilets: No.
Wheelchairs: Easy access, no steps.
Changing rooms: No.
Teas: Two pubs nearby; teas in Jarrow.
Groups: Coach parties welcome to shop; contact Mr Heads, mentioning this guide.
Transport: Next to Bede Metro station.
Mail order: No.
Catalogue: Yes.

Warner's

Tassagh Road BT60 3TU
(01861) 531301

Ladies' lingerie: bras in all sizes, briefs, body suits and cami tops. Ladies' blouses, skirts, jackets and nightwear. Children's clothing, including nightwear, baby to toddlers. Gentlemen's shirts, boxer shorts, vests, T-shirts and socks. *'End of range perfects. Seconds at 40% discount. Specialist fitting available. Please phone for details of special weekend sales.'*

....

Seven miles south of Armagh; nearly 20 miles north-west of Newry.
 From Armagh: you need the A29 south. Continue for seven miles. When you reach Keady, go left after fire station on left. Factory is facing you; the shop is at the back.
 From Newry: take the A25 west then A29 north. Go through Keady. Go right in front of fire station. Factory is facing you; the shop is at the back.

Open: Tues, Wed, Fri and Sat 11–4; Thur 2–8. Please phone for special Christmas shopping hours.
Closed: Monday; two weeks July; Christmas week.
Cards: Most major credit cards.
Cars: Own car-park.
Toilets: Ask if required.
Wheelchairs: Ramp access available.
Changing rooms: Two.
Teas: Restaurants and tea shops in village.
Groups: Groups of shoppers welcome.
Transport: Bus no. 69 from Armagh; also 278 Dublin Express.
Mail order: Yes.

Ian M Roberts Ltd.

57–75 St Peters Avenue NN16 0EL
(01536) 518846

Men's good quality suits, sports jackets, overcoats (wool/cashmere), trousers, pure wool blazers, ladies' skirts. Jackets and suit sizes 36"–58"; trousers 30"–48" waist.

....

Near the cemetery south of the town centre.
 Via A6 from the south: pass St Mary's Hospital on right. Go over next traffic lights, then take first right (St Peters Avenue). *
 From the north: go through town centre. As you emerge from the one-way system, go left after the church into St Peters Ave. *
 From the west (A43 and A6): stay on A6 for Bedford. Go right at traffic lights (George Hotel on left) then left at next lights (swimming pool on left). Take next right, St Peters Avenue. *
 **Ignore the 'No Through Road' sign. Shop is behind long wooden fence 200 yds on left; go in 'IN' gate.*

Open: Tues–Fri 12.30–4.30; Sat 10–4.
Closed: Monday; Christmas–New Year. Phone for possible holiday closures.
Cards: Access, Visa.
Cars: Large car-park next to shop.
Toilets: Yes.
Wheelchairs: Very easy access; spacious shop.
Changing rooms: Yes.
Teas: In Kettering.
Groups: Groups welcome to visit shop – please phone to arrange time.
Transport: Short walk from town centre.
Mail order: No.

Jaeger

15 Munro Place, Bonnyton Industrial Estate KA1 2NR
(01563) 526511

Large range of ladies' blouses, skirts, jackets, coats, knitwear etc. Men's suits, jackets, trousers, knitwear, shirts, ties, socks. Household goods.
'Quality merchandise at reduced prices.'

Open: Mon, Thur 9–12 and 2–4; Tues, Wed, Fri 9–4; Sat, Sun 10–4.
Closed: First two weeks July. Please phone about Bank Holidays and Christmas.
Cards: Access, Switch, Visa.
Cars: Own car-park.
Toilets: No.
Wheelchairs: Stairs to large shop upstairs.
Changing rooms: Yes.
Teas: In town.
Groups: No factory tours. Shopping groups welcome with prior phone call.
Transport: None.
Mail order: No.

West-north-west of town.
From town centre: take A735 for Kilmaurs. At roundabout with B7064, go left and left again after railway bridge.*
From the north on A77: turn on to B7038 for Kilmarnock. At first roundabout fork right on to B7064, go straight at next roundabout, then go left after railway bridge.*
From all south-east and easterly directions get on or stay on A71 for Irvine. At roundabout take B7064 for Crosshouse.**
From Irvine on A71: turn left for Crosshouse on to B7081.**
**At next roundabout go right; go left at lights. Take first right after dual carriageway section starts.*
*Shop clearly signed at bottom of hill.

Jaeger

1 Hansa Road, Hardwick Industrial Estate PE30 4HY
(01553) 691111

Ladies' coats, dresses, blouses, skirts, knitwear. Men's suits, jackets, trousers, knitwear, shirts etc. Also household goods, hosiery, wool.
'Quality merchandise at reduced prices.'

Open: Mon–Fri 10–4.30; Sat 9–3.30.
Closed: Please phone for holiday closures.
Cards: Access, Amex, Delta, Diners, Switch, Visa.
Cars: Outside shop.
Toilets: Nearby.
Wheelchairs: Easy access, ramp to large shop.
Changing rooms: Yes.
Teas: Plenty of places in town; Caithness Crystal; Little Chef nearby.
Groups: Shopping groups welcome with prior phone call.
Transport: Swaffham and Downham Market buses.
Mail order: No.

Easy to find on southern outskirts of town.
From town centre: go south towards A10 and Downham Market. Look for Campbell Soups on right; Jaeger is on left.
From south on A10 or Norwich on A47: get on to King's Lynn southern bypass (A47/A149); exit for King's Lynn at large roundabout.*
From west: continue on southern bypass to major roundabout where A10 joins.*
From north: go left on to the southern bypass from wherever you hit the ring road. At major roundabout go to King's Lynn.*
*Go along Hardwick Road towards King's Lynn. Take second right (Hansa Road). Shop is on the left.

Lochleven Mill Shop

Lochleven Mill, Bridgend KY13 7DI
(01577) 863528

Extensive range of luxury knits in cashmere and lambswool including cardigans, sweaters, jackets, coats, skirts, kilts, scarves, travelling rugs etc. Custom built *Pringle* shop-within-a-shop for wide range of ladies and gents sportswear and accessories. Shop also stocks an extensive range of fashionwear from prestigious names such as *Daks Simpson, Barrie, Burberrys, McGeorge, Finn Karelia, Henry White* etc. *'Genuine end of lines from Pringle and other leading names at amazing bargain prices. Cashmere jumpers priced from only £50.'*

....

At southern end of town.

From M90 exit 6 and Kincardine Bridge via A977: enter Kinross and go right at T-junction. Continue on road to Lochleven Mills (last building on left before leaving town).

From north-east on A91: take B996 through Kinross; Mill Shop is located on left, after hump bridge over river.

Open: Mon–Wed and Fri–Sat 9–5.30. Bank Holidays.
Closed: Thursday; Christmas–New Year.
Cards: Amex, Diners, Mastercard, Visa.
Cars: Own car-park. Coaches by arrangement.
Toilets: Yes.
Wheelchairs: Three steps down to spacious shop.
Changing rooms: Yes.
Teas: Good selection of hotels and cafés.
Groups: No factory tours. Groups welcome to shop. Please contact Ellen Anderson (Manageress).
Transport: Regular bus service from Edinburgh, Perth and Glenrothes.
Mail order: No.

Babygro

Hayfield Industrial Estate KY2 5DM
(01592) 261177

Baby and children's wear, sleepwear, ladies' wear, leisurewear and underwear.

....

On the north side of the town centre.

From M90 exit 3: follow signs to Kirkcaldy West. At first roundabout follow sign to 'Industrial Estates'. Pass Esso and Gulf petrol. At next traffic lights go right (for Hayfield Ind Est), then take first left just before Shell petrol.*

From town centre: pass railway station and go left at traffic lights over railway bridge. At next two roundabouts take second exits; at third roundabout go straight. Turn right immediately after Shell petrol station on right.*

***Shop is in first building on left.**

Open: Mon 10.30–4.30; Tues–Sat 9.30–4.30; Sun 12.30–4.30. Bank Holidays.
Closed: For Christmas opening times please check.
Cards: All major credit cards.
Cars: Beside factory and in street.
Toilets: No.
Wheelchairs: Three steps to sizeable shop.
Changing rooms: No.
Teas: In town.
Groups: No factory tours but groups of shoppers welcome if they phone first.
Transport: Buses from centre stop opposite factory.
Mail order: No.

Debut Group Ltd.
North Street NG16 4BR
(01773) 717171

Cotton/lycra, supplex/lycra fitnesswear from children's to ladies' size 24. Leotards, leggings, cycle shorts. Also wide range of bodies in plain and ribbed fabrics.

'High quality perfects and seconds with substantial reductions on normal high street prices.'

....

A short distance off the main road (A608) which links Heanor and the M1.

From Heanor: take A608 downhill towards Langley Mill/ Eastwood. Pass Langley Mill garage, go over pedestrian lights and go left into North Street (sign to railway station). *

From the Eastwood/M1: go uphill into Langley Mill, under the railway bridge and take the first right (opposite the large stone church), North Street. *

*Shop entrance is in Ebenezer Street, fourth road on the left. Shop is a few yards on right.

Open: Tues–Fri 11.30–5; Sat 10–3.
Closed: Monday; Bank Holidays; Christmas–New Year.
Cards: Access, Visa.
Cars: In street.
Toilets: Yes.
Wheelchairs: Access difficult; six steps.
Changing rooms: Yes.
Teas: Local pubs in Langley Mill 100 yds away.
Groups: Shopping groups welcome, but large groups please phone first. No factory tours.
Transport: Bus nos. 120, 125 from Derby and R11 from Nottingham; or to Langley Mill BR station.
Mail order: No.

Into Clothing
144 The Parade CV32 4AC
(01926) 430407

Ladies' quality clothing. Massive selection includes knitwear in wool and angora, silk blouses, jackets in wool and cashmere, skirts, trousers, lingerie etc.

'We buy ends of lines and overmakes from factories – well known "brand names for less". Prices 50%–70% less than high street prices.'

....

In the town centre.

Shop is in main shopping parade opposite the town hall and next to Pizza Hut.

Open: Mon–Sat 9–5.30 (also four Sundays before Christmas).
Closed: Christmas and Boxing Days.
Cards: Access, Amex, Eurocard, Mastercard, Switch, Visa.
Cars: Opposite, and in multi-storey at rear of shop in Bedford Street.
Toilets: Across the road.
Wheelchairs: Level access, wide door.
Changing rooms: Yes.
Teas: Regency Arcade café four doors away; lots of places in town.
Groups: Shopping groups welcome, no need to book.
Transport: BR station and buses in town.
Mail order: No.

Joshua Wardle Ltd.
Cheadle Road, Leekbrook ST13 7AY
(01538) 382451

Ladies' wear, men's wear, children's wear, underwear and lingerie; homewares. In-store Dannimac shop sells off-price merchandise.

'Famous name chainstore perfects, seconds, ends of lines at reduced prices. Phone to check current range details.'

....

A mile and a half south of Leek.

From Leek: take A520 south towards Stone. After you pass under the railway bridge, shop is on factory site about 600 yds on right.

From the south: take A520 towards Leek. Go through Cheddleton and pass St Edwards Hospital. 200 yds after you go over railway bridge, clearly marked shop is on left, opposite farms and The Travellers Rest.

Open: Mon–Fri 9.30–4;
Sat 10–3.
Closed: Easter; Christmas, New Year and Bank Holidays. Also 22 July–6 August.
Cards: Access, Switch, Visa.
Cars: Own car-park for 100 cars. Spaces reserved for disabled.
Toilets: On site at the canteen.
Wheelchairs: Ramps leading to shop, no steps.
Changing rooms: Yes.
Teas: On site at the canteen or at the Travellers Rest.
Groups: No.
Transport: Buses from Leek, Hanley and Cheadle pass front of factory.
Mail order: No.

The Mill Shop
Shoobridge Mill, Haywood Street ST13 5LA
(01538) 399796

Nightdresses, housecoats, nightshirts; ladies', children's, men's and boys' briefs; vests, boxer shorts; babywear; men's dressing gowns. Also sell tracksuits, underwear, children's dressing gowns.

'Special offers most weeks. Sales in January and August.'

....

Close to the centre of town, this is a conspicuous mill on the main road near Normid (Co-op).

Coming north on the A520 from Cheddleton/Longton: at traffic lights as you reach Leek, go right.*

Coming north on the A53 from the Stoke area: go straight at traffic lights in town.*

*Clearly marked shop is shortly on the right in a large mill on the near corner of a small side road (Shoobridge Street).

Open: Mon–Sat 9–5.
Occasional Bank Holidays, please phone to ask.
Closed: Christmas–New Year.
Cards: Access, Visa.
Cars: Car-park and in street.
Toilets: Nearby.
Wheelchairs: No access (four steps), but large shop.
Changing rooms: Yes.
Teas: In Leek.
Groups: No factory tours but coach parties welcome to shop.
Transport: Any bus to Leek.
Mail order: No.
Catalogue: No.

Gossard

Grovebury Road LU7 8SM
(01525) 851122

Gossard and *Berlei* bras, underwear and lingerie.

'Gossard and Berlei bras and lingerie at 1/3 to 2/3 of original retail price on perfect discontinued lines only. Seconds in all ranges. Please phone this genuine factory shop for occasional Saturday sales with special prices, mentioning this book.'

....

South of the town centre.
From Leighton Buzzard: take A4146 south for Hemel Hempstead. Go right at mini-roundabout into Grovebury Road. *
From Hemel Hempstead: go north on A4146 for Leighton Buzzard. Keep going straight to town outskirts. Go left by mini-roundabout into Grovebury Road. *
***Look for Gossard 500 yds on left.**

Open: Mon–Sat 9.30–5.30.
Closed: Bank Holidays; Christmas–New Year.
Cards: No.
Cars: Car-park in front of building.
Toilets: In town.
Wheelchairs: Ramp to shop.
Changing rooms: Yes.
Teas: In town; farmhouse along road.
Groups: No factory tours but pre-booked shopping groups welcome.
Transport: 10 minutes' walk from town centre.
Mail order: Yes.

Nicole Farhi/French Connection

75–83 Fairfield Road E3 3QP
(0181) 981 3931

Nicole Farhi jackets, skirts, trousers, blouses, knitwear; *French Connection* knitwear, blouses, skirts etc.

'Previous season's stock plus samples and some seconds.'

....

In Bow, just north of the A11/A12 (Bow Road).
From London going east along Bow Road: pass Bow Road tube station on right then go left at traffic lights immediately after white concrete old Poplar Town Hall (and in front of NatWest bank) into Fairfield Road. Go under railway bridge: shop on left.
Going west towards London on A12: from large roundabout/overpass on A12 where Blackwall Tunnel road goes south, go north on to A102 (ie do NOT take overpass); take left slip road (A1030) for Old Ford; at top of slip road go left into Tredegar Road; after 150 yds go left into Fairfield Road. Company on right, 50 yds before railway bridge.

Open: Tues and Wed 10–3; Thur 11–6.30; Fri 10–5.30; Sat 10–3.
Closed: Mondays; Bank Holidays; Christmas–New Year.
Cards: Access, Visa.
Cars: In street outside.
Toilets: No.
Wheelchairs: No step, small shop.
Changing rooms: Yes.
Teas: Local pubs and cafés.
Groups: Shopping groups welcome if you phone first.
Transport: Local buses. Bow Road tube station. Bow Church station on Docklands Light Railway.
Mail order: No.

Burberrys

29–53 Chatham Place E9 6LR
(0181) 985 3344

Men's and women's raincoats, trenchcoats, knitwear, shirts, skirts; accessories including umbrellas, scarves, bags. Some children's clothes. Golf items. Jams, teas, coffee, sauces, vinegar; fragrances etc.

....

Just east of Mare Street (A107), the main north–south road through Hackney.

Going south along Mare Street: go under railway bridge, go left at traffic lights (Morning Lane) for Bow/Leyton.*

Coming north on Mare Street: pass Hackney Central Library (stone building with classical columns on right corner site); go right at traffic lights for Bow/Leyton (B113).*

*After 400 yds pass Duke of Wellington pub on right; immediately go right (Chatham Place). Shop entrance 30 yds on right.

Open: Mon–Fri 12–6; Sat 9–3.
Closed: Please check with company.
Cards: Yes..
Cars: Local streets.
Toilets: No.
Wheelchairs: Ramps to and in huge shop.
Teas: Some pubs and cafés in Hackney.
Groups: Please telephone first.
Transport: Buses and trains to Mare Street.

In-Wear

100 Garratt Lane SW18 4DI
(0181) 871 2155

Wide range of ladies' and men's fashion jackets, trousers, dresses, shirts, skirts, jeans etc., from the *In-Wear, Matinique* and *Part Two* collections.

'Samples, ends of lines and slightly imperfect merchandise.'

....

South of Wandsworth on A217, just off South Circular Road (A205).

From all directions: go to Wandsworth then go clockwise round one-way system. Pass town hall on right, staying in left lane. Go left at traffic lights (before Arndale Centre). Clearly marked company is 300 yds on right (beyond Sainsbury's on left). Go right into car-park.

Coming north into Wandsworth on A217: look for clearly marked building on left, after the Old Sergeant pub on left.

Open: Mon–Fri 10–5; Sat 10–4.
Closed: Bank Holidays; Christmas–New Year.
Cards: Access, Amex, Transax, Visa.
Cars: Own car-park.
Toilets: Yes.
Wheelchairs: Easy access, no steps, large ground floor shop.
Changing rooms: Yes.
Teas: In the Arndale Centre.
Groups: Shopping groups welcome – please phone first.
Transport: Several buses, including nos. 35, 37, 44; 10 minutes' ride from Wandsworth Town BR station.
Mail order: No.

Charnos
Nottingham Road NG9 6GE
(0115) 973 0345

Ladies' lingerie, hosiery, underwear, knitwear, dresses, skirts and blouses; children's wear; men's wear; sportswear; household linens.

See our display advertisement inside back cover

....

One of the easiest shops to find!
It is on the main road (A6005) from Long Eaton to Nottingham, about 300 yds east of the town centre.
From Long Eaton: go over railway: shop is immediately on left, in clearly marked red-brick building.

Open: Tues–Fri 10–5; Sat 9.30–1; Sun 10–4.
Closed: Monday; Christmas–New Year.
Cards: Access, Visa.
Cars: On side road.
Toilets: No.
Wheelchairs: Access to large shop through rear door.
Changing rooms: Yes.
Teas: In Long Eaton (easy walking distance).
Groups: Groups of shoppers always welcome – prior phone call appreciated. For tours of the Ilkeston factory for organised groups – please contact Louise Robinson (0115) 932 2191.
Transport: Within easy walking distance of town centre so take any bus to Long Eaton.
Mail order: No.

Towles plc
Nottingham Road LE11 1HF
(01509) 213555

Men's and children's sweaters, cardigans, underwear, socks; schoolwear; T-shirts; men's and ladies' leisurewear. Wool and cotton items.

'Slightly imperfect goods or ends of ranges on sale at competitive prices. Occasional special sales. Free privilege card gives extra 10% discount – ask for it on your next visit. All goods made in our own factories in North Leics.'

See our display advertisement on p. *345*

....

On the north-east side of town.
From Nottingham on A60: pass the railway station, go straight at traffic lights and over hump bridge; shop is 50 yds on left.
From town centre: take A60 to Nottingham. From Clarence Street you see this clearly marked shop facing you at far end of road. Once out of the one-way system, look for the hump bridge: shop is just before it on the right.
From Leicester via A6: turn right at traffic lights on to A60 for Nottingham; at next traffic lights turn right. Shop is a short way on the right but not visible as it is set back; look for the Jack O'Lantern pub on the left, directly opposite.

Open: Mon–Fri 10–4; Sat 10–5; Sun 10–4.
Closed: Easter Sunday; Christmas Day.
Cards: Access, Delta, Switch, Visa.
Cars: Car-park behind shop (access to the right of shop).
Toilets: Yes.
Wheelchairs: Easy access.
Changing rooms: No.
Teas: In town.
Groups: No tours of the factory but groups welcomed to fairly small shop. Be sure to phone first.
Transport: BR station close by; bus station 1/2 mile.
Mail order: No.

Designer Warehouse

Paradise Mill, Park Lane
(01625) 511169

Ends of lines and samples of up-to-the-minute designer wear: coats, skirts, dresses, evening wear, blouses. Top designer labels from British manufacturers, Italian, German, French, Danish, Finnish.

'Clothing for that special occasion. At least 50% off normal retail prices.'

....

In the town centre, next to Paradise Mill Silk Museum which is well signed.

From Leek on A523: **as you come into town, at traffic lights with the Sun Inn on left, go left; at next traffic lights, go straight. After the Register Office on left, go left into Park Lane.**

From Stockport/Manchester via A523: **at roundabout (Tesco on left) keep straight; follow new Silk Road; go right at lights, under railway lines, to station.***

From Buxton on A537: **at traffic lights at bottom of hill, go straight under railway for station.***

*Pass station on your left; continue to traffic lights, go right. After the Register Office on left, go left into Park Lane. Shop is 150 yds on left.

Open: Mon–Sat 9.30–5.30.
Closed: Bank Holidays; Christmas, Boxing and New Year's Days.
Cards: Access, Switch, Visa.
Cars: In street.
Toilets: No.
Wheelchairs: One step, large ground floor shop.
Changing rooms: Yes.
Teas: Café 200 yds via walkway.
Groups: Groups welcome to shop if they arrange visit first.
Transport: 10 minutes' walk from BR station; 5 minutes from bus station. Regular services from all routes.
Mail order: No.

Beck Mill Factory Shop

Kings Road LE13 1QE
(01664) 480147

Range of designer clothes from: *Feminella, Barry Sherrard, Jeffrey Brownleader, Di Tardo, Elsie Whiteley, Astraka, Wolsey, Cavvalini, Dannimac, Roman Originals, Warners, Double Two, Farah, Lee Cooper, James Barry, Lancers, Dior, Hathaway, Nautica* plus many more. Also many famous chainstore surplus and seconds.

'Come and see our exciting selection of top quality brands at up to 70% discount. Perfects and seconds at factory shop prices.'

....

A short distance north of town centre off the A607.

From Leicester on A607: **cross the river, go towards Grantham. You come into Norman Way. Pass Raymond Mays' Rover Garage on left; take second left.***

From Grantham on A607: **pass Jet petrol station on left and go right at first traffic lights, then take first right.***

From Nottingham via A606: **pass modern Council Offices on right and cattle market on left. At next lights go left for Grantham, Norman Way. Pass Raymond Mays' Rover Garage on left, take the second left.***

*In Kings Road go around S-bend; arched door to shop 50 yds on left.

Open: Mon–Sat 10–5; Fri late night to 6; Sun 10–4.
Closed: Christmas Day only.
Cards: Access, Visa.
Cars: Own large car-park.
Toilets: Yes.
Wheelchairs: Easy access to large shop.
Changing rooms: Yes.
Teas: Refreshment area in shop.
Groups: Coach parties and groups welcome to shop anytime. Regular open evenings – please phone for details.
Transport: Local buses.
Mail order: No.

Pendor (Clothing) Ltd.

Mayphil Buildings, Goat Mill Road, Dowlais CF48 3TF
(01685) 722681

Wide range of clothing for all the family: ladies' lingerie, corsetry and all outerwear; children's wear; sports and leisure wear for all the family; men's blazers, trousers, shirts etc; leather goods and sports bags.

'Most goods, half normal retail price or less, nearly all perfects.'
....

Just off A4102 on north-eastern edge of town.
Via Heads of the Valley road (A465): at roundabout (with Asda/large BP garage) turn off downhill (A4102) for Merthyr. Go left at next roundabout into Goat Mill Road.*
From town centre: take A4102 for Abergavenny. Go uphill for about a mile then go right at unmarked roundabout (OP Chocolate high up above far right side) into Goat Mill Road.*
*Mayphil Buildings are few hundred yards on right.
From the south: stay on A470 dual carriageway to Merthyr to the end. Take third exit at roundabout (A4060 to Abergavenny). Go uphill for 1 mile, go left into Dowlais Ind. Estate. Follow road round; shop on left.

Open: Mon, Tues, Fri, Sat 9.30–5.30; Wed, Thur 9.30–8; for Sunday openings please check. All Bank Holidays.
Closed: Christmas, Boxing and New Year's Days.
Cards: Access, Visa.
Cars: Large car-park.
Toilets: Yes.
Wheelchairs: Easy access to large, spacious shop on ground floor.
Changing rooms: Yes.
Teas: In Merthyr.
Groups: Day, evening and weekend visits to shop arranged for groups. Coaches welcome any time. A phone call in advance is helpful.
Transport: Local buses stop outside.
Mail order: No.

TDP Textiles Ltd.

TDP House, Rawdon Road DE12 6DF
(01283) 550400

Fashions for ladies; men, teenage boys, girls, younger brother and sister, babies; character underwear, nightwear; T-shirts, denim jeans etc.

'The majority of our goods are manufactured under contract for major chainstores and mail order companies. This is a new look factory shop with a children's play area.'
....

Moira is a small village; this shop is on the north side, on the former pottery site.
From the traffic lights at the main crossroad in the centre of Moira (where B5003 crosses B586): take B586 north for Swadlincote. Go under the railway: drive to shop is on the right after 100 yds.
From Swadlincote/Woodville: go south on B586 towards Moira; go left into factory yard (100 yds before the railway bridge).
Entrance to ground floor shop is clearly signed.

Open: Tues–Sat 10–6; Sun 10–4. Some Bank Holidays, please phone to check.
Closed: Monday; Christmas–New Year.
Cards: All major cards except Diners and Amex.
Cars: Own car-park beside shop.
Toilets: Yes.
Wheelchairs: Easy access to large ground floor shop.
Changing rooms: Yes.
Teas: Available on premises.
Groups: Shopping groups welcome: please phone first. No factory tours.
Transport: Own transport necessary.
Mail order: No.

Cudworth of Norden

Baitings Mill OL12 7TQ
(01706) 41771

Outdoor and heavy-duty clothing, mainly for adults;
children's wax-jackets. High quality moleskin and corduroy
garments – trousers, breeches, shirts. Bodywarmers, jackets. New ranges, eg short sleeved summer shirts, lightweight walking trousers.

'Most stock perfect; some seconds. Orders taken by phone.
See us at many summer country shows around Britain
(April–Sept).'

....

Going north-west from Rochdale on A680: In Norden, go right
immediately after The White Lion into private road.
  Coming south-east on A680 towards Rochdale: go through
double-bend at beginning of Norden. Slow down as you see tall
square chimney, go left in front of The White Lion into private
road. Shop is immediately behind pub.

Open: Sat 10.30–2. Usually in
shop Mon–Fri too, but phone
to confirm. Happy to open
other times, including
Sundays, by arrangement.
Closed: Saturdays through-
out August.
Cards: Access, Visa.
Cars: Outside shop.
Toilets: Yes.
Wheelchairs: Access to small
shop not really possible.
Changing rooms: Yes.
Teas: Cafés in vicinity. Pub
in front of shop.
Groups: No mill tours.
Shopping groups welcome if
they phone first.
Transport: Local buses stop
just across main road.
Mail order: Yes.
Catalogue: Write or phone for
catalogue, mentioning this
guide.

Big L Factory Outlet (Levi's)

Commercial Street NN1 1PK
(01604) 603022

Large range of jeans for all the family; T-shirts, sweatshirts,
shirts and jackets.

'Most items slightly substandard with price reductions of about
a third. Some perfect ends of lines. Men's jeans from £15.99
instead of £49.99; T-shirts from £9.99 (£15) and sweatshirts
from £16.99 (usually £21).'

....

Off St Peter's Way roundabout, on the south side of town centre.
  From M1 exit 15: go towards Northampton. At roundabout, go
left on to ring road West (A45 for (A43)). At next roundabout,
go right for town centre (A508). Go over next roundabout and
railway, then go right at roundabout for Bedford A428. Take first
left, Commercial Street. *
  Coming south from Market Harborough and from town centre:
follow signs for M1 South, going anti-clockwise round town.
When you turn left at roundabout, look for Carlsberg brewery on
right then take next left, Commercial Street. *
  *Shop is 100 yds ahead.

Open: Mon, Tues 10–5.30;
Wed, Thur, Fri 9.30–5.30;
Sat 9–6. Bank Holidays.
Closed: Christmas and
Boxing Days.
Cards: Access, Visa.
Cars: Own car-park by shop.
Toilets: Town centre.
Wheelchairs: Small ramp,
wide doors, huge ground
floor shop.
Changing rooms: Yes, lots.
Teas: Lots of places in
Northampton.
Groups: Shoppers very
welcome. Prior phone call
appreciated.
Transport: 5 minutes' walk
from town centre.
Mail order: No.

Dewhirst plc

5 Welham Road
(01653) 690141

Men's quality suits, sports jackets and blazers, trousers, shirts, casual jackets, coats. Ladies' blouses, skirts, trousers, dresses, fashion jackets, blazers, suits, coats, underwear. Children's shirts, blouses, skirts, trousers, dresses, jackets, coats.

'Wide selection of famous name high quality seconds & perfects for all the family. Bargain prices. Men's suits from £80.'

Malton and Norton are adjoining towns on either side of river. This shop is south of the river.

Coming north from York on A64: turn off right for Malton town centre. At two centre traffic lights, go right into Castlegate; keep straight, cross river then level-crossing and immediately bear right into Welham Road. *

Coming south from Scarborough on A64: turn left off A64 for Norton. Go along main shopping road; turn left immediately before level-crossing into Welham Road. *

***Shop is on left (after Barker's garage).**

Open: Mon–Fr. Sat 9–5; Sun 11–5.
Closed: Easter Sun, Christmas and Boxing.
Cards: Access, Master c..d, Switch, Visa.
Cars: On site outside shop.
Toilets: Public toilets nearby.
Wheelchairs: Ramps. Small shop, but space for one wheelchair at a time.
Changing rooms: Three.
Teas: Cafés nearby.
Groups: Please phone in advance.
Transport: BR and bus stations five minutes walk.
Mail order: No.

Warner's

Dabell Avenue, Blenheim Ind. Estate NG6 8WA
(0115) 979 5796

Ladies' lingerie: bras, pants, suspenders, half skirts, teddies. Ladies' jumpers, tights, socks, nightwear, some outerwear, eg jackets. Men's shirts, ties, sweaters, T-shirts, underwear, socks. Children's socks.

'Firsts and seconds sold here, including chainstore items, at approximately 40% reductions. Special weekend sales throughout the year. Please phone for details.'

On the north-west side of Nottingham, near M1 exit 26.

From M1 exit 26: take A610 for Nottingham. At next roundabout, take second exit (Low Wood Road) for 'Bullwell 2 1/2' & Blenheim Ind. Estate. *

From Nottingham: take A610. Cross ring road. Go over first roundabout marked 'Bulwell 1'; pass BP petrol station on left. At next huge roundabout, take fifth exit (Low Wood Road) for 'Bulwell 2 1/2' & Blenheim Ind. Estate. *

***At next roundabout go left (Seller's Wood Drive) and right at next (Bennerley Road). Take first left, Dabell Avenue: company in large grey building on left with large letter W.**

Open: Wed, Fri and Sat 10–5; Thur 10–7.
Closed: Monday and Tuesday; Bank Holidays.
Cards: Yes.
Cars: Outside shop.
Toilets: Ask if desperate.
Wheelchairs: Small slope to medium sized ground floor shop.
Changing rooms: Yes.
Teas: Yes.
Groups: Groups of shoppers welcome.
Transport: Bus no. 84 from Nottingham city centre then 8 minutes' walk.
Mail order: No.

K & M (Leather Clothing) Mnfg. Co. Ltd.

Wesley Street NG5 2BJ
(0115) 960 3124/960 9474

Wide range of sheepskin and leather coats, jackets, slippers, gloves etc.

'Items all made by this company. Made-to-measure service. Professional garment alterations and repair. Post-Christmas sale.'

....

About 1.5 miles north of city, behind Bristol Street Motors in Mansfield Road.

From Nottingham centre: go north on Mansfield Road (A60). At first roundabout, follow signs to Mansfield. At next major junction, go left into Hucknall Road (A611). Take first right (Jenner Street), then first left (Wesley Street).

From the ring road: turn off by City Hospital into Hucknall Road (A611) to city centre. After a mile (100 yds before traffic lights), go left into Jenner Street, then left into Wesley Street.

Open: Mon–Sat 10–4; *also* Oct–Jan Sun 11-4; New Year's Day 11–2.30.
Closed: Bank Holiday Mondays; Whit week; Christmas and Boxing Days.
Cards: Access, Eurocheque, Visa.
Cars: Easy parking.
Toilets: Please ask if necessary.
Wheelchairs: Easy access to large shop.
Changing rooms: No.
Teas: Hot drinks available if required.
Groups: Coach parties welcome – please arrange in advance, mentioning this guide.
Transport: Plenty of buses along Mansfield Road.
Mail order: No.

670 Nottingham : Sherwood

The Factory Shop

313 Hucknall Road NG5 1FJ
(0115) 962 0821

Ladies' wear: blouses, skirts, jackets, trousers, ski pants, knitwear, coats and leisurewear. Items mainly produced in own factories.

'Perfects and seconds on sale. We aim to be cheaper than our main rivals.'

....

On the north side of city centre.

From Nottingham: take Mansfield Road (A60) north. Go over first large roundabout and turn left at traffic lights (A611 for Hucknall). Pass Sunblest Bakery; go over traffic lights at Haydn Road. Shop is 100 yds on left.

From the ring road: turn south by City Hospital on to A611 (Hucknall Road) for city centre; go over first traffic lights and downhill. Shop is on right, 100 yds before traffic lights (at Haydn Road).

Open: Mon–Sat 9.30–4.30; Sun 10–4.
Closed: Bank Holidays; Christmas–New Year.
Cards: No.
Cars: Outside shop plus limited off street parking.
Toilets: No.
Wheelchairs: One step to medium sized shop.
Changing rooms: Yes.
Teas: Cafés within easy walking distance.
Groups: No factory tours, but shopping groups welcome. No need to pre-book.
Transport: Bus nos. 15, 16, 17, 18, 19 from Trinity Square. All stop almost directly outside shop.
Mail order: No.

Abbey Textiles Ltd.

Robinson House, Avenue Road CV11 4LV
(01203) 374141

Wide range of clothing with something for all the family.
Famous chainstore items at very reasonable prices.

'Genuine factory shop with a lot of goods made on premises.
Also by buying from other manufacturers and clearance outlets
the range has been increased to supply customer demand.'

....

About 3/4 mile south of Nuneaton town centre.
From the ring road round the central Nuneaton shopping area:
turn off at the large roundabout on to the B4113 for Coventry
(Coton Road). At the large roundabout with railway viaduct
across it, turn left into Avenue Road (A4254). Company is 300
yds on right, opposite a school.
From the A5 north-east of Nuneaton: turn south on to the A47;
at the roundabout turn left on to A4254 (Eastern Relief Road/
Eastborough Way). Virtually keep straight, pass the Pingles
Leisure Centre on the right; this company is shortly on the left.

Open: Tues–Sat 9–5;
Sun 10–4.
Closed: Monday; Christmas,
Boxing and New Year's Days.
Cards: Access, Visa.
Cars: Own car-park.
Toilets: No.
Wheelchairs: Easy access.
Changing rooms: Yes.
Teas: In town.
Groups: Shopping groups
at any time, but essential to
phone first.
Transport: Nuneaton–
Coventry Midland Red bus
no. 658 stops in Coton Road.

A & J Carter Ltd.

65a London Road LE2 5DN   Closed
(0116) 271 2939

Large selection of babies' and children's wear – terry, cotton
and velour sleepsuits and pyjamas; fleece walkers, sleeping
bags, dressing gowns. Sweatshirts, jogging suits, trousers,
dresses, dungarees. T-shirts, shorts, sundresses, underwear,
socks and much more.

'Perfects, seconds and designer samples. A real factory shop,
everything British-made.'

....

Going north along A6 into Oadby: go left at first traffic lights
and immediately right into London Road. Shop is on right, set
back from road and opposite first shops on the left.
From Leicester on A6: pass race course on right, cross next
traffic lights and go right at next lights to Wigston (A5096). At
mini-roundabout (London Road) go straight – shop is 150 yds
on left.
From Wigston: turn right at the mini-roundabout in the centre
of Oadby (London Road) and shop is 150 yds on left.

Open: Mon, Tues, Thur
1.30–4.30; Wed 9–12 and
1.30–4.30; Fri, Sat 9–12.
Closed: Bank Holidays; local
industrial holidays. Please
phone prior to journey.
Cards: Access, Visa.
Cars: In forecourt and rear
of premises.
Toilets: No.
Wheelchairs: No access for
chairs, although shop is on
ground floor without steps.
Changing rooms: No.
Teas: In Asda at Leicester
end of village. Also pubs.
Groups: No factory tours, but
coach parties welcome to shop;
please phone first mentioning
this guide. Special opening by
arrangement.
Transport: From BR London
Road Station in Leicester, take
Midland Fox bus nos. 30 or 31
to London Road, Oadby.

The Market Place at Chanterelle

97–99 Station Road East RH8 OAY
(01883) 714389

Comprehensive range of ladies' fashions: jackets, suits, blouses, knitwear and dresses.

'Most of the collections are current season's top quality famous name brands. Discounts up to 50% off normal retail prices, with new collections arriving weekly.'

....

In the centre of Oxted, two minutes from the station.
Follow signs to town centre and railway station. With the station on your right, continue down Station Road East: the shop (called Chanterelle) is 100 yds on the right.

Open: Mon–Sat 9.30–5.30.
Closed: Bank Holidays.
Cards: Access, Switch, Visa.
Cars: Town car-parks.
Toilets: Ask if desperate.
Wheelchairs: Easy access to main floor (for full price current ranges); unfortunately no lift to first floor Market Place (for discounted garments).
Changing rooms: Yes.
Teas: Tea and coffee available. Local cafés.
Groups: Shopping groups welcome.
Transport: Two minutes' walk from Oxted BR station. Local buses.
Mail order: No.

Town & Country Manner

Penrith Industrial Estate CA11 9EO
(01768) 890986

Large range of outdoor clothing; country wear and quality classic fashion for all the family. Up to 50" waist, 20" collar for gents, size 30 for ladies. Skirts, trousers and jackets with some exclusive lines. Shoes, boots, socks, waterproofs, workwear and home linens. Mail order ends of lines, one-offs from bargain cloth buys, overmakes and seconds.

'Traditional quality at realistic prices. Most garments made specifically for this shop, including very large sizes to order. Always special offers. Skirts usually under £20; other items up to 40% off.'

....

West of Penrith close to the motorway.
From town centre: aim for M6/Keswick. At roundabout with Shell petrol station on right, follow signs to Penrith Industrial Estates.*
From M6 exit 40: aim for Penrith. At first mini-roundabout (Shell petrol station on left), go left following signs to Penrith Industrial Estates.*
*Go under railway bridge; shop is 200 yds, clearly signed on left.

Open: Mon–Sat 9–5; Sun 10–5.
Closed: Christmas Day; usually open New Year's Day, please check.
Cards: Access, Visa.
Cars: Own car-park at rear.
Toilets: Yes.
Wheelchairs: One step to large warehouse; assistance gladly given.
Changing rooms: Yes.
Teas: Café opposite and hotel nearby; tea shops in town.
Groups: Shopping groups welcome, but larger groups please phone first.
Transport: Penrith BR 15 minutes' walk, buses to Penrith.
Mail order: Yes. From brochure range only. Phone 01768 899111, mentioning this guide, for free mail order brochure to view small selection of range.
Catalogue: Free.

675 Peterborough Cambs

Jaeger Sale Shop
3 Cumbergate PE1 1YS
(01733) 63114

Previous season's Jaeger ladies' collection from UK and export.

'All stock perfect but one season behind. Sales twice yearly for extra bargains. Ask to go on mailing list, mentioning this book.'

In the town centre.

From A1: take A605 into Peterborough. Pass Rover garage on left, go over railway; go left at roundabout on to A15. Cross river and stay on A15, for Sleaford/Lincoln. At large roundabout with footbridges over it, go into Queensgate Shopping Centre car-park. *

Via A47 from Leicester or Wisbech: turn on to A15 for Peterborough Centre; go into Queensgate Shopping Centre car-park opposite station. *

*Go down to ground floor of car-park and walk almost to end: go right into Cumbergate. Jaeger shortly on right.

Open: Mon–Sat 9.30–5.30.
Closed: Bank Holidays; Christmas, Boxing and New Year's Days.
Cards: Access, Amex, Diners, Jaeger Credit Card, Visa.
Cars: In town centre.
Toilets: No.
Wheelchairs: Wheelchairs can be collected from 11th floor of Queensgate car-park, please book first to ensure availability.
Changing rooms: Yes.
Teas: Hot and cold drinks willingly made! Toy box for children.
Groups: Shopping groups welcome, but phone call appreciated.
Transport: In town centre; near bus and train stations.
Mail order: No.

676 Peterlee Co. Durham

Claremont Garments
2 Doxford Drive, South West Industrial Estate SR8 2RL
(0191) 518 3026

Ladies' wear: lingerie, swimwear, casualwear (bodies, leggings etc), dresses, blouses, skirts, trousers, and tailored suits, coats and jackets. Schoolwear: boys' trousers and shirts; girls' skirts and shirts. Boys' wear: a limited range of casual shirts and trousers.

'All garments are leading chainstore perfects, seconds or ends of lines, and are offered at greatly reduced prices.'

See our display advertisement on p. 347

In large industrial estate west of the A19.

From A19 exit for 'Peterlee/Horden' B1320. Follow signs to South West Industrial Estate into Shotton Road; at next roundabout (bank on far right corner) go left and next left again. The shop is in second building on left.

Open: Mon–Fri 10–4.30; Sat 10–4. Good Friday.
Closed: All Bank Holidays except Good Friday. Christmas to be arranged, please phone.
Cards: Most major credit cards.
Cars: Own car-park.
Toilets: No; in town centre.
Wheelchairs: Ramp; easy access.
Changing rooms: Yes.
Teas: In town centre.
Groups: Shopping groups welcome, but large groups please phone first.
Transport: Bus to Peterlee town centre.
Mail order: No.

Dewhirst Ltd.
Mill Hill, North West Industrial Estate SR8 5AB
(0191) 586 4525

New purpose-built spacious shop for men's quality suits, sports jackets and blazers, trousers, formal and casual shirts, casual jackets, coats. Ladies' blouses, skirts, trousers, jeans dresses, fashion jackets, blazers, suits, coats. Children's shirts, blouses, skirts, trousers, dresses, jackets, coats, schoolwear.

'Premier factory shop in the Dewhirst Group with the largest display of goods for all the family. Men's quality suits from £80. High quality famous chainstore slight seconds.'

In large industrial estate west of the A19.
  From A19 exit for 'Peterlee/Horden' B1320. From this exit roundabout follow signs to North West Industrial Estate. The shop is in the first factory on the right.

Open: Mon–Wed 9–5.30; Thur 9–7; Fri 9–6; Sat 9–5; Sun 11–5.
Closed: Easter Sunday; Christmas, Boxing and New Year's Days.
Cards: Access, Connect, Switch, Visa.
Cars: Outside shop.
Toilets: On request.
Wheelchairs: Ramps to huge shop.
Changing rooms: Yes.
Teas: About 1 mile in Peterlee.
Groups: No factory tours; shopping groups welcome, please phone first.
Transport: Buses from Sunderland, Hartlepool, Durham stop outside.
Mail order: No.

Jaeger Sale Shop
Unit 7 The Armada Shopping Centre
Mayflower Street PL1 1QJ
(01752) 668315   Closed

Large range of ladies' wear including knitwear, blouses, skirts, trousers, jackets, suits. Men's knitwear, shirts, ties and socks.

'Ladies' and men's wear at bargain prices.'

In the city centre within Armada Shopping Centre.
  From any direction into Plymouth: follow signs to city centre and park in city centre car-parks then short walk.

Open: Mon–Sat 9–5.30 (Tues 9.30–5.30).
Closed: Please phone about holidays.
Cards: Access, Switch, Visa.
Cars: Sainsbury/Armada car-park nearest for wheel-chairs and pushchairs.
Toilets: Armada Centre.
Wheelchairs: Easy access by lift.
Changing rooms: Yes.
Teas: Coffee shop in Centre.
Groups: Shoppers welcome by appointment.
Transport: Local buses.
Mail order: No.

The Brown's Factory Shop

Beast Fair Service Road, off Ropergate WF8 1DL
(01977) 602563

Men's suits, trousers, jackets and waistcoats; jeans, shirts, boots, padded shirts. Some ladies' wear: leggings, blouses, skirts, trouser suits.

'We manufacture for major high street shops. We sell overcuts, cancelled orders or items with slight damage. Sample prices: jacket seconds from £12.99, suits (mostly perfect) from £39.99, shirts from £7.99.'

In the centre of town near Market Square.

From M62 exit 32: take (A639) to Pontefract, go past the race course on the right. Follow road for another 1/4 mile onto dual carriage-way. Just after the pelican crossing fork left into Front Street, then first right immediately after Greyhound public house on the right. Follow road round and shop is on the right opposite Keyzers Restaurant.

From town centre (Market Square): shop is behind Marks & Spencers and Boots.

Open: Mon, Tues, Wed, Fri 10–5.30; Sat 10–5.
Closed: Thursday; Bank Holidays; for Christmas–New Year opening please phone.
Cards: None.
Cars: Pay-&-display at rear; limited meter parking; free parking on site Saturdays.
Toilets: Ask if required.
Wheelchairs: Unfortunately too difficult: two flights of stairs.
Changing rooms: Yes, two.
Teas: Café opposite and pubs in town.
Groups: No factory tours; shopping groups welcome but please phone first.
Transport: Bus station 7 minutes' walk.
Mail order: No.

Falmer Jeans Ltd.

24–26 Brook Road SS6 7XF
(01268) 773633

Wide range of men's and ladies' jeans and casual wear: shorts, T-shirts, blouses etc.

'All items are ends of lines, previous year's ranges or slightly substandard stock at reduced prices.'

On south side of Rayleigh, just off Southend Arterial Road (A127).

Going east on A127 to Southend: go left at Rayleigh Weir overpass/roundabout. At huge roundabout, take second left (The Weir pub on left) as if going back on to A127.*

From Southend on A127: go to major roundabout as above, then double back as if going back along dual carriageway.*

*Take first left, following signs to Industrial estate; go right into Brook Road. Company clearly marked on right.

Open: Mon–Sat 9–5.30. Phone for Bank Holidays. Some days between Christmas–New Year.
Closed: Some Bank Holidays.
Cards: Access, Switch, Visa.
Cars: Outside shop.
Toilets: Ask if necessary.
Wheelchairs: Assistance into sizeable shop by prior arrangement.
Changing rooms: Yes.
Teas: In Rayleigh.
Groups: Shopping groups welcome if they phone first.
Transport: Buses to Rayleigh Weir then 1/4 mile walk.
Mail order: No.

Dewhirst Ltd.

Junction of West Coatham Lane & Limerick Road
TS10 5QC
(01642) 472391/2

Men's quality suits, sports jackets and blazers, trousers, formal and casual shirts, casual jackets, coats. Ladies' blouses, skirts, trousers, jeans, dresses, fashion jackets and blazers, suits, casual jackets, coats. Children's shirts, blouses, skirts, trousers, dresses, jackets, coats, schoolwear.

'Products are high quality famous chainstore slight seconds. Men's quality suits from £80.'

West of Redcar, close to ICI Wilton works and British Steel.
From Middlesbrough or Redcar on the trunk road A1085: at roundabout, turn towards Dormanstown Industrial Estate where signed. Dewhirst is first factory on left (Limerick Road), clearly marked.

From Middlesbrough on A66: go towards Redcar and you come on to A1085. At roundabout, turn towards Dormanstown Industrial Estate where signed. Dewhirst is first factory on left (Limerick Road), clearly marked.

Open: Mon–Fri 9–5.30; Sat 9–5; Sun 10.30–4.30. Bank Holidays.
Closed: Good Friday; Easter Sunday; Christmas, Boxing and New Year's Days.
Cards: Access, Connect, Switch, Visa.
Cars: Own car-park.
Toilets: No.
Wheelchairs: One small step.
Changing rooms: Yes.
Teas: No.
Groups: No factory tours, but groups of shoppers always welcome (prior phone call appreciated).
Transport: Cleveland Transit and United buses operate Redcar–Middlesbrough services via Dormanstown; all stop outside factory.
Mail order: No.

Jaeger Knitwear

c/o Arrow Auctions, Bartleet Road, Washford B98 1LV
(01527) 529029

High quality ladies' knitwear, blouses, skirts, dresses, jackets etc. High quality men's knitwear, suits, jackets, trousers, shirts, ties and socks.

'Quality merchandise at reduced prices.'

In a new location south-east side of Redditch, just off the B4497 (Icknield Street Drive).
From M42 exit 3/Birmingham: take A435 south for Redditch/ Evesham.*

From Redditch town: aim east for 'Birmingham/Coventry (A435)' on A4023 Coventry Highway; keep straight until you meet the A435. Then go south for Alcester/Evesham.*

*Stay on this partly dual carriageway road (do not go right for Redditch town centre) through Mappleborough Green. Pass the Boot Inn on left; after about 1/2 mile, go right on to B4497 (Icknield Street Drive). Pass Washford Mill pub on left, go over roundabout, take second right (Bartleet Road). Go immediately right into Arrow Auction site. Shop on right.

Open: Mon–Fri 10–4.30; Sat 10–3.30.
Closed: Bank Holidays; Christmas and New Year, please phone for dates.
Cards: Access, Connect, Switch, Visa.
Cars: Parking spaces directly outside shop.
Toilets: On-site.
Wheelchairs: One step into medium sized shop.
Changing rooms: Yes.
Teas: Café on-site weekdays; also in Redditch.
Groups: Shopping parties welcome – prior phone call appreciated.
Transport: None.
Mail order: No.
Catalogue: No.

Keeping up with Fashion

Criticism of modern fashion trends is by no means a new phenomenon. When crinolines, and the new bright aniline dyes, made their appearance in mid 1800s, critics called them prime examples of the immorality of modern dress. A contemporary fashion columnist stated in a family journal that 'all men whose opinion is worth having prefer the simple and genuine girl of the past, with her tender little ways and pretty bashful modesties, to this loud and rampant modernization'. Caricaturists had a field day depicting the absurdity of ladies trying to squeeze through narrow doorways and blocking up pavements.

The volume of the skirt was initially achieved by an ever increasing number of under-petticoats and careful pleating, until technology made it possible to replace these heavy layers with a steel-framed support. By 1862 it was estimated that between 130 and 150 tons of steel were used weekly for the manufacture of crinolines.

But keeping up with changes in fashion as they occurred demanded money (then as now!) and resourcefulness. Our nineteenth century forebears were confronted with the taxing problem of stretching their old narrow dresses over their new fangled crinolines. Advice was often given on how to insert additional fabric to make this possible.

The crinoline had a relatively short life. It had its heyday in the 1860s, but by the end of the decade no amount of advertising could sustain it at the centre of fashionable interest, and manufacturers were forced to diversify into bustle and corset production. Huge lengths of skirt had begun to be bunched up towards the back over bustles until, by the end of the 1870s, the much softer princess line made skirt support unnecessary.

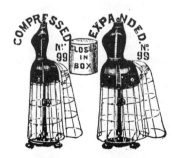

*With thanks to Manchester University Press
for permission to use information from Christopher Breward's
The Culture of Fashion.*

Charnos

Greenhill Industrial Estate, Greenhill Lane DE55 4BP
(01773) 540408

Ladies' lingerie, hosiery, underwear, knitwear, dresses, skirts and blouses; children's wear; men's wear; sportswear; household linens.

See our display advertisement inside back cover

Entrance to estate is in Greenhill Lane, main road through Riddings.

From Somercotes: go downhill; clear entrance to estate is on right.

If you go uphill towards Somercotes: look for entrance to Greenhill Industrial Estate on left.

Charnos is at far end of first large building on right, beyond huge car-park.

Open: Tues–Fri 10–4; Sat 9.30–1.
Closed: Mondays; Christmas–New Year.
Cards: Access, Visa.
Cars: Own car-park.
Toilets: No.
Wheelchairs: Easy access to large shop.
Changing rooms: Yes.
Teas: Cafés in town.
Groups: Groups of shoppers welcome, prior phone call appreciated. For tours of Ilkeston factory for organised groups, please contact Louise Robinson (0115) 932 2191.
Transport: Trent bus nos. 148 (Ripley–Mansfield), 330 (Heanor–Alfreton), 333 (Alfreton–Nottingham) pass through Riddings.
Mail order: No.

Claremont Garments

Tenter Street S60 1L6
(01709) 828668

Ladies' wear: lingerie, swimwear, casualwear (bodies, leggings etc), dresses, blouses, skirts, trousers, and tailored suits, coats and jackets. Schoolwear: boys' trousers and shirts; girls' skirts and shirts. Boys' wear: a limited range of casual shirts and trousers.

'All garments are leading chainstore perfects, seconds or ends of lines, and are offered at greatly reduced prices.'

See our display advertisement on p. 347

Close to B&Q which is just off the inner ring road (A630) by the College Road roundabout.

From Doncaster or Sheffield on the A630: continue to the roundabout with B&Q on the outside of the ring road. Turn off onto the B6089 (to Barnsley) and take the first left in front of 'The Stag's Head' into Tenter Street. Take the next right into Hope Street and the shop is 100 yds on the left, clearly signed.

Open: Mon–Fri 9–4.30; Sat 9–2.30.
Closed: Bank Holidays.
Cards: Most major credit cards.
Cars: In street.
Toilets: In town centre.
Wheelchairs: Two steps to medium-sized shop.
Changing rooms: Yes.
Teas: In town centre.
Groups: Shopping groups welcome, but large groups please phone first.
Transport: Rotherham Bus Station.
Mail order: No.

Cooper & Roe

Pasture Lane NG11 6AJ
(0115) 921 6766

Large range of all-wool knitwear for men and women. Ladies' clothing – blouses, skirts, underwear, lingerie, hosiery; children's wear, leisurewear etc.

'Almost all items are made by this company. Seconds and export overmakes. Extended opening before Christmas.'

....

South of Nottingham, between Ruddington and Clifton.
From West Bridgford/Nottingham: easiest to take A60 south towards Loughborough and go right at traffic lights to Ruddington. Then go right along main street towards West Bridgford (but not along A60); shortly turn left opposite The Victoria Tavern for Clifton. After 1/4 mile go over old railway bridge, then left into Pasture Lane. Shop clearly signposted.
From Clifton: follow Green Lane, go over brook; Pasture Lane is on right after about 1/3 mile.

Open: Mon–Thur 9–5; Fri 9–6; Sat 9–1.
Closed: Bank Holidays; Christmas–New Year.
Cards: None.
Cars: Car-park behind factory.
Toilets: Yes.
Wheelchairs: Easy access to large shop. Special opening times can be arranged.
Changing rooms: Yes.
Teas: Tea rooms and small restaurant in village.
Groups: No tours of works but groups always welcome to shop – no need to book but phone call appreciated.
Transport: Bus no. 14 (from Broadmarsh Centre, Nottingham, to Ruddington) then 1/2 mile walk or no. 54 (Nottingham–Ruddington–Clifton).
Mail order: No.

John Partridge Ltd.

Power Station Road, Trent Meadows WS15 2HS
(01889) 584438

John Partridge waxed cotton jackets, trenchcoats, waistcoats. Showerproof classic town coats, casual coats, *Goretex* coats, tweed coats, quilted jackets and waistcoats; children's waxed jackets, quilted jackets and waistcoats. Ladies' fashions. *Aigle* wellingtons, *Christy* hats, moleskin and cord trousers; waterproof trousers and leggings, shooting sticks.

'All garments sold here either slightly imperfect or discontinued lines. Spring and Autumn clearance sales held in marquee by factory – phone for details.'

....

From Uttoxeter: go under the railway bridge, over river bridge and take first left into Power Station Road. Shop is 100 yds on left.
From Stafford: fork left at first roundabout as you enter town. Go to double roundabout; turn left on to B5013 for Uttoxeter.*
From Cannock, Lichfield and Armitage: go to first roundabout. Turn into Elmore Lane (B5013 but not signposted) with The Globe on right and Little Chef on left. Pass police station on left, go straight at double roundabout.*
*Pass church on right, take first right (Power Station Road). Shop is 100 yds on left.

Open: Mon–Fri 9–5; Sat 9–4. Good Friday, Easter Monday and some other Bank Holidays – phone to check.
Closed: Christmas and Boxing Days.
Cards: Access, Amex, Visa. During clearance sales cheques and cash only.
Cars: Outside shop.
Toilets: Yes.
Wheelchairs: One small step to medium sized shop.
Changing rooms: Yes.
Teas: Hot drinks machine.
Groups: No tours but groups of shoppers welcome.
Transport: None.
Mail order: No.

imore Fashions Ltd.

r icow Farm Road WA7 4UJ
(01928) 560169

Ladies' wear: skirts, dresses, jackets, trousers, suits, shorts.
'Leading chainstore seconds only sold here, at factory shop prices.'

··

Just off the A557 on the west side of Runcorn.
From M56 exit 12: take A557 north towards Runcorn.
From either Liverpool or Chester: turn off A557 (Runcorn Expressway) at sign 'Westfield Docks/Runcorn Station'.
From Liverpool direction: go left at top of slip road; large factory is clearly visible, 200 yds on right.
From Chester: turn right at end of slipway, go over a small bridge; factory is 200 yds on right.

Open: Tues, Thur, Fri 10.30–3.
Closed: Monday and Wednesday; Bank Holidays; last week July and 2 weeks in Aug; Christmas–New Year. Phone first to check dates.
Cards: Access, Switch, Visa.
Cars: Own car-park.
Toilets: In Runcorn.
Wheelchairs: 12 steps to shop.
Changing rooms: No.
Teas: In Runcorn.
Groups: Groups welcome to shop but must phone first.
Transport: None.

---

688 Saffron Walden Essex

Swaine Adeney Brigg

Nursery Road, Great Chesterford CB10 1QV
(01799) 530521

Luxury country clothing: ladies' and men's tailored jackets, trousers, skirts, jumpers, blouses, shirts, scarves, gloves and wax and cotton outerwear; English bridle hide leather goods; gifts, toiletries and the famous Brigg umbrella.
'Perfect ends of lines etc. Usually at least 30% off London retail prices.'

··

About four miles north-west of Saffron Walden and near M11 exit 9.
Going north on M11: take exit 9 (for A11 Norwich). At first roundabout (junction with A1301 for Sawston and Cambridge, and B184 for Saffron Walden) take exit for Saffron Walden.*
Going south on M11: take exit 10 then A505 towards Sawston. After 1.5 miles turn right on to A1301 for Saffron Walden. At roundabout with A11, take B184 for Saffron Walden.*
***At roundabout go right for Great Chesterford. Continue around sweeping left bend, pass glass house (nursery) on right and turn right immediately. Shop is at the end, straight ahead.**

Open: Tues–Sat 10.30–4.
Closed: Monday; Good Friday; Christmas–New Year.
Cards: Access, Amex, Switch, Visa.
Cars: Factory car park.
Toilets: Yes.
Wheelchairs: One step to small shop.
Changing rooms: Yes.
Teas: Gluttons Café in Saffron Walden.
Transport: Great Chesterford BR station behind factory.
Mail order: No.

Glen Alva Ltd.

Hallpark Mill, Whins Road FK10 3PK
(01259) 723024

Wide selection of babywear and children's garments, all knitted: shawls, layettes, matinée jackets, jumpers etc, for all ages up to 10. Also some adults' designer knitwear.

'Perfects, seconds and overmakes at low mill shop prices from 50p. Always a half-price rail.'

....

On A908 at southern end of Sauchie.

From A907 roundabout by Alloa Brewery in Alloa: take A908 north towards Tillicoultry. Mill is about 1/4 mile on left after next roundabout and immediately after Beaton's DIY.

From Tillicoultry coming south on A908 and from Alva on B908: go through Sauchie and these two roads join. Pass Rover showroom on left; shop entrance at far end of the factory on right, well signposted.

Open: Mon–Sat 10–4; Sun 12–4; Bank Holidays.
Closed: Christmas, Boxing and New Year's Days; 2 Jan.
Cards: No.
Cars: Own car-park.
Toilets: No.
Changing rooms: Yes.
Teas: In Alloa.
Groups: Viewing window into factory. Groups of shoppers welcome, prior phone call unnecessary. No guided tours.
Transport: Alloa–Sauchie/Hillfoot buses stop near by.

Hide Park Leather Co.

38c Hoylake Road, Southpark Industrial Estate
DN17 2AY
(01724) 280375

Massive selection of leather, suede and sheepskin coats, jackets, trousers and skirts, mostly made here. Larger sizes available. Made-to-measure service. Repairs and some alterations. Large range of motorbike clothing.

'Some clearance lines and seconds available at knock-down prices, but mainly perfects.'

....

In Industrial Estate south-west of Scunthorpe.

From M180: turn on to M181, go right at first roundabout, and right at second roundabout (large pub on near left corner). Go over next roundabout, then go left into Southpark Road. Take the first right into Hoylake Road: factory is 1/4 mile on left, clearly signposted.

Open: Mon–Sat 10–5; most Sundays. Bank Holidays.
Closed: Christmas and Boxing Days.
Cards: Access, Visa.
Cars: Own car-park.
Toilets: Yes.
Wheelchairs: One step to small shop.
Changing rooms: Yes.
Teas: In Scunthorpe.
Groups: You can see the garments being made, and select your own skins. Groups welcome to shop – please telephone first.
Transport: None.
Mail order: No.

691 Sedbergh Cumbria

Farfield Clothing
Farfield Mill LA10 5LW
Phone (015396) 20169 Fax (015396) 21716

Soft warm quality British polar fleece jackets and jumpers in a paintbox range of colours and styles for all ages. Children's wear from own 'Tough Customer' collection and own 'Original' fibre pile jackets and jerkins.

'A real factory shop selling own brands. Firsts and seconds. At least 25% reduction over the whole range. Example: seconds of polar fleece adult jackets and jumpers £19.99. '

....

About 1 mile south-east of Sedbergh.
   From Sedbergh: follow signs to Hawes (A684). This shop, clearly signed, is on the left. Go along the drive to the mill.
   From Hawes along the A684: pass the Frostow Methodist Chapel on the left, and the mill is just over 1/2 mile on the right. Go slowly as you have to turn quite sharply into the drive.

Open: Mon–Fri 9–5; Sat 9–1.
Closed: Christmas and New Year.
Cards: Access, Mastercard, Visa.
Cars: In the mill yard.
Toilets: Yes.
Wheelchairs: No steps, easy access.
Changing rooms: No, but welcome to try things on.
Teas: Posthorn or Copper Kettle café in Sedbergh, 1 mile away.
Groups: For group visits to mill or shop please book with Mrs Jean Pearson. Maximum 10; no charge.
Transport: Bus Kendal–Sedbergh town; or Settle–Carlisle railway to Garsdale Station (6 miles).
Mail order: 'Farfield' and 'Tough Customer' clothing available by mail order.
Catalogue: Free brochure, please telephone.

692 Selkirk Borders

Brenire
Unit 3, Linglie Mill, Riverside Industrial Estate TD7 5DV
(01750) 21836

Heavy-knit outdoor hand-framed knitwear made in locally spun 100% pure new wool; army-style sweaters.

'Perfects and seconds on sale.'

....

To the north of town.
   From Peebles/Innerleithen on A707 and from Moffat on A708: cross river into Selkirk and immediately turn left into Buccleuch Road. After 1.25 miles, turn left into Level Crossing Road; shop is 100 yds on right.
   From Hawick on A7: go through Selkirk and turn left after Exacta and before the Selkirk Glass Factory.*
   From Edinburgh and Galashiels on A7 take the first right after Selkirk Glass, for Peebles, Moffat.*
   *After 300 yds take first right (Level Crossing Road) for North Riverside Ind. Area; shop is 100 yds on right.

Open: Mon–Fri 9–4.45; Sat 9–12.
Closed: Last week July and first week August; Christmas–New Year.
Cards: Visa.
Cars: Own car-park in front of factory.
Toilets: Ask if desperate.
Wheelchairs: Yes.
Changing rooms: No.
Teas: Shop on estate does sandwiches etc.
Groups: You are always welcome to watch garment production but company cannot cater for groups. Shopping groups welcome, prior phone call please.
Transport: Bus from Galashiels or Hawick to Selkirk square, then 10 minutes' walk.
Mail order: Yes.

Gardiner of Selkirk Ltd.

Tweed Mills, Dunsdale Road TD7 5DZ
(01750) 20735

Men's and ladies' tweeds in different weights and designs; co-ordinating Shetland hand and machine knitting wool and knitwear; Aran knitting wool; skirts, ties and travel rugs; sometimes jackets and coats. Also weaving yarn; ties, shirts, socks, sewing accessories, pottery.

'Genuine mill shop with most items produced in own factory next to shop. All at mill prices. Firsts and seconds. Tweeds from £5.50 per m (150 cm wide); yarn from 25p per oz; knitwear from £14.95; pottery from £6.95.'

···

On north side of town.

From Peebles/Innerleithen on A707 and Moffat on A708: cross river into Selkirk and go left into Buccleuch Road. Shop clearly marked on left after half a mile.

From Hawick on A7: go through Selkirk, go left after Exacta and before Selkirk Glass.*

From Edinburgh & Galashiels on A7: take first right immediately after Selkirk Glass, signposted to Peebles, Moffat.*

*Shop half a mile on right.

Open: Mon–Sat 9–5; Bank Holidays.
Closed: Christmas–New Year.
Cards: Access, Visa.
Cars: Ample parking adjacent to shop.
Toilets: Yes.
Wheelchairs: Two steps to large shop.
Changing rooms: No.
Teas: Hot & cold drinks machine, snack machine in factory (50 yds).
Groups: Groups to shop or mill please phone Mr D Weir (01750) 20283.
Transport: None.
Mail order: Yes.
Catalogue: No. Will send small samples of fabric or yarn from current stock trying to match customers verbal description of requirement.

Mulberry

The Old School House, Kilver Street BA4 5NF
(01749) 340583

Men's and women's outer garments and stylish casual wear; straw hats; wide range of leather bags, rucksacks, belts, organisers, wallets etc. Some dressmaking and upholstery fabrics. Household items, eg furniture (settees, tables etc), china and glass.

'Last season's goods, some seconds.'

···

This company has moved about 10 miles south. It is now on the north-east side of Shepton Mallet.

Coming south on the A37: pass the Downside Inn on the right then the right turn-off to Shepton town centre. Shop is a short distance on left, clearly visible. It is opposite Showerings.

From traffic lights at the junction of A361 (Frome–Wells road) and A37: take A37 north for Bristol. Clearly visible shop is a few hundred yards on right (opposite Showerings on left).

Open: Mon–Sat 10–6; Sun 11–4.
Closed: Christmas, Boxing and New Year's Days.
Cards: Access, Amex, Connect, Diners, Eurocard, JCB, Switch, Visa.
Cars: Clearly marked free car-park adjacent to shop.
Toilets: Yes, including for disabled. Baby changing facilities.
Wheelchairs: Side entrance; no steps. Huge shop.
Changing rooms: Yes.
Teas: Tea room in shop opening shortly.
Groups: By prior appointment only with manageress.
Transport: Castle Cary BR station then taxi (about 6 miles).
Mail order: No.

Durham Clothing Co. Ltd.

Dabble Duck Industrial Estate DL4 2QK
(01388) 777226

Men's suits, jackets and trousers; ladies' jackets, trousers and skirts. Dinner suits, shirts, ties. *Dannimac* coats and anoraks.

'First quality goods at factory prices. '

....

On the south side of Shildon.
From A1(M): take A68 then A6072, following signs to Shildon. As you approach Shildon, go left at first roundabout, right at second roundabout, and right again at next roundabout.*
From Bishop Auckland on A6072: cross first roundabout, go left at second roundabout and right at next roundabout.*
*Take first left on to Dabble Duck Industrial Estate: factory is second on left.

Open: Mon–Thur 10–3; Fri 12–5; Sat 10–4; Bank Holidays 10–4.
Closed: Christmas Day.
Cards: None.
Cars: Own parking.
Toilets: Yes.
Wheelchairs: Stairs to medium sized shop on first floor.
Changing rooms: Yes.
Teas: In Shildon.
Groups: Shopping groups welcome; please telephone first.
Transport: Local buses stop 100 yds away; 5 minutes' walk from station.
Mail order: No.

Claremont Garments

26 Dolphin Road BN43 6PR
(01273) 461571

Ladies' and girls' underwear and nightwear; also ladies' and children's outerwear and leisurewear.

'Seconds and ends of lines, including chainstore items, sold here. Range of stock much wider now. Newly refurbished shop.'

See our display advertisement on p. 347

....

Beside the railway line, a couple of hundred yards off the coast road, on the east side of the town centre.
From M23/Brighton: drive along seafront through Portslade and Southwick into Shoreham. Pass B&Q and Halfords on right; go right at traffic lights after Courts.*
From Worthing on coast road (A259): at roundabout go right for Shoreham town centre; drive through Shoreham. Pass large Esso petrol station on right then go left at traffic lights for Dolphin Industrial Estate.
*Cross level crossing, go right into Dolphin Road (parallel to railway); well marked building on left. Go up drive on left.

Open: Mon–Fri 9–4.30; Sat 9–3.
Closed: Phone for details.
Cards: Yes.
Cars: Own car-park.
Toilets: Ask if desperate!
Wheelchairs: Showroom on first floor (no lift).
Changing rooms: No.
Teas: Welcome to use factory canteen (8 am–2 pm).
Groups: Groups welcome to shop, but essential to phone Sue Cush first.
Transport: 10 minutes' walk from centre of Shoreham.
Mail order: No.

Skipton Mill Shop Ltd.
Albion House, Rope Walk BD23 1EE
(01756) 791149

Clothing for men, women and children: including leisure–
wear, shoes, jackets, dresses, blouses etc. Also cosmetics,
toilet bags, pottery, gifts and home furnishings.
'Perfects and seconds often with 30–50% price reductions.'

....

Easy to find in town centre, next to bowling green near town hall.

*In the town centre, go into High Street (main shopping street)
which has a church, castle and roundabout at top end.*

*Coming uphill, ie towards church/castle: go right into car-park
just before town hall on right and 50 yds before roundabout.**

*From top end, ie by church: go down High Street for 50 yds,
turn left to car-park immediately after town hall.**

**Once in car-park, go down to public toilets and go right
around the building to entrance.*

Open: Mon–Sat 9–5.30;
Sun 11–5.30; Bank Holidays.
Closed: Christmas and
Boxing days only.
Cards: Access, Visa.
Cars: Pay-and-display car-
park. Coach park.
Toilets: By car-park.
Wheelchairs: No steps.
Changing rooms: Yes.
Teas: Several attractive
places in town.
Groups: Shopping groups
welcome – please contact
Richard Tankard.
Transport: Any bus or train
to Skipton.
Mail order: No.

Mexx Factory Outlet
132 Fairlie Road, Slough Trading Estate SL1 4PY
(01753) 525450

Huge range of men's, ladies', kids' and teens' fashion
clothing – sweatshirts, jeans, shorts, T-shirts, skirts etc.
All standard ranges plus a few samples. Also major high
street brand concessions at heavily discounted prices.

*'All first quality, previous season's items and some samples.
Substantial discounts on previous high street prices. Ask to go
on mailing list for special sales. Factory outlet information
line for current promotions.'*

....

*On the huge and well-marked Slough Trading Estate, north-west
of Slough.*

*From M4 exit 6: go towards Slough then follow signs to
Trading Estate. At traffic lights (Office World on near left, Do-It-
All on far left) go left (Buckingham Avenue). At second traffic
lights go right then continue to clearly marked company on
right. Car-park and entrance at back.*

Open: Mon–Sat 9.30–5.30
(Thur late night to 7);
Sun 10–4.
Closed: Phone to check
Christmas–New Year.
Cards: Access, Connect,
Switch, Visa.
Cars: Own car-park at rear.
Toilets: Yes.
Wheelchairs: No steps to
vast shop.
Changing rooms: Yes.
Teas: Vending machine for
cold drinks in seating area.
Groups: Shopping groups of
all sizes welcome. Children's
play, drawing and competition
area with television.

Coats Viyella

Nottingham Road DE55 4JM
(01773) 727590

Large range of men's shirts, trousers, knitwear; Viyella and Jaeger ladies' knitwear, skirts, blouses, jackets etc; children's wear, high quality household linens.

'Seconds, ends of lines etc from several companies in this group.'

The factory is on the B600, between Alfreton and Somercotes.

From Leabrooks going north towards Alfreton: pass large factory on left, then turn left into Hockley Way. *

From Alfreton coming south: pass slip road to A38 on the left, then take first right (Hockley Way). *

*Turn left through first gate into grounds and go round to clearly marked shop at rear.

Open: Mon–Fri 10–4; Sat 9–4.
Closed: Bank Holidays. Please phone for Christmas closures.
Cards: Access, Visa.
Cars: Close to shop in factory yard.
Toilets: Yes.
Wheelchairs: Ramp to huge shop on ground floor.
Changing rooms: Yes.
Teas: In Alfreton.
Groups: Coach parties welcome to shop. Prior phone call appreciated.
Transport: Leabrooks–Alfreton buses stop outside.
Mail order: No.

Claremont Garments

Rekendyke Ind. Est., Eldon Street NE33 5BT (0191) 454 8822

Ladies' wear: lingerie, swimwear, casualwear (bodies, leggings etc), dresses, blouses, skirts, trousers, and tailored suits, coats and jackets. Schoolwear: boys' trousers and shirts; girls' skirts and shirts. Boys' wear: a limited range of casual shirts and trousers.

'All garments are leading chainstore perfects, seconds or ends of lines, and are offered at greatly reduced prices.'

See our display advertisement on p. 347

About 1/2 mile south-west of the town centre.

From Sth Shields town centre: take any road north towards the river (cranes at the docks); turn left for 'Riverside B1302'. At a roundabout where the (A194) branches left keep following signs to 'Riverside'. Pass large Halfords on left; & the 'Tyne Lodge' pub on the right, follow road round to the left and turn right opposite the mosque into Eldon St. Take 2nd right into West Walpole St. *

From Tyne Tunnel south entrance: follow signs to Sth Shields. Go under railway bridge immediately after roundabout, turn left at 2nd roundabout signed 'Riverside B1302' (still dual carriage). At small roundabout in front of Tyne Dock pub turn right into Sth Eldon St. Continue over next crossing, take first left into West Walpole St. *

*Claremont shop is in the third building on the right.

Open: Mon–Fri 9–4.30; Sat 9.30–2.30.
Closed: Most Bank Holidays, please phone to check.
Cards: Most major credit cards.
Cars: Own car-park.
Toilets: In Frederick Street in town.
Wheelchairs: No steps; easy access.
Changing rooms: Yes.
Teas: In Frederick Street in town.
Groups: Shopping groups welcome, but large groups please phone first.
Transport: Chichester Metro station.
Mail order: No.

Tweedmill

Llanerch Park LL17 0UV
(01745) 730072

Quality fashion clothing for men and women direct from UK and Europe's leading manufacturers. Over 10,000 perfect garments; also handbags, luggage, accessories etc. Hats, scarves and picnic rugs woven at the mill.

'This season's overmakes, cancelled orders, designer samples etc. Take delivery of over 1000 garments a week; most with 30% off and 100's at half price.'

....

Two miles south of St Asaph, just off the A525 (St Asaph–Denbigh road).

From St Asaph: take A525 south for Denbigh. Go left at brown signs to Golf Driving Range.*

From Denbigh: go north on A525. In Trefnant, go straight over traffic lights. Follow road round then go right at conspicuous brown sign to Golf Driving Range.*

***After 50 yds, go straight through gates then left to large building.**

Open: Mon–Sat 10–6; Sun 11–5.
Closed: Christmas Day
Cards: Access, Switch, Visa.
Cars: Large car and coach park.
Toilets: Yes.
Wheelchairs: Ramp to vast shop.
Changing rooms: Yes.
Teas: Own café open till 5.
Groups: Shopping groups always welcome. Large groups please book first.
Transport: Bus stop at end of lane.

LS & J Sussman Ltd.

Daniels Lane, Holmbush Industrial Estate PL25 3HP
(01726) 70030

Men's, ladies', boys' and girls' clothing; bedding and towels.

'Sell both end-of-range stock and good seconds.'

....

To the east of St Austell, off A390 (St Austell–Liskeard road).

From town centre: go over roundabout near Asda, heading for Lostwithiel; go under a railway bridge, go left at first traffic lights into Daniel's Lane.*

From Liskeard on A390: follow brown signs to 'Cornish Coliseum and Leisure World', cross the first traffic lights, and go right at the next set into Daniel's Lane.*

***Turn right into Stennack Rd; shop is through first entrance on left.**

Open: Mon, Thur 9–1 and 2–4.45; Tues, Wed, Fri 9–1 and 1.30–4.45; Sat 9–12.
Closed: Bank Holidays; Christmas–New Year.
Cards: Access, Visa.
Cars: Yes.
Toilets: In Asda on the bypass.
Wheelchairs: Yes.
Changing rooms: Yes.
Teas: In Asda.
Groups: No factory tours. Shopping groups by appointment with the shop manageress please.
Transport: Hopper bus from bus station to Holmbush Industrial Estate. Plymouth–Lostwithiel buses along A390.
Mail order: No.

Dewhirst Ltd.

Pennywell Industrial Estate, Pennywell SR4 9EM
(0191) 534 7928

Men's quality suits, sports jackets and blazers, trousers, shirts, casual jackets, coats. Ladies' blouses, skirts, trousers, dresses, fashion jackets, blazers, suits, casual jackets, coats. Children's shirts, blouses, skirts, trousers, dresses, jackets, coats, schoolwear.

'Products high quality famous chainstore slight seconds. Men's quality suits from £80.'

West of Sunderland, just off A19 Sunderland by-pass at junction with A183 (Chester-le-Street road).

From this junction turn towards Sunderland and into Pennywell Industrial Estate at first roundabout. Take first right and go right again to go around Dewhirst building. Shop is on left, clearly signed.

Open: Mon–Fri 9–5.30; Sat 9–5; Sun 11–5. Bank Holidays.
Closed: Good Friday; Easter Sunday; Christmas, Boxing and New Year's Days.
Cards: Access, Connect, Switch, Visa.
Cars: In factory grounds.
Toilets: No.
Wheelchairs: One step then four steps to large shop.
Changing rooms: Yes.
Teas: No.
Groups: Welcome – please phone first.
Transport: Buses to Sunderland from Consett, Chester-le-Street, Wrighton stop outside shop.
Mail order: No.

Claremont Garments

Bowne Street NG17 4BJ   *(01623) 442466*

Ladies' wear: lingerie, swimwear, casualwear (bodies, leggings etc), dresses, blouses, skirts, trousers, and tailored suits, coats and jackets. Schoolwear: boys' trousers and shirts; girls' skirts and shirts. Boys' wear: a limited range of casual shirts and trousers.

'All garments are leading chainstore perfects, seconds or ends of lines, and are offered at greatly reduced prices.'

See our display advertisement on p. 347

In the centre of town, in a small street parallel to Outram Street.

From Mansfield: take A38 west for M1; at roundabout (King's Mill Hospital on right) go straight; pass Blue Bell pub on right and Citroen showroom on left. At traffic lights, take second exit (Outram Street). Take third left (Stoney Street) then first right (Bowne Street). Shop is on left.

From M1 exit 28: take A38 for Mansfield. After several traffic lights go left (Station Road, B6022). Pass Wickes on left. Go straight at traffic lights; pass KwikSave on right. At mini-roundabout, go right into Outram Street. Pass Asda on left, go over mini-roundabout, over bridge then right into Penn Street. Take first left, Bowne Street. Shop is on right.

Open: Mon–Fri 9–4.30; Sat 9–3.
Closed: Please phone about Bank Holidays.
Cards: Most major credit cards.
Cars: Own car-park.
Toilets: Nearest are in Asda, or in town.
Wheelchairs: No steps; easy access.
Changing rooms: Yes.
Teas: Two local cafés in Outram Street (5 minutes' walk)
Groups: Shopping groups welcome, but large groups please phone first.
Transport: Lots of buses to Sutton.
Mail order: No.

705 Sutton-in-Ashfield

Cooper & Roe
Kirkby Road NG17 1GP
(01623) 554026

Huge range of clothing – all-wool knitwear for men and women; ladies' blouses, skirts, underwear, lingerie, hosiery; children's wear; leisurewear etc.

'Almost all items are made by this company. Seconds and export overmakes. Extended opening before Christmas. New children's play area.'

··

About 3/4 mile south of Sutton centre, on the road to Kirkby (B6018).

From Sutton: factory is on right (large clear sign). Shop is at back.

From Kirkby via B6018: pass Ashfield Comprehensive School (on left) and Ashfield Hotel (on right). Factory, clearly marked, is on left.

The new A38 runs 150 yds south of this company. Turn off at traffic lights on to B6018 for Sutton. Factory is 150 yds on left.

Open: Mon–Thur 9–5; Fri 9–6; Sat 9–1.
Closed: Bank Holidays; Christmas–New Year.
Cards: None.
Cars: Private car-park.
Toilets: Yes.
Wheelchairs: Ramp to huge shop now on first floor.
Changing rooms: Yes.
Teas: In Sutton.
Groups: No factory tours but groups always welcome to shop by appointment.
Transport: Buses to Sutton and Kirkby pass the factory.
Mail order: No.

---

706 Swansea : Fforestfach

Dewhirst Ltd.
Unit 22, The Kingsway, Fforestfach Industrial Estate
(01792) 584621

Men's quality suits, sports jackets & blazers, trousers, formal and casual shirts, casual jackets, coats. Ladies' blouses, skirts, trousers, jeans, dresses, fashion jackets, blazers, suits, coats. Children's shirts, blouses, skirts, trousers, dresses, jackets, coats, schoolwear.

'High quality famous chainstore slight seconds. Men's suits from £80; boys' shirts and trousers, and girls' blouses and dresses from £4.99; ladies' blouses, trousers and skirts from £7.99; Men's shirts and trousers from £7.99. About 50–60% discount from high street prices.'

··

Fforestfach is about 1.5 m north-west of Swansea town centre.

From Swansea: take road to Carmarthen (A483), follow signs to Fforestfach. These die out, so then follow sign to 'Swansea Ind. Park' – go left at traffic lights when you see this sign (also sign to Dewhirst). You will be in The Kingsway.*

From M4 exit 47: follow signs to Swansea Ind Park. Go right at traffic lights after Shell petrol station into Kingsway.*

*Go downhill; clearly marked shop is several hundred yards on left, after the brow of the hill.

Open: Mon–Fri 9–5.30; Sat 9–5; Sun 11–5.
Closed: Easter Sunday; Christmas, Boxing and New Year's Days.
Cards: Access, Connect, Switch, Visa.
Cars: At shop.
Toilets: Yes.
Wheelchairs: Level access into large shop. Easy for the disabled.
Changing rooms: Yes.
Teas: Lots of places in Swansea. Tesco 1/4 mile.
Groups: No factory tours; shopping groups welcome – please phone first.
Transport: Main bus routes along Carmarthen Raod or Ystrad Road, which are at either end of The Kingsway.
Mail order: No.

Triumph International
Arkwright Road, Groundwell SN2 5BF
(01793) 720213

Large selection of underwear, swimwear and nightwear for ladies and men. Maternity bras available. Bra fittings available, mastectomy fittings by appointment.
'Many perfect discontinued styles at reduced prices.'
See our display advertisement opposite.

....

On northern side of Swindon, off A419 (M4–Cricklade road).
From M4 exit15: go north on Swindon bypass (A419) for 6+ miles. Go left on to A4311 for Swindon centre at Turnpike roundabout. At first mini-roundabout go left into Arkwright Rd. Entrance on right.
From town centre going north: leave railway station on left. Go under railway bridge, follow signs to Gorse Hill, Penhill & Groundwell on A4311 (A345 on some maps!). Go under footbridge in Penhill; go right at next roundabout (Arkwright Road).

Open: Mon-Sat 10–4.
Closed: Bank Holidays; Christmas–New Year.
Cards: Access, Switch, Visa.
Cars: Own car-park.
Toilets: No.
Wheelchairs: Four steps to shop – help available.
Changing rooms: Yes.
Teas: In service area 5 minutes away.
Groups: Shopping groups welcome; please call Dianne Harris first.
Transport: Bus no. 16 bus to Penhill Estate, 1/2 mile away.
Mail order: No.

Jaeger Sale Shop
43 Church Street B79 7DF
(01827) 52828

High quality ladies' and men's wear including ladies' jackets, skirts and blouses; men's suits, jackets, trousers, shirts, ties and socks etc. Ladies' and men's knitwear.
'High quality merchandise at greatly reduced prices.'
....

Easy to find in the pedestrianised area of the town centre opposite the church.

Open: Mon-Sat 9.30–5.30.
Closed: Bank Holidays; Christmas and New Year.
Cards: Amex, Access, Visa, Switch and Jaeger Accounts.
Cars: Car-parks nearby.
Toilets: In town.
Wheelchairs: Yes, no steps.
Changing rooms: Yes.
Teas: In town.
Groups: Bus parties welcome by prior arrangement.
Transport: Tamworth BR station 1/2 mile. Shop near bus station.
Mail order: No.

FOR VALUE-FOR-MONEY CALL AT OUR FACTORY SHOP FOR AN EXCITING RANGE OF UNDERWEAR, SWIMWEAR AND NIGHTWEAR FOR LADIES AND MEN!

For details see our entry no. 707

709 Telford Salop

Fruit of the Loom
Halesfield 10G TF7 4QR
(01952) 587123 ext 207

T-shirts, sweatshirts, jogging bottoms and polo shirts.
'Firsts, seconds and ends of line sold here from factory in Ireland at discounted prices; minimum discount 25%.'

On the south-east side of Telford, Halesfield is off the A442 (Telford–Bridgnorth road).
*From Telford town centre or M54 exit 5: get on to A442 (Queensway) for Bridgnorth. At the Brockton roundabout turn left for Shifnal, then second right into Halesfield 10G. ***
*From Ironbridge: follow the A4169 for Madeley and Shifnal. Go through Madeley, turn right at the Coppice Farm roundabout and take the first left after the next roundabout into Halesfield 10G. ***
*From Kidderminster and Bridgnorth via A442: at the Brockton roundabout turn right for Shifnal into Halesfield 10 and then take second right into Halesfield 10G. ***
*Shop is at far end of this road clearly signed.

Open: Mon–Thur 9.30–4; Fri 9.30–3.30; Sat 9.30–12.30.
Closed: Bank Holidays; Christmas–New Year.
Cards: Access, Switch, Visa.
Cars: Car-park.
Toilets: Yes.
Wheelchairs: Level access, wide door
Changing rooms: Yes.
Teas: In Telford.
Groups: Yes, please phone first.
Mail order: No.

Callant of Scotland (Knitwear) Ltd.
Devonpark Mills, Devonside FK13 6HR
(01259) 752353

High quality fully fashioned knitwear for men and ladies in cashmere, lambswool and Shetland; embroidery service for clubs.

'Perfects and seconds. At least 40% below shop prices on most goods.'

....

On A908 south of Tillicoultry.
From Alloa on A908: turn left into drive shortly after you enter town.
From Alva/Dollar on A91: turn towards Aloa on A908 by clock-tower. Continue over river and after the right hand bend, go right into drive.

Open: Mon–Fri 9–4; Sat and Sun 11–4.30. Bank Holidays.
Closed: Christmas, Boxing and New Year's Days; 2 Jan.
Cards: Access, Visa.
Cars: Own car park.
Wheelchairs: Easy access; ramp to shop.
Changing rooms: Yes.
Teas: In town.
Groups: Shopping groups welcome – prior phone call essential.
Transport: Buses every 1/2 hour from Stirling and Alloa.
Mail order: Yes.

Lindsay Allan Designs Ltd.
Barn Park Drive FK13 6BX
(01259) 752772

Designer leisurewear, in a variety of fabrics including fleece and lycra, for ladies and children; sweatshirts, waistcoats, jogging suits etc. Designs are all unique, colourful and co-ordinated.

'Ends of lines and slight rejects at affordable and attractive prices. High quality fibres means that products wash well and need minimum ironing.'

....

At south-west end of town.
From Alva: take first right at the beginning of town just after the hump-backed bridge and in front of Castlecraig Hotel. *
From the east: go through town, pass Bank of Scotland on left and then turn left immediately after the Castlecraig Hotel on left (opposite road leads to Tourist Information Centre). *
*The factory is in the corner of the second left turn.

Open: Mon–Fri 9–5.
Closed: Christmas–New Year; Easter.
Cards: No.
Cars: Own car-park.
Toilets: Yes.
Wheelchairs: Easy access.
Changing rooms: Yes.
Teas: Within easy walking distance.
Groups: Shopping groups welcome.
Transport: Buses every 1/2 hour from Stirling and Alloa.
Mail order: No.

S R Leisure

2 Phoenix Road, Crowther Industrial Estate, District 3
NE38 0AD
(0191) 415 3344

Active sportswear. Suppliers to professional skiers, walkers, golfers, fishermen, sailors, canoeists, rowers, rally drivers etc. Large selection of polar fleece, waterproofs, ski wear and accessories from gaiters to *Gore-tex* boots. Ski clothing hire. Tent/awning repairs and alterations, caravan re-upholstery.

'Corporate leisure wear from baseball caps to waterproofs made to individual requirements. Full embroidery facilities and made-to-measure service.'

....

On north-west edge of town, near junction of A1(M) and A1.
   From A194(M) south or northbound: exit on to A182 to Washington; go right on to A1231. Take next exit; at roundabout go into Crowther Industrial Estate.*
   From A1 Western Bypass southbound: go left on to A1231 for Washington. Go right at first roundabout and turn off at next exit into Crowther Industrial Estate.*
   ***Go to end of Crowther Road, go right and follow road around to left, going uphill. Phoenix Road is shortly on right, shop clearly visible.**

Open: Mon–Fri 9–4.45; Sat 9–2.30.
Closed: All Bank Holidays; Christmas–New Year.
Cards: Access, Delta, Eurocard, Mastercard, Switch, Visa.
Cars: Outside shop.
Toilets: No.
Wheelchairs: One step, easy access.
Changing rooms: Yes.
Teas: In town centre.
Groups: Group of shoppers always welcome! Please phone first.
Transport: Very difficult.
Mail order: Yes.
Catalogue: Please phone for price list.

Next 2 Choice

44-46 High Street WD1 2BR
(01923) 233255

Surplus stocks, *Next plc, Next Directory*. Specialising in ladies' and men's wear.

'Save up to 50% off normal Next first quality prices; seconds sold from 1/3 of normal retail price. Special sales Jan and Sept.'

....

Easy to find in the pedestrianised High Street, almost opposite WH Smith and next to Dixons.
   Driving clockwise round the inner ring road: take the right slip-road for Church multi-storey car-park. Go to High Street and turn left, then 300 yds walk and the shop is on left just after Dixons.

Open: Mon–Sat 9–5.30.
Closed: Christmas and Boxing Days.
Cards: Access, Amex, Switch, Visa.
Cars: Car-park in town centre.
Toilets: Church car-park.
Wheelchairs: No steps to large shop.
Changing rooms: No, but refund if items returned in perfect condition within 28 days.
Teas: In town centre.
Groups: Shopping groups welcome! Book with store manager.
Transport: Watford BR station.
Mail order: No.

Fashion Factory

37 Park Street TF1 3AF
(01952) 260489

A variety of constantly changing, quality branded ladies' wear.

'Savings of between 40–70% off high street prices. Stock always perfect unless indicated (99% first quality). No chainstore items. Summer and winter sales. Personal shoppers only.'

··

In Wellington town centre.
   From M54 exit 6: take A442 north. At the third roundabout (Telford hospital on far right), go left into Apley Avenue. At T-junction (school on right corner), go left in to Whitchurch Road which becomes Park Street. Large shop is on right.

Open: Mon–Sat 9.30–5.30; Sun 10–4.
Closed: Christmas Day and Easter Sunday.
Cards: Access, Visa.
Cars: At Red Lion Inn next door.
Toilets: Nearest at Red Lion Inn next door.
Wheelchairs: Shop on two floors, access to ground floor only (no steps).
Changing rooms: Yes, on both floors.
Teas: At Red Lion Inn next door.
Groups: Evening shopping by appointment. Please contact Denise Wagg.
Mail order: No.

East Quay Knitwear

6 Station Road, corner of Buttlands NR23 1AE
(01328) 710891

Large selection of men's and ladies' knitwear in natural fibres, much of it previously seen in leading international stores.

'From traditional to chic, for outdoor pursuits to cocktail parties, we have a sweater for you. Lots of bargains including ends of lines, samples and seconds at greatly reduced prices, and good selection of current stock. Prices £10–£100.'

··

Wells is on the north coast of Norfolk, nine miles north of Fakenham.
   From all directions: follow signs to town centre. The main shopping street is pedestrianised so continue driving till you see the Buttlands (large grassed area) where you can park. Well marked shop is on the corner almost facing the Buttlands.

Open: Seven days July, Aug, Sept 10–6. Winter times may vary, please check.
Closed: Christmas and Boxing Days.
Cards: None.
Cars: Easy, in street outside shop.
Toilets: Public toilets opposite.
Wheelchairs: Ground floor, no steps but small shop.
Changing rooms: Yes.
Teas: Excellent facilities nearby.
Groups: No factory tours; shopping groups welcome, but please phone first.
Transport: Buses from Norwich, Kings Lynn or Fakenham stop opposite.
Mail order: Yes. Only current stock lines by mail order.
Catalogue: Free.

BOYS' SULTAN TWEED SUITS   "ROYAL NAVY" SERGE   CHILDREN'S SERGE KILT SUITS   "ROYAL NAVY" VELVET SUITS   BOYS "PARK" TWEED SUITS

716   West Auckland   Co. Durham

Claremont Garments

Greenfields Industrial Estate, Tindale Crescent DL14 9TR
(01388) 661703

Ladies' wear: lingerie, swimwear, casualwear (bodies, leggings etc), dresses, blouses, skirts, trousers, and tailored suits, coats and jackets. Schoolwear: boys' trousers and shirts; girls' skirts and shirts. Boys' wear: a limited range of casual shirts and trousers.

'All garments are leading chainstore perfects, seconds or ends of lines, and are offered at greatly reduced prices.'

See our display advertisement on p. 347

....

North-east of West Auckland and south-west of Bishop Auckland (these two towns are hard to differentiate!) Just off A688 almost opposite Tindale Crescent Hospital.

   From Bishop Auckland on A688 (towards West Auckland/Barnard Castle): go right at traffic lights (signs to Tindale Cres Hosp). *

   From centre of West Auckland: take A688 for Bishop Auckland. At traffic lights with signs to Tindale Crescent Hospital go left. *

   From A1(M)/Darlington: turn on to A68; at next roundabout take A6072. Follow signs to West Auckland. Go straight at traffic lights. *

   *Industrial estate is 200 yds on left; shop first on left.

Open: Mon–Fri 10–4.30; Sat 10–4. Good Friday.
Closed: Bank Holidays (except Good Friday); Christmas and New Year please check.
Cards: Most major credit cards.
Cars: Own car-park.
Toilets: In Bishop Auckland, 1 mile.
Wheelchairs: One small step to large shop.
Changing rooms: Yes.
Teas: In Morrison's super-market.
Groups: Shopping groups welcome, but large groups please phone first.
Transport: Buses to Evenwood from Bishop Auckland bus station; stop at Tindale Crescent (traffic lights).
Mail order: No.

Next 2 Choice

10–11 Ladygate Centre, High Street SS12 9AK
(01268) 764893

Surplus stocks including men's, women's and children's fashions from *Next plc, Next Directory* and other high street fashions. *Next* footwear.

'Save up to 50% off normal Next first quality prices; seconds sold from 1/3 of normal retail price. Special sales Jan and Sept.'

....

Near southern end of High Street.

From A127: turn onto A132 towards Wickford. Stay on A132 to large roundabout where A129 goes left (and Somerfield is on far left). From this roundabout exit to Somerfield and Ladygate Centre. Shop is in this centre.

From the north on A132: stay on A132 as far as Somerfield on right (by roundabout where A129 turns right for Billericay). Exit this roundabout for Somerfield and Ladygate Centre.

Open: Mon–Thur 9–5.30; Fri 9–6; Sat 9–5.30.
Closed: Christmas and Boxing Days.
Cards: Access, Amex, Switch, Visa.
Cars: In town centre car-park.
Toilets: No.
Wheelchairs: Easy access. No steps.
Changing rooms: No, but refund if goods returned in perfect condition within 28 days.
Teas: In town centre.
Groups: Shopping groups welcome! Book with store manager.
Transport: Wickford BR station.
Mail order: No.

Benco Hosiery

Cemetery Lane DE4 4FG
(01629) 824731

Men's, ladies', children's and babywear including: underwear, nightwear, casualwear, schoolwear, sportswear, outdoorwear and selected footwear; hats, gloves and scarves. A large range of hosiery including socks, tights, stockings, worksocks and legwarmers. Household linens and babylinen.

'Very large shop on ground floor. Huge range of perfects and seconds at very low prices.'

See our display advertisement on p. 331

....

At the northern end of Wirksworth.

If you are going out of Wirksworth towards Matlock: pass the Jet petrol station on left, then turn right and immediately left (by the village school) where you see 'Factory Shop' sign.

Coming into town from Matlock direction: Cemetery Lane is first turning on left (sign to 'Whatstandwell, Crich (B5035)').

Open: Mon–Sat 9–5; (Thur late opening to 8.30). Sun 10–5.
Closed: Christmas and Boxing Days only.
Cards: Access, Delta, Eurocard, Mastercard, Switch, Visa.
Cars: Large car-park behind shop.
Toilets: Yes, very clean.
Wheelchairs: Easy access to huge shop.
Changing rooms: Yes.
Teas: Self-service drinks and snacks including seating and children's play area.
Groups: Can arrange coach parties to the shop after hours – visit can include pie and pea supper in nearby pub! Please arrange in advance, mentioning this Guide.
Transport: Trent Bus nos. 152, 153, 154 (Derby–Matlock).
Mail order: No.

Velmore Fashions Ltd.
Holt Road LL13 9DY
(01978) 363456

Ladies' wear; dresses, suits, jackets, skirts, trousers, shorts. *'Leading chainstore seconds only sold here, at factory shop prices.'*

....

On east side of Wrexham.
From Wrexham: take road east for Holt and Nantwich (A534)/ Wrexham Ind. Est. Pass The Hand on left; Velmore is 400 yds on left.
From Chester via A483: take slip road for Wrexham Ind. Est. (A534); at first roundabout take first turn 'Wrexham Ind. Est.'. Follow road to end; at next roundabout take second exit ('Town Centre'). Go over mini-roundabout (Greyhound Inn on corner).*
Going west on A534: keep straight, look for mini-roundabout with Greyhound Inn.*
*Pass Brooklands garage on left – clearly marked factory 200 yds on right.

Open: Mon, Wed, Fri 10.30–3.
Closed: Tuesday and Thursday; Bank Holidays; last week July and 2 weeks Aug; Christmas–New Year. Phone to check.
Cards: Access, Switch, Visa.
Cars: Yes.
Toilets: In Wrexham.
Wheelchairs: Eight steps to shop.
Changing rooms: No.
Teas: In Wrexham.
Groups: Groups welcome to shop but must telephone first.
Transport: Local buses.

Bridge of York
3 Main Street, Fulford YO1 4HJ
(01904) 634508

Ladies' skirts and blouses (sizes 10–24; long/short sleeves) in wide range of Viyella fabrics, cotton lawn prints, viscose in many designs. Men's shirts: traditional styles (sizes 14 1/2–19 1/2) – fuller fit and longer body in long/short/extra-long sleeves. Fashion shirts in polycotton, 100% cotton, viscose. Ties.

'Excellent quality, competitive prices. Satisfied customers at home and abroad! Fax (01904) 631624.'

....

A short way south of York.
From A64: take A19 towards York. Go through two sets of traffic lights, pass church on right then this factory is on right, next to Adam's House Hotel.
From York: take road (A19) south for Selby; pass Fulford Barracks. Go over one set of lights then factory is 150 yds on left, down the drive. Look for wrought iron sign.

Open: Mon–Sat 9–4.30.
Closed: Christmas and New Year; Bank Holidays.
Cards: Access, Visa.
Cars: Beside factory.
Toilets: Yes.
Changing rooms: Can be arranged.
Teas: In town.
Groups: Tours for groups by appointment. Groups welcome to shop – please phone first.
Transport: York–Fulford buses.
Mail order: Yes. No seconds sent.

ATTRACTIVE
NEW SPRING
TEA
FROCKS
AT SPECIAL PRICES

THE value of these Tea Frocks is quite exceptional. They are made by our own skilled workers, and they follow the latest trend of fashion as expressed in the newest French Models.

" GRACE "

Charming Old World Tea Frock, in good quality chiffon taffetas. The long bodice is lined silk, and has inset short sleeves and a full scalloped skirt, which is daintily trimmed picot, edged goffered silk.

In a large range of colours and black,

SPECIAL PRICE

£5 17 6

Sent on Approval.

Footwear

There is a vast number of factory shops selling footwear and the choice is enormous. This is the industry in which factory shops have increased in number most.

In 1642 Oliver Cromwell placed an order in Northampton for 4,600 pairs of boots for his army, and the reputation of this already thriving community of shoemakers spread far and wide. Northampton was one of the places which had the prerequisites for the trade: an active tanning industry, hides from local cattle and oak bark from local woodlands.

The industrialisation of the shoe trade began in mid-nineteenth century. Britain's factory-made footwear was soon being worn all over the Empire, providing employment for a large number of people in this country. In the twentieth century Northamptonshire once again profited from the demands of war: of the seventy million pairs of footwear produced for the British and Allied forces in the First World War, over two thirds were made in this area.

This century has seen many changes in technology and materials, and in the organisation of the industry as a whole. Many independent firms have, unfortunately, closed down or been taken over, and much footwear sold in Britain is made abroad. Even well known brand name companies find it cheaper to place production in developing countries, in eastern Europe and in the far east. But so long as some minor process is carried out in the UK, such footwear can be sold as if made in Britain.

The range of factory shops covers every conceivable type of footwear: shoes, pumps, boots, slippers, trainers and sports shoes from top of the market for men and women to beach shoes for the children. You can have shoes made to fit, and you can order shoes by mail order.

Briggs & Shoe Mines	721	**Ambleside** Cumbria	
Crockers of Arnold	722	**Arnold** Notts	
K Shoes	723	**Askam-in-Furness** Cumbria	
De Bradelei Mill Shops	318*	**Belper** Derbys	
Clarks	324*	**Bicester** Oxon	
Converse	325*	**Bicester** Oxon	
Hobbs	332*	**Bicester** Oxon	
Joan & David	338*	**Bicester** Oxon	
Kurt Geiger	344*	**Bicester** Oxon	
K Shoes	724	**Blackpool** Lancs	
Wynsors World of Shoes	725	**Bradford** W Yorks	
Crockers of Bridgwater	726	**Bridgwater** Somerset	
Sedgemoor Shoes	727	**Bridgwater** Somerset	
Crockers of Burnham	728	**Burnham-on-Sea** Somerset	
Lambert Howarth & Sons	729	**Burnley** Lancs	
Whitfords Bury Boot & Shoe Co.	730	**Bury** Lancs	
Peaklander Footwear	731	**Calver** Derbys	
Briggs & Shoe Mines	732	**Carlisle** Cumbria	
Wynsors World of Shoes	733	**Castleford** W Yorks	
Wynsors World of Shoes	734	**Chesterfield** Derbys	
Wynsors World of Shoes	735	**Cleckheaton** W Yorks	
Boundary Mill Shop	373*	**Colne** Lancs	
Mansfield Shoes	736	**Cumnock** Ayrshire	
Furness Footwear	737	**Dalton-in-Furness** Cumbria	
Hall & Son	738	**Darlington** Co. Durham	
White and Co. (Earls Barton)	739	**Daventry** Northants	
Shoe Factory Shop, The	740	**Derby** Derbys	
K Shoes	741	**Dundee** Tayside	
Factory Shoe Company	742	**Earl Shilton** Leics	
Barker Shoes	743	**Earls Barton** Northants	
Famous Footwear	387*	**Ellesmere Port** Cheshire	
Kurt Geiger	394*	**Ellesmere Port** Cheshire	
Timberland	405*	**Ellesmere Port** Cheshire	
Crockers	744	**Glasgow : Parkhead** Strathclyde	
Morlands	745	**Glastonbury** Somerset	
Richard Draper	746	**Glastonbury** Somerset	
Priestley Footwear	747	**Great Harwood** Lancs	
Shoe Factory Shop, The	748	**Grimsby** Humberside	
Wynsors World of Shoes	749	**Grimsby** Humberside	
Charles Clinkards	411*	**Hartlepool** Cleveland	
Wynsors World of Shoes	750	**Hazel Grove** Gr Manchester	
Peter Newman	751	**Herne Bay** Kent	
Shoe Factory Shop, The	752	**Hull** Humberside	
Broughton Shoe Warehouse	753	**Ipswich** Suffolk	

* Please see full details in relevant chapter

K Shoes Factory Shop, Sports Factory and Baggage Factory	755	**Kendal**	Cumbria
K Shoes Full Price	438*	**Kendal**	Cumbria
Barker Shoes	756	**Keswick**	Cumbria
Wynsors World of Shoes	757	**Leeds**	W Yorks
Lotus Shoes	758	**Leek**	Staffs
Shoe Factory Shop, The	759	**Leicester**	Leics
New Balance Athletic Shoes (UK)	760	**Maryport**	Cumbria
Matlock Shoe Sales	761	**Matlock Green**	Derbys
K Shoe Mines	762	**Morecambe**	Lancs
Crockett & Jones	763	**Northampton**	Northants
J. L. & Co.	764	**Northampton**	Northants
Piggly-Wiggly Shoe Store	765	**Northampton**	Northants
Tricker's	766	**Northampton**	Northants
Bally Factory Shop, The	767	**Norwich**	Norfolk
Factory Shoe Shop, The	768	**Norwich**	Norfolk
Robert Cole Shoes	769	**Norwich**	Norfolk
Shoe Factory Shop, The	770	**Nottingham**	Notts
Wynsors World of Shoes	771	**Penketh**	Lancs
Briggs & Shoe Mines	772	**Penrith**	Cumbria
T Groocock & Co. (Rothwell)	773	**Rothwell**	Northants
K Shoes	774	**Shap**	Cumbria
Wynsors World of Shoes	775	**Sheffield**	S Yorks
K Shoes	776	**Southport**	Merseyside
Sundaes	777	**Spalding**	Lincs
Wynsors World of Shoes	778	**St Helens**	Merseyside
Lotus Factory Shop	779	**Stafford**	Staffs
Shoe Shed, The	780	**Stafford**	Staffs
Famous Fashion Discounts	451*	**Stockton-on-Tees**	Cleveland
Wynsors World of Shoes	781	**Stockton-on-Tees**	Cleveland
Lotus Shoes	782	**Stone**	Staffs
Clarks Factory Shop	783	**Street**	Somerset
Clarks Shop, The	459*	**Street**	Somerset
Crockers of Street	784	**Street**	Somerset
Denby Pottery	463*	**Street**	Somerset
Crockers of Swindon	785	**Swindon**	Wilts
Wynsors World of Shoes	786	**Thurcroft near Rotherham**	S Yorks
Gaghills Mill & Footwear Museum	787	**Waterfoot**	Lancs
K Shoes	788	**Watford**	Herts
Crockers of Worle	789	**Worle**	Somerset
Factory Outlet Shopping Centre	491*	**York**	N Yorks
Wynsors World of Shoes	790	**York**	N Yorks

* Please see full details in relevant chapter

FOOTWEAR

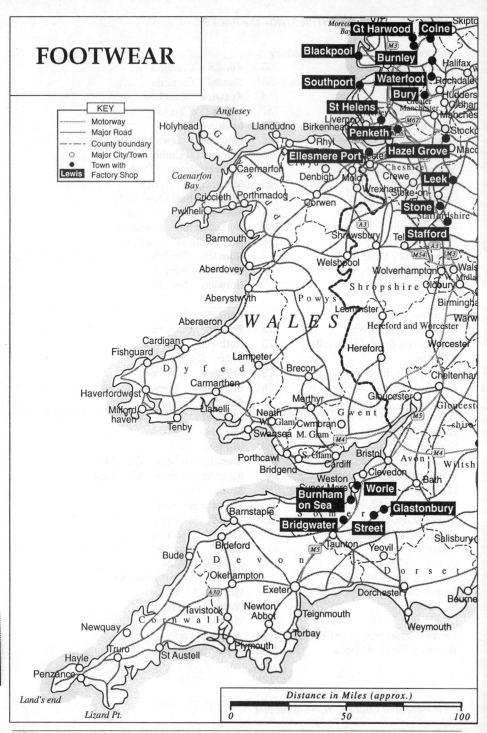

KEY

.... Motorway
———— Major Road
– – – County boundary
○ Major City/Town
● Town with
Lewis Factory Shop

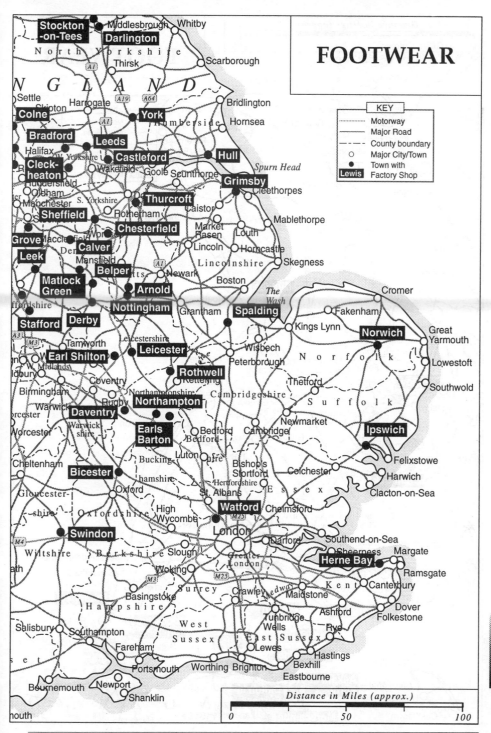

FOOTWEAR

KEY
.... Motorway
———— Major Road
— · — County boundary
○ Major City/Town
● Town with
Lewis Factory Shop

Distance in Miles (approx.)

0   50   100

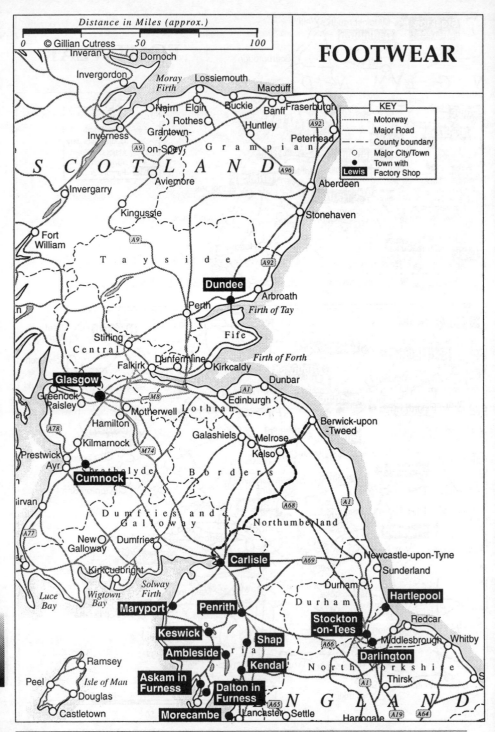

FOOTWEAR

Distance in Miles (approx.)

© Gillian Cutress

0   50   100

KEY

....	Motorway
———	Major Road
– – –	County boundary
○	Major City/Town
●	Town with
Lewis	Factory Shop

Inveran
Dornoch
Invergordon
Moray Firth
Lossiemouth
Macduff
Nairn Elgin
Buckie
Banff Fraserburgh
Rothes
Huntley
Inverness
Grantown-on-Spey
A9
Peterhead
G r a m p i a n
A96
S C O T L A N D
Invergarry
Aviemore
Aberdeen
Kingussie
Stonehaven
Fort William
A9
T a y s i d e
A92
Dundee
Perth
Arbroath
Firth of Tay
Stirling
F i f e
Central
Dunfermline
Firth of Forth
Falkirk
Kirkcaldy
Glasgow
Dunbar
Greenock
Paisley
M8
A1
Edinburgh
Motherwell
L o t h i a n
Hamilton
A78
Berwick-upon-Tweed
Kilmarnock
Galashiels
Melrose
M74
Kelso
Prestwick
Ayr
Strathclyde
B o r d e r s
Cumnock
irvan
D u m f r i e s a n d
G a l l o w a y
A68
A1
N o r t h u m b e r l a n d
A77
New Galloway
Dumfries
Kirkcudbright
Solway Firth
Carlisle
A69
Newcastle-upon-Tyne
Luce Bay
Wigtown Bay
Sunderland
Durham
D u r h a m
Hartlepool
Maryport
Penrith
Stockton-on-Tees
Redcar
Keswick
Shap
A66
Middlesbrough
Whitby
Ramsey
Ambleside
Darlington
Peel
Isle of Man
Kendal
N o r t h   Y o r k s h i r e
Douglas
Askam in Furness
Dalton in Furness
A1
Thirsk
Castletown
Morecambe
Lancaster
Settle
A65
E N G L A N D
A19
A64
Harrogate

721 Ambleside Cumbria

Briggs & Shoe Mines

The Annex, Salutation Hotel LA22 9BY
(015394) 32757

Wide range of sub-standard and clearance footwear of all types for men, women and children.
'All stock made by branded manufacturers.'

See our display advertisement on p. 445

....

Close to the centre of this small town.
From Kendal: get into the one-way system and go around, following signs first to 'Town Centre' then continue towards Kendal again. *
  From Keswick: turn left immediately after Jumpers on the left. *
  ***The shop is behind the large and conspicuous Salutation Hotel on the left, on the first floor.**

Open: *Nov–Easter:* daily 9.30–5.30;
Easter–Oct: daily 9.30–7.30.
Closed: Christmas Day.
Cards: Access, Connect, Switch, Visa.
Cars: Own coach and car-park.
Toilets: Behind Bertrams Restaurant, 30 yds downhill towards Kendal.
Wheelchairs: Unfortunately no access to first floor shop.
Teas: In Ambleside.
Groups: Coach parties welcome to shop. Drivers can obtain a £1 voucher for each passenger.
Transport: Bus stops opposite shop. Local transport and buses from further afield.
Mail order: Yes.
Catalogue: Pleased to supply by mail order items in stock if customers know size, fitting and style. Ask for the manager.

722 Arnold Notts

Crockers of Arnold

111 Front Street NG5 7ED
(0115) 967 4212

Huge selection of *Clarks* and *K Shoes* discontinued lines and slight sub-standards for men, women and children. Self-select from *Clarks, K Shoes, Springers, CICA, Hi-Tec, Nike, Puma, Dr. Martens.*

'An average of 30% saving on normal High Street prices for perfect shoes. Fully trained Clarks fitters for confidence when buying your children's shoes. Big savings on luggage, bags and accessories.'

....

About 3.5 miles north of Nottingham in the centre of Arnold.
  From Nottingham: take A60 (Mansfield Road) north. At Daybrook Square go right at traffic lights signposted Arnold Town Centre (Grove Pub on left). Go over traffic lights (Sainsbury's on right). Go over pedestrian lights, take next right (Croft Road), go left into public car-park. Shop is in Front Street (on left), next to Asda.

Open: Mon–Sat 9–6; Sun 10–4; Bank Holidays 10–5.
Closed: Christmas, Boxing and New Year's Days; Easter Sunday.
Cards: Access, Switch, Visa.
Cars: Huge free car-park next to Asda.
Toilets: In Asda.
Wheelchairs: Easy level access to large shop.
Teas: In Asda.
Groups: Coach parties welcome, concessions for drivers and organisers. £1 voucher per passenger towards purchases.
Transport: Bus nos. 56, 57, 58, 59, 90.
Mail order: No.

K Shoes

James Street LA16 7BA
(01229) 462267

Extensive range of shoes, sandals, boots, slippers and trainers including a wide selection of footwear from *Clarks, Dr Martens, Hi-Tec, Merrell, Puma* and many other famous brands. Good choice of handbags and gifts.

'Average of 30% saving on normal high street prices for perfect shoes. Also wide range of K Shoes discontinued lines and slight substandards for men, women and children. Self-select store but trained staff on hand to measure feet and give assistance if needed. '

....

Askam is 6 miles north of Barrow. Shop in centre of Askam near station.

From the south: take Barrow-in-Furness road to Dalton-in-Furness (A590); at mini-roundabout at end of town go straight, up hill for Askam (A595).*

From the north (Workington, Sellafield, Muncaster, Ravenglass Railway): follow A595.*

*Turn off A595 (Workington–Dalton road) in Askam by station. Go over level crossing and straight into James Street. The drive to shop is 50 yds on right, just after K Shoes factory complex.

Open: Mon–Fri 10–5.30; Sat 9–5; Bank Holidays 10–5.
Closed: Christmas, Boxing and New Year's Days. Easter Sunday.
Cards: Access, Switch, Visa.
Cars: Free parking within factory complex and adjacent to the shop.
Toilets: Yes.
Wheelchairs: Easy access.
Teas: In town.
Tours: Free tour of the large adjoining factory available for groups by advance arrangement. Coach parties welcome; concessions for drivers and organisers. £1 voucher per passenger towards purchases.
Transport: Any bus or train to Askam-in-Furness then walk.
Mail order: No.

K Shoes

Unit 3, Clifton Road Retail Park FY4 4RB
(01253) 699380

Huge selection of *K Shoes* and *Clarks* discontinued lines and slight sub-standards for men, women and children. Self-select from over 8000 pairs of big name brands on display - *Clarks, CICA, K Shoes, Springers Mercury* and *Hi-Tec.*

'An average of 30% saving on normal High Street prices for perfect shoes. Fully trained Clark fitters for confidence when buying your children's shoes. Big savings on luggage, bags and accessories.'

....

Clifton Road Retail Park is close to the end of M55 exit 4 on the outskirts of Blackpool.

From M55: follow town centre signs (A583). At first traffic lights turn left and at mini-roundabout turn left into Retail Park (signed for Tesco Superstore). K Shoes Factory Shop is between Tesco and Matalan.

Open: Mon–Fri 9.30–7.30; Sat 9–6; Sun 10–4; Bank Holidays 9.30–7.30.
Closed: Christmas Day and Easter Sunday.
Cards: Access, Switch, Visa.
Cars: Adjacent free car-park.
Toilets: In-store in adjacent retail units.
Wheelchairs: Easy level access to single floor sales area.
Teas: Café in Tesco.
Groups: Coach parties welcome: please mention this guide; concessions for drivers and organisers. £1 voucher per passenger towards purchases.
Transport: Bus nos. 6, 23, 24, 25, 33 and 44A (Tesco at Marton).
Mail order: No.

Wynsors World of Shoes

339 Thornton Road BB8 9BM

(01274) 495016

Men's, ladies' and children's fashion shoes in leather and synthetic materials.

'Massive range of branded footwear from own factory and all over the world. Stock changes daily. Prices from £1 to £100. Special lines at lowest prices in the country. January and July sales.'

See our display advertisement on p. 435

....

NB This shop, on the west side of Bradford, has moved down Thornton Road B6154 and is now just inside ring road (A6177).

From the city centre: take B6154 (Thornton Road) for Allerton and Thornton. After 1.25 miles, this clearly marked shop is on the right, on the corner of Weetwood Road.

Going east along Thornton Road B6154 towards Bradford: pass Morrison's on the right. Cross the outer ring road (A6177). The shop is shortly on the left, on the corner of Weetwood Road.

From the ring road (A6177): at traffic lights, turn on to Thornton Road B6145 for Bradford city centre. The shop is shortly on the left, on the corner of Weetwood Road.

Open: Mon–Wed and Sat 9–5.30; Thur, Fri 9–8; Sun 10–4; Bank Holidays 10–4.
Closed: Christmas, Boxing and New Year's Days.
Cards: Access, Style, Visa.
Cars: Large car-park outside door.
Toilets: In supermarket opposite.
Wheelchairs: One entrance has ramp/handrail to large shop.
Teas: Café in shopping centre.
Groups: No factory tours. Groups of shoppers always welcome without booking.
Transport: From Bradford Interchange: bus nos. 605, 616 (to Allerton); 607 (Thornton); 692 (Bingley); 697 (Keighley); 698 (Oxenhope).

Crockers of Bridgwater

2 Eastover TA6 5AA

(01278) 452617

Good selection of *Clarks* discontinued lines and slight sub-standards for men, women and children. Self-select from big name brands on display – *K Shoes, Springers, CICA, Hi-Tec, Nike, Puma, Kangaroos, LA Gear* and *Fila.*

'Fully trained Clarks fitters are on hand to measure feet and give assistance where it is needed. An average of 30% saving on normal High Street prices for perfect shoes. Big savings on luggage, bags and accessories.'

....

On east side of town centre, on east side of river.

Bridgwater has a main road (A39) skirting south side of town centre. Coming east from coast direction: go round town, over river and left at traffic lights into Salmon Parade.*

Coming west on A39/A38 into town: at roundabout, go straight, staying on A39. Go over first traffic lights and right at next, into Salmon Parade.*

*Salmon Parade runs along river bank. Eastover is first right: shop is by corner.

Open: Mon–Sat 9–5.30.
Closed: Sunday; Bank Holidays; Christmas, Boxing, New Year's Days.
Cards: Access, Switch, Visa.
Cars: Car-parks in town centre.
Toilets: In town centre and car-parks.
Wheelchairs: Easy access – one step. Staff are available to help.
Teas: In town centre.
Groups: Coach parties welcome, concessions for drivers and organisers. 10% discount for each passenger.
Transport: Local buses and trains.

Sedgemoor Shoes Ltd.

River Lane, Dunwear TA7 OAB
(01278) 427662

Made-to-measure shoes in wide range of leathers, colours, styles and fittings. Free measuring and quotations. Some ready-made shoes.
'Small business specialising in problem feet. Personal service. Occasional seconds.'

....

To the east of Bridgwater off A372 (Bridgwater–Weston Zoyland road).

From Bridgwater on A372: pass signs to college on left; as open country begins follow sign to Dunwear on right. Travel by the river under motorway; after you round a corner with phone kiosk on right, industrial estate is on left.

From Weston Zoyland going north-west for Bridgwater: after 1.5 miles take left turn to Dunwear; after 1 mile, company is on right.

Open: Mon–Fri 9–5.
Closed: Bank Holidays; Spring Bank Holiday week; last week July/first week August; 2 weeks at Christmas.
Cards: No.
Cars: In front of shop.
Toilets: Yes.
Wheelchairs: Easy access, small ground floor shop.
Teas: In Bridgwater.
Groups: Offer personal service so not really suitable for groups. Individuals may be able to see shoes being made.
Transport: Taxi from Bridgwater.
Mail order: Yes.
Catalogue: Colour brochure available.

Crockers of Burnham

10 High Street TA8 1NY
(01278) 794668

Good selection of *Clarks* discontinued lines and slight sub-standards for men, women and children. Self-select from big name brands on display – *K Shoes, Springers, CICA, Hi-Tec, Puma, Kangaroos, LA Gear* and *Fila*.
'Fully trained Clarks fitters are on hand to measure feet and give assistance where it is needed. An average of 30% saving on normal High Street prices for perfect shoes. Big savings on luggage, bags and accessories.'

....

One road off the sea-front, parallel to shore.

From M5 exit 22 and A38: go west into Burnham. You come into town on Love Lane. (Be careful, one-way streets.) Go over into Princess Street; left into Victoria Street; right into College Street; left into High Street. Shop is further along on right, on corner of South Street.

From Esplanade: go into South Street – shop at far end.

Open: Mon–Sat 9–5.30; Sun 11–5. Bank Holidays 10–5.
Closed: Christmas and Boxing Days.
Cards: Access, Switch, Visa.
Cars: Large car-park on seafront.
Toilets: In car-park.
Wheelchairs: Easy access.
Teas: In town centre.
Groups: 10% discount for coach passengers.
Transport: Local buses.
Mail order: No.

Lambert Howarth & Sons Ltd.

Finsley Mill, Finsley Gate BB11 2HI
(01282) 425641 switchboard, 471283 shop.

Men's, ladies' and children's shoes, boots, slippers, training shoes. Towels, bags. Ladies', men's and children's wear, and accessories.

'Boat people (from Burnley Canal) can step off their boat into our new, redesigned shop! Seconds and ends of lines at considerably reduced prices.'

....

Close to town centre, backing on to canal. Probably easiest to look for tall black chimney with red stripes and water tank on roof with large sign 'Osbornia Shoes'.

Finsley Gate runs under the A56 overpass. Shop is opposite Super Bowl.

From town centre: go up Manchester Road, pass Mechanics Institute on right, go left at next traffic lights into Finsley Gate..

From M65 exit 10: take A671 to Town Centre (Happy Eater on right). Get in right lane for 'Through traffic'. At lights, go straight (The Mitre on right) into Trafalgar Street. By next roundabout go left (Manchester Street); at lights go right into Finsley Gate. *

***Go under A56: shop on right opposite Superbowl.**

Open: Mon–Fri 9.30–5; Sat 9–4. Some Bank Holidays, phone to check.
Closed: Good Fri–Easter Mon; Christmas–New Year.
Cards: Yes.
Cars: Parking available.
Toilets: Ask if desperate.
Wheelchairs: Ramp to sizeable shop.
Changing rooms: Yes.
Teas: Coffee in superbowl across the road. Cafés in town.
Groups: No factory tours. Shopping groups always welcome with prior phone call.
Transport: Easy walking distance from centre of town.

Whitfords Bury Boot & Shoe Co.

Brandlesholme Road BL8 1BQ
(0161) 764 6964

Shoes for people who have difficulty finding correctly fitting footwear: wide fittings D, E–EEEE in sizes 3–9 for ladies; ultra wide for men in sizes 6–12. Heavy duty corsetry. Dresses, coats, underwear and nightwear. Also items for people with disabilities eg clothing with velcro fastening and button through, long handled toe-nail scissors, incontinence pants/pads/mattress covers, heat pads for arthritic pain, bedding, curtains and travel goods.

'Slippers and shoes from £6.99–£40. Sales in January and July with prices reduced by 25–50%.'

....

On the B6214 north-west of Bury.

From M66 exit 2: take slip road for Bury/Heywood. At end of slip-road follow signs on Bury bypass for Bolton, Ramsbottom, Tottington. Go along dual carriageway, signposted A58 Bolton. Get into outside lane. Follow Ramsbottom signs. At traffic lights take right fork for A676 Tottington/Ramsbottom; pass B&Q; at next lights go right for Ramsbottom (Dusty Miller pub on left). Go along Brandlesholme Road, and immediately before Mobil garage on right, go right. Company is on right (car-park at end).

Open: Mon–Sat 9–5; Bank Holidays 10–4.
Closed: Christmas–New Year period.
Cards: Access, Visa.
Cars: Own car-park.
Toilets: Yes.
Wheelchairs: Wheelchair available from shop if required.
Changing rooms: Yes.
Teas: In town.
Groups: No guided tours, but shopping groups welcome – phone Mrs Pam Bill, especially for 52-seater coaches.
Transport: Bus no. 474 (to Ramsbottom) from Bury Interchange: ask for Whitfords Bury Boots.
Mail order: Yes.
Catalogue: Free on request. No seconds by mail order.

Peaklander Footwear (Heginbotham Bros. Ltd.)

Peaklander Works S30 1XH
(01433) 630317

Wide range of footwear for men, women and children – safety boots and shoes, hiking boots and shoes, casual and formal shoes, casual boots, slippers, trainers, wellingtons, sandals etc. Brands include *Dr Martens, Regatta, Padders, Sterling & Hunt, Equity* and *Rieker*. Also anoraks, country clothing etc.

'We buy in bulk from factories both local and worldwide and pass the savings on to our customers. 90% of stock comprises perfect current seasonal items.'

....

Five miles north of Bakewell and 15 miles south-west of Sheffield at crossroads of A623 and B6001.

From Sheffield: take A625 to Hathersage. Turn left on to B6001. Keep going for four miles; at traffic lights go right on to A623. Shop entrance is a few yards on left.

From Bakewell town centre: cross river, going north on A619 for Chesterfield. Shortly go left on to B6001 for Hassop. Stay on this road for about five miles. At traffic lights in Calver, go left on to A623: shop is a few yards on left.

Open: Mon–Sat 9–5; Sun, Bank Holidays 10–5.
Closed: Christmas and Boxing Days.
Cards: Access, Switch, Visa.
Cars: Own large car-park at the side of the factory.
Toilets: No; nearest 100 yds.
Wheelchairs: Access with no steps from car-park; one small step inside medium-sized shop, assistance gladly given.
Changing rooms: One.
Teas: Across the road.
Groups: Groups welcome to shop, booking not necessary; no factory tours.
Transport: Bus nos. 65, 66, 67, 175, 460, 795, X67 stop outside shop.
Mail order: Yes.
Catalogue: Free leaflets. Only hiking and shooting boots, and *Equity* shoes sent.

Briggs & Shoe Mines

Drovers Lane CA3 8DT
(01228) 819315

Clearance and sub-standard footwear for all the family. Self selection with expert help and advice available. Small range of clothing and sports apparel.

'Family footwear by famous makers at clearance, reduced or sub-standard prices.'

See our display advertisement on p. 445

....

Near river bridge north of town centre.

Follow directions to any town centre car-park. Briggs & Shoe Mines is to be found 50 yds from the Civic Centre (Carlisle's tallest building), diagonally opposite the Police Station.

Open: Mon–Sat 9–5.30 (Tues 10–5.30); Bank Holidays 10–5.
Closed: Christmas Day.
Cards: Access, Connect, Switch, Visa.
Cars: Numerous car-parks in town centre.
Toilets: Yes.
Wheelchairs: No steps, easy access.
Teas: Many cafés in town centre.
Groups: Shopping groups welcome, please contact manager to book. £1 reduction per member of a coach party on purchase.
Transport: Bus stop about 200 yds away outside town market hall.
Mail order: Yes.
Catalogue: No. Pleased to supply items in stock if customer knows size, fitting and style. Ask for shop manager.

Wynsors World of Shoes

Enterprise Way (01977) 514774

Children's, ladies' and men' shoes: sport and leisure styles; range of comfort fit & wider shoes; leather brogues; excellent range of leather and fashion handbags; branded sports bags.

'99% perfects. Average 30% less than high street prices; specials and promotions offering at least 50% off. Sales in Jan & July.'

See our display advertisement on p 435

In the town centre between the bus and railway stations, on the new retail park by Netto, Aldi etc.

From M62 exit 32: exit for Castleford. Pass Shell on left. At roundabout exit left for Castleford.*

From Ferrybridge: at roundabout as you reach town, go right for Castleford. *Pass Fina petrol on right: at roundabout immediately after it, go straight for Leeds A639. Keep straight. Go over level-crossing. At traffic lights (King William IV pub on far right corner) go right (Akerton Road). Pass swimming pool on left. At far end, turn right for Town Centre (A655).**

From M62: take exit 31 for Castleford. At roundabout, go straight uphill on A655 for Castleford.**

**Go over level-crossing (by Castleford Gates Junction box). Pass Do It All on right. At roundabout take third exit left into Enterprise Way (in front of Netto). Shop visible ahead on right.

Open: Mon, Tues, Sat 9–5.30; Wed, Thur, Fri 9–8; Sun 10–4. Bank Holidays 10–4.
Closed: Christmas, Boxing and New Year's Days only.
Cards: Access, Style, Visa.
Cars: Own large car-park.
Toilets: In bus station opposite.
Wheelchairs: Easy access to large shop.
Teas: Café 59 yds; pub next door.
Groups: Welcome with prior phone call to shop manager.
Transport: Near BR station. Any bus to or from town centre.
Mail order: No.

Wynsors World of Shoes

Netto Retail Development, Sheffield Road S41 8JT (01246) 276690

Men's, ladies' and children's fashion shoes in both leather and synthetic fabrics.

'Major sales January and July. Mainly perfects, a few seconds. 30% less than high street prices. Promotions every 6 weeks offering at least 50% off.'

See our display advertisement on p. 435

About 3/4 mile north of town.

From town: take A61T north for Sheffield: go left at roundabout (Tesco on right) for Newbold/Stonegavels. Keep straight for 1/2 mile to roundabout: go right on to B6057. Shop is on left, past Mobil and Netto.

Coming south on A61T: at roundabout with Tesco on left, go right for Whittington Moor. Follow road for 1/2 mile to roundabout: go right on to B6057. Shop is on left, past Mobil and Netto.

From large one-way system (Holywell Cross) on north side of town centre: take old Sheffield Road (B6057), following signs north to Whittington Moor. After roundabout, shop is on left, past Mobil and Netto.

Open: Mon, Tues, Wed, Sat 9–5.30; Thur, Fri 9–8; Sun 10–4.
Closed: Christmas and Boxing Days.
Cards: Access, Style, Visa.
Cars: Large car-park at shop.
Toilets: No.
Wheelchairs: Easy access, no steps.
Teas: Café 200 yds from shop.
Groups: Shopping groups welcome with prior phone call.
Transport: Chesterfield bus nos. 14, 15, 19, 20, 21, 22, 36; Sheffield bus nos. 203, 204, X11 stop outside shop.
Mail order: No.

Wynsors World of Shoes

Unit B, Horncastle Street, Castle Mills BD19 3HH
(01274) 851366

Men's, ladies' and children's fashion shoes in both leather and synthetic fabrics.

'Massive range of branded footwear from own factory and all over the world. Stock changes daily. Prices from £1 to £100. Special lines at lowest prices in country. January and July sales.'

See our display advertisement on opposite page.

....

From M62 exit 26: take A638 into Cleckheaton. After 1 mile pass big church on left; take second right, Horncastle Street.*
From town centre and Heckmondwike: take A638 for Bradford. After crossing A643, pass Yorkshire Bank on right and take first left, Horncastle Street.*
*Shop 50 yds on right.

Open: Mon–Wed and Sat 9–5.30; Thur, Fri 9–8. Bank Holidays 10–4.
Closed: Christmas, Boxing and New Year's Days.
Cards: Access, Style, Visa.
Cars: Behind building and on street.
Toilets: Opposite in market.
Wheelchairs: No steps, large shop.
Teas: Cafés and good fish & chip shop.
Groups: Groups of shoppers always welcome. No need to book.
Transport: Any bus to Cleckheaton (500 yds).
Mail order: No.

Mansfield Shoes/Factory Shoe Shop

Craigens Road, KA18 3AM
(01290) 420860

Large range of shoes for all the family.

....

At the south end of town by roundabout where B7083 leads off the A76 for Cumnock town centre.
From south: exit for Cumnock on B7083.*
From A70 westbound and town centre: go towards Dumfries. As you leave town pass Pace petrol on right and after 50 yds turn left for shop.
From Ayr on A70: turn onto A76 going to Dumfries and from Kilmarnock going south on the A76 bypass Cumnock and at roundabout with B7083 turn left towards Cumnock.*
*After 100 yds turn right for shop which is clearly signposted.

Open: Mon–Fri 9.30–5.30; Sat 10–5; Sun 12–5.
Closed: Christmas and Boxing Days.
Cards: Access, Switch, Visa.
Cars: Own car-park.
Toilets: No.
Wheelchairs: Easy access to big shop.
Teas: Local cafés.
Groups: Shopping groups please telephone in advance.
Transport: Local buses.

Furness Footwear

Long Lane, off Mill Brow
(01229) 462744

Men's, ladies' and children's fashion shoes, both leather and synthetic.

'Vast range of branded footwear from own factory and all over the world. Stock changes daily. Prices from £1 to £100.'

....

Off the A590 south of Dalton-in-Furness.
From town centre, Ulverston and Askam-in-Furness: go towards Barrow-in-Furness at roundabout. Go out of town, pass Burmah petrol station on right, take next left (Long Lane). Shop in second building on right.
From Barrow-in-Furness via A590: pass Furness General Hospital, go straight at roundabout, go right after 500 yds towards Stainton. Shop in second building on right.

Open: Mon–Sat 9–5.30 (Fri late night to 8). Bank Holidays.
Closed: Christmas, Boxing and New Year's Days.
Cards: Access, Switch, Visa.
Cars: Factory car-park.
Toilets: Ask if desperate.
Wheelchairs: Easy access to large shop.
Teas: Hot-drinks machine; sweets, crisps, biscuits on sale.
Groups: Welcome to shop.
Transport: Main Barrow–Ulverston buses stop at shop.
Mail order: No.

Hall & Son – a Lotus Shoes factory shop

6 Blackwellgate DL1 6HL
(01325) 466009

Ladies' court shoes and sling backs, sandals, leather casuals, fashion shoes. Men's city styles, casuals and sandals. Also seasonal footwear such as slippers and ladies' fashion boots. Handbags.

'This is a factory shop belonging to Lotus Shoes. A visit here could be part of a day's shopping trip.'

....

In the centre of town near the Market Hall (with a large clock-tower).
From the top end of the Market Hall: go left of Binns department store and keep going around it. Hall & Son are on the same side of the road, 50 yds beyond Binns.

Open: Mon–Sat 9–5.30. Bank Holiday Mondays.*
Closed: *Tuesdays after Bank Holiday Mondays. Christmas and New Year.
Cards: Access, Switch, Visa.
Cars: Double yellow lines. Large car-park at lower end of the Market Hall. Also Skinnergate.
Toilets: Below Market Hall.
Wheelchairs: Easy access, some steps to the back of the shop.
Teas: In town.
Groups: Coach parties welcome: please contact Mrs L Kell.
Transport: About 300 yds from main bus stop in town.
Mail order: No.

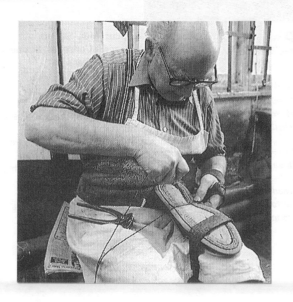

White and Co. (Earls Barton) Ltd.
11 New Street NN11 4BO
(01327) 702291

Footwear, mainly *Dr Martens*: boots, motorbike boots, steel capped shoes, fashion shoes, loafers, brogues etc in various colours, many not available elsewhere in UK as most produced for export; small range of leather-soled shoes. *'Won Queen's Award for Exports 1990.'*

....

In the centre of town about 100 yds south of the cross in market square.

From M1 exit 16: follow A45 to Daventry. At the first round-about with the hotel on left take second exit and go right at second roundabout. Pass Waitrose on left and shop is directly on right.

From all other directions: follow signs to Town Centre and you end up in New Street. Pass Waitrose on left and shop is directly on right.

Open: Tues, Fri, Sat 10–4. Some Bank Holidays: please phone to check.
Closed: Easter; Spring Bank Holiday week; last week in July; first week in August; third week September; Christmas–New Year.
Cards: No.
Cars: Free public car-park adjacent.
Toilets: In town.
Wheelchairs: Easy access.
Teas: Cafés in town.
Tours: Welcome to shop and look round factory (max 20 people). Please book first with reception, mentioning this book. No young children please.
Transport: Buses from station.
Mail order: No.

The Shoe Factory Shop
Unit 6, Eagle Centre, Traffic Street DE1 2NL
(01332) 372823

7,000 pairs of men's, ladies' and children's shoes in stock.
'Ladies' young fashion shoes and boots from £10. Ends of lines £5–£20. Men's perfect shoes and trainers from £10. Quality footwear at well below normal retail prices. Some branded footwear for men.'

....

This large, conspicuous shop is close to city centre, immediately behind the Eagle Centre.
   By car: go round the inner ring road until you come to round-about with London Road (A6). Turn towards city centre, then take first right into this new development of shops.

Open: Mon–Sat 9–5.
Closed: Christmas, Boxing and New Year's Days.
Cards: Access, Switch, Visa.
Cars: Car-park opposite.
Toilets: City centre.
Wheelchairs: Easy access to huge, spacious shop.
Teas: Plenty of places to eat in the city centre.
Groups: No factory tours but always welcome shopping groups.
Transport: 5 minutes' walk from bus and BR stations.
Mail order: No.

K Shoes
Unit 26A Wellgate Centre DD1 2DB
(01382) 322048

Huge selection of K seconds and clearance lines for men and women including shoes, sandals, boots, slippers and handbags.
'All goods are seconds and discontinued lines.'

....

The Wellgate Centre is in the town centre (between Victoria Road/Murraygate).
   From all directions: follow signs to town centre. Park in any car-park then walk into pedestrianised area. Shop is on third floor, beside the library.

Open: Mon–Sat 9–5.30; Sun 12–4.30.
Closed: Christmas and New Year's Days.
Cards: Access, Switch, Visa.
Cars: Town centre car-parks.
Toilets: Several close by.
Wheelchairs: Level access to sizeable shop.
Teas: Nearby cafés.
Groups: Small groups to shop only (no factory tours).
Transport: Any train or bus to town centre.

742 Earl Shilton Leics

The Factory Shoe Co. (Hill Top Shoes Ltd.)

Hill Top Shoe Works LE9 7DS
(01455) 844416

Ladies' leather fashion court shoes, sandals, fashion boots, ankle boots. Men's all-leather shoes. Leather jodhpur boots for ladies and children.

'Wide range of shoes with leather uppers including high fashion designer ranges and present catalogue shoes.'

··

This shop is on the A47 at the Leicester end of the village.

   From Leicester: the shop is 100 yds on the right after the Thurlaston turn-off (to the left).

   From Hinckley: go through Earl Shilton: shop is 100 yds after the Ultramar Petrol Station (both on the left).

Open: Mon 12–5.30; Thur, Fri 12–5.30; Sat 10–2.
Closed: Tuesday; Wednesday; second week in July; Christmas–New Year.
Cards: No.
Cars: Own car-park, and public car-park across the road.
Toilets: Ask if desperate.
Wheelchairs: No steps.
Teas: In town.
Groups: No.
Transport: Leicester –Hinckley buses pass the shop.
Mail order: No.

743 Earls Barton Northants

Barker Shoes

Station Road NN6 0NS
(01604) 810387

Imperfect and discontinued ranges of high quality shoes for men and women. Also narrow (AA) ladies' shoes and larger sizes. All shoes are made by this company on site except for a few continental fashion shoes.

'Excellent value quality footwear.'

··

From the A4500 or A45 (both going from Northampton to Wellingborough): go into the centre of Earls Barton. Turn off towards 'Village only' opposite the church: factory entrance is about 100 yds on right. The shop is clearly visible, straight ahead in the factory yard.

Open: Mon–Sat 10–5; Sun and Bank Holidays 10–4.
Closed: Christmas–New Year.
Cards: Access, Switch, Visa.
Cars: Ample car-park adjacent to shop.
Toilets: Yes.
Wheelchairs: Very easy access to huge, spacious shop – no steps, wide doors.
Teas: Restaurant, pub and coffee shop on village green.
Groups: No factory tours but groups/coaches welcome to shop on weekdays. Be sure to book.
Transport: Local buses from Northampton & Wellingborough; ask for Earls Barton Square. Short walk to shop.
Mail order: No.
Catalogue: For full price shoes only.

Crockers of Glasgow

Unit 26, The Forge Shopping Centre G31 4EC
(0141) 556 5290

Good selection of *Clarks* discontinued lines and slight sub-standard footwear for men, women and children. Self-select from big brands on display – *K Shoes, Springers, CICA, Hi-Tec, Puma* and *Mercury.*

'An average of 30% saving on normal high street prices for perfect shoes. Fully trained Clarks fitters to measure feet and give assistance. Big savings on luggage, bags and accessories.'

....

About two miles east of Glasgow city centre, in a well marked shopping centre.

From the city centre: take Gallowgate (A89) or Duke Street eastwards. Turn off into this shopping centre where you see it marked.

From M8 exit 13: you need to go about a mile south of here, aiming for Parkhead Cross. Enter the shopping centre from Duke Street.

Open: Mon–Sat 9–5.30; Sun 12–4.30; Bank Holidays 12–4.30.
Closed: Christmas and New Year's Days; 2 January.
Cards: Access, Switch, Visa.
Cars: Adjacent car-park (free).
Toilets: In shopping centre.
Wheelchairs: Easy access, no steps to large ground floor shop.
Teas: In shopping centre.
Transport: Any bus from the centre of Glasgow.
Mail order: No.

Morlands

Northover BA6 9YB
(01458) 835042

Traditional designs in quality men's, women's, children's sheepskin garments. Rugs, mittens, hats, renowned sheepskin slippers, boots and other footwear; small leather goods, gifts of local interest.

'Largest supplier of Morlands' products, all at factory prices. Perfects and seconds.'

....

Northover is on A39 between Glastonbury and Street.

Leave Glastonbury on A39 for Street; continue past roundabout by B&Q. Factory is clearly signed on right after about 1/2 mile.

From M5 exit 23: follow signs to Glastonbury on A39. In Street, at roundabout where B3151 comes in, continue left on A39 – factory is short distance on left.

Open: Mon–Sat 9.30–5; Bank Holidays 10–4.
Closed: Christmas and Boxing Days; Good Friday.
Cards: Access, Amex, Diners, Visa.
Cars: Opposite in visitors' car park.
Toilets: Street or Glastonbury.
Wheelchairs: Three flights of stairs.
Teas: Street and Glastonbury.
Groups: Coach parties welcome.
Transport: No.

Richard Draper

Chilkwell Street BA6 8YA
(01458) 831118

Footwear manufacturers – *Draper* brand sheepskin boots and slippers. Traditional shoes and sandals. Also sheepskin rugs, mittens, hats, scarves, knitwear, small leathergoods, gifts, etc.

'Largest suppliers of Draper products. Quality footwear including ladies' walking shoes in wide fittings and large sizes. All at competitive factory prices.'

....

On south-west side of Glastonbury.
   From Glastonbury centre: follow signs to Shepton Mallet on A361, in direction of the Tor. Pass Museum of Rural Life on corner of Chilkwell Street; shop is on right, past the Rifleman's Arms pub.
   From Shepton Mallet on A361: large factory is clearly signposted on left as you reach Glastonbury.

Open: Mon–Sat 9.30–5.30; some Bank Holidays – please phone to check.
Closed: Christmas, Boxing and New Year's Days.
Cards: Access, Amex, Diners, Visa.
Cars: Large car-park.
Toilets: Yes.
Wheelchairs: Two small steps, large ground floor shop. Stairs to upper showroom.
Teas: Tea rooms by Abbey.
Groups: Groups welcome to shop; please book in advance with Frances Draper, mentioning this book. No factory tours.
Transport: Local buses to Glastonbury.
Mail order: Yes.
Catalogue: Free mailing list for customers. Free catalogues twice a year. Write or phone. No seconds by mail order.

Priestley Footwear Ltd.

Albion Mill, Water Street BB6 7QT   *Closed*
(01254) 886241

Fashion shoes for ladies, men and children: shoes, boots, slippers and training shoes. Assorted ladies' clothing, including branded clearance lines. Other bargains.

'Perfects, seconds and ends of lines (many branded) on sale.'

....

Close to the centre of town, on the north side.
   From M65 exit 7: take A680 (Accrington–Clitheroe road) then follow the first sign into Great Harwood. This road becomes Queen Street after gasometer on right. Turn right off Queen Street, the main shopping street, beside large classical building (swimming baths) set back from road. Go right just before main factory: shop at end of building.

Open: Mon–Sat 9–5; Bank Holidays 9–5.
Closed: Easter; Christmas-New Year.
Cards: None.
Cars: Adjacent to shop.
Toilets: In town centre.
Wheelchairs: One small step, large shop.
Teas: In Great Harwood.
Groups: Shopping groups welcome if they phone first.
Transport: Any bus to Great Harwood.
Mail order: No.

The Shoe Factory Shop
21 Wellowgate DN32 0RA
(01472) 342415

7,000 pairs of men's, ladies' and children's shoes in stock.
'Ladies' perfect court shoes from £10; rejects from £8; ends of lines £5–£20. Men's perfect shoes from classic styles, made in England, to canvas, wellies etc. Children's leather and synthetic shoes from £5.'

....

In the centre of town, just behind the station.

Coming south from M18 on A180: go straight at first two roundabouts; at third roundabout (Texas on near right corner), go right for 'Town Centre, A16, National Fishing Heritage Centre'. At traffic lights go straight for town centre. Pass MFI on right. At next lights, go straight for 'Town Hall Courts'. Follow the one-way system to left (Pasture Street) then right (round the back of the town hall). At traffic lights go straight into Osborne Street which becomes Bethlehem Street. With stone church on right, go left after The White Hart into Wellowgate. After level-crossing, go straight. Shop is 150 yds on left.

Open: Mon–Sat 9–5 (Thur late night to 7).
Closed: Bank Holidays; Christmas, Boxing and New Year's Days.
Cards: Access, Visa, Switch.
Cars: Large car-park behind shop.
Toilets: In town.
Wheelchairs: Easy access to large, spacious shop.
Teas: Two doors away.
Groups: Coach parties to shop please contact the manageress in advance.
Transport: Any train or bus to Grimsby.
Mail order: No.

Wynsors World of Shoes
123 Cromwell Road DN31 2BC   *(01472) 251627*

Ladies' and girls' fashion shoes, sandals and boots in leather and synthetic materials. Many chainstore and branded items from cancelled orders and shoes for all the family from all over the world. Top brands especially in sports shoes, all at cut prices

'99% perfects. Average 30% less than high street; special buys & promotions offering at least 50% off. Major sales in Jan & July.'

See our display advertisement on p. 435

....

From M82/M180: take A180 towards town centre. Go over first roundabout, then at second roundabout go right into Pyewipe Road. Continue straight at traffic lights, down Boulevard Avenue to Market Hotel roundabout. Go left into Cromwell Road (A1136) (Presto on your right). Shop is 200 yds on right.

From town hall in town centre (follow signs to town hall, then you should be in the one-way road which goes behind the town hall): at traffic lights go straight into Osborne Street which becomes Bethlehem Street. This is a one-way road. Pass stone church on right then bear left. At traffic lights, go right into Dudley Street (A1136). Cross over Littlefield Lane into Cromwell Road. Shop is 300 yds on left.

Open: Mon, Tues, Wed, Sat 9–5.30; Thur, Fri 9–8; Sun 10–4.
Closed: Christmas, Boxing and New Years's days.
Cards: Access, Style, Visa.
Cars: Own car-park.
Toilets: No.
Wheelchairs: Easy access to large shop.
Teas: Cold drinks available; good fish & chip shop across the road.
Groups: Shopping groups welcome with prior phone call to shop manager.
Transport: Bus nos. 4, 4X, 16, 45 from town centre; X21 Cleethorpes–Hull stops outside.
Mail order: No.

Wynsors World of Shoes

56/57 London Road SK12 1LF
(0161) 456 2632

Men's, ladies' and children's fashion shoes in both leather and synthetic fabrics.

'Massive range of branded footwear from own factory and all over world. Stock changes daily; monthly offers at lowest prices in the country. Shoes from £1 to £100.'

See our display advertisement on p.435

In the centre of Hazel Grove.

Coming south from Stockport via A6: look for Shopping Giant and Gospel Church on right; go left into Angel Street to park; Kwik Save car-park behind well marked shop.

Coming north from Macclesfield via A523(T) and Sheffield via A6015: these roads become the A6. Look for Shopping Giant and Gospel Church on left: turn right into Angel Street to park in the Kwik Save car-park behind the well marked shop.

Open: Mon–Wed 9–5.30; Thur, Fri 9–8; Sat 9–5.30; Sun and Bank Holidays 10–4.
Closed: Christmas and New Year's Days.
Cards: Access, Style, Visa.
Cars: In Kwik Save car-park adjacent.
Toilets: Opposite.
Wheelchairs: Easy access to large shop. No steps.
Teas: In Co-Op Shopping Giant.
Groups: Shopping groups welcome
Transport: Hazel Grove BR Station; bus no. 192 stops outside shop.
Mail order: No.

Peter Newman

Eddington Park, Thanet Way CT6 5TS
(01227) 741112

10,000+ shoes for all the family on display: *Clarks, K, Rohde, Equity, Lotus.* Shoes, boots, trainers and slippers.

'Branded shoes at factory prices. This company does not manufacture but these shoes are ends of ranges etc from their other retail shops. Prices considerably reduced.'

Large conspicuous shop on the A229 (Thanet Way) on the south side of Herne Bay.

Shop is on the left, next to Texas, if you are going east towards Ramsgate.

Open: Mon–Sat 9–5.30.
Closed: Christmas and Boxing Days.
Cards: Access, Connect, Switch, Visa.
Cars: Car-park outside shop.
Toilets: Available on site.
Wheelchairs: No steps, huge shop.
Teas: Refreshment area with tea/coffee/soft drinks machines in store. Tea rooms in Herne Bay.
Groups: No factory tours. Shopping groups and coach parties welcome – prior phone call appreciated.
Transport: Herne Bay BR station close by: go out of station, turn right, through alleyway to rear of factory shop.
Mail order: No.

The Shoe Factory Shop

6 Oslo Road, Sutton Fields Ind Est HU8 0YN
(01482) 839292

7,000 pairs of men's, ladies' and children's shoes in stock .

'Ladies' perfect court shoes from £10; rejects from £8; ends of lines £5–£20. Men's perfect shoes, from classic styles made in England to canvas, wellies etc. Children's leather and synthetic shoes from £5.'

....

About 3.5 miles north of city centre.
  Going north or south along Beverley Road (A1079): turn east at traffic lights when you see signs to Outer Ring Road. After bridge, go right at new roundabout into Stockholm Road. Take second left, Oslo Road. Shop is at far end on left, adjacent to Do-It-All.

Open: Mon, Tues, Wed, Sat 9–5; Thur, Fri 9–7. Bank Holidays.
Closed: Christmas, Boxing and New Year's Days.
Cards: Access, Switch, Visa.
Cars: Huge car-park.
Toilets: No.
Wheelchairs: Easy access to large shop on ground floor.
Teas: Café three doors away.
Groups: Shopping groups welcome to shop: please contact the manageress first.
Transport: Bus no. 10 (to Bransholme) from town centre.
Mail order: No.

Broughton Shoe Warehouse

Tudor Place, off Woodbridge Road IP4 2DP
(01473) 233522

High quality Italian and Spanish men's and ladies' shoes.

'Save up to 50% on high street prices.'

....

Few hundred yards north-east of city centre.
  From Colchester: follow signs to town centre. At roundabout with Civic Hall straight ahead, go left; go right at next roundabout on to A1156 eastbound. *
  From south and east: follow 'Through Traffic' signs; at roundabout with Civic Hall on right, go straight; at next roundabout go right on to A1156 (Crown Street). *
  *Pass bus station on right, swimming pool on left. Pass Odeon on right; after 50 yds turn left into car-park.
  From Norwich/Stowmarket: go left on to A1156 for Ipswich; stay on it to Odeon on right. After 50 yds turn left into car-park.

Open: Mon–Sat 9–5; Sun 10–4.
Closed: Christmas and New Year's Days. Phone to check Bank Holidays.
Cards: Access, Switch, Visa.
Cars: Own car-park.
Toilets: No.
Wheelchairs: No steps.
Teas: Locals pubs and cafes.
Groups: Welcome.
Transport: Short walk from town centre and bus station.

754 Kendal Cumbria

Briggs & Shoe Mines
Sandes Avenue LA9 4SG
(01539) 721335

Over 10,000 sq ft sales area with 100,000 pairs of boots and shoes for all the family. Wide range of sports and walking footwear. Handbags, socks, accessories etc.

'Half of shop sells reduced-price major branded, sub-standard and clearance lines, including K Shoes directly from K factories in Kendal. 60 major international brands at regular price. Measurement and fitting by qualified staff.'

See our display advertisement above.

Within the town centre.
Sandes Avenue is the northern link in the busy one-way system round town. From the A6 (Stricklandgate), the main road which goes from south to north through Kendal: turn right towards Penrith. This large conspicuous shop is on the right, 25 yards from the corner.

Open: *Summer:* Mon–Sat 9–7; Sun 11–5. *Winter (Nov–Easter):* Mon–Sat 9–5.30; Sun 11–5. Bank Holidays10–5.
Closed: Xmas Day, Easter Sun.
Cards: Access, Connect, Switch, Visa.
Cars: Own car-park; multi-storey behind shop (car-park ticket gives you reductions on footwear). Free coach park 120 yds away (with bus washing!).
Toilets: Yes.
Wheelchairs: Easy access to huge shop.
Teas: Café next door.
Groups: Coaches welcome – mention this guide. Parties receive £1 vouchers per person towards purchases.
Transport: 150 yds to Kendal BR; Kendal mini link bus network.
Mail order: Pleased to supply items in stock if customers know size, fitting and style.

K Shoes Factory Shop, Sports Factory and Baggage Factory

Netherfield LA9 7DA
(01539) 721892

Extensive range of quality shoes, sandals, boots, walking boots, slippers, trainers, handbags, luggage, sports clothing, sports equipment, outdoor clothing, accessories and gifts.

'Exciting new K Shoes factory shop. Great savings averaging 30% less than in the high street from K Shoes, Clarks, Springers, CICA and other famous brands. Self-select store with trained staff to measure feet and give assistance where needed.'

On the A65 on south-east side of town.

From town centre: take A6 south signposted to M6. When you see signs to A65, follow these until you see K Village on right. Entrance at far end of complex: follow signs to shop.

From south via A65: as you come into Kendal, clearly signposted complex and shop are on the left shortly after you reach river (on left).

From A591(T) northbound (Kendal bypass): take A6 for Kendal and turn right at first traffic lights signposted to K Factories. Take first left after bridge then first left into car-park. (This is quickest way from M6 exit 36.)

Open: Mon–Fri 9.30–6; Sat 9–6; Sun 11–5. Bank Hols 9–6.
Closed: Christmas Day and Easter Sunday.
Cards: Access, Switch, Visa.
Cars: Free parking at the rear of the building (places for disabled drivers).
Toilets: Yes, including disabled; baby changing facilities.
Wheelchairs: Most entrances and exits have ramps for wheelchairs & shopping aisles are wide enough for easy access.
Teas: Leith's at the Food Factory Restaurant. Also sandwich bar.
Groups: Coaches welcome, concessions for drivers and organisers. £1 voucher per passenger towards purchases. Play area for children.
Transport: Ten minutes' walk from town centre.

Barker Shoes Factory Shop at Pattinsons

Lupton Court CA12 5JD
(017687) 72016

High quality shoes for men and women. All perfects. Cater for extreme sizes and fittings. All shoes made by Barker Shoes.

'Barkers unique quality at direct factory prices. No rejects.'

....

This shop is at the rear of Pattisons Shoes which is on Main Street in the centre of Keswick.

Open: Mon–Sat 9–5.30.
Bank Holidays.
Closed: Phone to check Christmas and New Year opening.
Cards: Access, Switch, Visa.
Cars: In car-park opposite.
Toilets: In town.
Wheelchairs: One step to ground floor shop.
Teas: Lots of pubs and cafés.
Groups: Small shopping groups welcome.
Transport: Any bus to Keswick.
Mail order: Yes.
Catalogue: Free.

Wynsors World of Shoes

1A Middleton District Shopping Centre LS10 3NK
(0113) 271 0849

Men's, ladies' and children's fashion shoes in both leather and synthetic fabrics.

'Massive range of branded footwear from own factory and all over the world. Stock changes daily; monthly offers at probably lowest prices in the country. Shoes from £1–£100. Sales in January and July.'

See our display advertisement on p. 435

....

From Leeds: take M1 south. Take exit 44 to Middleton. At end of slip road, go right to Belle Isle Road (dual carriageway). Go straight at Belle Isle Circus; at next roundabout, take second exit. Take second exit at next roundabout; shop is clearly visible.
  From M62 exit 28: take A650 to Ardsley; after 1/2 mile go left on to A654. Go over motorway, turn left at roundabout to Middleton (Middleton Park Avenue). At large Middleton Circus, turn right on to Middleton Park Road; go right at next roundabout.

Open: Mon–Wed, Sat 9–5.30;
Thur, Fri 9–8.
Bank Holidays 10–4.
Closed: Christmas, Boxing and New Year's Days.
Cards: Access, Style, Visa, .
Cars: Large car-park outside shop.
Toilets: Yes.
Wheelchairs: No steps, easy access to very large shop.
Teas: Lots of places in Leeds.
Groups: Shopping groups always welcome without booking.
Transport: Buses from Leeds nos. 8, 9,10, 19, 21, 23, 77, 86, 87.
Mail order: No.

Lotus Shoes

36 Derby Street ST13 5AB
(01538) 383700

Shoes: ladies' courts, sandals, leather casuals. Men's city shoes, top grade all-leather men's welted brogues and golf shoes, leather casuals, sandals. Also seasonal products such as slippers, ladies' fashion boots, warm-lined boots. Handbags, purses and shoe cleaning products.

'Quality footwear at discounted prices. Occasional sales on selected footwear.'

In the centre of town, in the main shopping street.

Derby Street leads from the lower end of the Market Place to the war memorial. If you come from the Market Place, the shop will be on your right.

Open: Mon–Sat 9–5.30 (except Thur closed all day). Good Friday.
Closed: Thursday; Bank Holidays; Christmas, Boxing and New Year's Days.
Cards: Access, Visa.
Cars: Town car-parks.
Toilets: In the Market Place.
Wheelchairs: Difficult – two steps, but easy access to shop in Stafford.
Teas: Several cafés, pubs and eating places in town.
Groups: No factory tours as not on factory site, but groups of shoppers welcome. Prior phone call appreciated.
Transport: Easy walking distance from bus station.
Mail order: No.
Catalogue: The branded catalogue can be viewed in shop but is not for distribution.

Kid boots (17/11d), jet beaded shoes (10/9d), men's dancing and dinner pumps (5/11d) and other fine footwear advertised by Peter Robinson in the January sale 1902

The Shoe Factory Shop
Constance Road, North Evington LE5 5EB
(0116) 249 0114

Huge selection (over 5,000 pairs) of ladies', men's and children's shoes at discount prices. Fashion shoes and boots from own factory.

'Rejects (only slightly imperfect), perfects, ends of lines, special purchases. Ladies' shoes from £5, boots from £10; children's from £4; men's shoes from £10.'

··

About 1.5 miles east of the city centre.

From Leicester centre: take the A47 towards Uppingham. At huge Humberstone roundabout stay on A47 then turn right at fourth set of traffic lights into St Barnabas Road (which becomes East Park Road). Turn left at the second traffic lights into St Saviour's Road. Take the seventh right into Gedding Road, then first right into Linden Street and go right into Constance Road. Shop is 50 yds on the left within the factory premises (wide entrance to the car-park).

Open: Mon–Fri 10–5
(Thur 10–6); Sat 9–5.
Some Bank Holidays.
Closed: Christmas, Boxing and New Year's Days.
Cards: Access, Visa, Switch.
Cars: Own car-park.
Toilets: No.
Wheelchairs: Small ramp to large, spacious shop on ground floor.
Teas: Plenty of places to eat in city centre.
Groups: No facilities for showing visitors around the factory but shop always welcomes clubs, groups etc – contact the manageress first, mentioning this book.
Transport: Leicester City bus nos. 31 and 33 from outside Woolworths in town centre (Humberstone Gate).
Mail order: No.

New Balance Athletic Shoes (UK) Ltd.
St Helen's Lane, Flimby CA15 8RY
(01900) 602850

Running shoes, football boots, hiking boots, basketball boots, tennis and squash shoes, cross trainers, fitness shoes, walking shoes, sports clothing, sports bags.

'First quality as well as seconds sold here.'

··

Off the A596, south of Flimby between Maryport and Workington.

From Maryport: go south through Flimby, turn left after Armstrong Ltd.*

From Workington: go north, pass Ectona and turn right after Laing.*

***Take first right and New Balance is at end of drive.**

Open: Mon–Fri 9.30–5.30;
Sat 9–4. Bank Holidays.
Closed: Christmas, Boxing and New Year's Days.
Cards: Access, Delta, Electron, Switch, Visa.
Cars: Outside shop in factory car-park.
Toilets: In Workington.
Wheelchairs: Easy access to medium sized shop.
Changing rooms: Yes.
Teas: In Workington.
Groups: Parties welcome to shop; please contact Chris Mintoft, mentioning this book.
Transport: Maryport–Workington buses stop outside.
Mail order: No.
Catalogue: Yes.

Matlock Shoe Sales
Paxton Warehouse DE4 3BX
(01629) 583105

Men's and women's footwear including fashion and designer shoes, casuals, boots, slippers, trainers, hiking boots, wellingtons, sandals etc.

'We buy in bulk from factories all over the world and pass the savings on to our customers. 90% of stock current season and perfect. Shop is bigger and better for 1995.'

See our display advertisement opposite

....

On the A615, half a mile east of Matlock town centre (ie, from roundabout at end of bridge).

From Matlock: take A615 for Alfreton. Continue for 1/2 mile; pass Total petrol station on right and after 100 yds go sharp left into company drive (signposted).

Coming into Matlock on A615: pass Matlock town sign on left; after 200 yds go sharp right into private drive (100 yds before Total petrol station on left). Shop clearly marked.

Open: Mon–Sat 9–6; Sun 10–5; Bank Holidays 9–6.
Closed: Christmas, Boxing and New Year's Days.
Cards: Access, Visa.
Cars: Own large car-park behind shop.
Toilets: Yes.
Wheelchairs: Easy access, parking for disabled by door.
Teas: Lots of places locally.
Groups: Large shopping groups welcome, but please phone first.
Transport: 10 minutes' walk from town centre and Matlock station.
Mail order: No.

K Shoe Mines
46 Regent Road LA3 1TE
(01524) 419293

Boots and shoes for men, women and children. Other footwear, handbags, socks etc.

'Sub-standard and clearance goods directly from K factories in Kendal. About 60 other famous brand products at substandard and clearance prices.'

See our display advertisement on p.445

....

Regent Road leads off at right angles from the southern end of Morecambe Prom (traffic lights at this junction, signs to 'Lancaster M6 South'). Shop on left, on fourth corner from sea-front.

From Lancaster: at third large roundabout at beginning of town, go left into Westgate for 'Heysham'. The Shrimp is on right. Westgate becomes Regent Road. Pass Shell petrol station on right, go through two traffic lights; shop on corner site on right.

Open: Mon–Sat 9–5.30; Bank Holidays 10–5.
Closed: Christmas Day.
Cards: Access, Connect, Switch, Visa.
Cars: Adjacent streets – free. Coaches 800 yds.
Toilets: On the sea front.
Wheelchairs: Unsuitable.
Teas: Many cafés.
Groups: Coach parties welcome: please mention this Guide. Organised parties get £1 voucher per person towards purchases.
Transport: Bus nos. 2, 2A (Lancaster–Heysham Towers) to corner Westminster Road/Regent Road. Mini bus nos. 6A, 6B pass door. Buses 3 & 4 (Lancaster–Prom) stop at Promenade/Regent Road.
Mail order: Gladly supply items in stock if customers know size, fitting and style. Always ask for shop manager.

763 Northampton
see map on page 453

Crockett & Jones Ltd.
Perry Street NN1 4HN
(01604) 31515

Top grade men's shoes, ladies' mid-heel and walking shoes.
'Factory seconds from renowned quality shoe manufacturers.'

From Kettering via A43: pass the first parade of shops on your
right, go across traffic lights and pass the park on the right.
When the park ends take first left after pedestrian traffic lights
into Derby Street.*

From town centre: go towards Kettering on A43. Once on
Kettering Road pass two churches on the left then go right
opposite the Post Office shortly before pedestrian lights into
Derby Street.*

*Take next right then second left around church into Perry
Street. The factory is 20 yds on left after next crossing. Enter
through the main door: shop on right.*

Open: Fri 3–6; Sat 9.30–2.
Closed: Easter; week at
Christmas.
Cards: No.
Cars: In street.
Toilets: Ask if you are
desperate!
Wheelchairs: One step.
Teas: In town.
Groups: Groups are welcome
to the shop.
Transport: Buses from town
centre to Kettering Road, then
5 minutes' walk.
Mail order: No.

J. L. & Co. Ltd.

Westminster Works, Oliver Street NN2 7JL
(01604) 715011

Producing the finest quality 'Goodyear' welted men's leather shoes for *John Lobb, Paris* and *Edward Green*. A wide range of slight seconds always in stock – brogues, loafers, lace-ups and ankle boots etc. for town and country.

'Top quality men's shoes about half usual retail prices, from £100. A company owned by Hermes International and sister company to John Lobb, Paris.'

....

North-north east of town centre just off A43 to Kettering.
From Kettering via A43: look for first parade of shops on right. Turn right immediately after Lloyds Bank in this parade – factory is 40 yds on the left.
From town centre: go towards Kettering on A43. Once on Kettering Road, pass the park on left and go straight at lights (White Elephant pub on far left corner) at end of this park. Take first left after these lights and the factory is 40 yds on left. Ring at front door and ask for shop.

Open: Mon–Fri 9.30–5; Sat 9.30–12.30; 'A phone call to let us know the timing of your visit would be most helpful.'
Closed: Bank Holidays; last week July; first week Aug; third week Sept; Christmas-New Year.
Cards: Access, Amex, Visa.
Cars: In street.
Toilets: Yes.
Wheelchairs: Lift to third floor.
Teas: In town.
Groups: Groups of shoppers welcome, prior phone call appreciated. No factory tours.
Transport: Local buses.
Mail order: Yes.
Catalogue: No.

---

765 Northampton *see map on page 453*

Piggly-Wiggly Shoe Store Ltd. (Hawkins)

178 Kettering Road NN1 4BH
(01604) 32798

Unisex *Hawkins* leather walking boots and shoes, including a large selection of *Hawkins* fashion footwear and work boots.

'One section of shop sells constantly changing selection of seconds and ends of lines at huge discounts; the other maintains standard stock range at discounted prices.'

....

On the A43 on north-west side of town.
Coming south to town centre from Kettering on A43: cross traffic lights (White Elephant Junction) with The Kingsley Park Tavern on right; keep straight, passing tennis courts on right. Shop is on left, just before traffic lights.
From other directions: get on to inner ring road, clockwise or anti-clockwise. Go round till you see detached stone Chronicle and Echo office, turn right if going clockwise or right from other direction. At traffic lights by newspaper, turn off for Kettering, Corby (A43)/St Michael's Car Park. At far end, go left. Go over traffic lights at Talbot Road: shop is third on right (yellow fascia).

Open: Mon–Tues 10–5; Wed–Sat 9.30–5.30.
Closed: Bank Holidays. Please phone for Easter and Christmas openings.
Cards: Access, Visa.
Cars: Local streets (double yellow lines immediately outside).
Toilets: Ask if desperate!
Wheelchairs: One step into shop; one step inside. Medium sized shop.
Changing rooms: You are welcome to try footwear on.
Teas: Lots of places in town.
Groups: Shopping groups/walking clubs please phone first if over five people.
Transport: Bus nos. 3, 7, 11, 45 pass by. 15 minutes' walk from town centre.
Mail order: Please phone to enquire.

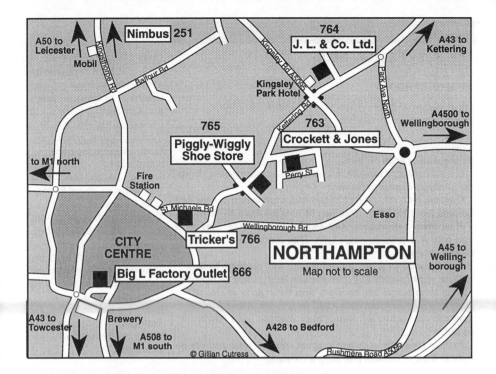

see map above

766 Northampton

Tricker's

50–60 St Michael's Road NN1 3JY
(01604) 30595

Men's high class shoes; brogues, oxfords, heavy walking shoes and boots. Velvet slippers.

'High quality men's shoes. End of lines, seconds and perfects. Discount offered on perfect shoes. Shoes made to special measure, in a variety of leathers of your choice.'

....

Short distance north of town centre.
   From all directions: get on to the inner ring road.
   Going clockwise pass huge fire station on the left (multi storey car-park and shopping centre on right) and then go left immediately after the Chronicle and Echo Newspaper offices at traffic lights following signs to Kettering.
   St Michaels Road starts here and is a one-way street. The factory is located on right hand side (just past the car-park) 150 yds down in a distinctive brown glazed tiled building. Shop (signposted) is just through main entrance.

Open: Mon–Fri 9–12 & 2–4.
Closed: Dec 22–Jan 2 and all factory holidays. Please phone to check.
Cards: Access, Amex, Diners, Visa.
Cars: In street outside; also multi-storey car-park (entrance on right, 20 yds before factory).
Toilets: Yes, on premises.
Wheelchairs: One step up to shop.
Teas: In town centre.
Groups: No.
Transport: Bus depot 200 yds away; Northampton BR station 1 mile away.
Mail order: Yes.
Catalogue: Free.

The Bally Factory Shop

Hall Road NR32 2LM
(01603) 760590

Large range of ladies', men's and children's footwear.
Handbags and accessories.

'Factory shop in factory complex.'

....

Near southern edge of town.
    The A47 (Kings Lynn–Great Yarmouth dual carriageway) forms the southern bypass of Norwich.
    From the A47, B1108 B1172 and A11: stay on or turn onto A47 towards Great Yarmouth. Then turn off onto the A140 for Norwich.*
    From Great Yarmouth on A47 and Beccles on A146: stay on or turn onto A47 towards Kings Lynn. Then turn off onto A140 towards Norwich.*
    From Ipswich on A140: go underneath A47 southern bypass.*
    Turn right immediately after the Lex Ford garage on right.*
    From town centre and northerly directions: go to or around inner ring road and turn onto A140 for Ipswich. About 2 miles from city centre turn left immediately after the Forte Posthouse on left.**
    ****Pass Toyota, Nissan and Peugeot on right: after 200 yds go right in front of bollards into Bally's car-park.**

Open: Mon–Fri 9.30–5.30;
Sat 9–5.30. Most Bank Holidays
– phone first to check.
Closed: Christmas, Boxing
and New Year's Days.
Cards: Access, Amex,
Connect, Diners, Switch, Visa.
Cars: Ample free parking
outside shop.
Toilets: Yes, and for disabled.
Wheelchairs: Ramp for easy
access to huge shop.
Teas: Coffee shop for coffee,
tea, cold drinks, light lunches,
cream teas.
Groups: No factory tours but
shopping groups and coaches
always welcome by prior
arrangement. Contact Sally
Jackson or Debbie Wicks.
Transport: Cityline bus no. 11
stops virtually opposite.
Catalogue: No.

The Factory Shoe Shop

Esdelle Works, Drayton Road NR3 4RP
(01603) 425907

Ladies' and men's quality footwear from own Norwich
factories and associated continental factories. Slim to wide
fittings usually in stock. Brands include *Van-Dal, Holmes,
Jenny* and *Gallus*. Also stock quality handbags.

*'Over 4,000 pairs of slight seconds and ends of ranges at
reduced prices.'*

....

About 3/4 mile north-west of inner ring road (A147).
    From large roundabout on St Crispin's Road (inner ring road): turn off due north into Pitt Street (A140 and A1067), for 'Swimming Pool, Cromer, Fakenham'; after 1/2 mile, fork left into Drayton Rd (A1067); pass Wensum Park. Factory on left; shop 50 yds down drive past factory.
    From north-west section of outer ring road (A140): at traffic lights by Asda, go into Drayton Road (A1067) for city centre. Go over large roundabout, look for Wickes DIY on right; shop is just beyond, on right, down drive before factory, well marked.

Open: Mon–Sat 10–4.
Closed: Bank Holidays;
Christmas–New Year.
Cards: Access, Switch, Visa.
Cars: Own large car-park.
Toilets: Nearby.
Wheelchairs: No steps to
large shop.
Teas: Many places in Norwich.
Groups: Shopping groups
welcome; book with Mrs Green
and ask for discount details.
For factory tour call Personnel
on (01603) 426341.
Transport: Cityline bus no. 11
stops outside.
Mail order: No.

Robert Cole Shoes
90 Catton Grove Road
NR3 3AA
(01603) 487757

Shoes from local, UK and worldwide factories. Over 4,000 shoes on display in all makes, sizes, styles and colours. Major brands, chainstore seconds, discontinued lines, samples.

'The quality footwear discount shop of East Anglia. All stock sold at very competitive prices. Men's shoes from £13–£60; ladies' shoes from £8–£60; children's shoes from £6–£30.'

....

On the northern section of the main Norwich ring road between the Cromer Road (A140) and the North Walsham Road (B1150).
   Shop is clearly visible at junction of Catton Grove Road and the ring road.

Open: Mon–Sat 9–5.30; Sun 10.30–4.30; Bank Holidays.
Closed: Christmas and Boxing Days.
Cards: Access, Visa.
Cars: Own well signposted car-park.
Toilets: No.
Wheelchairs: One step.
Teas: In Norwich.
Groups: Shopping groups please book first with Robert Cole or Denise West.
Transport: Several local buses stop outside door.
Mail order: Yes.
Catalogue: No.

The Shoe Factory Shop
20 Broad Street NG1 3AL
(0115) 924 2390

Over 2,000 pairs of ladies', men's and youths' footwear at discount prices. Fashion shoes and boots from own factory.
'Perfects and ends of lines from £10–£30. Men's shoes from £10–£50.'

....

In Lace Market, a fascinating conservation area in city centre. Possibly easiest to park in Victoria Centre car-park and walk.
   By car from Broadmarsh Centre: get in second to left lane of one-way system (go under footbridge; pass entrance to car-park on right) and go right then left for Trent Bridge. At large round-about go left.*
   From Trent Bridge: go towards city centre and over railway; at large roundabout go right.*
   ***Stay in left lane. Keep going round. Look for Gas Showroom on right side then turn left into George Street. At top, go left then left again into one-way Broad Street. Shop 100 yds on right after Broadway Cinema.**

Open: Mon–Fri 10–5; Sat 9–5.
Closed: Bank Holidays; Christmas, Boxing and New Year's Days.
Cards: Access, Switch, Visa.
Cars: In street and nearby public car-park.
Toilets: City centre.
Wheelchairs: Four steps to large shop.
Teas: Lots of places in town.
Groups: Shopping groups very welcome with prior phone call.
Transport: Any bus or train to Nottingham then short interesting walk.
Mail order: No.

Wynsors World of Shoes

74 Warrington Road WA5 2EV
(01925) 727481

Men's, ladies' and children's fashion shoes, both leather and synthetic.

'Massive range of branded footwear from own factory and all over the world. Stock changes daily. Prices from £1 to £100. Special lines at lowest prices in the country.'

See our display advertisement on p. 435

....

Warrington Road is the main A562, linking Widnes to Warrington. From Warrington: take A57. At roundabout in Great Sankey take left fork for Widnes. Continue into Warrington Road. Shop on left, on same forecourt as Mobil petrol station.

Open: Mon, Tues, Wed, Sat 9–5.30; Thur, Fri 9–8; Sun 10–4. Bank Holidays 10–4.
Closed: Christmas, Boxing and New Year's Days.
Cards: Access, Style, Visa.
Cars: Own car park in front and behind shop.
Toilets: Locally.
Wheelchairs: Easy access, no steps to large shop.
Teas: Take-away 100 yds. Many places in Warrington.
Groups: Welcome to shop.
Transport: Stop nearby for bus nos. 12, P1, P2, 302, T10, A1, A2.
Mail order: No.

Briggs & Shoe Mines

Southend Road CA11 8JH
(01768) 899001

Shoes for all the family. Self selection, with expert help and advice available. Small range of clothing and sports apparel, accessories, socks etc.

'3,000 sq ft of sales area for family footwear by famous makers, all at clearance, reduced or sub-standard prices.'

See our display advertisement on p. 445

....

South of the town centre.

From the town centre: take the A6 for Kendal and turn right opposite Shell petrol station (signpost to 'Swimming Baths'), then follow signs to car-park. Shop is adjacent to car-park.

From M6 exit 40: take A66 east; turn left at roundabout on to A6 for Penrith. Turn left opposite Shell petrol station and follow signs to car-park.

Open: Mon–Sat 9.30–5.30; Bank Holidays 10–5.
Closed: Christmas Day.
Cards: Access, Connect, Switch, Visa.
Cars: By shop or in adjacent car-park.
Toilets: In car-park.
Wheelchairs: Difficult access as 5 stairs to main shop floor.
Teas: In town.
Groups: Shoppers welcome. £1 reduction per member of a coach party on purchase. Pre-booked meals for parties at Caesar's Restaurant. Driver's gratuity; company pays for coach parking.
Transport: Buses pass by.
Mail order: Pleased to supply by mail order items in stock if customers know size, fitting and style. Ask for manager.

GROOCOCK of Rothwell

Padders
A treat for feet

773 Rothwell Northants

T Groocock & Co. (Rothwell) Ltd.
Gordon Street NN14 6EH
(01536) 418416

HIgh quality men's and ladies' leather shoes. Comfortable and stylish leisure/walking shoes. Ladies sizes 3–8, men's sizes 6–14 including wide fittings.

'All made in our own factory established in 1914. Some discontinued lines and slightly imperfects at greatly reduced prices.'

See our display advertisement above.

....

Near the southern end of town.

From Kettering: coming north on A14 leave at first roundabout to Rothwell on to A6. After you enter Rothwell take second right (Gordon Street) (Factory Shop sign on the wall facing you). *

Coming south on A6 from Desborough / Market Harborough: weave through the town until you see the right turn-off to Lamport Hall (but don't turn off!); after 150 yds, down the hill, take first left (Gordon Street). *

*The shop is immediately on the left, clearly signed.

Open: Mon–Fri 10–5; Sat 9–1.
Closed: Bank Holidays; Christmas–New Year.
Cards: Access, Switch, Visa,
Cars: Outside shop.
Toilets: No.
Wheelchairs: Four steps but wide doors.
Teas: In town.
Groups: Welcome to shop – not necessary to book.
Transport: Buses from Kettering stop on the A6 near the shop.
Mail order: No.

K Shoes

Closed

Main Street CA10 3NL
(01931) 716648

Wide choice of shoes, sandals, walking boots, slippers and trainers including a good selection of footwear from *K Shoes, Springers, Clarks, CICA, Dr Martens, Puma* and *Hi-Tec.* Also handbags and luggage.

'Average saving of 30% on normal high street prices for perfect shoes. Discontinued lines and slight sub-standards for men, women and children. Self-select store but trained staff to measure feet and give assistance where needed. '

....

On A6, 12 miles south of Penrith and 18 miles north of Kendal, in centre of Shap.

From M6 exit 39: go right at road junction into village. Well marked shop is on left opposite school.

From Penrith on A6: pass Shell petrol station on left: shop is 400 yds on right.

From Kendal: pass King's Arms Hotel on left: shop is 400 yds on left just past NatWest Bank.

Open: Mon–Sat 9–5; Bank Holidays 10–5.
Closed: Christmas, Boxing and New Year's Days.
Cards: Access, Switch, Visa.
Cars: Outside shop; public car-park across street 80 yds south.
Toilets: In public car-park.
Wheelchairs: Easy access to small shop.
Teas: In Shap.
Groups: Coach parties welcome, concessions for drivers and organisers. £1 voucher per passenger towards purchases.
Transport: Any bus to Shap.
Mail order: No.

Wynsors World of Shoes

108 Infirmary Road S6 3DC
(0114) 273 7903

Men's, ladies' and children's fashion shoes in both leather and synthetic fabrics.

'Massive range of branded footwear from own factory and all over world. Stock changes daily; monthly offers at lowest prices in the country. Shoes from £1–£100; January and July sales.'

See our display advertisement on p. 435

....

On the north-west side of town.

From town centre: take A61 for Penistone/Huddersfield. Fork left on to B6079 for Hillsborough. Shop is on right, opposite huge Safeway.

From the north on A61: pass Sheffield Wednesday football ground on right. After 1 mile go right at traffic lights with Great Mills on far left corner. Shop is on right corner at next crossing.

Open: Mon, Tues, Wed, Sat 9–5.30; Thur, Fri 9–8; Sun 10–4. Bank Holidays 10–4.
Closed: Christmas, Boxing and New Year's Days.
Cards: Access, Style, Visa.
Cars: Own car-park.
Toilets: Opposite.
Wheelchairs: No steps, large shop.
Teas: Café 100 yds. In Sheffield.
Groups: Shopping groups always welcome without prior notice.
Transport: Bus nos. 13, 14, 57, 58, 66, 67, 81–84, 86 stop outside.
Mail order: No.

K Shoes

9–11 Chapel Street PR8 1AF Closed
(01704) 531583

Good selection of *K Shoes* discontinued lines and slight sub-standards for men, women and children. Excellent choice for all the family from the following big name brands – *K Shoes, Springers, CICA, Puma, Mercury, Hi-Tec, Dr Martens.*

'An average of 30% saving on normal High Street prices for perfect shoes. Fully trained fitters for confidence when buying your children's shoes. Big savings on luggage, bags and accessories.'

....

In town centre, diagonally opposite BR Station.

Open: Mon–Sat 9–5.30; Sun 11–5; (*winter months*: Sun 11–4); Bank Holidays 10–5.
Closed: Christmas and Boxing Days.
Cards: Access, Switch, Visa.
Cars: Use multi-storey car-parks.
Toilets: In town.
Wheelchairs: Easy access to self-select shop.
Teas: Numerous cafés in town.
Groups: Coach parties welcome: please mention this guide; concessions for drivers and organisers. £1 voucher per passenger towards purchases.
Transport: Close to BR station. Buses to Liverpool, Wigan, Manchester, Preston.

Sundaes

The Chase, 18 High Street, Moulton PE12 6QB
(01406) 371370

Leather sandals handmade on premises using finest materials; leather linings and insoles. All handlasted to give proper fit. Wide choice of styles mainly for ladies, some for men and children. Amazing choice of colours.

'Always some discontinued lines and colours and slight seconds, some at half price. All guaranteed. Phone for details of our special fittings service.'

....

Moulton is about 5 miles east of Spalding, south of the A151. Go into Moulton to the village green. Look for The Chase, a gravel drive between the butcher and post office. Sundaes workshop is at the far end of The Chase (parking and turning possible).

Open: *April to end Sept:* Mon–Fri 9–3; *Oct to end Mar* by appointment. Sat 9–12 in summer (phone to confirm opening times).
Closed: Bank Holidays; 22 Dec–2 Jan.
Cards: Access, Switch, Visa.
Cars: Own car-park.
Toilets: Yes.
Wheelchairs: Easy access.
Changing rooms: Fitting area and small showroom.
Teas: In Spalding.
Groups: Shopping groups welcome by appointment.
Transport: Infrequent local buses from Spalding.
Mail order: Yes.
Catalogue: Free colour catalogue. Mention this book when requesting it. Send current range only.

Wynsors World of Shoes
Boundary Road WA10 2PV
(01744) 454983

Men's, ladies' and children's fashion shoes in both leather and synthetic fabrics.

'Massive range of branded footwear from own factory and all over the world. Stock changes daily; monthly offers reduced at least 50%.'

See our display advertisement on p. 435

....

A short distance west of town centre.

From town centre: take Westfield Street towards Prescot; after first roundabout take first right, Eccleston Street.*

From Prescot on A58: pass Pilkington offices on right, go left into Boundary Road just as you enter one-way system. Shop 200 yds on right.

From east on A58: go over railway, go left at third roundabout. Take first right, Eccleston Street, just before TA centre.*

From A580 (Liverpool – Manchester road): take A570 into St Helens. At first roundabout go right and next right again, Eccleston Street.*

*At traffic lights go left around Nags Head. Shop in third building on left.

Open: Mon, Tues, Wed 9–5.30; Thur, Fri 9–8; Sat 9–5.30; Sun 10–4. Bank Holidays 10–4.
Closed: Christmas, Boxing and New Year's Days.
Cards: Access, Style, Visa.
Cars: Own large car-park.
Toilets: Locally.
Wheelchairs: Easy access (no steps) to large shop.
Teas: Pub and café within 150 yds.
Groups: Groups welcome to shop. No need to book but prior phone call appreciated.
Transport: 5 minutes from town centre by local bus.
Mail order: No.

Lotus Factory Shop
Freemen Street ST16 3JA
(01785) 223200

Ladies' court shoes, sandals, leather casuals. Men's city shoes, leather casuals, sandals, top grade all-leather welted brogues and golf shoes. Seasonal footwear – slippers, ladies' fashion boots, warm-lined boots. Handbags, purses and shoe cleaning products.

'Large selection of quality footwear at discounted prices. Occasional sales on selected footwear.'

....

Just north of Stafford centre.

From the ring road around town: turn off to Stone (A34). But don't go to Stone – take second exit at this major roundabout to Sandon (B5066). Pass the gaol, then go right at first significant cross-roads into Sandon Road. After a few hundred yds, large Lotus factory is on right; turn right just before it into Freemen Street, then left into own car-park.

Coming south on A34 from Stone: turn left at first major round-about on outskirts of Stafford. Follow road round for 1 mile: look for Stafford sign near RAF Station. Turn right: after 1/2 mile Lotus is on left.

Open: Mon–Sat 9–5. Good Friday and May Day Bank Hol.
Closed: Easter Monday; Bank Holidays (but open May Day Bank Holiday); Christmas, Boxing and New Year's Days.
Cards: Access, Visa.
Cars: Large car-park. Parking for disabled beside shop door.
Toilets: In gatehouse.
Wheelchairs: Ramp to fire exit.
Teas: In Stafford.
Groups: No tours of the works but coach parties welcome to shop – book with Mrs Mills in shop, mentioning this Guide.
Transport: Bus no. 72 every 1/2 hour from Stafford stops outside.
Mail order: No.
Catalogue: Branded catalogue can be viewed in shop but is not for distribution.

The Shoe Shed

Castlefields, Newport Road ST16 1BQ
(01785) 211311

One of UK's largest footwear distributors with shoes bought in from the UK and all over the world. Current perfect merchandise at competitive prices (many reduced by up to 30%): ladies' shoes and sandals from £5, men's shoes from £10.
'Regular special offers.'

....

On the south-west side of town, near the railway station.

From Newport, going into Stafford on A518: pass sign on left (pointing right) to Rowley Hall Hospital; turn left after pillar box on left. *

From other directions and ring road: follow signs to A518 for Telford/Newport. Pass station on right, turn right (from town centre) or go straight (from the ring road) and cross railway line; after 200 yds turn right in front of pillar box. *

*Clearly marked company is at end of lane; shop at back right.

Open: Seven days a week 10–4. Some Bank Holidays.
Closed: Christmas and Boxing Days.
Cards: None.
Cars: Large car-park.
Toilets: Yes.
Wheelchairs: One step; help willingly given. Huge spacious shop.
Teas: Refreshments for pre-booked groups.
Groups: Shopping groups please contact manageress first.
Transport: 5 minutes' walk from station; 10 minutes' walk from town centre. Bus nos. 9, 11, 12, 13.

Wynsors World of Shoes

Parkfield Road, off Bridge Road TS18 3DJ
(01642) 672525

Men's, ladies' and girls' leather and synthetic fashion shoes, bags and sundries from all over the world, including many famous names.
'Special monthly offers with at least 50% reductions. Major sales in January and July.'

See our display advertisement on p. 435

....

On south side of town centre, in new small retail park.

From A19 going north or south: go on to A66 towards Darlington. *

*From Darlington or Middlesbrough on A66: exit for A135 for Stockton west and Yarm. At end of slip road follow signs to Stockton. At T-junction with lights go right, pass the Lord's Tavern on left; at small roundabout fork right and at second roundabout turn right into Parkfield Road. **

On foot from town: with WH Smith on left, go along Bridge Street. Cross over roundabout into Parkfield Road. **

**Take second left into retail estate. Shop first on left.

Open: Mon–Wed 9–5.30; Thur–Fri 9–8.00; Sat 9–5.30; Sun 10–4. Bank Holidays.
Closed: Christmas, Boxing and New Year's Days.
Cards: Access, Style, Switch, Visa.
Cars: Own large car-park.
Toilets: No.
Wheelchairs: Easy access
Teas: Lots of places in Stockton High Street.
Groups: Shopping groups welcome. Prior phone call appreciated.
Transport: Any bus or train to Stockton.
Mail order: No.

Lotus Shoes
27 High Street ST15 8AJ
(01785) 812915

Shoes: ladies' courts, sandals, leather casuals. Men's city shoes, top grade all-leather welted brogues and golf shoes, leather casuals, sandals. Also seasonal products such as slippers, ladies' fashion boots and warm-lined boots. Handbags, purses and shoe cleaning products.

'Quality footwear at discounted prices. Occasional sales on selected footwear.'

....

This shop is in the main shopping street (now pedestrianised) of Stone opposite the Crown Hotel. If you go down the High Street, the shop is on the left.

Via A34 from Stafford: you come into the one-way system. Park in car-park on left then walk through Adie's Alley into High Street: Lotus is directly opposite.

Open: Mon–Sat 9–5.30. Good Friday. **Closed:** Easter Monday and other Bank Holidays. **Cards:** Access, Visa. **Cars:** In town car-parks. **Toilets:** In Stone. **Wheelchairs:** Easy access, no steps into medium sized shop. **Teas:** Pubs and cafés in Stone. **Groups:** No factory tours (not on factory site) but coaches welcome to other Lotus shop (Stafford). Prior phone call please. **Transport:** Any bus or train to Stone. **Mail order:** No. **Catalogue:** Branded catalogue can be viewed in shop but is not for distribution.

Clarks Factory Shop
Clarks Village, Farm Road BA16 0BB
(01458) 843161

Extensive range of quality shoes, sandals, boots, walking boots, slippers, trainers, handbags, luggage, sports clothing, sports equipment, outdoor clothing, accessories and gifts.

'Self-select store with trained staff to measure feet and give assistance.'

....

In Clarks Village, easy to find and clearly marked off the Street by-pass.

Open: *1 April–31 Oct:* Mon– Sat incl. Bank Hols 9–6; Sun 11–5. *1 Nov–31 March:* Mon– Sat incl. Bank Hols 9–5.30; Sun 11–5. **Closed:** Easter Sun., Xmas Day. **Cards:** Access, Delta, Switch, Visa. **Cars:** Ample parking, places set aside for disabled drivers. **Toilets:** Yes, including disabled and baby facilities. **Wheelchairs:** Most entrances & exits have ramps, & shopping aisles are wide for easy access. **Changing rooms:** Yes. **Teas:** Leith's at the Food Factory Restaurant. Burger King takeaway, plus sandwich and pizza kiosks. Picnic area. **Groups:** Groups welcome. Please contact ext. 2746 for details of special events. Free entry to Shoe Museum. **Transport:** Short distance from town centre.

Crockers of Street

112/114 High Street BA16 0EV
(01458) 442055

Good selection of *Clarks* discontinued lines and slight sub-standards for men, women and children. Self-select from big brands on display – *K Shoes, Springers, CICA, Hi-Tec, Puma, Kangaroos, Mercury* and *Fila*.
'Fully trained Clarks fitters are on hand to measure feet and give assistance where it is needed. An average of 30% saving on normal High Street prices for perfect shoes. Big savings on luggage, bags and accessories.'

....

Easy to find in the middle of main street, on right if you come from Glastonbury direction.

Open: Mon–Sat 9–5.30; Sun 11–5; Bank Holidays 9–5.30.
Closed: Christmas Day, Easter Sunday.
Cards: Access, Switch, Visa.
Cars: Parking in town centre.
Toilets: In town centre.
Wheelchairs: Easy access, no steps.
Teas: In town centre.
Groups: 10% discount for coach passengers.
Transport: Local buses.
Mail order: No.

Can you take shoes back?

Return of goods by the customer is some-times a matter of some contention in the footwear business. No doubt misunder-standings arise on both sides but shops report that more people are complaining. One factory shop tells us that some teenagers buy shoes before the weekend, wear them once, purposely damage them then demand a replacement pair next week. 'They even choose the replacement pair before returning the first ones!'

The Office of Fair Trading recognizes the potential for problems and publishes a leaflet with a four-step plan to returning shoes. First, go back to the shop at once and explain your problem to the manager. If you return unworn faulty shoes you may insist on a cash refund or a refund on your credit card account. If you are offered a credit note, you do not have to accept it.

If you delay, or have used the shoes, how-ever, you may be offered only a partial refund; or a repair or replacement. You can ask for the shoes to be sent to the Footwear Testing Centre for an indepen-dent opinion. This costs £21 of which you contribute £7. The shop must stick by whatever the report says; if your com-plaint is upheld your costs are refunded.

Remember however that there are cases where you may not be entitled to any-thing, for example if the shoes were marked 'seconds'. You are not entitled to a refund if you simply decide later that you no longer like the shoes, or they do not fit; or if you yourself caused a fault. Nor will you be entitled to any comeback if you ignore the shop's advice; for example, 'if you were told that the trainers were not machine washable, but went ahead and washed them that way anyway'.

Crockers of Swindon

West Swindon Centre SN5 7DI
(01793) 873662

Good selection of *Clarks* discontinued lines and slight sub-standards for men, women and children. Self-select from big brands on display – *K Shoes, Springers, CICA, Hi-Tec, Puma, Kangaroos, Mizuno, Mercury, LA Gear* and *Fila.*

'Fully trained Clarks fitters to measure feet and give assistance where it is needed. An average saving of 30% on high street prices for perfect shoes. Big savings on luggage, bags and accessories.'

....

From M4 exit 16: go into Swindon, following signs for Link Centre and West Swindon District Centre. Pass the Link Centre (large white building on the right) then turn right into car-park C of the West Swindon Centre. Crockers is next door to Asda.

Open: Mon–Fri 9–8; Sat 9–6; Sun 10–4; Bank Holidays 10–5.
Closed: Christmas and New Year's Days. Easter Sunday.
Cards: Access, Switch, Visa.
Cars: Adjacent car-park (free).
Toilets: In shopping centre.
Wheelchairs: Easy access, no steps.
Teas: In shopping centre.
Groups: 10% discount for coach passengers.
Transport: Any bus to West Swindon.
Mail order: No.

Wynsors World of Shoes

Wynsor House, Woodhouse Green S66 9AM
(01709) 540876

Men's, ladies' and children's fashion shoes in both leather and synthetic fabrics.

'Massive range of branded footwear from own factory and all over the world. Stock changes daily; monthly offers at lowest prices in the country. Shoes from £1 to £100. January and July sales.'

See our display advertisement on p. 435

....

From Rotherham: take the A6021 for Maltby then join A631 at the Stag roundabout. Follow this dual carriageway to next roundabout with The Mason on the left and turn right on to the B6060 (Morthen Road).*

From M18 exit 1: go towards Rotherham on A631. At next roundabout (The Mason on far right), turn left on to the B6060 (Morthen Road).*

*The B6060 takes you over the motorway to Thurcroft. Pass garage on right: shop is on right after The Double Barrel.

Open: Mon, Tues, Wed, Sat 9–5.30; Thur, Fri 9–8; Sun 10–4. Bank Holidays 10–4.
Closed: Christmas, Boxing and New Year's Days.
Cards: Access, Style, Visa.
Cars: At front of shop.
Toilets: Locally.
Wheelchairs: No steps, large shop.
Teas: Pub next door. Café and fish & chips 1/2 mile.
Groups: Shopping groups always welcome without prior booking.
Transport: Bus nos. 19, 19a, and 208 from Rotherham.
Mail order: No.

Gaghills Mill & Footwear Museum

Burnley Road East BB4 9AS
(01706) 215417

Men's, ladies' and children's shoes, boots, slippers and training shoes. Towels, bags and ladies', men's and children's wear and accessories.

'Perfects and ends of lines.'

....

Burnley Road East (B6328) is only road going north along the valley from Waterfoot towards Burnley.

From traffic lights in Waterfoot: at this T-junction, turn off Bacup Road (A681) into Burnley Road East (B6328). Go north for 400 yds then turn right at sign to 'Gaghills Factory Shop & Museum'. Clearly marked company is 50 yds on right.

Coming south from Burnley on Burnley Road East (B6328): go downhill towards Waterfoot. Pass Edge Side Post Office on the left; after several hundred yards go left at sign 'Gaghills Factory Shop & Museum'.

Open: Mon–Thu 10.30–5; Fri 10–1; Sat 9.30–3.30; Bank Holiday Mon 10–5.
Closed: Easter; Christmas–New Year.
Cards: None.
Cars: Large car-park.
Toilets: Yes.
Wheelchairs: Lift available.
Changing rooms: Yes.
Teas: Locally.
Groups: Groups welcome to shop, please phone first. Allow extra time to visit fascinating small museum in original shoe company premises.
Transport: Buses: Rochdale–Accrington and Rawtenstall–Todmorden go to main bus stop in Waterfoot (4 minutes' walk from mill). Rawtenstall–Burnley and Blackburn–Burnley (via Rawtenstall) stop at top of drive.

K Shoes

100 The Parade WD1 5B2
(01923) 243251

Huge selection of *K* seconds and clearance lines for men, women and children including shoes, sandals, trainers, boots, slippers, handbags.

'All goods are seconds and discontinued lines.'

....

In the town centre, inside the inner ring road near Maples and Clements Department Store and opposite Kudos (formerly Paradise Lost) night club.

Go round the inner road and park in Roslynn Road multi-storey car-park; then walk.

Open: Mon–Sat 9–5.30; most Bank Holidays, but please phone to check.
Closed: Christmas and Boxing Days.
Cards: Access, Visa.
Cars: Local car-parks.
Toilets: Nearby.
Wheelchairs: Easy access to large shop.
Teas: Various places in Watford.
Groups: Small groups of shoppers welcome with prior phone call please.
Transport: Local trains and buses.
Mail order: No.

Crockers of Worle

Queensway Shopping Centre BS22 0BT
(01934) 521693

Good selection of *Clarks* discontinued lines and slight sub-standards for men, women and children. Self-select from big name brands on display – *K Shoes, Springers, CICA, Hi-Tec, Puma, Kangaroos, Mizuno, Mercury, LA Gear* and *Fila*.

'Fully trained Clarks fitters on hand to measure feet and give assistance. An average of 30% saving on normal high street prices for perfect shoes. Big savings on luggage, bags and accessories.'

....

Easy to find in huge retail park on east side of Weston-super-Mare.
From M5 exit 21: go west along A370 for Weston and go downhill. Go right for Sainsbury's and park there.
From Weston: take A370 towards M5. Go left for Sainsbury's into retail park.

Open: Mon–Fri 9–8; Sat 9–6; Sun 10.30–4.30. Bank Holidays 9–5.
Closed: Christmas Day, Easter Sunday.
Cards: Access, Switch, Visa.
Cars: Adjacent car-park (free).
Toilets: In car-park.
Wheelchairs: Easy access, no steps.
Teas: Nearby.
Groups: 10% discount for coach passengers.
Transport: Worle Station; plenty of buses from Weston.
Mail order: No.

Wynsors World of Shoes

Clarence Street YO3 7EV
(01904) 637611

Ladies' and girls' fashion shoes, sandals and boots in leather and synthetic materials. Mnay chainstore and branded items from cancelled orders and shoes for all the family from all over the world. Top brands especially sports shoes, all at cut prices.

'99% perfects. Average 30% less than in high street; special buys; promotions with at least 50% off. January and July sales.'

See our display advertisement on p. 435

....

Close to York Minster, outside the walls on the north side of the city.
From the minster: walk along High Petergate and through Bootham Bar. Turn right into Gillygate. Continue straight in Clarence Street; shop and car-park are on right on the corner (with Lord Mayor's Walk).

Open: Mon, Tues, Wed, Sat 9–5.30; Thur, Fri 9–8; Sun 10–4.
Closed: Christmas, Boxing and New Year's Days.
Cards: Access, Style, Visa.
Cars: Own car-park and large public car-park opposite.
Toilets: Facilities across the road.
Wheelchairs: Easy access to large shop.
Teas: Cold drinks available; four cafés and two pubs within 100 yds.
Groups: Shopping groups welcome with prior phone call to shop manager.
Transport: Any bus to town centre.
Mail order: No.

Illustrations

The illustrations show:

One of the most enjoyable yet totally unexpected aspects of producing these guides is the large number of letters we receive from readers. Some letters recount funny shopping experiences; many provide wonderful information about shops which we ourselves have not yet caught up with; others ask us for specific details.

A recurring request is that we indicate the quality of items sold in the shops. We personally feel unable to provide such information because our opinion would be too subjective. We also know, from the questionnaires which many people are kind enough to return, that views on any one shop vary according to what the customer is looking for. If you require cheap clothing for an economical family beach holiday in Spain, you will be looking for something different from that needed for a luxury cruise in the Cayman Islands. You can obtain both ranges of clothing when you buy direct from the maker and both can be excellent value for money – but how you judge the shop will depend on whether it stocked what you were looking for on the day you went and whether the service was what you expected.

However, in the best traditions of other guide books, we welcome the chance to continue building up information about those shops which you, the shopper, consider offer top value for money, good service, wide ranges of goods – or the reverse! Shopping is much more than just a question of spending money. It is a pleasure – an enjoyable aspect of a day's outing – an essential feature of a holiday. (Would you believe that 50% of money spent on holiday goes on shopping?) When you buy items from shops like the ones described in these books, there is also the 'fun of the chase'.

Wth your help we would like to build up a list of the best factory and mill shops. Please complete the form opposite. Unless you request otherwise, we might use your name in connection with a good report.

We need to know:

the name and address of the shop you visited; when you shopped there; what you bought; the amount you spent; and how you considered the following aspects: How welcoming were the staff? Was the service good/bad/unmemorable? What did you think of the products for sale? Did you consider the items represented good value for money? What was especially good or bad about your shopping trip?

To: Gill Cutress, The Factory Shop Guide, FREEPOST (SW 8510), London SW2 4BR

I should like to comment on the following shop

Name and address of the shop visited ....

....

....

Date of visit .... How much you spent ....

What you bought ....

Comments, anecdotes etc on the shop, service, parking, goods for sale – or whatever attracted your attention!

Where did you buy your guide?...

Your name ....

Your address ....

....

Post code ....

Phone number .... Date ....

If you would like more copies of this form, please give us a ring and we'll post them.
Phone (0181) 678 0593 Fax (0181) 674 1594

To: Gill Cutress, The Factory Shop Guide, FREEPOST (SW 8510), London SW2 4BR

I should like to comment on the following shop

Name and address of the shop visited ....

....

....

Date of visit .... How much you spent ....

What you bought ....

**Comments, anecdotes etc on the shop, service, parking, goods for sale –
or whatever attracted your attention!**

Where did you buy your guide?...

Your name ....

Your address ....

....

Post code ....

Phone number .... Date ....

*If you would like more copies of this form, please give us a ring and we'll post them.
Phone (0181) 678 0593 Fax (0181) 674 1594*

Would you like a free book next year?

More manufacturers are opening factory shops. If you have enjoyed visiting other shops, either here, or in France or elsewhere in the world, we should be delighted to hear about them. If you are the first person to send us new details which are published next year, we shall be happy to send you a free copy of the new guide.

Name of company ....
Address ....
What do they sell? ....

Name of company ....
Address ....
What do they sell? ....

Name of company ....
Address ....
What do they sell? ....

Name of company ....
Address ....
What do they sell? ....

Where did you buy your copy of this guide? ....
How did you hear about it? ....

Your name ....
Your address ....
....
Town ....
Post code ....
Your phone no. ....
Date ....

Readers in Britain only, please send to:
Factory Shop Guide, FREEPOST (SW 8510) London SW2 4BR
(0181) 678 0593   fax (0181) 674 0594

How can we make this guide even more useful?

To help us give you the information you are looking for, please fill in this questionnaire.

SPECIAL OFFER – SAVE 60p ON YOUR NEXT ORDER! Send (no stamp needed) this fully completed form back to us and we will send you a 60p voucher to use when you next order any of our titles from us.

Why do you like Factory Shopping?

Is there anything you don't like about Factory Shops?

Which shops do you prefer? (please tick only one answer)
a. Shops which sell only those goods which they make themselves
b. Shops with a mixture of items, including related bought-in goods
c. Shops which sell anything, including imported items, if they are cheap
d. No preferences
e. Factory outlet centres
Any other comments?

How much did you spend at the last Factory Shop you visited?
a. Less than £10
b. £10 or over but under £15
c. £15 or over but under £20
d. £20 and over
e. £30 and over
f. £100 and over
g. £200 and over

Which items in Factory Shops interest you in particular?
a. Knitting wools
b. Sewing materials
c. Craft materials
d. Pottery & porcelain
e. Glassware
f. Children's clothing
g. Household linens, furnishings
h. General clothing
i. Designer clothing
j. Carpets
k. Furniture
l. What else?

Have you visited Factory Shops
a. While on holiday? — Often / Sometimes / Not at all
b. While travelling on business? — Often / Sometimes / Not at all
c. When visiting relatives? — Often / Sometimes / Not at all
d. During day trips from home? — Often / Sometimes / Not at all

Have you visited any of the 'factory outlet centres'? Yes / Not yet
If yes, which one(s)?

On the day you last went to a Factory Shop, how many individual Factory Shops did you visit in total?

Provided you have time, do you enjoy touring the factory itself when you visit a Factory Shop?
Very much / it's OK / not much / no thanks
What is the furthest you have travelled especially to go to a particular Factory Shop?

Did you buy your own copy of this Guide? Yes / No   **Was the book a present?** Yes / No
Have you given a copy to anyone else? Yes / No
Have you previously bought other Factory Shop Guides? Yes / No   If yes, which?

How many of the shops, mentioned in this book, were new to you? Just a few / Quite a lot / Almost all
How many people have looked through your copy of this Guide? (include yourself!)
Are you male / female?
Which age bracket are you in?   Under 20   20–29   30–39   40–49   50–59   60–69   70+
Which newspaper(s) do you read?   Sun   Mail   Express   Telegraph   Times   Independent   Guardian
Mirror   Observer   Sunday Times   Others

Which weekly and monthly magazines do you see regularly?

What other information would you like this guide to give?

Any other comments?

Please send the following books to me:

.....copy(ies) of the **Derbys/Notts/Lincs Guide** at £4.50 each   £   .

.....copy(ies) of the **Staffordshire & the Potteries Guide** at £3.95 each   £   .

.....copy(ies) of the **Yorks/Humberside Guide** at £3.95 each   £   .

.....copy(ies) of the **Northern England Guide** at £3.95 each   £   .

.....copy(ies) of the **Leics/Northants/Bedford Guide** at £3.95 each   £   .

.....copy(ies) of the **Western Midlands Guide** at £4.50 each   £   .

.....copy(ies) of the **North-West England/North Wales Guide** £4.50   £   .

.....copy(ies) of the **Scotland Guide** at £4.50 each   £   .

.....copy(ies) of the **E Anglia & SE England Guide** at £4.50 each   £   .

.....copy(ies) of the **SW England & S Wales Guide** at £4.50 each   £   .

     P&p within UK: 60p each above book, max £3.50   £   .

.....copy(ies) of the **Italian Guide** at £12.95 each   £   .

.....copy(ies) of the **Great British Factory Shop Guide** at £14.95 each   £   .

.....copy(ies) of the **Northern France Guide** at £9.95 each   £   .

.....copy(ies) of the **Sweden Guide** at £8.95 each   £   .

.....copy(ies) **Gardeners' Atlas (Notts/Derbys/S Yorks)** at £6.95   £   .

.....copy(ies) **Gardeners' Atlas (Surrey, Sussex, Middx)** at £6.95   £   .

     P&p within UK: £1 each above book, max £3.50   £   .

I enclose a cheque *or* please debit my **Access / MasterCard / Visa**
Cheques made payable to G. Cutress   **GRAND TOTAL**   £   .

Credit card **Access / MasterCard / Visa**

No. .... **Expiry date** ....

Name .... **Tel. no.** ....

Address ....

....

Town .... **Post code** ....

Signed .... **Date** ....

Readers in Britain only, please send to: The Factory Shop Guide,
FREEPOST (SW 8510) London SW2 4BR   Phone (0181) 678 0593   Fax (0181) 674 1594

Overseas readers, please send your credit card details to:
The Factory Shop Guide, 1 Rosebery Mews, Rosebery Road, London SW2 4DQ
for airmail delivery (actual postage plus small packing fee).

SPECIAL MESSAGE TO READERS WHO HAVE PREVIOUSLY SENT US THE FULLY
COMPLETED FORM ON p. 472: DON'T FORGET TO ENCLOSE
YOUR 60p 'THANK YOU' VOUCHER!

I would like to send a gift to the following person:

Name...

Address ....

Town... Post Code ....

.....copy(ies) of the **Derbys/Notts/Lincs Guide** at £4.50 each £ .

.....copy(ies) of the **Staffordshire & the Potteries Guide** at £3.95 each £ .

.....copy(ies) of the **Yorks/Humberside Guide** at £3.95 each £ .

.....copy(ies) of the **Northern England Guide** at £3.95 each £ .

.....copy(ies) of the **Leics/Northants/Bedford Guide** at £3.95 each £ .

.....copy(ies) of the **Western Midlands Guide** at £4.50 each £ .

.....copy(ies) of the **North-West England/North Wales Guide** £4.50 £ .

.....copy(ies) of the **Scotland Guide** at £4.50 each £ .

.....copy(ies) of the **E Anglia & SE England Guide** at £4.50 each £ .

.....copy(ies) of the **SW England & S Wales Guide** at £4.50 each £ .

P&p within UK: 60p each above book, max £3.50 £ .

.....copy(ies) of the **Italian Guide** at £12.95 each £ .

.....copy(ies) of the **Great British Factory Shop Guide** at £14.95 each £ .

.....copy(ies) of the **Northern France Guide** at £9.95 each £ .

.....copy(ies) of the **Sweden Guide** at £8.95 each £ .

.....copy(ies) **Gardeners' Atlas (Notts/Derbys/S Yorks)** at £6.95 £ .

.....copy(ies) **Gardeners' Atlas (Surrey, Sussex, Middx)** at £6.95 £ .

P&p within UK: £1 each above book, max £3.50 £ .

I enclose a cheque *or* please debit my Access / MasterCard / Visa
Cheques made payable to G. Cutress **GRAND TOTAL** £ .

Credit card Access / MasterCard / Visa

No. .... Expiry date ....

Your name .... Tel. no. ....

Your address ....

....

Town .... Post code ....

Signed .... Date ....

Readers in Britain only, please send to: The Factory Shop Guide,
FREEPOST (SW 8510) London SW2 4BR Phone (0181) 678 0593 Fax (0181) 674 1594

Overseas readers, please send your credit card details to:
The Factory Shop Guide, 1 Rosebery Mews, Rosebery Road, London SW2 4DQ
for airmail delivery (actual postage plus small packing fee).

Scotland

From the Islands and John O'Groats to Hadrian's Wall: about 100 enticing shops for superb cashmere knitwear and international designer woven cashmere; wools and co-ordinated knitwear; tartans and kilts. Taste and buy top quality Scottish jams & soups, shortbread & biscuits, and find out which whisky distilleries are open to visitors. Several super potteries for cookware and animal figurines, decorative boxes, cut and engraved crystal glassware, coloured glass paperweights, curtaining; shiny fashion raincoats, designer sweatshirts, brand name jeans, well known brands of ladies' skirts, jackets, coats, workwear, beds, bedding, garden furniture, terracotta pots, giant casseroles, household linens, sheeting, silk scarves, body-warmers, lightweight raincoats, sheepskin jackets, stylish children's leisurewear and family clothing. From the Shetlands and Hebrides to Wick, Lochinver, Ullapool, Oban, Inverness, Aberdeen, Perth, Kinross, Dundee, Alva, Stirling, Dunfermline, Bo'ness, Edinburgh, Glasgow area, Kilmarnock, Dunoon, Campbeltown, Ayr, Galashiels, Selkirk and Hawick.

Northern England

This part of the country is rich in shops selling outdoor wear and sports clothes (wetsuits, beach wear, fishing gear, trainers). Track down about 70 shops: for the home – beds and mattresses, oven-to-table glass cookware, curtain fabrics and furniture; to wear – men's trousers, women's jackets, underwear, stylish country wear, quality shoes, hats for all occasions – plus an extraordinarily diverse assortment of products including leather briefcases, lighters, shoehorns, caviar spoons, artists' supplies. Find well known names in rainwear, clothing, oiled cotton jackets, top quality leather and canvas bags, curtains, colourful (sweet smelling!) candles, children's clothing, bedding galore, caravan upholstery, stretch car seat covers, carpets, electric tools, crafts materials, fitness shoes, branded leather shoes, vast ranges of family footwear, outstanding quality tweeds, and hand-woven woollen fabrics, huge ranges of men's jackets, trousers and suits, garden pots and stationery. Washington, Peterlee, Hartlepool (new factory outlet centre), Newcastle, Gateshead, Redcar, Middlesbrough, Stockton, Darlington; Carlisle, Wigton, Maryport, Cleator, Penrith, Keswick, Kendal, Ambleside, Furness area and south to Carnforth.

Other Factory Shop Guides in the series

Ten regional guides show you how to find top value for money in mill and factory shops in specific areas of the country. Set out in alphabetical order by town, these books contain many detailed street maps together with background information on the regions.

These regional guides are ideal for shoppers who wish to discover the factory shops in their own vicinity and for people who are going on holiday to a specific region. They make good presents for people living there too!

Guides are available in good bookshops, WH Smith, Waterstone's, James Thin etc and by mail directly from us.

If you would like to have up-to-date details about current books, please send an SAE or give us a ring for a free leaflet.

Ninety-eight shops for carpets, towels, blouses, children's and family clothing, furnishing fabrics, sofa beds, skiwear, high quality knitwear, co-ordinated home furnishings, lightweight fleece outdoor clothing, garden furniture, knitting yarns (mail order too) and sports wear. Humberside has trousers, jackets, chainstore clothing, table lamps, pottery, footwear, leather and sheepskin coats in Bridlington, Driffield, Hull, Immingham, Scunthorpe, Grimsby (for fresh and smoked fish and Danish specialities). Yorkshire for furnishing fabrics, wallpapers, underwear, shoes, hand-made sprung beds, country furniture, left-handed scissors, cutlery, silverware, glassware, woollen & worsted fabrics, woollen clothing, tapestry kits, craft materials, tablecloths, hats, gloves, dress and curtain velvets. Three factory shop centres. Whitby, York, Ripon, Harrogate, Addingham, Keighley, Skipton, Leeds, Bradford area, Hebden Bridge, Halifax, Holmfirth, Huddersfield, Sheffield, Rotherham, Doncaster.

Yorkshire & Humberside

Nearly 120 shops sell great value spectacles, high performance waterproof clothing, famous name high street fashion garments, outstanding selections of curtain fabrics, every possible style in blinds, unusually wide shoes for people who have difficulty in finding comfortable footwear, useful items for the disabled, all styles of lighting, carpets galore, Christmas cards and wrapping paper, Welsh quarry tiles and caviar spoons. An extraordinary area for bedding, curtain and furnishing fabrics and tiles, including famous brand names. Many make curtains at reasonable cost. Also a wide range of family clothing, rucksacks, sleeping bags, bedding, knitwear, pond liners, garden equipment, lampshades and bases, small electrical items, toys and sewing threads. From Lancaster, Blackpool, Runcorn, Wrexham and Liverpool south to Glossop, including the entire Manchester area.

North-West England & North Wales

The ONLY publication that tells you how to find the world-famous potteries – plus some small ones which you have probably not come across before, including a company making traditional Staffordshire dogs. If you wish to go round the potteries, to watch china made and decorated, or simply want to find excellent value for money, this book tells you where, when and how. Staffordshire companies make much more than china! This book lets you into the secrets of other companies, some with equally famous names, for exquisite enamelled boxes, clothing, wax jackets, hand-cut crystal, countrywear, shoes, lingerie and knitwear. Wilmslow, Leek, Biddulph, Stafford, Rugeley, Tutbury, Burton & Tamworth. 39 potteries in Stoke. Specially drawn maps of individual towns. Information for overseas visitors on how to get china home.

Staffordshire & The Potteries

Nowhere else will you find such detailed information, along with specially drawn maps, of the traditional hand-cut full lead crystal companies in the Stourbridge area, west of Birmingham. Also for the fascinating Jewellery Quarter in Birmingham offering hand-crafted individual jewellery at excellent prices, and skilled repairs. One of the best areas for superb selections of carpets, natural fibre floor coverings, curtains, children's outdoor toys, leather shoes, vibrant hand painted scarves and ties, ladies' clothing, trousers, pottery, tableware (Royal Worcester), hair dryers, small electrical items, Christmas tree lights, fitted kitchens, silver plated cutlery and trays etc, brass and copper items, house nameplates, all styles in hats and headwear, designer T-shirts, top branded knitwear, leather items, garden pots, lamp-shades and lights. Craven Arms, Telford, Shrewsbury, Stourbridge, Stourport, Walsall, Ross-on-Wye, Kidderminster, Wolverhampton, Birmingham, Tewkesbury, Worcester, Stratford.

Western Midlands

What an amazing area for factory shops! Enticing shops sell knitwear, lingerie, shoes, underwear, lighting, leisurewear, curtains, pottery, earthenware tableware, glassware, terracotta, garden pots, tableware, lace, bridal fabrics, cutlery and an unbelievable range of products previously available from catalogue companies by post. Shops in Lincolnshire for family clothing, excellent knitwear, net curtains, and hand-made sandals. Buy made-to-measure large sized leisurewear, vast variety of clothing for all the family and all activities, including fishing and golfing; baby and chainstore children's wear, luggage, bath cubes and soaps, sweets, silks, marvellous selections of dress fabrics, cooking and kitchenware, curtains and curtaining, decanters, fashion shoes, sports shoes and trainers, cane and a very broad range of upholstered and leather furniture, a huge range of knitwear, hosiery, leather jackets, light fittings, men's suits, jackets and trousers, paperweights, pillows, shirts, stocking fillers, toys, tablecloths, towels, wallcoverings, Welsh dressers and wrapping paper! About 100 shops from Sheffield south to Shepshed.

Derbyshire, Nottinghamshire & Lincolnshire

For shops selling curtains, women's knitwear, sewing machines and spare parts, furnishing fabrics, furniture, walking boots, and garden urns, columns and statues. You can buy super value lighting, lampshades, soaps and shampoos, family shoes and men's leather footwear, Doc Marten's boots, ladies' and family clothing. Also boys' underwear, football boots and a terrific selection of sports clothing, schoolwear, knitting yarns, dress and curtain fabrics, 100% wool sweaters, carpets, bermuda shorts, men's suits, ladies' jackets, safety footwear, socks and Stilton

Leicestershire, Northamptonshire & Bedford

cheese. Also cosmetics, soaps, toiletries, kitchen and home accessories, oven-to-tableware, bedding, handbags, leather goods, curtains, lamp shades, luggage, tablemats, tables, chairs. Ashby, Moira, Shepshed, Coalville, Loughborough, Leicester, Sileby, Wigston, Hinckley, Nuneaton, Oakham; Kettering, Northampton, Wellingborough, Earls Barton; Bedford (for furnishing fabrics) and many other places.

South-West England & South Wales

From Oxfordshire south and west: offering basketware, bedding, family clothing, carpets, floor and wall tiles, famous cider, garden pots and lots of sheepskin products. Kitchenware, fitted kitchens, designer silk wear, some fabrics, lots of footwear (incl. made-to-measure), safety clothing, furniture, crystal glass, handmade paper, knitwear, lamp bases & shades, model animals and houses, a great range of pottery, ribbons, rugs, soft and wooden toys, schoolwear, wools and yarns. From the Channel Islands, thro' Cornwall & Devon to Gloucestershire (tablemats, carpets, tiles) and Oxfordshire (carpets, pottery, furnishing fabrics); Christchurch and Poole; Wiltshire (carpets, underwear, table mats, tiles, ladies' clothing); many shops in Somerset (Clarks Village), Bristol; 29 shops in South Wales for superb cashmere, cut glass, traditional woollen fabrics, cakes, body warmers, boiled sweets, diabetic chocolate, household textiles, ladies' quality clothing.

East Anglia & South-East England

Manufacturers and shoppers are catching on fast in southern England. This edition features 103 shops from Norfolk (sweets, country knitwear, shoes, handbags, famous brand clothing); Suffolk (terracotta kitchen jars, silk, pottery, basketware, leather coats); Cambridgeshire (top quality leather cases and briefcases, famous ladies' wear, mail-order returns); Essex (quality furniture and repairs, dried flowers, jeans, chainstore ends of lines); the Home Counties north of London (world-famous ladies' clothing, designer wear, furnishing fabrics, lingerie, carpets, glass); Bedfordshire (curtaining and furnishing fabrics); London (candles, tableware, stylish shoes, sofa beds, original clock designs, lighting, teak furniture, furnishing fabrics, model kits); Kent (garden pots and furniture, silk ties, shoes, dried flowers); Sussex (lingerie, pots, sewing/knitting supplies, fashion jewellery, trugs, tiles, designer wear); Surrey (cashmere, knitwear, furniture); Hampshire (electric toasters, stainless steel tableware, sportswear, carpets); the Isle of Wight (pottery and glass). Also fish smokeries and an enormous selection of other items!

Northern France

Cross the Channel and discover a little known shopping trail, or 'How to make the most of enticing French products at less than traditional French prices!'. Our innovative and information-packed guide (in English and French) is the first of its kind, ideal for day-trippers and weekenders travelling to France, along with serious Francophiles who have more time in which to seek out the great array of factory shops. Expect to pay about a third less than normal French prices. From Calais and Boulogne east to St Omer and Lille, into Belgium, then south to Cambrai, Laon, Reims, St Quentin and Troyes, the major factory shopping town in France. Enjoy all those tempting French items with that certain French je ne sais quoi – such as outstanding ranges of co-ordinated household linens by leading international names; *Le Creuset* ovenware (seconds can cost as little as a third of the normal UK retail price!); *Cristal d'Arques* tableware; sumptuous *YSL, Daniel Hechter, Descamps, Primrose Bordier* and *Olivier Desforges* designer name bathrobes; exquisite lacy lingerie; *Le Bourget, DD* and *Zanzi* hosiery; stylish women's wear (including *Weill of Paris* and *Paul Mausner*); *Levi's* and *Wrangler* leisurewear; *Le Coq Sportif* and *Adidas* sportswear; *Bally* shoes; ski clothing; hand-made chocolate; traditional French pottery including snail plates!; children's clothes, including *Petit Bateau, Catimini* and *Osh Kosh*; and outstanding men's jackets and suits. With 234 shops, including four interesting factory outlet centres, this guide gives detailed directions to and a photo of each shop. The price guide indicates what you can expect to pay. Champagne trails near Rheims add fizz to your shopping!

Bargain Hunting in Italy

This personally researched book is by a shopping fiend living in Milan. 'Italy produces and exports many beautiful luxury goods, be it silks, shoes, furniture or household wares', so she has explored the world of seconds, close-outs, showroom models, samples, ends of lines, bargain basements and secondhand shops. In English and Italian, this 320-page guide details 600 places set out by province (38 shops around Como, 33 in Florence area, seven near Perugia, 41 entries for Rome, 5 for Bologna, 5 for Verona, 134 in Milan etc). This 'extremely useful guide for the intelligent consumer in search of expensive goods at less expensive prices ...' is available in the UK only from *The Factory Shop Guide*.

South Africa

There are 300 factory shops in the Cape Town area. If you are going there on holiday, take advantage of the low Rand. You can find good buys in men's clothing and explore a wide variety of shops selling women's clothing, shoes, sportswear etc. If searching out the shops by yourself seems too daunting, you can join a tour and be guided round the shops by expert shopper Pam Black. For a free leaflet about Pam's books *The A—Z of Factory Shops* for the Cape area or Natal please send us an SAE. By credit card, you can arrange for a book to be sent to yourself or directly to friends in South Africa.

Sweden

We have discovered a book which tells you how to save money at Swedish factory shops! With world-famous names in glass, such as *Boda, Orrefors* and *Kosta Boda*, and in household articles, such as *Dorre* and *Scandia* – all of which offer items at 30–50% below normal retail prices – this book should soon cover its cost even if you use it just a few times on your Swedish holiday. For people who admire Swedish design but who are reluctant to pay traditional Swedish prices. Available in the UK only from *The Factory Shop Guide*.

Abakhan Fabrics	140	Mostyn Clwyd
Abbey Horn of Lakeland	241	Carnforth (Holme) Lancashire
Abbey Textiles	671	Nuneaton Warwickshire
Abbey Woollen Mill	557	Swansea West Glamorgan
Abrovian Factory Shop	631	Hebden Bridge West Yorkshire
Acced	378	Ellesmere Port Cheshire
Ahmad Textiles	118	Bradford West Yorkshire
Alan Paine Knitwear	566	Ammanford Dyfed
Alan Paine Knitwear	616	Godalming Surrey
Alexon/Eastex/Dash	454	Street Somerset
Alfred Enderby	268	Grimsby Humberside
Appliance Centre	161	Leicester Leicestershire
Aquascutum	320	Bicester Oxfordshire
Aquascutum	632	Hemel Hempstead Hertfordshire
Armstrong, J B	639	Ilkeston Derbyshire
Art Candles	238	Bodmin Cornwall
Arthur Price of England	2	Lichfield Staffordshire
Ashlie Craft	285	Long Eaton Nottinghamshire
Ashtons	105	Hyde Greater Manchester
Astbury Lighting	158	Congleton Cheshire
Aynsley China	63	Stoke-on-Trent Staffordshire
Aynsley China	66	Stoke-on-Trent Staffordshire
Babygro	594	Cowdenbeath Fife
Babygro	650	Kirkcaldy Fife
Baggage Factory	455	Street Somerset
Baker, GP & J/Parkertex Fabrics	127	High Wycombe Bucks
Bally	767	Norwich Norfolk
Balmoral Knitwear	611	Galston Strathclyde
Barbour	644	Jarrow Tyne & Wear
Barden Mill Shop	587	Burnley Lancashire
Bargain Baggage	286	North Shields Tyne & Wear
Barker Shoes	743	Earls Barton Northamptonshire
Barker Shoes	756	Keswick Cumbria
Barnett, C & R	303	Bradford West Yorkshire
Barracks Fabrics	134	Macclesfield Cheshire
Bateman, Ogden & Co.	302	Bradford West Yorkshire
Baxters Visitor Centre	266	Fochabers Grampian
Beck Mill	662	Melton Mowbray Leicestershire
Bedding Box, The	100	Great Harwood Lancashire
Beevers of Whitby	233	Whitby North Yorkshire
Begg of Ayr	570	Ayr Strathclyde
Belinda Robertson Cashmere	608	Edinburgh Lothian
Benco Hosiery	718	Wirksworth Derbyshire
Benetton	321	Bicester Oxfordshire
Benetton	379	Ellesmere Port Cheshire
Benetton	409	Hartlepool Cleveland
Benetton	456	Street Somerset
Bicester Outlet Shopping Village	319	Bicester Oxfordshire
Big Dog	322	Bicester Oxfordshire
Big L	606	East Kilbride Strathclyde
Big L	666	Northampton Northamptonshire
Big L	380	Ellesmere Port Cheshire
Black & Decker	457	Street Somerset
Black Dyke	312	Queensbury West Yorkshire
Blackwell Bros.	91	Swindon Wiltshire
Blakeney Pottery	78	Stoke-on-Trent Staffordshire
Blindcraft	204	Ayr Strathclyde
Blindcraft Edinburgh	211	Edinburgh : Craigmillar Lothian
Bond, R L & C M	294	Farsley West Yorkshire
Bookscene	364	Brighton E Sussex
Bookscene	410	Hartlepool Cleveland
Bottoms Mill	108	Todmorden Lancashire

Boundary Mill	373	Colne Lancashire
Boynett Fabrics	115	Bedford Bedfordshire
Brannam, C H	83	Barnstaple Devon
Brass and Copper Shop	236	Birmingham West Midlands
Brenire	692	Selkirk Borders
Bretby Art Pottery	50	Woodville Staffordshire
Bridge of York	720	York North Yorkshire
Brierley Hill Glass Co.	23	Brierley Hill West Midlands
Briggs & Shoe Mines	721	Ambleside Cumbria
Briggs & Shoe Mines	732	Carlisle Cumbria
Briggs & Shoe Mines	754	Kendal Cumbria
Briggs & Shoe Mines	772	Penrith Cumbria
Bristol Carpets	172	Bristol : St George Avon
Britannia Products	492	Bradford West Yorkshire
British Mohair Spinners	290	Bradford West Yorkshire
British Mohair Spinners	299	Shipley West Yorkshire
BRK Crystal	12	Gildersome South Yorkshire
Brookhouse Pottery	35	Denbigh Clwyd
Brooks Mill	376	Elland West Yorkshire
Broughton Shoe Warehouse	753	Ipswich Suffolk
Brown's Factory Shop, The	679	Pontefract West Yorkshire
Brunel (By Testall) Upholstery	232	Westhoughton Gr Manchester
BTM Fabrics	316	Wigston Leicestershire
Burt Marshall, Lumsden	107	Perth Tayside
Caithness Crystal	14	King's Lynn Norfolk
Caithness Glass	18	Perth Tayside
Caithness Glass	31	Wick Highland
Callant of Scotland (Knitwear)	710	Tillicoultry Central
Candy & Co	190	Newton Abbot : Heathfield Devon
Carlton House	79	Stoke-on-Trent Staffordshire
Carpet Bags	281	Bury St Edmunds Suffolk
Carpet Company, The	198	Westhoughton Gr Manchester
Carpet Shop (Carpets of Worth)	196	Stroud Gloucestershire
Carpets of Worth	195	Stourport-on-Severn Hrfd & Worcs
Carrington Curtains	123	Harrogate North Yorkshire
Carrington Curtains	152	York North Yorkshire
Carter, A & J	672	Oadby Leicestershire
Catalogue Bargain Shop	497	Bilston West Midlands
Catalogue Bargain Shop	498	Bradford West Yorkshire
Catalogue Bargain Shop	499	Bridgnorth Shropshire
Catalogue Bargain Shop	500	Burnley Lancashire
Catalogue Bargain Shop	501	Caerphilly Mid Glamorgan
Catalogue Bargain Shop	502	Chorley Lancashire
Catalogue Bargain Shop	503	Cowdenbeath Fife
Catalogue Bargain Shop	504	Doncaster South Yorkshire
Catalogue Bargain Shop	505	Droitwich Hereford & Worcester
Catalogue Bargain Shop	506	Ebbw Vale Gwent
Catalogue Bargain Shop	507	Eccles Greater Manchester
Catalogue Bargain Shop	508	Farnworth Greater Manchester
Catalogue Bargain Shop	509	Faversham Kent
Catalogue Bargain Shop	510	Gainsborough Lincolnshire
Catalogue Bargain Shop	511	Glasgow : City Centre Strathclyde
Catalogue Bargain Shop	512	Glasgow : Parkhead Strathclyde
Catalogue Bargain Shop	513	Gloucester Gloucestershire
Catalogue Bargain Shop	514	Gravesend Kent
Catalogue Bargain Shop	515	Hamilton Strathclyde
Catalogue Bargain Shop	516	Heckmondwike West Yorkshire
Catalogue Bargain Shop	517	High Barnet Hertfordshire
Catalogue Bargain Shop	518	Huddersfield West Yorkshire
Catalogue Bargain Shop	519	Lincoln Lincolnshire
Catalogue Bargain Shop	520	Llandudno Gwynedd
Catalogue Bargain Shop	521	London : Hounslow London
Catalogue Bargain Shop	522	London : Palmers Green London
Catalogue Bargain Shop	523	London : Peckham London
Catalogue Bargain Shop	524	Malvern Hereford & Worcester
Catalogue Bargain Shop	525	Manchester Greater Manchester

Please note that the NUMBERS refer to the ENTRIES, NOT the PAGES

Companies with Factory Shops
continued

Colston Bassett Dairy	264	Colston Bassett Nottinghamshire
Consortium Jewellery	551	Birmingham West Midlands
Converse	325	Bicester Oxfordshire
Cooper & Roe	685	Ruddington Nottinghamshire
Cooper & Roe	705	Sutton-in-Ashfield Notts
Corcoran & May	132	London : Ealing
Corcoran & May	133	London : Putney
Corcoran & May	145	Sevenoaks Kent
Corgi Hosiery	567	Ammanford Dyfed
Courtaulds Textiles Homeware	109	Wigan Greater Manchester
Crabtree & Evelyn	433	Kendal Cumbria
Crabtree & Evelyn	461	Street Somerset
Craft Collection Mill Shop	296	Horbury West Yorkshire
Creative Carpets	179	Enderby Leicestershire
Crockers of Arnold	722	Arnold Nottinghamshire
Crockers of Bridgwater	726	Bridgwater Somerset
Crockers of Burnham	728	Burnham-on-Sea Somerset
Crockers of Glasgow	744	Glasgow : Parkhead Strathclyde
Crockers of Street	784	Street Somerset
Crockers of Swindon	785	Swindon Wiltshire
Crockers of Worle	789	Worle Somerset
Crockett & Jones	763	Northampton Northamptonshire
Crown Burslem Pottery	54	Stoke-on-Trent Staffordshire
Croydex	203	Andover Hampshire
Croydex	205	Barnstaple Devon
Croydex	209	Dartford Kent
Crucial Trading	176	Craven Arms Shropshire
Crucial Trading	188	London : Bermondsey
Crystal Art	15	Luton Bedfordshire
Cudworth of Norden	665	Norden Greater Manchester
Curtain Choice	121	Chorley Lancashire
Curtain Factory Shop, The	131	Lincoln Lincolnshire
Custom Carpets	182	Frome Somerset
Dainty Supplies	301	Washington Tyne & Wear
Daleswear	642	Ingleton North Yorkshire
Dalgliesh, D C	556	Selkirk Borders
Dalkeith Mill Shop	597	Dalkeith Lothian
Danish Food Centre	269	Grimsby Humberside
Darley Mill Centre	407	Harrogate North Yorkshire
Dartington Crystal	10	Denby Derbyshire
Dartington Crystal	434	Kendal Cumbria
Dartington Crystal	462	Street Somerset
Dartington Crystal	13	Great Torrington Devon
Dartmouth Pottery	34	Dartmouth Devon
David Evans	305	Crayford Kent
David Mellor Cutlery	1	Hathersage Derbyshire
David Nieper	564	Alfreton Derbyshire
De Bradelei Mill Shops	318	Belper Derbyshire
Debut Group	651	Langley Mill Nottinghamshire
Dema International	9	Chesterfield Derbyshire
Den-Home Cushioning	126	Heckmondwike West Yorkshire
Denby Factory Shop	44	Matlock Bath Derbyshire
Denby Factory Shop	45	Nottingham Nottinghamshire
Denby Pottery	36	Denby Derbyshire
Denby Pottery	41	Kendal Cumbria
Denby Pottery	48	Street Somerset
Denholme Velvets	306	Denholme West Yorkshire
Dennis Hall Tudor Crystal	26	Stourbridge West Midlands
Dennis of Ruabon	200	Wrexham Clwyd
Dent's	558	Warminster Wiltshire
Derwent Crystal	6	Ashbourne Derbyshire
Derwent Crystal	11	Derby Derbyshire
Descamps	326	Bicester Oxfordshire
Designer Warehouse	661	Macclesfield Cheshire
Dewhirst	569	Ashington Northumberland
Dewhirst	604	Driffield Humberside

**Companies with
Factory Shops**
continued

Company	No.	Location
Dewhirst	637	Hull Humberside
Dewhirst	677	Peterlee Co Durham
Dewhirst	681	Redcar (Dormanstown) Cleveland
Dewhirst	703	Sunderland Tyne & Wear
Dewhirst	706	Swansea West Glamorgan
Dewhirst	667	Norton, Malton North Yorkshire
Dexam International	250	Midhurst W Sussex
Dim	383	Ellesmere Port Cheshire
Dovetail Enterprises	210	Dundee Tayside
Durham Clothing	695	Shildon Co Durham
Early's of Witney	110	Witney Oxfordshire
East Lancashire Towel Co.	94	Barrowford Lancashire
East Quay Knitwear	715	Wells-next-the-Sea Norfolk
Edinburgh Crystal	327	Bicester Oxfordshire
Edinburgh Crystal	365	Brighton E Sussex
Edinburgh Crystal	384	Ellesmere Port Cheshire
Edinburgh Crystal	413	Hartlepool Cleveland
Edinburgh Crystal	17	Penicuik Lothian
Elite Factory Clothes Shop	568	Ashbourne Derbyshire
Embsay Mills Needlecraft	300	Skipton North Yorkshire
Eminence	385	Ellesmere Port Cheshire
Empress Mills	293	Colne Lancashire
End of the Line Furniture	202	Ambergate Derbyshire
Equator	328	Bicester Oxfordshire
Equator	386	Ellesmere Port Cheshire
Equator	414	Hartlepool Cleveland
Esprit	464	Street Somerset
Essentially Hops	240	Canterbury Kent
Ethos Candles	249	Mere Wiltshire
Ettrick Forest Interiors	144	Selkirk Borders
F W Needham	237	Birmingham West Midlands
Fabric Design	138	Matlock Bath Derbyshire
Fabric Factory, The	125	Heanor Derbyshire
Fabric Mill Shop, The	136	Manchester Greater Manchester
Fabric Shop, The	113	Addingham West Yorkshire
Fabric World	148	South Croydon Surrey
Fabric World	150	Sutton Surrey
Factory Bedding & Fabrics	99	Carlisle Cumbria
Factory Fabric Shop, The	309	Leeds West Yorkshire
Factory Fabrics	116	Blaydon on Tyne Tyne & Wear
Factory Outlet Shopping Centre	491	York North Yorkshire
Factory Shoe Company, The	742	Earl Shilton Leicestershire
Factory Shoe Shop, The	768	Norwich Norfolk
Factory Shop Ltd, The	366	Brighton E Sussex
Factory Shop Ltd, The	371	Bristol Avon
Factory Shop Ltd, The	372	Bury St Edmunds Suffolk
Factory Shop Ltd, The	374	East Dereham Norfolk
Factory Shop Ltd, The	375	Egremont Cumbria
Factory Shop Ltd, The	428	Holbeach Lincolnshire
Factory Shop Ltd, The	429	Horley Surrey
Factory Shop Ltd, The	431	Keighley West Yorkshire
Factory Shop Ltd, The	439	Lancaster Lancashire
Factory Shop Ltd, The	440	Liverpool Merseyside
Factory Shop Ltd, The	441	Minehead Somerset
Factory Shop Ltd, The	442	Morley West Yorkshire
Factory Shop Ltd, The	444	Pershore Hereford & Worcester
Factory Shop Ltd, The	446	Ripon North Yorkshire
Factory Shop Ltd, The	448	Rugby Warwickshire
Factory Shop Ltd, The	450	Sileby Leicestershire
Factory Shop Ltd, The	452	Newcastle under Lyme Staffs
Factory Shop Ltd, The	487	Stroud Gloucestershire
Factory Shop Ltd, The	488	Tiptree Essex
Factory Shop Ltd, The	489	Trowbridge Wiltshire
Factory Shop Ltd, The	490	Warminster Wiltshire
Factory Shop, The	317	Basildon Essex
Factory Shop, The	601	Doncaster South Yorkshire

Companies with Factory Shops

continued

Factory Shop, The	670	Nottingham Nottinghamshire
Falmer Jeans	596	Cumnock Strathclyde
Falmer Jeans	680	Rayleigh Essex
Famous Fashion Discounts	451	Stockton-on-Tees Cleveland
Famous Footwear	387	Ellesmere Port Cheshire
Farfield Clothing	691	Sedbergh Cumbria
Fashion Factory	589	Cannock Staffordshire
Fashion Factory	714	Wellington Shropshire
Fent Shop, The	297	Macclesfield Cheshire
Filigree	149	South Normanton Derbyshire
Fine Fabrics	307	Derby Derbyshire
Florentine Trading Co.	141	Nottingham Nottinghamshire
Frank Knighton & Sons	219	Ilkeston Derbyshire
Fred Lawton & Son	183	Huddersfield West Yorkshire
Fred Perry	329	Bicester Oxfordshire
Fred Perry	388	Ellesmere Port Cheshire
Fred Perry	465	Street Somerset
Frenni Furniture	208	Crymych Dyfed
Fruit of the Loom	607	East Kilbride Strathclyde
Fruit of the Loom	389	Ellesmere Port Cheshire
Fruit of the Loom	709	Telford Shropshire
Furness Footwear	737	Dalton-in-Furness Cumbria
Furniture Direct	217	High Wycombe Buckinghamshire
Gaghills Mill & Footwear Museum	787	Waterfoot Lancashire
Galleria, The	426	Hatfield Hertfordshire
Galt Toys	277	Cheadle Cheshire
Gardiner of Selkirk	693	Selkirk Borders
George Brettle	576	Belper Derbyshire
George Butler of Sheffield	3	Sheffield South Yorkshire
Georgian Crystal (Tutbury)	29	Tutbury Staffordshire
Giovanna	367	Brighton E Sussex
Gladstone Pottery Museum	68	Stoke-on-Trent Staffordshire
Glen Alva	689	Sauchie by Alloa Central
Gleneagles Crystal	8	Broxburn Lothian
Glenpatrick Mill Shop	178	Johnstone Strathclyde
Golden Shuttle	584	Bradford West Yorkshire
Goodson Lighting	166	Stafford Staffordshire
Goodwood MetalCraft	242	Chichester W Sussex
Gorse Mill Lighting	157	Chadderton Greater Manchester
Gossard	579	Blackwood Gwent
Gossard	655	Leighton Buzzard Bedfordshire
Graham & Brown	170	Blackburn Lancashire
Grandford Carpet Mills	180	Fareham Hampshire
Green, T G, Pottery	33	Church Gresley Derbyshire
Groocock & Co.	773	Rothwell Northamptonshire
Guernsey Woollens	620	Guernsey Channel Islands
Haddonstone	85	Brixworth Northamptonshire
Hadida, M R	69	Stoke-on-Trent Staffordshire
Hall & Son	738	Darlington Co Durham
Hallmark	415	Hartlepool Cleveland
Hallmark	466	Street Somerset
Hamilton McBride	92	Accrington Lancashire
Hartleys (Mail Order) Shop	122	Colne Lancashire
Harvergrange / Spartan Luggage	288	Tibshelf Derbyshire
Hat Shop, The	549	Atherstone Warwickshire
Hawick Cashmere Company	626	Hawick Borders
Hawk Cycles	278	Cradley Heath West Midlands
Helix Lighting	164	Rushden Northamptonshire
Helly Hansen	330	Bicester Oxfordshire
Henry Watson's Potteries	49	Wattisfield Suffolk
Heyford's Upholstery	206	Bicester Oxfordshire
Hico	331	Bicester Oxfordshire
Hide Park Leather Co.	690	Scunthorpe Humberside
Highland Society for the Blind	220	Inverness Highland
Highland Stoneware Pottery	42	Lochinver Highland
Hiram Wild	4	Sheffield South Yorkshire

Please note that the NUMBERS refer to the ENTRIES, NOT the PAGES

Companies with factory shops

continued

486   *The Official Great British Factory Shop Guide*

History Craft	252	Oxford Oxfordshire
History Craft	256	Stratford-upon-Avon Warwickshire
History Craft	260	York North Yorkshire
Hobbs	332	Bicester Oxfordshire
Hole Farm Dried Flowers	259	Witham Essex
Holland Studio Craft	60	Stoke-on-Trentn Staffordshire
Hom	333	Bicester Oxfordshire
Homebirds	137	Market Harborough Leicestershire
Homemaker Edging Services	197	Wakefield West Yorkshire
Honey	416	Hartlepool Cleveland
Hook Norton Pottery	39	Hook Norton Oxfordshire
Hornsea Freeport	430	Hornsea Humberside
Hornsea Pottery	368	Brighton E Sussex
House of Marbles/Teign Valley Glass	276	Bovey Tracey Devon
Hubbinet Reproductions	226	Romford Essex
Hudson & Middleton	70	Stoke-on-Trent Staffordshire
Ian M Roberts	646	Kettering Northamptonshire
In-Wear	658	London : Wandsworth
Into Clothing	652	Leamington Spa Warwickshire
Jackson's Landing	408	Hartlepool Cleveland
J L & Co.	764	Northampton Northamptonshire
Jaeger	565	Alloa Central
Jaeger	577	Belper Derbyshire
Jaeger	334	Bicester Oxfordshire
Jaeger	591	Cleckheaton West Yorkshire
Jaeger	592	Coalville Leicestershire
Jaeger	635	Hucknall Nottinghamshire
Jaeger	647	Kilmarnock Strathclyde
Jaeger	648	King's Lynn Norfolk
Jaeger Knitwear	682	Redditch Hereford & Worcester
Jaeger Sale Shop	675	Peterborough Cambridgeshire
Jaeger Sale Shop	678	Plymouth Devon
Jaeger Sale Shop	708	Tamworth Staffordshire
Jaeger/Jaeger Man	467	Street Somerset
James Barry	390	Ellesmere Port Cheshire
James Barry	417	Hartlepool Cleveland
James Barry	468	Street Somerset
Jamieson & Smith	298	Shetland : Lerwick
Jane Shilton	335	Bicester Oxfordshire
Jeff & Annabel's Diamond Gallery	552	Birmingham West Midlands
Jeffrey Rogers	336	Bicester Oxfordshire
Jeffrey Rogers	391	Ellesmere Port Cheshire
Jewellery Quarter Discovery Centre	553	Birmingham West Midlands
Jigsaw	337	Bicester Oxfordshire
Joan & David	338	Bicester Oxfordshire
Jockey	612	Gateshead Tyne & Wear
John Beswick	71	Stoke-on-Trent Staffordshire
John Chapman	282	Carlisle Cumbria
John Heathcoat	315	Tiverton Devon
John Jenkins	339	Bicester Oxfordshire
John Partridge	340	Bicester Oxfordshire
John Partridge	392	Ellesmere Port Cheshire
John Partridge	686	Rugeley Staffordshire
John Smedley	595	Cromford Derbyshire
John Smedley	602	Doncaster South Yorkshire
John Wilman	173	Burnley Lancashire
Johnson, H & R Tiles	194	Stoke-on-Trent Staffordshire
JoKids	341	Bicester Oxfordshire
JoKids	393	Ellesmere Port Cheshire
JoKids	418	Hartlepool Cleveland
JoKids	469	Street Somerset
Joman Manufacturing	142	Peterlee Co Durham
Jorgus Carpets	168	Anderton Cheshire
Joshua Wardle	653	Leek Staffordshire
Jumpers	436	Kendal Cumbria

Please note that the NUMBERS refer to the ENTRIES, NOT the PAGES

Companies with factory shops
continued

Jumpers	470	Street Somerset
Just Fabrics	119	Burford Oxfordshire
K & M (Leather Clothing)	669	Nottingham Nottinghamshire
K Shoe Mines	762	Morecambe Lancashire
K Shoes	723	Askam-in-Furness Cumbria
K Shoes	724	Blackpool Lancashire
K Shoes	741	Dundee Tayside
K Shoes	774	Shap Cumbria
K Shoes	776	Southport Merseyside
K Shoes	788	Watford Hertfordshire
K Shoes Factory Shop, Sports		
Factory & Baggage Factory	755	Kendal Cumbria
K Shoes Full Price	438	Kendal Cumbria
K Village	432	Kendal Cumbria
Karen Millen	342	Bicester Oxfordshire
Karrimor International	560	Accrington Lancashire
Katie Gray Factory Frock Shop	624	Halifax West Yorkshire
Kay & Son, Prime Fish Merchants	270	Grimsby Humberside
Keela International	615	Glenrothes Fife
Kemptown Terracotta	84	Brighton E Sussex
Kent & Curwen	617	Godalming Surrey
Kids Playfactory	343	Bicester Oxfordshire
Kurt Geiger	344	Bicester Oxfordshire
Kurt Geiger	394	Ellesmere Port Cheshire
Kyme Mill Shop	585	Bradford West Yorkshire
Lady Clare	248	Lutterworth Leicestershire
Lambert Howarth & Sons	729	Burnley Lancashire
Lambourne Clothing	643	Ipswich Suffolk
Lands' End Direct Merchants	495	Oakham Leicestershire
Langley Furniture	216	Heanor Derbyshire
LBS Polythene/Gardeners' Choice	86	Colne Lancashire
Le Tricoteur	621	Guernsey Channel Islands
Liberty	304	Burnley Lancashire
Lighting Bug	155	Cannock West Midlands
Lightwater Village Factory Outlets	447	Ripon North Yorkshire
Lincoln House Home Furnishings	229	Somercotes Derbyshire
Lindsay Allan Designs	711	Tillicoultry Central
Linen Cupboard, The	471	Street Somerset
Linen Mill Shop, The	104	Huddersfield West Yorkshire
Liz Claiborne	395	Ellesmere Port Cheshire
Liz Claiborne	472	Street Somerset
Lochleven Mill Shop	649	Kinross Tayside
Long Clawson Dairy	273	Long Clawson Leicestershire
Lotus Factory Shop	779	Stafford Staffordshire
Lotus Shoes	758	Leek Staffordshire
Lotus Shoes	782	Stone Staffordshire
Low Woods Furnishings	146	Shepshed Leicestershire
Lowe, R H	593	Congleton Cheshire
Lyles, S. Son & Co.	177	Dewsbury West Yorkshire
Lyndalware	235	Auchterarder Tayside
M & G Designer Fashions	633	Hickstead Village W Sussex
Maitland Enterprises	253	Preston Lancashire
Major Oak Clothing Company	580	Blidworth Nottinghamshire
Mansfield Shoes	736	Cumnock Strathclyde
Marden Furniture	231	Sutton-in-Ashfield Notts
Market Place, The	673	Oxted Surrey
Marlborough Tiles	174	Cheltenham Gloucestershire
Marlborough Tiles	189	Marlborough Wiltshire
Marlborough Tiles	192	Salisbury Wiltshire
Mascot Clothing	590	Clacton-on-Sea Essex
Match Leisurewear	640	Ilkeston Derbyshire
Material Things	135	Macclesfield Cheshire
Matlock Shoe Sales	761	Matlock Green Derbyshire
McArthur Glen Designer Outlet Village	377	Ellesmere Port Cheshire
McIntosh's	96	Blaydon on Tyne Tyne & Wear
Merchants Quay	363	Brighton E Sussex

Mexx	698	Slough Berkshire
Mill Fabric Shop, The	128	Hyde Greater Manchester
Mill Shop (Johnstons of Elgin)	609	Elgin Grampian
Mill Shop, The	559	Aberdeen Grampian
Mill Shop, The	599	Denby Dale West Yorkshire
Mill Shop, The	654	Leek Staffordshire
Minton	80	Stoke-on-Trent Staffordshire
Mister Mackenzie	613	Glasgow : Central Strathclyde
Modec Fine Arts	239	Bolton Greater Manchester
Monsoon	345	Bicester Oxfordshire
Monsoon/Accessorize	473	Street Somerset
Moorcroft, W	55	Stoke-on-Trent Staffordshire
Moorland Pottery	56	Stoke-on-Trent Staffordshire
Morlands	745	Glastonbury Somerset
Moulinex Swan	154	Birmingham West Midlands
Mulberry	694	Shepton Mallet Somerset
Musbury Fabrics	102	Helmshore Lancashire
Museum Merchandise	346	Bicester Oxfordshire
Nazeing Glassworks	7	Broxbourne Hertfordshire
New Balance Athletic Shoes	760	Maryport Cumbria
Next 2 Choice	713	Watford Hertfordshire
Next 2 Choice	717	Wickford Essex
Nicole Farhi	656	London : Bow Greater London
Nike	396	Ellesmere Port Cheshire
Nimbus	251	Northampton Northamptonshire
Northern Feather Home Furnishings	93	Ashton-in-Makerfield Gr Manch
Nottingham Laces & Trimmings	310	Long Eaton Nottinghamshire
Nova Garden Furniture	212	Faversham Kent
O P Chocolate	274	Merthyr Tydfil Mid Glamorgan
Oban Glass Studio	16	Oban Strathclyde
Oneida	347	Bicester Oxfordshire
Optical Direct (C-L-M)	548	Accrington Lancashire
Optical Direct	550	Bacup Lancashire
Origin	571	Bampton Devon
Original Book Works, The	243	Cirencester Glos
Osborne Silversmiths	5	Sheffield South Yorkshire
Osh Kosh B'Gosh	348	Bicester Oxfordshire
Oswaldtwistle Mills	443	Oswaldtwistle Lancashire
P B A Mill Shop	143	Rawtenstall Lancashire
P F Collections	222	Long Eaton Nottinghamshire
P J Gold Depot	554	Birmingham West Midlands
Paco	397	Ellesmere Port Cheshire
Palatine Products	223	Newcastle upon Tyne T & W
Papworth Travel Goods	287	Papworth Everard Cambridgeshire
Park Rose Pottery Leisure Park	32	Bridlington Humberside
Parker, V & F (Arden Jewellery)	555	Birmingham West Midlands
Paul Costelloe	398	Ellesmere Port Cheshire
Paul Steiger	129	Kirkby-in-Ashfield Notts
Peaklander Footwear	731	Calver Derbyshire
Peel Mill	445	Ramsbottom Greater Manchester
Pendor (Clothing)	663	Merthyr Tydfil Mid Glamorgan
Pepe Jeans	349	Bicester Oxfordshire
Peter MacArthur & Co.	308	Hamilton Strathclyde
Peter Newman	751	Herne Bay Kent
Peter Scott	627	Hawick Borders
Phoenix Carpets	187	Little Horwood Buckinghamshire
Pier, The	474	Street Somerset
Pifco Salton Carmen Russell Hobbs Tower	153	Birmingham W Mids
Pifco Salton Carmen Russell Hobbs Tower	159	Failsworth Gr Manch
Pifco Salton Carmen Russell Hobbs Tower	167	Wombourne W Mids
Piggly-Wiggly Shoe Store	765	Northampton Northamptonshire
Pilkington's Tiles	191	Poole Dorset
Playdri Products	279	Bury St Edmunds Suffolk
Ponden Mill	427	Haworth West Yorkshire
Portmeirion Potteries	72	Stoke-on-Trent Staffordshire
Portmeirion Seconds Shop	81	Stoke-on-Trent Staffordshire

Please note that the
NUMBERS refer to the
ENTRIES,
NOT the PAGES

Companies with
factory shops
continued

Potterton Cases	283	Leicester	Leicestershire
Price's Candles	350	Bicester	Oxfordshire
Price's Candles	246	London : Battersea	
Priestley Footwear	747	Great Harwood	Lancashire
Principles	351	Bicester	Oxfordshire
Principles	399	Ellesmere Port	Cheshire
Proud Fabrics	311	Nelson	Lancashire
Providence Reproductions	218	Hyde	Greater Manchester
Queen's Fine Bone China	73	Stoke-on-Trent	Staffordshire
R S Sports & Leisurewear	641	Ilkeston	Derbyshire
Racing Green	352	Bicester	Oxfordshire
Red Rose Carpets	181	Fleetwood	Lancashire
Red Rose Velvets	112	Accrington	Lancashire
Red/Green	353	Bicester	Oxfordshire
Regent Belt Co.	284	Long Buckby	Northamptonshire
Remington	400	Ellesmere Port	Cheshire
Remington	475	Street	Somerset
Richard Draper	746	Glastonbury	Somerset
Robert Cole Shoes	769	Norwich	Norfolk
Robin Hood Mill Shop	97	Bolton	Greater Manchester
Roger Lascelles Clocks	247	London : Fulham	Greater London
Rohan	476	Street	Somerset
Rookes Pottery	87	Hartington	Derbyshire
Rowe Carpets	184	Kidderminster	Hrfd & Worcester
Rowe Carpets	199	Worcester	Hereford & Worcester
Royal Aberdeen Blind Workshops	201	Aberdeen	Grampian
Royal Brierley	419	Hartlepool	Cleveland
Royal Brierley	477	Street	Somerset
Royal Brierley Crystal	24	Brierley Hill	West Midlands
Royal Brierley Crystal	27	Tipton	West Midlands
Royal Crown Derby	37	Derby	Derbyshire
Royal Doulton	52	Stoke-on-Trent	Staffordshire
Royal Doulton	57	Stoke-on-Trent	Staffordshire
Royal Doulton	61	Stoke-on-Trent	Staffordshire
Royal Doulton Crystal	22	Amblecote	West Midlands
Royal Grafton Fine Bone China	74	Stoke-on-Trent	Staffordshire
Royal Scot Crystal	28	Toddington	Bedfordshire
Royal Strathclyde Blindcraft	214	Glasgow	Strathclyde
Royal Worcester	64	Stoke-on-Trent	Staffordshire
Royal Worcester	478	Street	Somerset
Royal Worcester Porcelain	51	Worcester	Hereford & Worcester
Royal Worcester & Spode	46	Porth	Mid Glamorgan
Rubert of London	583	Borehamwood	Hertfordshire
Rutland Lighting	160	Grantham	Lincolnshire
Rutland Lighting	163	Market Overton	Leicestershire
Rye Pottery	47	Rye	E Sussex
S R Leisure	712	Washington	Tyne & Wear
Salisbury China	75	Stoke-on-Trent	Staffordshire
Sapphire Books	354	Bicester	Oxfordshire
Sapphire Books	401	Ellesmere Port	Cheshire
Schott-UK	20	Stafford	Staffordshire
Scotch House	402	Ellesmere Port	Cheshire
Sedgemoor Shoes	727	Bridgwater	Somerset
Selective Marketplace	494	Loughborough	Leicestershire
Selkirk Glass	19	Selkirk	Borders
Shark Group	275	Amble	Northumberland
Shaw Carpets	169	Barnsley (near)	South Yorkshire
Sheban Furniture	227	Seaford	E Sussex
Sheltered Workshop for Blind	95	Blackburn	Lancashire
Sherry's Towel Mill	106	Padiham	Lancashire
Shireburn Carpets	175	Clitheroe	Lancashire
Shoe Factory Shop, The	740	Derby	Derbyshire
Shoe Factory Shop, The	748	Grimsby	Humberside
Shoe Factory Shop, The	752	Hull	Humberside
Shoe Factory Shop, The	759	Leicester	Leicestershire
Shoe Factory Shop, The	770	Nottingham	Nottinghamshire

Please note that the NUMBERS refer to the ENTRIES, NOT the PAGES

Companies with factory shops
continued

Please note that the NUMBERS refer to the ENTRIES, NOT the PAGES

Companies with factory shops

continued

Vanners	314	Sudbury Suffolk
Vectase Lighting	156	Rochdale Greater Manchester
Velmore Fashions	610	Ellesmere Port Cheshire
Velmore Fashions	687	Runcorn Cheshire
Velmore Fashions	719	Wrexham Clwyd
Victoria Carpet Weavers Shop	185	Kidderminster Hrfd & Worcester
Village Gift Shop, The	482	Street Somerset
Villeroy & Boch	359	Bicester Oxfordshire
Villeroy & Boch	43	London : Wandsworth
Viyella	406	Ellesmere Port Cheshire
Viyella	483	Street Somerset
Vossen	111	Wrexham Clwyd
W W Wales/Burns Country Foods	272	Kilmarnock Strathclyde
Wade Ceramics	58	Stoke-on-Trent Staffordshire
Walkers Shortbread	261	Aberlour on Spey Grampian
Walsall Leather Museum	289	Walsall West Midlands
Walton's Mill Shop	124	Harrogate North Yorkshire
Ward Art & Crafty Warehouse	244	Gateshead Tyne & Wear
Warner's	575	Belmullet Co. Mayo, Eire
Warner's	605	Dromore Co Down, Ulster
Warner's	645	Keady Co Armagh, Ulster
Warner's	668	Nottingham Nottinghamshire
Warner's	360	Bicester Oxfordshire
Warwick Fabrics	117	Bourton-on-the-Water Gloucs
Weald Smokery, The	265	Flimwell E Sussex
Weavers Shop, The	171	Bloxham Oxfordshire
Weavers Shop, The	186	Kidderminster Hrfd & Worcester
Webb Ivory	493	Burton-on-Trent Staffordshire
Webb Ivory	496	Swadlincote Derbyshire
Wedgwood Best	53	Stoke-on-Trent Staffordshire
Wedgwood Group	62	Stoke-on-Trent Staffordshire
Welsh Whisky Co., The	263	Brecon Powys
Weston Mill Pottery	89	Newark Nottinghamshire
Wetherall	598	Denbigh Clwyd
Wetheriggs Country Pottery	90	Penrith Cumbria
White and Co. (Earls Barton)	739	Daventry Northamptonshire
Whitfords Bury Boot & Shoe Co.	730	Bury Lancashire
Wilton Carpets	193	Salisbury Wiltshire
Windsmoor	484	Street Somerset
Winfields	425	Haslingden Lancashire
Witham Contours	618	Grantham Lincolnshire
Woods of Windsor	361	Bicester Oxfordshire
Wookey Hole Caves & Papermill	258	Wells Somerset
Woolea	485	Street Somerset
Wrangler	362	Bicester Oxfordshire
Wrangler	424	Hartlepool Cleveland
Wrangler	486	Street Somerset
Wrangler Factory Outlet, The	588	Calverton Nottinghamshire
Wrights of Trowmill	630	Hawick Borders
Wynsors World of Shoes	725	Bradford West Yorkshire
Wynsors World of Shoes	733	Castleford West Yorkshire
Wynsors World of Shoes	734	Chesterfield Derbyshire
Wynsors World of Shoes	735	Cleckheaton West Yorkshire
Wynsors World of Shoes	749	Grimsby Humberside
Wynsors World of Shoes	750	Hazel Grove Greater Manchester
Wynsors World of Shoes	757	Leeds West Yorkshire
Wynsors World of Shoes	771	Penketh Lancashire
Wynsors World of Shoes	775	Sheffield South Yorkshire
Wynsors World of Shoes	778	St Helens Merseyside
Wynsors World of Shoes	781	Stockton-on-Tees Cleveland
Wynsors World of Shoes	786	Thurcroft South Yorkshire
Wynsors World of Shoes	790	York North Yorkshire
Yarnolds	151	Wolverhampton West Midlands
Yorkshire Outlet	page 286	Doncaster, South Yorkshire

Please note that the NUMBERS refer to the ENTRIES, NOT the PAGES

Companies with factory shops

Avon	Bristol	371	Factory Shop Ltd., The
	Bristol	172	Bristol Carpets
Bedfordshire	Bedford	115	Boynett Fabrics
	Leighton Buzzard	655	Gossard
	Luton	15	Crystal Art
	Toddington	28	Royal Scot Crystal
Berkshire	Slough	698	Mexx Factory Outlet
Borders	Hawick	626	Hawick Cashmere Company
	Hawick	627	Peter Scott & Co.
	Hawick	628	Short & Robertson Knitwear
	Hawick	101	Slumberdown Enterprises
	Hawick	629	Valerie Louthan & Country Store
	Hawick	630	Wrights of Trowmill
	Selkirk	692	Brenire
	Selkirk	313	Claridge Mills
	Selkirk	556	D C Dalgliesh
	Selkirk	144	Ettrick Forest Interiors
	Selkirk	693	Gardiner of Selkirk
	Selkirk	19	Selkirk Glass
Buckinghamshire	Aylesbury	262	Chiltern Brewery, The
	High Wycombe	217	Furniture Direct
	High Wycombe	127	GP & J Baker & Parkertex Fabrics
	Little Horwood	187	Phoenix Carpets
Cambridgeshire	Fenstanton	213	Table Place, The
	Papworth Everard	287	Papworth Travel Goods
	Peterborough	675	Jaeger Sale Shop
	Wisbech	545	Catalogue Bargain Shop
Central	Alloa	565	Jaeger
	Sauchie by Alloa	689	Glen Alva
	Tillicoultry	710	Callant of Scotland (Knitwear)
	Tillicoultry	711	Lindsay Allan Designs
Channel Islands	Guernsey	620	Guernsey Woollens
Channel Islands	Guernsey	621	Le Tricoteur
Cheshire	Cheadle	277	Galt Toys
	Congleton	158	Astbury Lighting
	Congleton	593	R H Lowe
	Ellesmere Port	377	**McArthur Glen Designer Outlet Village**
		378	Acced
		379	Benetton
		380	Big L, The
		381	Catamini
		382	Collective
		383	Dim
		384	Edinburgh Crystal
		385	Eminence
		386	Equator
		387	Famous Footwear
		388	Fred Perry
		389	Fruit of the Loom
		390	James Barry
		391	Jeffrey Rogers
		392	John Partridge
		393	JoKids
		394	Kurt Geiger
		395	Liz Claiborne
		396	Nike
		397	Paco
		398	Paul Costelloe
		399	Principles
		400	Remington
		401	Sapphire Books
		402	Scotch House

Factory shops by county
continued

Cheshire *contd.*	Ellesmere Port	403	Suits You
		404	Tie Rack
		405	Timberland
		406	Viyella
	Ellesmere Port	610	Velmore Fashions
	Macclesfield	134	Barracks Fabrics
	Macclesfield	661	Designer Warehouse
	Macclesfield	297	Fent Shop, The
	Macclesfield	135	Material Things
	Runcorn	687	Velmore Fashions
Cleveland	Hartlepool	408	**Jackson's Landing**
		409	Benetton
		410	Bookscene
		411	Charles Clinkards
		412	Chas N Whillans
		413	Edinburgh Crystal
		414	Equator
		415	Hallmark
		416	Honey
		417	James Barry
		418	JoKids
		419	Royal Brierley
		420	TOG 24
		421	Tom Sayers
		422	Toyworld
		423	Treasure Island
		424	Wrangler
	Middlesbrough	528	Catalogue Bargain Shop
	Redcar	681	Dewhirst
	Stockton-on-Tees	451	Famous Fashion Discounts
	Stockton-on-Tees	781	Wynsors World of Shoes
Clwyd	Denbigh	35	Brookhouse Pottery Workshop
	Denbigh	598	Wetherall
	Mostyn	140	Abakhan Fabrics
	St Asaph	701	Tweedmill
	Wrexham	200	Dennis of Ruabon
	Wrexham	719	Velmore Fashions
	Wrexham	111	Vossen
Co Armagh, NI	Keady	645	Warner's
Co Down, NI	Dromore	605	Warner's
Co Durham	Darlington	738	Hall & Son
	Peterlee	676	Claremont Garments
	Peterlee	677	Dewhirst
	Peterlee	142	Joman Manufacturing Co.
	Shildon	695	Durham Clothing Co.
	West Auckland	716	Claremont Garments
Co. Mayo, Eire	Belmullet	575	Warner's
Cornwall	Bodmin	238	Art Candles
	Bodmin	582	Silken Ladder Factory Outlet
	St Austell	702	LS & J Sussman
Cumbria	Ambleside	721	Briggs & Shoe Mines
	Askam-in-Furness	723	K Shoes
	Carlisle	732	Briggs & Shoe Mines
	Carlisle	99	Factory Bedding and Fabrics
	Carlisle	282	John Chapman
	Dalton-in-Furness	737	Furness Footwear
	Egremont	375	Factory Shop Ltd., The
	Kendal	754	Briggs & Shoe Mines
	Kendal	432	**K Village**
		433	Crabtree & Evelyn
		434	Dartington Crystal
		41	Denby Pottery
		436	Jumpers
		755	K Shoes Factory Shop, Sports Factory and Baggage Factory
		438	K Shoes Full Price
	Keswick	756	Barker Shoes

> **Please note that the NUMBERS refer to the ENTRIES, NOT the PAGES**

> *Factory shops by county*
> continued

494   *The Official Great British Factory Shop Guide*

County	Town	No.	Shop
Cumbria *contd.*	Lindal-in-Furness	245	Colony Country Store
	Maryport	760	New Balance Athletic Shoes
	Penrith	772	Briggs & Shoe Mines
	Penrith	674	Town & Country Manner
	Penrith	90	Wetheriggs Country Pottery
	Sedbergh	691	Farfield Clothing
	Shap	774	K Shoes
Derbyshire	Alfreton	564	David Nieper
	Ambergate	202	End of the Line Furniture
	Ashbourne	6	Derwent Crystal
	Ashbourne	568	Elite Factory Clothes Shop, The
	Belper	318	De Bradelei Mill Shops
	Belper	576	George Brettle and Co.
	Belper	577	Jaeger
	Calver	731	Peaklander Footwear
	Chesterfield	9	Dema International
	Chesterfield	734	Wynsors World of Shoes
	Church Gresley	33	T. G. Green Pottery
	Cromford	595	John Smedley
	Denby	10	Dartington Crystal
	Denby	36	Denby Pottery
	Derby	600	Claremont Garments
	Derby	11	Derwent Crystal
	Derby	307	Fine Fabrics
	Derby	37	Royal Crown Derby
	Derby	740	Shoe Factory Shop, The
	Hartington	87	Rookes Pottery
	Hathersage	1	David Mellor Cutlery
	Heanor	125	Fabric Factory, The
	Heanor	216	Langley Furniture
	Ilkeston	638	Charnos
	Ilkeston	219	Frank Knighton & Sons
	Ilkeston	639	J B Armstrong & Co.
	Ilkeston	640	Match Leisurewear
	Ilkeston	641	R S Sports & Leisurewear
	Matlock Bath	44	Denby Factory Shop
	Matlock Bath	138	Fabric Design
	Matlock Green	761	Matlock Shoe Sales
	Moira	664	TDP Textiles
	Riddings	683	Charnos
	Riddings	254	Standard Soap Co.
	Ripley	225	Chelsee Design
	Somercotes	699	Coats Viyella
	Somercotes	229	Lincoln House Home Furnishings
	South Normanton	149	Filigree
	Swadlincote	496	Webb Ivory
	Tibshelf	288	Harvergrange & Spartan Luggage
	Wirksworth	718	Benco Hosiery
Devon	Bampton	571	Origin
	Barnstaple	83	C H Brannam
	Barnstaple	205	Croydex
	Bovey Tracey	276	House of Marbles and Teign Valley Glass
	Dartmouth	34	Dartmouth Pottery
	Great Torrington	13	Dartington Crystal
	Newton Abbot	190	Candy & Co.
	Plymouth	678	Jaeger Sale Shop
	Tiverton	315	John Heathcoat & Co (Sales)
	Torquay	542	Catalogue Bargain Shop
Dorset	Poole	191	Pilkington's Tiles
Dyfed	Ammanford	566	Alan Paine Knitwear
	Ammanford	567	Corgi Hosiery
	Crymych	208	Frenni Furniture
	Haverfordwest	625	Thistle Trading Co.
East Sussex	Brighton	84	Kemptown Terracotta

Factory shops by county

continued

East Sussex *contd.*	Brighton	363	Merchants Quay
		364	Bookscene
		365	Edinburgh Crystal
		366	Factory Shop Ltd., The
		367	Giovanna
		368	Hornsea Pottery
		369	TOG 24
		370	Tom Sayers
	Flimwell	265	Weald Smokery, The
	Hastings	215	Collins and Hayes
	Rye	47	Rye Pottery
	Seaford	227	Sheban Furniture
Essex	Barkingside	572	Choice Discount Stores
	Basildon	573	Choice Discount Stores
	Basildon	317	Factory Shop, The
	Clacton-on-Sea	590	Mascot Clothing
	Grays	619	Choice Discount Stores
	Hadleigh	623	Choice Discount Stores
	Rayleigh	680	Falmer Jeans
	Romford	226	Hubbinet Reproductions
	Saffron Walden	688	Swaine Adeney Brigg
	Tiptree	488	Factory Shop Ltd., The
	Wickford	717	Next 2 Choice
	Witham	259	Hole Farm Dried Flowers
Fife	Cowdenbeath	594	Babygro
	Cowdenbeath	503	Catalogue Bargain Shop
	Glenrothes	615	Keela International
	Kirkcaldy	650	Babygro
Gloucestershire	Bourton-on-Water	117	Warwick Fabrics
	Cirencester	243	Original Book Works, The
	Cheltenham	174	Marlborough Tiles
	Gloucester	513	Catalogue Bargain Shop
	Stroud	196	Carpet Shop (Carpets of Worth)
	Stroud	538	Catalogue Bargain Shop
	Stroud	487	Factory Shop Ltd., The
Grampian	Aberdeen	559	Mill Shop, The
	Aberdeen	201	Royal Aberdeen Blind Workshops
	Aberlour on Spey	261	Walkers Shortbread
	Elgin	609	The Mill Shop (Johnstons of Elgin)
	Fochabers	266	Baxters Visitor Centre
Gr Manchester	Ashton-in-Makerfield	93	Northern Feather Home Furnishings
	Bolton	239	Modec Fine Arts
	Bolton	97	Robin Hood Mill Shop
	Broadbottom	98	Tiviot Prints
	Castleton	156	Vectase Lighting
	Chadderton	157	Gorse Mill Lighting
	Eccles	507	Catalogue Bargain Shop
	Failsworth	159	Pifco Salton Carmen Russell Hobbs Tower
	Farnworth	508	Catalogue Bargain Shop
	Hazel Grove	750	Wynsors World of Shoes
	Horwich	103	Towel Mill Shop, The
	Hyde	105	Ashtons
	Hyde	128	Mill Fabric Shop, The
	Hyde	218	Providence Reproductions
	Manchester	525	Catalogue Bargain Shop
	Manchester	136	Fabric Mill Shop, The
	Norden	665	Cudworth of Norden
	Ramsbottom	445	Peel Mill
	Walkden	543	Catalogue Bargain Shop
	Westhoughton	232	Brunel (By Testall) Upholstery
	Westhoughton	198	Carpet Company, The
	Wigan	109	Courtaulds Textiles Homeware
Gwent	Blackwood	579	Gossard
	Ebbw Vale	506	Catalogue Bargain Shop
Gwynedd	Llandudno	520	Catalogue Bargain Shop
Hampshire	Andover	203	Croydex
	Fareham	180	Grandford Carpet Mills

Please note that the NUMBERS refer to the ENTRIES, NOT the PAGES

Factory shops by county
continued

Hereford & Worcester	Droitwich	505	Catalogue Bargain Shop
	Kidderminster	184	Rowe Carpets
	Kidderminster	185	Victoria Carpet Weavers Shop
	Kidderminster	186	Weavers Shop, The
	Malvern	524	Catalogue Bargain Shop
	Pershore	444	Factory Shop Ltd., The
	Redditch	682	Jaeger Knitwear
	Stourport	195	Carpets of Worth
	Stourport	280	T P Activity Toys
	Worcester	547	Catalogue Bargain Shop
	Worcester	199	Rowe Carpets
	Worcester	51	Royal Worcester Porcelain
Hertfordshire	Borehamwood	583	Rubert of London
	Broxbourne	7	Nazeing Glassworks
	Hatfield	426	The Galleria
	Hemel Hempstead	632	Aquascutum
	High Barnet	517	Catalogue Bargain Shop
	Watford	788	K Shoes
	Watford	713	Next 2 Choice
Highland	Inverness	220	Highland Society for the Blind
Highland	Lochinver	42	Highland Stoneware Pottery
Highland	Wick	31	Caithness Glass
Humberside	Bridlington	32	Park Rose Pottery Leisure Park
	Driffield	604	Dewhirst
	Grimsby	268	Alfred Enderby
	Grimsby	269	Danish Food Centre
	Grimsby	270	Kay & Son, Prime Fish Merchants
	Grimsby	748	Shoe Factory Shop, The
	Grimsby	271	Van Smirren Seafoods
	Grimsby	749	Wynsors World of Shoes
	Hornsea	430	Hornsea Freeport
	Hull	637	Dewhirst
	Hull	752	Shoe Factory Shop, The
	Scunthorpe	690	Hide Park Leather Co.
Isle of Wight	Yarmouth	40	Chessell Pottery
Kent	Canterbury	240	Essentially Hops
	Crayford	305	David Evans and Co.
	Dartford	209	Croydex
	Faversham	509	Catalogue Bargain Shop
	Faversham	212	Nova Garden Furniture
	Gravesend	514	Catalogue Bargain Shop
	Herne Bay	751	Peter Newman
	Sevenoaks	145	Corcoran & May
Lancashire	Accrington	92	Hamilton McBride
	Accrington	560	Karrimor International
	Accrington	548	Optical Direct (C-L-M)
	Accrington	112	Red Rose Velvets
	Anderton	168	Jorgus Carpets
	Bacup	550	Optical Direct
	Barrowford	94	East Lancashire Towel Co.
	Blackburn	170	Graham & Brown
	Blackburn	95	Sheltered Workshop for the Blind
	Blackpool	724	K Shoes
	Burnley	587	Barden Mill Shop
	Burnley	500	Catalogue Bargain Shop
	Burnley	120	Color Blind
	Burnley	173	John Wilman
	Burnley	729	Lambert Howarth & Sons
	Burnley	304	Liberty
	Bury	730	Whitfords Bury Boot & Shoe Co.
	Carnforth (Holme)	241	Abbey Horn of Lakeland
	Chorley	502	Catalogue Bargain Shop
	Chorley	121	Curtain Choice
	Clitheroe	175	Shireburn Carpets
	Colne	373	Boundary Mill Shop
	Colne	293	Empress Mills

**Factory shops
by county**
continued

Please note that the NUMBERS refer to the ENTRIES, NOT the PAGES

Factory shops by county

continued

County	Town	No.	Shop
Mid Glamorgan	Caerphilly	501	Catalogue Bargain Shop
	Merthyr Tydfil	527	Catalogue Bargain Shop
	Merthyr Tydfil	274	O P Chocolate
	Merthyr Tydfil	663	Pendor (Clothing)
	Pontypridd	532	Catalogue Bargain Shop
	Porth	46	Royal Worcester & Spode
	Pyle Cross	534	Catalogue Bargain Shop
	Tonypandy	541	Catalogue Bargain Shop
Norfolk	East Dereham	374	Factory Shop Ltd., The
	Kenninghall	88	Suffolk Potteries
	King's Lynn	14	Caithness Crystal
	King's Lynn	648	Jaeger
	Norwich	767	Bally Factory Shop, The
	Norwich	768	Factory Shoe Shop, The
	Norwich	769	Robert Cole Shoes
	Wells-next-the-Sea	715	East Quay Knitwear
North Yorkshire	Harrogate	123	Carrington Curtains
	Harrogate	407	Darley Mill Centre
	Harrogate	124	Walton's Mill Shop
	Ingleton	642	Daleswear Factory Shop
	Norton, Malton	667	Dewhirst
	Ripon	446	Factory Shop Ltd., The
	Ripon	447	Lightwater Village Factory Outlets
	Scarborough	536	Catalogue Bargain Shop
	Skipton	300	Embsay Mills Needlecraft Centre
	Skipton	697	Skipton Mill Shop
	Whitby	233	Beevers of Whitby
	York	720	Bridge of York
	York	152	Carrington Curtains
	York	491	Factory Outlet Shopping Centre
	York	260	History Craft
	York	790	Wynsors World of Shoes
Northamptonshire	Brixworth	85	Haddonstone
	Daventry	739	White and Co. (Earls Barton)
	Earls Barton	743	Barker Shoes
	Kettering	646	Ian M Roberts
	Long Buckby	284	Regent Belt Co.
	Northampton	666	Big L Factory Outlet (Levi's)
	Northampton	763	Crockett & Jones
	Northampton	764	J. L. & Co.
	Northampton	251	Nimbus
	Northampton	765	Piggly-Wiggly Shoe Store
	Northampton	766	Tricker's
	Rothwell	773	T Groocock & Co. (Rothwell)
	Rushden	164	Helix Lighting
Northumberland	Amble	275	Shark Group
	Ashington	569	Dewhirst
	Blyth	581	Claremont Garments
Nottinghamshire	Arnold	722	Crockers of Arnold
	Blidworth	580	Major Oak Clothing Company
	Calverton	588	Wrangler Factory Outlet
	Colston Bassett	264	Colston Bassett & District Dairy
	Hucknall	635	Jaeger
	Kirkby-in-Ashfield	129	Paul Steiger
	Langley Mill	651	Debut Group
	Long Eaton	285	Ashlie Craft
	Long Eaton	659	Charnos
	Long Eaton	310	Nottingham Laces & Trimmings
	Long Eaton	222	P F Collections
Nottinghamshire	Mansfield	526	Catalogue Bargain Shop
	Newark	89	Weston Mill Pottery
	Nottingham	531	Catalogue Bargain Shop
	Nottingham	668	Warner's
	Nottingham	669	K & M (Leather Clothing) Mnfg.
	Nottingham	45	Denby Factory Shop
	Nottingham	770	Shoe Factory Shop, The
	Nottingham	670	Factory Shop, The

Please note that the NUMBERS refer to the ENTRIES, NOT the PAGES

Factory shops by county
continued

Nottinghamshire *contd.*	Nottingham	141	Florentine Trading Co.
	Ruddington	685	Cooper & Roe
	Sutton-in-Ashfield	704	Claremont Garments
	Sutton-in-Ashfield	705	Cooper & Roe
	Sutton-in-Ashfield	231	Marden Furniture
Oxfordshire	Bicester	206	Heyford's Upholstery
	Bicester	319	**Bicester Outlet Shopping Village**
		320	Aquascutum
		321	Benetton
		322	Big Dog
		323	Cerruti 1881 Femme
		324	Clarks
		325	Converse
		326	Descamps
		327	Edinburgh Crystal
		328	Equator
		329	Fred Perry
		330	Helly Hansen
		331	Hico
		332	Hobbs
		333	Hom
		334	Jaeger
		335	Jane Shilton
		336	Jeffrey Rogers
		337	Jigsaw
		338	Joan & David
		339	John Jenkins
		340	John Partridge
		341	JoKids
		342	Karen Millen
		343	Kids Playfactory
		344	Kurt Geiger
		345	Monsoon
		346	Museum Merchandise
		347	Oneida
		348	Osh Kosh B'Gosh
		350	Price's Candles
		351	Principles
		352	Racing Green
		353	Red/Green
		354	Sapphire Books
		355	Suit Company/Moss Bros Group
		356	The Scotch House
		357	TOG 24
		358	Triumph
		359	Villeroy & Boch
		360	Warner's
		361	Woods of Windsor
		362	Wrangler
	Bloxham	171	Weavers Shop, The
	Burford	119	Just Fabrics
	Hook Norton	39	Hook Norton Pottery
	Oxford	252	History Craft
	Witney	110	Early's of Witney
Powys	Brecon	263	Welsh Whisky Co. , The
	Newtown	530	Catalogue Bargain Shop
Shetland	Lerwick	298	Jamieson & Smith
Shropshire	Bridgnorth	499	Catalogue Bargain Shop
	Craven Arms	176	Crucial Trading
	Telford	709	Fruit of the Loom
	Wellington	714	Fashion Factory
Somerset	Bridgwater	726	Crockers of Bridgwater
	Bridgwater	727	Sedgemoor Shoes
	Burnham-on-Sea	728	Crockers of Burnham
	Frome	182	Custom Carpets Factory Shop
	Glastonbury	745	Morlands

Somerset *contd.*	Glastonbury	746	Richard Draper
	Minehead	441	Factory Shop Ltd., The
	Shepton Mallet	694	Mulberry
	Street	784	Crockers of Street
		453	**Clarks Village**
		454	Alexon/Eastex/Dash
		455	Baggage Factory
		456	Benetton
		457	Black & Decker
		458	Clarks Factory Shop
		783	Clarks Factory Shop
		459	Clarks Shop, The
		460	Claude Gill Books
		461	Crabtree & Evelyn
		462	Dartington Crystal
		48	Denby Pottery
		463	Denby Pottery
		464	Esprit
		465	Fred Perry
		466	Hallmark
		467	Jaeger/Jaeger Man
		468	James Barry
		469	JoKids
		470	Jumpers
		471	Linen Cupboard, The
		472	Liz Claiborne
		473	Monsoon/Accessorize
		474	Pier, The
		475	Remington
		476	Rohan
		477	Royal Brierley
		478	Royal Worcester
		479	Sports Factory
		480	Thorntons Chocolates
		481	Triumph/Hom
		482	Village Gift Shop, The
		483	Viyella
		484	Windsmoor
		485	Woolea
		486	Wrangler
	Wells	258	Wookey Hole Caves & Papermill
	Worle	789	Crockers of Worle
South Yorkshire	Adwick-le-Street	561	Stagslax Menswear
	Barnsley	169	Shaw Carpets
	Doncaster	504	Catalogue Bargain Shop
	Doncaster	601	Factory Shop, The
	Doncaster	602	John Smedley
	Doncaster	603	Topping Howard Enterprises
	Doncaster	*page* 286	Yorkshire Outlet, The
	Gildersome	12	BRK Crystal
	Rotherham	684	Claremont Garments
	Sheffield	3	George Butler of Sheffield
	Sheffield	4	Hiram Wild
	Sheffield	5	Osborne Silversmiths
	Sheffield	775	Wynsors World of Shoes
	Thurcroft	786	Wynsors World of Shoes
Staffordshire	Biddulph	578	Charnos
	Burton-on-Trent	493	Webb Ivory
	Cannock	589	Fashion Factory
	Leek	653	Joshua Wardle
	Leek	758	Lotus Shoes
	Leek	654	Mill Shop, The
	Lichfield	2	Arthur Price of England
	Rugeley	686	John Partridge
	Stafford	166	Goodson Lighting

Please note that the NUMBERS refer to the ENTRIES, NOT the PAGES

Factory shops by county
continued

Staffordshire contd.	Stafford	779	Lotus Factory Shop
	Stafford	20	Schott-UK
	Stafford	780	Shoe Shed, The
	Stoke-on-Trent	52	Royal Doulton
	Stoke-on-Trent	53	Wedgwood Best
	Stoke-on-Trent	54	Crown Burslem Pottery
	Stoke-on-Trent	55	Moorcroft, W
	Stoke-on-Trent	56	Moorland Pottery
	Stoke-on-Trent	57	Royal Doulton
	Stoke-on-Trent	58	Wade Ceramics
	Stoke-on-Trent	59	Churchill Tableware
	Stoke-on-Trent	60	Holland Studio Craft
	Stoke-on-Trent	61	Royal Doulton
	Stoke-on-Trent	62	Wedgwood Group Factory Shop
	Stoke-on-Trent	63	Aynsley China
	Stoke-on-Trent	64	Royal Worcester
	Stoke-on-Trent	65	St George's Fine Bone China
	Stoke-on-Trent	66	Aynsley China
	Stoke-on-Trent	67	Ceramic World
	Stoke-on-Trent	68	Gladstone Pottery Museum
	Stoke-on-Trent	69	Hadida, M R
	Stoke-on-Trent	70	Hudson & Middleton
	Stoke-on-Trent	71	John Beswick
	Stoke-on-Trent	72	Portmeirion Potteries
	Stoke-on-Trent	73	Queen's Fine Bone China
	Stoke-on-Trent	74	Royal Grafton Fine Bone China
	Stoke-on-Trent	75	Salisbury China
	Stoke-on-Trent	76	Sovereign Ceramics
	Stoke-on-Trent	21	Staffordshire Crystal
	Stoke-on-Trent	255	Staffordshire Enamels
	Stoke-on-Trent	77	Staffordshire Tableware
	Stoke-on-Trent	452	Factory Shop Ltd., The
	Stoke-on-Trent	78	Blakeney Pottery
	Stoke-on-Trent	79	Carlton House
	Stoke-on-Trent	80	Minton
	Stoke-on-Trent	81	Portmeirion Seconds Shop
	Stoke-on-Trent	82	Spode
	Stoke-on-Trent	194	Johnson, H & R Tiles
	Stone	782	Lotus Shoes
	Tamworth	708	Jaeger Sale Shop
	Tutbury	29	Georgian Crystal
	Tutbury	30	Tutbury Crystal Glass
	Woodville	50	Bretby Art Pottery
Strathclyde	Airdrie	562	Unique Fashions
	Alexandria	563	Cocoon Coats
	Ayr	570	Begg of Ayr
	Ayr	204	Blindcraft
	Cumnock	596	Falmer Jeans
	Cumnock	736	Mansfield Shoes
	East Kilbride	606	Big L
	East Kilbride	607	Fruit of the Loom
	Elderslie	178	Glenpatrick Mill Shop
	Galston	611	Balmoral Mill Shop
	Glasgow	613	Mister Mackenzie
	Glasgow	511	Catalogue Bargain Shop
	Glasgow	512	Catalogue Bargain Shop
	Glasgow	744	Crockers of Glasgow
	Glasgow	614	Claremont Garments
	Glasgow	214	Royal Strathclyde Blindcraft
	Hamilton	515	Catalogue Bargain Shop
	Hamilton	308	Peter MacArthur & Co.
	Kilmarnock	647	Jaeger
	Kilmarnock	272	W W Wales /Burns Country Foods
	Oban	16	Oban Glass Studio
Suffolk	Bury St Edmunds	281	Carpet Bags
	Bury St Edmunds	372	Factory Shop Ltd., The
	Bury St Edmunds	279	Playdri Products

Factory shops
by county
continued

Suffolk *contd.*	Ipswich	753	Broughton Shoe Warehouse
	Ipswich	643	Lambourne Clothing
	Sudbury	314	Vanners Mill Shop
	Wattisfield	49	Henry Watson's Potteries
Surrey	Godalming	616	Alan Paine Knitwear
	Godalming	617	Kent & Curwen
	Guildford	622	Susan Walker Classics
	Horley	429	Factory Shop Ltd., The
	Oxted	673	Market Place, The, at Chanterelle
	South Croydon	148	Fabric World
	Sutton	150	Fabric World
Tayside	Auchterarder	235	Lyndalware
	Dundee	210	Dovetail Enterprises
	Dundee	741	K Shoes
	Kinross	649	Lochleven Mill Shop
	Perth	107	Burt Marshall, Lumsden
	Perth	18	Caithness Glass
Tyne & Wear	Blaydon on Tyne	116	Factory Fabrics
	Blaydon on Tyne	96	McIntosh's Factory Shop
	Gateshead	244	Ward Art & Crafty Warehouse
	Gateshead	612	Jockey
	Howdon	634	Claremont Garments
	Jarrow	644	Barbour
	Newcastle	529	Catalogue Bargain Shop
	Newcastle	223	Palatine Products
	North Shields	286	Bargain Baggage Factory Shop
	South Shields	700	Claremont Garments
	Sunderland	703	Dewhirst
	Sunderland	230	Sunelm Products
	Washington	301	Dainty Supplies
	Washington	712	S R Leisure
Warwickshire	Atherstone	549	Hat Shop, The
	Kenilworth	221	Table Place, The
	Leamington Spa	652	Into Clothing
	Nuneaton	671	Abbey Textiles
	Rugby	448	Factory Shop Ltd., The
	Stratford-on-Avon	256	History Craft
West Glamorgan	Port Talbot	533	Catalogue Bargain Shop
	Swansea	557	Abbey Woollen Mill
	Swansea	540	Catalogue Bargain Shop
	Swansea	706	Dewhirst
West Midlands	Bilston	497	Catalogue Bargain Shop
	Birmingham	153	Pifco Salton Carmen Russell Hobbs Tower
	Birmingham	236	Brass and Copper Shop
	Birmingham	551	Consortium Jewellery
	Birmingham	237	F W Needham
	Birmingham	552	Jeff & Annabel's Diamond Gallery
	Birmingham	553	Jewellery Quarter Discovery Centre
	Birmingham	154	Moulinex Swan
	Birmingham	554	P J Gold Depot
	Birmingham	555	V & F Parker (Arden Jewellery)
	Birmingham	207	Treetops Pine Furniture
	Cannock	155	Lighting Bug
	Cradley Heath	278	Hawk Cycles
	Shirley, Solihull	165	Clutterbuck, A E
	Stourbridge	537	Catalogue Bargain Shop
	Stourbridge area	22	Royal Doulton Crystal
	Stourbridge area	23	Brierley Hill Glass Co.
	Stourbridge area	24	Royal Brierley Crystal
	Stourbridge area	25	Staffordshire Crystal
	Stourbridge area	26	Dennis Hall Tudor Crystal
	Sutton Coldfield	539	Catalogue Bargain Shop
	Tipton	27	Royal Brierley Crystal
	Walsall	544	Catalogue Bargain Shop
	Walsall	289	Walsall Leather Museum
	Wolverhampton	546	Catalogue Bargain Shop

Please note that the **NUMBERS** *refer to the* **ENTRIES,** **NOT the PAGES**

Factory shops by county continued

West Midlands *contd.*	Wolverhampton	151	Yarnolds
	Wombourne	167	Pifco Salton Carmen Russell Hobbs Tower
West Sussex	Burgess Hill	586	Jaeger Factory Sale Shop
	Chichester	242	Goodwood MetalCraft
	Fulking	267	Springs Postal Service
	Hickstead Village	633	M & G Designer Fashions
	Midhurst	250	Dexam International
	Shoreham-by-Sea	696	Claremont Garments
West Yorkshire	Addingham	113	Fabric Shop, The
	Batley	114	Skopos Mill Shop
	Batley	574	Tor Outdoor Products
	Bradford	118	Ahmad Textiles
	Bradford	302	Bateman, Ogden & Co.
	Bradford	492	Britannia Products
	Bradford	290	British Mohair Spinners
	Bradford	303	C & R Barnett
	Bradford	498	Catalogue Bargain Shop
	Bradford	584	Golden Shuttle
	Bradford	585	Kyme Mill Shop
	Bradford	291	Texere Yarns
	Bradford	725	Wynsors World of Shoes
	Bradford	292	Yorkshire Mohair Mill, The
	Castleford	733	Wynsors World of Shoes
	Cleckheaton	591	Jaeger
	Cleckheaton	735	Wynsors World of Shoes
	Denby Dale	599	Mill Shop, The
	Denholme	306	Denholme Velvets
	Dewsbury	177	S. Lyles, Son & Co.
	Elland	376	Brooks Mill
	Farsley	294	R L & C M Bond
	Farsley	295	Skep Mill Shop, The
	Halifax	624	Katie Gray Factory Frock Shop
	Haworth	427	Ponden Mill
	Hebden Bridge	631	Abrovian Factory Shop
	Heckmondwike	516	Catalogue Bargain Shop
	Heckmondwike	126	Den-Home Cushioning
	Holmfirth	38	China Ladies of Holmfirth, The
	Horbury	296	Craft Collection Mill Shop
	Huddersfield	518	Catalogue Bargain Shop
	Huddersfield	104	Linen Mill Shop, The
	Huddersfield	636	Shop at the Mill
	Huddersfield	183	Fred Lawton & Son
	Keighley	431	Factory Shop Ltd., The
	Leeds	309	Factory Fabric Shop, The
	Leeds	757	Wynsors World of Shoes
	Morley	442	Factory Shop Ltd., The
	Pontefract	679	Brown's Factory Shop, The
	Queensbury	312	Black Dyke Mill Shop
	Shipley	299	British Mohair Spinners
	Shipley	228	Skopos Furniture Gallery
	Shipley	147	Skopos Mill Shop
	Wakefield	197	Homemaker Edging Services
Wiltshire	Marlborough	189	Marlborough Tiles
	Mere	249	Ethos Candles
	Salisbury	192	Marlborough Tiles
	Salisbury	193	Wilton Carpet Factory
	Swindon	91	Blackwell Bros.
	Swindon	257	Clover Leaf Giftware
	Swindon	785	Crockers of Swindon
	Swindon	707	Triumph International
	Trowbridge	489	Factory Shop Ltd., The
	Warminster	558	Dent's
	Warminster	490	Factory Shop Ltd., The

Please note that the NUMBERS refer to the ENTRIES, NOT the PAGES

Factory shops by county